D1204748

NUCLEAR STRATEGY AND NATIONAL SECURITY

NUCLEAR STRATEGY AND NATIONAL SECURITY Points of View

Edited by Robert J. Pranger and Roger P. Labrie

American Enterprise Institute
for Public Policy Research
Washington, D.C.

ACKNOWLEDGMENTS

The publisher wishes to thank those who have given permission to reprint the following articles:

"Can Nuclear Deterrence Last Out the Century?" Reprinted by permission from *Foreign Affairs* (January 1973). Copyright 1972 by Council on Foreign Relations, Inc.

"The Mutual-Hostage Relationship Between America and Russia." Reprinted by permission from *Foreign Affairs* (October 1973). Copyright 1973 by Council on Foreign Relations, Inc.

"Strategic Adaptability" (Fall 1974). Reprinted with permission from *Orbis*, A Journal of World Affairs, published by the Foreign Policy Research Inst.

"Nuclear Strategy and Nuclear Weapons." Reprinted with permission from *Scientific American* (May 1974). Copyright 1974 by Scientific American, Inc. All rights reserved.

"Strategic Vulnerability: The Balance Between Prudence and Paranoia." Reprinted by permission from *International Security* vol. 1, no. 1 (Fall 1976). Copyright 1976 by the President and Fellows of Harvard College.

"Soviet-American Strategic Competition: Instruments, Doctrines, and Purposes." Reprinted with the acknowledgment of the National Defense University, Washington, D.C.

"NATO's Doctrinal Dilemma" (Summer 1975). Reprinted with permission from *Orbis*, A Journal of World Affairs, published by the Foreign Policy Research Institute.

"A Credible Nuclear-Emphasis Defense For NATO" (Summer 1973). Reprinted with permission from *Orbis*, A Journal of World Affairs, published by the Foreign Policy Research Institute.

"Civil Defense in Limited War—A Debate" (April 1976). Reprinted by permission from *Physics Today*. © American Institute of Physics.

"The Race to Control Nuclear Arms." Reprinted by permission from *Foreign Affairs* (October 1976). Copyright 1976 by Council on Foreign Relations, Inc.

"Technical Innovation and Arms Control." Reprinted with permission from *World Politics* (July 1974). Copyright 1974 by Princeton University Press.

Punctuation, capitalization, and other points of style have been altered in some instances for consistency or clarity.

AEI studies 175

Library of Congress Cataloging in Publication Data

Nuclear Strategy and National Security—Points of View

(AEI studies   ; 175)
1. United States—Defenses. 2. United States—Military policy. 3. Strategy. 4. Atomic weapons. I. Pranger, Robert J. II. Labrie, Roger P. III. Series: American Enterprise Institute for Public Policy Research. AEI studies; 175. UA 23.N78 355.03'3073 77-15624 ISBN 0-8447-3275-3

Printed in the United States of America

THE AEI PUBLIC POLICY PROJECT
ON NATIONAL DEFENSE

The American Enterprise Institute,
as part of its foreign policy and
related defense policy study program,
decided in 1976 to establish a defense project
in order to focus public debate on the array of
vital defense issues. The project sponsors research
into strategy, threat, force structure, defense economics,
civil-military relations, and other areas
and presents the results in publications such as
this one and the unique *AEI Defense Review* series.
In addition it sponsors forums, debates, and conferences,
some of which are televised nationally.

The project is chaired by Melvin R. Laird,
former congressman, secretary of defense,
domestic counsellor to the President, and
now senior counsellor of *Reader's Digest*.
The twenty-four member advisory council
represents a broad range of defense viewpoints.
The project director is Robert J. Pranger,
head of AEI's foreign and defense policy studies program.
General Bruce Palmer, Jr., U.S. Army (retired)
serves as consultant to the chairman.

Views expressed are those of the authors
and do not necessarily reflect the views either
of the advisory council and others associated with
the project or of the advisory panels,
staff, officers, and trustees of AEI.

CONTENTS

GENERAL INTRODUCTION

Robert J. Pranger and Roger P. Labrie

Since the end of World War II, much of the debate in the United States over national security policy has centered on issues pertaining to the acquisition of nuclear weapons, the refinement of existing delivery systems, and the manner in which they would be used should the need ever arise. Although public deliberation over these issues has for the most part not been directly affected by the changing status of U.S.–Soviet political relations, the advent of nuclear parity between the two superpowers has heightened awareness of the controversies surrounding nuclear policies and of the mutual dependency that unites the future of the two societies. This development in itself, however, cannot insure that a national consensus will emerge as to the proper role of nuclear weapons in America's national security strategy. Indeed, if recent history is any guide to the future, it is unlikely that any set of nuclear policies can satisfy all the participants in the debate. Given the nature of nuclear deterrence and military operations—that one cannot know which doctrines or weapons provide the most effective deterrent or what the consequences of a nuclear exchange would be—it is imperative that whatever assumptions underlie the conflicting opinions on nuclear policy be made explicit.

The determinants of nuclear policy are great in number and their relative influence is difficult to assess. Many are the product of political processes in various governmental and private institutions, and consequently reflect the interests and prejudices of their sponsors. Intelligence estimates of the size and characteristics of the Soviet nuclear arsenal, and the perceptions of Soviet intentions derived from this information, are the most obvious determinants of U.S. policy. This is not to suggest, however, that there is any unanimity on their validity. There is much controversy, for instance, over the magnitude of Soviet counterforce capability and the efficacy of its civil defense program;

even more contentious are assessments of Soviet intentions. Despite the uncertainty inherent in such analyses, they do represent major contributions to the final decision-making processes within the executive and legislative branches of the federal government.

A number of other factors have helped to determine the composition and purpose of our nuclear arsenal. Some of the most important of them derive from our military involvement in Southeast Asia and have their roots in the domestic economic and political turmoil of the war years, in the changing popular attitudes toward the legitimacy and efficacy of force, and in the lack of consensus on the role the United States should play in world affairs. These "legacies" of the Vietnam era help explain many of the changes in our nuclear strategy and doctrine.

The most obvious consequence of our involvement in Vietnam was the upheaval in almost every aspect of American life. The war drained not only national wealth, but also public confidence in elected officials and political institutions at virtually every level. Public demands for new priorities in government, together with growing skepticism as to the legitimacy of using force to secure national objectives in the world, were important considerations in the formulation of new directions in foreign and military policies. The war revealed the limits of our military power and political commitments, necessitating new policies in harmony with domestic realities. The result was what the Nixon administration called a strategy of "realistic deterrence."

Realistic deterrence endowed foreign and defense policies with the objective of making our international political commitments more consistent with our military capabilities. There were three major features of the strategy of realistic deterrence: (1) the Nixon Doctrine; (2) the "total force" concept for defense planning, originated by Secretary of Defense Melvin R. Laird ("realistic deterrence" was also his term); and (3) the détente relationship between the United States on the one hand, and the Soviet Union and the People's Republic of China on the other. Whereas the Nixon Doctrine defined American interests and the means to protect them, and "total force" provided a more comprehensive understanding of U.S. and allied power, the third feature, détente, provided the means whereby the incidence and the intensity of international conflict could be minimized. The objective of the new strategy was a less interventionist foreign policy, one dictated by domestic realities and a changing international environment.

In the international arena, another set of factors exerted conflicting pressures on America's new strategy. The year 1972 witnessed a number of unprecedented events, ushering in the era of superpower détente. In February, President Nixon visited Communist China, and in May the first Strategic Arms Limitation Talks (SALT) bore fruit in the agreements limiting U.S. and Soviet antiballistic missile installations and strategic offensive nuclear arms. To a large extent, these events were the outcome of an altered perception of adversary intentions and a common predicament in an age of nuclear parity. Détente became a means to an end—the realignment of American political commitments with American power—though its immediate impact on nuclear strategy and weapons policy was nominal. Détente allowed the United States to implement many of the provisions of the Nixon Doctrine.

The noninterventionist intent of the Nixon Doctrine, the loss of some faith in the efficacy of conventional forces, and the economic constraints on the defense budget created an atmosphere conducive to the traditional American faith in technological solutions to intractable nontechnical problems. Although U.S. interests and political commitments in other lands have not diminished as a result of the Vietnam experience and the Nixon Doctrine, the manner in which the commitments are to be realized and fulfilled has changed in deference to new domestic and international realities. One of the major features of the new policy was a shift of the primary burden for defense to regional allies. The United States would augment the increased efforts of friendly nations with material assistance and training, as well as air and naval combat support if necessary. It was in conjunction with this new policy that the United States also sought to strengthen its nuclear deterrent.

Dissatisfaction with prevailing nuclear strategy and planning concepts surfaced early in the Nixon administration. In July 1962 Secretary of Defense Robert McNamara had voiced similar concerns when he proposed a new doctrine for nuclear weapons, one which would place greater emphasis on *counterforce* targeting (that is, on a wide variety of enemy military targets), albeit as a means of damage-limitation. The counterforce idea came to a prominent place in strategic thinking in the Nixon administration and, together with the notion of limited nuclear war, was articulated as policy by Secretary of Defense James R. Schlesinger in March 1974. The purpose of this shift in doctrine was to provide the President with retaliatory means other than striking Soviet urban centers with large numbers of warheads, a *countervalue* option that was believed to lack credibility, if no other options existed as well, in an era when both the United States and Soviet Union possessed the means to destroy each other. It must be emphasized that this doctrinal shift would not rule out countervalue nuclear deterrence, but would, instead, expand the range of nuclear options. In Schlesinger's words, "No one who has thought much about these questions disagrees with the need, as a minimum, to maintain a conservatively designed reserve for the ultimate threat of large-scale destruction." Limited nuclear strike options, however, were seen as enhancing the credibility of nuclear retaliatory threats and therefore as deterring attacks against the United States and its allies. When the Soviet Union threatened to intervene in the 1973 Middle East war, and the United States went on nuclear alert, the value of a strengthened deterrence capability became apparent to a number of policy makers.

At least one other factor contributed to the change in strategy during this period—the development and deployment of more accurate delivery systems which, together with improved command and control facilities, were essential for limited nuclear strikes against military and other strategic targets. The extent to which technology contributed to the adoption of this new doctrine may be unknown, but there can be no doubt that science did provide the means of satisfying the perceived diplomatic and military requirements of a nation disillusioned with its defense establishment and fearful of involvement in wars. The relationship of technology to strategy may be symbiotic, with each lending legitimacy to the other. The degree to which either dominates the other may change with circumstances and the character of political leaders.

In the post-Vietnam debate over the future role of the United States in world affairs, new political and military strategies have been formulated to deal with new realities. That debate continues today, and its implications are as uncertain as the changing realities it seeks to comprehend. While there is virtually no disagreement that deterrence should be the primary purpose of nuclear arsenals, controversy continues to surround questions regarding their composition and use should deterrence fail. Increasingly, deterrence has been associated with a capability to employ nuclear weapons on the battlefield or in limited strategic exchanges; the traditional dichotomy between deterrence and war-fighting has today become ambiguous for many people. Yet, others would argue that by blurring the distinction between prevention and initiation of nuclear war there is at least some chance that such a war would become more "thinkable" than in the past. Contemporary debate on American nuclear strategy and national security policy is taking place between these two schools of thought. This volume is designed to present the major arguments in the debate and issues related to it.

PART ONE

AN OVERVIEW OF AMERICA'S CHANGING GLOBAL ROLE

1

U.S. FOREIGN AND DEFENSE POLICY

U.S. FOREIGN POLICY FOR THE 1970s:
A NEW STRATEGY FOR PEACE

Richard M. Nixon

In the first of his foreign policy reports to Congress, President Richard M. Nixon identified the changing nature of the international system and its implications for a realistic national security policy. New realities were seen as demanding a new approach or strategy for the preservation of peace and stability in an evolving world order.

While uncertainty is inherent in change, the durability of America's interests and security commitments must not be subject to doubt, according to the President. Only the manner in which those interests are to be protected must change, to take into account the new realities at home and abroad. A recognition that political, economic, and military resources are finite, together with a belief in the enduring value of international interests, led President Nixon to formulate a national security strategy entailing a new partnership with allies, adequate military strength, and the desire to resolve differences with adversaries through a process of negotiation and mutual accommodation.

A nation needs many qualities, but it needs faith and confidence above all. Skeptics do not build societies; the idealists are the builders. Only societies that believe in themselves can rise to their challenges. Let us not, then, pose a false choice between meeting our responsibilities abroad and meeting the

Source: *U.S. Foreign Policy for the 1970s: A New Strategy for Peace, A Report to the Congress by Richard Nixon, President of the United States*, February 18, 1970, pp. 1-13.

needs of our people at home. We shall meet both or we shall meet neither.

The President's remarks
at the Air Force Academy Commencement,
June 4, 1969

[In January of 1969] the most immediate problem facing our nation was the war in Vietnam. No question has more occupied our thoughts and energies during this past year.

Yet the fundamental task confronting us was more profound. We could see that the whole pattern of international politics was changing. Our challenge was to understand that change, to define America's goals for the next period, and to set in motion policies to achieve them. For all Americans must understand that because of its strength, its history and its concern for human dignity, this nation occupies a special place in the world. Peace and progress are impossible without a major American role.

*   *   *

A New Era

The postwar period in international relations has ended.

Then, we were the only great power whose society and economy had escaped World War II's massive destruction. Today, the ravages of that war have been overcome. Western Europe and Japan have recovered their economic strength, their political vitality, and their national self-confidence. Once the recipients of American aid, they have now begun to share their growing resources with the developing world. Once almost totally dependent on American military power, our European allies now play a greater role in our common policies, commensurate with their growing strength.

Then, new nations were being born, often in turmoil and uncertainty. Today, these nations have a new spirit and a growing strength of independence. Once, many feared that they would become simply a battleground of cold-war rivalry and fertile ground for Communist penetration. But this fear misjudged their pride in their national identities and their determination to preserve their newly won sovereignty.

Then, we were confronted by a monolithic Communist world. Today, the nature of that world has changed—the power of individual Communist nations has grown, but international Communist unity has been shattered. Once a unified bloc, its solidarity has been broken by the powerful forces of nationalism. The Soviet Union and Communist China, once bound by an alliance of friendship, had become bitter adversaries by the mid-1960s. The only times the Soviet Union has used the Red Army since World War II have been against its own allies—in East Germany in 1953, in Hungary in 1956, and in Czechoslovakia in 1968. The Marxist dream of international Communist unity has disintegrated.

Then, the United States had a monopoly of overwhelming superiority of nuclear weapons. Today, a revolution in the technology of war has altered the nature of the military balance of power. New types of weapons present new dangers. Communist China has acquired thermonuclear weapons. Both the Soviet Union and the United States have acquired the ability to inflict unacceptable damage on the other, no matter which strikes first. There can be no gain and certainly no victory for the power that provokes a thermonuclear exchange. Thus, both sides have recognized a vital mutual interest in halting the dangerous momentum of the nuclear arms race.

Then, the slogans formed in the past century were the ideological accessories of the intellectual debate. Today, the "isms" have lost their vitality—indeed the restlessness of youth on both sides of the dividing line testifies to the need for a new idealism and deeper purposes.

This is the challenge and the opportunity before America as it enters the 1970s.

The Framework for a Durable Peace

In the first postwar decades, American energies were absorbed in coping with a cycle of recurrent crises, whose fundamental origins lay in the destruction of World War II and the tensions attending the emergence of scores of new nations. Our opportunity today—and challenge—is to get at the causes of crises, to take a longer view, and to help build the international relationships that will provide the framework of a durable peace.

. . . Peace must be far more than the absence of war. Peace must provide a durable structure of international relationships which inhibits or removes the causes of war. Building a lasting peace requires a foreign policy guided by three basic principles:

- Peace requires partnership. Its obligations, like its benefits, must be shared. This concept of partnership guides our relations with all friendly nations.

- Peace requires strength. So long as there are those who would threaten our vital interests and those of our allies with military force, we must be strong. American weakness could tempt

9

would-be aggressors to make dangerous miscalculations. At the same time, our own strength is important only in relation to the strength of others. We—like others—must place high priority on enhancing our security through cooperative arms control.

- Peace requires a willingness to negotiate. All nations—and we are no exception—have important national interests to protect. But the most fundamental interest of all nations lies in building the structure of peace. In partnership with our allies, secure in our own strength, we will seek those areas in which we can agree among ourselves and with others to accommodate conflicts and overcome rivalries. We are working toward the day when *all* nations will have a stake in peace, and will therefore be partners in its maintenance.

Within such a structure, international disputes can be settled and clashes contained. The insecurity of nations, out of which so much conflict arises, will be eased, and the habits of moderation and compromise will be nurtured. Most important, a durable peace will give full opportunity to the powerful forces driving toward economic change and social justice.

This vision of a peace built on partnership, strength and willingness to negotiate is the unifying theme of this report. In the sections that follow, the first steps we have taken during this past year—the policies we have devised and the programs we have initiated to realize this vision—are placed in the context of these three principles.

1. Peace through Partnership—The Nixon Doctrine. As I said in my address of November 3, "We Americans are a do-it-yourself people— an impatient people. Instead of teaching someone else to do a job, we like to do it ourselves. This trait has been carried over into our foreign policy."

The postwar era of American foreign policy began in this vein in 1947 with the proclamation of the Truman Doctrine and the Marshall Plan, offering American economic and military assistance to countries threatened by aggression. Our policy held that democracy and prosperity, buttressed by American military strength and organized in a worldwide network of American-led alliances, would insure stability and peace. In the formative years of the postwar period, this great effort of international political and economic reconstruction was a triumph of American leadership and imagination, especially in Europe.

For two decades after the end of the Second World War, our foreign policy was guided by such a vision and inspired by its success. The vision was based on the fact that the United States was the richest and most stable country, without whose initiative and resources little security or progress was possible.

This impulse carried us through into the 1960s. The United States conceived programs and ran them. We devised strategies, and proposed them to our allies. We discerned dangers, and acted directly to combat them.

The world has dramatically changed since the days of the Marshall Plan. We deal now with a world of stronger allies, a community of independent developing nations, and a Communist world still hostile but now divided.

Others now have the ability and responsibility to deal with local disputes which once might have required our intervention. Our contribution and success will depend not on the frequency of our involvement in the affairs of others, but on the stamina of our policies. This is the approach which will best encourage other nations to do their part, and will most genuinely enlist the support of the American people.

This is the message of the doctrine I announced at Guam—the "Nixon Doctrine." Its central thesis is that the United States will participate in the defense and development of allies and friends, but that America cannot—and will not—conceive *all* the plans, design *all* the programs, execute *all* the decisions and undertake *all* the defense of the free nations of the world. We will help where it makes a real difference and is considered in our interest.

America cannot live in isolation if it expects to live in peace. We have no intention of withdrawing from the world. The only issue before us is how we can be most effective in meeting our responsibilities, protecting our interests, and thereby building peace.

A more responsible participation by our foreign friends in their own defense and progress means a more effective common effort toward the goals we all seek. Peace in the world will continue to require us to maintain our commitments—and we will. As I said at the United Nations, "It is not my belief that the way to peace is by giving up our friends or letting down our allies." But a more balanced and realistic American role in the world is essential if American commitments are to be sustained over the long pull. In my State of the Union Address, I affirmed that "to insist that other nations play a role is not a retreat from responsibility; it is a sharing of responsibility." This is not a way for America to withdraw from its indispensable role in the world. It is a way—the only way—we can carry out our responsibilities.

It is misleading, moreover, to pose the fundamental question so largely in terms of commitments. Our objective, in the first instance, is to support our *interests* over the long run with a sound foreign policy.

The more that policy is based on a realistic assessment of our and others' interests, the more effective our role in the world can be. We are not involved in the world because we have commitments; we have commitments because we are involved. Our interests must shape our commitments, rather than the other way around.

We will view new commitments in the light of a careful assessment of our own national interests and those of other countries, of the specific threats to those interests, and of our capacity to counter those threats at an acceptable risk and cost.

We have been guided by these concepts during the past year in our dealings with free nations throughout the world.

- In Europe, our policies embody precisely the three principles of a durable peace: partnership, continued strength to defend our common interests when challenged, and willingness to negotiate differences with adversaries.

- Here in the Western Hemisphere we seek to strengthen our special relationship with our sister republics through a new program of action for progress in which all voices are heard and none predominates.

- In Asia, where the Nixon Doctrine was enunciated, partnership will have special meaning for our policies—as evidenced by our strengthened ties with Japan. Our cooperation with Asian nations will be enhanced as they cooperate with one another and develop regional institutions.

*   *   *

- In the Middle East, we shall continue to work with others to establish a possible framework within which the parties to the Arab-Israeli conflict can negotiate the complicated and difficult questions at issue. Others must join us in recognizing that a settlement will require sacrifices and restraints by all concerned.

- Africa, with its historic ties to so many of our own citizens, must always retain a significant place in our partnership with the new nations. Africans will play the major role in fulfilling their just aspirations—an end to racialism, the building of new nations, freedom from outside interference, and cooperative economic development. But we will add our efforts to theirs to help realize Africa's great potential.

- In an ever more interdependent world economy, American foreign policy will emphasize the freer flow of capital and goods between nations. . . .

- The great effort of economic development must engage the cooperation of all nations. We are carefully studying the specific goals of our economic assistance programs and how most effectively to reach them.

- Unprecedented scientific and technological advances as well as explosions in population, communications, and knowledge require new forms of international cooperation. The United Nations, the symbol of international partnership, will receive our continued strong support. . . .

2. America's Strength. The second element of a durable peace must be America's strength. Peace, we have learned, cannot be gained by good will alone.

In determining the strength of our defenses, we must make precise and crucial judgments. We should spend no more than is necessary. But there is an irreducible minimum of essential military security: for if we are less strong than necessary, and if the worst happens, there will be no domestic society to look after. The magnitude of such a catastrophe, and the reality of the opposing military power that could threaten it, present a risk which requires of any President the most searching and careful attention to the state of our defenses.

The changes in the world since 1945 have altered the context and requirements of our defense policy. In this area, perhaps more than in any other, the need to reexamine our approaches is urgent and constant.

The last 25 years have seen a revolution in the nature of military power. In fact, there has been a series of transformations—from the atomic to the thermonuclear weapon, from the strategic bomber to the intercontinental ballistic missile, from the surface missile to the hardened silo and the missile-carrying submarine, from the single to the multiple warhead, and from air defense to missile defense. We are now entering an era in which the sophistication and destructiveness of weapons present more formidable and complex issues affecting our strategic posture.

The last 25 years have also seen an important change in the relative balance of strategic power. From 1945 to 1949, we were the only nation in the world possessing an arsenal of atomic weapons. From 1950 to 1966, we possessed an overwhelming superiority in strategic weapons. From 1967 to 1969, we retained a significant superiority. Today, the Soviet Union possesses a powerful and sophisticated strategic force approaching our own. We must consider, too, that Communist China will deploy its own intercontinental missiles during the coming decade, introducing new and complicating factors for our strategic planning and diplomacy.

In the light of these fateful changes, the Administration undertook a comprehensive and far-reaching reconsideration of the premises and procedures for designing our forces. We sought—and I believe we have achieved—a rational and coherent formulation of our defense strategy and requirements for the 1970s.

The importance of comprehensive planning of policy and objective scrutiny of programs is clear:

- Because of the lead-time in building new strategic systems, the decisions we make today substantially determine our military posture—and thus our security—five years from now. This places a premium on foresight and planning.

- Because the allocation of national resources between defense programs and other national programs is itself an issue of policy, it must be considered on a systematic basis at the early stages of the national security planning process.

- Because we are a leader of the Atlantic Alliance, our doctrine and forces are crucial to the policy and planning of NATO. The mutual confidence that holds the allies together depends on understanding, agreement, and coordination among the 15 sovereign nations of the Treaty.

- Because our security depends not only on our own strategic strength, but also on cooperative efforts to provide greater security for everyone through arms control, planning weapons systems and planning for arms control negotiations must be closely integrated.

For these reasons, this Administration has established procedures for the intensive scrutiny of defense issues in the light of overall national priorities. We have re-examined our strategic forces; we have reassessed our general purpose forces; and we have engaged in the most painstaking preparation ever undertaken by the United States Government for arms control negotiations.

3. Willingness to Negotiate—An Era of Negotiation. Partnership and strength are two of the pillars of the structure of a durable peace. Negotiation is the third. For our commitment to peace is most convincingly demonstrated in our willingness to negotiate our points of difference in a fair and businesslike manner with the Communist countries.

We are under no illusions. We know that there are enduring ideological differences. We are aware of the difficulty in moderating tensions that arise from the clash of national interests. These differences will not be dissipated by changes of atmosphere or dissolved in cordial personal relations between statesmen. They involve strong convictions and contrary philosophies, necessities of national security, and the deep-seated differences of perspectives formed by geography and history.

The United States, like any other nation, has interests of its own, and will defend those interests. But any nation today must define its interests with special concern for the interests of others. If some nations define their security in a manner that means insecurity for other nations, then peace is threatened and the security of all is diminished. This obligation is particularly great for the nuclear superpowers on whose decisions the survival of mankind may well depend.

The United States is confident that tensions can be eased and the danger of war reduced by patient and precise efforts to reconcile conflicting interests on concrete issues. Coexistence demands more than a spirit of good will. It requires the definition of positive goals which can be sought and achieved cooperatively. It requires real progress toward resolution of specific differences. This is our objective.

As . . . Secretary of State [William P. Rogers] said on December 6:

> We will continue to probe every available opening that offers a prospect for better East-West relations, for the resolution of problems large or small, for greater security for all.
> In this the United States will continue to play an active role in concert with our allies.

This is the spirit in which the United States ratified the Non-Proliferation Treaty and entered into negotiation with the Soviet Union on control of the military use of the seabeds, on the framework of a settlement in the Middle East, and on limitation of strategic arms. This is the basis on which we and our Atlantic allies have offered to negotiate on concrete issues affecting the security and future of Europe, and on which the United States took steps last year to improve our relations with nations of Eastern Europe. This is also the spirit in which we have resumed formal talks in Warsaw with Communist China. No nation need be our permanent enemy.

America's Purpose

These policies were conceived as a result of change, and we know they will be tested by the change that lies ahead. The world of 1970 was not predicted a decade ago, and we can be certain that the world of 1980 will render many current views obsolete.

The source of America's historic greatness has been our ability to see what had to be done, and then to do it. I believe America now has the chance to move the world closer to a durable peace. And I know that Americans working with each other and with other nations can make our vision real.

U.S. FOREIGN POLICY FOR THE 1970s:
SHAPING A DURABLE PEACE

Richard M. Nixon

The Nixon Doctrine established the broad outlines within which the foreign and defense policies of the United States have been formulated in the present decade. Taking into account the profound transformations in domestic and international circumstances which have occurred since the end of World War II, the doctrine was designed as a testimony to America's continued role in world affairs. While the United States would not abandon any of its overseas commitments and interests, it would delegate a greater share of the burden for their preservation to regional allies with similar interests.

In this excerpt from his 1973 foreign policy report to the Congress, President Nixon described the changing international situation and its implications not only for American interests but also for its national security policy. A balance of military forces must be preserved if the evolution of the international order is to be conducive to peace, he said, and the strategic nuclear power of the United States would play an important role in determining the direction of that evolution. U.S. strategic doctrine must be adapted to new realities, however, for its nuclear deterrence to be both effective and credible.

Defense Policy

Of all the changes in the international situation over the postwar period discussed in this report, one of the most fundamental has been the shift in our strategic position.

The Challenge We Faced. When I entered office [January 1969], we faced a situation unique in American postwar experience. An era was behind us. In the immediate aftermath of World War II challenges to our security could be met with the assurance that our strategic nuclear

Source: *U.S. Foreign Policy for the 1970s: Shaping a Durable Peace, A Report to the Congress by Richard Nixon*, May 3, 1973, pp. 178-86.

position was overwhelmingly superior. By January 1969, the United States no longer enjoyed this strategic preponderance.

The Soviet Union had embarked on a formidable expansion of its nuclear arsenal. We could chart with some certainty when the Soviet Union would surpass us in numbers of intercontinental and submarine-launched ballistic missiles; we could also project when they could close the technological gap in strategic weapons. Our own offensive building program had virtually ceased, as we had shifted our effort to qualitative improvements. We had developed a concept for ballistic missile defense of our territory, but had no active deployment. We faced a negotiation on strategic arms controls, but had only begun to analyze the relationship to strategic weapons decisions.

At the same time, our spending for defense had grown substantially. Almost all the increases, however, had been absorbed by the war in Vietnam. The costs of new weapons were escalating, as were the expenses of maintaining the men of our armed forces. In addition, we were bearing burdens abroad for the common defense that seemed out of proportion to those borne by our allies. More than a million Americans were stationed overseas, and our reserves at home were minimal.

Yet, I found that our strategic doctrine called for an American capability to fight in two major theaters simultaneously. The confrontation atmosphere of the cold war persisted in both Europe and Asia. But the international environment after 25 years suggested new opportunities for diplomacy and, accordingly, for adjustments in military planning. The rigidity of the confrontation between East and West was easing, and the conduct of nations could no longer be viewed in the simple bipolar context of military blocs.

The need for an urgent reexamination of our national security policy and programs was obvious. There were four overriding questions:

- What doctrine was appropriate for our strategic forces in an era when the threat of massive retaliation alone was no longer credible in all circumstances and decisive nuclear superiority was probably unattainable?

- What should the interrelationship be between the programs required for maintaining our strength and our proposals for limiting strategic arms through negotiations?

- How could we simultaneously satisfy pressing domestic needs, meet our responsibilities in Vietnam, and maintain the capabilities of our other forces in a period when non-nuclear challenges were an important dimension of the security problem?

- How could we, in coordination with our allies, strengthen our mutual defense in a manner that retained their confidence in our reliability but permitted them to play a more prominent role?

Early in my first term, I made a series of decisions that resulted in a new concept of national security, reflected in the Nixon Doctrine.

In strategic nuclear policy, we adopted the doctrine of sufficiency. We could no longer be complacent about the strategic status quo merely because we could cause a certain level of destruction in response to an attack. We therefore began to develop a sounder and more flexible doctrine for our forces that would provide other retaliatory options besides a direct attack on millions of people.

Concurrently, in order to reduce our vulnerability and to compensate for the Soviet buildup, we launched a program to modernize our strategic forces. We continued to convert our land- and sea-based missiles to multiple independently targetable warheads (MIRVs). Thus, our missiles which would survive an attack would be able in retaliation to strike their targets with greater assurance of eluding defenses. We laid plans for a new long-range missile and submarine that would reduce vulnerability by allowing operation in a larger ocean area while still in range of targets. In addition, to increase the survivability of our retaliatory forces, we began planning a new strategic bomber to replace the aging B-52 force. We also initiated the Safeguard anti-ballistic missile (ABM) program to protect our land-based retaliatory forces.

Each of these decisions was taken, however, with the full understanding that, as an integral part of our national security policy, we also would seriously pursue negotiations for arms limitations. We would offer the Soviet Union the opportunity to reach agreement on measures that would enhance the security of both sides.

Finally, we began to assess our security obligations to determine how our alliance defense posture might be strengthened through mutual effort. We examined whether U.S. forces in some forward areas might be reduced; in those regions where security required a strong and continuing American presence, as in Europe, we and our allies initiated new programs for sharing the defense burden.

In the past four years we have laid a solid foundation for safeguarding American security for the remainder of this decade. We are now entering a period of promising prospects for increasing international stability. But the outcome is by no means guaranteed. We are still in a challenging period of transition. We still face difficult decisions.

There have been a number of positive developments since 1969. Unprecedented progress has been made in strategic arms controls. For the first time in two decades there is a genuine possibility of mutual and balanced force reductions in Europe. Our allies in Western Europe and Asia have become stronger, both economically and militarily, and are contributing more to mutual defense. Tensions in these two regions have been easing. A Vietnam Peace Agreement has been signed and our force of a half million men has returned home.

On the other hand, we cannot ignore the negative trends that persist. Even though Vietnam is entering a new phase, conflict remains in Indochina and ferment persists in other key areas of the world such as the Middle East where the interests of major powers are involved. Modern weapons are still being delivered to areas of great instability. The Soviet Union is strengthening its armed forces in every major category, including those in which the United States traditionally has had a substantial margin of superiority. A Soviet military presence now has been established in many strategic areas of the world.

As we determine the requirements for our defense in these circumstances and approach ongoing arms control negotiations, five factors of the current situation are of particular importance:

- There is approximate parity between the strategic forces of the United States and the Soviet Union. Soviet numerical advantages are offset by superior American technology.

- In such an era greater reliance must be placed on non-nuclear forces.

- Technological change while creating new opportunities also poses a potential threat to existing strategic stability.

- Manpower costs have increased substantially. They now absorb more than 56 percent of our entire defense budget, compared with 42 percent a decade ago. Now that we have chosen to rely on all-volunteer forces, the proportion devoted to manpower is not likely to decrease.

- The costs of increasingly complex modern weapons are also spiralling, further constraining our ability to maintain conventional force levels.

At the same time, the political climate at home has changed. In spite of the adjustments we have already made to new conditions, we face intensified pressures for further withdrawals of our deployed forces and for greater reductions. In the post-Vietnam environment, some Americans seem eager to return to the prevalent philosophy of the 1930s, and resist U.S. involvement in world affairs. The consensus which sustained our national commitment to a strong American military posture over the postwar period is no longer unchallenged.

The emerging global order, however, has neither exact historical parallels nor a predestined outcome. American actions will be a deci-

19

sive determinant of its shape. In a period of developing detente, it is easy to be lulled into a false sense of security. Threats are less blatant; the temptation is greater to make unilateral reductions and neglect the realities of existing forces of potential adversaries.

In such a fluid period we have no responsible choice but to remain alert to the possibility that the current trend toward detente with the Soviet Union and China may not prove durable. We have only begun an area of negotiations. We must not now ignore fundamental changes in the balance of forces or in the potential strength of our adversaries in an era of rapid change. To do so would only tempt challenges to our security interests and jeopardize chances for achieving greater stability through further agreements.

Military adequacy is never permanently guaranteed. To maintain security requires a continuing effort. But faced with escalating costs of manpower and weapons and competing domestic demands, we must insure that defense spending is based on a realistic assessment of our security requirements, and we must endeavor to reduce expenditures through more effective management.

There is, however, an irreducible minimum below which we cannot go without jeopardizing the very foundations of our diplomacy, our interests, and our national security. This Nation cannot afford the cost of weakness. Our strength is an essential stabilizing element in a world of turmoil and change. Our friends rely on it; our adversaries respect it. It is the essential underpinning for our diplomacy, designed to increase international understanding and to lessen the risks of war.

While taking the necessary steps to maintain the sufficiency of our strength, we are seeking a sound basis for limiting arms competition. Both elements are fundamental to a national defense that insures a more stable structure of peace.

Strategic Policy. Deterrence of war is the primary goal of our strategic policy and the principal function of our nuclear forces. Thus, our objectives continue to be:

- to deter all-out attack on the United States or its allies;

- to face any potential aggressor contemplating less than all-out attack with unacceptable risks; and

- to maintain a stable political environment within which the threat of aggression or coercion against the United States or its allies is minimized.

Strategic forces are the central component of our military posture. It is on them that our security and that of our allies is most heavily dependent.

While our goals are unchanged, there have been fundamental changes in the strategic military environment. Approximate nuclear parity between the United States and the Soviet Union is now a strategic reality and has been confirmed in strategic arms control agreements. Certain technological advances, however, could become destabilizing. So it is, therefore, imperative that we continue to assess the adequacy of our strategic policy and programs in light of advances made by potential adversaries.

The task is greatly complicated by the long lead-time required to make significant changes in these forces. Because of the extended development phase for new systems, a lengthy period could pass before a nation perceived that it was falling dangerously behind. From that point, it would require another considerable period before the imbalance could be corrected.

We must plan now to have a strategic force that will be adequate to meet potential threats of the next decade. We must develop our programs in the context of an uncertain world situation and accelerating technological possibilities.

During the 1960s missiles were relatively inaccurate and single warheads were the rule. Today, accuracies have improved significantly and missiles carry multiple warheads that can be independently targeted. In the present environment it would be misleading to measure sufficiency only by calculating destructive power in megatonnage. The quality of weapons systems, and their survivability, are vital determinants of sufficiency.

The SALT Agreement of May 1972 halted the rapid numerical growth of Soviet strategic offensive systems. Within the limits of the current SALT Agreement, however, strategic modernization programs may continue. We must, therefore, carefully assess the efforts the Soviets are making to improve their capabilities and must pace our programs accordingly.

- At least three new Soviet intercontinental ballistic missiles (ICBMs) are being developed: a new, very large missile which could have greater capability than the SS-9, which is now the largest operational Soviet missile; a smaller ICBM, possibly intended as a follow-on to the SS-11 missile; and a solid propellant ICBM, probably designed to replace the SS-13 or possibly to provide a mobile capability.

- These new missiles may well carry MIRVs [multiple independently targetable reentry vehicles] with accuracies which would increase the vulnerability of our land-based missiles, thus jeopardizing the current strategic stability.

21

- The Soviet Union has begun deployment of a new submarine capable of submerged launch of a 4,000-mile-range missile.

- The Soviet ABM [anti-ballistic missile] research and development program continues unabated.

If present trends continue and we do not take remedial steps, the forces which we currently rely upon to survive an attack and to retaliate could be more vulnerable. At some time in the future we could face a situation in which during a crisis there could be a premium to the side that initiated nuclear war. This would be an unstable and dangerous strategic relationship. Such a strategic environment is unacceptable.

In the late 1960s the effectiveness of American strategic nuclear forces was measured by a criterion known as "assured destruction." This concept assumed that deterrence could be maintained if it were clear that following a large-scale nuclear strike the United States could retaliate and inflict an unacceptable level of damage on the population and industry of the attacker.

In the 1970s strategic doctrine must meet different criteria. While the specter of an unacceptable response is fundamental to deterrence, the ability to kill tens of millions of people is not the only or necessarily the most effective deterrent to every challenge. Such a drastic course can be credibly reserved only for the most overwhelming threats to national survival. Moreover, the measurement of the effectiveness of our strategic forces in terms of numbers of dead is inconsistent with American values.

A different strategic doctrine is required in this decade when potential adversaries possess large and more flexible nuclear forces. The threat of an all-out nuclear response involving the cities of both sides might not be as credible a deterrent as it was in the 1960s. An aggressor, in the unlikely event of nuclear war, might choose to employ nuclear weapons selectively and in limited numbers for limited objectives. No President should ever be in the position where his only option in meeting such aggression is an all-out nuclear response. To deal with a wide range of possible hostile actions, the President must maintain a broad choice of options.

Credible deterrence in the 1970s requires greater flexibility:

- Lack of flexibility on our part could tempt an aggressor to use nuclear weapons in a limited way in a crisis. If the United States has the ability to use its forces in a controlled way, the likelihood of nuclear response would be more credible, thereby making deterrence more effective and the initial use of nuclear weapons by an opponent less likely.

- Therefore, to extend deterrence over a wider spectrum of possible contingencies we should ensure that our forces are capable of executing a range of options.

- If war occurs—and there is no way we can absolutely guarantee that it will not—we should have means of preventing escalation while convincing an opponent of the futility of continued aggression.

Greater flexibility in the employment of our forces does not necessitate any drastic change in our nuclear programs. The fundamental objective of military forces remains deterrence. Potential aggressors must be aware that the United States will continue to have both the resolve and the capacity to act in the face of aggression in all circumstances.

Strategic Programs. Our weapons programs are planned within the framework of this strategic policy. We must also consider Soviet strategic developments, arms limitations, and the potential for technological change. In light of the current strategic situation, I have determined that the U.S. must continue its modernization programs to ensure the future sufficiency of our nuclear forces.

- We are therefore improving our ICBM force. Silos for Minuteman missiles are being hardened, and 550 Minuteman III missiles with multiple independently targeted warheads will be deployed by the mid-1970s.

- Development of a new strategic submarine, the Trident, has been undertaken to provide a highly survivable replacement for our current ballistic missile submarines.

- We are developing a generation of submarine launched missiles with substantially greater range. With these new missiles our Trident and Poseidon submarines will be able to operate in a much larger ocean area while still within range of targets, and thus will be less vulnerable.

- The survivability of B-52 bombers has been increased by decreasing the time required for take-off on warning of an attack and by developing new basing concepts. This will reduce the threat from the growing force of Soviet ballistic missile submarines.

- We have also begun engineering development of the B-1 bomber as a potential replacement for the aging B-52s. The B-1 would maintain our bomber force as an important element in our mix of retaliatory forces, providing assurance against technological

23

breakthroughs, complicating an enemy's offensive and defensive planning, and ensuring flexibility of response.

- The ABM facility at Grand Forks, North Dakota, is being completed. This installation will give us operational ABM experience while directly enhancing the survivability of Minuteman ICBMs. We will also continue our planning for the Washington, D.C. ABM site in order to provide additional security for the major control center of our forces.

- Similarly, we are improving facilities for command and communications to control our responses in crisis situations.

We cannot prudently ignore the long-term strategic requirements of our security. But at the same time we are conscious of a serious responsibility—to preserve an environment which enhances stability and encourages further efforts to limit nuclear arms. Our forces, therefore, are not designed to provide a capability for a disarming first strike. Moreover, our programs are not so substantial that our objectives could be misunderstood, conceivably spurring a Soviet building cycle. There is not necessarily a direct relationship between every change in the strategic forces of the two sides. Some changes reflect an action-reaction cycle in the strategic arms programs of the two nations. In other cases, the similarity between American and Soviet forces results simply from the fact that roughly the same technologies are employed.

TOWARD A NATIONAL SECURITY STRATEGY OF REALISTIC DETERRENCE

Melvin R. Laird

In the second of his annual reports to Congress, Secretary of Defense Melvin R. Laird examined some of the implications of the Nixon Doctrine as they pertained to the area of national security. The policies of previous administrations, wrote Mr. Laird, were focused primarily on the deterrence of nuclear aggression. Consequently, conventional capabilities to meet certain types of conflict, such as that prevalent in less developed regions of the world, were found to be deficient. The program outlined in the following excerpts was intended to re-

Source: *Toward a National Security Strategy of Realistic Deterrence, Statement of Secretary of Defense Melvin R. Laird on the Fiscal Year 1972–76 Defense Program and the 1972 Defense Budget* (Washington, D.C., March 9, 1971), pp. 11–43.

structure the military posture of the United States so as to extend the concept of deterrence to cover "all forms of war."

In order to meet new challenges to American interests throughout the world, and in recognition of the changing nature of future conflicts, Secretary Laird developed the total force approach to defense planning. Because nuclear weapons had proved ineffective in deterring most forms of aggression, the conventional capabilities of the United States and its allies had to be improved. By placing the utility of nuclear weapons in a different perspective, by viewing the economic and political stability of allies as critical elements of deterrence, and by transferring primary responsibility for defense to those nations facing threats, a more comprehensive and realistic approach to national security was established.

I.   Strategy Overview

In his first Report to Congress on Foreign Policy, on February 18, 1970, President Nixon enunciated a policy of peace and what is needed to achieve it. Based on the principles of partnership, strength, and a willingness to negotiate, this positive policy is designed to move our country and the rest of the world toward a generation of peace. This basic policy, reaffirmed in the President's second Report on Foreign Policy, on February 25, 1971, underlies and guides our new National Security Strategy of Realistic Deterrence.

The goal of peace and the need to maintain adequate combat capabilities are fully consistent. The President recognized this when he declared adequate strength to be one of the three pillars of his foreign policy; without adequate military power our nation could not attain or maintain peace.

From the President's Strategy for Peace, we derive this guideline for Defense planning:

> Our goal is to prevent wars, to maintain a realistic and ready military force aimed at deterring aggression—adequate to handle aggression should deterrence fail. As Secretary of Defense, I believe that in terms of force levels and expenditures, we can make the transition from war to lasting peace and expanding freedom with an efficient and modernized U.S. military force that, in peacetime, would require no more than seven percent of Gross National Product or less and be made up of no more than 2.5 million men and women who are volunteers. Combined with adequate strength, true partnership and constructive negotiations, such a force is designed to deter war.

*   *   *

A. Security Policy and Strategy in Perspective. The security a nation enjoys at any given time is, in great part, the result of past efforts, particularly in the area of technology. The United States and other Free World nations clearly enjoy greater security today than they would if the tremendous efforts of the past twenty years had not been made.

In the past two decades we achieved first place in nuclear capability, became pre-eminent in space, and substantially strengthened our conventional capabilities. Our military power was an important factor in preventing aggression and safeguarding peace in many parts of the world, notably Europe. However, it did not prevent aggression in Indochina.

One problem was that national security policies during the past decade did not focus sufficiently on lowering the probability of *all* forms of war through deterrence of aggressors. The effect of these policies on military planning was to create forces that lowered the probability of nuclear war while stressing a growing U.S. military capability to engage and to fight in other types of conflict.

That this military capability proved not to be an effective deterrent was due to a second major problem in national security planning. This was the failure to correlate closely and fully military strategy, national security strategy, and foreign policy, which embrace all elements of effective deterrence—non-military as well as military.

This Administration believes—and this is the foundation of President Nixon's Strategy for Peace—that our central national security objective is the prevention of war, and the movement toward a generation of peace. A realistic military strategy for the decade of the 1970s cannot be permitted to become an end in itself. It must be an inseparable part of a broader national strategy of deterrence, and meaningfully related to our pressing requirements in the domestic field.

*   *   *

B. The Changing Environment—Prelude to the 1970s. When the Nixon Administration assumed office in January 1969, it was clear that our complex national security problems demanded a basic rethinking of the existing policies in the light of changing world and domestic conditions. It was clear that new directions were needed. . . .

At least seven factors, taken together, indicate that the economic, political, military, and manpower realities existing now are significantly different from the situation just five years ago. These factors are:

- A growing Soviet military capability and technological momentum.

- An expanding Soviet influence around the world, as evidenced by worldwide deployment of its growing naval forces.

- An emerging Chinese Communist nuclear threat.

- The reordering of national priorities, with a reduced percentage of Gross National Product for defense spending.

- Sharply rising U.S. personnel costs and a start toward Zero-Draft and an All-Volunteer military force.

- A changing world economic environment because of vigorous growth, particularly among Free World nations.

- An increasing awareness among NATO members of the need for burden sharing and among many of our Asian friends of the need for regional support.

Confronted with this changing environment, we concluded after careful analysis in the National Security Council that we must, whatever else, assure the following criteria in national security planning for the decade of the 1970s:

1. Preservation by the United States of a sufficient strategic nuclear capability as the cornerstone of the Free World's nuclear deterrent.

2. Development and/or continued maintenance of Free World forces that are effective, and minimize the likelihood of requiring the employment of strategic nuclear forces should deterrence fail.

3. An International Security Assistance Program that will enhance effective self-defense capabilities throughout the Free World, and, when coupled with diplomatic and other actions, will encourage regional security agreements among our friends and allies.

C. Transition to a New National Security Strategy. . . . The two major initiatives undertaken in 1969 which have a strong impact on our future defense planning were . . . the Nixon Doctrine and the Strategic Arms Limitation Talks (SALT). The first emphasized our determination to instill a new basis for cooperation between us and our allies which takes into account their growing capabilities. The other demonstrated our commitment to serious and meaningful negotiations as the preferred path toward peace.

SALT is a crucial effort by the United States, in the field of negotiations, to seek agreement with the Soviet Union on strategic arms limitation. SALT represents an attempt (a) to reduce the likelihood of strategic nuclear war between the U.S. and the Soviet Union; and (b) to preserve U.S. strategic sufficiency through negotiations, rather than through competition in an arms race. SALT represents, among other things, an effort to avoid major increases in strategic force expenditures. . . .

The application of the Nixon Doctrine can provide Free World strength and security as a realistic way to support peace initiatives through meaningful negotiations.

* * *

Although both FY 1970 and 1971 were transitional with respect to program and budget levels, the FY 1971 plan contained many of the key elements of the President's Strategy for Peace. Among the elements distinguishing the FY 1971 plan from the previous strategy were:

- a concept of strategic sufficiency which is based on specific criteria for the design of our strategic capabilities;

- a strong conventional capability buttressed by increased burden sharing and improved defense capabilities of other Free World nations;

- adequate peacetime general purpose forces for simultaneously meeting a major Communist attack in either Europe or Asia, assisting allies against non-Chinese threats in Asia, and contending with a contingency elsewhere;

- smaller U.S. active forces, with great emphasis to be given to their readiness and effectiveness, including modernization;

- a re-emphasis on maintaining and using our technological superiority;

- increased international security assistance for the defense needs and roles of other Free World nations; and

- a new approach to U.S. military manpower, based on a goal of Zero Draft and an All-Volunteer active force, with increased reliance on National Guard and Reserve forces.

What has emerged from the review and decisions of the 1969-70 transition years is a new approach to national security planning concepts and a reformulation of older concepts. The new strategy is one of "Realistic Deterrence."

D. A Strategy of Realistic Deterrence. . . . the essential components of the President's Foreign Policy and the interrelated nature of the three pillars of peace—strength, partnership and negotiation—demonstrate in their broadest aspects the close relationship between the President's policy objectives on the one hand, and the close correlation of foreign policy activities guided by the State Department and those aspects of national security strategy which are the primary responsibility of the Department of Defense.

The President's foreign policy objectives concentrate on long-term objectives and long-term policies. He noted in describing the Nixon Doctrine that it is neither practical, nor the most effective way to build a lasting structure of peace, to rely solely upon the material and manpower resources of the United States to provide this capability. We have said, and I would repeat, that we do not intend to be the policeman of the world. Many of our allies are already prosperous; others are rapidly becoming so. Therefore, it is realistic and more effective that the burden of protecting peace and freedom should be shared more fully by our allies and friends.

We seek a structure of peace, in which free nations support each other against common threats according to their proportionate strengths and resources, while each bears the major responsibility for its own defense. The security of all is enhanced if each nation increasingly is able to rely upon itself for its own defense, particularly its own defense manpower.

The Nixon Doctrine, by fostering and encouraging the capabilities of our allies, will enhance world stability. It is designed to foster development of a more effective deterrent—and through it a more stable world—thereby increasing the prospects for meaningful negotiation from a posture of strength around the world.

This approach in defense planning to national and international security—through the pillars of strength and partnership, each nation in a significant role and bearing its appropriate portion of the burden, each committed to working for peace from a strong internal security base—is a strategy of Realistic Deterrence. It forms the foundation for the third pillar—meaningful negotiation.

Turning to the defense posture and force aspects of this strategy . . . I would point out that whatever the outcome of SALT, our strategic forces will remain the cornerstone of the Free World's deterrent against nuclear attack and must always be sufficient for this crucial role. While assuring an adequate deterrent at the strategic and tactical nuclear level, we and our allies also need to maintain strong conventional capabilities. Hence, for those levels in the deterrent spectrum below general nuclear war, the forces to deter Soviet and Chinese adventures clearly must have an adequate warfighting capability, both in limited nuclear and conventional options. This has been reaffirmed during the past two years by a comprehensive reexamination, together with our allies, of our national and our multilateral deterrent capabilities, most especially NATO's historic review of Alliance Defense for the 70s.

As we move toward the President's goal of peace in the decade of the 1970s, the deterrent to localized conflict, apart from large-scale Soviet or Chinese attack, increasingly will be provided by allies and friends who themselves have a capability and national will to defend themselves. Local security would be further enhanced by regional defense arrangements which provide and take advantage of shared capabilities.

1. *Regional variations.* Obviously, no single strategy can be applied in the same exact terms to situations which are sharply different. Therefore, we must fashion the elements of our strategy of Realistic Deterrence to match the various conditions we find in different regions. Let me cite several factors briefly. . . .

In NATO/Europe, U.S. national security strategy for the 1970s must include the objective of maintaining a strong NATO deterrent in Western Europe, including its northern and southern flanks, against a wide range of possible Soviet and Pact initiatives, short of strategic nuclear exchanges. Such initiatives could span a continuum, from border incursions and military-backed political threats to a full-scale conventional or tactical nuclear attack, including conflict at sea.

In Asia, our continuing nuclear superiority vis-à-vis the Chinese can contribute significantly to deterrence of Chinese nuclear attacks, or conventional attacks on our Asian allies, and would be strengthened further with an area ballistic missile defense effective against small attacks. However, there is a need for our Asian friends and allies to strengthen their conventional forces, both to defend themselves against non-Chinese attacks and, in regional conjunction, to build a defensive capability which would give Communist China increased pause before initiating hostilities. At the same time, we will maintain adequate forces to meet our commitments in Asia.

It is not realistic or efficient to expect each country to develop an independent self-defense capability against all levels of non-Chinese and non-Soviet attack. The drain on allied manpower and on their economies would inhibit the achievement of economic growth, and, therefore, the political stability which is essential to military security. At the same time, deep historical, social and political inhibitions to immediate and effective regional mutual security arrangements in some areas must be recognized. Thus, a careful balance must be achieved between independent capabilities and collective arrangements. One of the most important means available to the U.S. to stimulate and to help aid in the development of these capabilities and arrangements is the provision of appropriate security assistance to our allies.

In summary . . . the Strategy of Realistic Deterrence, emphasizing Free World strength and partnership, offers the most feasible approach toward our goal of achieving basic national and international security objectives. This strategy involves a shift in the direction [of] U.S. foreign and security policy. . . . Successful application of the President's Strategy for Peace requires a coordinated application of all foreign policy resources—military power, diplomacy, military and economic assistance, and foreign trade—and most importantly, the understanding and strong support of Congress and the American people.

As the President said in his Foreign Policy Report last month: "Gone for Americans is a foreign policy with the psychological simplicity of worrying primarily about what we want for others. In its place is a role that demands a new type of sustained effort with others."

II. Concepts for Defense Planning

. . . The basic objective of our Strategy of Realistic Deterrence is to prevent armed conflict and ultimately to eliminate its use as a means by which one nation tries to impose its will upon another. But so long as the threat persists that other nations may use force, adequate military power must remain an essential element of Free World strategy.

In defense planning, the Strategy of Realistic Deterrence emphasizes our need to plan for optimum use of all military and related resources available to meet the requirements of Free World security. These Free World military and related resources—which we call "Total Force"—include both active and reserve components of the U.S., those of our allies, and the additional military capabilities of our allies and friends that will be made available through local efforts, or through provision of appropriate security assistance programs.

A. The Total Force Approach.

It needs to be understood with total clarity . . . that defense programs are not infinitely adjustable. . . . There is an absolute point below which our security forces must never be allowed to go. That is the level of sufficiency. Above or at that level, our defense forces protect national security adequately. Below that level is one vast undifferentiated area of no secu-

31

rity at all. For it serves no purpose in conflicts between nations to have been almost strong enough.

President's Foreign Policy
Report to Congress,
February 25, 1971

.... In planning to meet [existing threats to the Free World], we intend to use the Total Force approach. We will plan to use *all* appropriate resources for deterrence—U.S. and Free World—to capitalize on the potential of available assets.

In considering the spectrum of potential conflict, we will be guided by the following principles in our defense planning:

- In deterring *strategic nuclear war*, primary reliance will continue to be placed on U.S. strategic deterrent forces.

- In deterring *theater nuclear war*, the U.S. also has primary responsibility, but certain of our allies are able to share this responsibility by virtue of their own nuclear capabilities.

- In deterring *theater conventional warfare*—for example, a major war in Europe—U.S. and allied forces share the responsibility.

- In deterring *sub-theater or localized warfare*, the country or ally which is threatened bears the primary burden, particularly for providing manpower; but when U.S. interests or obligations are at stake, we must be prepared to provide help as appropriate through military and economic assistance to those nations willing to assume their share of responsibility for their own defense. When required and appropriate, this help would consist essentially of backup logistical support and sea and air combat support. In some special cases, it could include ground combat support as well.

Moreover, U.S. involvement in world affairs is not based exclusively on our alliances, but rather, our formal and informal obligations derive from and are shaped by our own national interests. To protect our interests, we must insure free use of international air space and free access to the world's oceans. Thus, our future defense planning must also insure a U.S. capability to prevent an effective challenge to free use of international air space and the oceans of the world.

The significance of Total Force planning perhaps is best illustrated by examining its military application to NATO.

As has been stated, the U.S. bears primary responsibility in the field of strategic and theater nuclear weapons, although in the latter case certain of our allies also contribute significant forces. Our strategic forces must be sufficient now and in the future, since they are a cornerstone of the Free World's deterrent. By providing strong, effective and survivable strategic forces, reliable and effective intelligence and command and control, and other necessary capabilities in our strategic posture, we seek to convince potential opponents that recourse to the holocaust of general nuclear war will continue to be an irrational and unsuccessful option.

U.S. strategic forces relate primarily to the deterrence of a strategic nuclear attack. They also serve an important role, together with theater and tactical nuclear capabilities, in deterring conflict below the level of general nuclear war.

However, as the last two decades have demonstrated, reliance on a nuclear capability alone is by no means sufficient to inhibit or deter aggression. A sufficient nuclear capability must be coupled with a sufficient conventional capability in both our own forces and in those of our allies. This conventional capability must be adequate to meet aggression in the sophisticated environment which would be expected in a conflict with the Warsaw Pact. If these NATO forces are to deter this type of aggression, they must be capable of confronting it with such capabilities as strong armor and anti-tank forces, appropriate air power for air superiority and ground combat support, strong naval forces to support NATO's flanks, and other combat and support forces.

In addition, such a conflict would require reinforcement and augmentation from the U.S. and would undoubtedly involve conflict at sea. Therefore, we and our allies must be able to control wherever necessary the air and sea lanes needed to support U.S. and allied forces abroad.

Finally, because some of our NATO allies—for example, Greece and Turkey—do not have and cannot afford needed modern equipment, it is in our interest to help them modernize their forces, and to rely on them to man and operate those forces. Conversely, we must and do expect that those NATO allies who are able to do so will improve their contributions to the common defense through appropriate programs, financial participation, and force modernization.

In summary, through application of all resources across (1) the full spectrum of possible *conflict* and (2) the full spectrum of *capabilities,* we intend to maintain sufficient U.S. strength and to mesh this strength with that of other nations in a new order of partnership. If we are to achieve a lasting peace, we must work together to deter aggression, to prevent war.

We will apply the Total Force Concept in non-NATO areas as well. The President stated in his Foreign Policy Report to Congress last year, in a passage with particular application to Asia, that our friends and allies must bear an increasing responsibility for their own defense.

In his second annual Foreign Policy Report to Congress last month, he said:

> We will continue to provide elements of military strength and economic resources appropriate to our size and our interests. But it is no longer natural or possible in this age to argue that security or development around the globe is primarily America's concern. The defense and progress of other countries must be first their responsibility and second, a regional responsibility. Without the foundations of self-help and regional help, American help will not succeed. The United States can and will participate, where our interests dictate, but as *a* weight—not *the* weight—in the scale.

When the Nixon Administration assumed office in January, 1969, just the opposite was the case in Southeast Asia. U.S. forces were carrying the major part of the burden. Our first challenge under President Nixon's Strategy for Peace was to reverse the trend toward greater and greater involvement of Americans in ground combat. We set out to end American military involvement in the Indochina fighting.

A key element for the success of our new strategy is the need for Total Force planning in an even wider context than defense planning alone. This wider context embraces all Free World assets—military and non-military—which can help prevent the outbreak or continuation of conflict, while fostering freedom, peace, self-determination and cooperation among nations.

*   *   *

C. Total Force Planning and International Security Assistance. The challenging objectives of the Nixon Doctrine can be achieved . . . only if we and our allies both contribute to their achievement.

Each nation must do its share to contribute what it can appropriately provide: manpower from many of our allies; technology, material, specialized skills from the United States. By furnishing the materiel and related training support essential to develop and maintain such forces, the International Security Assistance Program serves as a key instrument of the Nixon Doctrine. It is for these reasons that security assistance assumes new importance for initiatives in the area of national security and foreign policy, through which the Administration seeks to reduce both the total cost of an adequate defense posture and our overseas involvement.

Many willing and potentially helpful friends and allies simply do not have the resources or technical capabilities to assume greater responsibility for their own defense. Unless we help them, the basic policy of diminishing the need for direct U.S. military involvement, without impairing Free World security, cannot be successful.

The better equipped our friends and allies are to provide for their own security, the more firm will be our own security. This is so because the probability of war and of U.S. involvement in war will be lowered.

An effective security assistance program can allow an increasing replacement of U.S. forces—particularly ground combat forces—with local forces. A vigorous and successful security assistance program can also help achieve a period of more meaningful negotiations and a less dangerous world environment as part of the program to attain our objectives: lasting peace and expanding freedom—that is our hope and that is our goal.

D. New Initiatives to Support a Strategy of Realistic Deterrence. The Strategy of Realistic Deterrence calls for new initiatives and new concepts to complement Total Force planning. Some of these initiatives will fall in areas where the U.S. bears the primary responsibility, while others will stem from closer integration of our planning with that of our friends and allies. Some may more properly be called new directions or redirections of effort, rather than initiatives. Regardless of what they may be called, we believe they are necessary—to modernize our forces, reshape them to future environments, and to provide for our security.

1. U.S. force planning initiatives. The Free World relies on U.S. strategic forces as the cornerstone of its deterrent. As President Nixon has stated, our strategic force policy is one of sufficiency. In addition to our diplomatic initiative in SALT, we believe that it is appropriate to explore a range of new concepts for future strategic force planning. Depending on progress in SALT or the growth in the military threat, particularly from the Soviet Union, we may or may not need to implement some of these concepts. . . .

Another difficult area in planning our forces for the future is the range of potential crisis situations which may require positioning of general purpose forces. In the past, these forces have been designed primarily for sophisticated conventional theater warfare, although provisions were included for minor contingency and limited war conflict situations. We are investigating possible modifications to selected portions of our existing forces, both to enhance overall capabilities and to improve the responsiveness of our forces.

One major step we have taken is our new policy with respect to

35

Reserve Forces. Members of the National Guard and Reserve, instead of draftees, will be the initial and primary source for augmentation of the active forces in any future emergency requiring a rapid and substantial expansion of the active forces.

Lower sustaining costs of non-active duty forces, as compared to the cost of maintaining larger active duty forces, make possible a greater flexibility in planning the Total Force structure. This lower cost of non-active forces allows more force units to be provided for the same cost as an all-active force structure, or the same number of force units to be maintained for lesser cost. However, it also requires that the capability and mobilization readiness of Guard and Reserve units be promptly and effectively enhanced. . . .

*   *   *

3. Force planning with our allies. The concept of force planning with our allies is not new; it is our objective to revitalize and improve this important military contribution to Free World security.

In NATO planning the United States must fully and effectively pursue detailed and integrated long-range planning and actions—including research and development, procurement, training and operations—that are appropriate for a total-NATO force. Our recent efforts represent major steps in the direction of making sure that NATO forces indeed do constitute a realistic deterrent to Warsaw Pact aggression.

The NATO Ministerial meetings in Brussels last December [1970] . . . evidenced a new spirit in NATO—one in which our Allies fully recognized the existing realities and resolved on their own to take more of the defense burden upon their own shoulders.

I believe that three items of particular significance emerged from these meetings. First, the Ministers approved the NATO AD-70 Study accomplished over the preceding six months. It highlighted the need for more conventional deterrence and pointed out specific inadequacies in existing NATO capabilities. There was a unanimous feeling that more must be done in the conventional field and that modern and sufficient NATO tactical and strategic capabilities must be maintained.

A second important area was that of detente. . . .

A third important area, that of burden sharing, set precedents which constitute a significant first step toward more equitable sharing of the NATO defense burden. Ten European nations agreed among themselves to provide almost a billion dollars of additional expenditures over the next five years, divided about equally between improvements to their own forces and contributions to an additional infrastructure program for better communications and aircraft shelters. This is the most tangible evidence yet of European recognition that Europe must do more in its own behalf. . . . It is the first important common move toward force improvement in the last 10-12 years. This demonstration of European awareness of the strategic, fiscal, manpower, and political realities and their determination to face them is good for both Europe and ourselves.

We are continuing our studies and planning to integrate more closely all the resources available within NATO, to improve our procedures for management and mobilization, and thereby enhance NATO's capabilities.

Other examples of closer cooperation include the modernization program for Korean armed forces, and of course, the entire Vietnamization program.

But there are additional steps we are taking or planning to improve both our own and allied capabilities. One area involves a more cooperative R&D effort. . . . we desire to eliminate any unnecessary duplication in weapons systems research and development activity. To the degree that such duplication can be reduced, our overall force capabilities can be improved at lower cost.

Although this plan is not without disadvantages, it has been carefully weighed. We believe that it is in our mutual interest to proceed along these lines with our allies.

Similarly, we believe that our R&D program has a definite role to play in implementing the Nixon Doctrine. Suitable military assistance to our allies is frequently limited both by the items in the U.S. inventory, which may not necessarily be appropriate to the situation at hand and, in some cases, by a lack of knowledge of the technical and economic problems facing these countries. There are several areas where appropriate effort can help insure that suitable equipment or assistance commensurate with allied capabilities is provided.

*   *   *

. . . Our goal is to provide equipment to reduce dependence upon U.S. forces, select equipment which offers an optimized military capability for the funds available, and provide options for more sophisticated U.S. general purpose equipment as appropriate and commensurate with the capabilities of a friend or ally.

POLITICAL REALISM AND THE "REALISTIC DETERRENCE" STRATEGY

A. Trofimenko

In the following article, published in the Soviet periodical Ekonomika, Politika, Ideologiya, *the Nixon Doctrine and its strategy of "realistic deterrence" are analyzed from a Marxist perspective. The author examines the "new realities" which shaped American national security policy in the 1970s and concludes that the strategy of realistic deterrence differs little from the Kennedy-Johnson strategy of "flexible response" and remains committed to the preservation of global imperialist interests.*

Trofimenko agrees with Nixon administration officials that changing circumstances in domestic and international politics necessitated a new American approach to world affairs. The emergence of new centers of power, such as Western Europe, Japan, and China, the achievement of nuclear parity between the United States and the Soviet Union, and the increasingly strident demands within the United States for a reordering of national priorities all contributed to a fundamental change in American security policy. The author believes the change was actually one of tactics, however, rather than of objectives, with the United States shifting the primary combat burden for its world "policeman" role onto the shoulders of its allies. The United States, aside from providing support for those allies, would attempt to enhance the utility of its nuclear arsenal in deterring lesser conflicts.

The author concludes that the strategy of realistic deterrence "only continues the futile search for ways and means of waging war which are without danger for the United States," and that there can be very little realism in such a policy.

Some two years after coming to power, Nixon's Republican administration officially announced that it had revised the "national security strategy" or, in other words, the U.S. military-political strategy. As a result of this revision—the fourth since the end of World War II—the "flexible response" strategy, the U.S. operational strategy in the sixties, was replaced by the "realistic deterrence" strategy. This new U.S. strategy was advanced by Defense Secretary M. Laird in his statement on the U.S. military program for 1972–1975 in the House of Representatives Armed Services Committee on March 9, 1971.

What, then, is the essence of the new strategy? In what way is it

Source: *Foreign Broadcast Information Service, Soviet Union* (10 December 1971), pp. H1-H13.

new? What demands does it make on the U.S. Armed Forces and armaments, and what ways and means of utilizing them does it outline? To answer these questions, it is necessary, above all, to investigate the logic of Washington's approach to this matter. First it is necessary to take a look at the process of changes, so to speak, from the "American ivory tower," and to ascertain which flaws in the former strategy—strictly from Washington's viewpoint—the new strategy is intended to remove. This is the only way to ascertain the direction in which the evolution of U.S. military-political strategy is going.

I

Above all, from the viewpoint of the present U.S. leaders, the basic weakness of the "flexible response" strategy was rooted in the fact that it was not realistic. By emphasizing the present "realism," the new formula itself—"realistic deterrence"—characterizes the previous course as unrealistic and impracticable. One can fully agree with this, the more so since, as the U.S. Vietnam fiasco has shown, the former U.S. strategic course really did not take into account many objective factors of the international situation; this is where its unrealistic nature showed through.

U.S. leaders and theoreticians give a quite specific interpretation of the negative, that is, unrealistic . . . aspects of the former strategy. Defense Secretary M. Laird points out that the "flexible response" strategy "was realistic from the viewpoint of deterring nuclear war." However, in its approach to conventional war it proved unsound and unrealistic; it "did not prevent us getting involved in the most prolonged conflict in our history."[1]

It is clear that in this case Laird is distressed not because of the very fact of involvement as such; . . . he is troubled by the duration of the conflict or, more precisely, by the lack of success of the overseas military operation undertaken by the United States in the hope of rapid success. To correct Washington's strategic course and breathe "realism" into it, it is necessary, according to Laird, in the first place to correct the basic shortcoming of the former course: its inability to prevent the United States from getting into impasse military situations of the Vietnam type.

Of course, it is undeniable that the new U.S. strategy does not absolutely reject the previous one on a broad plane but makes it more specific and develops it. As a strategy of the U.S. ruling class (and as any class strategy in general) it maintains, regardless of its specific formulations, the continuity of the fundamental aims and purposes of

---

[1]*Commanders Digest*, 1 May 1971, p. 2.

this class, which have been worked out over the decades, and the immutability of the general approach to the methods of achieving the aims. Emphasizing the deep roots of class strategy, V.I. Lenin said that to understand war it is necessary to place it in relation to the policy of the state and the class in question which has been pursued throughout the preceding decades.

Under modern conditions another factor, which reduces the possibility of implementing radical and rapid changes in strategy, has an increasingly strong effect. It is a question, first, of the enormous cost of the basic nucleus of the armed forces of large states—strategic weapons systems—and, second, the length of the cycle from "the conception of an idea to the combat deployment of a system," which is connected with the exceptional complexity of the above-mentioned systems. By virtue of this the U.S. military-political strategy is embodied not only in the already developed strategic armaments but also in those systems which still do not actually exist "in the flesh," that is, in metal, and which will become realities only in several years time. But they have already been ordered, and industry is working on them. Therefore, a fundamental change in theory, so radical that some of the previous systems would become unnecessary, is virtually impossible under the conditions of a capitalist economy.

This is why no subsequent U.S. strategy can signify a cardinal break with a previous one, particularly at the initial stage of a new strategic course. Above all, it is advanced as a declaration of what is desired and as a definition of the long-term prospects of building the armed forces and armaments and of methods of utilizing them in a new manner, but under conditions when the former strategy is still operating. Thus, the existing weapons systems were created according to the recipes of former strategy, but their gradual buildup created the precondition for a transition from quantity to quality, and this new quality exerts an influence on the development of strategic thinking and demands, as Nixon put it, "new definitions of strength."

In speaking of the qualitative changes in U.S. military strength throughout the sixties, it should be emphasized that these changes were not of the same stamp. Having increased in absolute significance both in its conventional and nuclear aspects, this strength did not create "supremacy." In 1969 R. Nixon unequivocally stated the fact of equality between the strategic arsenals of the United States and the Soviet Union. "The gap has been eliminated," he declared. "It will never again exist."

This further change in the alignment of forces between the chief power of imperialism and the leading socialist country in the latter's favor is the most important factor (even from the subjective viewpoint of Washington's leaders) among the "four realities" which Laird frequently and persistently speaks of as the chief motives for changing U.S. strategy.

"We," the U.S. defense secretary declares with regard to the new U.S. strategy, "call it realistic because it is intended to take into [account the] actual reality which the United States and the rest of the world are encountering in these difficult times. . . . The four chief factors of actual reality which led to the adoption of the new strategy are these: Strategic reality, financial reality, the manpower reality, and political reality. Strategic reality includes, above all, the colossal growth in military might of the Soviet Union, which was clearly inferior to us in strength at the start of the sixties and which has today almost achieved parity."[2]

Discussing other factors of "strategic reality," U.S. strategists also emphasize the acquisition by the People's Republic of China [P.R.C.] of a nuclear capability and the anti-Soviet direction of the present Peking leadership's policy. In planning U.S. strategy for the seventies, the Washington leaders clearly proceeded from the premise that, with the maintenance of the present situation in China, the P.R.C. leadership will not act in solidarity with the U.S.S.R. in one crisis situation or another connected with military provocation by the United States or its allies.

In general, U.S. strategists and leaders consider the intensification of the so-called multipolarity of the world to be a most important factor of strategic reality. When the U.S. theoreticians Kissinger, Morgenthau, Shulman, and Brzezinski, for example, discuss the replacement of the U.S.-U.S.S.R. "bipolar opposition" world by a multipolar world, this may appear to some to be merely another pseudo-scientific embellishment designed by the refined mind of one U.S. "policy maker" or another to impart greater credibility to his academic schemes. In fact the multipolarity concept is primarily a recognition by U.S. theoreticians of the limited nature of U.S. imperialism's potential in the modern world.

When the U.S. [advocates] of the policy of "strength" in the mid-fifties advanced the theory of the world's "bipolarity"—the theory of the decisive opposition of two "superpowers"—they left out of their reckoning all the remaining states as being secondary ones which may be virtually ignored in an analysis of the overall strategic balance. It suddenly turned out that Vietnam, which, according to all the U.S. calculations a "superpower" such as the United States ought not to take into account, disrupted all the plans of the Washington strategists. After six years of a most bloody war they were forced to

[2]*Commanders Digest*, 1 May 1971, p. 2.

"renounce the attempt to impose a purely military solution on the battlefield" as unattainable for the United States in Vietnam.[3]

The concept of the world's multipolarity, which is now being advanced by U.S. policy makers, is quite broad and comprehensive: it embraces a recognition of the appearance of new "centers of power" in the capitalist world such as the European Economic Community or Japan, realization of the well-known lack of convergence between the interests of the United States and the policies and interests of many of its chief capitalist allies, even with regard to the socialist countries, and understanding of the fact that the U.S. "strategic nuclear missile force" is not automatically a political influence and that in the majority of conflict situations in the "Third World" it cannot be used even as a real threat.

However, it is important to emphasize here that all these more or less correct statements began to be set forth in public by U.S. theoreticians only at the end of the sixties, after the failure of the U.S. military intervention in Indochina had become obvious to all the world, and U.S. ideologists had been faced with the necessity of explaining theoretically the fact of the nonomnipotence of U.S. imperialism in the world and, at the same time, somehow to prepare U.S. public opinion for a possible modification of the U.S. position in its approach to "local" or "counterinsurgent" wars.

One more conclusion is drawn from the same multipolarity concept by the U.S. leadership with respect to U.S. partners and allies. Washington is increasingly beginning to realize that, just as it cannot deal with "small opponents" "in its own way"—easily, quickly, and with impunity—so also it cannot very well manipulate its "junior partners" in the capitalist world from positions of the notorious "nuclear force," as it did more or less freely in the fifties. (However, even in the fifties Washington's *diktat* with respect to America's partners sometimes did not work—in those cases when the demands of the United States ran excessively counter to the national interests of its allies. One example of this is the refusal of the French National Assembly to ratify the treaty on the creation of the European Defense Community in August 1954.)

Since the United States is not omniscient and omnipotent (a fact, incidentally, recognized long ago by J. Kennedy, who, although having recognized the fact, drew from it few practical conclusions for U.S. foreign policy) to maintain its leadership in the pan-imperialist and anti-communist policy of the West, it is having to rely ever increasingly upon the assistance and cooperation of its capitalist partners (and, at

---

[3] See President Nixon's speech on Vietnam, 14 May 1969, *International Herald Tribune*, 16 May 1969.

the same time, competitors) and reckon with the latters' definite national interests.

The fact that the principle of partnership was the first strategic principle publicly formulated by the Republican administration (the "Nixon Doctrine") even before its proclamation of the new military-political strategy, confirms the extremely great importance which is attached to this principle by the present Washington leadership.

The need for new, more flexible forms of maintaining leadership in the imperialist camp, if indeed the United States intends making more extensive and active use of the forces of its allies in the class struggle in the world arena, is one of the factors of the "political reality" which the creators of the new U.S. strategy are having to take into account along with "strategic reality." The same category of political reality also includes the domestic policy situation in the United States itself, where the popular masses are demanding increasingly decisively and loudly the renunciation of military adventures abroad and the administration's turning to face the internal socioeconomic problems. Recognizing this reality, President Nixon said: "We must not undertake more abroad than the public opinion in our own country is capable of assessing positively."

Of course, this recognition by the President does not mean that the U.S. administration always attentively heeds public opinion when formulating its foreign policy. On the contrary, the optimum policy for any government of a bourgeois country is either to ignore public opinion or to create an artificial climate of support for official policy in the country by means of the propagandist manipulation of public opinion. However, as has been shown by the American people's reaction to the aggression in Vietnam, the possibilities for such manipulation are not infinite. Moments arise when the split between the sentiments and feelings of broad public circles and official policy proves so deep that a bourgeois government, wishing to remain in power, has either to correct official policy or to resign from power and hand over the reins of government to another grouping (party) of the ruling class, which puts forward one "alternative" or another.

*   *   *

The third "reality" is the direct result of the dollar crisis, which has been created by excessive U.S. military expenditures abroad throughout the period since World War II. On the foreign plane Washington is encountering the real problem of a lack of means to fulfill on its former scale its functions as the gendarme of the capitalist world. On the domestic plane financial reality is turning into permanent and increasing inflation, which is once again connected with the colossal military expenditures which lead to a chronic budget deficit.

In an attempt to take account of financial reality the U.S. administration, on the one hand, is striving by persuasion and exhortation and also by means of unilateral financial and economic measures to transfer part of its expenditures (including military expenditures) for maintaining the world capitalist economic system to its partners, loading onto their shoulders an additional financial burden. On the other hand, it is striving somehow to stabilize the level of U.S. military expenditures at least for the period of the present and the next presidential terms.

. . . This apology for stabilization will mean, first, a certain, although perhaps not very considerable, increase in the U.S. military budget in absolute figures; and, second—and this is very important—that the $30 billion which the administration has spent on the war in Vietnam and which, in the event of the withdrawal of the U.S. armed forces, could be wholly directed to the civilian economy for purposes, let us say, of public health, will go to modernize armaments and to raise the "quality" of the U.S. strategic arsenal, as the defense secretary has plainly stated.

Thus, on this question the certain realism connected with recognizing the paramount importance of internal civilian problems is brought to naught by militarism, which has become a way of life for many in the United States, for those who hope to continue to feed off the federal military pie.

The problem of manpower is yet another real problem for the U.S. leadership. According to Laird, there is a certain shortage of human resources and, in particular, of specialists with high qualifications, who would wish to link their career with the army. The problem also lies in the high cost of the personnel's maintenance, on which 52 percent of all expenditures of the military budget is spent.

The people's negative attitude toward the army, which manifests itself, in particular, in the fact that veterans of the war in Vietnam, as distinct from the heroes of the antifascist war [World War II], enjoy no honor and respect among the population, complicates the Pentagon's problem of recruiting cadres. . . .

The administration has advanced plans to end the call-up for military service by 1974 and to create a completely volunteer army, hoping to solve the manpower problem by granting servicemen certain privileges.

Finally, one more factor influencing the change in military strategy is the rapid development of military equipment under the conditions of the scientific and technical revolution. The decisive transformations in the means of waging war render inevitable the systematic revision of the methods of waging war and of the methods of utilizing armaments and the armed forces.

*   *   *

Thus, having established that the Republican administration took into account the combined effect of real factors when formulating the "realistic deterrence" strategy, we must recognize the novelty of this strategy with reservations regarding the class nature of U.S. military-political doctrine and its aims. To say that nothing new has appeared in the U.S. strategy means failing to take into account imperialism's attempts to adapt itself to the new situation in the world, which was spoken of at the 24th CPSU Congress.

II

Having ascertained which factors of actual reality are being taken into account by the Republican administration, one may also take a look at the realistic deterrence strategy itself and at its essence and see in which direction this strategy is evolving in comparison with the previous one—the Kennedy-Johnson flexible response strategy. A comparative analysis of these policies will make it possible to answer the question as to what new elements the realistic deterrence strategy introduces to the U.S. military position.

Since the present U.S. leaders and theoreticians believe that the Kennedy-Johnson line, as far as nuclear war is concerned, was completely realistic, it is evident that the changes being made by the realistic deterrence strategy to this aspect of the previous concept and, correspondingly, to the building of the U.S. nuclear forces, must be minimal. Indeed, as far as one can judge from the information published, the Nixon administration intends to continue to rely, at least for the next few years, on the same backbone of the strategic forces which were created by the decisions of the previous administrations, continuing, at the same time, to modernize these forces at the rate and in the direction outlined by the activities of the previous administrations. Thus, in this aspect—nuclear armaments—the flexible response strategy seems to the present Republican leadership quite realistic and in U.S. interests.

But of what, one wonders, does the realism of this aspect of the flexible response strategy consist—realism without quotation marks, not simply determined subjectively from Washington, but from the viewpoint of compliance by the U.S. strategic policy with the objective situation in the world and, primarily, with the alignment of forces between socialism and imperialism, the U.S.S.R. and the United States?

To get at the root of the question, the realism of the Kennedy-

Johnson administrations in the strategic forces sphere lay in the realization of the fact of the devaluation of the U.S. nuclear missile arsenal under the conditions of the growth in the U.S.S.R.'s military might. Kennedy and Johnson, McNamara and Clifford, understood the impossibility of the United States' achieving victory in a nuclear missile war against the U.S.S.R., for the United States would gain nothing politically in such a conflict but might lose everything. Therefore, J. Kennedy's administration, having repudiated the Dulles strategy of massive retaliation with its impossibly provocative nature (the threat to inflict nuclear strikes "at moments and in places" to be chosen by the United States), already virtually admitted the impossibility of using a big war as a means of policy, regarding the strategic nuclear missile potential as a means of restraining the other side from inflicting the first strike against the United States.

But since, in reality, it was a question all these years not of restraining the U.S.S.R. from attacking the United States but, on the contrary, of the U.S.S.R. restraining U.S. imperialism from unleashing a big thermonuclear war, the U.S. concept of deterrence signifies, in fact, a recognition that the Soviet Union possesses such strategic strength which effectively restrains the United States from direct use of its nuclear missile arsenal against the U.S.S.R. This is how the situation of the well-known nuclear balance between the U.S.S.R. and the United States arose, which is characterized by the second part of the formula of the new strategy, that is, by the word *deterrence*. Recognizing the colossal destructive nature of a central nuclear missile conflict and the reality of nuclear or strategic parity, the realistic deterrence strategy officially proceeds from U.S. reluctance to be the initiator of unleashing such a conflict and stipulates only the U.S. right and resolve to inflict a counterstrike in the event of an attack on itself.

The previous strategy of flexible response was also chiefly characterized by such an approach to the direct use of the U.S. strategic arsenal against the "chief opponent." The authors of the new strategy hope to raise the effectiveness of this arsenal not by direct means but with the help of indirect politico-psychological pressure. (The problem of the psychological effect of nuclear weapons not only on the field of battle—at the time of their physical use—but also under the conditions of "confrontation," is undoubtedly a problem which deserves the specialists' closest attention. The strategic concept of nuclear deterrence is, in its very essence, a concept of psychological influence on the opponent.) In this respect they perceive favorable possibilities for themselves in balancing between the U.S.S.R. and the People's Republic of China and in defending in this way their own imperialist interests.

It was not this new element of the realistic deterrence strategy which predetermined the appearance of the epithet *realistic* in its formulation. The Republican administration needed the adjective *realistic* to emphasize that, as distinct from the Kennedy-Johnson administrations, it demonstrates realism not only in the nuclear missile aspect of the strategy but also in its approach to conflict in general and, primarily, in its approach to conflicts of the conventional type, such as the Vietnam conflict.

But of what does the realism of the new strategic course consist in this second, conventional aspect?

According to Washington, the realistic deterrence strategy, as distinct from the previous one which dragged the United States into a bloody, costly, and hopeless war, promises to insure peace throughout the life of an entire generation.

In what way? Perhaps Washington has decided to renounce war as a means of policy?

It is clear to anyone who follows U.S. policy to the slightest degree that the present Washington leaders do not intend to implement anything like a renunciation of war. Having renounced for the most egoistic reasons possible—reasons of self-preservation—the initiative in unleashing a big nuclear missile war, they in no way intend to altogether repudiate war as a means of policy. The present Washington leaders' philosophy on this score is quite well known. President Nixon believes that "peace demands force."[4] Henry Kissinger, his leading adviser, the imprint of whose views is more than noticeable in the formulations of the new strategy, has repeatedly declared that "war must be made a utilized instrument of policy"[5] and that "the incapacity to use force may perpetuate all disputes."[6]

According to the new strategy, Washington is by no means thinking of excluding war altogether but of reducing the chances of the direct participation of U.S. manpower in conflicts. Herein lies the key to the so-called realism of the new strategy. "One of the chief aims of this strategy," Laird says, "is to prevent the participation of Americans in future Vietnams."[7]

There will not be a big war, at least in the next decade, between the United States and the U.S.S.R. or the United States and the P.R.C., the U.S. leaders reason, and we shall exclude a small war (for the Americans!) by shifting the waging of it onto the shoulders of the U.S. partners. This is the essence of Washington's new strategic approach,

---

[4]*Congressional Record*, 18 February 1970, p. H 925.

[5]*The Center Magazine*, vol. 4, no. 1, January-February 1971, p. 59.

[6]H. Kissinger, *Nuclear Weapons and Foreign Policy*, New York, 1957, p. 4.

[7]*Commanders Digest*, 1 May 1971, p. 7.

which is intended to correct the "nonrealism" of the former strategic policy.

The forms and direction of the building of the conventional branches of the U.S. armed forces, which find their main reflection in the concept of "combined force" [total force] formulated in Laird's report are determined in accordance with this new approach. Promoting this concept, Washington is trying increasingly to regard the armed forces of U.S. partners and allies as a direct continuation of the United States' own "military arm."

> Laird says: We intend to use the approach from the position of combined force with which it is possible to dispose of all the resources of the United States and of the free world for the purpose of deterrence. With the aid of the use of all forces within the limits of the whole spectrum of possible conflict and the complete enlistment of the capabilities of our friends and allies we shall maintain an adequate force for the United States and we shall couple this force with the other nations in a new system of partnership. For the U.S. forces the concept of combined force will mean to enhance the importance of our National Guard and reserve units.[8]

From the data published by the Pentagon on the U.S. general purpose forces it follows that the planned reductions in their numbers to achieve a certain stabilization of military expenditures, and to prepare for a transition to the voluntary principle of forming the armed forces, are not essentially reflected in the total number of U.S. units in a state of high mobilization readiness (including the trained reserve and National Guard units). At the same time, as before, the Pentagon intends to maintain the high combat readiness of the mobile forces, equipping them with the latest means of air and sea transport. The stress placed on building up the U.S. ground units testifies to the fact that they are intended, as before, for use in operations outside U.S. borders. The desire to insure for the United States great freedom of action in the use of U.S. armed forces in the world arena also dictates the increasingly great turn of the U.S. leadership to the "blue water strategy" or the "naval option," in the terminology of U.S. theorists.

However, the quantitative aspect of military preparations in the field of conventional forces is nonetheless now regarded by Washington as primarily a matter for U.S. partners and allies in various military blocs. Washington sees its fundamental task as improving the quality of the U.S. strategic nuclear missile arsenal—which is regarded as the

---

[8]Statement of Secretary of Defense Melvin R. Laird before the House Armed Service Committee on the fiscal year 1972–76 defense program and 1972 defense budget (Washington: 9 March 1971), p. 5.

nucleus of the armed forces, the main "deterrent factor,"—and also the modernization of the conventional U.S. Armed Forces on the basis of new equipment.

By expanding military partnership and promoting U.S. allies to the foreground as the main and, according to the optimum variation, the only suppliers of manpower for waging "local wars," the Washington leaders are trying to create freedom of action for themselves in critical situations, having to some extent freed themselves from the rigid obligations and concepts which required the indispensable military participation of the U.S. Armed Forces in any conflicts which threatened to change the social status quo to the advantage of the progressive, democratic, anti-imperialist forces. . . . This shifting of the load of waging local conflicts onto U.S. partners and allies also contains the "new realism" of the strategy of realistic deterrence and on it is founded the promise of "insuring peace for the present generation of Americans."

The new realism is an attempt to adapt Washington's former pragmatic philosophy to the conditions of the seventies. Washington has never removed from its foreign policy tools the principle of "don't do it yourself when others can do it for you." Guided by precisely this principle, the U.S. leaders began an anti-Communist crusade in the first years after World War II. They hastily knocked together various anti-Communist military blocs and alliances throughout the world, calculating that, under the general ideological leadership of the United States and with U.S. military aid, real battles on the "front borders" would be waged by others—U.S. military partners and allies.

However, Washington's gamble on the military force of others has proved a loser. From its interference in the civil war in Greece at the end of the forties to Vietnam, the United States has had to act basically alone. In Washington this is explained by the fact that for a long time U.S. partners and allies were weak, while its scornful attitude to its partners under the former U.S. leadership only intensified the latters' reluctance to offer their necks to defend "joint" but essentially American interests. Now, it is explained further, when the United States has changed its scornful attitude toward its allies for "an equal and just" attitude, when many of these allies have "stood on their own feet," Washington considers that U.S. partners will increase their "contribution to the common cause" (that is, to the common imperialist strategy) both by accelerating and expanding the scale of military building and by providing manpower for waging local and counterinsurgent wars.

How realistic is this aspect of the strategy of realistic deterrence, and how real is Washington's hope of waging local wars by foreign hands?

To the extent to which the interests of the United States and its "trusties" in local aggression coincide, there can be some grounds for such hope. The classic example on this plane is the activity of Israel, which by its aggressive policy has implemented both its own expansionist designs and the aims of U.S. imperialism in the Near East.

The practice of postwar years shows, however, that the interests of the United States and its possible local partners have fully or even essentially coincided in far from all conflict situations. Most often quite strong divergence of interests is observed even if one examines the regional policy of such states as, for instance, Great Britain, the Federal Republic of Germany, Portugal, Pakistan, Japan, and Australia which gave the most active support to the U.S. foreign policy course in the postwar epoch. All this makes the gamble of the strategy of realistic deterrence on the effective military force of U.S. partners, with the aim of using it against a "third party," extremely unsubstantiated and unrealistic.

Evidently Nixon, Laird, and Kissinger realize that there are few U.S. partners who will "just like that" risk thrusting their heads into a noose for the sake of maintaining friendship with Washington (surely the Vietnam lesson is obvious to all). Realizing this, the U.S. leaders hope by the determination and firmness of their position to arouse a policemanlike zeal in others. Demonstrating the firmness and determination of the United States toward the use of force "in the event of necessity," President Nixon declared in his second foreign policy message to Congress: "Potential enemies must know that in our retaliatory actions we shall choose any degree of intensiveness essential for protecting our interests." The Republican administration is thereby, as it were, giving us to understand that it rejects the "rotten" and "fallacious" principle of the "measured out use of force" which it regards as the most important characteristic of the strategy of "flexible response. . . ." This declared "rejection" by the new strategy of the principle of "measuring" must also be, according to Washington's designs, the basic factor insuring the effectiveness of realistic deterrence.

In this connection it is extremely important to understand what sort of measuring of force the flexible response strategy envisaged. As the practice of the sixties shows, the sense of the notorious "measuring" consisted in the fundamental and qualitative separation of nuclear warfare and nonnuclear warfare by U.S. theorists and politicians. By the very adoption of the formula of flexible response the Kennedy government determined the parameters of U.S. use of military force and admitted that in a new strategic situation they could make up their minds to use their nuclear force only in exceptional and specific cases—basically only in the event of retaliatory defense against an inconceivable direct nuclear attack by the Soviet Union on the United States or on their main allies in Europe. A U.S. nuclear attack on the U.S.S.R. (signifying the inevitability of a retaliatory Soviet strike) proved, as noted above, unattractive for Washington as a strategic prospect, and for this reason virtually impracticable, as R. McNamara was obliged to admit.

It was in this and nothing else that the essence of the Kennedy and Johnson principle of the "measured out use of force" consisted. When it was a matter of using conventional forces, then on this plane, as is shown by the barbaric actions of the U.S. aggressors in Indochina, U.S. imperialism carried out no measuring.

To resolve purely local tasks and for the struggle against "insurgent" formations, the Pentagon, in the matter of intensifying conventional, nonnuclear warfare, has reached a virtual ceiling, using B-52 bombers and aircraft carriers and resorting to massive, indiscriminate bombing and artillery bombardment.

So surely, you ask, the Republican administration does not intend to observe in fact this basic and only measuring, which was implemented by the Kennedy administration, which drew a strict distinction between nuclear and nonnuclear wars? When you start to seek a clear answer to this question in the utterances of the U.S. leaders you discover that an unambiguous answer is not given.

President Nixon's statements, particularly those addressed to the U.S.S.R. draw a very precise distinction between nuclear and nonnuclear wars and stress U.S. reluctance, as in previous years, to be the initiator in launching a global thermonuclear conflict in any event fraught with catastrophe for the United States itself.

In Defense Secretary Laird's statements, however, particularly those calculated for the ears of U.S. partners and allies, the question of the use of nuclear weapons is treated with such boastful courage: he says that the division of weapons into nuclear and nonnuclear has no fundamental significance—the United States will use the weapons best suited to the situation. To encourage others to aggressive adventures in the name of the interests of U.S. imperialism, the Pentagon bosses hasten to assure their partners that they can boldly undertake any local military action since it will be carried out under the cover of the U.S. "nuclear umbrella."

The duality in the position of the present U.S. leadership in the approach to the question of the feasibility of using nuclear weapons reflects the basic contradiction of all postwar U.S. strategic courses: the contradiction between the desire to preserve war as a political means and imperialism's ever narrowing opportunities for waging a success-

51

ful war which brings results. This contradiction appears in various forms and in various aspects—as in the contradiction between the violence of threats and a certain restraint of actions; as in the contradiction between the instinctive dislike of accepting any restrictions on U.S. force and the enforced necessity of taking into account the force of the enemies and showing caution in the practical use of force; or as in the contradiction between the desire to achieve a position of absolute force and the rational recognition of the inaccessibility of such a position under the conditions of the contemporary world.

Now the U.S. leaders, who have elaborated a new strategy, are striving, on the one hand, to demonstrate the hardening of the U.S. position and the United States' great readiness for the decisive use of military force, and the renunciation of "gradation" in the use of this force, and are striving, in a word, to make their strategy more of a deterrent for potential enemies and more encouraging for allies.

At the same time, setting themselves the aim of a great deterrent, the U.S. leaders are obliged to publicly acknowledge changes in the strategic situation which are unfavorable for the United States, and to take into account the growth in the U.S.S.R.'s might, and are obliged officially to replace the provoking concept of U.S. "strategic supremacy" with the concept of "sufficiency" of forces and to formulate their strategy in increasingly moderate expressions (compare the transition from massive retaliation to flexible response and realistic deterrence).

If one takes an objective look at how matters stand with the so-called measuring in the use of U.S. force, then it must be seen that the change in the strategic situation in the world is forcing the U.S. leadership toward not a lesser, but a greater measuring of force compared with those which occurred under Kennedy and Johnson.

The U.S. leadership is now obliged to discuss the question of the "price" (for the United States) of a conventional "local" conflict and not only of a global nuclear missile conflict.

Realizing to a certain degree the endlessness, and consequently the hopelessness, of the nuclear arms race, the U.S. leaders, by the very fact of the talks with the U.S.S.R. on strategic arms limitation, are now obliged, if only in concept, to agree with the need for setting a certain "ceiling" on strategic armaments. All this cannot but show the unsoundness of the hints made by the Pentagon leaders about the possibility of unrestrained U.S. use of its military force in the contemporary epoch.

This contradiction between the boundless desires of U.S. imperialism and the ever narrowing U.S. opportunities in the world arena is also reflected in U.S. strategy as the contradiction between its adventurist and realistic elements.

The new U.S. strategy of realistic deterrence, despite its name, is far from providing a deterrent against war. It only continues the futile search for ways and means of waging war which are without danger for the United States—a search which Washington has been carrying out for twenty-five years. This time "local war by proxy" is declared to be such a "safe war." The manpower of U.S. partners combined with U.S. military-technological force must also, according to Washington's thinking, open up new expanses and opportunities for manipulating military force in the international arena.

The strategy of realistic deterrence, like previous U.S. strategy, is aimed at restraining social changes in the world. For this reason it is reactionary in its essence and doomed to the same inevitable failure as the strategy of flexible response which suffered a fiasco in Vietnam, for it refuses to recognize the inevitability and irreversibility of the social changes dictated by the will of the peoples.

Recognizing the dangers connected with the stockpiling of nuclear weapons in the world (this recognition was expressed in particular in the U.S. signing of the nuclear nonproliferation treaty), the Washington leaders are trying to intensify the "politico-psychological" use of the U.S. nuclear missile arsenal, in connection with which the strategy of realistic deterrence again entails diplomatic talks with nuclear bluff and blackmail which can hardly promote an easing of international tension or promote the refusal of an even greater number of countries to choose the path of nuclear armament.

Finally, proceeding from the formal recognition of the strategic equality and parity of the United States and the U.S.S.R., this strategy nonetheless does not want to come to terms with the fact of this equality and is aimed nonetheless at searching for crafty, devious ways to achieve for the United States some military advantages compared with the U.S.S.R.

Thus, the "realism" of the new strategy is reduced to modifications of imperialist strategy and to attempts to combine certain "realities" which cannot be combined, while keeping unchanged its expansionist foreign policy aims and philosophy of force.

PART TWO
STRATEGIC DOCTRINE

2

THE CRITICAL ISSUES

CAN NUCLEAR DETERRENCE LAST OUT THE CENTURY?

Fred Charles Iklé

Fred C. Iklé argues that many of the assumptions upon which the strategy of mutual assured destruction (MAD) is based are obsolete and not conducive to effective arms control.

The McNamara notion of deterrence was predicated on the proposition that a rational adversary would never decide to launch a nuclear attack on the United States if he were confronted with a threat of massive retaliatory destruction. Iklé disputes this assumption; in addition, he expresses concern over the possibility that Soviet leaders may decide they could inflict a devastating first strike on America's strategic forces and deter any response whatsoever.

Together with the ever-present possibility of accidental missile firings and the moral implications of a nuclear doctrine based on the destruction of civilians, the above concerns led Iklé to propound a new strategy of flexible response. The author suggests an alternative doctrine for targeting nuclear weapons, as well as the means to minimize the possibility of surprise attack, in order to create a more stable and less threatening atmosphere for mutual deterrence and arms control.

The autumn of last year [1972] marked half the road from the beginning of the nuclear era to the year 2000. Mankind has been spared nuclear devastation since the annihilation of two Japanese cities by the only two nuclear weapons then existing. But the destructiveness of nuclear arsenals, now increased many thousandfold, has sunk into human consciousness like man's knowledge of his mortality.

Source: *Foreign Affairs*, vol. 51, no. 2 (January 1973), pp. 267-85.

We all turn away, however, from the thought that nuclear war may be as inescapable as death, and may end our lives and our society within this generation or the next. We plan and work every day for the twenty-first century—as parents educating our children, as young workers saving for retirement, as a nation that seeks to preserve its physical environment, its political traditions, its cultural heritage. For this larger horizon—encompassing for the younger generation simply the common expectation of a healthy life—we do in fact assume "nuclear immortality." We believe, or we act as if we believe, that thanks to a certain international order, the existing arsenals of nuclear weapons with their almost incomprehensible destructiveness will never be used.

Yet, this order is so constructed that it cannot move toward abolition of nuclear weapons. It demands, as the necessary condition for avoiding nuclear war, the very preservation of these arms, always ready to destroy entire nations.

This ever-present danger once caused great anguish among the informed public in Western countries and evoked a diffused anxiety everywhere. Since the mid-1960s, the concern of both the public and the specialists has become far less acute, even though Soviet strategic forces have grown dramatically. Since 1968, confidence has been encouraged by the prospect of agreement in the Strategic Arms Limitation Talks (SALT) and, in May 1972, by the Moscow accords.

These initial agreements are designed, at least from the American perspective, first to preserve mutual deterrence as the strategic relationship between the United States and the Soviet Union, and second, to stabilize it by curbing the build-up of nuclear forces. As seen by a majority of American government officials, congressional leaders and civilian experts, these two objectives should govern our strategic arms-control policy as well as our own force planning for the foreseeable future. Other objectives (such as protecting cities) are held to jeopardize deterrence, and massive arms reductions or general and complete disarmament are considered utopian as well as dangerous.

According to this view, there are no alternatives to our current approach to mutual deterrence that deserve serious consideration. Even though the military services, government agencies and experts may differ on particular points of doctrine and choices of weapons, the dominant view of the workings of mutual deterrence has come to uphold three far-reaching dogmas:

One: our nuclear forces must be designed almost exclusively for "retaliation" in response to a Soviet nuclear attack—particularly an attempt to disarm us through a sudden strike.

Two: our forces must be designed and operated in such a way that this "retaliation" can be swift, inflicted through a single, massive and—above all—prompt strike. What would happen after this strike is of little concern for strategic planning.

Three: the threatened "retaliation" must be the killing of a major fraction of the Soviet population; moreover, the same ability to kill our population must be guaranteed the Soviet government in order to eliminate its main incentive for increasing Soviet forces. Thus, deterrence is "stabilized" by keeping it mutual.

This third dogma dictates not only our desire that Russian cities should remain essentially undefended, but also our willingness to abstain from defending our cities and even to hobble our capability to destroy Soviet nuclear arms. Proponents of this arrangement argue that it will lead to "arms race stability"; critics maintain that guaranteeing capabilities for Mutual Assured Destruction is indeed a "MAD" strategy.

Soviet military writers, by and large, express other views. Above all, they reject the idea that their forces should be designed for retaliation only, stressing instead the need to be prepared for fighting a nuclear war. Among Americans interested in nuclear strategy, however, only a minority now oppose any of these dogmas, and fewer still would reject them all. Absence of any one of these three elements—it is widely believed—would undermine deterrence, stimulate an arms race, or both.

Yet, these assumed requirements of stable deterrence are to a large extent the heritage of strategic policies from prior decades, now obsolete. They are a perilous way to protect ourselves from nuclear catastrophe and harmful to the prospects of strategic disarmament. Happily, they are dispensable for deterrence. Over the decades to come, we can develop and put into effect a safer and more humane strategy to prevent nuclear war.

II

It was Winston Churchill who in 1955 first expounded the essential ideas of mutual deterrence to the world at large. In that celebrated "balance of terror" speech, he made a "formidable admission," as he himself called it: "The deterrent does not cover the case of lunatics or dictators in the mood of Hitler when he found himself in his final dugout. This is a blank." The most disturbing defect, today, in the prevalent thinking on nuclear strategy is the cavalier disregard for this blank.

An almost exclusive emphasis on deterrence could be defended as a satisfactory long-term policy if it could be convincingly argued that successful deterrence was tantamount to prevention of nuclear war.

There exists no rational basis for such an argument. No matter how cataclysmic the threatened "assured destruction," those calculated decisions which our deterrent seeks to prevent are not the sole processes that could lead to nuclear war. We simply cannot know which of the various potential causes is most probable—whether it be a coherently calculated decision to attack, or an "irrational" decision or technical accident. Yet the approach now prevailing puts almost all effort into preventing the "rational" decision.

Moreover, our current strategy explicitly selects for nearly exclusive emphasis a very special type of intended attack. It has thus become the overriding concern of American strategic analysts and force planners to ensure that our intercontinental arms would be capable of "retaliating" after a Soviet attack sought to destroy them. It so happens that the problem of deterring such an attack lends itself to rigorous analysis, *provided* one postulates that a particular type of rationality governs a Soviet decision whether or not to launch it. The fascinating opportunity for such intellectual rigor—so exceptional in military and political affairs—may partly explain why this problem has commanded so dominant a place in American strategic thinking.

This analysis has now become the canonical way of determining the adequacy of our strategic forces. It uses *our* ideas about how surprise attacks could be designed, our estimates of what weapons the Soviets have and how they would perform, our latest findings about the performance of our own weapons, and, as soon as we discover a mistake in these calculations, our corrections. That is to say, we impute to the Soviet military leadership our imaginativeness (or lack of it) in inventing "successful" attacks, our state of knowledge (or ignorance) of how the weapons on both sides would perform in the vortex of a thermonuclear war and our diligence (or carelessness) in calculations.

The results of such calculations are taken most seriously by American defense planners. Should they suggest a way in which our "retaliatory" capability might be jeopardized, we institute remedies: we harden, disperse or add penetration aids. Should they show that we could still inflict massive destruction, we conclude that all is well. To be sure, we must consider surprise strikes against us based on our understanding of how the relationship between the two strategic forces might be exploited. But we should not disregard all other risks.

Yet this is what the canonical analysis does. It makes a peculiar assumption about the "rationality" of the Soviet decision we need to deter. On the long slope descending from rationality to irrationality, it postulates that only a short stretch needs to be considered. We must prepare—it is argued—for the possibility that Soviet leaders might move so far down this slope as to be tempted to decide on a surprise attack, provided the calculations that we impute to their military staff indicate the attack would "succeed." That is, we prepare for the event that Soviet leaders might judge how a global nuclear war would turn out by relying on such largely untested calculations, trusting their military advisers to have used unbiased estimates and avoided gross mistakes. But we need not prepare for the possibility that Soviet leaders might be somewhat less "rational" and let a cabal of officers mislead them by twisting the enormously complicated data to show that a surprise attack could "succeed" even where our own analysis clearly indicates it would fail.

Or, to put it differently, our analysis implicitly argues that we have to prepare for a certain type of Soviet leader: a man who could be tempted to launch a surprise attack if the calculations we impute to them promise "success"; who would ignore the dangers of long-term radioactive fallout (which our analysis omits) and expect they could stay on top of the postwar chaos (about which our analysis says next to nothing). But we need not prepare—it is argued—for Soviet leaders who might be "less rational" in an acute crisis and who might rely on their ability to launch an attack so designed as to deter us from retaliating. Such a stratagem of "counter-deterrence" would seek to cripple our nuclear forces in a surprise attack while sparing our cities, in order to deter the U.S. President from reprisal against Russian cities lest withheld Soviet forces then devastate American cities.

When leaders of a powerful country are credited with a willingness to gamble on some scheme for nuclear surprise attack—a scheme whose calculations they cannot validate, whose assumptions they cannot test and whose failure would mean the end of their regime or even their country—how rational a decision are we assuming in our posture of deterrence? When the prevailing American view of mutual deterrence postulates that both the Russian nuclear posture and our own must be designed to deter an opponent of such degraded rationality, why stop at this particular degradation in judgment?

The narrowness of our canonical analysis of what it takes to keep deterrence stable can perhaps be traced to the traumatic American experience of the Pearl Harbor attack. By a few easy protective measures we could have denied the Japanese militarists their success in 1941. This lesson we have learned well, and with good reason. We should not permit such a surprise attack to become easy, lest we invite it during some crisis when our antagonist sees himself forced to choose among deadly alternatives.

To make a surprise attack unsuccessful, however, is not necessarily to deter it. By 1945, after all, the Japanese surprise attack had turned into a failure. Shortly before the attack was launched, Emperor

Hirohito anticipated such an outcome and asked his military leaders how they envisaged defeating the United States, given its superior industrial might. His question never received an answer.[1] Would hardening, dispersal and a higher alertness of the American forces in 1941 have made the Japanese military abstain, or merely have driven them to redesign their attack?

Pearl Harbor thus provides a lesson beyond that of the danger of forces vulnerable to surprise attack. The Japanese military evidently expected that the United States, if it were disarmed in the Pacific, would not mount the terribly costly effort of striking back. In choosing this gamble, they were even more "irrational" than future Soviet leaders would have to be to gamble on "counter-deterrence," since our striking back after Pearl Harbor did not invite the devastation of American cities. Yet today, our European-based nuclear arms, for instance, are vulnerable to a "counter-deterrence" attack.

Rather recent history reminds us that men can acquire positions of power who are willing to see their nation destroyed in pursuit of causes which only they and their henchmen espouse. In countries that tolerate a dictatorship, a leader might always rise to the top who deems it a virtue, perhaps part of his revolutionary creed, to live dangerously—*vivere pericolosamente,* as Benito Mussolini put it. What a sad irony that the nations that had to fight Hitler to his last bunker should now rely on an interlock of their military postures, making survival depend on the rationality of all future leaders in all major nuclear powers.

III

In the 1950s, prior to the missile age and Russia's massive build-up of her nuclear forces, one heard a great deal about the risk of accidental war. Now, when American and Soviet missiles by the thousands are poised in constant readiness, this concern has curiously diminished. To justify this more relaxed attitude, some might point to the fact that no unauthorized detonation has ever occurred, or cite the American-Soviet agreements of 1971 for improving the hotline or recall the elaborate safeguards with which the military seem to protect nuclear weapons.

But nobody can predict that the fatal accident or unauthorized act will never happen. The hazard is too elusive. It is inherent not only in the ineradicable possibility of technical defects, but also in the inevitable vulnerability to human error of all command and operational procedures—during periods of high alert as well as during the many years

---

[1] Many other examples can be found of aggressive wars that have been planned without at all considering how they were to end. See the author's *Every War Must End* (New York: Columbia University Press, 1971).

of quiet waiting. So exceedingly complex are modern weapons systems, both in their internal mechanisms and in their intricate interactions, that it seems doubtful whether any group of experts could ever ferret out every unintended ramification, discover every lurking danger. Indeed, the very word "system" misleads in that it suggests a clearly bounded combination of parts, their interactions all designed to serve the intended purpose.

The deadly danger is deepened by the fact that latent hazards can only be corrected if they are sought out. To look, day in and day out, for some hidden risk of accident is not a task, however, that captures the attention of top decision makers. It is far from unusual in military operations for serious oversights or occasional incompetence to go undetected or uncorrected until after a major disaster. For example, after the North Korean seizure in 1968 of the American reconnaissance ship *Pueblo,* when the crew had been unable to destroy all the cryptographic material before capture, destructive incendiary devices were suddenly permitted aboard ship. Previously, such devices had been prohibited because of the fire hazard, and the development of safer ones had been neglected. Safeguards rarely come without costs, and often appear to pose counteracting hazards.

Drastic shortcomings in the Defense Department's worldwide communications came to the attention of a congressional subcommittee after the Israeli attack in 1967 on the American ship *Liberty.* At the beginning of the Six-Day War, the Joint Chiefs of Staff decided to order the *Liberty* into safer waters. Over a period of 13 hours prior to the Israeli attack, they sent their order in at least four messages. Two of the messages were misrouted to the Philippines and one of these was thence sent to the National Security Agency in Maryland, there merely to be filed. Another message was routed over two paths to be doubly sure; in the first path it was lost in a relay station, in the second delayed until many hours after the attack. The fourth message also arrived too late. This failure in emergency communications occurred under almost perfect conditions: no facilities had been disabled, there was no enemy jamming, and no restrictions on the use of available communication modes had been imposed.

It can be argued that safeguards for nuclear arms are likely to be more stringent and more carefully designed than arrangements protecting cryptographic equipment or procedures for transmitting top-level emergency commands. But those Russians and Americans who monitor the safety of strategic arms cannot afford to learn from past accidents to probe for and correct critical hazards. When it comes to defects in safeguards that might lead to an accidental nuclear war, our societies cannot survive by learning through trial and error.

Polaris and Poseidon submarines suffer from communication difficulties so serious that "some of the messages never get delivered," as a senior naval officer put it. To permit "retaliation" after a massive surprise attack, officers on American and Russian missile-carrying submarines must be ready, presumably, to launch their enormously destructive loads even after military communications networks have been destroyed. Yet, they must never inadvertently or deliberately misconstrue an order to launch—during all the long years the submarines will cruise the oceans as part of the "stable" deterrent, as well as during the confusion and turmoil of a global crisis. Will this formidable requirement always be met?

The peril may well be greater on the Soviet side. Since the American military establishment is relatively open to outside scrutiny, pressures to ferret out safety hazards or institute perhaps costly remedies can come from civilians in the executive branch, congressional committees and even the public. Under the compartmentalized, pervasive secrecy of the Soviet military, however, past accidents and present hazards can be kept not only from the public but from senior civilian authorities as well.

Given that occasional incompetence or malfeasance is predictable in large institutions—whether military or civilian—the safety of nuclear armaments remains a constantly pressing uncertainty. Given the huge and far-flung missile forces, ready to be launched from land and sea on both sides, the scope for disaster by accident is immense. Given that our strategic dogmas demand the targeting of populations and denial of defensive measures, the carnage would be without restraint. And as if all this were not terrifying enough, some proponents of these dogmas want to push matters to the brink.

Various influential people have urged that the United States adopt procedures to launch its missile force upon receipt of a warning that a Soviet surprise attack is on the way. Senator Fulbright, for example, recommended in 1969 that our missiles should be launched "immediately" upon warning of a Soviet attack, "without any fiddling around about it, even without asking the computer what to do," even if the warning indicated a "light attack." Other American senators and government advisers have also advocated that, in the event our forces became more vulnerable, we adopt a policy of launching our missiles on warning. According to at least two of these advocates—Jerome Wiesner, President Kennedy's Science Adviser, and Richard Garwin, member of President Nixon's Science Advisory Committee—it might not even be necessary to wait for the first nuclear detonation before launching.

But what might appear as a deliberate attack within the few minutes before the expected impact could have been a false warning; even an actual nuclear explosion could have been accidental. The short time available to execute a "retaliatory" launch-on-warning of our missile forces would not be enough to resolve this uncertainty.

Advocacy of a launch-on-warning policy might be viewed as a passing aberration in a fluid debate, if it were not for institutional pressures among the military that will keep driving in the same direction. Those branches of American and Russian military services that believe they must continue to press the case for land-based missile forces will—because of the increasing vulnerability of these forces—be ever more tempted to stress launch-on-warning as an option. To make this option more acceptable, new warning systems would be acquired; these in turn would strengthen vested interests in favor of this policy.

In Russia, such pressures may be even more compelling, because Soviet strategic thinking continues to consider favorably "preemption," that is, striking at the enemy before he can complete—or even start—his attack. For instance, the 1968 edition of Marshal V. D. Sokolovskii's book on Soviet military strategy refers to surveillance systems for detecting "the adversary's immediate preparations for a nuclear attack" as well as his massive missile launch, making it possible "to bar an aggressor's surprise attack and deliver prompt nuclear strikes against him." As recently as 1971, Defense Minister Grechko stressed the importance of speed for "frustrating an aggressor's surprise blows and successfully carrying out those military tasks, especially by the rocket troops . . . which must be fulfilled in a matter of seconds." In a matter of seconds—through technical accident or human failure—mutual deterrence might thus collapse.

President Nixon, in his last two foreign policy messages, has rejected a launch-on-warning policy. However, should one side give the appearance of adopting it, the other might feel compelled to institute faster launch procedures, creating an "arms race" in reducing safeguards against accidental war. Under mounting pressures from Soviet "hawks," and from some American "doves" as well as "hawks," in both countries responsible people in the center may not keep enough influence to halt this race. The very fact that well-informed and well-intentioned advisers now recommend, in essence, that the balance of terror should rest on hair-triggered doomsday machines offers a chilling reminder that we cannot rely on unswerving rationality among those who might affect critical strategic decisions.

The launch-on-warning aberration is only the most conspicuous outgrowth of the belief that to prevent nuclear war we have but to deter it. Our present strategic policy aggravates the risk of accidental war through many less visible practices as well as by its grand design.

65

IV

While the current overemphasis on mutual deterrence against a "rational" surprise attack dates from the mid-1960s, the other two dogmas of our nuclear strategy are largely the legacy of earlier periods. This is particularly true of the dogma that "retaliation" must be swift, inflicted in an all-out strike.

The world's first nuclear force—the U.S. Strategic Air Command (SAC)—was established in a period when we did not have to deter nuclear attack, but seriously feared the Red Army might move into Western Europe with its preponderant conventional strength. SAC became the remedy for the weakness perceived in the United States because of our extensive unilateral disarmament following World War II. One cannot appreciate the thinking of American leaders at that time, unless one makes an effort to recall how imminent they judged the likelihood that the Russians would launch an all-out ground attack in Europe.

Accordingly, to fight a war seemed at least as important a mission for SAC as to deter one. And in planning to fight a war, American strategists took account of what they had learned from the bombing raids in World War II. Whereas they had found that urban societies could continue to support a war effort as long as the damage was partial and gradual, it still seemed possible that sudden and extensive destruction would produce a collapse. Thus, the strategy that had not fully succeeded against Hitler because of technological limitations now seemed feasible thanks to the atomic bomb. Our new weapons could administer the "knock-out blow" against Russia's cities—the industrial and political centers—in order to halt the Red Army's advance against Western Europe. Hence, to be an effective war-fighting strategy, atomic bombing had to be a concentrated, quick blow.

As the Russians also began to acquire a nuclear capability, American strategists came to fear attack on European or even American cities, as an act of "retaliation" should SAC carry out the attack that would leave the advancing Red Army without support from the homeland. Thus, the first priority for SAC in the mid-1950s became the destruction of the Soviet nuclear capability before it could be used. This priority provided a second reason for our nuclear strike to be prompt and massive.

Initially, our strategic forces for this disarming strike lacked intercontinental range; they had to be based in North Africa or Europe to reach their targets. Later, we assigned an increasingly large role in this mission to our growing intercontinental arms, which meant they had to be capable of reaching their targets early enough to prevent the launching of most of the Soviet weapons. Thanks to the new solid fuel technology, our U.S.-based missiles could be launched in minutes and Minuteman became our principal land-based missile force. The requirement for speed, stemming from the disarming mission of our forces protecting Western Europe and appropriate perhaps for the 1950s and early 1960s, was thereby transferred to the arms that were to remain a principal element in our intercontinental deterrent for the 1970s and beyond.

After 1963, however, our dominant strategic philosophy shifted from the emphasis on the disarming strike to the principle of "mutual assured destruction." This shift was primarily motivated by our view of the arms race: we feared that our efforts to maintain a capability for a disarming strike would stimulate a continuing build-up of Soviet forces; and conversely, we hoped that our restraint would be reciprocated. Accordingly, we began to deny ourselves the capability to defend against those Soviet forces that could escape our quick, disarming strike in behalf of NATO, and—further undermining this earlier mission of our strategic forces—we began to curtail our capability to hit Soviet forces. In 1971, for example, the Senate referred explicitly to this new arms-control thinking in voting against funds to improve the accuracy of our missiles.

As a result of these developments, our current strategic posture is afflicted by a deep but strangely concealed contradiction. Those of our forces that serve to protect our NATO allies are still largely designed and operated in accordance with the earlier strategy threatening, in response to a major conventional attack, a nuclear first strike that would seek to disarm. But our global deterrence posture now has to meet the opposite requirement: to eschew, and through agreement mutually to preclude, a nuclear disarming capability. Meanwhile, some of our allies have come to regard our nuclear forces based on their soil as the most tangible symbol committing our entire deterrent forces to their defense, so that our former technological reason for overseas basing has been replaced by a political one. In the midst of the incompatibility between our nuclear strategy for NATO and our global deterrence policy, our so-called "tactical" nuclear weapons—also a legacy of a bygone era—introduce yet another anachronism of obsolete posture and technology.

To make the historical evolution still more complex, starting about 1960 the growing Soviet nuclear capability seemed to threaten more than just vengeful destruction of our cities so as to deter NATO's nuclear "knock-out" response to a Red Army advance. Soviet intercontinental missiles began to pose the canonical threat that figures so prominently in our strategic analysis—the massive surprise attack to disarm the United States. Given that the major portion of our strategic forces had been designed primarily for the prompt disarming strike in response to a Soviet invasion of Europe, they had not been primarily designed to survive a Soviet nuclear attack. For this new mission—"retaliation" in response to the Soviet nuclear strike—our bombers and missiles had to be launched promptly, before they were all destroyed on the ground. Here was the third reason conspiring to keep our strategic thinking riveted to the notion that "retaliation" had to be swift.

V

Clearly distinguishable from the notion that "retaliation" must be a swift, massive strike in any strategy of mutual deterrence is the now equally prevalent dogma that this strike must be designed to kill millions of people. This dogma can also be traced to the technical and conceptual limitations of strategic bombing in World War II. One has to recall the emotions and theories behind Hitler's raids on Coventry and London, and the deliberate bombing of residential areas in Hamburg, Tokyo, Dresden and Hiroshima, to understand how we could have arrived where we are today. After World War II, military experts began to recognize that the immensely greater destructive power of nuclear weapons could compensate for the inaccuracy of aerial bombing, hence permitting destruction of small-sized military targets. But only if these targets were in unpopulated areas could they be destroyed without the killing of civilian populations. A nuclear weapon small enough to avoid vast civilian damage, yet accurate enough to hit most military targets, was not within the technology of the first nuclear decade.

As our strategic planners began to grapple with the role of nuclear weapons, not only was their vision confined by these technological limitations; but their sensitivity to the distinction between combatants and civilians—long cultivated through civilizing centuries—had become dulled by the strategic bombing in World War II. And given that we were then still planning how to fight—not to deter—a nuclear war, the mass killing of noncombatants came to be viewed as a "bonus effect," a useful by-product of the bombing campaign on which we relied to win in the event of World War III. Our "knock-out blow" would paralyze the Red Army not only by demolishing railroad yards, factories and party headquarters, but also by decimating urban populations and thus (perhaps) crushing Russia's "morale."

This history—not reasoned strategic analysis—led us into the habit of thinking that one had to threaten the killing of millions and millions of people in order to deter an "aggressor." Nonetheless, the question of whether or not cities should be the targets of the "retaliatory" strike remained unsettled. In the late 1950s, a few strategists began to make the case that we should avoid hitting Russian cities in our initial strike responding to Soviet aggression. Instead, we should seek to destroy whatever Soviet nuclear weapons had not yet been used as well as other military targets, holding Soviet cities "hostage" to deter attacks on our cities. This strategy, it was then argued, would not only serve us better if nuclear war should break out for whatever reason, but would be just as effective to deter it.

During his first two years in office, Secretary of Defense McNamara came out in support of this new strategy and advocated military efforts consistent with it, such as civil defense and "counterforce" capabilities. Yet, after 1963, he began to promote the concept of "assured destruction." Initially, he perhaps meant to use this concept primarily as a convenient bureaucratic tactic. By pointing out our overwhelming capability for "assured destruction," he had a precise, statistical measurement for arguing against budgetary pressures from the military services, that we had more than enough arms for deterrence.

What began as a budgetary device within the Defense Department, conveniently fitting the need to shift defense dollars from our strategic forces to Vietnam from 1965 on, ended up as one of the dogmas governing our strategic and arms-control policy. We came to view a "retaliatory" threat to kill a major fraction of the Russian population as necessary for deterrence. And we came to believe that forces tailored to this threat were the only alternative to forces that appeared to jeopardize Russia's nuclear deterrent and hence would stimulate an arms race.

As "assured destruction" became the yardstick of nuclear strategy, the underlying calculations adopted a brutally simplifying index of success. It considered only those hostages whose death from the retaliatory strike would be certain and exactly calculable—those killed by the direct blast and heat effect of our weapons. In gauging the excellence of our deterrent—as reflected in statistics presented to Congress —those Russians who would be killed or injured by fires, fallout and famine were excluded. Cognoscenti call this method of calculation the "cookie cutter"—nuclear weapons are assumed to "take out" hostages in a neat circle, like a piece of dough.

Such tasteless jargon helps to conceal the peculiar reasoning that is implicit in the modern approach to deterrence. We impute to the potential aggressor enough rationality or compassion to be reliably deterred by the prospect that calculable millions of his compatriots would meet prompt and certain death from "direct weapons effects"; we somehow do not trust him to be deterred by the prospect of the less easily measured millions who would suffer and die from radiation sickness, untreated injuries or starvation. And while destruction of industry has been mentioned as being part of our "assured destruction," the question whether one could spare people and target only industry has scarcely been raised. Yet, by permitting evacuation, for instance, separation of urban industries and populations might be accomplished.

The Nixon administration properly discontinued flaunting of these gruesome statistics to demonstrate the reliability of our deterrent. Nonetheless, most American strategic experts still use the same calculus.

Our arms-control experts and military planners insulate themselves from the potential implications of their labors by layers of dehumanizing abstractions and bland metaphors. Thus, "assured destruction" fails to indicate what is to be destroyed; but then "assured genocide" would reveal the truth too starkly. The common phrase, "deterring a potential aggressor," conveys a false simplicity about the processes that might lead to a nuclear attack, as if we had to worry only about some ambitious despot who sits calculating whether or not to start a nuclear war. A moral perversity lies hidden behind the standard formula: in the event this "aggressor" attacks, we must "retaliate by knocking out *his* cities." Tomas de Torquemada, who burned 10,000 heretics at the stake, could claim principles more humane than our nuclear strategy; for his tribunals found all his victims guilty of having knowingly committed mortal sin.

The jargon of American strategic analysis works like a narcotic. It dulls our sense of moral outrage about the tragic confrontation of nuclear arsenals, primed and constantly perfected to unleash widespread genocide. It fosters the current smug complacence regarding the soundness and stability of mutual deterrence. It blinds us to the fact that our method for preventing nuclear war rests on a form of warfare universally condemned since the Dark Ages—the mass killing of hostages.

Indeed, our nuclear strategy is supposed to work the better, the larger the number of hostages that would pay with their lives should the strategy fail. This view has become so ingrained that the number of hostages who could be killed through a "second strike" by either superpower is often used as a measure of the "stability" of deterrence. Our very motive behind the recent treaty curbing the deployment of missile defenses is to keep this number reliably high.

In the long run, preserving a mutual threat of genocide may impede the reduction of tension and distrust between the two nuclear superpowers that we all hope for. It is far better, of course, for major powers to maintain peace between them by planning for deterrence instead of for war. But to stabilize deterrence by keeping ready arsenals for instant and unrestrained slaughter of men, women and children is likely to impose a wrenching perspective on the officialdom of both nations. Such a "stabilization" perpetuates an arms-control philosophy that, at its core, is incredibly hostile. How would American-British relations have developed in the nineteenth century if, instead of the Rush-Bagot agreement, we had negotiated the establishment of armaments on each side permanently primed to destroy most cities in the United States and England?

Despite the arcane jargon of modern deterrence theory, ordinary Americans and Russians cannot escape the realization that their generation and their children's generation are destined to remain the chosen target of the nuclear forces on the other side. Toward each other as a people, Americans and Russians harbor practically no feelings of hostility, but by our theories they must indefinitely face each other as the most fearful threat to their future existence.

VI

Mercifully, no inhuman power condemns us to live perpetually in the grim jail of our own ideas. Alternatives can be found, although it may take decades to construct a better order for the prevention of nuclear war and the task will require the work of many minds. This is all the more reason for beginning today.

A good place to begin is to cast out the dogma that to deter nuclear attack, the threatened response must be the mass killing of people. By taking advantage of modern technology, we should be able to escape the evil dilemma that the strategic forces on both sides must either be designed to kill people or else jeopardize the opponent's confidence in his deterrent. The potential accuracy of "smart" bombs and missiles and current choices in weapon effects could enable both sides to avoid the killing of vast millions and yet to inflict assured destruction on military, industrial and transportation assets—the sinews and muscles of the regime initiating war. Combined with this change in concept and techniques of "retaliation," we must design solutions more stable than in the past to the problem of achieving invulnerable deterrent forces. No matter how accurately each side can aim its own weapons, we want to make it physically impossible for most of the strategic arms to be destroyed by sudden attack.

It is premature to judge whether such a change in capabilities and doctrine might eventually make it desirable for us and the Russians to permit active defenses for urban populations while prohibiting them for military assets other than the nuclear deterrent. If such discrimination were to become technically feasible, its desirability would depend

71

not only on American-Soviet relations at that time, but also on the danger of attack, if any, from other nuclear powers.

The second dogma we have to discard is that response to nuclear attack must be the prompt, even instant, launching of nearly the entire nuclear force. By eliminating the need to design our arms for instant launching, we can reduce vulnerability in many new ways. Precisely how to design forces that are far less vulnerable because they are not meant for instant reaction is a task for future research. We may not now see promising approaches; over all these years we have never made the effort. Arms buried thousands of feet underground come to mind, with provision for reaching the surface—and their targets—weeks or months after attack. By insisting that our strategic arms be capable of swift launch, we have restricted our engineers to such vulnerable arrangements as aircraft in delicately ready conditions and missiles exposed on or near the surface.

If we can eliminate the vulnerability of our strategic arms to surprise attack, we will have broken the vicious circle: that they must be ready for prompt launching because they are vulnerable, and that they are vulnerable because they must be ready. Furthermore, should the Russians come to agree with us, we could jointly decide to replace the doomsday catapults invented in the 1950s with arms that are incapable of being launched swiftly. If the strategic order could be transformed in this way, the dominant fear of surprise attack which drives our arms competition would loosen its grip. Weapons incapable of quick launching tend to be less suitable for surprise; and against truly invulnerable nuclear armaments, surprise would have lost its purpose.

Neither we nor the Russians will suddenly scuttle all our hair-triggered engines of destruction. By abandoning the dogma of speed, however, both of us can shift intellectual energies and budgetary resources to develop different nuclear armaments. Strategic weapons have a long lifetime; between the initial concept and the scrap heap, up to 25 years may elapse. What we engineer during this decade will have to prevent nuclear war into the next century.

Discarding the dogma of speed would result in another gain, perhaps even more important than reduced vulnerability. It would go a long way to reduce the danger of accidental war. By eliminating the requirement for launching entire missile forces in a matter of minutes, we can get rid of the triggering mechanisms and sensitive command procedures where some obscure malfunction might lead to cataclysm. Time is the best healer of mistakes, whether technical or human. The insistence on speed leaves insufficient time for double-checking; it denies opportunities for correction. If rapidity becomes the overriding concern, independent monitors tend to get pushed aside. Until about

1950, the Atomic Energy Commission shared in the custody of the nuclear weapons deployed by the military. But the notion that these weapons had to be ready for immediate use led President Truman to turn them over to the sole custody of the military.

Although avoiding the killing of hostages, these changes would not make nuclear war less unacceptable as an instrument of policy. Deterrence would remain: the conventional military might of the aggressor nation—its navy, army and air force with their logistics support—would be the first to suffer "assured destruction." Such a prospect would make even less tempting the planning of nuclear war than today's actual or imagined opportunities for a quick strike to deprive the opponent of his nuclear weapons. And the risk of the destruction of cities would still loom in the background.

Could the Soviet leaders be induced to accept such an evolution? We have lately devoted a major effort to teach our dogmas to the Russians—some feel with considerable success. Certain stubborn positions in Soviet strategic thought, however, manifest a less narrow view of deterrence by showing greater concern for dangers of a nuclear war that cannot be deterred, and reflect a longer time perspective than we have developed. Once freed from our dogmas, we may discover that the distance in strategic views between us and the Russians is less than it appears today.

The greatest obstacles to the necessary reconstruction of our strategic order may well be intellectual and institutional rigidities. We justify our old habits of thinking because we are so competently familiar with the arguments against change. We are disposed to reject suggestions for improvement by demanding a perfect solution at the outset.

Military services cling to the type of weapons to which they have become accustomed, seeking marginal improvements rather than radical innovation. For instance, the United States Navy in the 1950s was at first reluctant to press ahead with the Polaris program, preferring to stress the strategic mission of carrier-based aircraft. Similarly, the Soviet Strategic Rocket Forces and the United States Air Force will probably want to hold on to their land-based missile forces well beyond the 1970s. Much is made about the importance of preserving our "triad" of strategic forces, as if the fact that we happened to acquire bombers, missiles and submarines created some sacred trinity. Means outlive their ends among military organizations, for it is to the means that institutional loyalties and intellectual craftsmanship are devoted.

The scholasticism justifying our current policy is full of contradictions. On the one hand, we brush aside the immorality of threatening to kill millions of hostages, assuming that the threat will deter and that to deter means to prevent nuclear war. On the other hand, we argue that we must be poised to carry out "retaliation" swiftly and thus convey determination for irrational vengeance, since all rational purpose of retaliation would have disappeared when its time had come. We want to maintain a vague threat of using nuclear weapons first to deter massive conventional attack; yet, to stabilize mutual deterrence we must not threaten Soviet nuclear arms nor defend against them. . . .

The result of such contradictions is a cancelling out of good intentions. In some years, our arms policy is dominated by our preoccupation with the arms race and the view that we should therefore hobble our forces. In other years, we decide to refurbish our so-called options for attacking Russia's nuclear arms. Left to itself, this pulling and hauling between *yin* and *yang* will not lead the world into a safer era. On the contrary, the bureaucratic struggle may result in the worst compromise among the biases of contending factions. While luck has been with us so far, strategic thinking must and can find a new path into the twenty-first century.

THE MUTUAL-HOSTAGE RELATIONSHIP
BETWEEN AMERICA AND RUSSIA

Wolfgang K. H. Panofsky

Wolfgang K. H. Panofsky takes exception to Fred C. Iklé's assertion that deterrence based on threats to the existence of civilian society is outdated and harmful to stable deterrence and arms control. While agreeing with Dr. Iklé that MAD is a morally uncomfortable strategy, the author believes history has proven its efficacy as a doctrine for averting nuclear catastrophe.

Arguing that the mutual-hostage relationship of the United States and the Soviet Union is not a consequence of policy but rather of "physical fact," Panofsky asks the question: "How can we do better?" He criticizes the concept of limited nuclear war for not really altering the basic fact that the populations of the superpowers are indeed hostages to the will of their political leaders. In addition, he believes the deployed technology necessary for a counterforce response is virtually indistinguishable from that needed for a first-strike threat to the opponents' strategic forces. To reduce the risk of escalation to total nuclear war by adopting a strategy emphasizing limited nuclear options would, according to the author, actually remove one of the most essential fears at the heart of deterrence. Mere changes in targeting doctrine cannot negate the mutual-hostage relationship between adversary societies, nor can they decrease the danger of accidental or irrational war.

Source: *Foreign Affairs,* vol. 52, no. 1 (October 1973), pp. 109-18.

For nearly two decades the strategic nuclear armaments of the Soviet Union and the United States have been great enough for each to hold the other's civilian population as hostage against a devastating nuclear attack. Living with this situation has not been and will not be easy: it has become, quite simply, one of the major tensions of modern life. Yet the mutual-hostage relationship has been given credit, and probably justly so, for the prevention of massive world wars.

During the last few years, this relationship has been exposed to broader public scrutiny as a result of the SALT I negotiations and treaty, and a number of articles and statements have appeared criticizing U.S. policy with regard to the situation.[1] One critic, Donald Brennan, coined the acronym MAD, for Mutual Assured Destruction, to indicate his view of the policy underlying SALT. While others have not employed quite as harsh terms, they still assert that the terms of the SALT I treaty prohibiting extensive anti-ballistic missile (ABM) deployments do in fact signify a morally repugnant policy of leaving "mass slaughter" as the only option in case deterrence has failed in some way.

The recently named head of the Arms Control and Disarmament Agency, Fred Charles Iklé, cites three "far-reaching dogmas" as implied by current U.S. policies:

> One: our nuclear forces must be designed almost exclusively for "retaliation" in response to a Soviet nuclear attack—particularly an attempt to disarm us through a sudden strike.
>
> Two: our forces must be designed and operated in such a way that this retaliation can be swift, inflicted through a single, massive, and—above all—prompt strike. What would happen after this strike is of little concern for strategic planning.
>
> Three: the threatened "retaliation" must be the killing of a major fraction of the Soviet population; moreover, the same ability to kill our population must be guaranteed the Soviet government in order to eliminate its main incentive for increasing Soviet forces. Thus, deterrence is "stabilized" by keeping it mutual.[2]

The first of these "dogmas" conforms to the technical realities: in the post-SALT I era (and under conditions prevailing throughout the

---

[1]See, for instance: Michael May, *Orbis*, Summer 1970, pp. 271 ff., and Princeton Center of International Studies Research Monograph 37, 1972; W. R. Van Cleave, *Freedom at Issue*, no. 19, May-June 1973; D. G. Brennan, "The Case for Missile Defense," *Foreign Affairs*, April 1969, and *Survival*, September-October 1972; Fred Charles Iklé, "Can Nuclear Deterrence Last Out the Century?" *Foreign Affairs*, January 1973 (a more complete edition of that article appeared as a report of the California Arms Control and Foreign Policy Seminar as of January 1973).

[2]Iklé, "Can Nuclear Deterrence Last Out the Century?"

past decade!) our strategic forces must be designed primarily for retaliation in response to nuclear attack. However, I take strong exception to the second and third points, which claim that such a response, according to accepted doctrine underlying SALT, must be rapid and of massive proportion.

Naturally the present situation is far from ideal. We cannot be relieved of moral responsibility for having permitted a situation to develop in which large segments of the population of both West and East can in fact be sacrificed at the will of political leaders; neither is the situation free from acute danger in case of failure of mutual deterrence. Iklé aptly criticizes the mutual-hostage relationship which these policies imply by eloquently recalling that the threat of the killing of civilians has been condemned as immoral in the codes of both ancient and modern warfare, and by also pointing out the fragility of "stability through deterrence," for example in scenarios of accident and unauthorized nuclear attack.

Yet how can we do better? The critics seem to imply that the mutual-hostage relationship between the populations of the United States and the Soviet Union is a consequence of policy, and would therefore be subject to change if such a policy were modified. Yet this relationship is a matter of physical fact and is thus grossly insensitive to any change in strategic policy. The reason is simple: the destructiveness of today's offensive arsenal of nuclear weapons is so overwhelming that deaths would number in the many millions or even tens of millions if only a fraction of the available weapons were delivered against the opponent's homeland.

In the face of this physical reality much of the recent criticism has concentrated on extending a hope of "low-casualty" nuclear war by advocating a policy of strictly anti-military attacks, or of "controlled" nuclear attacks against selected targets only—either military or civilian.

Neither of these scenarios, however, solves the basic problem of the mutual-hostage relationship. For no one can be sure whether an opponent will, in fact, follow a similarly "restrained" policy; he may instead choose a full anti-population response. Moreover, civilian casualties as a result of any massive anti-military attacks would still be enormous. Finally, once the barriers against use of nuclear weapons are broken, escalation toward full-scale nuclear war is exceedingly difficult to prevent.

It is characteristic that none of the recent analyses meet these questions head-on. In essence these papers start with the premise that "there must be a better way" than mutual deterrence, but the viability, let alone the advantage, of other specific policies is not demonstrated.

If the only defect of the criticism deploring the state of mutual deterrence now extant between the United States and the Soviet Union were a failure to provide concrete alternative prescriptions that would be more likely to prevent nuclear war, this would be a matter of little concern. However, the problem is deeper. Any successful attempt to project an image—however ill-founded—of a "clean" nuclear war generating minimum civilian casualties could make the use of nuclear weapons in limited conflicts more acceptable. The fact remains— irrespective of the extent to which the strategies of either country include plans for deliberate retaliation against the opponent's population—that the peoples of both countries are in jeopardy in any kind of nuclear conflict.

This is not the first time these questions have been raised—far from it. After former Secretary of Defense McNamara took office, he proclaimed in 1962 a "city-avoiding" strategy designed to minimize civilian casualties in a nuclear war. But during his tenure in office he gradually became convinced that such a policy was unworkable, both on physical and military grounds: civilian casualties in connection with a purely anti-military attack were still apt to number in the many millions[3] and one could not be sure the opponent would also follow a city-avoiding strategy; instead he might choose to target centers of population! Accordingly, McNamara in his later years completely changed his position, moving toward a policy of deterrence and, more specifically, "assured destruction." Without going into the merit of McNamara's conversion, this history illustrates that throughout a period of major change in strategic policy the mutual-hostage relationship between the U.S. and Soviet populations remained a physical reality of central importance.

In the face of the unavoidable fact that the populations of both countries are exposed to overwhelming danger in case of nuclear war, emphasis has been placed on stabilizing the political, economic and military relationships between the two countries. In the purely military-strategic sense this search for stability has taken the form of an effort to remove any *rational* incentive for the initiation of nuclear war. In principle, such an incentive could be removed if technology permitted the evolution of active and passive defense measures which would either almost totally prevent the arrival of enemy nuclear weapons or else eliminate their devastating consequences. In view of the enormous destructiveness of each penetrating warhead and the low performance and high cost of feasible defensive measures, a state of

---

[3]Calculations indicate that an attack against all of the U.S. Minuteman silos would result in casualties (U.S. or Canadian) in the multi-million range from fallout alone; from all causes the actual numbers would be still larger.

defense-dominated stability appears unattainable. (Brennan remains the principal dissenter from this conclusion.) A defense deployed against a massive nuclear attack, using any technology now known or surmised, would be enormously expensive if it were designed to hold casualties to a small percentage of the population; moreover, a relatively less expensive increase in the opponents' offensive forces would cancel the protection provided by such a defense. These conclusions are valid even if highly optimistic assumptions are made regarding the performance of defense measures—which can never realistically be tested.

Once a tight defensive umbrella is ruled out, stability rests on deterrence achieved by protection of the strategic offensive forces against a totally disabling preemptive first strike. This, in turn, implies that the strategic nuclear weapons on either side have to be protected against initial attack through hardening, mobility or secrecy of location, and that any moves *on either side* which would impair these values would be considered destabilizing. Thus, in this situation, the deployment of weapons suitable for an effective attack against the strategic retaliatory forces of the opponent (often termed a "counterforce attack") detract from the margin of stability. However, stability as it has now been achieved does not imply that there is only one preordained option with which the strategic forces would retaliate if they were subject to attack. It is this latter point which apparently is frequently misunderstood by critics of the present situation.

II

What really are the choices which our strategic systems permit in the event the country is attacked? Once the technical nature of the forces is restricted, making them unsuitable for an effective first strike against the other side's strategic weapons, then certain types of counterforce responses to an enemy attack should no longer be considered real options. Thus, any response which could be interpreted as part of a first-strike posture is ruled out. Specifically, a counterforce attack, which by virtue of its explosive power, accuracy and number of warheads might endanger the land-based, hardened silos of the other side, would have to be explicitly ruled out because that same configuration would also be an essential component of a first-strike attack. However, this is the *only* restriction on the procedure which is not imposed by deliberate policy or by technical conditions subject to modification. This means that while I agree with Iklé's first point, "that our nuclear forces must be designed almost exclusively for retaliation," as correctly representing the cornerstone of stability in this epoch, the nature of such retaliation is given wide latitude; the other two points made by Iklé in his article seriously misrepresent the current situation by claiming that response is restricted to instant and massive retaliation.

In fact, there is no basic *technical* reason why any retaliation would have to be swift; a great deal of technical, political and diplomatic effort during the last two decades has gone into measures to prevent just that compulsion. The "hot line" which was first established by the Memorandum of Understanding of June 20, 1963, and whose character was upgraded during the SALT talks, is a case in point. The very purpose of that hot line is to permit an exchange of information among the parties in case a nuclear explosion has taken place on the territory of one of them, and this communication does not preclude subsequent retaliation. Similarly, efforts have been made to harden and diversify command-and-control systems so that no instantaneous "go" orders have to be sent out on first verification of nuclear attack, let alone on warning. Whether these measures on either side of the ocean are fully adequate technically is, of course, a matter about which residual doubt will always remain. Increased awareness of this problem and measures to improve the situation technically are certainly needed.

Those measures (such as improving the accuracy of strategic warheads, adding multiple warheads to intercontinental missiles, et cetera) which appear to threaten land-based missile silos are the main causes of arguments, albeit highly unpersuasive, for the need for rapid response, or even launch-on-warning. There has been a flood of calculations regarding the alleged vulnerability of the land-based Minuteman forces. Such projections use a range of numbers of enemy missiles that assume multiple Soviet warheads yet to be developed; these are to impact with assumed explosive powers and at various distances from the silos. Calculations on the survival of strategic aircraft under attack and estimates of their ability to deliver nuclear weapons are less numerous and more difficult; there are no meaningful calculations at all on the vulnerability of our strategic submarines.

Apparently, the reason for this disparity of calculational effort is that computations of Minuteman vulnerability can easily be made with a wide variety of models, even if the assumptions are difficult to justify; there is no specifically known physical vulnerability for nuclear missile submarines. However, calculations even for Minuteman are dubious since Minuteman vulnerability is very steeply dependent on the accuracy of the attacking missiles, and the performance of such missiles and hardened silos under actual combat conditions is uncertain. Moreover, it is very difficult to predict precisely how in a heavy attack one missile will affect another: dust or debris produced by one missile impact may destroy another incoming warhead and the radiation from one nuclear explosion can disable a companion missile. For these and other reasons

an attacker could have little confidence in his calculated ability to reduce the number of Minuteman survivors to the very small number
"negligible" as a retaliatory threat.[4] Thus, even though the more extreme projections of the Soviet threat beyond this decade (unless limited by future SALT agreements) indicate very few Minuteman survivors from a Soviet attack, Minuteman remains a substantial contributor to deterrence.

Whatever the vulnerability may be of each member of the "triad"
of strategic retaliatory forces (submarines, land-based missiles and
bombers), there is no technical method in view by which either side
could mount a fully disabling and synchronized attack against the *combination* of nuclear strategic forces of the other. Thus, neither the present nor the foreseeable technical situation creates a need for a rapid,
and possibly ill-considered, response to attack.

It is equally incorrect to state that such a counterattack must be a
single massive strike. With the exception of being denied a counterforce strike against the other side's hardened silos, the choice in numbers and kinds of targets—be they military or civilian—is governed
only by the technical features of the command-and-control system and
the doctrine which governs its application. Therefore, the answer to
the President's oft-quoted question: "Should a President, in the event
of a nuclear attack, be left with the single option of ordering the mass
destruction of enemy civilians, in the face of the certainty that it would
be followed by the mass slaughter of Americans?" delivered as part of
the State of the World message in 1970, is "No, he should not." And he
does indeed have many other choices. Thus, Iklé's third point—"The
threatened 'retaliation' must be the killing of a major fraction of the
Soviet population"—also does not correctly describe the current situation, either before SALT or after.

The President himself has now said, in his fourth foreign policy
message of May 1973: "An aggressor, in the unlikely event of nuclear
war, might choose to employ nuclear weapons selectively and in lim-

---

[4]A retaliatory attack would have to be very small indeed to be "negligible." Indeed,
neither leaders nor serious observers in either country should pay much attention to the
spuriously precise analyses cranked out by military computers to "determine" levels of
damage from nuclear attack. Such calculations usually take into account only "prompt"
casualties, that is those resulting from blast or prompt radiation. Few analyses consider
fallout, and none of those generally used take into account such post-attack effects as
fire, damage to food supplies, medical care and productivity, or epidemics. As Iklé
notes, the omission of such after-attack effects leads to substantial underestimates. It is
another instance of the way in which, in his words: "The jargon of American strategic
analysis works like a narcotic. It dulls our sense of moral outrage about the tragic confrontation of nuclear arsenals, primed and constantly perfected to unleash widespread
genocide."

ited numbers for limited objectives," and "If the United States has the ability to use its forces in a controlled way, the likelihood of nuclear response would be more credible, thereby making deterrence more effective and the initial use of nuclear weapons by an opponent less likely." These statements justify more convincingly the need for a large variety of nuclear options—not as a means to abolish the mutual-hostage relationship between U.S. and Soviet citizens but to strengthen deterrence against first use of nuclear weapons of *all* kinds. SALT has not impaired these more limited responses; on the contrary, the severe ABM restraints of the SALT treaty have assured penetration of even small missile attacks and therefore have broadened the range of possible retaliation.

III

Mankind has indeed succeeded in creating a situation in which the vast stockpiles of nuclear weapons in the world can no longer be "rationally" used. But is that enough? Although the above discussion clearly refutes the claim of Iklé and others that the present strategic doctrine requires a rapid and massive retaliatory response, the critics have performed a valuable service by shaking confidence in the long-range "stability" which the present arrangements imply. Whether or not credit has been given correctly to the role of nuclear weapons in having prevented large-scale war after World War II, it is true that this record may be broken at any time by a nuclear accident, by escalation of a war initiated by third powers, or by unauthorized attacks. There is no meaningful way to predict whether these "irrational" nuclear catastrophes can be avoided throughout this century and beyond as long as the enormous nuclear stockpiles grow, or even remain.

On the positive side, there is increasing pressure for more layers of safety devices, better communications, et cetera. Moreover, there may also be hope that Permissive Action Links (PALs)—devices which by mechanical means prevent one military echelon from executing a strike without permission from a higher level—may be used for strategic as well as tactical nuclear weapons systems. On the negative side, we have the ever-increasing complexity of nuclear delivery systems and the increasing destructive power at the command of a single submarine commander. Finally, there is the problem of maintaining high standards of diligence and responsibility on a routine basis for a protracted number of years.

A possible constructive step in arms-control negotiations would be an agreement on progressively tightening the political and technical command-and-control provisions over the strategic systems of the nuclear powers. This is clearly a move not subject to verification, but the incentive to violate such an accord appears small enough so that such a provision might be negotiable.

But in the last analysis, the risk of accidental war cannot be eliminated. Our hope for avoiding a nuclear catastrophe over the long range rests on continually reducing the product of the two variables that define the risk—the number of nuclear weapons in strategic stockpiles and the chance of any one of them being delivered through accidental launch or unauthorized use. Without a steady decrease in this index, the future is indeed dim.

In short, even though the present degree of stability is greater than the critics suggest, there can be no assurance that it will in fact prevent the outbreak of nuclear war either by accident or through conflict introduced by third countries. The critics of the present doctrine have done substantial harm by their unsubstantiated claim that some strategic policy—not accompanied by a dramatic reversal in the growth of nuclear armaments—can relieve the inhumanity of the present situation, even perhaps the risk of accidental war.

In another respect, the emphasis of the SALT critics on the use of nuclear weapons against military targets has given new incentives and justification for the procurement of counterforce weapons such as highly accurate nuclear warheads. Such developments would be destabilizing by being physically indistinguishable from weapons designed for a preemptive attack against the opponent's retaliatory forces. In addition there is the revival of the word "controlled." This refers to the military use of strategic nuclear weapons in actual warfighting, while presumably minimizing the risk of escalation to a full-scale nuclear conflict. Yet, if such a risk could really be minimized—a highly dubious assumption—then such a development would, in fact, remove a factor that now deters the outbreak of large-scale war.

IV

I do not know or foresee a solution to the problem which Iklé states: "By taking advantage of modern technology, we should be able to escape the evil dilemma that the strategic forces on both sides must either be designed to kill people or else jeopardize the opponent's confidence in his deterrent." In the absence of any specifically proposed, let alone established, resolution of this problem, statements such as these tend to mislead civilian policymakers and extend false hopes that technology will lead us out of the nuclear dilemma. Ill-founded attempts to "sanitize" nuclear war are a disservice to the maintenance of stability, as well as to efforts to reduce areas of risk.

In essence, the critics of a primarily deterrent posture and the advocates of "nuclear war-fighting" assume that scientific progress will somehow alter the existing realities. I can see no technological basis for this assumption. Specifically:

No technological distinction exists or can be created between those nuclear weapons endangering the deterrent forces of the opponent in a first or preemptive strike (and thus decreasing stability) and weapons designed to attack the same forces by retaliation.

There is no demonstrable break between nuclear weapons designed for limited attacks and those designed for "strategic" retaliation.

Anti-military nuclear attacks of substantial size will almost certainly generate enormous civilian casualties.

Whatever plans or technological preparations the United States may make to fight a "controlled" nuclear conflict, there can be no certain method to protect the U.S. population in case the opponent decides to respond with an anti-population attack.

Available casualty estimates understate the effects of large-scale nuclear war; such consequences as epidemics aggravated by maldistribution of medical care, fire, starvation, ecological damage and societal breakdown are well-nigh incalculable.

From these inescapable conditions it follows, in my judgment, that the only clear demarcation line giving a "fire-break" in the use of weapons in war will continue to be the boundary between non-nuclear and nuclear devices. Mere shifts in policy and strategic doctrine will neither eliminate the hostage role of the populations of the United States and the Soviet Union, nor decrease the danger of nuclear catastrophe through accident or through unauthorized attack. Nor will they, in Churchill's words, "cover the case of lunatics or dictators in the mood of Hitler when he found himself in his final dugout." Only the relaxation of political tensions, coupled with bold steps limiting and reducing the quality and quantity of arms, and with ever-increasing vigilance over the control, safety and nonproliferation of nuclear weapons, can offer hope that nuclear disaster can be avoided.

3

STRATEGIC DOCTRINE: OFFICIAL DOCUMENTS AND STATEMENTS

ANNUAL DEFENSE DEPARTMENT REPORT, FY 1975

James R. Schlesinger

Although President Nixon had originally expressed his displeasure with existing strategic doctrine in his first foreign policy report to the Congress in 1970, it was not until four years later that his administration announced a comprehensive program to adapt the nuclear arsenal to the changing circumstances and evolving threats of the 1970s. The first lengthy exposition of that program was contained in Secretary of Defense James R. Schlesinger's Annual Defense Department Report *on the fiscal year 1975 budget. It details the ramifications for defense programs to be subsequently presented in testimony before congressional committees, and it sheds light on basic threat perceptions and analyses of Soviet intentions. The statement led to the adoption of a strategy placing greater emphasis on limited nuclear options and counterforce targeting capabilities. It reveals both an appreciation of the diminishing utility of nuclear weapons for deterring war and a desire to compensate for it.*

America's nuclear strategy has failed to keep pace with technological developments, according to Secretary Schlesinger. Consequently, the strategic forces of the United States have been poised to deter a massive attack which has little probability of occurring, leaving the President with inadequate options to respond to more likely threats. In order for the United States to provide an adequate deterrent across "the entire spectrum" of possible threats, it must maintain the capability to respond in kind. Should deterrence fail and war occur, the United States must be capable of responding with options designed to terminate the conflict and prevent further escalation.

In contemplating what had previously been considered beyond human

---

Source: James R. Schlesinger, *Annual Defense Department Report, FY 1975* (Washington, D.C., March 4, 1974), pp. 25–45.

85

control, namely, the actual waging of nuclear war and the means of bringing it to an end, the strategy presented in this report goes further than any earlier annual report. It not only seeks to enhance the credibility of the nuclear threats which are the basis of deterrence, but provides an answer to the disconcerting question, What if deterrence fails?

II. Strategic Forces

Among the major capabilities in the defense arsenal of the United States, the strategic nuclear deterrent forces command the most attention. Yet compared with the general purpose forces, their costs are relatively small. And, with brief exceptions, their costs as a percent of the total defense budget have actually declined during the past decade.

*   *   *

A. The Basis for the Strategic Nuclear Forces. To underline the trends in these relatively modest costs is not to minimize the importance of the strategic nuclear deterrent forces. At the same time that the United States has necessarily become more engaged in world affairs than ever before in its history, it has become increasingly vulnerable to direct nuclear attack and to the possibility of unprecedented destruction. Nuclear weapons now cast their shadow over all of us, and even complete political isolation would no longer relieve us of their threat. The United States is too powerful to be ignored and no longer far enough away (measured by ICBM [intercontinental ballistic missiles] trajectories) to be out of hostile reach. It is understandable, therefore, why strategic nuclear forces should receive so much attention. Without a firm foundation of nuclear deterrent forces the rest of our power would not count for much in the modern world.

I cannot stress this last point too strongly. All wars since 1945 have been non-nuclear wars shadowed by the nuclear presence. The threat to use nuclear weapons has remained, for the most part, in the background, but belligerents and neutrals alike have known that, like the big stick in the closet, it was there. Perhaps we may hope that in the future, as in the past, the nuclear forces will act as a brake upon violence, and that wars will remain conventional or not begin at all. Perhaps we may even hope that the strategic nuclear forces, by contributing to a worldwide balance of power and international stability, will carry us well beyond detente to a more enduring peace and to a general reduction of armaments.

Not only are the strategic forces vitally important; they are controversial as well. Most of the major defense debates during the past thirty years have centered on them, and alarms have rung over such matters as the B-36, the bomber "gap," the missile "gap," MIRVs [multiple independently targetable reentry vehicles], and ABM [anti-ballistic missile] deployments. Much of the debate has centered on specific weapons systems. But issues have also arisen about the size and composition of the offensive and defensive forces, the nature of alternative target systems, and the desirability and feasibility of enhancing deterrence and limiting escalation by having the option to avoid destroying enemy cities.

Of equal concern has been the growth to maturity of Soviet strategic offensive forces. Only a decade ago these forces numbered in the hundreds; now we count them in the thousands, and they have a substantially greater throw-weight. As a consequence, the issue that faces us no longer is (if it ever was) how to avoid initiatives that might continue or accelerate the strategic competition, but how—in a situation of essential equivalence—to interpret and respond to a wide range of potential Soviet initiatives.

If we are to have informed and productive debate on these matters, it is important that the Congress and the public understand the evolutionary character of strategic force planning and doctrine. Accordingly, it is essential to review the factors that now shape our strategic nuclear forces, the assumptions we make about these factors in designing our posture, and the directions we propose to take in our Five-Year Defense Program. In undertaking this review, I will place particular emphasis on why we are maintaining such comparatively large and diversified offensive forces, why we are modifying our strategic doctrine, and why we are proposing the pursuit of a number of research and development projects as prudent hedges for the future.

What is generally accepted, as a minimum, is that we ourselves must not contribute to any failures of deterrence by making the strategic forces a tempting target for attack, or prone to accidents, unauthorized acts, or false alarms.

I should also stress that it is only in the process of examining why and how deterrence might fail that we can judge the adequacy of our plans and programs for deterrence. And once that analysis begins, it quickly becomes evident that there are many ways, other than a massive surprise attack, in which an enemy might be tempted to use, or threaten to use, his strategic forces to gain a major advantage or concession. It follows that our own strategic forces and doctrine must take a wide range of possibilities into account if they are successfully to perform their deterrent functions.

Nuclear proliferation represents another important factor. It is a complex process driven by many actions and considerations. But one element affecting its extent and velocity undoubtedly is the degree to which other countries believe that the U.S. strategic deterrent continues—or fails—to protect them. Accordingly, in support of our non-proliferation policy, we must take account of the concerns of other countries in our doctrine and force planning.

There is also an important relationship between the political behavior of many leaders of other nations and what they perceive the strategic nuclear balance to be. By no means do all of them engage in the dynamic calculations about the interaction of Soviet and U.S. forces that have so affected our own judgments in the past. However, many do react to the static measures of relative force size, number of warheads, equivalent megatonnage, and so forth. Hence, to the degree that we wish to influence the perceptions of others, we must take appropriate steps (by their lights) in the design of the strategic forces.

Finally, an important connection exists between U.S. arms control efforts and the size and composition of the strategic nuclear forces. Arms control agreements are, of course, designed deliberately to constrain the freedom of the parties in the planning of their offensive and defensive capabilities. Strategic programs, in turn, affect the prospects for arms control. And specific weapons systems are the coin of this particular realm. Not only are such systems the mediums of exchange; they are also the basis for expanding or contracting the forces. As a consequence, arms control objectives must have a major impact on our planning.

1. The problem of objectives. I believe it is well understood that the size and composition of our strategic nuclear forces must depend to some degree on the magnitude of the overall deterrent burden that we place upon them. It is also a matter of increasingly widespread appreciation that these forces cannot bear the entire burden by themselves, however fundamental their importance may be. Other capabilities, nuclear and non-nuclear, must be maintained in strength to cover the entire spectrum of deterrence. What still requires emphasis, however, is the diversity of roles that the strategic nuclear forces continue to play. Our ability to achieve major national security objectives continues to be hostage to the operational doctrine, size, and composition of these forces.

Deterrence has been and remains the fundamental objective of our strategic nuclear forces. But what precisely do we want these forces to deter? Clearly, we expect them to forestall direct attacks on the United States; at the same time, however, we accept the equally heavy responsibility to deter nuclear attacks on our allies. To some extent we also depend on the strategic forces to exercise a deterrent effect against massive non-nuclear assaults, although we now place the main emphasis on U.S. and allied theater forces for that purpose. We also view our strategic forces as inhibiting coercion of the U.S. by nuclear powers, and, in conjunction with other U.S. and allied forces, helping to inhibit coercion of our allies by such powers.

While deterrence is our fundamental objective, we cannot completely preclude the possibility that deterrence might fail. The objectives we would want our strategic forces to achieve in those circumstances remain an issue to which I shall return.

2. *U.S.S.R. and P.R.C. strategic objectives.* Despite the importance of these objectives, it is probably the present and prospective strategic nuclear forces of other nations that constitute the single most powerful influence on the design of our own capabilities. Most of our strategic objectives, in fact, are a function of these potential threats.

The most important nuclear capability facing the United States is that of the U.S.S.R. As we engage in our own planning, we need to understand better than we now do why this capability is evolving at such a rapid rate and what the Soviets hope to gain by such large expenditures and such ambitious programs. Only with an improved understanding can we decide judiciously what impact this capability should have on our own choice of strategic programs.

Primarily at issue are the answers to two major questions. To what extent have the Soviets simply responded to and tried to counter U.S. initiatives? And to what extent have they sought (and do they continue to seek) something more ambitious than a capability for second-strike massive retaliation against the United States?

Much has been written on both counts, at least in the United States. But the Soviets have not proved especially communicative about their programs and motives, and the evidence of what they are up to is, to say the least, fragmentary and conflicting. As so often is the case, we are faced with uncertainty. . . .

What does this evidence suggest?

First, the Soviets have proceeded with development of many strategic programs ahead of, rather than in reaction to, what the United States has done. It is worth recalling, in this connection, that they took the initiative in the deployment of MRBMs and IRBMs [medium-range and intermediate-range ballistic missiles], ICBMs, ABMs, and FOBS [fractional orbital bombardment systems]. At the present time, they have four new ICBMs that are actively being flight tested.

Second, the Soviets—through their medium-range (or peripheral attack) capabilities—may have initially intended to threaten Western Europe as their only response to the intercontinental U.S. threat to the U.S.S.R. in the early days of the strategic competition. But they have maintained and expanded that threat long after having acquired the capability to launch a direct attack on the United States. Indeed, the size of their medium-range force bears no evident relationship to the capability of its counterparts in Western Europe or even to any urban target system there.

Third, it is noteworthy that the Soviets are apparently not content with the SALT I agreements, which temporarily froze certain Soviet quantitative advantages (in ICBMs and SLBMs [submarine-launched ballistic missiles]) in compensation for certain U.S. advantages. They have decided, as far as we can judge, to strive for at least comparable qualitative capabilities as well.

To sum up, what we now have to face in our force planning is that the Soviets have:

- acquired better than numerical parity with the United States in terms of strategic nuclear launchers (counting bombers as well as missiles);

- continued their extensive threat to Western Europe even after having acquired a massive direct threat to the United States;

- begun to exploit the larger throw-weight of their ICBMs so as to permit the eventual deployment of as many as 7,000 potentially high-accuracy MIRVs with large yields;

- started production of the Backfire bomber which could well evolve into an intercontinental threat.

It is premature to assess confidently what objectives the Soviets have set for themselves with these active, expensive programs. However, it is certainly conceivable that they foresee both political and military advantage, not only in the growing numerical weight of their forces, but also in their potential to bring major portions of our own strategic arsenal into jeopardy.

The United States, for its part, cannot afford to stand idly by in the face of these developments. As I shall discuss later, we are recommending a number of quite specific research programs to hedge against any sustained drive to achieve what the Soviet Union may regard, however mistakenly, as meaningful, exploitable, superiority. Preferably by agreement or if necessary by unilateral action, we believe that we must maintain an essential equivalence with them. We are prepared to balance our strategic forces down if SALT succeeds, or to balance them up if we must match Soviet momentum.

The Soviet strategic capability no longer is the only one that we must take into account in our force planning. A second important force from the standpoint of the United States is that of the People's Republic of China (P.R.C.). During the past decade, the Chinese have moved steadily from a program of development and testing to a deployed nuclear capability. We now estimate that they already have on line a modest number of MRBMs, IRBMs, and nuclear-capable medium and light bombers.

Previous forecasts about the evolution of this capability have not proved particularly reliable, and I cannot guarantee any higher confidence in the current projections. Nevertheless, we estimate that the PRC could achieve an ICBM initial operating capability as early as 1976 and an SLBM initial operating capability at a somewhat later date.

We do not yet have much insight into the strategic and political objectives that the P.R.C. is seeking to achieve with these deployments. But certain interesting features about them are already evident.

- The Chinese are clearly sensitive to the importance of second-strike nuclear capabilities and are making a considerable effort to minimize the vulnerability of their strategic offensive forces.

- The range and location of their systems are such that they can already cover important targets in the eastern U.S.S.R. But they are also located so as to cover other countries on their periphery.

- With the deployment of the ICBM that they have under development (and later an SLBM), they will have the capability to reach targets throughout the U.S.S.R. and in the United States as well.

Our relations with the P.R.C. have, of course, improved very dramatically during the last four years. Moreover, the present Chinese leadership may well be striving for exclusively second-strike counter-city forces. Nonetheless, we must in prudence take these forces into account in our planning.

*   *   *

It is . . . [also] essential that we focus on the issues that could arise if and when several additional nations acquire nuclear weapons, not necessarily against the United States, but for possible use or pressure against one another. Such a development could have a considerable impact on our own policies, plans, and programs. Indeed, this prospect alone should make it evident that no single target system and no stereotyped scenario of mutual city-destruction will suffice as the basis for our strategic planning.

3. *Deterrence and assured destruction.* I frankly doubt that our thinking about deterrence and its requirements has kept pace with the evolution of these threats. Much of what passes as current theory wears a somewhat dated air—with its origins in the strategic bombing campaigns of World War II and the nuclear weapons technology of an earlier era when warheads were bigger and dirtier, delivery systems con-

siderably less accurate, and forces much more vulnerable to surprise attack.

The theory postulates that deterrence of a hostile act by another party results from a threat of retaliation. This retaliatory threat, explicit or implicit, must be of sufficient magnitude to make the goal of the hostile act appear unattainable, or excessively costly, or both. Moreover, in order to work, the retaliatory threat must be credible: that is, believable to the party being threatened. And it must be supported by visible, employable military capabilities.

The theory also recognizes that the effectiveness of a deterrent depends on a good deal more than peacetime declaratory statements about retaliation and the existence of a capability to do great damage. In addition, the deterrent must appear credible under conditions of crisis, stress, and even desperation or irrationality on the part of an opponent. And since, under a variety of conditions, the deterrent forces themselves could become the target of an attack, they must be capable of riding out such an attack in sufficient quantity and power to deliver the threatened retaliation in a second strike.

The principle that nuclear deterrence (or any form of deterrence, for that matter) must be based on a high-confidence capability for second-strike retaliation—even in the aftermath of a well-executed surprise attack—is now well established. A number of other issues remain outstanding, however. A massive, bolt-out-of-the-blue attack on our strategic forces may well be the worst possible case that could occur, and therefore extremely useful as part of the force sizing process. But it may not be the only, or even the most likely, contingency against which we should design our deterrent. Furthermore, depending upon the contingency, there has been a longstanding debate about the appropriate set of targets for a second strike which, in turn, can have implications both for the types of war plans we adopt and the composition of our forces.

This is not the place to explore the full history and details of that longstanding strategic debate. However, there is one point to note about its results. Although several targeting options, including military only and military plus urban-industrial variations, have been a part of U.S. strategic doctrine for quite some time, the concept that has dominated our rhetoric for most of the era since World War II has been massive retaliation against cities, or what is called assured destruction. As I hardly need emphasize, there is a certain terrifying elegance in the simplicity of the concept. For all that it postulates, in effect, is that deterrence will be adequately (indeed amply) served if, at all times, we possess the second-strike capability to destroy some percentage of the population and industry of a potential enemy. To be able to assure that destruction, even under the most unfavorable circumstances—so the argument goes—is to assure deterrence, since no possible gain could compensate an aggressor for this kind and magnitude of loss.

The concept of assured destruction has many attractive features from the standpoint of sizing the strategic offensive forces. Because nuclear weapons produce such awesome effects, they are ideally suited to the destruction of large, soft targets such as cities. Furthermore, since cities contain such easily measurable contents as people and industry, it is possible to establish convenient quantitative criteria and levels of desired effectiveness with which to measure the potential performance of the strategic offensive forces. And once these specific objectives are set, it becomes a relatively straightforward matter—given an authoritative estimate about the nature and weight of the enemy's surprise attack—to work back to the forces required for second-strike assured destruction.

The basic simplicity of the assured destruction calculation does not mean that the force planner is at a loss for issues. On the contrary, important questions continue to arise about the assumptions from which the calculations proceed. Where, for the sake of deterrence, should we set the level of destruction that we want to assure? Is it enough to guarantee the ruin of several major cities and their contents, or should we—to assure deterrence—move much further and upward on the curve of destruction? Since our planning must necessarily focus on the forces we will have five or even ten years hence, what should we assume about the threat—that is, the nature and weight of the enemy attack that our forces must be prepared to absorb? How pessimistic should we be about the performance of these forces in surviving the attack, penetrating enemy defenses (if they exist), and destroying their designated targets? How conservative should we be in buying insurance against possible failures in performance?

Generally speaking, national policy makers for more than a decade have chosen to answer these questions in a conservative fashion. Against the U.S.S.R., for example, we tended in the 1960s to talk in terms of levels of assured destruction at between a fifth and a third of the population and between half and three-quarters of the industrial capacity. We did so for two reasons:

- beyond these levels very rapidly diminishing increments of damage would be achieved for each additional dollar invested;

- it was thought that amounts of damage substantially below those levels might not suffice to deter irrational or desperate leaders.

We tended to look at a wide range of threats and possible attacks

93

on our strategic forces, and we tried to make these forces effective even after their having been attacked by high but realistically constrained threats. That is to say, we did not assume unlimited budgets or an untrammeled technology on the part of prospective opponents, but we were prudent about what they might accomplish within reasonable budgetary and technological constraints. Our choice of assumptions about these factors was governed not by a desire to exaggerate our own requirements but by the judgment that, with so much at stake, we should not make national survival a hostage to optimistic estimates of our opponents' capabilities.

In order to ensure the necessary survival and retaliatory effectiveness of our strategic offense, we have maintained a TRIAD of forces, each of which presents a different problem for an attacker, each of which causes a specialized and costly problem for his defense, and all of which together currently give us high confidence that the force as a whole can achieve the desired deterrent objective.

That, however, is only part of the explanation for the present force structure. We have arrived at the current size and mix of our strategic offensive forces not only because we want the ultimate threat of massive destruction to be really assured, but also because for more than a decade we have thought it advisable to test the force against the "higher-than-expected" threat. Given the built-in surplus of warheads generated by this force sizing calculation, we could allocate additional weapons to non-urban targets and thereby acquire a limited set of options, including the option to attack some hard targets.

President Nixon has strongly insisted on continuing this prudent policy of maintaining sufficiency. As a result, I can say with confidence that in 1974, even after a more brilliantly executed and devastating attack than we believe our potential adversaries could deliver, the United States would retain the capability to kill more than 30 percent of the Soviet population and destroy more than 75 percent of Soviet industry. At the same time we could hold in reserve a major capability against the P.R.C.

Such reassurances may bring solace to those who enjoy the simple but arcane calculations of assured destruction. But they are of no great comfort to policy makers who must face the actual decisions about the design and possible use of the strategic nuclear forces. Not only must those in power consider the morality of threatening such terrible retribution on the Soviet people for some ill-defined transgression by their leaders; in the most practical terms, they must also question the prudence and plausibility of such a response when the enemy is able, even after some sort of first strike, to maintain the capability of destroying our cities. The wisdom and credibility of relying simply on the preplanned strikes of assured destruction are even more in doubt when allies rather than the United States itself face the threat of a nuclear war.

4. The need for options. President Nixon underlined the drawbacks to sole reliance on assured destruction in 1970 when he asked:

> Should a President, in the event of a nuclear attack, be left with the single option of ordering the mass destruction of enemy civilians, in the face of the certainty that it would be followed by the mass slaughter of Americans? Should the concept of assured destruction be narrowly defined and should it be the only measure of our ability to deter the variety of threats we may face?

The questions are not new. They have arisen many times during the nuclear era, and a number of efforts have been made to answer them. We actually added several response options to our contingency plans in 1961 and undertook the retargeting necessary for them. However, they all involved large numbers of weapons. In addition, we publicly adopted to some degree the philosophies of counterforce and damage-limiting. Although differences existed between those two concepts as then formulated, particularly in their diverging assumptions about cities as likely targets of attack, both had a number of features in common.

- Each required the maintenance of a capability to destroy urban-industrial targets, but as a reserve to deter attacks on U.S. and allied cities rather than as the main instrument of retaliation.

- Both recognized that contingencies other than a massive surprise attack on the United States might arise and should be deterred; both argued that the ability and willingness to attack military targets were prerequisites to deterrence.

- Each stressed that a major objective, in the event that deterrence should fail, would be to avoid to the extent possible causing collateral damage in the U.S.S.R., and to limit damage to the societies of the United States and its allies.

- Neither contained a clear-cut vision of how a nuclear war might end, or what role the strategic forces would play in their termination.

- Both were considered by critics to be open-ended in their requirement for forces, very threatening to the retaliatory capabilities of the U.S.S.R., and therefore dangerously stimulating to the arms race and the chances of preemptive war.

95

- The military tasks that each involved, whether offensive counter-force or defensive damage-limiting, became increasingly costly, complex, and difficult as Soviet strategic forces grew in size, diversity, and survivability.

Of the two concepts, damage-limiting was the more demanding and costly because it required both active and passive defenses as well as a counterforce capability to attack hard targets and other strategic delivery systems. Added to this was the assumption (at least for planning purposes) that an enemy would divide his initial attack between our cities and our retaliatory forces, or switch his fire to our cities at some later stage in the attack. Whatever the realism of that assumption, it placed an enormous burden on our active and passive defenses—and particularly on anti-ballistic missile (ABM) systems—for the limitation of damage.

With the ratification of the ABM Treaty in 1972, and the limitation it imposes on both the United States and the Soviet Union to construct no more than two widely separated ABM sites (with no more than 100 interceptors at each), an essential building-block in the entire damage-limiting concept has now been removed. . . . The treaty has also brought into question the utility of large, dedicated anti-bomber defenses, since without a defense against missiles, it is clear that an active defense against bombers has little value in protecting our cities. The salient point, however, is that the ABM Treaty has effectively removed the concept of defensive damage limitation (at least as it was defined in the 1960s) from contention as a major strategic option.*

Does all of this mean that we have no choice but to rely solely on the threat of destroying cities? Does it even matter if we do? What is wrong, in the final analysis, with staking everything on this massive deterrent and pressing ahead with a further limitation of these devastating arsenals?

No one who has thought much about these questions disagrees with the need, as a minimum, to maintain a conservatively designed reserve for the ultimate threat of large-scale destruction. Even more, if we could all be guaranteed that this threat would prove fully credible (to friend and foe alike) across the relevant range of contingencies—and that deterrence would never be severely tested or fail—we might also agree that nothing more in the way of options would ever be needed. The difficulty is that no such guarantee can be given. There are several reasons why any assurance on this score is impossible.

---

*Editors' Note: On July 3, 1974, President Nixon and Secretary Brezhnev signed in Moscow the "Protocol to the Treaty between the United States of America and the Union of Soviet Socialist Republics on the Limitation of Anti-Ballistic Missile Systems" which further restricted deployment of ABMs to one site in each country.

Since we ourselves find it difficult to believe that we would actually implement the threat of assured destruction in response to a limited attack on military targets that caused relatively few civilian casualties, there can be no certainty that, in a crisis, prospective opponents would be deterred from testing our resolve. Allied concern about the credibility of this particular threat has been evident for more than a decade. In any event, the actuality of such a response would be utter folly except where our own or allied cities were attacked.

Today, such a massive retaliation against cities, in response to anything less than an all-out attack on the U.S. and its cities, appears less and less credible. Yet as pointed out above, deterrence can fail in many ways. What we need is a series of measured responses to aggression which bear some relation to the provocation, have prospects of terminating hostilities before general nuclear war breaks out, and leave some possibility for restoring deterrence. It has been this problem of not having sufficient options between massive response and doing nothing, as the Soviets built up their strategic forces, that has prompted the President's concerns and those of our Allies.

Threats against allied forces, to the extent that they could be deterred by the prospect of nuclear retaliation, demand both more limited responses than destroying cities and advanced planning tailored to such lesser responses. Nuclear threats to our strategic forces, whether limited or large-scale, might well call for an option to respond in kind against the attacker's military forces. In other words, to be credible, and hence effective over the range of possible contingencies, deterrence must rest on many options and on a spectrum of capabilities (within the constraints of SALT) to support these options. Certainly such complex matters as response options cannot be left hanging until a crisis. They must be thought through beforehand. Moreover, appropriate sensors to assist in determining the nature of the attack, and adequately responsive command-control arrangements, must also be available. And a venturesome opponent must know that we have all of these capabilities.

Flexibility of response is also essential because, despite our best efforts, we cannot guarantee that deterrence will never fail; nor can we forecast the situations that would cause it to fail. Accidents and unauthorized acts could occur, especially if nuclear proliferation should increase. Conventional conflicts could escalate into nuclear exchanges; indeed, some observers believe that this is precisely what would happen should a major war break out in Europe. Ill-informed or cornered and desperate leaders might challenge us to a nuclear test of wills. We cannot even totally preclude the massive surprise attack on our forces which we use to test the design of our second-strike forces, although I regard the probability of such an attack as close to zero under existing conditions. To the extent that we have selective response options—smaller and more precisely focused than in the past—we should be able to deter such challenges. But if deterrence fails, we may be able to bring all but the largest nuclear conflicts to a rapid conclusion before cities are struck. Damage may thus be limited and further escalation avoided.

I should point out in this connection that the critics of options cannot have the argument both ways. If the nuclear balance is no longer delicate and if substantial force asymmetries are quite tolerable, then the kinds of changes I have been discussing here will neither perturb the balance nor stimulate an arms race. If, on the other hand, asymmetries do matter (despite the existence of some highly survivable forces), then the critics themselves should consider seriously what responses we should make to the major programs that the Soviets currently have underway to exploit their advantages in numbers of missiles and payload. Whichever argument the critics prefer, they should recognize that:

- inertia is hardly an appropriate policy for the United States in these vital areas;

- we have had some large-scale preplanned options other than attacking cities for many years, despite the rhetoric of assured destruction;

- adding more selective, relatively small-scale options is not necessarily synonymous with adding forces, even though we may wish to change their mix and improve our command, control, and communications.

However strong in principle the case for selective options, several questions about it remain. What kinds of options are feasible? To what extent would their collateral effects be distinguishable from those of attacks deliberately aimed at cities? And what are their implications for the future size and composition of our strategic forces and hence for our arms control objectives in this realm?

Many of the factors bearing on these questions will become more evident later in this statement. It is worth stressing at this point, however, that targets for nuclear weapons may include not only cities and silos, but also airfields, many other types of military installations, and a variety of other important assets that are not necessarily collocated with urban populations. We already have a long list of such possible targets; now we are grouping them into operational plans which would be more responsive to the range of challenges that might face us. To the extent necessary, we are retargeting our forces accordingly.

Which among these options we might choose in a crisis would depend on the nature of an enemy's attack and on his objectives. Many types of targets can be preprogrammed as options—cities, other targets of value, military installations of many different kinds, soft strategic targets, hard strategic targets. A number of so-called counterforce targets, such as airfields, are quite soft and can be destroyed without pinpoint accuracy. The fact that we are able to knock out these targets—counterforce though it may be—does not appear to be the subject of much concern.

In some circumstances, however, a set of hard targets might be the most appropriate objective for our retaliation, and this I realize is a subject fraught with great emotion. Even so, several points about it need to be made.

- The destruction of a hardened target is not simply a function of accuracy; it results from the combined effects of accuracy, nuclear yield, and the number of warheads applied to the target.

- Both the United States and the Soviet Union already have the necessary combinations of accuracy, yield, and numbers in their missile forces to provide them with some hard-target-kill capability, but it is not a particularly efficient capability.

- Neither the United States nor the Soviet Union now has a disarming first-strike capability, nor are they in any position to acquire such a capability in the foreseeable future, since each side has large numbers of strategic offensive systems that remain untargetable by the other side. Moreover, the ABM Treaty forecloses a defense against missiles. As I have already noted in public: "The Soviets, under the Interim Offensive Agreement, are allowed 62 submarines and 950 SLBM launchers. In addition, they have many other nuclear forces. Any reasonable calculation would demonstrate, I believe, that it is not possible for us even to begin to eliminate the city-destruction potential embodied in their ICBMs, let alone their SLBM force."

The moral of all this is that we should not single out accuracy as some sort of unilateral or key culprit in the hard-target-kill controversy. To the extent that we want to minimize unintended civilian damage from attacks on even soft targets, as I believe we should, we will want to emphasize high accuracy, low yields, and airburst weapons.

To enhance deterrence, we may also want a more efficient hard-target-kill capability than we now possess: both to threaten specialized sets of targets (possibly of concern to allies) with a greater economy of force, and to make it clear to a potential enemy that he cannot proceed with impunity to jeopardize our own system of hard targets.

Thus, the real issue is how much hard-target-kill capability we need, rather than the development of new combinations of accuracy and yield per se. Resolution of the quantitative issue . . . depends directly on the further evolution of the Soviet strategic offensive forces and on progress in the current phase of the Strategic Arms Limitation Talks.

In the meantime, I would be remiss if I did not recommend further research and development on both better accuracy and improved yield-to-weight ratios in our warheads. Both are essential whether we decide primarily on high accuracy and low yields or whether we move toward an improved accuracy-yield combination for a more efficient hard-target-kill capability than we now deploy in our missiles and bombers. Whichever way we go, we have more need than the Soviets for increased accuracy because of our constrained payloads and low-yield MIRVs which have resulted from our lower missile throw-weights.

With a reserve capability for threatening urban-industrial targets, with offensive systems capable of increased flexibility and discrimination in targeting, and with concomitant improvements in sensors, surveillance, and command-control, we could implement response options that cause far less civilian damage than would now be the case. For those who consider such changes potentially destabilizing because of their fear that the options might be used, let me emphasize that without substantially more of an effort in other directions than we have any intention of proposing, there is simply no possibility of reducing civilian damage from a large-scale nuclear exchange sufficiently to make it a tempting prospect for any sane leader. But that is not what we are talking about here. At the present time, we are acquiring selective and discriminating options that are intended to deter another power from exercising any form of nuclear pressure. Simultaneously . . . we and our allies are improving our general purpose forces precisely so as to raise the threshold against the use of any nuclear forces.

5. *Separability of targeting doctrine and sizing of forces.* The evolution in targeting doctrine is quite separable from, and need not affect the sizing of, the strategic forces. It is quite feasible to have the foregoing options within the limits set by the ABM Treaty and the Interim Agreement on offensive forces. What is more, none of the options we are adopting and none of the programs we are proposing for research and development need preclude further mutually agreed constraints

on or reductions in strategic offensive systems through SALT. If the Soviets are prepared to reduce these arsenals in an equitable fashion, we are prepared to accommodate them. In fact, I can say that we would join in such an effort with enthusiasm and alacrity.

To stress changes in targeting doctrine and new options does not mean radical departures from past practice. Nor does it imply any possibility of acquiring a first-strike disarming capability. As I have repeatedly stated, both the United States and the Soviet Union now have and will continue to have large, invulnerable second-strike forces. If both powers continue to behave intelligently and perceptively, the likelihood that they would unleash the strategic forces is so low that it approaches zero. We are determined, nonetheless, to have credible responses at hand for any nuclear contingency that might arise and to maintain the clear ability to prevent any potential enemy from achieving objectives against us that he might consider meaningful. The availability of carefully tailored, preplanned options will contribute to that end. They do not invite nuclear war; they discourage it.

I repeat, we are eager to begin a reduction of the strategic forces by mutual agreement and on terms of parity. That is our first preference. We would be quite content if both the United States and the Soviet Union avoided the acquisition of major counterforce capabilities. But we are troubled by Soviet weapons momentum, and we simply cannot ignore the prospect of a growing disparity between the two major nuclear powers. We do not propose to let an opponent threaten a major component of our forces without our being able to pose a comparable threat. We do not propose to let an enemy put us in a position where we are left with no more than a capability to hold his cities hostage after the first phase of a nuclear conflict. And certainly we do not propose to see an enemy threaten one or more of our allies with his nuclear capabilities in the expectation that we would lack the flexibility and resolve to strike back at his assets (and those of any countries supporting the threat) in such a way as to make his effort both high in cost and ultimately unsuccessful.

How we proceed on these counts will depend on the U.S.S.R. But I do not believe that we can any longer delay putting our potential countermeasures into research and development. The Soviets must be under no illusion about our determination to proceed with whatever responses their actions may require. And if we undertake the programs that I shall discuss later, the prospects for misunderstanding should be low. More sensible arrangements for both parties may then be feasible.

6. *Strategic balance and international stability.* Until the late 1960s, U.S. superiority in launchers, warheads, and equivalent megatonnage

was so great that we could ignore or disparage the importance of such "static" measures in comparing our forces with those of the U.S.S.R. Now, however, our numerical superiority has disappeared in almost every category except that of warheads, and it could dwindle very rapidly there as well.

Whether the Soviets believe that with the shift in these indicators they have achieved any meaningful, exploitable advantage is not clear. However, they have not been reticent in stressing to a variety of audiences their superiority over the United States in numbers of ICBMs and other strategic capabilities. Their words, at least, have suggested that they see these asymmetries as giving them diplomatic if not military leverage.

As far as we can judge, moreover, the Soviets now seem determined to exploit the asymmetries in ICBMs, SLBMs, and payload we conceded to them at Moscow [in the SALT I Interim Agreement of May 26, 1972]. Apparently, they are considering the deployment of large numbers of heavy and possibly very accurate MIRVs. As I have already indicated, this kind of deployment could in time come to threaten both our bombers and our ICBMs. Admittedly, we would still retain immense residual power in our deployed SLBM force, and the Soviets would surely know it. But to many interested observers, the actual and potential asymmetries (as measured by these "static" criteria) would look even more pronounced in favor of the U.S.S.R.

In such circumstances we cannot exclude the possibility that future Soviet leaders might be misled into believing that such apparently favorable asymmetries could, at the very least, be exploited for diplomatic advantage. Pressure, confrontation, and crisis could easily follow from a miscalculation of this nature.

It is all well and good to assert that the Soviet leaders, faced by an adamant and unified America, would come to their senses in time to avoid fatal mistakes in such a situation and would recognize the illusory nature of their advantages. But a crisis might already be too late for such an awakening. It is worth a price in research and development hedges to prevent such illusions from arising in the first place.

None of this should be taken to mean that exact symmetry must exist between the two offensive forces. The United States is willing to tolerate the existence of asymmetries provided that, in an era of alleged parity, they do not all favor one party. But we are not prepared to accept a situation in which all the visible asymmetries point in one direction. And we know from experience that the Soviets are not prepared to do so either. The potential for misunderstanding, miscalculation, and diplomatic error is too great to risk. A more equitable and stable arrangement would be one in which both sides maintain survivable second-strike reserves, in which there is symmetry in the ability of each side to threaten the other and in which there is a perceived equality between the offensive forces of both sides.

Accordingly, not only must our strategic force structure contain a reserve for threatening urban-industrial targets, the ability to execute a number of options, and the command-control necessary to evaluate attacks and order the appropriate responses; it must also exhibit sufficient and dynamic countervailing power so that no potential opponent or combination of opponents can labor under any illusion about the feasibility of gaining diplomatic or military advantage over the United States. Allied observers must be equally persuaded as well. In this sense, the sizing of our strategic arsenal, as distinct from our targeting doctrine, will depend on the outcome of SALT. In default of a satisfactory replacement for the Interim Agreement on strategic offensive forces, we will have to incorporate "static" measures and balancing criteria into the planning of our strategic offensive forces.

7. *Principal features of the proposed posture.* This review of the factors that necessarily shape the planning and programming of the strategic nuclear forces should also indicate the principal features that we propose to maintain and improve in our strategic posture. They are:

- a capability sufficiently large, diversified, and survivable so that it will provide us at all times with high confidence of riding out even a massive surprise attack and of penetrating enemy defenses, and with the ability to withhold an assured destruction reserve for an extended period of time;

- sufficient warning to ensure the survival of our heavy bombers together with the bomb alarm systems and command-control capabilities required by our National Command Authorities to direct the employment of the strategic forces in a controlled, selective, and restrained fashion;

- the forces to execute a wide range of options in response to potential actions by an enemy, including a capability for precise attacks on both soft and hard targets, while at the same time minimizing unintended collateral damage;

- the avoidance of any combination of forces that could be taken as an effort to acquire the ability to execute a first-strike disarming attack against the U.S.S.R.;

- an offensive capability of such size and composition that all will perceive it as in overall balance with the strategic forces of any potential opponent;

- offensive and defensive capabilities and programs that conform with the provisions of current arms control agreements and at the same time facilitate the conclusion of more permanent treaties to control and, if possible, reduce the main nuclear arsenals.

U.S.–U.S.S.R. STRATEGIC POLICIES

Testimony of Secretary of Defense James R. Schlesinger

As the principal spokesman on strategic policy for the second Nixon administration, Secretary of Defense James R. Schlesinger outlined the new selective targeting doctrine, emphasizing limited-strike options, to a subcommittee of the Senate Foreign Relations Committee, on March 4, 1974. The transcript of that testimony, now declassified, reveals that doctrinal changes had been contemplated under previous administrations and that estimates of actual and anticipated Soviet strategic capabilities compelled the United States to adopt a doctrine of flexible nuclear options.

One of the primary concerns expressed by the members of the subcommittee was that the acquisition of improved counterforce capabilities and targeting flexibility might lessen inhibitions against using nuclear weapons. Schlesinger emphasized that the primary intention of the change in targeting doctrine was to increase the credibility of the retaliatory threat inherent in deterrence. In this way, America's strategic nuclear weapons would be more useful in deterring a limited attack on the United States, or a massive conventional attack on Western Europe. The doctrinal modifications articulated by Schlesinger thus were to serve a dual purpose: to adapt U.S. strategic forces to the changing threat resulting from evolving Soviet technology, and to make more credible the nuclear umbrella the United States has extended over its European allies.

Secretary SCHLESINGER: The issue of retargeting, Mr. Chairman— which I prefer to refer to as a change in targeting doctrine—does not require any change in our force structure. The purpose of the change in the targeting doctrine, which emphasizes flexibility and selectivity, is to shore up deterrence. We believe, for reasons that I can lay out in considerable length, that the change in targeting doctrine serves to shore up deterrence across the entire spectrum of risk and consequently reduces the likelihood, which is fortunately already very

Source: *U.S.–U.S.S.R. Strategic Policies,* Hearing before the Subcommittee on Arms Control, International Law and Organizations of the Committee on Foreign Relations, United States Senate, 93rd Congress, 2d session, March 4, 1974.

low, of any outbreak of nuclear war. We want to keep recourse to nu-clear weapons as far away as possible. Our objective in all of these matters is, if conflict were to come, to keep that conflict at as low a level of violence as possible. We are using the strategic forces, as it were, to establish a framework within which conflict, if it comes, would be fought at a low level, in terms of the violence of the weapons involved.

It is our judgment that this change in targeting doctrine shores up deterrence. A targeting doctrine which stresses going only against cities is not an adequate deterrent for most purposes when the Soviet Union, as is the case today, has a counter-deterrent which is beyond the capacity and, I believe, the desire of the United States to take away. In fact, this is not the way the forces were targeted, but the overt public doctrine stressed only going against cities.

If the United States were to strike at the urban industrial base of the Soviet Union, the Soviet Union could and presumably would fire back destroying the urban industrial base of the United States. Con-sequently, the Soviet Union, under those circumstances, might believe that the United States would be self-deterred from making use of its strategic forces. Thus, they might regard themselves as relatively risk-free if our deterrent doctrine, our targeting doctrine, were to stress only going against cities.

Now, in my judgment, the effect of the emphasis on selectivity and flexibility, which I separate from any issue of sizing, is to improve deterrence across the spectrum of risk.

Mr. Chairman, as you know from our previous discussions about NATO, there has been a declining credibility, as the Europeans see it, in the relationship of U.S. strategic forces to European security.

The decline in that credibility was based upon the belief that the Americans would not use their strategic forces if, for example, New York and Chicago were placed at risk in order to protect Western Europe. Consequently, NATO, which is undergoing many travails, was also undergoing the travail of growing European disbelief that the U.S. strategic forces were locked into the security of Europe, despite our having made that pledge repeatedly over a period of many years.

The reaction in Europe to change in targeting doctrine has been uniformly welcoming, even joyous, because they recognize that this means U.S. strategic forces are still credibly part of the overall deterrent for Europe. That deterrent is based upon three components: strategic forces, tactical nuclear forces, and a satisfactory conventional capa-bility.

The change in targeting doctrine does not require new capabilities. There are some aspects for which we are asking the Congress this year for additional funding, but the change in doctrine is not dependent upon the additional funding. We are asking money in this budget for improved command and control, and for some improvement in accuracy, but the change in targeting doctrine does not depend for its efficacy upon our getting this money.

Mr. Chairman, I think that I have distinguished between the sizing of the forces and the purposes for which we have changed our targeting doctrine. I hope these comments are useful at the outset, and I am here to respond.

Senator MUSKIE: They are indeed useful.

With respect to the targeting doctrine, you speak of it as representing a change of doctrine. The actuality of our targeting practice already includes military targets as well as cities, doesn't it?

Secretary SCHLESINGER: Yes, sir.

Senator MUSKIE: How will this new doctrine change the actuality of our targeting?

Secretary SCHLESINGER: The change in targeting doctrine comes about in the following way: Of course, all our delivery vehicles are targeted against specific targets. The point that is different about the targeting doctrine that I have outlined to you is the emphasis on selectivity and flexibility. In the past we have had massive preplanned strikes in which one would be dumping literally thousands of weapons on the Soviet Union. Some of those strikes could to some extent be withheld from going directly against cities, but that was limited even then.

With massive strikes of that sort, it would be impossible to ascertain whether the purpose of a strategic strike was limited or not. It was virtually indistinguishable from an attack on cities. One would not have had blast damage in the cities, but one would have considerable fallout and the rest of it.

So what the change in targeting does is give the President of the United States, whoever he may be, the option of limiting strikes down to a few weapons. It is to be understood that, if the United States were to strike the Soviet Union in response to some hypothetical act on their part, this would not have to be a massive response. The credibility of a massive response was understandable in the fifties and even in the sixties when the United States had virtually a nuclear monopoly with regard to intercontinental strike forces. But the massiveness of those strikes has reduced the credibility of the deterrent since about 1967–68, when the Soviets began to introduce large numbers of missiles into their force structure.

They now have a deterrent posture that is beyond the capacity of the United States to take away. Some welcome that, some do not welcome that. But I think it is a fact of life. There is no way that the United States can limit damage to itself against a well coordinated strike by the Soviet Union.

Senator MUSKIE: Are you saying that the President does not now have the option of a limited strike against missile silos?

Secretary SCHLESINGER: He does hypothetically in that he could ask SAC [Strategic Air Command] to construct such a strike in an emergency. [Deleted.]

But in order to have that kind of capacity one has to do the indoctrination and the planning in anticipation of the difficulties involved. It is ill-advised to attempt to do that under the press of circumstances. Rather one should think through the problems in advance and put together relevant, small packages which a President could choose under the circumstances in which they might be required—which I stress I do not think will arise.

I think that this will shore up deterrence in those few areas in which there is weakness.

Senator MUSKIE: So what you are saying is that our preoperational strategic plan is a massive attack on cities and missile silos and other limited targets alike, and what you are proposing is a range of options which would range from attack on missile sites up to a massive attack on cities.

Secretary SCHLESINGER: Yes, sir.

Let me see if I can help your questioning and the questioning of the other members of the committee, if I may.

There are three aspects of this issue: the first is the sizing question. Then with regard to targeting there are two questions: first, is selectivity and flexibility, a desirable thing, and, second, are the particular programs which we of the Department of Defense are advocating this year with regard to accuracy and command control, desirable?

I would like to separate those two items because in talking with many people in the arms control community I find that to the extent that we are talking about greater selectivity and flexibility they are quite content. In fact, they think that this is a step forward in a moral and a practical sense. What they are concerned about are the inferences that the Soviets might draw from a program for greater accuracy. I emphasize this because when you get down to the hard rock of selectivity and flexibility in targeting plans, there really is very little criticism of that. Across the entire spectrum of people who have thought about this issue, there is relatively little criticism.

Senator MUSKIE: You seem to imply that if we establish this range of options for the President that this would somehow be reassuring to the Soviets, and they would assume from the fact he has this range that he would not use the option of massive attack against the cities.

Secretary SCHLESINGER: I am not sure it would be reassuring to the Soviets, Mr. Chairman.

Senator MUSKIE: Well, reassuring in the sense of influencing their own selection of a response or their own decision with respect to a first strike and so on.

Secretary SCHLESINGER: Yes, sir.

It might. The reassurance that I mentioned was in terms of the perspective taken by third parties toward the general deterrent effect of the two major strategic forces in the world.

The Soviets would not necessarily draw reassurance from this. It is not our objective to give them reassurance. In order to have deterrence one must have a credible threat. To the extent that this makes the possible use of U.S. strategic forces more credible, it has a beneficial effect on deterrence; but it does not necessarily reassure the Soviets.

What would be the psychological reaction by the Soviets to the announcement of this kind of strategy? They can go in one of two directions: they can, as some fear, say that limited strikes are feasible. That fear has been around for some years. There is no indication that the Soviets really believe that.

On the other hand, they may continue to believe that all wars must inevitably escalate to the highest level. If they believe the latter, then they will continue to be deterred from any action that would conceivably precipitate the start of the use of nuclear weapons which would have this escalatory effect.

Senator CASE: Mustn't they believe either one or the other? Aren't there just two choices, as you said previously? . . .

They will either believe one thing, which you say—as I understand it—that there is, it is possible to have less or there is not. Once you start with nuclear weapons it will inevitably go up.

Secretary SCHLESINGER: In logic they must believe one or the other, but there are relatively few people who take that precise a view of these problems. Many people believe that in all likelihood it must go all the way, but that there is some possibility that nuclear war could be constrained at a lower level. Other people argue that, once three or four or five nuclear weapons are employed, sensible political leaders would look around aghast at the consequences—at the most agonizing consequences—and say, "Let's stop right here."

Senator CASE: This is the part that I think has to be stressed because I think it is the heart of anything new you have brought into this thing. But, in fact, there isn't anything new because already we have targets, we have weapons targeted, individual targets that can be selected.

Secretary SCHLESINGER: Yes.

Senator CASE: It is just a matter of thinking about it, isn't it?

Secretary SCHLESINGER: Right. That is why I referred to it as targeting doctrine rather than the term retargeting that has been employed. It is the question of firing doctrine, and how you view the problem. You are quite right, Senator, to stress that aspect.

Senator HUMPHREY: And the indoctrination of our own people, isn't it?

Secretary SCHLESINGER: That is right.

Senator MUSKIE: In other words, you have to position our hardware and command organization to accord with this targeting doctrine. If circumstances should arise tomorrow that would justify selective targeting, how much of an inhibition would we have as a result of our failure to have programmed the selective? How much of an inhibition in terms of time constraints and so on?

[Discussion off the record.]

Senator FULBRIGHT: In answer to Senator Case, do you think it is possible to have a limited nuclear war, just to exchange a couple of weapons?

Secretary SCHLESINGER: I believe so, Senator.

Senator FULBRIGHT: You do? Why do you believe that?

Senator CASE: On this ground, that there is a *locus penitentiae* at a time when before it reaches the maximum, both sides would say, "Whoops, boys."

Secretary SCHLESINGER: Yes.

Senator CASE: Maybe so, and this is extremely important to discuss, because unless you have nuclear weapons used in such relatively small things that they are really not nuclear weapons, if you can imagine such, any destruction of a city is going to be an event that will inevitably, it seems to me, prevent any further rational discussion.

Senator FULBRIGHT: I am not as aware on this as some of the others. Could you visualize the circumstances that would result in a limited war?

*   *   *

Secretary SCHLESINGER: As your question implies, this is not a decision that any President or any political leader of the Soviet Union is likely to take lightly. It is an agonizing situation. It is very difficult to think of circumstances under which nuclear weapons will be employed. I am delighted to say that is the case.

What I am saying is that it is easier to think of the circumstances in which limited use might occur than it would be to think of a massive all-out strike against the urban industrial base of another nation which has the capability of striking back.

One circumstance I can think of is the possibility of the overrunning of Western Europe. This would be a major defeat for the NATO alliance and for the United States. I don't know what we would do under those circumstances in terms of the strategic forces, but I believe that it is necessary for our strategic forces to continue to be locked into the defense of Europe in the minds of the Europeans and of the Soviet Union.

That would be one of the circumstances. It is very hard for me, Senator, to think of other circumstances in which the advantages involved in the use of nuclear weapons could in any way be commensurate with the risks. We are talking about a very low probability about an extremely great horror and, therefore, I cannot think of many circumstances in which this would be the appropriate response.

Senator HUMPHREY: Let me see if I understand the chairman's view.

Are you asking him to give us a situation in which there would be a limited response?

Senator FULBRIGHT: In other words, where you would only drop a couple.

Senator HUMPHREY: Yes; and that would not trigger the escalatory process.

Senator FULBRIGHT: I can't think of any. I wonder what circumstances you can think of. You don't think Europe would be a case like that, do you?

Secretary SCHLESINGER: When I think of our overseas interests, Europe is the one preeminent place in which this could conceivably arise. But let me give you an illustration of that.

Senator FULBRIGHT: I don't understand the question. Do you mean that after they have made the decision all-out full force to overrun Europe, that you think one bomb would deter them and they would stop and say, "I am sorry"?

Secretary SCHLESINGER: I was not saying what weapons.

Senator FULBRIGHT: Or two bombs or six bombs?

Secretary SCHLESINGER: What we are talking about is an individual target set. If, for example, under those circumstances, one were to go after their oil production capacity—just take that as an illustration of a target set—the removal of that capacity would have a crippling effect on the Soviet ability to wage war against Western Europe.

Senator FULBRIGHT: Do you mean that if we did, that you don't think they would respond with nuclear weapons against us?

Secretary SCHLESINGER: They might well. I think that they would.

Senator FULBRIGHT: Sure they would.

Secretary SCHLESINGER: But I believe, Senator, if we were to maintain continued communications with the Soviet leaders during the war, and if we were to describe precisely and meticulously the limited nature of our actions, including the desire to avoid attacking their urban industrial base, that in spite of whatever one says historically in advance that everything must go all out, when the existential circumstances arise, political leaders on both sides will be under powerful pressure to continue to be sensible. Both sides under those circumstances will continue to have the capacity at any time to destroy the urban industrial base of the others. The leaders on both sides will know that. Those are circumstances in which I believe that leaders will be rational and prudent. I hope I am not being too optimistic.

Senator CASE: And you argue further that because this is a possibility, therefore, the Russians won't go into Western Europe with massive conventional force?

Secretary SCHESLINGER: That is our hope.

Senator FULBRIGHT: They won't anyway with our present forces unless they have lost their minds. If they are completely irrational, why none of the theories would hold up. I don't see how it changes that.

Senator CASE: I think he says this is a more credible deterrent than the present situation.

Secretary SCHLESINGER: At the present time our forces in Western Europe really in no way threaten the territory of the Soviet Union. The Soviets might perceive it differently.

*   *   *

Senator MUSKIE: . . . are you saying that our massive retaliatory capability has lost credibility with respect to our commitment to Europe from the Soviet point of view, and that if we have this more limited targeting capability, that the Soviets might regard that as a more credible deterrent?

Secretary SCHLESINGER: Yes, sir; I think that is very briefly it.

Senator MUSKIE: That is your position?

Secretary SCHLESINGER: Massive retaliation, of course, existed in the fifties. It was a somewhat different doctrine from assured destruction in the sixties. Massive retaliation, as adopted by Mr. Dulles, involved the use of strategic weaponry in response to a whole array of possible actions. It involved striking back at any times and places we chose. Assured destruction, to the extent it was elaborated in the sixties, tended to be described primarily in terms of going against cities.

Once the Soviet Union built up a counter-deterrent, assured destruction became a logically incredible kind of threat. It is not necessarily psychologically incredible, but it is logically incredible. That is our problem and that is why we are shifting the targeting doctrine to make it more credible. I believe as long as we have a credible threat there are not going to be hostilities of major dimensions.

Senator HUMPHREY: Mr. Secretary, I tend to agree with you, but you open up an option that I think is fraught with some danger, namely that you can have an exchange of one or two nuclear weapons on what is called a more sensible and selective doctrine and that would be it. In other words, the commander in chief of the Soviet Union, or the United States or any country could say, "I have reason to believe that I could use as commander in chief now three to four nuclear weapons on a selected target," and that this would have a deterrent effect because the horror of all-out nuclear war is just too much, and that the selective doctrine and this new targeting concept would give the President of the United States better and more efficient use of our existing weaponry.

The problem, as I see it, goes right back to Senator Fulbright's original question. Suppose once you have let loose that first bomb and it hits the Hiroshima or the Nagasaki of the Soviet Union, that instead of terrorizing the population, instead of bringing it to its knees, or even causing them to stop, look and think, what I would venture would be the immediate reaction is, "Well, we can really let them have it." I mean that is the danger. I don't say it will happen. I say this is one we have to think through.

Are we in a sense making it easier to trigger the holocaust or are we, in our doctrine, making more efficient use of our existing weaponry with the same deterrent effect that we had during the fifties and sixties with the massive deterrence? . . .

112

Secretary SCHLESINGER: I think your question goes to the heart of it.

Senator SYMINGTON: As a member of the Armed Services Committee, Mr. Secretary, last week I received a copy of your classified defense posture statement in which you discussed the strategic doctrine and from which I would now ask the following questions. On page 69 you gave a list of the principal features of the proposed strategic posture. The fourth item is the objective and I quote, "The avoidance of any combination of forces that could be taken as an effort to acquire the ability to execute a first-strike disarming attack against the U.S.S.R."

Because this restriction has to be interpreted in the eyes of the conservative Soviet analyst who looks with the same suspicion at the long-range evolution of the U.S. forces as we do at Soviet military developments, why do you believe that the development of a hard target kill capability by the United States will not be interpreted by Soviet analysts to point to the evolution of a United States first-strike capability against Soviet land-based forces?

Kindly note in your reply that the Soviets have concentrated a very much larger fraction of their retaliatory power in land-based ICBM's [intercontinental ballistic missile] than has the United States.

Secretary SCHLESINGER: Yes, sir.

That concentration, by the way, is undergoing change. They now have over 650 SLBM's [submarine-launched ballistic missiles] at sea, so the proportion of their forces that we cannot get at is increasing. . . .

I believe that there is some misunderstanding about the degree of reliability and accuracy of missiles. . . . it is impossible for either side to acquire the degree of accuracy that would give them a high confidence first strike because we will not know what the actual accuracy will be like in a real-world context.

As you know, we have acquired from the western test range a fairly precise accuracy, but in the real world we would have to fly from operational bases to targets in the Soviet Union. The parameters of the flight from the western test range are not really very helpful in determining those accuracies to the Soviet Union.

We can never know what degrees of accuracy would be achieved in the real world. I think that that probably is advantageous for the reasons that your question hints at.

The effect of this is that there will always be degradation in accuracy as one shifts from R. & D. [Research and Development] testing, which is essentially what we have at the western test range, to operational silos. . . .

*   *   *

The point that I would like to make, Senator, is that if you have any degradation in operational accuracy, American counter-force capability goes to the dogs very rapidly.

We know that and the Soviets should know it, and that is one of the reasons that I can publicly state that neither side can acquire a high confidence first-strike capability. I want the President of the United States to know that for all the future years, and I want the Soviet leadership to know that for all the future years. If the Soviet planners sit down and make exactly the same calculations, they will see that even after a U.S. first-to-strike, their ICBM force would have sufficient ability to strike back and destroy the industrial base of the United States.

* * *

Senator SYMINGTON: Now, on page 56 you make a persuasive case that the United States should have other options in response to a nuclear attack against the U.S. mainland, other than a massive all-out nuclear attack. But then, on page 60, you identify that requirement with a requirement for the need of attacking hard silos.

To what extent do we have an option now to withhold retaliation for an appropriate time of deliberation and to what extent now do we have the option of delivering less than a massive response?

Secretary SCHLESINGER: At the present time, we have the hypothetical option. That is why I indicated that we should separate the change in targeting doctrine from certain funding requests that we are making this year. I think that those funding requests will improve the doctrine, but the doctrine is not dependent on them. We can devise selective, flexible strikes with our existing array of weaponry.

* * *

Senator SYMINGTON: On page 62 you make what I believe is your intended case for adding hard target capability to future U.S. strategic forces when you state:

> To enhance deterrence we may also want a more efficient hard target kill capability than we now possess. Both [to threaten] specialized sets of targets possibly of concern to allies, with the greater economy of force, and to make it clear to a potential enemy that he cannot proceed with impunity to jeopardize our own system of hard targets.

What type of targets of possible concern to our allies are you referring to?

Secretary SCHLESINGER: IRBM [intermediate-range ballistic missile] sites, to take one example. Conceivably—underscoring the conceivably—we might be talking about certain hardened command and control facilities or weapons storage sites, those kinds of targets.

Senator SYMINGTON: What do you mean when you say the possible enemy "cannot proceed with impunity to jeopardize our own system of hard targets"?

Secretary SCHLESINGER: That that underscores one of my major concerns which goes back to the sizing and opportunity issue I discussed before. I do not think that it would be advisable for the United States to be in a position in which a potential foe has or had a counter-force capability that was markedly superior to that of the United States. I do not urge the United States to acquire a major counter-force capability, but there is built into the Soviet program, given the recent R. & D. activity, the potential net throw weight for a major counter-force capability. If they move in that direction, I think we simply cannot allow that marked superiority to develop. I stress again that I am not advocating that for either side.

Senator HUMPHREY: Would you permit a clarification? When you say counter-force, are you really talking first-strike capability?

Secretary SCHLESINGER: No, sir. We have to distinguish among disarming first strike, no first use, and counter-force. Counter-force can go against any military target. It can go against IRBM sites as opposed to ICBM sites. It would go against airfields or army camps. It has a range, and one can go counter-force rather than counter-value without necessarily putting himself into a position of having a disarming first-strike capability. In fact with our capabilities we cannot put ourselves in a position to have a disarming first strike unless we have, not [deleted] of a nautical mile CEP [circle of equal probability], which we have not achieved yet, but a fraction of [deleted].

Senator CASE: Well, there is a difference between counter-force in the sense of going against small or particular targets as your intermediate range sites or your control for target, missiles targeted to Europe, for instance. You are still for this?

Secretary SCHLESINGER: Yes, sir.

Senator CASE: You are not for an all-out effort?

Secretary SCHLESINGER: Right. We cannot, and we should not, put in the minds of any political leaders the notion that they have got a serious potentiality for a disarming first strike.

*   *   *

115

Senator SYMINGTON: On page 56, you talk about a "response to a limited attack on military targets that caused relatively few civilian casualties."

Do you really believe that such an attack against the United States is possible, and just what do you mean in numbers by relatively few civilian casualties?

Secretary SCHLESINGER: I think that hundreds of thousands of casualties, as opposed to tens and hundreds of millions, must be regarded as relatively few in number. But I am talking here about casualties of 15,000, 20,000, 25,000—a horrendous event, as we all recognize, but one far better than the alternative.

Senator SYMINGTON: Could not public statements by U.S. civilian leaders like yourself that "military attacks on military targets would cause relatively few civilian casualties," actually decrease the deterrent value of our nuclear forces?

Secretary SCHLESINGER: No, sir, I do not believe so. The reason I do not believe so is that the United States would retain all of the capabilities embodied in the assured destruction notion.

The point is that we would hopefully restrain the use of those capabilities during this hypothetical wartime period so that our potential opponent would continue to have reason to desist from attack on the urban industrial base of the United States.

*   *   *

Senator FULBRIGHT: . . . I realize, the way you explained it to the committee, you do not intend it that way, but there is a very general impression that this is an oblique manner of approaching first strike. Your predecessor came up and on the first day of hearings before this committee said, yes, he knew Russia was going for a first strike. That was the justification for the ABM [anti-ballistic missile system].

We went on with that for a year. . . . there is definitely a feeling that this new doctrine as you call it, is designed to accomplish at least what used to be considered a first strike. You have new rhetoric for all these things now, but it used to be—

Secretary SCHLESINGER: No, sir, I think the rhetoric reflects some very real differences. The change of targeting doctrine is intended simply to shore up deterrence. If we can deter war, that is the result that we all want. We distinguish, as I attempted to do at the outset in the discussion with Senator Muskie, between the change in targeting doctrine and the size of our force. The change in doctrine requires no changes in our force structure, and it even permits a reduction in our force structure if the Soviets would collaborate.

116

We do not want to expand our forces. We hope through SALT, which is a feature of détente, to restrain the growth of forces on both sides.

* * *

Senator SYMINGTON: Has the type of selective and flexible targeting capability that you are now proposing ever been proposed in the past; and if so, why was it not adopted?

Secretary SCHLESINGER: It has been stated by several Secretaries of Defense. We could probably break out the particular passages of past Defense reports. But nobody at the political level from 1961 to 1971 has put the energy behind developing the doctrine and the plans. Many statements can be found saying that flexibility or selectivity would be desirable. But before this time it has been sort of an aspiration. Now we are consciously basing our deterrent strategy upon the achievement of flexibility and selectivity in the way that was discussed earlier.

[The following information was subsequently supplied:]

Statements From Previous Defense Reports, Some of Which Were the Classified Versions

[Supplied by Department of Defense]

Extract From FY 1963 Posture Statement of Secretary of Defense Robert S. McNamara

"Furthermore, it is possible that the Soviet's initial strike might be directed solely at our military installations, leaving our cities as hostages for later negotiations. In that event, we might find it to our advantage to direct our immediate retaliatory blow against their military installations, and to withhold our attack on their cities, keeping the forces required to destroy their urban-industrial complex in a protected reserve for some kind of period of time.

"Accordingly, we should plan for the 1965-1967 time period a force which could: 1. Strike back decisively at the entire Soviet target system simultaneously; or 2. Strike back, first, at the Soviet bomber bases, missiles sites and other military installations associated with their long-range nuclear forces to reduce the power of any follow-on attack—and then, if necessary, strike back at the Soviet urban and industrial complex in a controlled and deliberate way. Such a force would give us the needed flexibility to meet a wide range of possible general war situations."

*Extract From FY 1966 Posture Statement of Secretary of Defense
Robert S. McNamara*

"For purposes of this discussion, we can define general nuclear war as a war in which strategic nuclear weapons are launched against the homelands of the United States and the Soviet Union. Such attacks might be directed against military targets only, against cities only, or against both types of targets, either simultaneously or with a delay. They might be selective in terms of specific targets attacked or they might be general."

"NATO should not only have an improved capability to meet major non-nuclear assaults with non-nuclear means and forces prepared for that option, but it should also achieve a true *tactical* nuclear capability which should include a broad, flexible range of nuclear options, short of general nuclear war, and the means to implement them."

*Extract from FY 1973 Posture Statement of Secretary of Defense
Melvin R. Laird*

"In order to maintain needed flexibility, we design our forces so that we have strategic alternatives available for use depending on the nature or level of provocation. This means capabilities that enable us to carry out an appropriate response without necessarily resorting to mass urban and industrial destruction."

*Extract from FY 1974 Posture Statement of Secretary of Defense
Elliot L. Richardson*

"U.S. strategic offensive forces have long been designed to carry out retaliatory options appropriate to the nature and level of provocation as well as to maintain an assured destruction capability. Our planning objectives and the sufficiency criteria for deterrence of direct strategic nuclear attack against the United States are currently under intensive review, following the conclusion of the Strategic Arms Limitation agreements and President Nixon's request for a more flexible capability in the application of our strategic forces. In particular, it is our goal to be able to respond to a nuclear attack without having to resort to mass urban and industrial destruction in retaliation. At the same time, we are seeking to maintain a deterrent posture that will not jeopardize the stability of the strategic balance."

*   *   *

Senator MUSKIE: I would like to put to you some of the questions that have been raised by the arms control community on your new strategic concept, and I am referring to a recent New York *Times* article by John Baker and Robert Berman, who raised these points and I would like to go through it in sequence so we can have your responses for the record.

* * *

The first problem raised by Baker and Berman in their February 22d article is this:

> The capability to destroy the adversary's nuclear forces will lower the nuclear threshold of deterrence by making nuclear weapons appear more useable in the form of surgical or precision nuclear strikes. Such capability will also increase the likelihood that some strategic planners will unrealistically perceive such strikes as an acceptable policy option of the President.

Secretary SCHLESINGER: As I have indicated, I trust there is not much built into that word "acceptable option." I think the decision to use nuclear weapons, either strategic or tactical, would be an agonizing decision for any political leader and certainly for the NATO Alliance collectively.

What I have stressed is that there must be a belief in the credibility of the threat. If you managed to persuade your opponent that you have a threat that is not implementable in practice, then you have lost the deterrent effect of your weaponry. It is my judgment that the fact that one makes one's opponent believe that something is possible diminishes the likelihood of clashes, that is, it improves deterrence.

Senator MUSKIE: Is this strategy, in your view, one which ought to be attractive to the Soviets as well?

Secretary SCHLESINGER: Their position, I think, is somewhat different from our own. One could say that they have the proximate objective of the domination of Western Europe. They can have a contribution toward the achievement of that objective if they can successfully decouple American strategic forces from Western European security. Our strategy tends to recouple strategic forces with Western European security, so our objectives are somewhat different from theirs. Consequently, this strategy must be far more attractive to us than it is to them.

They would like to isolate the United States in the North American Continent. Through this strategy we foreclose that possibility. Therefore, we have a more powerful incentive for going in this direction than do they.

Senator MUSKIE: Nevertheless, if we were to adopt this strategy, could they not counter it?

Secretary SCHLESINGER: Yes, sir.

Senator MUSKIE: And use it as a cloak for developing a first-strike capability?

Secretary SCHLESINGER: I do not think they need this strategy as a cloak. The potentiality for a perceived major first-strike capability against our ICBM's is built into the weapons that they have under test at the present time, plus the throw weight and numbers that they have as a result of SALT I. They do not have to have recourse to this kind of strategy.

In any event, this strategy is open to them. Part of the problem, of course, is the difference between an open and a closed society. We are more or less obligated to explain to the American public as well as to the Soviets and to third audiences, the calculations on which American security and the security of our alliances rest. The Soviets are under no such pressure. Nobody knows what calculations lie behind Soviet strategic planning.

Senator MUSKIE: Let me get to the next point made by Berman and Baker. They say:

> Although a disarming first strike by one nation upon the other's strategic forces is technically impossible because of the existence of sea-based missiles neither side will find a vulnerable land-based missile force acceptable. In addition, an incentive will exist for both sides to seize the initiative to strike first since the attractiveness of hitting counterforce targets in the second strike could never equal that of the first strike.

Secretary SCHLESINGER: I would like to develop that for you sometime, but I think that is a decade or more off, and so I will confine myself to the first part of that question.

That is one of our concerns. We are hopeful that through SALT we will avoid the buildup of armaments on both sides. That is destabilizing. If one deals with the ICBM components alone, the growth of throw weights has the potentiality for the sort of destabilization that the gentlemen refer to.

Our objective in SALT should be to retain as limited a vulnerability of the ICBM force as is possible, and we are hopeful that we may accomplish that in SALT. But one has to look at deterrence in terms of the overall strategic forces on both sides. In that context, there will never be a powerful incentive for a strike against land-based strategic forces taken by themselves.

I think that there is a danger of irrationality, but these will be agonizing decisions. We agree with the logic and we do not want to go very far in that direction. The authors of the article tend to over-emphasize the ease with which people might slip into the notion of going for a first strike counter-force of the sort which has been described.

Senator MUSKIE: Is the SLBM currently adaptable to the selective strategy of which you speak?

Secretary SCHLESINGER: It is not as adaptable as ICBM's at the present time.

Senator MUSKIE: Is that because of the accuracy question?

Secretary SCHLESINGER: It is a complex question. It is not primarily accuracy.

Senator MUSKIE: The submarine?

Secretary SCHLESINGER: A submarine like the Poseidon is hard to adapt to it because you have so many MIRV's [multiple independently targetable reentry vehicles] permissible and so many missiles per boat. As soon as you fire, you expose the boat. Consequently, the ICBM is a far more useful instrument for this kind of strategy than is the SLBM. I should not exclude SLBM's in principle but they are far less attractive in this regard than ICBM's.

Senator MUSKIE: What you are saying then, is that SLBM's still have to be an anti-city missile.

Secretary SCHLESINGER: I think that overstates it. You can go against soft targets with them but you would not have as high a degree of selectivity and flexibility at the present time in the SLBM force as in the ICBM force, because of greater accuracy and controllability of an ICBM. They would be a better weapon, but your statement, I think, is a little too restrictive about SLBM. It points in the direction you are saying, but it is not a preferred weapon.

Senator MUSKIE: And there has been, I think, a growing tendency in recent years to regard the SLBM as the weapon of the future and perhaps to reduce reliance on the land-based missile. Could your strategy buy that?

Secretary SCHLESINGER: No, sir. I have never agreed with that point of view. One can talk about a higher proportion of forces at sea, but I do not think we would be well-advised to eliminate the land-based component.

Senator MUSKIE: Let me get to the next point made by Baker and Berman.

> Counterforce doctrines will encourage arms competition since various factions in each government will push for more sophisticated strategic systems requried by a range of exotic war-fighting scenarios.

Secretary SCHLESINGER: I think there is some truth in that. I think we have to go after that issue head-on. . . . We would do this to limit the tendencies to move in that direction through the SALT negotiations by seeking limitations on both the aggregation and on certain qualitative features.

But I do not think the doctrine itself leads in that direction. Rather, it is the potentialities in the force structure which do, particularly the potentialities that I have outlined for the Soviet Union.

Senator MUSKIE: The next point is this one.

> A counterforce capability to destroy the foe's nuclear forces would impede the progress of certain arms control efforts such as limitations of multiple independently targeted vehicles, on MIRVs, and the confidence in test ban which would inhibit further developments of war-fighting capabilities.

Secretary SCHLESINGER: There the cart is before the horse. Once again we should be attempting to limit the incentive of both sides to go in this direction. But it is not a limited counter-force capability that does that. It is the potentiality built into the new Soviet systems that gives you the kind of counter-force capability that they are describing.

Let me underscore, Mr. Chairman, once again, that neither side can achieve the kind of counter-force capabilities that the authors are implicitly assuming. There is just no possibility that a high confidence disarming first strike is attainable for either side, even against the ICBM components of the strategic forces on both sides and certainly not against both sets of forces, SLBM's and ICBM's.

*   *   *

Senator MUSKIE: This might be a good point in the record to ask you to define what you mean by "essential equivalence." It is a new phrase. We have heard other phrases during the debate on the first [SALT] treaty, and it might be helpful if we had a definition of this new concept.

Secretary SCHLESINGER: Essential equivalence is a phrase that was used in the President's foreign policy report of last year. What it means is, first, that we do not plan to have our side a mirror image of their strategic forces. We do not have to have a match for everything in their arsenal. They do not have to have a match for everything in our arsenal. But in the gross characteristics of the forces, in terms of overall number and overall throw weight or payload, there should be some degree of equivalency between the two. That does not even mean they have to be precisely the same in terms of throw weight. But, as I indicated earlier, the Soviets have the potential for 12 million pounds of throw weight in their ICBM force as opposed to 2 million pounds in our projected forces. A discrepancy of 6 to 1 in their favor is not essential equivalence. If it were 3 to 2 it might be quite different.

Senator MUSKIE: That does not mean, then, we have to have the same numbers with respect to each category of nuclear weapons?

Secretary SCHLESINGER: Not for military reasons. Perhaps for political reasons in terms of perceived equality between the two forces, that may be desirable. But from a military standpoint . . . it is ideal. If we can control throw weight it would be better to proliferate the number of ICBM sites, driving each site down to a lower level of throw weight. It is better to have 2,000 weapons or 2,000 launchers with a thousand pounds of throw weight at each site (that is quite stable) than it is to have, say, 500 launchers with 5 or 10,000 pounds of throw weight on each site (that is less stable). That is the essence of armed civility. We would concentrate in the long run on the throw weight issue rather than on the numbers issue.

The Soviets and ourselves would both have an interest, if we could control throw weight, in adding to the numbers of launchers and reducing the amount of throw weight and destructive potential at each launcher.

*   *   *

Senator MUSKIE: On this business of making nuclear war seem more respectable, maybe that troubles me more than any other aspect of this proposal of yours—

Secretary SCHLESINGER: I think we have got to make the underlying calculations about nuclear war intellectually respectable. If we understand the underlying calculations rather than avoiding hard thought in this area, I think we can diminish the probability of nuclear war. But if we avoid that and, therefore, do not think through our deterrent strategy somebody might be tempted to do something. We are attempting to remove whatever temptation, however low, to start nuclear war; our objective is to shore up deterrence. If we are effective in that regard and at the same time have made thinking through the underlying

123

calculations respectable, we have reduced the probability of anyone actually using nuclear weapons.

Senator MUSKIE: Do you get any challenge to this thesis of the defense establishment?

Secretary SCHLESINGER: I think basically the answer is "No." I think that everybody has recognized that there are deficiencies in the doctrines that had been sort of carried over willy-nilly from past years. There was a gradual transformation of the tests of the adequate size of our forces—which was the origin of assured destruction—into belief somehow that that was a deterrent. The assured destruction logic serves to deter attacks against our urban industrial base. But we should not in our own mind feel that it is more effective as a deterrent than is actually the case.

*   *   *

Senator MUSKIE: . . . . At a news conference on January 24, Mr. Secretary, you said the United States is not seeking to develop a major counter-force capability but in the fiscal year 1975 defense budget, you have included a wide range of programs which will upgrade the counter-force effectiveness in American ICBM's, submarine missiles and even the bomber force. Consequently at what point do you differentiate a major counter-force capability from a lesser one?

Semantics I know.

Secretary SCHLESINGER: The distinction I have attempted to stress from the first is that if you look carefully at the numbers, even with a [deleted] of a nautical mile CEP [circle of equal probability] . . . we could not have a disarming first strike against even the Soviet ICBM's, even if we have that [deleted] of a nautical mile in operational practice.

Therefore, I continue stressing that neither side has such massive capabilities that they can have a high-confidence first strike. Such capability is just beyond achievement and no rational leader will have recourse to such a thing.

Senator HUMPHREY: Furthermore, once we began upgrading the accuracy of only a portion of our missile force, and I gather that is what you are contemplating now—

Secretary SCHLESINGER: Yes, sir.

Senator HUMPHREY [continuing]: Will not the Soviet Union assume that our entire missile force thus has this improved accuracy?

Secretary SCHLESINGER: Yes, sir, but as I indicated before, even if they were to make that assumption, even with the [deleted] of a nautical mile—

124

Senator HUMPHREY: We still leave them with 280 missiles.

Secretary SCHLESINGER: If there is no degradation in our operational accuracy, which they must assume, I would assume—and I will assume it for the Soviet Union—they still would have the ability to destroy the urban industrial base of the United States.

Senator HUMPHREY: In other words, what you are saying is if we had the best of all things happen for us they still have over 200 of these land-based ICBM's that they can use against us.

Secretary SCHLESINGER: That is right. And I hope they would not drive us into larger programs.

As I attempted to say to Senator Muskie before, it is disadvantageous for both sides to go for a great deal of throw weight. If one side can obtain it unilaterally it's advantageous for it but if it is matched by the other side both sides achieve greater instability, which is in the interest of neither side.

Senator HUMPHREY: Your predecessor, Secretary Laird, on several occasions disavowed any intention to develop counter-force capabilities which the Soviet Union could construe as having first-strike potential.

Has this policy been changed at all?

Secretary SCHLESINGER: No, sir. I think what I have indicated is we just don't have the potential for a first-strike disarming capability. Of course, we have always had counter-force disarming against soft targets, or, if we used larger weapons such as the Minuteman II, we have always had a counter-force capability against a limited number of hard targets. But we cannot destroy large numbers of hard targets.

Senator HUMPHREY: In your statement you mentioned the United States presently has a limited counter-force capability.

Secretary SCHLESINGER: Yes, sir.

Senator HUMPHREY: Does the United States presently have a greater or lesser counter-force capability compared to the Soviet Union?

Secretary SCHLESINGER: It is a very hard judgment to make. There are so many uncertainties. If you believe the results from our own test ranges would be applicable in operational conditions and if you infer what you must infer about present Soviet accuracies, I think one would conclude that we now have greater operational counter-force capabilities than they have. But those are quite a number of iffy assumptions. They do have this massive megatonnage in their force that we do not have, which compensates for inaccuracy.

125

SCHLESINGER TESTIMONY

Senator HUMPHREY: If we had a greater capability at this time what strategic and political advantages do we presently gain from such a capability that we may lose in the future? I mean assuming that we had it.

Secretary SCHLESINGER: We do not obtain an advantage from that mild edge in counter-force capability, if it exists. If there is a vast disproportion to the benefit of the Soviet Union—given the fact that the United States has pledged its strategic forces for a variety of functions around the world, to NATO and to other allies, and in pursuit of the nonproliferation agreement in which both parties pledge if other nations will not acquire nuclear capabilities that they will come to their assistance— then a major disproportion to the benefit of the Soviet Union and against the United States could lead to a weakening of resolve and a dissolution of our alliances overseas.

ANALYSES OF EFFECTS OF LIMITED NUCLEAR WARFARE

Testimony of James R. Schlesinger

and Analysis by the Office of Technology Assessment

In the following testimony of September 1974 before a subcommittee of the Senate Foreign Relations Committee, Secretary of Defense James R. Schlesinger provides estimates of likely casualties resulting from a counterforce exchange between the United States and the Soviet Union. In a limited nuclear war, such counterforce strikes could be targeted against U.S. ICBM fields, Strategic Air Command and strategic nuclear submarine bases, and command, control, and communications facilities. Schlesinger develops the notion of "self-deterrence" and states that the primary concern behind the change in targeting doctrine is to provide the President with nuclear response options which the Soviet Union would perceive as credible under any circumstances.

Following Secretary Schlesinger's testimony a number of questions were raised as to the validity of strike scenarios and assumptions used by the Defense Department in preparing its casualty estimates. Consequently, the Senate Foreign Relations Committee commissioned the Office of Technology Assessment (OTA) to study the issues raised in the Schlesinger testimony. OTA's critical analysis of the new strategic doctrine and its possible implications follows the Schlesinger testimony.

Source: *Analyses of Effects of Limited Nuclear Warfare,* prepared for the Subcommittee on Arms Control, International Organizations and Security Agreements of the Committee on Foreign Relations, United States Senate, September 1975.

126

Briefing on Counterforce Attacks,
Wednesday, September 11, 1974

Secretary SCHLESINGER: . . . Let me make some introductory remarks with regard to the change in targeting doctrine. I think . . . that the change in targeting doctrine is, of course, both broader and more limited than counterforce attacks.

We have no desire to develop a unilateral counterforce capability against the Soviet Union. [Deleted.] What we wish to avoid is the Soviet Union having a counterforce capability against the United States without our being able to have a comparable capability. I continue to be hopeful that the SALT [Strategic Arms Limitation Talks] talks will permit both sides to restrain themselves.

*   *   *

The purpose of our changing our targeting doctrine has been to enhance deterrence. We are dealing with very low probability events, in my judgment, and in the judgment of other people. By enhancing deterrence we reduce further the already low probability of others being tempted to take actions which are devastating to the major interests of the United States, including an attack on American soil of the sort that has been hypothesized.

The question of the role that this change in targeting doctrine plays in deterrence is associated with the question that frequently arises—will this change in doctrine lower the nuclear threshold?

I would submit that it would not. In my judgment, the way to keep the nuclear threshold high is by the maintenance of a stalwart conventional defense establishment. Lowering the level of our general purpose forces is what reduces the nuclear threshold. It drives us to early recourse, either through threat or actual employment of nuclear weapons, be they tactical or strategic. In order to hold up that threshold, in our judgment, we must have ample conventional capability.

Finally, I should emphasize that we have studied these matters for many years, but the reason that we carefully study these matters is so that we can avoid circumstances in which nuclear weapons would be employed. Careful study leads, in our judgment, to the avoidance of the kinds of unanticipated crises or situations that could, through miscalculation, bring us to nuclear war.

*   *   *

Deterrence, in our judgment, has certain characteristics: one, the opponent should see no vulnerabilities or asymmetries in the force balance between the two sides that he can exploit; two, we should have the ability to clearly indicate the strength of our resolve and, three . . . if for some reason deterrence should fail, we should have the ability to terminate that conflict at the lowest possible level of violence. The last is, of course, the issue . . .[of] whether the kinds of counter-military attacks that have been hypothesized really constitute a level of violence significantly different from large scale attacks involving both military and urban industrial targets.

*   *   *

The point that has been made by us . . . is that the ability of the United States to respond to [a Soviet limited nuclear] attack contributes to the deterrence of such an attack. If our only option were to be able to launch massive strikes against the Soviet urban industrial base, the Soviets in these hypothetical circumstances—and I continue to stress that they are hypothetical—might believe that the United States would be self-deterred and that, therefore, they could with relatively low risk selectively attack the interior of the United States.

If the United States possesses the ability to respond in kind, then the Soviet planner is faced with the prospect that the United States would respond and leave him in a no-gain situation and, therefore, he would continue to be deterred. Deterrence remains the name of the game.

*   *   *

As you know, the Soviets will be improving their capabilities. We would hope through SALT negotiations to control the rate of build-up of Soviet warheads that would have counterforce capabilities.

At the present time the Soviets have a couple of thousand warheads. As you look out beyond 1975 they probably will start a process of deployment of MIRVed [multiple independently targetable reentry vehicle] missiles which we would expect to number about 200 ICBM's [intercontinental ballistic missile] a year if they conform to previous trends. These deployments will involve some of the collection of new missiles that I discussed with you previously. So, roughly 7 or 8 years from now they could have on the order of 7,000 MIRVed reentry bodies deployed.

*   *   *

The number of fatalities that would be imposed on the American public by a massive strike of the sort that we have contemplated historically in the SIOP [Single Integrated Operation Plan] . . . would give us prompt plus fallout fatalities on the order of 95-100 million. . . .

[In] a selective counterforce strike by the Soviet Union—in which they attack SSBN [nuclear powered ballistic missile submarine] bases and SAC [Strategic Air Command] bases, as well as the ICBM silos—

the mortalities could be as high as, say 5 or 6 million. In an attack on the ICBM's alone, the mortalities would run on the order of a million; and for SAC bases, the mortalities would be less than that—on the order of 500,000.

Once again, these are prompt plus fallout fatalities. Also, please note that this hypothetical attack includes two reentry vehicles per silo and a mixed Soviet arsenal containing various weapon yields. . . .

[Another attack option could entail] a strike on the ICBM fields alone . . . involving one 1-megaton reentry vehicle per silo. For five of the six Minuteman fields, the total number of casualties would approach half a million and the total number of fatalities would be on the order of 300,000. An attack on Whiteman Air Force Base . . . because of its westerly proximity to a major urban/rural population complex, would drive the number of fatalities up to about 800,000. The number of casualties including people who fall ill as a result of radiation sickness coming from fallout would approach a million and a half.

* * *

We would emphasize the fact that these are highly undesirable circumstances and that we continue to believe that such an attack will be deterred. But the number of fatalities here is a relatively small fraction, less than 1 percent, of the fatalities associated with a massive attack against the United States which includes direct attacks on our cities.

. . . Significant variations in most of the parameters associated with such a strike on Minuteman would result in relatively modest changes in the number of casualties or fatalities, with the major exception being whether a burst is on the surface or in the air. If the Soviets chose to surface burst their weapons rather than airburst their weapons, it would drive the number of fatalities or casualties to a significantly higher level, something on the order of 3 million.

If the Soviets were contemplating such a strike, it is assumed that they would avoid surface bursting their weapons. But, if one assumes that they did not avoid surface bursts, then, of course, the casualty levels would be much higher.

. . . In this case, we also assume one 1-megaton weapon per target, optimum height of burst, and August, that is prevailing winds. We would utilize whatever civil defense facilities are available. At the present time they are fair, but you will see that attacking the roughly 45 operational SAC bomber bases would result in fatalities of around 300,000 Americans, and total casualties of around 700,000. So if that target system is attacked, once again one is talking about casualties of under a million.

* * *

[We can now examine] the fatalities associated with strikes against command and control facilities, or strikes against fleet ballistic missile submarine support bases, or against naval shipyards, or against other naval bases. These, of course, represent individual target systems. [Deleted.]

Attacks on those two command and control facilities would result in fatalities on the order of 40,000 to 45,000 people.

If the Soviets were to attack the CONUS—Continental United States—SSBN support bases, Charleston and Bremerton, possible fatalities could number on the order of 100,000.

*   *   *

The Soviets have a capability, which will increase as they deploy MIRV missiles, to conduct selective and limited strikes against the United States. To the extent that they improve their accuracies and lower their yields, of course, the fatalities associated with large yield weapons would diminish.

I regard the likelihood of a nuclear war getting started between the United States and the Soviet Union as very low. I find it difficult to conceive of the circumstances under which either side would attack the urban industrial base of the other out of the blue. It just does not make sense, unless a government has gone mad. So we would say that the likelihood of a nuclear exchange starting with a selective strike, however low, is still higher than the likelihood of such an exchange starting with a strike at the urban industrial centers of the United States.

Senator SYMINGTON: Could I ask you why you think that?

Secretary SCHLESINGER: Because a strike at the urban industrial centers of the United States would result in fatalities of 95 or 100 million people, possibly higher. Under those circumstances there would be no reason for the United States, in any Soviet calculation, to restrain itself from responding to such an attack in kind, thus destroying most of the urban industrial base of the Soviet Union. They themselves would lose the equivalent population of approximately 100 million people.

Senator CASE: Then we would lose the remaining 100 million?

Secretary SCHLESINGER: No, sir, I think that when one talks about this kind of strike one should recognize that it is the urban population that is the target not the small town or rural area.

Senator CASE: The enemy would exhaust its capacity the first time?

Secretary SCHLESINGER: Reasonably, you have a curve which indicates the population at risk and if they were to strike at our urban industrial base they would be moving up to the knee of the curve. I find it difficult to conceive of the circumstances under which any rational leader would consider such a strike to be to the advantage of his nation, given all that the attacker would have at risk under those circumstances.

Senator SYMINGTON: I personally cannot conceive of any country using nuclear weapons at any level today, because if I may say so, with great respect, you talk as if the Joint Chiefs of Staff of the Soviet Union and the Joint Chiefs of Staff of the United States were together in this thing and started to play a game of chess. It would be difficult for me, especially considering the casualties that you say would come around my State, and Senator Pearson's State, to think that the United States would take a relatively low position because only 1 million people have been killed, as it would be if there was 5, 10 or 15 million people killed. I cannot quite understand the gradation.

Secretary SCHLESINGER: I agree entirely with the thrust of your remarks. Any recourse to nuclear weapons is going to be a very agonizing choice for the political leadership. I trust it will remain that way, and even grow more agonizing for them to contemplate such a recourse. The point I am making is that however unlikely one regards these kinds of selective strikes, it is even more unlikely, unless one has a mad leadership, that any nation would attack, "out of the blue," the urban industrial base of any other nation that has significant nuclear retaliatory capability.

Senator SYMINGTON: So what we are really talking about is real insanity?

Secretary SCHLESINGER: I am not sure I would employ those words. I think we are talking about relative likelihood and unlikelihood.

Senator MUSKIE: By accepting the notion of limited nuclear involvement of this kind, don't we raise the possibility of reducing the resistance to using nuclear weapons and make it more likely?

Secretary SCHLESINGER: I do not think so, Senator.

Senator MUSKIE: Why not?

Secretary SCHLESINGER: I think the possibility has always been there, and has been recognized to be there, when one has adequate command and control facilities and an adequate supply of weapons. . . . So I am not trying to argue that these are likely events. I hope that we will keep the probabilities of their occurence exceedingly low. . . .

The point is that we should deter nuclear attacks on the United States across the spectrum. If an opponent were to decide that we would be self-deterred because the President of the United States lacked adequate response options, and if an opponent were a risk-taker, then such a selective nuclear attack becomes conceivable.

Senator PEARSON: Mr. Secretary, the urban industrial centers in the Soviet Union are fewer in number and smaller in size, are they not, than in the United States?

Secretary SCHLESINGER: I think the number is approximately the same.

Senator PEARSON: It is sort of silly to talk about numbers or arithmetic when you are dealing with 95 or 100 million people, but all of the comparisons that I have seen heretofore put the Soviets at a much lower figure. . . .

A few minutes ago, you set the Soviet fatalities at a higher figure than the United States.

Secretary SCHLESINGER: That was a rough approximation. I said around 100 million. I think the fatality figures are roughly comparable. There is a slightly higher vulnerability for the United States because our population is more urbanized than the Soviet population. That circumstance is to some extent offset by the fact that in the United States the concentration of populations in the urban areas themselves is lower than in comparable Soviet cities.

For example, Los Angeles has an urban population of about 6,000 per square mile, whereas Moscow has a population concentration of about 16,000 per square mile.

American cities are more spread out than Soviet cities and this tends to counteract the higher degree of urbanization. But, by and large, there is a somewhat higher relative vulnerability of the American population.

Senator PEARSON: Is changing targets an inflexible thing? Can you change a missile target within a relatively short period of time, or is it a fixed mechanism?

Secretary SCHLESINGER: In the past we have taken 16 to 24 hours, say, to change a target tape on a missile. One had to enter the missile in the silo to change the target tape. . . . Now, we are installing what we call the Command Data Buffer system in all Minuteman III wings, which permits us to change target sets in the missile computer in 36 minutes remotely from the launch control center.

Senator PEARSON: Even at 36 minutes, you do not get the flexibility of deciding whether you are going to hit industrial or urban industrial centers or whether you are going to hit missile sites?

Secretary SCHLESINGER: That permits greater flexibility with the employment of individual weapons, but the question of whether one is going against urban industrial sites or not depends upon preplanning and other elements of command and control. A major change which results from the change in targeting doctrine is that we are paying much more attention than previously to planning for the possibility of these kinds of selective strikes we have been talking about, and from which collateral damage would be low.

*   *   *

Senator MUSKIE: How many missiles would such a launch for limited purposes minimally involve?

Secretary SCHLESINGER: It would be as few as one or two missiles.

Senator CASE: You would use two missiles, would you not, Mr. Secretary, for each target?

Secretary SCHLESINGER: No, I do not think that you would need to do that. In the cases that we outlined, for example, against a soft target such as a SAC air base, we used a single reentry body; against Minuteman silos, we used as examples one and two warheads per silo.

Senator MUSKIE: Would you outline a scenario that would justify in the mind of an enemy the launching of a limited strike of this kind? Against what kind of targets and for what kind of purposes would it be, considering the risks that we might misread it and not be self-deterred but launch a massive response? I am trying to read the mind of a Soviet political leader in the future who would be tempted to launch a limited strike.

Secretary SCHLESINGER: We have to be quite hypothetical about this. I was attempting to respond to the questions . . . asked about what the mortalities would be from such selective attacks, rather than predicting that such a set of circumstances would arise.

Senator MUSKIE: In order to do that, Mr. Secretary, would you not have to see what combination of targets there would be in a postulated limited strike? . . .

Secretary SCHLESINGER: . . . As you know, there has been a great deal of worry about Minuteman vulnerability over the past few years. The concern that has been expressed is about crisis stability and the arranging of circumstances so that neither side has a strong incentive to strike first in a counterforce mode in such crisis. The worst set of circumstances arises where both sides are relatively vulnerable to such strikes since that places a higher premium on a first strike and that, in turn, drives both sides in the direction of preparing for a first strike. We have attempted to resist this tendency over the years by developing a high degree of invulnerability in our forces and so has the Soviet Union. Now a drawback, it is feared, of fixed land based systems is that as accuracy improves and reliability improves, one side or the other might be tempted in a crisis to attempt to reduce the weight of the potential attack of the other side by a major preemptive strike against these relatively vulnerable systems.

We attempt to avoid that situation by reducing vulnerabilities, by avoiding crises, and by maintaining stability in a strategic balance between the United States and the U.S.S.R. But those are the circumstances which could give rise to a Soviet counterforce attack on the United States in a crisis.

If you had, for example, an invasion of Western Europe and the Soviet Union under those circumstances is informed by the American Government that we are prepared to use our nuclear capabilities unless it desists, the Soviet Union at that time may conclude that the option for it to pursue would be to wipe out as much of America's nuclear retaliatory forces as it can and degrade its command-control system. In effect, the Soviet Union would be sending a message to the United States that it had badly crippled our military strength and that we had better desist from the war—that the Soviet Union has won its objectives. Those are the kinds of circumstances that one could hypothesize.

I am not saying that such a development is highly probable, but rather that those are circumstances that we have to consider.

Senator CASE: Did not that example—or did I misunderstand you, in that example—did you not say that the Soviet Union might attack the missile force?

Secretary SCHLESINGER: Yes, sir.

Senator CASE: And try to knock it out. That means a complete attack against the missile force?

Secretary SCHLESINGER: Yes, and my recollection is that we were talking about 2 million fatalities from some types of attacks.

Mr. KING [Office of the Secretary of Defense]: About 800,000 fatalities if he attacks the Minuteman force with just one 1-megaton air-burst weapon per silo.

Senator CASE: That is direct fatalities?

Mr. KING: And fallout fatalities.

Senator CASE: Against a full attack by two missiles against each of our Minutemen?

Secretary SCHLESINGER: Let me give you those calculations.

Senator CASE: At simultaneous times? So you are not picking the weather and you have to take a chance it is going to be bad.

Secretary SCHLESINGER: Yes, sir.

Senator CASE: Only 800,000?

Mr. KING: That is with just one 1-megaton air-burst weapon on each silo. It is a conceivable attack if accuracy is good enough.

Senator CASE: It is not conceivable to me that that would not be regarded by the United States as the kind of attack which required all-out response.

Secretary SCHLESINGER: Well, of course, the President would have such an option under any circumstances but—

Senator CASE: Of course, he has that now, too.

Secretary SCHLESINGER: He has that option now [deleted]. But one is talking under these circumstances of the possible survival of about 95 million people who would otherwise be vulnerable. A President of the United States under those circumstances where, as a result of an attack against the ICBM sites, there are already approximately 800,000 fatalities, would know that if he responds by destroying the urban industrial base of the Soviet Union approximately 95 million American fatalities would be added to that number.

Now, I am not suggesting that he might not order an all-out attack against the Soviet Union. But that is precisely the question that Mr. Nixon raised and the Senate Preparedness Investigating Subcommittee previously raised—that he might well choose not to respond with an urban industrial attack against the Soviet Union but rather to respond selectively.

Senator CASE: What would we be able to do now with our present capacity and targeting ability against such an attack? Could we make a counterattack against their weapons?

Secretary SCHLESINGER: The answer is that we could make such a counterattack, but not very effectively. However, such an exchange at the present time is unlikely to take place for two reasons. First, the Soviets just do not have the required force structure at the present time. We would hope that they will stay in that position and not acquire the kind of force structure needed to make this kind of attack effectively.

135

Second, although the United States has the number of weapons, we do not have the accuracy and high confidence hard target kill capability to initiate such an attack ourselves. That happens to be a very, very reassuring situation.

*   *   *

Senator MUSKIE: Mr. Secretary, the notion that somehow it is possible to develop limiting parameters among the consequences of various degrees of nuclear involvement seems to me unreal.

For example, on the very hypothesis that Senator Case posed to you about taking out our Minuteman force with two warheads per Minuteman silo, we have this memorandum from the Arms Control Agency. I quote:

> Consider the following bounds on the uncertainty relative to casualties resulting from an attack against Minuteman silos if the P-95 population protection factor is unknown, and the weather is not selected to minimize covering populated areas without fallout. The urban casualties can range from 145,000 to 50 million for two one-megaton warheads arriving at each Minuteman silo. Note this does not include casualties among the rural population.

I do not know enough to evaluate their judgment any more than to evaluate the opinion you have stressed. But these are two opinions expressed by people presumably more knowledgeable than I in this field. It seems to me that suggests the difficulty of developing parameters which can assure the Soviet general staff or our general staff that in order to deter the other side from a massive response it is safe to launch a minimal attack assuring that you will only get a minimal response in return. In the situation which you hypothesized, if the President of the United States knows the possibility is not that the damage to our population will be only 800,000 but that it could be 50 million, why should he limit his response? He sees these missiles launched. He does not know at that point whether the damage here would be on the lower range or the upper range. Given those uncertainties, should he give the Soviet Union any encouragement to believe that our response will be less than maximum?

Secretary SCHLESINGER: I think that the question that you raise is a good one, Mr. Chairman.

Let me deal with the technical parameters first.

We would have to go back and see just what kind of assumptions lay behind those calculations. Our calculations have assumed 450 REM's [roentgen equivalent man], I believe, as the fatal dose for members of the population or, alternatively, something on the order of seven PSI [pounds per square inch] overpressure. Of course, this assumes that there is no evacuation of population or change in our civil defense programs; the fatalities could be substantially reduced if we had such new programs.

But I find it very hard, Mr. Chairman, to conceive of a set of believable circumstances in which the fatalities would be 50 million from an attack on the Minuteman force alone.

Now, I would also mention that our figures include consideration of two warheads targeted on each silo, although the Soviets are not obligated to drop 2,000-odd one-megaton warheads on American soil.

There is, of course, a significant range of uncertainty. I think that underlying your comments was one of, what shall I say, the reassuring aspects of that uncertainty. To the extent that there are these uncertainties, and they are perceived by the leadership on both sides, they do impose restraint, and they contribute to deterrence. In other words, one cannot be sure, and to the extent that one cannot be sure, it makes a decision to launch such an attack more agonizing. To the extent that one has these high yield weapons which we have assumed in the data that we have presented, of course, one cannot say that the mortalities will be restricted to a certain level.

In a carefully planned attack, however, one can reduce those collateral mortalities significantly, if that is one of the attacker's objectives.

Senator MUSKIE: But with respect to the other side, the decision maker responsible for determining the nature of the response, he will not know what the limitations are until the strike is over.

Secretary SCHLESINGER: Quite right, Mr. Chairman.

Senator MUSKIE: What concerns me about all of this, is that to the extent that you arm the United States with a range of responses and to the extent that you encourage the Soviet Union to believe that the United States might be tempted to use the lesser than the greater response, do you not to that extent encourage the Soviet Union to consider the possibility of a limited strike?

Secretary SCHLESINGER: I do not think "encourage" is the right word. If the Soviet Union is prepared to consider these possibilities, and one must infer from the weapons developments and deployments that are already underway that they will be prepared to consider them, then what the United States does, I think, will have relatively little impact on the various strike alternatives that they might consider.

*   *   *

Senator MUSKIE: . . . Why are we talking about building this limited response capability, if, as you say, what we do is not going to matter much in influencing the other side?

Secretary SCHLESINGER: With regard to their planning of their options, our ability to respond in kind, if they were contemplating such a limited strike, would tend to deter it. If the only option we had under the circumstances were a massive urban strike against the Soviet Union, they might feel that because of the hundred million fatalities involved on our side, that we would be self-deterred and that they could obtain political benefit, political-military benefit by either threatening or conceivably employing such a limited strike against the United States.

Senator MUSKIE: What that line of argument implies is that there can be several exchanges between the two adversaries, using limited responses, on the assumption that no one of those exchanges is going to bring the other side to respond with a massive strike?

Secretary SCHLESINGER: The question here is whether they might not go all the way, or probably would not go all the way. There is always the possibility that one or both sides would go massively, and that the limited exchange could escalate to all-out strikes. We have continually underscored that possibility.

What we are saying here is that although we can give no assurance that one can avoid escalating to all-out exchanges, there is a possibility that one can avoid such escalation. With the hundreds of millions of fatalities involved in an all-out nuclear exchange, both sides have a very powerful incentive to avoid escalation if a nuclear exchange should ever start.

Senator MUSKIE: What concerns me is that in building these limited responses we cloak the possibility of massive exchanges, whereas if we are going to continue to rely on the doctrine of massive retaliation, then that possibility should always be clear and evident or we abandon it for something else.

Secretary SCHLESINGER: That capability is always there and the President, any President, can stress either the possibility or his determination to proceed with such a strike.

*   *   *

The advantage of [acquiring limited options] is that you close off any kind of ambition that you can speculate on on the part of the Soviet leadership. You are deterring across the entire spectrum of risk. If they regard the United States as prepared to go for a massive strike in retaliation, our ability to retaliate more selectively does not weaken that deterrent. If they consider the United States as prepared to contemplate selective strikes in retaliation, once again they seek risks that affect their judgments. The whole purpose here is to create the uncertainties that we can with high confidence assume will continue to deter them.

Senator MUSKIE: May I say I understand the need for a conventional deterrence in Europe as well, but that in-between is where I cannot get the feeling—

Secretary SCHLESINGER: Of course, we have an in-between deterrent in the sense that we have war plans that contemplate the employment of tactical nuclear weapons in Europe.

What we are doing here is to apply the same selectivity with regard to the strategic forces as has been historically contemplated with regard to the tactical nuclear force.

*   *   *

Senator CASE: . . . You started this whole razzle dazzle, as I recall it, at least to my thinking, when you made a couple of speeches about how we had to have a more effective capacity to engage in limited strategic warfare. . . . It immediately aroused concern among a number of people, including me, as to whether this really is something new, and if it was, would it not suggest to the Soviet Union, for example, that we intended to concentrate more on preparing for attacks less than those involved in all-out destruction.

This raised questions in the minds of a number of us whether this would not be perceived as, for example, an effort to acquire a counterforce strategy.

Secretary SCHLESINGER: Right.

Senator CASE: And related to this was the damage that that perception would create in the way of increased armament on the other side. This is what we are talking about.

Secretary SCHLESINGER: Yes, sir.

Senator CASE: Counter to this is the suggestion that some scientists have made, [that] there is not any real possibility of a low-level nuclear exchange.

*   *   *

The end question, Mr. Secretary, is whether you were really asking for anything new, or whether you were just making a speech for a useful purpose—a propaganda purpose—designed to scare the Russians into thinking that they had better make a deal with us now or we would get pretty tough. Now, that is not an unworthy purpose, but did these speeches represent strategy, or rhetoric?

Secretary SCHLESINGER: It is a strategy, Senator Case. The President of the United States should possess these options.

Senator CASE: But does he not now?

Secretary SCHLESINGER: Let me try and go through these questions. . . . The first question you raised is whether we possess options at the present time or possessed options previously. The answer to that question is, "Yes"; we had a number of options that had been built into our war plans, but all of these options were at a very high level which would have caused major fatalities in the Soviet Union. So we had options, but all of them that had been specified in the SIOP [Single Integrated Operational Plan] were at a fairly high level. . . . In practice, we had a very limited number of massive options. What we are trying to do now is to broaden the spectrum and particularly to provide some options at the lower end of the spectrum. That is, I think, the major difference between the options that we are developing now and the situation that existed previously.

Another question that you raised . . . had to do with inevitability of a small nuclear exchange escalating to the top. . . . I think that is a good question. It certainly is a possibility, as you indicated. We can give no assurance that a small exchange would not escalate to a higher level. We simply are stating that because there is a possibility of a small exchange escalating to the top, that is no reason why we must make it a certainty by going all the way to the top ourselves. Just because you reach that pessimistic conclusion at the outset does not mean that you must go and bash up the urban industrial base of your opponent, knowing full well that he will do the same thing to you. That is making a certainty of what would otherwise be an uncertainty.

You mentioned the possibility of tens of thousands of fatalities and that we ought not to base any strategy . . . on the possibility of that number of fatalities. I think that one must recognize that the assured destruction strategy that we have advertised for many years is based upon the threat of inflicting 100 million fatalities on the Soviet Union in retaliation and there are questions, moral questions indeed, about whether we ought to base our national strategy on the contemplation of the certainty of 100 million fatalities on the other side.

One must be as demanding and scrutinizing of the emphasis on assured destruction as the sole resource of American strategy, as one is of the more limited options. One has got to deal with them in a balanced way. I would suggest that when one gets through with such an examination, one comes to the conclusion that deterrence is enhanced by having the broader range of retaliatory options.

You asked, Senator Case, whether the Soviet Union would perceive our quests for accuracy and higher yield weapons as representing a threat to their own force structure, and that because of these perceptions, whether they would take actions which could otherwise be avoided.

There are two aspects to the answer to that question. The first aspect is that the Soviet Union, much to our astonishment, had proceeded last year with a set of development initiatives that are surprising in their depth and strength. Their new land-based missiles possess throw weights which on the average are three times that of the previous array of missiles. They appear to be acquiring on the order of 7,000 or 8,000 MIRV's just in their ICBM force, let alone their SLBM force. [Deleted.] I would hope that we would be able to persuade them not to deploy those new missiles up to the limit of the Interim Agreement, but they continue to say that they have spent the money on development on the SS–17, SS–18, and SS–19, and they are going to deploy them.

We have very carefully distinguished, Senator Case, and I hope that you will join in explaining this distinction, between the change in targeting doctrine and the set of strategic initiatives that we are proposing. The change in targeting doctrine can be implemented without the procurement of any additional weapons. Accuracy contributes somewhat to the effectiveness of the new targeting doctrine, but it is not essential for the implementation of that doctrine. We do not have to acquire a single additional weapon. We could have selective responses even if we had a smaller force structure than we presently have, and with no greater yields.

The change in targeting doctrine can be abstracted from any change in our force structure. The only thing that we need here is improved planning, which we can do at low cost or no additional cost, and improved command, control and communications.

So the change in targeting doctrine should be separated from any changes with regard to development, procurement, and deployment of new weapon systems.

* * *

In addition to that, we have sent up to the Hill requests for certain other things. We have sent up to the Hill a request for a new, heavier throw weight ICBM. We have requested money for Trident.

Senator CASE: In what statement is that request? Is this for research?

Secretary SCHLESINGER: The new ICBM is R. & D. We have stated unequivocably that we would prefer not to deploy that heavier throw weight ICBM and that we hope that the Soviet Union will refrain from the full deployment of their heavier throw weight ICBM's.

When I submitted to the Congress last year a request for money for a new SSBN, which would have smaller tubes than the Trident submarine, I made the point that this would limit our throw weight and that we were prepared to restrain ourselves if the Soviets were prepared to restrain themselves. So the strategic initiatives, which you correctly stated might lead the Soviets to perceive a risk to their force structure, are something that can be separated from the change in targeting doctrine.

We are prepared to renounce any one of those strategic initiatives, provided that we get reciprocation by the Soviet Union. It is advantageous to the Soviet Union not to proceed with these new developments because they will drive us into matching actions and both sides will be worse off. Accordingly, I would like to distinguish very sharply between the strategic initiatives that could lead to the perceptions that you mentioned, but which we are prepared to withhold, and the change in targeting doctrine which I think contributes to deterrence overall. By and large, I think that most individuals in the arms control community agree that greater flexibility by itself is a desirable change. They were rather unhappy being anchored to the notion that the only thing we could do in retaliation to even a small nuclear attack was to bust up the urban industrial base in the Soviet Union.

*   *   *

Senator CASE: . . . I really think what we may be coming down to, it seems to me, is whether on the other end of the scale what you are suggesting is a strategy which would make more likely the use of nuclear weapons and as a part of our regular military force. My conception is getting more strong that—except that nuclear weapons pose a deterrent against other nuclear weapons—we ought not to have strategy based upon their contemplated use. The more adequate our conventional forces, the higher the nuclear threshold—I agree with that, the latter proposition, as you know. . . . But, in addition to the possible concern people have had about the change in our strategy being provocative in respect to the Russian perception of what we have in mind, is there not a danger that many people might think that limited nuclear war is a reasonable and perhaps less expensive option than that involving conventional forces?

Secretary SCHLESINGER: Right. Well, those are all good questions, once again, Senator Case. I am like the ancient mariner, I seem to stop one of three of your questions, but let me take a crack at them. I strongly believe that these improvements in our deterrent posture will reduce the chances of recourse to nuclear weapons. I think the only way a nuclear war is likely to get started is by miscalculation, where the other side believes that the United States might be self-deterred and that it is worth running a risk. Principally, I think the risk would be in Europe.

If they are persuaded that the United States is prepared to respond at any level, a war will not be started.

As you know, for many years there has been talk of decoupling the United States from Europe. It is part of the problem General DeGaulle had. To the extent that we have changed our targeting doctrine, we have recoupled U.S. strategic forces with the security of Western Europe, and as long as we have that coupling action, I think that we have strengthened deterrence and, therefore, reduced the risk of nuclear war.

Part of the answer, I think, is to maintain those strong conventional forces, and once again, since you have endorsed my plea, let me embrace your position that the way to keep the nuclear threshold high is to maintain good conventional capabilities. We increase the likelihood of recourse to nuclear weapons when we weaken our conventional force structure.

Senator CASE: I could not agree with you more on that point.

Secretary SCHLESINGER: Good.

Senator CASE: But I do express the concern that what you have advocated in some quarters has made people think that you would rather readily move into low-level nuclear exchanges.

Secretary SCHLESINGER: Of course, I have spent much of my life trying to find ways of avoiding getting into nuclear war. I have repeatedly stressed . . . the need to maintain those conventional forces in Europe and maintain a balance with the Warsaw Pact forces. That is the area in which we risk actually coming to a nuclear exchange with the Soviet Union if we lose that balance. If we hold the nuclear threshold high I do not worry about it.

Senator PEARSON: How do the Soviets view the flexible strategy and do they have a view?

Secretary SCHLESINGER: They have responded to our commentary. We do not know whether they have talked internally about the possibility of these options. All that we are suggesting is that the prospective improvements in the Soviet force structure will give them the physical capabilities to consider selective options.

Now, their reaction to our position has been something of this sort—concern and surprise. The reason for surprise, as expressed to some of our people [deleted] is that they always assumed that we would target this way, therefore, why do we now say so, what is the purpose of all of this fanfare?

Senator CASE: Something like the questions you have received in Senate committees.

Secretary SCHLESINGER: I think the point that you can draw from this is that the change in the actual targeting doctrine is not so surprising to them. They may have been surprised that we had less targeting flexibility, or indicated we had less targeting flexibility, than they had thought.

* * *

Senator JAVITS: I have one question. . . . In the report of the Committee of Nine on NATO they had a paragraph which related to this very matter, that is, the utilization of the nuclear deterrent, both tactical and strategic, and an assessment of the facts which in effect said that if you are not ready to use it, forget it and that you have got to take the position that if you have to, you are ready to use it. That is what it is for. That is why it inhibits a conventional effort to overrun Europe. This is not a game; if the Soviets have prevailed and are in the ascendency, what you have is a supporting commitment not to use nuclear weapons?

* * *

Secretary SCHLESINGER: . . . You have touched upon the heart of the question, that in order to deter you must have a threat that you are prepared to implement, and that your opponent must perceive that you are prepared to implement that threat.

The reason for the change in targeting doctrine is that we know that we can persuade the Soviet Union that we are prepared to implement that threat, whereas reliance on the assured destruction doctrine could well lead the Soviet Union to believe that we are not prepared to implement the threat. It is for that reason that the changes in targeting doctrine have successfully eliminated doubts about the coupling of U.S. strategic forces with the defense of Western Europe.

Office of Technology Assessment—Response of the Ad Hoc Panel on Nuclear Effects*

I. BACKGROUND

The ad hoc panel on Nuclear Weapons Effects was formed so that the Technology Assessment Advisory Council could advise the OTA Board

---

*Transmitted to the Committee on Foreign Relations on March 5, 1975.

on how to respond to a request for an assessment made to OTA by the Senate Committee on Foreign Relations. The Committee had asked OTA to determine whether the Department of Defense had adequately analyzed the effects of possible limited exchanges of nuclear weapons which resulted in detonations of weapons on or over U.S. territory.

* * *

II. SUMMARY OF CONCLUSIONS

The panel members examined the results of the analyses of nuclear attacks which were given the Senate Foreign Relations Committee by the Department of Defense [DOD] and the assumptions which went into these analyses, in some detail. They concluded that the casualties calculated were substantially too low for the attacks in question as a result of a lack of attention to intermediate and long-term effects. They also concluded that the studies did not adequately reflect the large uncertainties inherent in any attempt to determine the civilian damage which might result from a nuclear attack.

The panel could not determine from the DOD testimony any consistent set of hypothetical Soviet objectives in the strikes analyzed. The attacks studied were evidently not designed to maximize destruction of U.S. ICBM's and bombers even though all ICBM's and large numbers of bomber bases were attacked. It seems apparent, however, even from the data now available, that if the Soviets used weapons now deployed or under development in an attack designed to maximize damage to U.S. strategic offensive forces, they would inflict massive damage on U.S. society. On the other hand, if the Soviet objective was something other than a desire to maximize damage to military targets, this objective was never made clear. It is evident that a small number of nuclear weapons could be detonated over isolated areas in the U.S. without causing significant civilian damage. It is not clear, however, that the Soviet Union could benefit in any way from such an attack particularly since they would be running the risk of a massive U.S. repsonse. The panel's assessment of the material presented does not, therefore, intend to imply that its members feel that the attacks analyzed are sensible or realistic.

The panel also noticed that the material examined did not contain any estimates of the intermediate or long-term effects of attacks smaller than a "comprehensive military attack" although this was requested in the original inquiries of the Foreign Relations Committee. The panel was informed that the Office of the Secretary of Defense had been contacted about this issue and had responded by saying that this analysis had not been done and would require several weeks or

145

months to perform. To the extent that policy will be based on this analysis, the panel finds this to be a serious deficiency particularly since the secondary effects of limited attacks on relatively remote installations are likely to represent a more substantial fraction of the total effects of such an attack than would be the case in a large attack near population centers.

The panel did not feel that it had enough information about DOD techniques for determining long-term effects to comment on the adequacy of these techniques.

While the panel believes that it is important that a realistic assessment of civilian effects be available for analysis of proposed changes in our target strategy and our attitude toward counterforce, they wish to emphasize that such analysis is only one and perhaps not the most important element of a much larger set of considerations affecting policy in this area. Such issues include: the effect, if any, on U.S. weapons acquisition, particularly weapons for hard-target counterforce attacks; the extent to which the new strategies could be executed without escalating into general nuclear war; the effect on deterrence of nuclear war; the degree to which such policy increases or decreases our reliance on nuclear weapons; the extent to which it raises or lowers the threshold of nuclear first use; and the effect on the perception of our allies about the credibility of our commitment to them.

*   *   *

[EDITORS' NOTE: *The Office of Technology Assessment's Ad Hoc Panel on Nuclear Effects was subsequently asked by Senator Clifford Case, of the Senate Foreign Relations Committee, to identify and analyze possible ramifications of the change in strategic doctrine proposed by Secretary Schlesinger. The panel's report, transmitted to the Subcommittee on Arms Control on May 6, 1975, follows.*]

I. COMMENTARY ON THE NEW DOCTRINE FOR STRATEGIC NUCLEAR WEAPONS

For more than ten years strategic nuclear weapons policy has been dominated by a recognition that: (1) neither the U.S. nor the Soviet Union can protect its populations and industry from an attack by the other side even by using its entire inventory of weapons in a preemptive first strike; (2) once a nuclear weapon is detonated on the territory of either the U.S., or the U.S.S.R., there would be a substantial probability that the exchange could not be terminated before both nations were destroyed. However unpleasant this "balance of terror" may be, there has never been any real prospect of changing the situation in a fundamental way by purchasing new weapons or by adopting new tactics. It is essential that we not lose sight of this fact during complex arguments about the need to prepare for "limited" nuclear warfare.

U.S. objectives for its strategic forces are revealed in:

• Statements by the President, the Secretary of Defense, the Secretary of State and other high officials.

• Actual acquisition of new military systems and priorities in military research and development.

• Actual plans for using existing strategic forces.

The objectives indicated in this way are not always consistent. In particular, our present forces cannot be explained entirely by a close reading of past statements by high officials on procurement objectives. The forces actually purchased often represent the effects of overreactions to Soviet initiatives, institutional momentum, inter-service rivalries, or the "manifest destiny" of an emerging technology. It would be unrealistic to expect a great deal of consistency from this history.

Secretary McNamara
Early in his term of office, Secretary of Defense McNamara stated that we should have a "flexible" strategic force which could be used in at least two ways: (1) to attack Soviet ICBMs and intercontinental bombers (avoiding civilian populations as much as possible) with the objective of limiting damage to the U.S.; and (2) to attack the "entire Soviet target system simultaneously." It soon became obvious, however, that limiting damage to the U.S. from a Soviet attack was a futile pursuit given the technical limitations of ABM, the difficulty of destroying Soviet strategic forces and the complex and costly problems presented by a program for effective civil defense. Acknowledging this state of affairs, McNamara later focused on one major objective:

. . . our forces must be sufficiently large to possess an "Assured Destruction" capability. By this I mean an ability to inflict at all times and under all foreseeable conditions an unacceptable degree of damage upon any single aggressor, or combination of aggressors—even after absorbing a surprise attack . . . In the case of the Soviet Union, I would judge that a capability on our part to destroy, say, one-fifth to one-fourth of her population and one-half of her industrial capability would serve as an effective deterrent. (FY 69-73 Defense Program, pages 47 and 50.)

147

This was, of course, only a declared objective for procurement—it did not necessarily imply that the U.S. would only use its weapons to attack Soviet population although it clearly had the effect of threatening that we would use our weapons for this purpose.

Secretary Laird

Secretary Laird replaced McNamara's criteria with a list of four "objectives" for force planning:

(1) Maintaining an adequate second strike capability to deter all-out surprise attack on our strategic forces.

(2) Providing no incentive for the Soviet Union to strike the United States first in a crisis.

(3) Preventing the Soviet Union from gaining the ability to cause considerably greater urban/industrial destruction than the United States could inflict on the Soviets in a nuclear war.

(4) Defending against damage from small attacks or accidental launches.

This list did not represent a major change from the goals which had already been established. However, it made our interest in reducing Soviet incentives for a first strike an explicit element of planning. Later the ABM Treaty had the effect of eliminating objective 4 and making objective 1 much easier to attain since without a Soviet ABM, fewer and less sophisticated weapons are required for an "assured destruction" capability.

Secretary Schlesinger

Secretary Schlesinger's new doctrine consists of satisfying four major requirements:

> First, we must maintain an essential equivalence with the Soviet Union in the basic factors that determine force effectiveness. Because of uncertainty about the future and the shape that the strategic competition could take, we cannot allow major asymmetries to develop in throw-weight, accuracy, yield-to-weight ratios, reliability and other factors that contribute to the effectiveness of strategic weapons and to the perceptions of the non-superpower nations. At the same time, our own forces should promote nuclear stability both by reducing incentives for a first use of nuclear weapons and by deterring and avoiding increased nuclear deployments by other powers.
>
> The second requirement is for a highly survivable force that can be withheld at all times and targeted against the economic base of an opponent so as to deter coercive or desperation attacks on the economic and population targets of the United States and its allies.

The third requirement is for a force that, in response to Soviet actions, could implement a variety of limited pre-planned options and react rapidly to retargeting orders so as to deter any range of further attacks that a potential enemy might contemplate. This force should have some ability to destroy hard targets, even though we would prefer to see both sides avoid major counterforce capabilities. We do not propose, however, to concede to the Soviets a unilateral advantage in this realm. Accordingly, our programs will depend on how far the Soviets go in developing a counterforce capability of their own. It should also have the accuracy to attack—with low-yield weapons—soft point targets without causing large-scale collateral damage. And it should be supported by a program of fallout shelters and population relocation to offer protection to our population primarily in the event that military targets become the object of attack.

The fourth requirement is for a range and magnitude of capabilities such that everyone—friend, foe, and domestic audiences alike—will perceive that we are the equal of our strongest competitors. We should not take the chance that in this most hazardous of areas, misperceptions could lead to miscalculation, confrontation, and crisis. (pp. I–13 and I–14)[1]

In the following sections we will attempt to be more specific about how the new doctrine differs from stated U.S. policy in previous years and to indicate how this new policy could affect our efforts to constrain nuclear competition through arms control. Primary attention will, therefore, be paid to those elements of this policy which may lead to requirements for new U.S. weapons or which could stimulate acquisition of new weapons by the Soviets.

A. ASSURED DESTRUCTION

1. *Current Policy.*—An assured destruction force remains an objective of the current DoD doctrine although it is no longer first in the new list of "requirements."

This is not to say that a highly survivable force which can be withheld for substantial periods of time, if need be, and targeted against an enemy's major economic and political assets is irrelevant. Most of us can agree on the need for such a force to serve, at a minimum, as a deterrent to attacks on the cities of the United States and its allies. But to treat such a reserve force as an all-purpose deterrent, as a sovereign remedy for the problems we face, would be the height of folly. (p. II–3)

[1]Unless otherwise noted, all page citations refer to the *Annual Defense Department Report* for FY 1976 and FY 197T.

Mr. Kissinger also seems to feel that an "assured destruction" policy is flawed. Secretary Kissinger told the press in 1972 that

. . . the simplistic notion of the early 1960s which measured deterrent by the amount of civilian carnage that could be inflicted by one side on the other [was] always wrong; hence to consider the mass use of nuclear weapons in terms of the destruction of civilian populations, one faces a political impossibility, not to speak of a moral impossibility. But this has been a fact, now, for five or six years. (Moscow, May 27, 1972)

* * *

Despite the reduced emphasis on assured destruction in recent administration statements, the major programs requested in the current budget (e.g., B–1 and Trident) are justified on the basis of the need to maintain a capability for "assured destruction."

2. *Background.*—The capability for "assured destruction" has been a primary and consistent element of U.S. strategic policy and has been used to justify the development of a "triad" of strategic arms that would be able to survive a Soviet attack and still retain a potential for attacking the Soviet population and economic base: missiles deployed on highly survivable Polaris submarines, ICBMs deployed in blast resistant underground "silos" (both equipped with MIRVs and penetration aids capable of defeating possible enemy defenses), and a sophisticated bomber force capable of taking off before an enemy attack could reach it and of penetrating Soviet air defenses.

Assured destruction was the primary procurement requirement from the mid-1960s through the tenure of Secretary Laird.

3. *Interpretation.*—(a) Previous statements about "assured destruction" mentioned attacks on both "urban" and "industrial" targets. The current formulation of "assured destruction" deals almost exclusively with plans for attacking the Soviet economic base, suggesting that weapons can and should be developed which can heavily damage industry and yet not kill many Soviets. If we can develop weapons with accuracies far greater than any currently available, we could (at least in paper calculations) attack some fraction of Soviet industry with low yield weapons and keep Soviet civilian casualties relatively low (by the standards of nuclear conflict). A large part of the Soviet industrial base, however, could not be attacked in this way. The extent to which this new formulation of "assured destruction" will translate into requirements for new weapons is not clear at this time.

(b) The new DoD report makes it clear that our assured destruction forces are not being jeopardized: "Neither side, for the foreseeable future, is likely to acquire a disarming first strike capability against the

STRATEGIC DOCTRINE: DOCUMENTS

other, even if the fixed, hard ICBM forces become more vulnerable in the 1980s." (p. II–3)

On the other hand, it expresses concern about the continued *credibility* of our deterrent capability:

> With a continuation of these "initiatives," and with the other programs outlined herein, I am confident that we can maintain a balance with the Soviet Union and assure a highly credible second-strike strategic deterrent within the framework of existing and future SALT agreements. *Without these programs, however, I can give no such assurance.* [Emphasis supplied.] (p. I–17)

B. CRISIS STABILITY

1. *Current Policy.*—The current DoD Report, like previous statements, notes U.S. interest in insuring that in a crisis neither side will be tempted to initiate a nuclear war because of fear that waiting for the other side to strike would put it in a less desirable position:

> . . . our own forces should promote nuclear stability both by reducing incentives for a first use of nuclear weapons and by deterring and avoiding increased nuclear deployments by other powers. (p. I–13)
>
> . . . neither that (counterforce) capability nor the improvements we are proposing for it should raise the specter in the minds of the Soviets that their ICBM force is in jeopardy . . . this improved hard-target-kill capability will not threaten the growing Soviet SLBM force. . . . It follows that we do not have and cannot acquire a disarming first-strike capability against the Soviet Union. In fact, it is our decided preference that neither side attempt to acquire such a capability. (pp. I–15 and I–16)

Since the current DoD Report argues that neither side could disarm the other, concern about "counterforce" capabilities must be put in perspective. The concern is apparently due more to the possible political and psychological costs of permitting one side to develop weapons theoretically capable of eliminating a fraction of the other's strategic forces than it is due to a fear that the core of either side's deterrent forces would be eliminated.

To the extent that these political and psychological concerns are taken seriously by either side, however, efforts might be made to overcome them (through new weapons programs or doctrine) which would have the effect of destabilizing an otherwise stable military situation. For example, if either side believed that its ICBMs might not survive a first strike, in a crisis, pressures could develop to use these weapons first rather than to lose them. In addition, plans could be developed for launching ICBMs on warning of an attack.

If either side believed that a major part of its strategic forces were vulnerable to a preemptive attack, great pressures would develop to replace these systems with more survivable forces—such as mobile ICBMs.

The current DoD Report suggests that matching Soviet "counter-force" capabilities for political purposes and for added "flexibility" is important enough to justify the risk of the Soviets interpreting these efforts as the first steps towards the development of a U.S. force capable of destroying the Soviet ICBM force.

The current DoD Report implies that we will attempt to challenge the Soviet deterrent forces if the provocation is sufficient: ". . . our planning objectives should be to . . . leave unchallenged the Soviet capability for deterrence provided that our interests are respected and the traditional norms of international behavior are accepted." (p. I-10)

It later suggests that we are at least keeping open the option of developing a force capable (in theory at least) of attacking their ICBM force: ". . . I must stress that we are not *now* seeking to develop the capability to destroy the Soviet ICBM force. [Emphasis supplied.]" (p. II–5)

The requested program appears indistinguishable from the early stages of a program for developing a capability to attack (on paper at least) a significant fraction of the Soviet ICBM force. The Soviets could not know the extent to which we might deploy improvements in our system to give us substantial counterforce capability against their fixed land based ICBMs; thus any force capable of "limited" counterforce could well have the same impact on Soviet attitudes, strategies and programs as a more ambitious project. The Soviets may be particularly sensitive about maintaining the survivability of their ICBMs since roughly 75% of their strategic weapons are deployed on their land based ICBM force in contrast to the U.S. which has only 25% of its strategic weapons on land-based ICBMs.

C. ESSENTIAL EQUIVALENCE AND POLITICAL PERCEPTIONS

1. *Current Policy.*—The discussion of the issue of "essential equivalence" found in the current DoD Report is unique in four ways:

(a) it makes the achievement of "perceived" equality with the Soviet Union the first objective of our strategic forces. This is justified as follows:

> . . . equality is also important for symbolic purposes, in large part because the strategic offensive forces have come to be seen by many—however, regrettably—as important to the

status and stature of a major power . . . the lack of equality can become a source of serious diplomatic and military miscalculation. Opponents may feel that they can exploit a favorable imbalance by means of political pressure. . . . (p. II–7)

(*b*) the need for equality is defined in such a way that it seems independent of military requirements;

(*c*) it notes that the "perceptions" of "non-superpower" nations are also of central importance; and

(*d*) it is much more specific than previous statements about how to define "essential equivalence." It includes such detailed measures as "throw-weight, accuracy, yield-to-weight ratios, reliability, and other such factors that determine force effectiveness." (p. I–13) It also includes appearance of counterforce capability. "No opponent should think that he could fire at some of our Minuteman or SAC bases without being subjected to, at the very least, a response in kind." (p. II–4)

The extent to which Secretary of State Kissinger endorses this policy is not clear. On the one hand, he told the Senate Foreign Relations Committee on September 9, 1974, that "failure to maintain equivalence could jeopardize not only our freedom but our very survival."

> . . . While a decisive advantage is hard to calculate, the *appearance* of inferiority—its actual significance—can have serious political consequences. With weapons that are unlikely to be used and for which there is no operational experience, the psychological impact can be crucial. Thus each side has a high incentive to achieve not only the reality but the appearance of reality. In a very real sense each side shapes the military establishment of the other.

On the other hand, he told a press conference on November 25 of that year that, "We are not going to build weapons just to match every large thing the Soviets have. We are going to build weapons for our purposes, not for an exact competition." He explained elsewhere that:

> When nuclear arsenals reach levels involving thousands of launchers and over ten thousand warheads, and when the characteristics of the weapons of the two sides are so incommensurable, it becomes difficult to determine what combination of numbers of strategic weapons and performance capabilities would give one side a militarily and politically useful superiority. (Senate Foreign Relations Committee, September 19, 1974)

> Throughout history the essential task of national security was to accumulate military power. It would have seemed

inconceivable even a generation ago that such power once gained could not be translated directly into foreign policy advantage. . . . When two nations are already capable of destroying each other, an upper limit exists beyond which additional weapons lose their political significance. The overwhelming destructiveness of nuclear weapons makes it difficult to relate their use to specific political objectives and may indeed generate new political problems. (Speech to American Legion, August 20, 1974)

2. *Previous Policy.*—The requirement for equality with the Soviet Union in a variety of strategic weapon characteristics has been noted in the past but never with as much emphasis as it is given in the most recent Annual Report. This may have been because the U.S. enjoyed a clear superiority in most aspects of strategic offensive weaponry until very recently. In 1968, Secretary McNamara argued that once both sides had deployed enough weapons to achieve an assured destruction capability, the concept of superiority became meaningless. In that year, however, the U.S. had nearly twice as many strategic delivery vehicles as the Soviet Union.

3. *Interpretation.*—(a) Considerable ambiguity remains about the extent to which we will be willing to tolerate "asymmetries" in force characteristics under the new doctrine. The current Annual Report states:

> . . . we have a good second-strike deterrent, but so does the Soviet Union. Although the two forces differ in a number of important respects, no one doubts that they are in approximate balance. There are, in short, no immediate grounds for fears about bomber or missile gaps. (p. I–16)
>
> We may need to maintain an offsetting advantage in some areas to compensate for Soviet advantages in others. For example, the United States should seek to stay ahead in accuracy to offset the large and apparently growing Soviet advantage in throw-weight. (p. II–8)
>
> Fortunately, the question of perceptions may to a large extent have been resolved by the understanding at Vladivostok . . . we shall plan for deployment of approximately 2,400 strategic delivery vehicles and 1,320 MIRVed missiles. (p. II–8)

(b) The forces of the U.S. and the Soviet Union differ considerably and a precise matching of all aspects of Soviet forces would require substantial changes in the current U.S. force. On the other hand, if we are willing to accept imbalances in detail, it is difficult to show that either side will have a clear overall advantage either now or in the near future. For example, the size and number of the Soviet ICBMs is matched by the technological superiority of U.S. ICBMs as well as by the large number and greater capability of U.S. long range bombers. The Soviets are building a large SLBM force but the U.S. has a significant lead in submarine and SLBM technology.

(c) A distinction must be made between matching capabilities and matching details of hardware. The differences in the technology base, geography, relationship to non-superpowers, and strategic doctrine of the two countries place ultimate limits to how symmetrical the strategic forces of both sides can be.

(d) Perceptions about military capabilities depend on a variety of judgments including (i) perception of the overall balance in military hardware; (ii) perception of general technological prowess; and (iii) perception of the intent and determination of the political leadership. Since most of these judgments are necessarily subjective, and since they can change rapidly, we can never be confident that we have achieved "perceived equivalence." It is also not clear that we can compensate for subjective political judgments by adjusting our deployments of strategic weapons. The strategic forces of the U.S. and U.S.S.R. are now roughly equal (although they differ significantly in detail and scenarios can always be constructed which show an advantage for one side or the other) and in technology, the U.S. with the accomplishments of its space program and its clear lead in aeronautics and electronics is surely perceived by the world at large to be ahead of the Soviets.

To some extent, perceptions are influenced by the importance which the U.S. gives to various indicators of strategic strength. We may therefore be able to change these perceptions by emphasizing different aspects of the strategic balance.

D. FLEXIBILITY FOR LIMITED NUCLEAR OPTIONS

1. *Current Policy.*—The current Defense Department Report establishes as a central objective of our strategic forces a requirement for "a force that, in response to Soviet actions, could implement a variety of limited preplanned options and react rapidly to retargeting orders so as to deter any range of further attacks." (p. I–13) The term "limited" is never strictly defined but it appears to include all attacks short of attacks on cities. It is unclear whether this requirement necessarily leads to a need for substantial improvement of current U.S. counterforce capabilities. However, the current DoD Report notes at several points that "limited preplanned options" will require "some ability to destroy hard targets" (p. I–13) and funds for weapons designed to support this capability are requested in this year's DoD budget.

155

The requirement for these new options is justified primarily by the argument that by having a capability for a full spectrum of nuclear attacks, the U.S. will improve the effectiveness and credibility of its deterrent:

> . . . even if there is only a small probability that limited response options would deter an attack or bring a nuclear war to a rapid conclusion, without large-scale damage to cities, it is a probability which, for the sake of our citizens, we should not foreclose. (p. II-7)
> . . . (an opponent) must be persuaded that in the face of a sufficient provocation, we will actually execute the retaliatory attacks. (p. II–1)
> It is intended to make nuclear war of any kind less, not more, likely. (p. II–6)
> . . . all of the evidence available to us suggests that very limited and quickly terminated nuclear exchanges could result in fatalities and casualties much lower than from some of the traditional conflicts. . . . (p. II–7)

2. *Background.*—Concern about developing strategic nuclear forces capable of strikes other than city attacks has been a consistent part of the debate about U.S. nuclear policy. This concern has, until recently, seldom been reflected in public statements about our plans for using or our objectives for purchasing nuclear weapons. For at least a decade, however, U.S. forces have been physically capable of executing a wide variety of limited attacks which avoided cities. The ABM Treaty assured flexibility in our forces since, as a result of that treaty, the large numbers of weapons which we had developed for penetrating postulated ABM systems were no longer required for "assured destruction." Former President Nixon renewed public interest in the subject by calling repeatedly for alternatives to "assured destruction" strategies early in his administration, but this was not publicly reflected in Defense Department planning until 1974.

In his first Annual Report, Secretary Schlesinger explained that a major effort would be made to develop "limited" nuclear options. He explained the difference between his new policy and previous plans as follows:

> It is true that in addition to retaliatory targeting against urban and industrial centers, our war plans have always included military targets. . . . In the past, most of these options—whether the principal targets were cities, industrial facilities, or military installations—have involved relatively massive responses. Rather than massive options, we now want to provide the President with a wider set of much more selective targeting options. Through the possession of such a

visible capability, we hope to reinforce deterrence. . . . (Annual Report for FY 75, pages 4–5)

3. *Interpretation.*—(*a*) The discussion of the doctrine of "limited preplanned options" contained in the current Report implies several things not explicitly stated. First, it suggests that we must be able to match a wide range of Soviet capabilities (as we perceive them), implying that the only way to deter a limited attack is to threaten similar attack in return. Secondly, it suggests that one of the attacks which we must be able to match is a massive Soviet strike at our strategic offensive forces—ICBM silos and SAC bases. Finally, it implies that flexibility may extend to options for using strategic nuclear weapons first:

> No opponent should think that he could fire at some of our Minuteman or SAC bases without being subjected to, at the very least, a response in kind. No opponent should believe that he could attack other U.S. targets of military or economic value without finding similar or other appropriate targets in his own homeland under attack. *No opponent should believe that he could blackmail our allies without risking his very capability for blackmail.* (pp. II–4 and II–5) [Emphasis added.]

(*b*) The Report also suggests that one of the important elements of the strategy will be to develop a capability for targeting Soviet industry and military facilities without causing large numbers of civilian casualties:

> In some circumstances, we might wish to retaliate against non-collocated, small soft targets, or facilities near large population centers; high accuracy and a low-yield, air-burst weapon would be the most appropriate combination for those targets. (p. II–5)
> . . . all of the evidence available to us suggests that very limited and quickly terminated nuclear exchanges could result in fatalities and casualties much lower than from some of the traditional conflicts we have experienced. And even if a nuclear exchange were to expand to all strategic nuclear targets in the United States, we would probably suffer at least 100 million fewer fatalities than if our cities were attacked. (p. II–7)

The real benefits of "limited preplanned options" are not made clear in the current DoD Report. Given that we could not limit damage to ourselves by executing any attack, however large, we must expect that the value of threatening limited attacks will not be military but political or psychological. It is difficult to distinguish between the political and psychological value of different "limited attacks." The

157

DoD Report gives us no way to judge whether the capability to attack industrial facilities near major cities would be more effective as a deterrent than a capability to attack an isolated military installation or even a capability for a demonstrative attack on an uninhabited region. Also, the potential benefits of any "limited attack" must be weighed against the clear risk that the Soviet response to such attacks could be very large. In this regard, it is interesting to note that the current DoD Report gives no indication that the Soviets are attempting to develop small weapons capable of limiting damage to the U.S. population in a counterforce attack.

(c) The current Report also seems to establish a requirement for an ability to strike back with complete flexibility even after absorbing a massive Soviet first strike which had destroyed a large fraction of our ICBM force and suggests that SLBMs and bombers are not adequate for flexible response:

> Since both we and the Soviet Union are investing so much of our capability for flexible and controlled responses in our ICBM forces, these forces could become tempting targets, assuming that one or both sides acquire much more substantial hard-target kill capabilities than they currently possess. If one side could remove the other's capability for flexible and controlled responses, he might find ways of exercising coercion and extracting concessions without triggering the final holocaust. (p. II–4)

(d) The impact of the new flexible response requirements on U.S. plans for buying new weapons is not clear at present. A year ago Secretary Schlesinger indicated that no new weapons need be developed for added flexibility:

> We have very carefully distinguished, Senator Case, and I hope that you will join in explaining this distinction, between the change in targeting doctrine and the set of strategic initiatives that we are proposing. The change in targeting doctrine can be implemented without the procurement of any additional weapons. Accuracy contributes somewhat to the effectiveness of the new targeting doctrine, but it is not essential for the implementation of that doctrine. We do not have to acquire a single additional weapon. We could have selective responses even if we had a smaller force structure than we presently have, and with no greater yields. (Senate Foreign Relations Committee, March, 1974)

However, since the FY 76 statement calls for hard target kill capability, it implies that new weapons with higher yields and better accuracy will have to be developed (e.g., a new ICBM such as the M-X, a large throw weight SLBM such as Trident II, and accuracy improvements including terminal homing MaRVs [maneuverable reentry vehicles]).

4. *Capabilities of Current and Improved Forces for "Limited Employment Options."*—A brief examination of what can be done to current forces to provide flexibility can put the new requirement in perspective.

(a) Our current strategic forces have the physical capability to attack nearly every significant Soviet industrial and military target (except for Soviet ICBM and SLBM forces) with a high probability of success. By mid-1975 we will have 8,500 independently targetable weapons only a small fraction of which could destroy a quarter (or more) of the Soviet population. Our current weapons could also destroy specific targets such as Soviet airfields, dams, submarine support facilities, isolated industrial facilities, etc. Our ability to attack any of these facilities in a limited strike with current command and control systems depends on several factors. If the target is already in our target inventory (which is very large given the enormous number of independently targetable weapons) and a specific weapon has been programmed for that target, the only thing that need be done is to establish a procedure for releasing the weapon. If this procedure is preplanned, the time delay in execution can be very short, a matter of minutes. In the unlikely event that the target is not already programmed, new targeting instructions must be developed for our ICBMs. This would require a number of days. To the extent that limited options require single weapons or single targets, we may also be limited by the fact that a large fraction of our forces carry MIRVs. Command Data Buffer, planned for Minuteman III, can reduce emergency retargeting time for a single Minuteman III missile from 16-24 hours to 36 minutes.

Improved command and control systems alone would, of course, not increase our chances of destroying ICBM silos but would decrease the time required to execute limited attacks (involving one or very few missiles) if our current systems are not already targeted on the desired facilities.

(b) A substantial improvement in missile accuracy with current or increased yields would significantly raise the calculated probability of destroying ICBM silos but it would (for reasons discussed elsewhere) not lead to an operational capability for destroying the entire Soviet ICBM force. An operational capability could not be achieved in view of the problems of coordinating a massive attack, uncertainties about operational reliabilities and accuracies (our missiles have never been tested in operational trajectories), uncertainties about interference between multiple weapons targeted on a single silo (fractricide), and uncertainty about whether the Soviets would launch their ICBMs on warning of an attack.

Given very precise accuracies, extremely small nuclear weapons could, in theory, be used to attack specific sites (such as individual industrial centers) with a great reduction in loss of civilian lives. However, none of the weapons requested in the current budget seem to be designed to reduce civilian casualties; no new weapon system is mentioned as having smaller yields than its predecessor.

E. CIVIL DEFENSE

1. *Current Policy.*—The current Annual Report has made Civil Defense a central element of strategic nuclear policy:

> . . . one would expect that the recent shift in emphasis towards a more flexible strategic response policy, which I discussed earlier in this section of the Defense Report, would be reflected in our Civil Defense Program. (p. II-54)
>
> . . . our very modest civil defense program should continue; it makes clear to a prospective opponent contemplating a limited strike that, since we can protect our citizens against fallout, we have a credible choice between an all-out response and no response at all. (p. II-5)
>
> Accordingly, we propose to continue our efforts, within the limits of the resources available, to improve our ability to protect the population in place against fallout and to develop in an orderly way two major options for the relocation of the population in a crisis. The first option, which would be designed against the threat of a Soviet counterforce attack, would involve the relocation of the population from high risk areas near key military installations. . . . The second option, which would be designed against an all-out Soviet nuclear attack, would involve the evacuation of the population from cities, as well as from near key military installations. (p. II-55)

*   *   *

2. *Interpretation.*—A modest, but well planned civil defense program, involving some training and storage of medical supplies, could be beneficial in the event of a highly limited nuclear attack (as well as during peacetime emergencies) and would not require prohibitive investments or raise the political and social complications associated with a major program. However, we have no way of knowing where a Soviet limited attack would occur, and it should be remembered that even a single megaton size weapon could cover regions hundreds of miles from its target (depending on height of detonation and meteorological conditions) with substantial levels of fallout. A much

greater area would become radioactive at a level which could result in serious long-term health effects for the affected population.

As a consequence, a Civil Defense system that has any reasonable chance of protecting civilians against a large nuclear attack would require a very large investment in new equipment (e.g., large numbers of shelters with sophisticated access and entrances). If relocation is to become a part of our *flexible* nuclear response, drills and exercises would be required involving nearly the entire U.S. population. Implementing such a program could lead to an increase in international and domestic tensions.

F. INTERACTION WITH SOVIET PROGRAMS

1. *Current Policy.*—The new doctrine makes an explicit connection between U.S. plans for new programs and our perception of Soviet behavior. We apparently hope to persuade the Soviets to exercise restraint by implying that if they do not, we will invest heavily in new programs of our own. The FY 76 Report states:

> Assuming that the Soviet leaders exhibit restraint in their application of the (Vladivostok) agreement's principles, we are prepared to exercise restraint as well. However until we obtain solid evidence of Soviet restraint, we shall plan (to build up to the Vladivostok levels) . . . How we proceed on these accounts will depend essentially on the actions of the Soviet Union. They currently have the initiative, and it is up to them to decide how much additional effort the two sides should put into these programs. (p. II-8)
>
> The Soviets have already begun what will be a very substantial, indeed unprecedented, deployment of large new ICBMs in the first quarter of this year. However, if the principles and spirit of Vladivostok prevail, our response can be quite restrained. (p. I-14)

The kind of Soviet restraint which we will require if we are to have a "restrained" response of our own to their new ICBM programs is not made clear. It does not appear to mean that we require them to stop MIRV deployment short of the 1320 MIRVs on new systems as permitted by Vladivostok.

2. *Interpretation.*—This policy goes beyond attempting to enforce restraint in Soviet foreign policy by achieving "perceived equality." It attempts to constrain further advances in Soviet forces by promising to match any of their advances.

Given the ambiguity about who has the initiative in many programs, there is danger that this policy could lead to increased competition instead of mutual restraint. For example, the Soviets may not feel that they have the initiative; in fact, they may believe that they must react to new U.S. programs (such as M-X, U.S. improved accuracy programs, Trident, and B-1) with systems of their own designed to enforce U.S. restraint. A choice must be made as to whether the small military and political risks involved in exercising restraint outweighs possible benefits in restricting the arms race.

II. THE VLADIVOSTOK AGREEMENT

The Vladivostok agreement has two basic elements:

A. It limits both sides to 2,400 "strategic delivery vehicles" (SDVs) for a period of ten years. This total will consist of all ICBMs, submarine-launched missiles (SLBMs) and "intercontinental bombers." Other systems which the Soviets had previously wanted us to count in the U.S. totals, such as U.S. aircraft in overseas bases and the British and French missile launching submarines, are not counted.

The number 2,400 is approximately 50 less than the number of "strategic delivery vehicles" which the [FY 1976-197T] DoD Report (page II-19) expects the Soviets to have operational by mid 1975. The agreement will thus require some reduction in Soviet forces. The U.S. will have 2,208 "strategic delivery vehicles" by mid 1975 and the ceiling would thus permit us to construct 192 additional SDVs before 1985. We could do this by constructing B-1s or Trident submarines without retiring older systems or constructing both and retiring some older systems (such as older Polaris boats, Titans, and B-52s).

B. The Vladivostok accords also permit each side 1,320 missiles equipped with multiple independently targetable reentry vehicles (MIRVs).

The U.S. currently has 1,046 MIRVed missiles operational or planned for conversion. If the Trident submarine is constructed along present plans, we will have 1,286 MIRVs by the time the agreement expires in 1985 (550 MMIII, 31 subs with 496 Poseidon or Trident I missiles and 10 Trident subs with 240 Trident missiles).

The 1,320 limit is substantially below the number of MIRVs which the Soviets could deploy by 1985 in the absence of an agreement.

The significant arms control benefits from Vladivostok are:

- It has established simple measures of equality in strategic forces.

- It extends the interim strategic offensive agreement thus protecting the AMB Treaty.

- It places an upperbound on worst case projections of the number of strategic delivery vehicles which the Soviets might deploy.

- It sets the framework for reductions and other arms control measures.

- It has overcome, for the time being at least, a serious obstacle in negotiations—the Soviets have for the first time agreed to exclude U.S. forward based systems and French and British SLBMs from the count.

Skepticism about the value of the Vladivostok agreement stems [from] arguments that:

- The numerical limits are set very high so that planned U.S. procurements are not affected and even Soviet procurements may remain as planned.

- MIRV limits are too high to decrease whatever threat MIRV deployment may appear to pose for the strategic balance.

- There are no restraints for qualitative improvements so that the arms competition can continue unabated in spite of Vladivostok.

- The agreement does not redress the current asymmetry in ICBM throw weight unless the U.S. plans to build new ICBMs to match Soviet levels.

- The high limits may provide both sides a license and justification to build eventually to higher limits than they might otherwise have.

There are several important issues that must be resolved before the Vladivostok agreement can be converted to a treaty.

- What methods, acceptable on political and technical grounds, can be used to verify the number of deployed MIRVed missiles?

- Will long-range, air-launched cruise missiles (ALCMs) be covered by the agreement? (Secretary Kissinger has told the press that the aggregate of SDVs would include "air-launched missiles" with ranges greater than 600 km (373 miles) but he did not specify whether cruise missiles were included.)

- Will long-range, submarine-launched cruise missiles (SLCMs) be covered by the agreement?

- Will the Soviet Backfire (currently in production) and the U.S. FB-111 (of which we have about 75) be included in the aggregate of SDVs?

- Can we adequately verify the number of deployed mobile ICBMs which are apparently permitted under the agreement?

163

III. Some Arms Control Issues Raised by the New Policy for Nuclear Weapons

A. How does the desire for "perceived" equality in all characteristics of strategic nuclear forces (including those areas where there are currently major asymmetries) affect the prospects for competition in strategic arms under Vladivostok? How does this requirement affect prospects for subsequent reductions and qualitative constraints?

Comments

1. Several fundamental U.S. and Soviet asymmetries cannot be eliminated: very different geography, technology, and a different constellation of allies and potential opponents. Consequently, it will probably only be possible to achieve overall equality and not equality in the details of weapons systems.

2. In defining essential equivalence it is difficult to determine whose judgment is important and what affects these judgments. This confusion could lead to attempts by both sides to match what it fears the other side might deploy for both military and political reasons. This could easily result in an arms race particularly given the time delay between initial intelligence on a new opposing system and full deployment of that system.

3. Weapons purchased for "political" purposes might undermine the stability of the military balance. For example, if either side develops a silo killing capability to enhance the "perceived" capabilities of its force, it could cause the other side to fear the military capability which this force had for a preemptive attack.

B. Will the current emphasis on added flexibility make arms control more difficult by leading to requirements for new weapons?

Comments

1. Our current strategic forces can be given great flexibility simply by changing existing plans and procedures. New missile payloads and improved guidance would be needed to destroy ICBM silos (even in principle) with high probability. Development of a high-accuracy, low-yield weapon could permit us to attack a greater number of "soft" targets with relatively few civilian casualties.

2. Given the considerable capabilities of our current force, it is not clear the added "flexibility" which could be achieved by purchasing new weapons would improve our ability to demonstrate resolve, to exert political or psychological pressure, or to reduce the likelihood of a massive Soviet response. If we determine, for example, that possible small Soviet attacks on our ICBM forces could be adequately deterred by U.S. capabilities to attack Soviet air-defense installations or other

STRATEGIC DOCTRINE: DOCUMENTS

military or economic targets, we would not require any forces beyond those currently available.

C. Could the flexible response doctrine indicated in the current Annual Report lead to greater U.S. reliance on nuclear weapons? Could this increase the probability of the introduction of nuclear weapons in a conflict or that once these weapons were used, the "firebreaks" between "tactical," "theatre," and "strategic" use of nuclear weapons would be lost?

Comments

1. Emphasizing our ability and willingness to employ limited nuclear strikes with our strategic forces may be of some political value in reassuring our allies of our nuclear commitment and of our willingness to use all available resources to defend them. Such assurances might also serve to deter extreme non-nuclear provocations.

2. On the other hand, there is a risk that the distinction between nuclear and non-nuclear conflict could be lost if we convince ourselves that there is no operational distinction between the two types of war and that nuclear weapons (particularly "strategic" nuclear weapons) can be introduced without seriously risking escalation to an all-out nuclear exchange. It is important to note, however, that the current DoD Report emphasizes the importance of conventional forces for meeting the security needs of ourselves and of our allies.

3. Extreme non-nuclear provocations might be more credibly deterred by political actions and by improving our conventional forces rather than by extending the flexibility of our strategic nuclear force. Budgetary constraints, of course, limit our ability to expand our conventional forces.

D. Would the development of a credible capability to destroy some of an opponent's hard missile silos affect the nuclear balance?

Comments

1. Currently neither side has a credible capability to destroy a large fraction of the other's fixed, hard ICBM silos.

2. If we develop a force with a credible capability to destroy some part of the Soviet ICBM force for the purpose of increasing the flexibility of our strategic forces, this force may be perceived as an important first step towards the development of a force capable of destroying all opposing ICBMs. Such a program could therefore risk the same Soviet response as a major U.S. counterforce program.

3. Perceived vulnerability of fixed, land-based ICBMs would reduce stability in a crisis and could lead to acquisition of more survivable replacement systems (thus motivating new generations of weapons).

E. Should restraint in the development and deployment of new types of strategic weapon systems be dependent on Soviet initiatives?
Comments

1. While the current Annual Report suggests that the initiatives in strategic weapon development are in the hands of the Soviets, the Soviets might not view the situation in the same light. From their perspective, the U.S. is responsible for many initiatives in strategic nuclear weapons (i.e., MIRVs, advanced missile guidance, advanced submarine technology, etc.).

2. The present momentum of military technology may limit arms control possibilities unless some restraint is exercised. Deployment of long range cruise missiles and mobiles could make verification difficult or impossible. It would be difficult to negotiate an agreement which both sides could accept as providing overall equality if new types of systems were being deployed at a rapid rate.

F. How would the development of mobile ICBMs or long-range cruise missiles (launched from submarines or aircraft) by either side affect the prospects for future arms control?

Comments

1. Mobiles could offer a technique for overcoming the possible vulnerability of our fixed ICBM force but they could be difficult to count with precision since they depend for survival on denying the other side information about their location.

2. Air-launched cruise missiles of long range could contribute to the survivability of our bomber force by assisting bombers to penetrate air defenses or even by eliminating the need for the aircraft to fly over hostile territory. Long-range missiles could be fired well outside enemy borders.

3. Long-range cruise missiles launched from submarines do not appear to add any important capability to U.S. strategic forces which our SLBMs do not already have.

Either system probably could be used to convert launchers designed for conventional warfare (such as attack submarines and transport aircraft) into strategic launchers without any visible modifications. This could prevent us from being able to count the number of deployed "strategic delivery vehicles" with any acceptable precision. However, before any such systems were deployed, many full-range flight tests would probably have to be conducted. This would run a risk of detection.

G. Where is the competition in strategic weaponry likely to be the most intense in the next ten years? Can we identify any developments in the foreseeable future which would be likely to lead to an intensification of the competition or which could complicate or preclude follow-on negotiations?

Comments

1. Emphasis on improving the qualitative characteristics of strategic weaponry is likely to replace emphasis on the numbers of delivery vehicles even on the Soviet side during the next decade. This will be particularly true under a SALT agreement which places an upper limit on numbers of launchers.

2. Improved accuracy (using terminal guidance and other techniques), cruise missiles, and mobile ICBMs are likely candidates for future competition.

3. Banning a new technology becomes much more difficult once flight testing of that technology has been completed. Not only are limits more difficult to verify after system testing has been completed; a tested system often acquires a degree of institutional commitment which can be difficult to overcome.

4. Once innovations in strategic weaponry are deployed by one side, it is difficult to limit these systems without permitting the side which is behind to catch up. This is true not only for new types of strategic systems but also for new generations of existing weapons systems.

THE THEATER NUCLEAR FORCE POSTURE IN EUROPE

James R. Schlesinger

In this April 1975 report to the Congress, Secretary of Defense James R. Schlesinger describes the deployment of theater nuclear weapons by the United States in the European region and the doctrine governing their possible use. Mr. Schlesinger notes that with the advent of strategic parity between the United States and the Soviet Union the deterrent role of theater nuclear forces has gained in importance. Should deterrence fail, NATO must be capable of fighting effectively at any level of conflict in order to repel an attack and terminate hostilities on a basis favorable to the West. The author concludes his report with a summary of current and anticipated force improvement and doctrinal refinement programs to enhance the credibility and effectiveness of NATO's defense and deterrent capabilities.

Source: James R. Schlesinger, *The Theater Nuclear Force Posture in Europe, A Report to the United States Congress* (Washington, D.C., April 1975).

A. Deterrence and NATO's Military Forces

1. NATO Objectives. The military forces of the North Atlantic Treaty Organization (NATO) have several objectives. First and foremost, they should deter armed attacks on the NATO Allies. If deterrence fails, these forces should be able to deny the enemy's military objectives and terminate the conflict quickly, at the lowest level of violence consistent with NATO's objectives. Achievement of these objectives requires the clear capability to fight effectively at any level of conflict threatened by the Warsaw Pact (WP). Equally important, these objectives can be achieved only if the NATO Alliance continues to manifest the political resolve to fight as necessary to maintain the political and territorial integrity of its member nations.

The resolve and cohesiveness of the NATO Alliance is essential if other important peacetime objectives are to be achieved:

- Deterrence of attempts to coerce members of the Alliance.

- Maintenance of a stable political, military, and economic environment to minimize the risk of crises or confrontations.

- Improvement of NATO security and increased stability in the critical central region.

2. Theater Nuclear Forces. The military postures of both NATO and the WP consist of three major elements—strategic forces, theater nuclear forces, and conventional forces. On the NATO side the posture is referred to as the NATO Triad and is the means of deterrence and defense. The conventional forces of that Triad deter and defend against conventional attacks. Theater nuclear forces deter and defend against theater nuclear attacks; help deter and, if necessary, defend against conventional attack; and help deter conflict escalation. The final leg of the Triad, strategic forces, deter and defend in general nuclear war, deter conflict escalation, and reinforce theater nuclear forces if needed. During the 1970's, the Soviets achieved overall parity in strategic forces with the United States. The threat of mutual annihilation limits the range of hostile actions which can be deterred by strategic forces and places more emphasis on the deterrent roles of theater nuclear and conventional forces. Even during a generation of great U. S. strategic nuclear superiority, the theater nuclear and conventional forces had important roles to play. Now, in the era of strategic equivalence, their importance has further increased.

Since the mid-1960's, NATO has been making substantial improvements in conventional forces. But the WP has also improved the quality and quantity of its conventional forces. While the range of actions which are deterred by NATO conventional forces is increasing, a successful conventional defense in Europe depends critically upon many assumptions—e.g., timely NATO mobilization, keeping pace with WP mobilization, continued deployment of Soviet conventional forces to the Sino-Soviet border, the maintenance of an adequate NATO support and logistics base. Theater nuclear forces which act in direct deterrence of WP theater nuclear attacks are also an essential part of the deterrent of conventional attacks because they hedge against failure—or WP perception of failure—of one or more of these assumptions.

Operational Soviet military doctrine apparently does not subscribe to a strategy of graduated nuclear response; however, a few press articles have indicated that limited use of nuclear weapons is possible, but fraught with the danger of escalation. WP forces, current doctrine and training indicate a readiness, however, for conducting a war in Europe with theater-wide, large-scale nuclear strikes. Their large armored forces are postured to exploit these nuclear attacks with rapid, massive penetrations of NATO lines. To deter such attacks, the WP must perceive that sufficient NATO theater nuclear forces can survive initial conventional and nuclear attacks and, in conjunction with surviving conventional forces, blunt WP armored attacks and attack remaining WP theater nuclear forces. If deterrence fails, NATO forces must be able to achieve these objectives and reverse the tactical situation, thus changing the assessment of WP political leaders regarding their prospects for early victory. This should create conditions whereby the conflict could be terminated relatively quickly and on terms acceptable to the Allies.

3. The Process of Changing the NATO Military Posture. U.S. analyses indicate a need for change in the theater nuclear force posture, as in other elements of the NATO Triad. Recent analyses by NATO military authorities tend to support the U.S. conclusion. It is vital, however, that the process of change be recognized as equal in importance to the changes themselves, so that the military posture is improved while maintaining the political cohesiveness of NATO.

U.S. theater nuclear forces deployed in Europe have been for years a major symbol of the earnest U.S. commitment to the common defense of the Alliance. Consequently, possible changes in the theater nuclear force posture must be carefully evaluated from both the military perspective and with an eye to the message these changes convey to Allies and adversaries about the future U.S. commitment to this common defense.

For many years the United States has strongly encouraged its Allies to depend on U.S. nuclear weapons, rather than developing and deploying their own. The United States has deployed nuclear weapons in Europe, with the cognizance of the Congress, for potential use in wartime by U.S. and Allied forces. It has worked closely over the years with the Allies to develop detailed doctrine and plans for use of these nuclear forces.

The following broad actions must continue to be carried out in close partnership with the NATO Allies:

- Pursuit of a more stable balance of forces in Europe through arms control negotiations.

- Modernization and improvement of NATO's conventional forces, to provide improved deterrence and defense against conventional attacks.

- Structuring of NATO's theater nuclear forces to improve survivability, provide for greater military effectiveness in combined conventional-nuclear conflict, improve command and control, reduce collateral damage, and increase the security of nuclear weapons in peacetime.

- Updating of doctrine and plans for theater nuclear operations in light of improved WP forces and NATO's conventional force improvements.

- Revision of plans and doctrine for employing strategic forces, to improve the deterrence of escalation in limited conflicts and to increase the military support which strategic forces can render to NATO for limited conflict.

B. NATO Strategy and Force Posture

1. Basic NATO Strategy. Since NATO was established in 1949, the overall Alliance strategy, which is the basis for defense planning, has evolved through three basic phases. Each phase has had deterrence of war as the primary objective.

The first phase was predicated on building and maintaining a large conventional force structure to match that of the U.S.S.R. and its allies. This strategy proved to be beyond that which NATO could economically support. It then evolved into the so-called "trip-wire" response, stated in Military Committee Document 14/2 (MC14/2), during the period of unquestioned United States nuclear superiority. MC14/2 emphasized deterrence through the threat of massive retaliation with nuclear weapons in lieu of large conventional forces. The inherent unsuitability to lower level threats of aggression and the inflexibility of this strategy, coupled with the growth of U.S.S.R. strategic and tactical nuclear capabilities, eventually eroded its credibility. Accordingly, NATO's current strategy of "flexible response" (MC14/3) was approved in 1967 by NATO as essential to redress these inadequacies.

MC14/3 emphasizes a spectrum of military capabilities to provide numerous defensive alternatives ranging from conventional warfare to the use or the threat of use of strategic nuclear weapons. A potential enemy is faced with great uncertainty as to which response might be selected.

The flexible response strategy calls for conventional and nuclear forces, doctrine, and planning which can accomplish the following objectives:

- To deter WP aggression.

- If deterrence fails, to defeat aggression at any level of attack (conventional or nuclear) made by the enemy.

- If direct defense fails, to use deliberately increased military force as necessary to make the cost and risk disproportionate to the enemy's objectives and cause him to cease his aggression and withdraw.

- In the event of general nuclear war, to inflict extensive damage on the Soviet Union and other WP countries. This objective would be accomplished in conjunction with the strategic forces of the NATO nuclear powers.

2. Elements for Implementing the NATO Strategy. Military forces, coordinated planning among the NATO nations, nuclear weapons and positive political control of nuclear forces are essential to implement the NATO strategy. The current status of these elements is:

a. NATO military forces. An examination of NATO and WP conventional forces shows some important asymmetries. The WP has a large numerical superiority in tanks. However, for NATO defensive operations, these advantages are offset, in part, by NATO's large number of anti-tank weapons and more extensive support structure. NATO has a small numerical advantage in aircraft if U.S. reinforcements are considered. NATO's aircraft are of higher quality and could contribute to the defense against armored attacks.

NATO and WP theater nuclear force postures differ. There are large numbers of IR/MRBM's [intermediate-range/medium-range ballistic missiles], medium bombers, and ballistic missile submarines based in the U.S.S.R. which are capable of conducting strikes on

NATO. NATO forward-deployed nuclear forces consist of battlefield support systems (artillery, short-range surface-to-surface missiles [SSM's] and atomic demolition munitions [ADM's]), nuclear air defense systems (Nike Hercules) and longer range systems (air delivered bombs, long range SSM's and submarine-launched ballistic missiles [SLBM's]). WP battlefield nuclear support systems consist of FROG and SCUD SSM's which could be equipped with nuclear, chemical, or non-nuclear warheads. WP forces also include nuclear-capable tactical aircraft.

b. Coordinated planning. Coordinated planning to support the NATO force posture and defense plans is carried out primarily through the following mechanisms:

- General policy and broad political-military planning is provided by the NATO Defense Planning Committee and the NATO Military Committee.

- Nuclear policy and broad political-military nuclear planning is provided by the Nuclear Planning Group (NPG) and its parent organization, the Nuclear Defense Affairs Committee (NDAC), for approval by the Defense Planning Committee.

- Coordination of NATO nuclear plans with U.S. nuclear employment plans is provided by a detachment of NATO officers at the U.S. Joint Strategic Target Planning Staff (JSTPS) at the U.S. Strategic Air Command (SAC) Headquarters.

*   *   *

c. Nuclear weapons. The Soviet Union maintains what are believed to be nuclear weapon storage sites to support Soviet and other WP forces.

. . . [In] August 1974, the United States had about 7,000 nuclear warheads deployed in Europe. Except for a small number of anti-submarine warfare (ASW) weapons for U.S. and Allied long-range patrol aircraft, these weapons support U.S. and Allied air force and army units. NATO is also supported by aircraft carriers with tactical nuclear bombs and by other naval forces with SLBM's [submarine-launched ballistic missiles], nuclear ASW weapons, and nulcear air defense weapons.

A substantial proportion of the U.S. warheads in Europe are deployed for use by allied delivery vehicles under Programs of Cooperation (POC's) and stockpile agreements. These are formal bilateral agreements between the United States and other nations which involve transfer of delivery vehicles capable of nuclear delivery or deployment of nuclear weapons for use by the host nation under the direction of SACEUR [Supreme Allied Commander Europe] or

SACLANT [Supreme Allied Commander Atlantic]. Host nations provide support for U.S. weapons and weapons provided for their use. The nuclear warheads remain in U.S. custody until released by the U.S. President in time of war.

*   *   *

d. Political control of NATO nuclear weapons. The United States maintains positive control in peace and war over all NATO nuclear weapons except those belonging to the United Kingdom and France. The U.S. President alone can release U.S. nuclear weapons in Europe for use, following appropriate consultation with Allies. Weapons for both U.S. and Allied forces are maintained under the positive, two-man control of U.S. personnel until released by the U.S. President. Additionally, all U.S. nuclear weapons deployed in Europe are locked with coded devices (Permissive Action Links—PAL's) which physically enforce this U.S. control.

*   *   *

3. Evolution of NATO Nuclear Doctrine and Force Posture. Many changes in the global strategic environment have occurred since 1967 when NATO adopted MC14/3, the strategy of flexible response. The more significant are:

- The achievement by the Soviets of parity of strategic forces with the U.S., which places greater emphasis on the deterrent role of conventional and theater nuclear forces.

- The evolution of U.S. doctrine for employing nuclear weapons which sets as the primary objective for the use of nuclear weapons the termination of war on terms acceptable to the United States and its Allies at the lowest feasible level of conflict.

- Continued improvement of the conventional forces on both sides and the gradual growth of confidence in the conventional forces' contribution to overall NATO deterrence.

- New technology for improving both nuclear (e.g., survivability improvements) and conventional forces, the adoption of which will serve to raise the nuclear threshold, consistent with NATO strategy.

- Prospects for bringing greater stability between the East and West through negotiations, including strategic limitations and force reductions in Europe.

- The increase in peacetime threats to the security of forward-deployed nuclear weapons.

The flexible response strategy remains a sound basic approach to NATO defense planning in the 1970's. Within this overall strategy, however, NATO's nuclear doctrine and force posture have been evolving since the inception of MC14/3. They must continue to evolve in order to increase effectiveness under changing conditions.

C. Interdependence of Conventional, Theater Nuclear, and Strategic Forces

What is the overall concept for use of tactical nuclear weapons in Europe?

How does the use of such weapons relate to deterrence and to a strong conventional defense?

To put these questions into perspective, we first discuss WP strategy, doctrine and forces. Then follows a review of the roles of the three elements of the NATO Triad—conventional forces, theater nuclear forces, and strategic forces. Overall concepts for use of theater nuclear forces are considered and the section concludes with an evaluation of the current NATO theater nuclear force posture.

1. Warsaw Pact Strategy, Doctrine, and Force Posture. U.S. and NATO understanding of Warsaw Pact strategy and doctrine is based on observations for many years of Soviet and WP policy declarations and writings, training exercises, and the organization and structure of WP forces.[1]

In Soviet and WP strategy, military forces are viewed first and foremost as instruments for achieving political goals. The primary Soviet aim is to create a "correlation of forces," in Soviet terminology, which favors them. This, along with political initiatives, they believe will lead, in the long term, to increased divisiveness among the NATO nations and increased Soviet influence, if not dominance, over Western Europe.

The Soviets do not view this policy as inconsistent with detente—they continue to modernize and improve all elements of their military forces. While most attention has been focused on Soviet strategic force developments and deployments, they have remarkably increased their capabilities in theater nuclear and conventional forces.

WP strategy emphasizes defense of the WP territory through a strong offensive capability for counterattacks and destruction of NATO forces. NATO is pictured as the aggressor in WP exercises, but after a brief defensive phase, WP exercises are devoted mainly to tactics

---

[1]For Soviet exposition of this strategy and doctrine see, for example, A. A. Sidorenko, *The Offensive (A Soviet View).* (Washington, D.C., 1970), pp. 221–22.

for massive offensive penetrations. WP objectives are to deter NATO attacks and, if deterrence fails, drive to victory through destruction of NATO military forces and seizure of NATO territory.

These objectives apply to both nuclear and conventional conflict. The WP does not think of conventional and nuclear war as separate entities. Despite a recent trend to improve its conventional forces and to recognize that a conventional war in Europe need not escalate to nuclear war, the WP strategy, doctrine, and forces are still strongly oriented towards nuclear operations.[2] The Soviets apparently see escalation of war in Europe to nuclear conflict as likely.

The WP poses air, ground, and naval threats to all areas of NATO Europe—the Northern flank region, the Central region, and the Southern flank area. While there are differences in WP forces for each region, the WP doctrine emphasizes surprise, shock, and rapid exploitation of nuclear attacks with conventional forces in all areas. Wherever possible, armored forces and their immediate support (artillery, tactical air, and SAMs [surface-to-air missiles]) play a key role in WP tactics.

- Surprise. Soviet declarations indicate that if the WP believes NATO is about to launch a major nuclear attack, it will seek to preempt with nuclear strikes on military targets.

- Shock. Massive concentration of nuclear and conventional firepower on key military targets is a strong tenet of WP doctrine. The objective is to rapidly disrupt and demoralize NATO's forces, creating opportunities for armored blitzkrieg attacks. Prime targets for WP attacks are NATO nuclear delivery units, military bases, ground combat forces, command posts and support units.

- Exploitation. WP armored forces and their immediate support (artillery, tactical air, SAM's) are postured and trained to exploit nuclear attacks by rapid, deep, multiple thrusts to destroy remaining NATO forces and seize NATO territory. These armored forces are equipped for operations in a nuclear and chemical environment, so as to maintain movement and keep constant pressure on NATO forces.

National leaders are not, of course, constrained to follow the doctrine their military forces use to guide training or exercise forces in peacetime. In fact, in past crises in which the United States or NATO nations have shown a determination to use the force necessary to protect their interests, Soviet leaders have reacted very cautiously. Nevertheless, WP forces are postured primarily for the type of

---

[2]Evidence suggests that the WP thinks in terms of employing *all* "weapons of mass destruction," nuclear, chemical, and biological, concurrent with conventional force use.

theater-wide nuclear strikes pictured in the doctrine and exercises, as evidenced, for example, by their strong dependence on SSM's estimated to have relatively poor accuracy and large yields.

2. The NATO Triad. The NATO Triad provides:

- Conventional forces to deter and defend against conventional attacks.

- Theater nuclear forces to deter and defend against theater nuclear attacks; help deter and, if necessary, defend against conventional attack; and help deter conflict escalation.

- Strategic forces to deter and defend in general nuclear war, deter conflict escalation, and reinforce theater nuclear forces if needed.

The roles of each of the three forces are complementary and strengthened by the others. An important example is the mutual support of conventional and theater nuclear forces. WP conventional air and ground forces would likely have to mass to penetrate NATO defenses successfully. However, NATO theater nuclear forces deter this massing, thus enhancing NATO conventional defense capabilities. Generally, NATO theater nuclear forces introduce major uncertainties into WP planning, complicate the tactical problems of the WP, and increase the risks in any WP attack on NATO.

Some important general principles are associated with the NATO Triad.

- The WP should not be allowed to perceive opportunities for successful military action at any point in the spectrum of potential conflict. A strong deterrent extending across this spectrum will discourage crises or minor conflicts which could escalate. In the event of major conflict, there will be downward pressures to contain the war and move to negotiations, rather than pressures for escalation, if the prospects are dim for successful military action by the Soviets at higher levels.

- We would prefer where possible to deter through provision of direct defense and denial of WP military gains (e.g., seizure of territory), rather than deterrence only through the threat of escalation and all-out retaliatory attacks on WP resources—though these latter options will be maintained.

- In the interest of minimizing possible wartime destruction in NATO Europe, it is highly desirable to maintain a high nuclear threshold and use nuclear weapons only if absolutely necessary (e.g., in response to WP use of nuclear weapons or to prevent major loss of NATO territory or forces if conventional defense fails).

- U.S. strategic forces continue to be coupled to deterrence of attacks on Europe, both through the threat of escalation of any conflict to general nuclear war and the provision of operational plans for limited use, as necessary, of strategic forces in support of theater conflict.

Stalwart conventional forces are an essential element of deterrence and the primary initial means of defense against conventional attacks. U.S. conventional forces are planned in concert with those of our NATO allies to provide a credible deterrent and a strong, immediate defense capability against conventional attacks considered most likely under current assumptions about the threat, mobilization, and other critical factors affecting the outcome of a war in Europe. A credible conventional capability is one perceived as sufficient to hold well forward without early recourse to theater nuclear weapons. Such a strong conventional defense raises the nuclear threshold and NATO continues to strive toward this goal.

Theater nuclear forces deter WP use of nuclear weapons in Europe by providing a capability for credible retaliatory responses. Theater nuclear forces, because they do not pose a major threat to the Soviet homeland, constitute a retaliatory capability which carries a perceptively lower risk of escalation than the use of strategic nuclear forces. Theater nuclear forces also help deter conventional attacks by posing a threat of nuclear use should the conventional situation warrant. NATO planning must also consider the possibility that conventional attacks against NATO could take place under conditions more favorable to the WP than are reflected in the planning assumptions. For example, NATO may not be able to mobilize as quickly as necessary or the Soviets may draw divisions from the Sino-Soviet border. Theater nuclear forces, in limited use, to complement conventional forces, could serve the political purposes of showing NATO's resolve and creating a situation conducive to negotiations, and could help avert major loss of NATO territory.

Strategic forces have utility in limited attacks to support theater forces—e.g., SLBM's provide highly survivable means for striking WP air bases in response to WP nuclear attacks on NATO air bases. Strategic forces are also the primary capability for extensive attacks against Eastern Europe and the Soviet Union in general nuclear war. The strategic forces, coupled in this way to the defense of Europe, help deter all levels of conflict and, if deterrence fails, could help to contain the conflict and move it to negotiations by deterring WP escalation.

3. Overall Concept for Use of Theater Nuclear Forces. The NATO strategy of flexible response requires the capability to employ nuclear options at various levels of conflict. These potential options range from limited use against enemy forces on the battlefield to extended use in the theater, or to general nuclear response. Of the various levels of NATO theater nuclear force employment which might be considered, two are especially important—(a) response to a theater-wide, preemptive nuclear attack by the Warsaw Pact and (b) response to an overwhelming WP conventional attack.

a. WP theater-wide nuclear attacks. As previously discussed, the WP forces are generally structured for offensive rather than defensive operations. While there are indications that WP strategists have accepted the concept of a possible initial conventional phase, WP forces are in fact postured and trained for theater-wide nuclear strikes against NATO nuclear and conventional military forces and for follow-on attacks by their armored conventional forces to exploit the nuclear attack and rapidly seize NATO territory. A primary purpose of NATO theater forces is to provide credible retaliatory responses to such attacks and thereby to deter them. The objective for employment of NATO theater nuclear forces in this situation is as follows:

- In conjunction with surviving conventional forces, to blunt the WP armored exploitation, to attack WP theater nuclear forces which continue to threaten NATO, and to attack or threaten WP targets of value.

- To achieve this objective with shock effect and decisiveness, so as to dramatically change the tactical situation, change the assessment of WP political leaders regarding early or cheap victory, and create a situation conducive to negotiations in which NATO has some tactical advantages.

- To accomplish the above while trying to avoid escalation to general nuclear war. Such escalation would not be in the interest of either the United States or its European Allies, nor the WP for that matter. Efforts would be made to control escalation in such desperate circumstances by a combination of clearly perceivable limits on the NATO nuclear response and the threat of more extensive strikes with theater and strategic forces if the WP chooses to escalate.

This objective, as well as a more detailed consideration of WP threats faced by NATO in the flank areas and the center region, implies some general characteristics for NATO forces. First, the theater nuclear forces and their essential support (e.g., warheads, delivery systems, intelligence, command, control and communications (C³) and logistics) must be sufficiently survivable to have credible retaliatory capability. Deterrence is enhanced and the nuclear threshold is raised if the WP nuclear forces are unable to destroy a significant portion of any leg of the NATO Triad without carrying out an attack of such large proportions that it threatens to precipitate an equally damaging attack against the WP by U.S. and NATO nuclear forces. The theater nuclear forces should also be highly survivable under conventional attacks, so as to avoid situations in which NATO is forced to choose between early use of theater nuclear forces or losing this capability.

Second, NATO conventional forces should be able to operate satisfactorily in a nuclear environment. The theater nuclear forces should be capable of complementing the conventional forces in combined conventional-nuclear operations. The force posture, operational plans, and command and control must reflect this objective.

Third, the level, mix, and characteristics of NATO theater nuclear forces should provide capabilities (in combination with surviving conventional forces) to destroy targets such as front line and second echelon WP armored units and their immediate tactical support—surface-to-surface missiles and rockets, artillery and tactical air capabilities. Armored forces for exploitation of both conventional and nuclear attacks and their supporting units are key elements in the WP strategy and doctrine. The ability to destroy these forces after a nuclear attack is believed to contribute to deterrence of such attacks. The threat of nuclear retaliation against urban-industrial targets or rear-based forces in Eastern Europe or the U.S.S.R. is probably less stable in a crisis and a less credible deterrent. If deterrence fails, such retaliation would be less effective in removing the threat to NATO territory. Nevertheless, the threat of such retaliation must certainly provide a strong deterrent to WP planners contemplating massive nuclear strikes.

Fourth, while theater nuclear forces for deep interdiction have less immediately decisive effects on the tactical situation, such forces are needed in the event that nuclear attacks on WP forward armored units and their support are not sufficient. They also provide counters to WP interdiction attacks. Such threats against East European countries may also diminish their willingness to cooperate with the Soviets, thus weakening WP solidarity.

b. Overwhelming WP conventional attack. NATO conventional forces are structured for a range of likely conditions of NATO and WP mobilization, likely assumptions about the number of Soviet divisions committed against NATO, and expected performance of forces of both sides. It is possible to envision significantly worse circumstances than those planning assumptions, in which NATO conventional forces are unable to hold under conventional attack. Consequently, such a contingency makes it impossible to rule out NATO first use of theater nuclear forces.

The first use of theater nuclear forces, even in very limited ways, carries grave risks of escalation and should be considered only when the consequences of conventional defeat would be even more serious. If the alternative is, for example, major loss of NATO territory or forces, NATO political leaders may choose to accept the risks of first use.

As is the case with retaliatory theater nuclear attacks, NATO should have a wide range of nuclear options to provide responses suitable to the provocation. First use should be clearly limited and defensive in nature, so as to reduce the risks of escalation. However, the attack should be delivered with sufficient shock and decisiveness to forcibly change the perceptions of WP leaders and create a situation conducive to negotiations.

Theater nuclear forces which fulfill the retaliatory objectives described above also are generally well suited for hedging against conventional force failures. They are designed to attack the same targets—WP armor and its immediate tactical support—that pose the most immediate threat to NATO forces. They are survivable under conventional attacks and thus need not be used early to avoid their loss to enemy action. While they cannot substitute for adequate conventional forces, they could temporarily reverse the tactical situation and create a stalemate or NATO advantage which could be used to induce negotiations. It should also be noted that conventional forces cannot substitute for an adequate theater nuclear force.

In addition to these characteristics, the credibility of the use of theater nuclear weapons on NATO territory is enhanced if the targeting and characteristics of these weapons reduce collateral damage to civilian structures and population, without removing the ultimate deterrent value of the fear of escalation, involving U. S. strategic forces.

4. Evaluation of the Current Theater Nuclear Force Posture. NATO theater nuclear forces in Europe consist of SSM's, artillery, tactical aircraft, SAM's, ADM's, and SLBM's. This section evaluates the current posture and forces including their target acquisition, command, control and communications, survivability and effects of collateral damage.

a. Theater nuclear weapons systems. (1) Surface-to-surface missiles: NATO's SSM's consist primarily of Pershing, Sergeant and Lance, with Lance currently being deployed to replace the older Sergeant missile and Honest John rocket. The primary role of Pershing is attack of fixed targets; Lance, Sergeant and Honest John provide tactical support to the battlefield.

Some Pershing missiles are on peacetime Quick Reaction Alert (QRA) at fixed locations. QRA missiles are designated against specific WP high priority, time sensitive targets.

As compared with Sergeant and Honest John, Lance is more survivable and more responsive. It has better peacetime security through an improved Permissive Action Link (PAL) system (coded locks on the warhead). Because of these improvements, Honest John rockets and Sergeant SSM's are being replaced with Lance in most NATO countries.

(2) Nuclear artillery: Artillery's high accuracy, low yield, rapid responsiveness, and ease of control by local commanders should provide for effective attacks against targets in proximity to friendly troops. Because of its relatively short range, confining nuclear effects to the immediate battle area, it is judged that use of nuclear artillery in limited nuclear conflict probably has less chance of resulting in escalation to theater-wide nuclear war than longer range SSM's or tactical aircraft.

Ways to improve the effectiveness of nuclear artillery projectiles are under study. . . .

(3) Nuclear-capable tactical aircraft: Some of NATO's tactical aircraft are completely nuclear-capable, that is, configured to carry nuclear weapons, supported by nuclear weapons, and with crews designated and trained for nuclear missions. Other aircraft are technically capable of delivering nuclear weapons, but are not all supported with nuclear weapons and crews trained for nuclear delivery. All of these aircraft can also carry conventional weapons. A small number of U.S. and Allied tactical aircraft are kept on peacetime QRA, launchable within a short period of time. More could be generated in a time of tension or hostilities.

Nuclear-capable tactical aircraft will continue to have a place in the NATO theater nuclear posture. They provide a means of rapidly concentrating nuclear firepower anywhere in the area of NATO operations. Against non-fixed targets well beyond the front lines, the manned aircraft has a potential advantage over current missiles in that the pilot could make last minute changes in his aim point, to correct for target movement, providing in effect a form of terminal guidance.

(4) Nuclear-capable surface-to-air missiles: Nike Hercules is a dual-capable SAM system deployed in NATO Europe which can counter extremely high altitude/high speed WP aircraft. Nuclear warheads for Nike Hercules deter massed air attacks and significantly increase the single-shot kill probability against aircraft at high al-

titudes, where collateral damage to NATO territory would be neglibible.

(5) Atomic demolition munitions: ADM's are nuclear demolition devices which are manually emplaced and detonated by timer or command. They can be used to destroy bridges, cave in tunnels or defiles, cut roads, and otherwise create barriers to slow enemy movement or induce concentrations of his forces. These actions could produce lucrative targets for attack by conventional or nuclear forces, and buy time for conventional reinforcements. Being defensive weapons and most likely to be used on NATO territory, they probably have lower escalation potential than most other theater nuclear weapons, often without direct casualties.

Studies are under way to examine alternatives in the form of earth penetrators delivered by missiles or aircraft.

(6) Submarine-launched ballistic missiles: Currently the United States is committed to share with NATO a portion of its sea-based strategic nuclear deterrent system in support of the Alliance. The highly survivable Poseidon RVs [reentry vehicles] provide high confidence that they will be available under all conditions of war initiation. Since these RVs are relatively ineffective against hard targets, other systems are required, such as Pershing with its higher yield and tactical aircraft with a higher yield capability and greater accuracy. Because of its relatively low yield, Poseidon will produce a low level of collateral damage except when employed against military installations collocated with urban areas. Here, weapons with lower yields and greater accuracies such as those currently deliverable by tactical aircraft would be used.

b. Command, control and communications. Command, control and communications (C^3) support is essential to both deterrence and flexible employment of theater nuclear forces. The wartime operational command of the forces, delivery vehicles and units, would be exercised by the NATO international military command structure (e.g., Allied Command Europe [ACE]). The United States maintains positive control of the nuclear warheads in both peace and war.

The United States and NATO are continuing to upgrade situation reporting and message handling procedures, and are continuing a series of communications improvements, including the NATO Integrated Communications System (NICS), which are intended to improve the overall flexible response capability.

*　*　*

c. Target acquisition. Successful target acquisition requires:

- Detection and identification of threatening targets before they can inflict significant damage on NATO forces.

182

- Location of the target to an accuracy consistent with weapon delivery accuracy and effects radius.

- Communication of this information in time for attacks to be made before the target is lost or the military benefits of attacking the target are substantially reduced.

Good target acquisition is important for all military operations. Special attention must be given to target acquisition for theater nuclear forces, because these forces should be employed against the most threatening of enemy targets in ways which best complement the conventional operation. Improved target acquisition will make more targets available for consideration and permit greater selectivity in targeting by NATO nuclear forces. Target acquisition for theater nuclear forces must also take into account that enemy nuclear attacks may degrade many of the usual means of acquiring targets.

*   *   *

d. Survivability. Survivability of NATO theater nuclear capabilities under both conventional and nuclear attack is a major requirement. This particularly means that alerted, dispersed units and their essential support (e.g., warheads, intelligence, C^3, logistics) should be survivable. Early and persuasive warning of imminent attack, conventional or nuclear, is essential to ensure alerting and dispersal measures can be taken.

It has not been possible in the past to assess quantitatively the survivability of dispersed theater nuclear elements of NATO ground forces. Generally it is judged that the maneuverability of these elements enhances their survivability. Past DoD theater nuclear force modernization programs were not fully keyed to specific threats to their survivability. To reduce these uncertainties and improve our modernization programs, a theater nuclear force "security" R&D program has been initiated with the following objectives:

- To assess the survivability of these elements under conventional and nuclear attack, identify deficiencies and develop improvements.

- To develop technology to counter possible future threats to the survivability of these theater nuclear elements.

As NATO continues to improve its air defenses and construct aircraft shelters, the nuclear-capable tactical aircraft are becoming more survivable to conventional attacks on their bases. However, NATO air bases remain vulnerable to WP nuclear attack. Studies are in progress to find ways of improving survivability under nuclear attack.

e. Collateral damage. Since the tactical use of nuclear weapons may involve detonation on NATO territory, reduction of collateral damage should make it more credible to the WP that the Alliance will use nuclear weapons. Further, if deterrence fails, weapons with low collateral damage would reduce civilian casualties and perhaps reduce the risks of uncontrolled escalation. The current stockpile has a large number of low yield weapons. SACEUR's targeting is intended to limit the collateral damage from use of NATO's current stockpile of nuclear weapons. Recent studies indicate that collateral damage could be further reduced, with acceptable reduction in military effects, by changing tactical procedures now in use for selecting weapon-target combinations and utilizing to a greater extent the current low-yield weapons.

Further reductions in collateral damage can be made by improvements in weapon systems (e.g., reduced yields, special warhead effects such as enhanced radiation, improved delivery system accuracy). However, it is necessary to keep in mind that NATO attempts to reduce collateral damage might not be matched by corresponding changes in WP capabilities or targeting doctrine.

D. Deployment of Weapons to Support Theater Nuclear Force Policy

* * *

1. Alliance Political Considerations. Our NATO Allies attach considerable importance to U.S. theater nuclear weapons in Europe because of their military value and also because of their political and psychological significance. To our Allies and the WP, the weapons are concrete evidence of the U.S. nuclear commitment to NATO. That commitment is an essential part of the NATO flexible response strategy and thus of a credible deterrent. Both we and our Allies are highly conscious of the fact that the tactical nuclear role in NATO strategy is a shared one. The U.S. has encouraged, and the Allies value highly, the shared responsibility for planning and participation in the possible employment of theater nuclear weapons within NATO's strategy. These political and psychological considerations must be taken fully into account in any assessment of the U.S. nuclear posture in Europe and in determining whether adjustments in that posture are desirable.

Another area of major concern to our Allies, and one which needs careful attention, is that any reductions and adjustments must flow from a careful military assessment of the NATO force posture.

In view of the foregoing, any possible adjustments to theater nuclear forces should be made for the purpose of strengthening the theater nuclear leg of the NATO Triad and preserving an important nuclear role for the Allies. In this way it should be possible to ensure continued Allied confidence in the U.S. nuclear commitment, the viability of a common defense through the NATO structure, and a general reinforcement of U.S./NATO deterrence objectives.

2. The Need for Nuclear Weapons in Europe. While arguments can be made against the deployment of nuclear weapons in Europe, the United States and its NATO Allies continue to hold that such deployments are an essential part of a credible NATO military posture.

The most important reason for this conclusion is that U.S. nuclear weapons in Europe are a visible symbol to Allies and adversaries of the U.S. commitment to provide for Europe's nuclear defense. Deterrence is enhanced by the presence of these weapons in the theater, because WP conventional or nuclear attack plans must take into account the possibility of early NATO nuclear responses. If deterrence fails, the responsiveness of NATO theater nuclear forces is greater if the weapons are collocated with delivery forces and readily available for use.

U.S. nuclear weapons in Europe for Allied delivery vehicles increase NATO cohesiveness by allowing the Allies to share the risks and responsibilities of Europe's nuclear deterrent. Moreover, the familiarity of U.S. and Allied troops with the nuclear weapons is increased if weapons are deployed in Europe and are part of the normal training practices.

There are disadvantages to having nuclear weapons deployed overseas, but the United States and its Allies believe there are sufficient reasons to continue such deployments in Europe. In their peacetime locations, the nuclear weapons are vulnerable to attack by WP theater nuclear forces, as are almost all of NATO's military forces. However, a surprise nuclear attack on NATO in the absence of a crisis or other warning sufficient to permit dispersal of many of the weapons is regarded as very unlikely.

Nuclear weapons in Europe would be vulnerable to overrun and capture by WP conventional forces, if they were deployed too far forward and the NATO conventional defense was insufficient. But NATO has taken care to minimize the number of such forward sites. The United States is currently studying closure of sites and consolidation of weapons into more secure locations, where this may be warranted.

*   *   *

3. U.S./NATO Review of Nuclear Warheads in Europe. The size, composition and deployment of the theater nuclear stockpile are matters of political as well as military importance since the continued security and stability of Europe are at stake. There must be full consultation with the Allies in both the military and political deliberations that could lead to any changes in posture.

A preliminary and general analysis of the currently authorized nuclear stockpile has been made in NATO which considers current strategy, associated war plans, the characteristics and numbers of weapons, and related logistics factors. The United States is asking NATO to conduct more detailed analyses of the present posture based on the following considerations identified in the NATO study and in related U.S. studies:

- The impact of modernized theater nuclear weapons on deployments.

- Deployment of modern conventional air munitions (e.g., Maverick and laser-guided bombs).

- Changes in employment policy.

*   *   *

E. Improvement in the NATO Military Posture

*   *   *

b. NATO theater nuclear forces. If NATO is to improve its deterrent posture for the future, the following major conditions must be met for theater nuclear forces:

First, we must reduce their vulnerability to sabotage, seizure, and conventional assault. Measures are already underway to ensure this condition in cooperation with our Allies.

Second, the vulnerability of these forces to surprise attack should be reduced, and the more exposed systems should have the capability to disperse quickly so as to match a surprise dispersal by the Warsaw Pact. The introduction of the Lance missile with its improved munitions should also increase the survivability, controllability, and effectiveness of the forces.

Third, we need to improve our command and control and situation reporting capabilities to the point where reliable and comprehensive information about both non-nuclear and nuclear attacks, and the status of defending forces, can be more rapidly and reliably communicated to those political leaders and military commanders who are involved in nuclear decisions and the release of nuclear weapons.

Fourth, target acquisition systems that can survive at least the first phase of any nuclear use still remain essential if we are to be able to implement a range of selective and controlled options, and at the same time limit the collateral damage from their implementation.

Fifth, we should continue to develop selective, carefully controlled options that will permit us: (a) to enhance our ability to deal with major penetrations of a sector and achieve a quick, decisive reversal of the tactical situation; and (b) to engage, if necessary, in a highly discriminating interdiction campaign against enemy lines of communication or forces behind the FEBA [forward edge of battle area]. Both options are designed to minimize the incentives for the enemy to reply at all or to respond with uncontrolled attacks.

It should be evident that these are demanding conditions, and that they will be difficult to satisfy. For many reasons we cannot regard our theater nuclear forces as a substitute for powerful conventional capabilities. They have a unique role to play in the spectrum of deterrence, and we should continue to maintain and improve them. But they should not be viewed as a crutch that can replace a strong conventional leg of the deterrent Triad.

*   *   *

2. Future Goals. . . . The following specific goals have been discussed throughout this report and are summarized below.

a. Theater nuclear force improvements which are under review include the following:

- Improved survivability of nuclear forces and weapons under conventional and nuclear attack.

- Commitment of more Poseidon RV's to NATO.

- Modernization of the theater nuclear forces to enhance and maintain the deterrent and war termination capabilities.

- Improved target acquisition capabilities.

- Continued improvement in security of nuclear weapon storage sites and, where militarily sound and economically advantageous, consolidation of sites.

b. Improvements in capabilities to employ nuclear forces are being pursued as follows:

- Upgrading of communications capabilities for command and control of nuclear forces.

- Improvements in command, control, and planning for combined conventional-nuclear operations. . . .

- Continuation of NATO employment planning efforts for limited use of theater nuclear weapons to complement conventional battlefield operations.

c. Conventional force improvements must continue to be made by the United States and its NATO Allies. At the recent meeting of Defense Ministers in Brussels, all agreed that conventional forces constitute the weakest leg of the NATO Triad and must continue to be given priority over nuclear weapons improvements. Adequate conventional force capabilities are a necessary foundation of total NATO deterrence.

*　　*　　*

At the same time, WP conventional forces continue to improve as well. Furthermore, the WP nations have shown no predisposition to reduce the strength of their nuclear capabilities. At the same time that they improve conventional forces, they are improving their nuclear capabilities. For this reason alone, theater nuclear weapons remain essential to the NATO deterrent posture in Europe.

ANNUAL DEFENSE DEPARTMENT REPORT, FY 1978

Donald H. Rumsfeld

In the following excerpt from his Annual Defense Department Report, *Secretary of Defense Donald H. Rumsfeld examines the strategic and tactical nuclear relationship between the United States and the Soviet Union. Two major themes are apparent: America's strategic force posture must maintain an assured retaliatory capability in order to deter attack, and the nature of that retaliation, in terms of objectives to be attained, must have some relationship to Soviet objectives should nuclear war occur.*

While the proper size and composition of our strategic arsenal are still subjects of debate, Rumsfeld notes that the more significant issues pertain to the role of nuclear weapons in national security policy. Deterrence, the primary objective of that policy, is seen as being strengthened by credible retaliatory threats and the maintenance of military capabilities equivalent to those of the Soviet Union.

After examining the current and projected capabilities and missions of Soviet weapons, Rumsfeld concludes that the United States must improve its capability to destroy hardened targets and respond to potential threats in a flexible manner. The function of nuclear weapons is no longer seen as simply to deter, but also to ensure that should war occur the Soviet Union will not emerge with a greater military capability or a greater potential for economic and political recovery than the United States.

Source: Donald H. Rumsfeld, *Annual Defense Department Report, FY 1978* (Washington, D.C., January 17, 1977), pp. 66-84.

STRATEGIC DOCTRINE: DOCUMENTS

Strategic Nuclear Forces

D. The Triad. The most efficient way to preserve a responsive, controllable, retaliatory capability is by means of a mixed force of ICBMs, SLBMs and bombers—namely the Triad. Maintenance of a second-strike Triad continues to be justifiable on a number of grounds. First, history shows that no system, however ingeniously designed, is ever entirely invulnerable for an indefinite period of time. For most measures, there tend to be countermeasures. And the countermeasures may show up with little advance warning, especially when one of the contestants operates in a closed society. Considering the fundamental importance of the tasks assigned to the U.S. strategic retaliatory forces, it is not unduly conservative to maintain three capabilities with differing characteristics, differing challenges to an opponent bent on countering them, and differing rates at which their vulnerability is likely to become critical. To take a less conservative approach is to risk precisely the instabilities which arise from claims of "bomber gaps" and "missile gaps." The Triad minimizes those risks because when vulnerabilities do begin to appear, they can be dealt with in an orderly fashion rather than with costly crash programs.

Another advantage of the Triad is that the three forces interact to promote the survivability of them all. While the survivability of the SLBMs does not depend directly on the ICBMs and bombers, the Soviets could concentrate much larger resources on countering ballistic missile submarines if they did not have to worry about the other two components. The ICBMs and bombers, on the other hand, interact strongly for their mutual benefit. A simultaneous attack against ICBMs and bombers through U.S. warning screens would enable the alert bombers to launch even if the ICBMs were withheld. An effort to slip under the warning screens and attack the bombers would give the ICBMs unambiguous evidence of the attack through the prior detonation of weapons on airfields. And any attempt to pin down the ICBMs while attacking the bombers would run into such delicate problems of communication and timing that it would risk triggering both forces.

*   *   *

As long as the ABM Treaty is observed, the ICBMs and SLBMs surviving a Soviet first-strike should be reliable enough to reach and attack their targets. Bomber penetration is less certain, although the great majority of the bombers should reach their targets, and planned modernization of the force will preserve that confidence in the future.

A second-strike by such a mixed force, approaching enemy targets at differing speeds, trajectories, and azimuths of attack, not only would complicate the problem of the defense; it would also permit a particular target to be attacked with delivery systems and weapons of differing characteristics. Cross-targeting increases the probability that even after a highly effective enemy first-strike, and even after some system failures, targets of importance to the enemy would come under attack from at least one element of the Triad.

For all these reasons, I believe we must continue with a Triad of bombers, land-based missiles, and sea-based missiles.

The overall size and composition of the Triad must necessarily depend on a variety of factors. I should point out in this connection that the peacetime inventory of delivery systems, weapons, and megatonnage is only one datum, and by itself not the most important, in indicating whether and in what ways U.S. forces need to be strengthened. What counts from the standpoint of force planning is how much of a given peacetime inventory would survive a first-strike, penetrate the enemy's defenses, and destroy a designated set of targets. It matters very little if we have an arsenal of 3,000 delivery systems, 8,500 warheads, and thousands of megatons if only a few of those systems could survive a surprise attack and reach their targets. . . . In short, a premium must be paid for the safety and stability of an assured retaliatory force. Such a premium should not be mistaken for overkill.

E. Assured Retaliation. Force size and composition will also be sensitive to the types of missions this retaliatory capability must perform. It is on this score, in fact, that the most significant issues arise concerning U.S. strategic nuclear forces. Widespread agreement exists that, at a minimum, the U.S. second-strike capability should be able to execute the mission of assured retaliation as the prime condition of deterrence. But even here, arguments persist as to specific targets and the damage to be assured. According to one approach, planners could simply target major cities, assume that population and industry are strongly correlated with them, and measure effectiveness as a function of the number of people killed and cities destroyed. Thus, as one example, prompt Soviet fatalities of about 30 percent and 200 cities destroyed would constitute a level of retaliation sufficient to assure deterrence.

A different approach views assured retaliation as the effort to prevent or retard an enemy's military, political, and economic recovery from a nuclear exchange. Specific military forces and industries would be targeted. The effectiveness of the retaliation would be measured in two ways:

- by the size and composition of the enemy's military capability surviving for postwar use;

- by his ability to recover politically and economically from the exchange.

If the Soviet Union could emerge from such an exchange with superior military power, and could recuperate from the effects more rapidly than the United States, the U.S. capability for assured retaliation would be considered inadequate.

Both approaches can obviously be carried to absurd lengths. The point, however, is that whichever approach is taken, the number, yield, and accuracy of the weapons needed in the U.S. inventory will depend to an important degree on the level of damage required of the assured retaliation mission. The ability to destroy only 10 cities on a second-strike makes one kind of demand on the posture; the requirement to destroy 200 makes quite another.

The present planning objective of the Defense Department is clear. We believe that a substantial number of military forces and critical industries in the Soviet Union should be directly targeted, and that an important objective of the assured retaliation mission should be to retard significantly the ability of the U.S.S.R. to recover from a nuclear exchange and regain the status of a 20th-century military and industrial power more rapidly than the United States.

This objective has been set for a number of reasons. With the growth and diversification of the Soviet economy, and with continued Soviet efforts to disperse and protect vital industries, the practice of simply targeting the largest cities might no longer produce the effects previously assumed. More specific and precisely designated aiming points are needed, especially for the lower-yield weapons now in the U.S. strategic inventory. The number of targets must be substantial because low levels of damage would not necessarily deter a desperate leadership, whereas high levels of damage and a low probability of recuperation might do so. Where the assured retaliation mission is concerned, any prospective enemy must understand at all times that the United States has a second-strike capability which can do him, not significant or serious, but virtually irreparable damage as a modern nation and great power.

F. Options. For some, a second-strike capability for counter-city retaliation is the essential and sole condition of strategic nuclear deterrence. To go beyond this minimal capability, as they see it, is to invite trouble: further competition, arms race and crisis instability, an increased risk of nuclear war, and a decreased probability of progress toward arms control and disarmament. For the United States, however, the deterrence of nuclear war requires a different approach than is embodied in the concept of counter-city retaliation.

1. Soviet capabilities. As previous Defense Reports have emphasized, the Soviet Union has now developed a strategic nuclear offensive capability of such size and diversity that a number of options must be taken into account. One could begin with an attack on the theater-based forces of the United States and its allies, after which the Soviets might seek to deter retaliation with their large strategic nuclear reserve capability. Second, a creeping attack on SSBNs [missile-launching nuclear submarines] at sea, selected military facilities in a theater, or even silos in the continental United States itself, could be launched to demonstrate their resolve and to force the United States into major concessions. A third example would be an attempt to destroy U.S. bombers and ICBMs, disrupt our command-control-communications, and avoid major damage to U.S. cities and people, while at the same time holding in reserve a large follow-on capability targeted against other U.S. assets and available for successive waves of attack. Such a campaign would not necessarily disarm the United States, but it could leave us with only the forces and the plans for partial coverage of the enemy target system. With them, the United States might be able to cause heavy damage to the industrial base of the Soviet Union and even to its people. But the withheld Soviet force would be able to do equal or greater damage to an equivalent target system in the United States.

2. The problem of deterrence. The credibility of a deterrent based solely on the capability and doctrine of counter-city retaliation, however large or small the programmed response, is likely to be low in the face of such contingencies. The Soviets might be skeptical about the threat contained in such a posture, and inclined to test U.S. resolve to defend allies by these means. Even though we might delude ourselves about the credibility of the threat under normal peacetime conditions, we might find that we were more deterred by it than the Russians in a crisis.

These examples admittedly raise contingencies which, as far as can be judged, have a low probability of occurrence. However, we should not forget the risks that accompanied the Soviet deployment of missiles to Cuba in the autumn of 1962. And even the surprise attack everyone agrees should be deterred tends to fall into this same category of low probability and high risk. Why then should the United States be any less concerned about equally rational and more limited attacks?

3. Options and escalation. Less than full attack contingencies raise enormous uncertainties. We are totally lacking in any relevant experience of them. Yet we know that once nuclear weapons are used, calamity of an unprecedented nature will lurk in the wings. In these circumstances, even if the probability of nuclear escalation is high, it seems appropriate to have available for the President some options rather than only the full response of assured retaliation. Accordingly, the U.S. posture should include the ability both to implement some preplanned options and to improvise responses to events not anticipated in contingency planning.

4. Options and hard targets. It should be evident that once the possibility of some options is admitted, the range of targets becomes wide. Many targets important to a society's economy and political system are separated to some degree from heavy concentrations of people. That tends also to be the case with a number of military targets, including general purpose as well as strategic nuclear facilities. To attack relatively soft targets, and to minimize collateral damage, relatively low-yield weapons with high accuracies are required. In previous years, because of these considerations, it has been U.S. policy to seek improved command and control, higher accuracy, and an increased variety of warhead yields in order to implement an effective range of options.

Last year I stated we would be making system improvements such as increased accuracy so as to ensure that any attack could be met by a deliberate and credible response. Certainly the need for more than a limited hard-target-kill capability was not foreseen. The costs of such a capability are substantial, in part because the phenomenon of fratricide limits the number of weapons that can be usefully applied to a hard target and therefore imposes heavy demands for accuracy, reliability, and command-control. A major effort to acquire a comprehensive hard-target-kill capability is likely to raise apprehensions about crisis and arms race stability.

The United States has continued to hope that the Soviets would have a similar outlook and comparable concerns. Today, however, it is much less certain that they see the wisdom of abstaining from comprehensive hard-target-kill capability. Not only have they failed to give serious consideration to U.S. proposals for reductions in throw-weight; they are actually in the process of increasing their own throw-weight by a substantial amount. In addition, they are making rapid improvements in the accuracy of their ICBMs.

It is uncertain how rapidly these programs will come to fruition. But there is now an increasing probability that before the mid-1980s, the Soviets could have the capability, with a small fraction of their ICBMs, to destroy a substantial portion of the Minuteman/Titan force as well as non-alert bombers and submarines in port. This potential would in no way give the Soviets a disarming first-strike. But it could enable them to create a dangerous asymmetry. As previous Defense

Reports have emphasized, much of the U.S. capability for deliberate, controlled, selective responses resides in the Minuteman force. If much of that force were eliminated, the Soviets would preserve their flexibility while that of the United States would be substantially reduced. The Kremlin would still have options; the choices open to a President would be limited.

This is not an acceptable prospect. It would be preferable to see the life of the fixed ICBM forces on both sides prolonged a good deal longer. Eventually, however, even with foreseeable arms control measures, improvements in accuracy combined with large throw-weights could make such systems vulnerable, and thus unreliable as second-strike forces. But additional time in which to negotiate and make deliberate decisions about reasonable substitutes would be valuable. That is the course the United States would still like to see both sides follow. But, we cannot permit the major degradation in the Triad that the growing Soviet capabilities threaten. And the United States must not permit the development of a major asymmetry in potential outcomes, with all the political and military hazards accompanying such a prospect.

If the life of the fixed, hard ICBMs cannot be extended, then stability requires both sides to improve their land-based forces enough so that they are more difficult to target by the other side. The United States should not accept a strategic relationship in which we must bear the heavier costs of alternative basing while the Soviets are allowed the luxury of retaining their fixed ICBMs. Since high accuracies can be built into mobile as well as fixed systems, the Soviet leadership should be aware that if the United States moves toward mobility, the Soviets will have strong incentives to go mobile as well.

5. *Options and first-strike.* The United States is not interested in creating a first-strike capability, acting provocatively, or threatening stability. The Congress will surely recognize that it is the Soviet Union and not the United States which has taken the initiative in creating this prospect. Members will also notice that the same critics who oppose the necessary U.S. counter-measures argue that the strategic nuclear balance is stable, not delicate, and that major asymmetries do not matter. Perhaps critics can live with these inconsistencies. The United States cannot.

The U.S. position is straightforward and consistent. We do not believe either side can achieve a serious, high-confidence, disarming first-strike capability, and we do not seek to attain one. To that extent, the strategic nuclear balance can be said to be stable. But significant asymmetries in the outcome of a strategic nuclear exchange can be created, and these asymmetries could give—and would be seen to have given—a meaningful advantage to one side over the other. As long as so much of the U.S. capability for flexibility is invested in the ICBM force, and as long as some options continue to be desirable, such an asymmetry could arise if one side eliminated most of the other's ICBMs. The United States should not permit that eventuality to develop.

6. *Options and stability.* This line of reasoning tends to be opposed only by those who, despite the evidence, cling to the view that there is only one condition of stability, namely mutual assured destruction; that the Soviets faithfully subscribe to that doctrine; and that the Kremlin will respond cooperatively to U.S. restraint. The same opponents contend that any options are provocative and increase the probability of nuclear war. More or less simultaneously, they assert that having options (and the limits on destruction implied by them) [is] infeasible because any nuclear exchange is bound to escalate to an all-out attack on cities, and because the collateral damage from nuclear detonations on military targets, especially hard targets, would make even a limited exchange indistinguishable from an all-out conflict. The conclusion from this reasoning is inexorable: the maintenance of options is both destabilizing and infeasible. Presumably, the prospective loss of the U.S. capability need be of no concern, while any threat to a comparable Soviet capability is provocative.

This is not a persuasive position. It depends upon assumptions about Soviet beliefs and behavior that are not borne out by the facts. It applies different standards of conduct to the United States than to the Soviet Union. And it is inconsistent. None of the allegations—about the provocative and damaging consequences of options—have any basis in experience. U.S. strategic plans have contained options for many years, yet no one has been provoked or tempted in a crisis. Indeed, to attach such importance to options, which are little different from other contingency plans, is to ignore how decisions about peace and war are made. Far more important than options in the choice of capabilities is the degree of U.S. conventional strength. If the nuclear threshold has been kept high, conventional responses will be given first priority in a crisis (at least by the United States) regardless of whether nuclear options are available. Experience should make that evident.

7. *Options and collateral damage.* As for the argument that anything less than a full-scale response would be indistinguishable from direct attacks on population, data and analyses indicate the contrary. In every case considered, both the short-term and the longer-run collateral damage from attacks on a comprehensive list of military targets

(including ICBM silos) has been dramatically lower than the fatalities from direct attacks on population targets. It must be emphasized, however, that the results, even in limited and controlled exchanges, could be appalling. They could involve the potential for millions of fatalities, even though the distinction between 10 million and 100 million fatalities is great and worth preserving. No U.S. decision maker is likely to be tempted by this prospect, especially in view of the dangers of nuclear escalation.

It is no inconsistency to recognize those dangers and still see the desirability of having some options short of full retaliation. The other side is fully capable of inventing and considering options. And precisely because we are uncertain about the course and ultimate consequence of a nuclear exchange beginning with less than a full response, surely all would want to avoid bringing about a holocaust by U.S. actions and would want any President to have at least the option to respond in a deliberate and controlled fashion. Just as surely, if such were actually to be the U.S. response in the terrible event of an attack, it is a response that must be available for the purposes of deterrence. To depend on irrational behavior by the Soviets, and to depend equally on an irrational response by us, is to put nuclear deterrence in double jeopardy. The Soviets, by their activities, indicate that they are not interested in mutual assured destruction. Accordingly, they must be accepted for what they are, not for what we want them to be. Their actions indicate that they take nuclear war seriously; the United States must do no less. Part of taking it seriously is responses short of full-scale retaliation in our strategic nuclear capabilities. It is a condition of stable deterrence.

G. Equivalence. Satisfaction of the fundamental requirements of second-strike survivability, Triad insurance, assured retaliation, and options should ensure stable deterrence under most circumstances. These requirements, in fact, underlie the current U.S. strategic nuclear posture. There is, however, one other factor we must consider in our planning.

It is generally recognized that world stability depends to a remarkable extent on the strength of the U.S. strategic nuclear deterrent. Unfortunately, not everyone assesses the effectiveness of that deterrent in the same way. It is the subject of many and differing perceptions which, in turn, can affect the behavior of prospective enemies, allies, neutrals, and attentive publics in the United States itself. If friends see the balance as favoring the Soviet Union rather than the United States, their independence and firmness may give way to adjustment, accommodation, and subordination. If potential enemies have a similar perception, they could misjudge the situation and make demands leading to confrontation, crisis, and unnecessary dangers. If domestic audiences see real or imaginary imbalances, they could insist on excessive and costly crash programs to restore the equilibrium. One has only to recall the reaction of Mao Tse-tung to the appearances of Soviet missile superiority after the Sputnik demonstrations, and the response in the United States to charges of a "missile gap," to recognize the impact of such perceptions on international affairs.

However much one might wish otherwise, popular and even some governmental perceptions of the strategic nuclear balance tend to be influenced less by detailed analyses than by such static indicators of relative nuclear strengths as launchers, warheads, megatonnage, accuracy, throw-weight and the like. If all or most of these indicators were to favor the Soviet Union, a number of observers might conclude that the United States was not equivalent to the U.S.S.R. in strategic power and that the balance was now weighted in favor of the Soviet Union.

It is to be hoped that, in designing the U.S. strategic posture to meet the requirements of adequate and stable deterrence, the perception as well as the reality of a strong deterrent will be created. U.S. programs of research and development should be expected to be, and be seen to be, sufficient to offset the dynamism of the Soviet Union in this realm. But to the extent that rough equivalence is not credited to the United States in these two respects, actions to create the necessary perception of equivalence could be required.

At the present time, it is widely agreed that the United States is seen as having "rough equivalence" with the Soviet Union, even though, up to now, we have not added to our strategic posture for that purpose. The United States should also continue to stress the effectiveness of its strategic forces in the performance of their missions as the basis for judging their adequacy. But the Congress and common sense require that the United States not be inferior to the Soviet Union, and the Vladivostok Understanding postulates equality between the two sides in central offensive systems. Accordingly, U.S. plans and programs for future U.S. offensive capabilities must be geared to those of the U.S.S.R.

*   *   *

Theater Nuclear Forces

A. Functions. Since the detonation of the first Soviet atomic device, there has been a growing recognition that U.S. strategic nuclear forces would not be able to bear the entire burden of credible deterrence by themselves. Some may have questioned that judgment in the past; no serious person doubts it today. The need for other forces to provide a credible response to contingencies less than a direct strategic attack on the United States or its allies is no longer an issue. Clearly, theater nuclear forces must constitute a part of that spectrum of deterrence and response.

Further, as strategic nuclear forces have become less dependent on overseas basing, adequate U.S. theater nuclear forces must be available as part of the deterrent. It has been generally accepted that the theater nuclear forces are not interchangeable with U.S. and allied conventional forces, and that nuclear firepower is no convenient substitute for manpower on the ground. But there should be no question about their importance as a backup to strong conventional defenses and as a major hedge against a failure of those defenses.

The United States has never ruled out a first use of nuclear weapons. If an enemy, whether by stealth and deception or by large-scale mobilization, should attempt to defeat U.S. and allied conventional forces, it is NATO and U.S. policy to take whatever action is necessary to restore the situation. Thus, the theater nuclear forces provide a source of options and flexibility that would be difficult and perhaps inadvisable to incorporate exclusively into strategic nuclear forces. Accordingly, to the extent that a nuclear response may be required locally, theater nuclear forces have an indispensable function to perform in defense and deterrence.

Perhaps most important of all, because other nations—and most particularly the Soviet Union—have developed theater nuclear capabilities, a U.S. deployment of such forces is required to deter and if necessary counter them. The United States no longer has the choice of whether or not to deploy strategic or theater nuclear capabilities.

B. Foreign Capabilities. It is true that the United States set the example in the deployment of theater nuclear forces. Postwar planners clearly misjudged the length of the U.S. nuclear monopoly and the amount of time it would take the Soviets to acquire theater nuclear forces of their own. Neither the value of stolen secrets nor the level of Soviet investment was fully anticipated. The size of the Soviet conventional forces oriented toward Europe was overestimated. At the same time, it was assumed that the less costly theater nuclear firepower could make up for shortfalls in NATO manpower, and that there would be an enduring U.S. advantage in tactical nuclear forces. But as early as 1956, the Soviets began deploying MRBMs [medium-range ballistic missiles] and nuclear-capable light and medium bombers. Nuclear-capable missiles organic to the ground forces were deployed to Soviet forces by the early 1960s. Today their theater nuclear forces contain a greater variety of missile delivery systems and more launchers (including those based in the U.S.S.R.) than those of the United States. The current Soviet capability ranges from the variable-range ICBMs and the new SS-X-20 . . . to short-range tactical rockets deployed with Soviet forces in the Far East as well as in Eastern Europe and with other Warsaw Pact units. All in all, so large and diversified is this capability that it has become difficult to deduce the target system used by the Soviets to justify it.

Much of this force is based outside the NATO Guidelines Area; accordingly, it does not come within the purview of the negotiations on Mutual and Balanced Force Reductions. This is disturbing because the Soviets continue not only to maintain and modernize their force, but also to articulate a military doctrine which permits an early use of nuclear weapons in a European war—initiated either by NATO to avert a conventional defeat, or by the Warsaw Pact to pre-empt NATO first use. On balance, however, the Soviets would seemingly prefer to wage a purely conventional campaign in Western Europe; they appear to see their growing theater nuclear capabilities both as a deterrent and as a countercapability to the nuclear forces of NATO.

The U.S.S.R. is not the only other nation besides the United States with theater nuclear forces. The P.R.C. officially entered the nuclear lists only in 1964. But it has now deployed a medium-bomber force of over 70 Tu-16s which is nuclear-capable, and a small complement of MRBMs and IRBMs [intermediate-range ballistic missiles]. We also believe that the Chinese are now conducting a research and development effort to acquire nuclear weapons of various yields along with differing types of delivery means for direct support of their ground forces. This effort underlines the possibility that any major clash between the Soviet Union and the P.R.C. could involve nuclear weapons at an early stage. For the foreseeable future, however, Soviet tactical nuclear forces will greatly outnumber those of the P.R.C.

This is not the only possibility for nuclear conflict. Other nations continue to show a strong interest in acquiring theater nuclear forces. Both Great Britain and France have long-standing nuclear capabilities. Not only is the United States obliged to maintain major theater nuclear forces in these difficult circumstances; we must also recognize that neither we nor the Soviets are any longer necessarily the sole judges of where, when, and how nuclear weapons will be used. To pretend that by unilateral restraint alone, the United States can control this situation or decide whether other nations will deploy nuclear weapons in a sensitive and important region of the world is to ignore the realities, however unpleasant they may be.

Foreign nuclear capabilities are bound to have an impact on the size and composition of U.S. theater forces. But here as elsewhere, the goal is not to make U.S. forces a mirror-image of what others deploy. Instead, planners must consider what is needed as a function of specific theaters, threats, contingencies, and missions. And because accidents, unauthorized acts and terrorist activities must be of concern where nuclear weapons are involved, we must ensure that security and control over the necessary nuclear warheads are maintained with high confidence at all times.

C. Contingencies. The main planning contingencies to consider in determining a preferred theater nuclear posture are an attack by the Warsaw Pact in Central Europe and an offensive launched against South Korea by North Korean forces logistically reinforced from the outside. Enough nuclear warheads should be maintained for both theaters, since the weapons required for the one would not be available for the other. For planning purposes, an assumption is made that a U.S. decision to use theater nuclear forces would be determined either by an overwhelming enemy conventional breakthrough or by his first use of nuclear weapons.

Within the framework of these planning contingencies, a number of factors determine the conditions of deterrence and hence an appropriate U.S. theater nuclear posture. Since planning allows for the possibility that an enemy might strike first with theater nuclear forces, U.S. capabilities must be sufficiently survivable to absorb such an attack and still have enough surviving launchers and weapons of the appropriate yields to perform their assigned missions. This means not only a proper mix of forces, but also—because of the relatively short distances between opposing battlefield systems—an emphasis for survivability on mobility and concealment. Sophisticated and survivable command-control-communications networks are an integral part of these forces as well.

D. Missions and Forces. The types of missions assigned to the theater nuclear forces will have a major impact on their size and composition. It is noteworthy in this connection that the U.S. theater nuclear forces are programmed against military targets. In fact, although there is no less interest in deterrence and stability here than in the strategic realm, the United States plans its theater nuclear forces on the basis of war-fighting missions. Both the posture and the contingency plans place proper emphasis on restraint rather than on indiscriminate damage, and on the achievement of traditional military and political objectives, rather than on the destruction of an enemy's society.

The principal missions needed to achieve these traditional ends are:

- limited nuclear strikes designed to destroy selectively important, fixed military targets and at the same time demonstrate a determination to resist the enemy's attack by whatever means necessary;

- regional nuclear strikes intended, as one example, to destroy an attacking enemy force before it achieves a major breakthrough;

- and theaterwide strikes directed at counter-air and counter-missile targets, lines of communication, and troop concentrations both at the front and in reserve.

Various methods exist for computing the number of theater nuclear weapons needed to perform these missions with an acceptable level of confidence. Owing to the transient nature of many tactical targets, the most reasonable approach is to develop options keyed to likely military targets—such as ground force units, airfields, bridges, or ships—and determine the number of weapons required to achieve a high probability of significant damage to them on a second-strike. It is on this basis that consideration should be given to whether the number of nuclear weapons deployed to key theaters and at sea is sufficient for the performance of the three vital main missions of the theater nuclear forces.

E. Modernization. Numbers alone, however, do not provide a satisfactory basis for judging the adequacy of the theater nuclear forces. Since it is policy to minimize collateral damage in any theater nuclear employment, an effort is made to tailor warheads and delivery systems to their targets, and to plan the use of yields no greater than necessary for the destruction of designated targets. As nuclear and guidance technologies advance, lower yields can be incorporated into the theater nuclear forces. Where it is done, there is neither a plan nor an intention to blur or erase the distinction between nuclear and non-nuclear weapons. The objective has been and remains to increase kill probabilities, reduce collateral damage, and economize in the use of scarce nuclear materials.

Some opposition, even now, remains both to the current theater nuclear posture and to its modernization. Some critics question the feasibility of conducting a theater nuclear campaign resembling a conventional conflict in any way, and doubt that the damage from such a campaign could be kept below catastrophic levels. They express skepticism about the stability of less than theater-wide nuclear options; they suggest that any use of nuclear weapons would escalate rapidly to a strategic nuclear exchange. With these reservations in mind, proposals are made to reduce the U.S. overseas deployments of nuclear weapons and to halt any procurement of the newer generation of nuclear weapons.

The difficulty with these proposals is that they seem to treat as known what is intrinsically uncertain. That theater nuclear warfare would resemble a traditional conflict can be described as a contradiction in terms: damage might be unprecedented; chaos could ensue; rapid escalation might follow. But the fact is, we do not know what the outcome would be. Therefore, as long as theater nuclear capabilities exist—and hardly anyone in a position of responsibility favors unilaterally doing away with them—the United States must surely insist on exercising control over them and having the option to use them in as selective and deliberate a manner as possible. Uncertainty is no excuse for irresponsibility, and the possibility of disaster is no reason to make certain that it occurs.

*　　*　　*

Allies deserve to see the U.S. determination to collaborate in their defense by available means. Critics are entitled to know that the currently deployed nuclear forces are not simply dangerous relics from a previous decade. Friend and foe, supporter and skeptic, need to recognize that U.S. theater nuclear forces, even though they may evolve in size and composition as technology advances, constitute an integral part of the overall U.S. deterrent.

4

LIMITED NUCLEAR OPTIONS— TWO VIEWS

STRATEGIC ADAPTABILITY

William R. Van Cleave and Roger W. Barnett

The authors of this article present the case for increased flexibility in the use of nuclear weapons should deterrence collapse. Viewing "assured destruction" as essentially a force planning tool that has been raised to the level of strategy, Van Cleave and Barnett believe it has acquired the aura of unassailable dogma. As such, it has become a static strategy of sorts, incapable of dealing with what the authors perceive to be the evolutionary nature of the strategic nuclear threat. Strategy has failed to keep pace with the new possibilities for weapons employment derived from technological advances.

The Schlesinger strategy of limited nuclear response, with its flexible targeting doctrine, is seen by the authors as being dynamic and adaptive, responding to the evolving threat from the Soviet Union. They believe that the debate over U.S. strategic nuclear policies should concern itself with the question of whether we need more or fewer limited options, retargeting capabilities, or counterforce weapons. Viewing assured destruction as a shortsighted strategy that ignores the consequences of a failure of deterrence, Van Cleave and Barnett believe the Schlesinger strategy provides the means whereby the mutual destruction of societies need not inevitably occur. In addition, it is seen as providing political leaders with the means to employ nuclear weapons for political and military advantage in a nuclear exchange.

The advent of nuclear weapons and long-range delivery systems altered and bifurcated the concept of war. Superimposed upon the

Source: *Orbis*, vol. 18, no. 3 (Fall 1974), pp. 655-76. The opinions and assertions contained herein are those of the authors. They are not to be construed as official or as reflecting the views of the Navy Department.

traditional image was one of a long-range nuclear duel between "superpowers," which came to dominate modern discussions of strategy. In *this* image, when the possibility of massive civilian destruction was considered, the notion of "winning" seemed to become obsolescent: victors and vanquished would be indistinguishable; there could be no winners, only losers.

Deterrence of war between nuclear powers thus came to be considered the only appropriate objective. As if to make this image of war a self-fulfilling prophecy, a "strategy" of deterrence developed that had as its aim, not winning, but assuring that all would be losers. No longer could a chief of armed forces approach his political leadership and proclaim palindromically, "Now, Sir, a war is won!"

If it is allowed, on the other hand, that "winning" may mean "not losing," or alternatively "securing an objective," pursuing relative advantage, or improving the outcome of a war, the term does not seem intrinsically evil or necessarily obsolescent—assuming that one cares who wins. "Winning" in this sense lies at the core of strategic policy-making and planning for national defense.

Participation in a strategic nuclear exchange, the "success" of which is measured in devastated cities and tens of millions of deaths, must be excluded entirely from all definitions of "winning." Preventing such an exchange must also unequivocally be classified as "not losing," or winning. But ensuring that nuclear war takes the form of such an exchange does not qualify as strategy; strategy does not seek to guarantee that both sides lose, that there will be no winners.

Deterrence of a strategic nuclear attack on the United States must certainly comprise the cornerstone of U.S. strategic policy. On this untarnished principle there is no debate. But the matter clearly does not end there. Deterrence is not static, either in what must be deterred or in the way deterrence is to be accomplished. Nor is deterrence alone the sum total of strategy. In brief, the key to strategy is *adaptability*, and adaptability is the key to recent changes in U.S. strategic nuclear doctrine.

Strategic adaptability presumes, in agreement with Professor Donald Zoll, that "strategy reduces itself to the arts of war designed to achieve objectives short of the vital interests of states—for whose protection, presumably, the full national power of the state must be unleashed—coupled with those plans necessary to deal with the contingency of a nuclear strike of irrevocable dimensions."[1] This hearkens back to the dual nature of winning—that if one wants to win, more is required than the ability simply to assure massive destruction in the name of forestalling a catastrophic nuclear exchange.

---

[1] Donald A. Zoll, "New Aspects of Strategy," *Strategic Review*, Fall 1973, p. 43.

A New Debate?

A new great debate over strategy, expected from Defense Secretary Schlesinger's espousal of what we are here calling strategic adaptability, and from Secretary of State Kissinger's later appeal for a national debate on strategy, has yet to bloom despite a smattering of journalistic articles largely denouncing or decrying the "Schlesinger strategy," and a lesser number of more scholarly treatments.[2] The principal reason for this is that there appears to be little latitude for such a dramatic debate if the issues and alternatives are accurately defined; and when the issues are dramatically but erroneously posed, and strawman alternatives are drawn, only a false and futile debate can result. Yet even if no great debate takes place, one notes intellectual ferment and a rethinking of established strategic and arms control precepts, a new skeptical look at what has been for a long time orthodox wisdom, accompanied by substantial—though hardly mass—apostasy. As two scholars writing on this renaissance of thought correctly pointed out, a "widespread and deep-seated dissatisfaction today with many of the fundamental premises underlying American strategic weapons policy" has been brought about by disillusionment with SALT and Soviet intransigence therein, by the vigor of Soviet strategic weapons programs, and by other manifestations of Soviet strategic doctrine and policy that have combined to produce a "general skepticism of Russian intentions."[3]

It is ironic that counterforce was eschewed as a major U.S. objective in order to exercise a self-restraint that, it was assumed, would induce similar self-restraint on the part of the Soviets; but it must now be seriously reconsidered because the lack of Kremlin restraint has produced a Soviet strategic capability rendering "assured destruction"—or any massive strike option—questionable as a planned response. In other words, the reconsideration has been necessitated not so much by our own volition or acumen as by the determination of our major adversary. The doctrine of assured destruction and the concept of "mutual assured destruction" might have remained the dual cyno-

---

[2]Examples of the latter include Colin S. Gray, "Rethinking Nuclear Strategy," *Orbis,* Winter 1974, and the relevant parts of Albert Wohlstetter's article in the same issue, "Threats and Promises of Peace: Europe and America in the New Era." Also, Colin S. Gray, "The Urge to Compete: Rationales for Arms Racing," *World Politics,* January 1974; Ted Greenwood and Michael L. Nacht, "The New Nuclear Debate: Sense or Nonsense?," *Foreign Affairs,* July 1974; and Bruce M. Russett, "Short of Nuclear Madness," *Worldview,* April 1973.

[3]Greenwood and Nacht, "New Nuclear Debate." For a description of these factors, see the testimony of Defense Secretary Schlesinger, *U.S.-U.S.S.R. Strategic Policies,* Hearing before the Subcommittee on Arms Control, International Law and Organization of the Committee on Foreign Relations, U.S. Senate, 93rd Congress, 2nd Session, March 4, 1974, made public on April 4, 1974.

sure of U.S. strategic and arms control thought had not steady growth of Soviet strategic offensive capabilities and steadfast Soviet rejection of those notions forced a rethinking of our doctrine and concepts.

*   *   *

A debate on matters of national strategy, subject to strong emotions in such areas as strategic force planning and targeting, may by its very nature muddle issues rather than clarify them. Alternatives become dramatically, if not apocalyptically, cast in spurious either-or terms, which themselves are seldom descriptive or analytic but polemic. Carrying normative or pejorative connotations, these often imprecise terms are employed as missile words to be launched against one's opponents: arms control, stability, arms race, overkill, first strike.

In actuality the choices—and the modifications represented by Schlesinger's announcements—are matters of degree, not of either-or. In many cases they merely involve clearer thinking, and tuning declaratory policy more closely to actual policies for acquisition, deployment and employment of forces. Some would have the choices defined sharply as being between "counterforce" and "assured destruction," between "war-fighting capability" and "deterrence," even though these can never be contrasted, have never been either-or choices, and never will be. Any modern strategic force has *some* inherent counterforce capability, whether against soft, hard or hardest military targets.[4] Any plan for the use of such forces will necessarily include some military targets: for example, defenses may have to be suppressed before other attacks take place. Any force, to deter, must be capable of being used. Does anyone seriously suggest that a military force have *no* war-fighting capability?

Whether U.S. strategic offensive forces have had and have now the ability to attack enemy military targets—even hardened ICBM

---

[4]It may be useful to emphasize here that counterforce is not synonymous with hard-target kill. Some counterforce targets have been hardened to nuclear and blast effects, some have not, and some cannot be. To use counterforce to describe only missile silo destruction is an impoverishment of the term; using it solely in that sense is a distortion. Counterforce targets may be soft, hard, harder and hardest, from an ability to withstand only a few pounds per square inch additional overpressure to perhaps 1,000 psi, with only silos and some command facilities in the last category. Moreover, even for hard-target capability, its significance resides in the degree to which it exists. Statistically, there is some hard-target counterforce capability in all ICBM forces. The measurement of accuracy (CEP) is a statistical expression of where we may expect 50 per cent of the weapons to detonate relative to the target, and hard-target-kill probability is a function of the number of weapons one is willing to dedicate to a single target, as well as of the accuracy and yields of those weapons. If one is willing to dedicate a large number to a single target, high or significant kill probabilities may be achieved; but this may not be an efficient use of that number of weapons, it may not result in anything close to a favorable exchange ratio, and it may be far from a first-strike capability.

silos—is no real issue. They have had and do have *some* such capability. The question is whether that capability is sufficient. Our present capability, even if improved to a great extent by major force programs not now planned, would not provide a first-strike disarming capability against Soviet land-based strategic forces, much less a preclusive disarming capability, as the Secretary of Defense has explained.[5] Thus, there is no real issue concerning possibly unsettling effects of a first-strike capability.

Indeed, it is difficult to make an issue of "flexibility," per se. As Schlesinger observed, "when you get down to the hard rock of selectivity and flexibility in targeting plans, there really is very little criticism of that."[6] (However, as Professor Wohlstetter points out, there is a strong tendency among those who accept flexibility in principle to argue that "fortuitously, we have just the right amount of flexibility that we need and, it seems by good luck, exactly the right degree of accuracy."[7])

Hence, the issues are not either-or as frequently suggested, but more or less: more or less enhanced flexibility; more or less selectivity; more or fewer options; more or less emphasis in planning on limited strikes, on restraint, on precision, on military targets.

The questions related to those issues are simple ones that need not be confounded by resort to polemical jargon or dramatic descriptions of alternatives and consequences. Will the adjustments proposed mean that we will be more or less able to deter various threats and to negate the effectiveness of threats to the United States and its allies? Are the adjustments more likely to increase or decrease our chances for controlling escalation in the event of war? Does deterrence, if it fails initially, also have to fail totally? Do we wish to be more or less able to discriminate between military targets and civilian ones, to attack militarily relevant targets selectively without the necessity of widespread urban and population destruction? To what extent do we want that capability? Do we wish to improve it principally by changes in targeting plans, or to improve it still further by changes in the physical capabilities of our forces?

---

[5]*U.S.-U.S.S.R. Strategic Policies,* and *Report of Secretary of Defense James R. Schlesinger to the Congress on the FY 1975 Defense Budget and FY 1975-1979 Defense Program,* 93rd Congress, 2nd Session, March 4, 1974. See page citations from the latter below, referred to as *FY 75 DOD Report.*
[6]*U.S.-U.S.S.R. Strategic Policies,* p. 10.
[7]Wohlstetter, "Threats and Promises of Peace," p. 1135. Greenwood and Nacht, "New Nuclear Debate," take essentially this approach, as does Wolfgang Panofsky in "The Mutual-Hostage Relationship between America and Russia," *Foreign Affairs,* October 1973, though Panofsky seems to reverse himself, from first arguing that high levels of population destruction are inherent in any strategic strike to suggesting that we have sufficient flexibility and options other than civilian destruction.

Answers to such questions, because they signify decisions on strategies and on force programs, must be derived on balance since considerations on both sides must be weighed. But the choices are unlikely to be as stark as they are editorially presented. The issues are more a matter of the general direction to take in strategic policy, the direction that will guide research and development, force acquisition and deployment, the planning of options for employment, and, finally, declaratory policy, since it is clearly a purpose of the Defense Secretary to have declaratory policy somewhat more consistent with actual policies than it may have been in the past.

Even in the matter of direction, however, there has been some confusion. Many accounts, in the guise of arguing against a putative movement away from assured destruction toward counterforce, actually would have U.S. planning move toward a more rigid and pure adherence to urban assured destruction. An inflexible Catonic strategy of city destruction, which would in all likelihood be mutual, would be substituted for continuing force improvements and plans enhancing the ability to use forces selectively in a manner that might induce restraint in an adversary—i.e., to hit and to confine damage essentially to point targets other than population concentrations.

It is always necessary to ask first what we want our strategic forces to *do*. Some would answer simply, to deter. But to deter what? How? Until those answers are determined, the capabilities we wish our forces to have and the strategies to be followed cannot be established. The tendency has been to try to isolate "deterrence" from usefulness of nuclear forces, from flexibility, "warfighting," denial of an adversary's objectives, and damage limitation. Concurrently, deterrence, undifferentiated by considerations of varied threats and tailored ways of countering those threats, has been seen by many as exclusively associated with the infliction of retaliatory punishment. In this view, the greater or more "assured" the destructiveness, the surer the deterrent; the more "usable" the forces, the more likely they were to be used, thereby presumably weakening deterrence. Destructive capability was emphasized over credibility. In the nuclear sphere at least, this was a direct reversal of the criticisms of "massive retaliation" that grew and became widely accepted in the late 1950s.

Presumably, in such thinking, the overriding objective is not deterrence, per se, much less defense, but avoidance at all costs of the use of nuclear weapons: our use to be deterred as much as enemy use. But if that is one's primary value, one should be candid about it and not disguise it under the rubric of deterrence. Such a posture evokes questions: Should deterrence be based upon *unusable* weapons? Can it be?

Inherently high levels of destructiveness do not constitute an optimum deterrent or even a satisfactory policy against some kinds of threats—at the tactical nuclear weapons level, for example, and where deterrence might best be accomplished by the credible ability to defend or to respond with restraint rather than to threaten mass destruction reflexively. Now, for military or political coercion, there are varieties of strategic nuclear threat possible, against which assured destruction or massive retaliation is not as credible as *measured* retaliation. Since deterrence is some product of capability and credibility, the capability to use nuclear forces in a rational and nonapocalyptic fashion, when compared with the credibility of massive strikes in response to non-massive attacks, and when the adversary has his own massive capabilities in reserve, may become a better—and infinitely safer—deterrent. Contrary to what many seem to believe, increasing the credibility of use does not promote a breakdown of deterrence and the ultimate use of nuclear weapons. The objective is deterrence, and if both capability and credibility of the use of strategic weapons are sufficient, deterrence will be strengthened.

But deterrence may fail in any case, and the weapons may have to be used. The ability to conduct selective and limited nuclear strikes for express and restricted purposes while holding major retaliatory forces in reserve (where they are of more value for coercion than if used for urban-industrial destruction) provides an important hedge against the inability to predict deterrence thresholds for a range of situations, promotes the possibility of escalation control, and increases opportunities for war termination without major urban damage. Flexibility in the application of strategic weapons thus supports the requirement of adaptability in strategic policy.

Hence, while it is true that strategic flexibility has been considered and debated in the past, it is timely to consider it again. Despite the similarity of some points in Secretary McNamara's June 1962 Ann Arbor speech and Schlesinger's current proposals, there are issues and considerations about limited strategic options and flexibility that are unique to the 1970s: for example, both technology and the strategic balance have changed in ways that prompt a re-examination of the utility of flexible and limited options.

Genesis of Assured Destruction

Through the 1960s "assured destruction" grew from an analytical tool to the principal criterion for gauging U.S. retaliatory force sufficiency, to the dominant strategic concept among the intellectual defense community and even among official planners, to a philosophy for arms control and mutual deterrence. After early flirtations with strategic flexibility, counterforce and damage limitation, "assured destruction" became the "badly needed" theory of requirements, the "conceptual framework for measuring the need and adequacy of our strategic forces."[8]

Strategically, assured destruction came to be measured in terms of destroying arbitrarily determined percentages of population and civil industry: (a) because of a lingering association of "strategic" bombing with city bombing; (b) because during the formative years of the concept the combination of yield and inaccuracy then characteristic of strategic forces failed to lend itself to discriminate attacks avoiding major collateral damage, at least on targets in or near urban areas; (c) because many regarded, and continue to regard, such destruction as inevitable (Panofsky asserts it to be "a physical fact" insensitive to policy) or at least easily accomplished, so that—if both sides designed their strategic forces on this premise—costs of strategic forces could be decreased, mutual deterrence would increase, and arms limitation agreements could be brought about; and (d) because population fatalities and gross urban-industrial destruction, given a few assumptions, seemed readily calculable and thus a fine accounting or measuring device.

However, the linkage of strategic bombing to city bombing need not be so rigid. Accuracies have been achieved that allow discriminate attacks without the accompaniment of widespread civilian collateral damage. There is nothing inevitable in massive population destruction or escalation. Likewise, there is a significant distinction among numbers killed, even at high levels. Strategic forces, even in the heyday of assured destruction, have been designed for capabilities and missions other than city busting.[9] Furthermore, there is ample evidence that the Soviets reject the concept outright. It has neither reduced arms competition nor produced meaningful arms control; to the contrary, it may have contributed to Soviet incentives for a strategic buildup to the extent that it provided them first with an opportunity to gain strategic parity, and then with an opportunity for measurable superiority.

The term assured destruction connotes a misleading simplicity and certainty: it reduces strategic calculations to the easily grasped tenets of a Catonic strategy and implies that this destruction is not only calculable but easy. Neither is the case. Nothing is "assured"; certainly not that the United States would so respond, not even that the planned

---

[8] Alain C. Enthoven and K. Wayne Smith, *How Much Is Enough?* (New York: Harper & Row, 1971), p. 170. This process is described in Chapters 5 and 6.

[9] Ibid., p. 195. "United States strategic offensive forces have been designed with the additional system characteristics . . . needed to perform missions other than assured destruction, such as limited and controlled retaliation."

or assumed destruction would take place if the United States did so respond.[10] In a situation where such use of U.S. forces would in all probability bring about condign destruction of U.S. cities—and thus amount to an act of self-destruction—it is hardly "assured" that U.S. forces would be put to that use.

In view of the rhetoric of assured destruction, the dominant role the concept has assumed in strategic intellectualizing, and its importance in guiding strategic force decisions and evaluating strategic arms limitation packages, it is essential to keep repeating that it is basically an analytical test, and not necessarily strategy. At least, if it is the "cornerstone of U.S. deterrence strategy," it exists in variations other than deliberate and methodical destruction of urban population. Ultimate reliance on assured destruction, however defined, does not preclude other options or prohibit all other strategies of employment. Even so primary an advocate as Alain Enthoven acknowledged: "The assured-destruction test did not, of course, indicate how these forces would actually be used in a nuclear war."[11]

For the most part, the arms control community in the United States has been the driving force for converting what was originally one analytical tool to aid evaluation of strategic retaliatory sufficiency into unidimensional strategic policy. The success of that endeavor has been largely in the realm of academic theorizing and declaratory policy (and even that has usually been hedged to include other possibilities)—although assured destruction calculations *did* become the predominant test of strategic forces and of various arms limitation packages considered for SALT from 1968 to 1972.[12] The staggering notion that the United States would actually wage a war, should that become necessary, according to criteria the analysts found useful and the academics beguiling—however monstrous in execution—was allowed to grow and harden into conviction without adequate objection. Pursuit of "stable deterrence" and arms control could not be interrupted by distinctions regarding what was to be deterred, or by questions about what should happen if deterrence failed. Stripped of its trimmings, the response was simply: It *won't* fail.

Even an argument that large-scale destruction is a by-product of

---

[10]See the article on "Population Vulnerability," by Conrad V. Chester and Eugene P. Wigner, in this issue of *Orbis* [Fall 1974], pp. 763-769.

[11]Enthoven and Smith, *How Much Is Enough?*, p. 195.

[12]As one of the present authors has pointed out in Congressional testimony, assured destruction calculations were almost exclusively the test of various SALT limitations packages. Statement of William R. Van Cleave, *Military Implications of the Treaty on the Limitations of Anti-Ballistic Missile Systems and the Interim Agreement on Limitation of Strategic Offensive Arms*, Hearing before the Committee on Armed Services, U.S. Senate, 92nd Congress, 2nd Session, July 1972, pp. 569-92.

large strategic attacks[13] is much different from judging the adequacy of strategic forces by population destruction, and the latter is a far cry from basing force employment strategy on deliberate attempts to achieve such results. As Albert Wohlstetter wrote:

... a policy of unrestrained, indiscriminate attack on Russian civilians, executed without reserve, with no attempt to induce restraint in the Soviet leadership, can serve no purpose of state under any circumstances. If "Mutual Assured Destruction" means a policy of using strategic force only as a reflex to kill population, it calls for a course of action under every circumstance of attack that makes sense in none.[14]

Thus, we are conscious of persistent questions: Is threatening massive urban and population destruction necessary to deter Soviet attacks on the United States? Is it an effective deterrent against limited threats? Even against the most extreme threats to the United States, is it a better deterrent than the threat of large-scale attacks on the enemy's military capability, natural resources or basic industries?

Exodus of Assured Destruction

Strategic doctrine in the interim between the McNamara era and the present was officially based on assured destruction, but the so-called sufficiency principle neither expressed the assured destruction criterion explicitly in terms of population fatalities nor made assured destruction equivalent to sufficiency. Resulting from an interagency study in 1969, the four criteria for strategic sufficiency insofar as a direct threat to the United States was concerned were:

Maintaining an adequate second-strike capability to deter an all-out surprise attack on our strategic forces.

Providing no incentive for the Soviet Union to strike the United States first in a crisis.

Preventing the Soviet Union from gaining the ability to cause considerably greater urban/industrial destruction than the United States could inflict on the Soviets in nuclear war.

Defending against damage from small attacks or accidental launches.[15]

---

[13]Panofsky's "physical fact" levels are much lower than those used by McNamara for hypothetical city targeting, and limited strikes—depending on the limitations and civil defense effectiveness—may reduce casualties further yet. Improvements in accuracy and Soviet civil defense plans combine to make possible discriminate attacks not accompanied by the high levels of population fatalities commonly postulated.
[14]Wohlstetter, "Threats and Promises of Peace," p. 1133.
[15]*Statement of Secretary of Defense Melvin R. Laird before the House Armed Services Committee on the FY 1972-1976 Defense Program and the FY 1972 Defense Budget*, 92nd Congress, 1st Session, March 9, 1971.

Overall, these criteria—which have not been repealed publicly—clearly announced that assured destruction is not enough and that "how much is enough?" in strategic forces must be judged by additional considerations. However, certain changes in wording in the current (FY 75) Department of Defense Report seem to imply a new set of sufficiency criteria.

In March 1974 the Secretary of Defense described the "principal features that we propose to maintain and improve in our strategic posture" as, *inter alia:*

. . . a capability sufficiently large, diversified, and survivable so that it will provide us at all times with high confidence of riding out even a massive surprise attack and of penetrating enemy defenses, and *with the ability to withhold an assured destruction* reserve for an extended period of time.

. . . command-control capabilities required by our National Command Authorities to direct the employment of the strategic forces in a *controlled, selective, and restrained* fashion.

. . . the forces to execute a *wide range of options* in response to potential actions by an enemy, including a *capability for precise attacks on both soft and hard targets, while at the same time minimizing collateral damage.*

. . . an offensive capability of such size and composition that all will perceive it as in overall balance with the strategic forces of any potential opponent.[16]

This formula calls for:

(1) Not only an assured destruction capability, but the ability to withhold it in reserve for an extended period of time. The assured destruction force becomes a last-ditch deterrent threat, its primary value resting in its influence on an enemy's restraint while it is not used, rather than in the principal employment option.

(2) A wide range of employment options enabling controlled, selective, restrained and precise attacks against both urban and nonurban targets, soft and hard, in a manner to limit collateral damage.

(3) "Essential equivalence" with the strategic forces of any enemy, both actually and perceptually. This equivalence refers not only to observables such as the relative size of strategic forces, but also to counterforce capabilities. It does not, however, require force symmetry or the matching of all opponent capabilities. Rather, it requires "overall balance" wherein enemy advantages may be canceled by U.S. advantages in other areas.

---

[16]*FY 75 DOD Report,* pp. 44-45. (Emphasis added.)

The problem then is not so much assured destruction. As an analytical tool, it may be useful if not overdone. As a force capability, it is necessary—but insufficient. Nor is the change proposed a move entirely away from it. There are two differences: (1) Instead of relying on assured destruction as our primary response capability and allowing it to dominate all other options, we now want more planned limited-strike options, some of which would be quite discriminate, while the assured destruction capability would be held in reserve with the objective of dampening escalation. Such a reserve would serve to make even clearer the limited nature of the other options. (2) In view of President Nixon's charge that measuring population fatalities is inconsistent with American values, and similar comments by Secretary Schlesinger, we may now prefer to judge the adequacy of the assured destruction capability with regard not so much to population fatalities and urban destruction as to objectives of greater political-military relevance to a war and its aftermath—such as (a) reduction of the enemy's military capability, both to prosecute the war and to exert postwar power beyond his borders (or, for that matter, to maintain domestic control and protect his own borders), (b) destruction of elements critical to his post-attack recovery capability, and (c) disruption of political control mechanisms.

To conduct a reasonable discussion of what changes are suggested for U.S. strategic doctrine and what are not, and of the reasons for the changes, it is best to understand exactly what the Secretary of Defense has said.

Adaptability: Measured Deterrence

On January 10, 1974, Secretary Schlesinger first announced that there has taken place "a change in the strategies of the United States with regard to the hypothetical employment of central strategic forces. A change in targeting strategy as it were."[17] (He did not say it was a thorough change.) He went on:

> To a large extent the American doctrinal position has been wrapped around something called "assured destruction" which implies a tendency to target Soviet cities initially and massively and that this is the principal option that the President would have. It is our intention that this not be the only option and possibly not the principal option.

---

[17]Remarks by Secretary of Defense James R. Schlesinger, Overseas Writers Association Luncheon, International Club, Washington, D.C., January 10, 1974. Mimeo. Transcript, Office of the Assistant Secretary of Defense for Public Affairs (OASD/PA).

Because of the growth of Soviet force capabilities, "the range of circumstances in which an all-out strike against an opponent's cities can be contemplated has narrowed considerably and one wishes to have alternatives for the employment of strategic forces other than what would be a suicidal strike against the cities of the other side."

That a broadening of the options available in U.S. targeting plans (the SIOP—Single Integrated Operational Plan) was in the wind should have come as no surprise. Concern had been expressed about overly restricted options and changes had been suggested in each of President Nixon's four previous annual messages on U.S. foreign policy.

In a news conference on January 24, Schlesinger explained his earlier remarks. In the first place, he said, the key to understanding the modifications—rather than focusing on counterforce versus assured destruction—is to recognize that the "emphasis is upon selectivity and flexibility; that does not necessarily involve what is referred to as major counterforce capabilities. . . . The emphasis is on the selection of targets." Nor does this selectivity necessarily require new force programs. More important, the Secretary emphasized, is a change in attitude and planning. "In order to have a strategy of selectivity and flexibility one must consciously adopt that and adjust plans to doctrine. That is a considerable change."[18]

In his annual report to Congress in March, Schlesinger elaborated on the changes and the reasons for them.[19] U.S. thinking about strategic deterrence, he said, has not kept pace with the evolution of the threat. "The scope of the Soviet program as it has now emerged is far more comprehensive than estimated even a year ago . . . a truly massive effort." It has developed "ahead of rather than in reaction to what the United States has done," and it will pose a much broader range of real threats to the United States and its allies than in the past.

To counter the more extreme views of assured destruction advocates, the Secretary reiterated that the United States has had targeting options in the past:

> Although several targeting options, including military only and military plus urban/industrial variations, have been part of U.S. strategic doctrine for quite some time, the concept that has dominated our rhetoric for most of the era since World War II has been massive retaliation against cities, or what is called assured destruction.[20]

---

[18]News Conference by Secretary of Defense James R. Schlesinger at the Pentagon, January 24, 1974. Mimeo. transcript, OASD/PA.
[19]FY 75 DOD Report, especially pp. 32-45.
[20]Ibid., p. 33.

Concurrently he explained to the Muskie Subcommittee of the Senate Committee on Foreign Relations:

> Of course, all our delivery vehicles are targeted against specific targets. The point that is different about the targeting doctrine that I have outlined to you is the emphasis on selectivity and flexibility. In the past we have had massive preplanned strikes in which one would be dumping literally thousands of weapons on the Soviet Union. Some of those strikes could to some extent be withheld from going directly against cities, but that was limited even then.
>
> With massive strikes of that sort, it would be impossible to ascertain whether the purpose of a strategic strike was limited or not. It was virtually indistinguishable from an attack on cities.[21]

We have, then, had options. However, they have (a) required the release of a very large number of weapons and therefore involved high levels of destruction; (b) been too few in number and insufficiently selective or limited to suit future requirements—we have made no real effort to develop adequate limited options either in planning or in force capabilities;[22] and (c) not been precise enough against military targets or, as Schlesinger later testified, particularly efficient against harder military targets.

We still plan to have an assured destruction capability, but today that is neither sufficient nor reassuring:

> Such reassurances may bring solace to those who enjoy the simple but arcane calculations of assured destruction. But they are of no great comfort to policymakers who must face the actual decisions about the design and possible use of the strategic nuclear forces. Not only must those in power consider the morality of threatening such terrible retribution on the Soviet people for some ill-defined transgression by their leaders; in the most practical terms, they must also question the prudence and plausibility of such a response when the enemy is able, even after some sort of first strike, to maintain the capability of destroying our cities.
>
> Since we ourselves find it difficult to believe that we would actually implement the threat of assured destruction in response to a limited attack on military targets that caused relatively few civilian casualties, there can be no certainty that, in

---

[21]*U.S.-U.S.S.R. Strategic Policies*, p. 9.
[22]Whatever has been said about options before, "nobody at the political level from 1961 to 1971 has put the energy behind developing the doctrine and the plans. . . . Now we are consciously basing our deterrent strategy upon the achievement of flexibility and selectivity." Ibid., p. 26.

a crisis, prospective opponents would be deterred from testing our resolve.

Today, such a massive retaliation against cities, in response to anything less than an all-out attack on the U.S. and its cities, appears less and less credible.[23]

Yet, deterrence may fail in many ways; the problem, therefore, is a lack of sufficient options between no response and large-scale responses. The requirement stipulated is for a series of measured responses as more credible deterrents to a range of threats, and more rational responses to limited failures in deterrence, responses that

bear some relation to the provocation, have prospects of terminating hostilities before general nuclear war breaks out, and leave some possibility for restoring deterrence.

Flexibility of response is also essential because, despite our best efforts, we cannot guarantee that deterrence will never fail; nor can we forecast the situations that would cause it to fail. . . . To the extent that we have selected response options—smaller and more precisely focused than in the past—we should be able to deter such challenges. But if deterrence fails, we may be able to bring all but the largest nuclear conflicts to a more rapid conclusion before cities are struck. Damage may thus be limited and further escalation avoided.[24]

It is important to note that, in contrast to ideas of damage limiting that would seek to deprive the enemy of his strategic capabilities through major counterforce operations and active defenses, the emphasis here is on *targeting restraint*. Restraint is characteristic of limiting and terminating conflict once deterrence has failed.

In discussing limited-strike options, Schlesinger indicated that:

targets for nuclear weapons may include not only cities and silos, but also airfields, many other types of military installations, and a variety of other important assets that are not necessarily collocated with urban populations. We already have a long list of such possible targets; now we are grouping them into operation plans. . . . To the extent necessary, we are retargeting our forces accordingly.

The choice of options would depend on the nature of an enemy's attack and his objectives. In addition, he acknowledged that "we may also want a more efficient hard-target-kill capability than we now possess" in order to enhance deterrence. "The real issue is how much

---

[23]*FY 75 DOD Report*, pp. 35, 37-38.
[24]Ibid., p. 38.

hard-target-kill capability we need."[25] The latter must be determined not only by our own assessment of the requirements of flexibility and selectivity, but also in light of the continued development of Soviet strategic force capabilities.

The Secretary stated candidly that we want to improve our counterforce capability somewhat, particularly through better accuracies. Although he requested research and development funding for a follow-on Minuteman warhead with larger yield, as well as improved accuracy, it is clear that the fundamental vehicle will be the removal of past restrictions on accuracy and other improvements to make selective targeting and retargeting possible. These improvements do not constitute expensive or major programs. . . .

In separating targeting changes and new programs, the Secretary went even further:

The change in targeting doctrine does not require new capabilities. There are some aspects for which we are asking the Congress this year for additional funding, but the change in doctrine is not dependent upon the additional funding. We are asking money in this budget for improved command and control, and for some improvement in accuracy, but the change in targeting doctrine does not depend for its efficacy upon our getting this money.[26]

While the door may be left open for future requests for program funding, these will be determined in view of developments in SALT and in the Soviet Union, as well as from continued assessments of our own requirements. In any case, that issue would be one of more-or-less, over which—including requests for funding—Congress and the public will have a say.

Essential Equivalence

There are, of course, new program requirements established for other reasons; e.g., to replace aging systems, to maintain necessary survivability and penetrability, and to prevent the United States from slipping into a position of actual or perceptible strategic inferiority to the Soviet Union. The last has been referred to as the requirement for "essential equivalence," which should be considered separately from the targeting issue, although it is somewhat related. Retargeting and improvement of strategic flexibility are desirable goals regardless of the size and throw-weight of our strategic missile forces and their comparison with

[25]Ibid., pp. 39-41.
[26]*U.S.-U.S.S.R. Strategic Policies*, p. 8.

those of the U.S.S.R. A policy of strategic adaptability requires enhanced flexibility in whatever strategic force we have. Whether this force may be reduced or must be increased depends upon SALT, Soviet activities, and the principle of essential equivalence, which insists that our forces not be significantly inferior to the strategic forces of the Soviet Union in numbers, throw-weight or counterforce capability.

Since equivalence includes counterforce capability as well as size, improved targeting flexibility is related to it to the extent that it also involves counterforce improvements. In fact, if essential equivalence is to guide U.S. force decisions it will demand greater hard-target counterforce capability than will the more flexible targeting, simply because of the enormous hard-target counterforce potential inherent in the Soviet ICBM force now being developed.

Essential equivalence thus has to do with the sizing of forces and depends upon Soviet force developments;[27] targeting improvement has to do with neither. Similarly, improving targeting flexibility has nothing to do with SALT or with any attempt to coerce or influence the Soviet Union. Essential equivalence is directly related to SALT—we hope to establish it by agreement to hold forces down equally—and may also be an attempt to gain leverage in the negotiations and to induce the Soviets to exercise greater restraint in their programs.

To be realistic, however, it must be acknowledged that essential equivalence may go the way of many other labeled policies and become little more than flummery. While it is an admirable goal, it is not an exact one and may become more elastic over time, as it grows clearer that equivalence in the three properties so far defined will be most difficult to attain if limited to those central strategic offensive forces contained in strategic arms limitation agreements. Taken literally, the term looks a bit stranger when juxtaposed with projections of ten to twelve million pounds of ICBM throw-weight and 7,000 to 15,000 ICBM MIRV's [intercontinental ballistic missile multiple independently targetable reentry vehicles] for the Soviet Union, against two million pounds' throw-weight and 2,000 to 3,000 MIRV's, respectively, for the United States.[28] Even if applied to the launcher limits established by the SALT I agreement, equivalence requires that we go up or they come down.

To attain essential equivalence, the forces to be included may have

---

[27]This does not mean to imply that essential equivalence is not promoted through advanced capabilities and the quality of technology, which is obvious in its counterforce criterion. Nor is it to suggest that technological advantages may not make up in important respects for quantitative disadvantages. Technological advance is probably the most fruitful route for the United States to take *if* it is pushed vigorously enough to offset Soviet quantitative advantages.

[28]*U.S.-U.S.S.R. Strategic Policies*, pp. 5-7.

to be so defined as to render the concept sterile: by including more U.S. systems (bombers, noncentral systems) while excluding comparable Soviet systems by comparing noncomparables such as bomber payload (carefully restricted to "heavy bomber" payload) and missile throw-weight, and by weighing (exaggerating?) alleged advantages in U.S. technology and in nonlimited systems.[29]

The conclusion is ineluctable that we can achieve improved targeting flexibility, selectivity and discrimination more easily than essential equivalence (in any meaningful sense of the term) and without any necessary association of the two. Enhanced flexibility of U.S. strategic forces may promote equivalence in targeting capability, but it does not depend upon "essential equivalence," however defined. It is an objective in and of itself, unrelated to the sizing of forces.

This is important to understand in view of expressed concerns that increasing our ability to plan more flexible and selective attacks and to strike targets more discriminately will somehow provoke a Soviet reaction, thereby fueling an "arms race," and/or destabilizing the strategic balance.

But how could this be? As the Secretary of Defense has pointed out, critics of options cannot have it both ways:

> If the nuclear balance is no longer delicate and if substantial force asymmetries are quite tolerable, then the kinds of changes I have been discussing here will neither perturb the balance nor stimulate an arms race. If, on the other hand, asymmetries do matter (despite the existence of some highly survivable forces), then the critics themselves should consider seriously what responses we should make to the major programs that the Soviets currently have underway to exploit their advantages in numbers of missiles and payload.[30]

There has been a tendency on the part of many advocates of mutual assured destruction and critics of counterforce, limited strategic options, and arms modernization, to argue at the same time that strategic deterrence is inherently stable (because of the impossibility of disarming first strikes and the inevitability of great civil devastation from even a small number of strikes in retaliation), but that improvements in counterforce, damage limiting, or flexibility would be destabilizing and increase the risk of nuclear war. They also argue that the in-

---

[29]One is reminded here of Dr. Edward Teller's comment, in Congressional testimony eleven years ago, on intelligence concerning capabilities easily seen and those not so easily assessed. "I am disturbed by the fact that in the region which is easily observed, we admit the Russians are ahead. Whereas in those regions where observation is more difficult we still claim superiority." *Nuclear Test Ban Treaty*, Hearings before the Committee on Foreign Relations, U.S. Senate, 88th Congress, 1st Session, August 1963.
[30]*FY 75 DOD Report*, p. 39.

evitability of great population destruction—essentially, assured destruction—is insensitive to policy (Panofsky), but that a change in policy away from reliance on that principal option toward more limited and selective options would, again, be destabilizing. If deterrence is so stable and population devastation so certain, if counterforce and damage-limiting measures are so meaningless, how can qualitative improvements in weaponry and adjustments of targeting policy be so destabilizing?

On the one hand, it seems, we have reached a plateau from which there is no escape; on the other hand, the merest hint of escape is bad. Man has devised a situation where, in the event of strategic nuclear warfare, excessively high levels of destruction are unavoidable; yet any attempt to relieve or to escape from this inflexible situation is both bad and a priori doomed to failure. We are eternal captives of what we ourselves have devised, according to the advocates of the inflexible mutual hostage strategy. (One might ask why, if such a condition is inevitable, it is necessary to advocate it.) Yet, they fear that changes will be upsetting. Of what?

At the same time it is argued that the proposed changes will be destabilizing in another sense: they will provoke major Soviet reactions and produce, or propel, an arms race. This concern seems to trouble even some who reject the mutual hostage theory or the notion that deterrence will be destabilized by the proposed changes, and who may on balance favor the changes. But (leaving aside for the moment that an "arms race"—or more accurately some increased arms competition—may be preferable to continuation of the existing situation and of recent trends in strategic arms relations) this reservation, as remarked by the Secretary of Defense, in reality is as baseless as the first concern, for the reasons cited in the next section.

Arms Pacing

In the first place, it is not proposed that the United States increase its forces, but that the flexibility and capability of the forces we have be improved; and for the most part the changes necessary do not now seem to involve major programs. Ensuring viable and adequately survivable forces in the future probably *will* involve major programs, and the test of essential equivalence *may* do so, but these requirements depend upon what the Soviets do. In the second place, while the Soviets have been arms racing, the United States has been arms walking or crawling;[31] with SALT's failure to meet our expectations, the problem

---

[31]See the two-part article by Albert Wohlstetter, "Is There a Strategic Arms Race?," *Foreign Policy*, Spring and Fall 1974; also Gray, "The Urge to Compete."

is now one of pacing, and the less pacing we do immediately, the sooner we will be placed in the position of having to catch up.

Moreover, war winning and counterforce capability have been consistent keynotes of Soviet strategic doctrine and strategic force development for some time, and it is abundantly clear that American pedagogy and restraint have not succeeded in steering Moscow away from such objectives. As two writers recently observed, "the Soviet Union has or will have great targeting flexibility and counterforce capability in its own strategic forces. . . . Soviet writers have consistently advocated a capability to engage in and to win a strategic nuclear war."[32]

Critics of increased flexibility, which they interpret to signify increased counterforce capability on the part of the United States, include among their arguments the assertion that the U.S.S.R. would be seriously concerned about any indication of increased hard-target-kill capability in U.S. strategic forces. At the same time they assert that the United States, by dint of its triad of mutually supporting strategic forces, need not fear a Soviet disarming first strike, since attack timing problems, the fratricide factor, and the assured survival of a large number of U.S. weapons would deter it. In view of the prevailing strategic balance (the significantly larger numbers of Soviet ICBM's and SLBM's [submarine launched ballistic missile] and the potentially great number of RV's [reentry vehicles]), the mix of strategic forces on both sides, and the natures of the two different political systems involved, this alleged concern over U.S. intentions and Soviet reactions becomes "curiouser and curiouser."

Even if improvements in U.S. targeting capability were to mean substantial improvements in counterforce capability, one must ask: What more can the Soviets do to develop *their* counterforce capability? It is most difficult to see what they could do beyond what they are already doing. And if there is a reaction, *to the extent that* the Soviets become concerned with U.S. hard-target counterforce capability, their reaction must be in the direction of improving the survivability of their own forces. Is that bad for the United States? Efforts and resources the Soviets must put into survivability measures are efforts and resources unavailable for a quest for strategic superiority, for their own menacing counterforce capabilities, or for other purposes more detrimental to U.S. interests.

Down the Up Escalator

In conclusion, this article expresses the conviction that the enhanced targeting flexibility proposed by Secretary of Defense Schlesinger is a

---

[32]Greenwood and Nacht, "New Nuclear Debate."

step in the right strategic direction. By promoting strategic adaptability and credibility with restraint, it will strengthen deterrence and promote U.S. interests in the event of war without increasing the risk of long-term detriments about which many are concerned. It is not a proper goal of strategy to increase war's destructiveness, particularly so meaninglessly; the object is, rather, to avoid losing; to preserve and to pursue U.S. interests; to control escalation, and to promote a more satisfactory war termination than that implied by assured destruction. An attempt to limit war damage, while maintaining or improving pre-war and intrawar deterrence, is laudable and an essential objective of both national military strategy and arms control. To insist that deterrence depends upon maximizing—or inflicting very high levels of—civil destruction as a necessary consequence of retaliation is execrable.

The programs suggested to improve current targeting capabilities are not costly and hardly constitute a "first-strike" threat. The degree of further improvement through future programs will be a matter of Congressional (and thereby public) approval. No increase in force levels is contemplated, but that, too, is an option for future consideration, depending upon the need to adapt to Soviet capabilities and upon the outcome of SALT.

In essence, advocates of strategic adaptability merely call for a return to more traditional, sensible, time-tested and proven strategic thinking—a return from a bizarre detour to a path with origins as far back as Sun Tzu:

What is of supreme importance in war is to attack the enemy's strategy. . . .

Next best is to disrupt his alliances. . . .

The next best is to attack his army. . . .

The worst policy is to attack cities. Attack cities only when there is no alternative.[33]

NUCLEAR STRATEGY AND NUCLEAR WEAPONS

Barry Carter

Barry Carter presents the case against the acquisition of nuclear weapons capable of threatening hardened military targets in the Soviet Union. While

---

[33]Sun Tzu, *The Art of War*, Translated and with an introduction by Samuel B. Griffith (Oxford, England: Oxford University Press Paperback, 1971), pp. 77-78.

agreeing with Secretary of Defense Schlesinger that the United States should have a broader range of options for selective retaliation, Carter maintains that proposed weapons programs would provide the United States with a capability to destroy Soviet missile silos. He sees the extension of Schlesinger's notion of "essential equivalence" to include weapons capabilities (as distinct from force levels) as destabilizing to deterrence and harmful to arms control efforts.

The current inventory of strategic weapons in the United States is more than sufficient for providing flexibility of targeting and limited strike options. As accuracy and yield-to-weight ratios are improved, however, Carter believes attitudes toward nuclear warfare will change and the inhibitions to limited war will diminish. The author concludes by stating that "the primary objective of nuclear strategy is to avoid nuclear wars, not to fight them," and he suggests certain provisions for SALT that would restrain the drive toward counterforce weapons.

"Should a President, in the event of a nuclear attack, be left with the single option of ordering the mass destruction of enemy civilians, in the face of the certainty that it would be followed by the mass slaughter of Americans? Should the concept of assured destruction be narrowly defined and should it be the only measure of our ability to deter the variety of threats we may face?"

The questions asked in the preceding quotation, taken from President Nixon's first foreign-policy report in 1970, have been cited repeatedly in the past few months by Administration spokesmen in an effort to explain and justify some significant changes that are being made in U.S. policy regarding its strategic military forces. The new strategy, spelled out most clearly in Secretary of Defense James R. Schlesinger's annual report for the fiscal year 1975, released in March, seeks "to provide the President with a wider set of much more selective targeting options," and hence greater "flexibility," in choosing an appropriate response to "any kind of nuclear attack."

As the opening quotation illustrates, much of the official rhetoric concerning this new development in U.S. strategic policy has been more misleading than illuminating. To criticize the "assured destruction" doctrine of the past decade or so as planning only for massive retaliation against Russian cities ignores the fact (belatedly acknowledged by Schlesinger) that U.S. strategic forces have for years had the capability, both in weapons and in planning, for a "flexible response." More important, the broad hypothetical issues invoked by such public statements have tended to obscure the more immediate real issues presented by this Administration's recent actions.

The real issues are serious ones. The primary operational question at present is whether or not the U.S. should develop missiles with an improved capability for attacking "hardened" targets in the U.S.S.R. The main rationale offered for developing such an improved "counterforce" capability (so called because it is aimed at an opponent's military forces) is that it is "impermissible" for the U.S. not to "match" certain Russian counterforce developments. There is also the suggestion that these missiles would minimize "unintended collateral damage."

The preceding question in turn raises the subtler issue of how the active promotion of such programs for improved counterforce capabilities affects the stability of the strategic nuclear deterrent and hence the likelihood that there will be a nuclear war. Before one can address these two issues one must understand why public debate should properly focus on such questions and not (at this time anyway) on the kind of questions posed in President Nixon's 1970 remarks.

In the late 1950s and early 1960s U.S. strategic policy went through a series of transformations. By 1962 American military planners recognized that the U.S. would have many more missiles than the U.S.S.R. could have for several years and in fact many more missiles than were required to devastate every major city in the U.S.S.R. A counterforce strategy therefore held out the attractive option of limiting damage to U.S. cities by destroying a substantial part of the Russian strategic forces. In language that sounds remarkably familiar today, Secretary of Defense Robert S. McNamara said in a speech in Ann Arbor, Mich.:

> The United States has come to the conclusion that, to the extent feasible, basic military strategy in a possible general nuclear war should be approached in much the same way that more conventional military operations have been regarded in the past. That is to say, principal military objectives, in the event of a nuclear war stemming from a major attack on the alliance, should be the destruction of the enemy's military forces, not of his civilian population.

The Russians, however, continued to deploy land-based intercontinental ballistic missiles (ICBM's) and submarine-launched ballistic missiles (SLBM's). As a result, even if the U.S. sought to limit damage to itself by the partial destruction of the Russian strategic forces, there would still be more than enough Russian forces left to kill tens of millions of Americans. Recognizing this fact, McNamara increasingly emphasized by the mid-1960s the concept of "assured destruction," which he said in 1968 meant the "ability, even after absorbing a well-coordinated surprise first strike, to inflict unacceptable damage on the attacker." This criterion he defined explicitly: "In the case of the Soviet Union, I would judge that a capability on our part to destroy, say, one-fifth to one-fourth of her population and one-half of her industrial capacity would serve as an effective deterrent."

Few concepts have been as maligned or misunderstood as that of assured destruction. Critics label it genocide or use the acronym of "mutual assured destruction" to call it MAD. In fact, the concept seems well designed to serve two purposes. First, by planning the size of U.S. forces on the basis of the "worst case" scenario of an all-out Russian surprise attack, it ensures that the U.S. possesses the ultimate threat: to be able to wipe out the U.S.S.R. or any attacker in retaliation. Second, since the destruction criterion is reasonably precise, the concept provides a useful basis for limiting strategic-weapons procurement and for evaluating arms-control proposals.

While retaining the assured-destruction concept, McNamara and his successor, Clark Clifford, supervised the development of the wide array of weapons that constitutes today's U.S. strategic arsenal. Both the numbers and the characteristics of many of these weapons were consistent with the assured-destruction concept, partly because the U.S. possesses a "triad" of strategic offensive forces and partly because of the hedge against the "highest expected threat." The triad approach seeks to maintain a major retaliatory capability in each component of our strategic offensive forces: ICBM's, SLBM's and long-range bombers. Justified on the grounds that each component presents a different problem for an attacker, difficult and costly problems for his defense and a hedge against unexpected failures in one or both of the other components, the net result of the triad approach is to provide in the aggregate a high degree of confidence that the assured-destruction mission could be carried out.

The hedge against the highest expected threat, as projected in the National Intelligence Estimates, meant that weapons would be developed and sometimes procured as a cushion against Russian developments that, although not considered likely, were possible. The predictable result was that the U.S. came to possess much more powerful forces than were shown by subsequent events to be required for assured destruction. For example, one of the main justifications offered for developing multiple independently targeted reentry vehicles (MIRV's) was to hedge against a greater-than-expected Russian deployment of an anti-ballistic-missile (ABM) system, on the theory that increasing the number of incoming warheads would enable the U.S. offense to penetrate the Russian defense more easily.

Of course, some of the development and procurement decisions also reflected inevitable political and bureaucratic pressures. For example, faced with pressures from the military and from Congress, McNamara apparently thought he could not ask for fewer than 1,000 Minuteman ICBM's.

Finally, the proponents of the assured-destruction concept in the latter half of the 1960s quietly subscribed to secondary strategic objectives, in particular the desire to retain some ability to respond flexibly in the case of an actual attack. If the U.S. were subjected to a "limited" nuclear attack—possibly with a small number of missiles or because of an accidental launch—most thought the President should have a range of options from which to choose. This factor helps to explain why, for example, the Minuteman II warhead, which was first deployed in 1966, could be programmed for up to eight alternative targets, and why there was flexibility in the actual targeting plans.

As a result the U.S. ended up with strategic-war capabilities considerably greater than the assured-destruction concept required. That this situation was rarely acknowledged publicly was a serious mistake, the results of which we are now reaping in public misunderstanding of the policies of the past and, more important, in the sometimes surprising ignorance about the present capabilities of the U.S. strategic forces. The simple fact, which cannot be stressed too strongly, is that the U.S. strategic forces are now capable of carrying out a large array of alternative missions, far in excess of assured destruction.

To begin with, assured destruction does not require many forces. Assuming zero or low Russian ABM levels (a reasonable assumption given the 1972 Moscow Treaty limiting ABM systems), the delivered warheads of 220 Minuteman III ICBM's could kill about 21 percent of the Russian population from immediate effects alone and destroy about 72 percent of the Russian industrial capacity. The delivered warheads from 170 Poseidon missiles (which is fewer than the total carried by 12 submarines) could cause a similar level of damage. Projections of bomber survivability vary greatly, but most experts would estimate that enough B-52s could reach their targets to satisfy easily the traditional assured-destruction criterion.

The total of U.S. strategic forces is, of course, much larger. There are at present 1,054 ICBM's, of which 1,000 are Minuteman missiles and 54 are the older, larger Titans. Of the Minuteman missiles 550 have been or are in the process of being converted to the Minuteman III, which can carry up to three warheads. These MIRV's are estimated to have an accuracy of 1,500 feet or less (expressed in terms of "circular error probable," which means that 50 percent of the warheads are expected to fall within a radius of 1,500 feet of the target). The explosive power, or yield, of each warhead is equivalent to between 170 and 200 kilotons of TNT, or at least 11 times the size of the 15-kiloton bomb dropped on Hiroshima. Rapid retargeting of the Minuteman III will be possible soon with the advent of new computer-software systems, such as the Command Data Buffer system. (All estimates of the numbers and characteristics of U.S. forces used in this article are taken from the statements of U.S. officials, from publications of the International Institute of Strategic Studies and from other reliable publications.)

In addition the U.S. arsenal includes 656 SLBM's, 496 of which are scheduled to become Poseidon missiles. The Poseidon can carry up to 14 MIRV's, but it is usually deployed with 10. Although accuracy might be reduced by uncertainties about the submarine's location, it still is probably less than 3,000 feet. Moreover, even though each warhead is smaller than Minuteman's, there are many more of them and each is still about three times the size of the Hiroshima bomb. Like the Minuteman III warheads, the Poseidon warheads can be retargeted quickly.

Bombers are often viewed as the stepchild of the U.S. strategic triad. The approximately 400 B-52s and 65 FB-111s are unaccountably ignored in many comparative tables of American and Russian strategic forces, notably in President Nixon's first three foreign-policy reports. This is surprising given the fact than an estimated 40 percent of the U.S. budget for strategic offensive forces is spent on bombers. Moreover, from the standpoint of nuclear strikes the per-sortie attrition rate of about 3 percent suffered by the B-52s in their attacks on heavily defended Hanoi demonstrated high survivability. Indeed, most places in the U.S.S.R. would not be as heavily defended as Hanoi, the B-52s would not be making the more vulnerable high-altitude attacks they made there and the bombers would use nuclear warheads to silence air-defense batteries. Each B-52 carries between four and 24 nuclear weapons, the load being a variable mix of gravity bombs and air-to-surface missiles. The bombs can be in the megaton range (that is, equal to 1,000 kilotons) and can be delivered with very high accuracy.

(This accounting of the U.S. strategic forces does not include the extensive U.S. "tactical" nuclear forces, many of which could attack targets in the U.S.S.R. In addition to the more than 7,000 tactical nuclear weapons in Europe, many such weapons are deployed in Asia and on forward-deployed ships in the Atlantic and the Pacific.)

In short, the U.S. already has a considerable potential for "limited" strategic strikes. Exactly how much capability depends on the critical assumption of who strikes first and how, as well as on one's assumptions about the nature of the Russian threat. In any case three important factors should be remembered about potential targets in the U.S.S.R.:

1. There are many nonmilitary, industrial targets outside urban centers that would require only one or two nuclear warheads each; such targets include manufacturing plants, power plants and the two construction yards for missile submarines.

2. Except for "hardened" targets, most military targets could be destroyed by only one or two warheads each; such targets include air-defense sites, military airfields, major army bases and submarine bases.

3. Even for hard targets such as missile silos, nuclear-weapons storage facilities and command posts, the use of small numbers of warheads will create a high probability of destruction. For instance, three Minuteman III warheads delivered against three Russian missile silos with a "hardness" about the same as that of the U.S. silos when they were first built would have approximately an 80 percent chance of destroying one silo, whereas seven Minuteman III warheads would have a similar 80 percent probability of knocking out one silo three times as hard. Presumably many Russian missile silos have a hardness in this range.

As a result, even with existing missiles, a limited strike by the U.S. that employed 100 missiles or fewer could do substantial damage to the U.S.S.R. and could knock out some Russian ICBM's.

In calculating the sufficiency of our strategic forces, one should not forget the Chinese. For any conceivable "crisis scenario" the total expenditure of U.S. warheads against China could easily come from the present surplus exceeding the weapons needed for the assured-destruction mission against the U.S.S.R. Not only could the U.S. destroy most of the nascent Chinese nuclear forces, but also it has been estimated that a few warheads detonated over 50 Chinese urban centers would destroy half of the urban population (more than 50 million people), more than half of the industrial capacity and most of the key governmental, technical and managerial personnel. Indeed, against fixed targets such as cities, the U.S. could use its B-52s, which could return to their bases for other missions.

Not only does the U.S. have this multifaceted capability but also its nuclear strategy has always included plans for attacks other than massive ones on Russian cities. This conclusion is logically inescapable when one realizes that the U.S. has had thousands of strategic warheads since the mid-1960s, has about 7,500 now and is expected to have almost 10,000 by 1977. There are only about 200 major cities in the U.S.S.R. Either the U.S. has aimed a superfluously large number of warheads at each major city or it has planned for other targets all along. Any doubts on this score were resolved by Secretary Schlesinger's statement in March that "our war plans have always included military targets."

President Nixon . . . made it very clear from the early days of his Administration that he wanted changes in U.S. strategic policy. Neither he nor any other high official, including Secretary Schlesinger, has ever rejected the assured-destruction concept. Rather they have defined assured destruction narrowly to mean only massive retaliation against cities and have said that more options are needed. To date the Nixon Administration has really presented two different sets of what "more" is needed. First there were the "sufficiency criteria," which were publicized in the period from 1970 to 1972. This past year has seen the emergence of a new set of criteria.

The sufficiency criteria, which President Nixon first hinted at in 1970, were spelled out by Secretary of Defense Melvin R. Laird in 1971. They are:

1. "Maintaining an adequate second-strike capability to deter an all-out surprise attack on our strategic forces."

2. "Providing no incentive for the Soviet Union to strike the United States first in a crisis."

3. "Preventing the Soviet Union from gaining the ability to cause considerably greater urban/industrial destruction than the United States could inflict on the Soviets in a nuclear war."

4. "Defending against damage from small attacks or accidental launches."

These four criteria have been explained further, including the fact that the deterrence is for the benefit of U.S. allies as well as the U.S.

The publication of the sufficiency criteria at least moved the public debate off the misleading view that U.S. policies and forces only envisioned massive retaliation against cities, but beyond that there is little new in the criteria. This is partly because they were never clearly explained; accordingly they remained more Delphic than definitive.

The first criterion is simply a basic statement of the assured-destruction concept. The third is a result of the assured-destruction assumption at meaningful levels of destruction; beyond the ability of either side to inflict 75 million fatalities and between 50 and 75 percent industrial damage—levels that would finish either country as a viable society—relative differences in the ability to inflict urban or industrial damage seem insignificant. Besides, much higher levels of destruction can only be achieved with considerable difficulty, since either country soon reaches a point of rapidly diminishing returns in terms of urban or industrial destruction per additional warhead.

The fourth criterion was clearly justification for the Safeguard ABM system. Without getting into the debate over such issues as whether or not the advantage of damage limitation against small attacks or accidental launches outweighs the disadvantage of the Russians' misinterpreting the purposes of any ABM deployment, suffice it to say that the Administration as early as May 1971, was committed to insignificant ABM levels in the ongoing Strategic Arms Limitation Talks (SALT). The fourth criterion thus became "inoperative."

That leaves the second criterion. It clearly enunciates a desirable objective in strategic policy: to avoid strategic forces or actions that would be destabilizing in a crisis. Although this objective was not explicit before, it was inherent in the assured-destruction objective of providing highly survivable forces that would thereby reduce the incentive for a first strike. The second sufficiency criterion fails to delineate what more, if anything, was needed.

The criteria are silent about the kinds of option other than assured destruction that the President was so concerned about. Moreover, should the U.S. react to protect its allies (still undefined) in the same way that it would to protect its own territory? And what are U.S. strategic objectives with regard to China? In short, except for the flirtation with the ABM possibility, the sufficiency criteria only hinted at new strategic policies rather than establishing them.

Instead of trying to amend the sufficiency criteria, the Administration decided about a year ago simply to scrap them and to start anew in redefining strategic policies. This time Secretary Schlesinger has been the principal spokesman. After some of his press conferences late in 1973 and early in 1974 led to confusion among journalists and other observers as to what the new policies encompassed, the appearance of Schlesinger's annual report in March clarified the issues considerably. At one place in that report the "Principal Features of the Proposed Posture" (a posture Schlesinger clearly likes to refer to as "essential equivalence") are listed:

1. "a capability sufficiently large, diversified, and survivable so that it will provide us at all times with high confidence of riding out even a massive surprise attack and of penetrating enemy defenses, and with the ability to withhold an assured destruction reserve for an extended period of time."

2. "sufficient warning to ensure the survival of our heavy bombers together with the bomb alarm systems and command-control capabilities required by our National Command Authorities to direct the employment of the strategic forces in a controlled, selective, and restrained fashion."

3. "the forces to execute a wide range of options in response to potential actions by an enemy, including a capability for precise attacks on both soft and hard targets, while at the same time minimizing unintended collateral damage."

4. "the avoidance of any combination of forces that could be taken as an effort to acquire the ability to execute a first-strike disarming attack against the U.S.S.R."

5. "an offensive capability of such size and composition that all will perceive it as in overall balance with the strategic forces of any potential opponent."

6. "offensive and defensive capabilities and programs that conform with the provisions of current arms control agreements and at the same time facilitate the conclusion of more permanent treaties to control and, if possible, reduce the main nuclear arsenals."

These factors plus the accompanying text in the report provide the best available insight into the proposed new policies. The first factor, combined with the second's requirement of bomber survivability, constitutes essentially a restatement of the assured-destruction concept. It needs no further elaboration here except to note that assured destruction does not require immediate response; indeed, the emphasis on a "second strike" capability and on the survivability of U.S. forces reflects the goal of having time in which to consider what the appropriate response should be.

Skipping briefly to the fourth, fifth and sixth factors, they raise a host of diverse issues—touching on all offensive and defensive strategic programs. There is not sufficient space to treat them comprehensively here; instead the focus will be on their impact on the Administration's concepts of strategic flexibility and limited nuclear war.

The third factor and the balance of the second address the questions of flexibility and limited strategic war directly. The underlying questions can best be summarized as follows: (1) Should the U.S. have a number of response options? (2) Should the U.S. develop missiles with improved counterforce capabilities? (3) Should the U.S. actively promote the idea of improving counterforce capabilities for fighting, if necessary, a limited nuclear war? Since the first question is essentially noncontroversial, the remaining two define the immediate issues.

Schlesinger reports that most of the targeting options in the past have involved "relatively massive responses." He wants to provide the President with a "wider set of much more selective targeting options." There is general agreement among strategic analysts that the U.S. should have a variety of response options other than massive retaliation against cities. These options could be useful, for example, in deterring a limited strategic attack. As Paul C. Warnke, a former Assistant Secretary of Defense, has put it: "There can . . . be little objection to the concept that our targeting plans should be sufficiently flexible to provide the President with a variety of options in the event of a nuclear attack." Warnke believes "we might be better positioned to deter a less than all-out Soviet attack if we have the refinement of command and

control to push only one or a few buttons rather than the entire console
. . . to respond with less than our Sunday punch."

This broad consensus includes those options that draw on the capabilities of present forces and those already well along in development. As we have seen, our present forces already have the accuracy-yield combinations to be used effectively to destroy almost anything except hard targets. Even against such hard targets as ICBM silos these forces could destroy large numbers of targets, but they would not do it "efficiently."

Schlesinger makes it clear, however, that he wants more than flexibility, that he wants counterforce options that require new or improved weapons. The incremental options are ones "minimizing unintended collateral damage" and providing a hard-target kill capability that "matches" that of the Russians. To be able to achieve these options Schlesinger seeks programs to develop missiles with improved counterforce capabilities.

The proposed defense budget for the fiscal year 1975 includes a number of such programs. The programs appear to fall into two categories.

First, there are the short-term programs, the ones that involve relatively minor changes and for which initial deployment might easily begin by the late 1970s. The major programs in this category include procurement of more Minuteman III missiles; refinement of the existing guidance system of the Minuteman III to increase accuracy (probably from 1,500 feet down to 700 feet or less); a higher-yield warhead for the Minuteman III identical in configuration with the existing warhead, and a general program to improve and measure the accuracy of SLBM's. The proposed budget also includes funds to flight-test a Minuteman III with a larger number of smaller reentry vehicles. Whether this program will increase counterforce capabilities or not depends on the accuracy and yield of the new warheads.

Second, there are two major long-term programs. Both will require considerable development time, and initial deployment would seem unlikely before 1980. Advanced development will be initiated for a terminally guided "maneuverable reentry vehicle" (MARV) for possible "retrofit" into both ICBM's and SLBM's. Although a MARV warhead has been programmed for some time for the advanced Trident I SLBM, it is not to be terminally guided, being designed for evasion of ABM interceptors rather than for improved accuracy. A new terminally guided MARV, however, will presumably have an accuracy of a few hundred feet. This would give even warheads the size of the Poseidon's a very effective hard-target kill capability.

Further research and development is needed to decide exactly how the new MARV will work. By definition, after the MARV has separated from the "bus," or postboost vehicle, that holds all a missile's warheads, it can maneuver almost up to impact in order to correct its flight path. The corrections could be accomplished in two ways. The most likely development is the homing MARV, what some call the true MARV. A sensor in the warhead would acquire an image or images of the target or of prominent terrain features nearby (or perhaps would simply acquire an "altitude profile" of the terrain along its flight path). An on-board matching device would match this information with a map stored in its memory. The warhead's flight path would then be corrected either by gas jets or by aerodynamic vanes.

An alternative approach is to use an inertial guidance system in the warhead as well as in the bus. Since the reentry vehicle often separates from the bus early in its flight, an on-board guidance system would allow much later changes in trajectory. The information on position would come, however, from the system's gyroscopes, from stars or even from satellites and not from the target area itself. As a result this approach in theory would probably not be as accurate as the homing approach.

The second long-term program is the development of an entirely new ICBM for the 1980s. This missile, which may even be an air-mobile missile, would include a new guidance system (presumably a terminally guided MARV), which Schlesinger says would give it "a very good capability against hard targets."

How reasonable or necessary is it to develop missiles with improved counterforce capabilities in order to minimize collateral damage or to match the Russians' hard-target kill capability?

It is particularly difficult to understand how these missiles will minimize collateral damage. The warheads Secretary Schlesinger is proposing will probably have at least the yield of the present Minuteman III and Poseidon warheads. Such warheads would cause extensive damage over a wide area. For example, a "small" 100-kiloton bomb exploding in the air over a target would cause substantial fatalities and damage from immediate effects alone over a circle with a radius of 2.5 miles. Since the possible improvement in accuracy for the Minuteman, for example, is at most about 1,000 feet even in the long run, the number of civilian fatalities will hardly be reduced significantly if a warhead at least three to 11 times the size of the Hiroshima bomb lands a few hundred feet closer to the intended target.

A substantially smaller warhead that still provides an improved hard-target kill capability is unlikely to be ready for deployment until the 1980s, since a very accurate terminally guided MARV is needed to allow a significant "trade-off" between lower yield and higher accuracy. Furthermore, the value of much smaller warheads in saving lives must be put in perspective.

First, the way to minimize fatalities, if nuclear weapons must be used, is careful target selection, in other words aiming at targets distant from urban centers. Air-defense sites or air bases in the Arctic and isolated army posts or industrial sites are good examples. For a very limited exchange the differences in fatality levels from an attack on such targets with warheads of, say, 50 kilotons as against five kilotons would not be significant.

Second, if there is a large-scale nuclear exchange, then there simply is no way of keeping civilian damage at a low level. The effects not only of immediate blast but also of radioactivity would kill millions.

Third, in an actual nuclear exchange the successful continuation of a U.S. policy aimed at minimizing civilian casualties depends in large part on what the Russians do, and the Russians have never seemed much attracted to this objective. Their strategic warheads have always been large. Even though they necessarily reduced the size of individual warheads on their ICBM's in order to deploy MIRV's on them, some if not all of the warheads are still in the megaton range.

Schlesinger's main justification for the new counterforce programs is that the U.S. needs an "efficient" hard-target capability to match that of the U.S.S.R. This seems a questionable refinement of the broader theme of "essential equivalence." Schlesinger has on occasion defined essential equivalence to suggest overall balance. For example, he recently testified: "We do not have to have a match for everything in their arsenal. They do not have to have a match for everything in our arsenal."

Whether or not such an overall balance exists today and for the foreseeable future is a question that deserves public debate; a good case can be made for the affirmative. Most important, both the U.S. and the U.S.S.R. have a high-confidence ability to carry out a wide variety of retaliatory options. In terms of static indicators the Russians do have more missiles and greater missile "throw weight." The U.S., however, has more bombers, more warheads (now and for the rest of the decade) and about equal overall throw weight (if bombers are included in the calculations). In terms of qualitative factors U.S. missile submarines are much quieter and hence harder to find than the Russian ones, and U.S. bombers are more modern. Finally, to maintain or even enhance some of its capabilities, the U.S. already has a number of strategic programs well along: the conversion of older missiles to larger Minuteman III and Poseidon missiles, the B-1 bomber and the Trident submarine with its advanced missiles.

235

Schlesinger, however, avoids the complex question of whether the general U.S.-U.S.S.R. strategic picture is one of overall balance— of essential equivalence. Rather, he selectively focuses on relative counterforce capabilities against ICBM silos. Selective vision is not exactly a new tactic in military analysis. The "missile gap" of 1960 is a classic case; the heated debate over the number of U.S. ICBM's compared with the number of Russian ICBM's ignored the massive U.S. bomber force. Schlesinger's selective vision is even blurred within its own field. Although the Russians are clearly developing new missiles and MIRV's, they apparently have not pursued the accuracy aspect of a counterforce strategy with much zeal. As General George S. Brown, the chief of staff of the Air Force, recently remarked about the new Russian programs, "MIRVing alone won't [take out the Minuteman force]. Accuracy is the other key element and we haven't seen evidence of accuracy improvement in their work which we would expect to see."

Is there some reason why the U.S. and the U.S.S.R. should have essential equivalence in the capability to destroy missile silos? The arguments against this course of action seem persuasive. There is no benefit in terms of traditional strategic analysis in being able to kill efficiently very large numbers of the other side's silos. As we have established, the U.S. can already destroy some silos, although at a cost of a few U.S. missiles each. Inefficient, limited destruction of silos should suffice for the war scenarios that some envision, in which the U.S. feels it necessary to destroy silos as a way of showing its "resolve." Killing many more silos would not minimize damage to the U.S.; everyone agrees that the U.S. cannot expect to destroy a large enough fraction of the silos or other strategic offensive forces of the U.S.S.R. to limit damage to this country in any meaningful way.

Finally, a critical assumption underlying the preceding discussion is that the silos will have missiles in them when they are destroyed. In fact, the flight time of a Minuteman missile to the Russian missile fields is about 30 minutes. If the Russians were to deploy early-warning satellites, they could detect almost instantaneously the launch of U.S. missiles, which means that the U.S.S.R. could probably have the option of launching many, if not all, of its missiles before the U.S. warheads arrived. Using U.S. warheads against empty silos in empty fields seems a particularly questionable policy.

The full cost of these new programs is unclear. Much depends on the size of the deployments and the extensiveness of the modifications. A useful bench mark is the Minuteman III program; the conversion of 550 older Minuteman missiles into Minuteman III's will cost between $5 billion and $6 billion. Although the costs of some of the new counterforce programs might be comparatively small, the total cost of all the new programs would greatly exceed the Minuteman III costs.

Added to the questions about the analytical reason for the new counterforce programs and the inevitable costs must be the distinct possibility that these programs will be destabilizing and will make arms limitations more difficult to negotiate.

Assuming a crisis situation, a substantial U.S. counterforce capability against Russian ICBM's is more likely to create an incentive for the U.S.S.R. to adopt a hair-trigger, launch-on-warning posture; the Russian leadership would fear that the U.S. might attack first in an attempt to limit damage to itself. These fears would make it even more likely for the U.S.S.R. to attack first in a crisis in order to destroy some of the U.S. ICBM's that had become more tempting targets as a result of the new U.S. counterforce programs.

Schlesinger deplores this instability (as in his fourth feature, cited above, of the new posture), but he and other high officials say that the new U.S. programs are not extensive enough to create such Russian fears. The conceivable accuracy and yield improvements on 1,000 Minuteman missiles, however, even without the terminally guided MARV, could give the U.S. the capability, on paper at least, of destroying between 80 and 90 percent of the Russian ICBM force. The deployment of the MARV or the use of improved SLBM's against the Russian missiles would push that percentage even higher.

The Russian leadership, moreover, might be more conservative than the U.S. leadership in assessing Russian strengths and weaknesses. This conservatism would be based at least partly on the fact that, unlike the balanced reliance in the U.S. on all three elements of the strategic triad, in the U.S.S.R. ICBM's are the primary component of the strategic offensive forces. The U.S.S.R. is allowed up to 1,618 ICBM's under the SALT I Interim Agreement (compared with 1,054 for the U.S.), and the Russians are actively developing four new ICBM's. Moreover, these missiles are under the command of the Strategic Rocket Forces, which since it was created in about 1960 has been one of the most important branches, if not the most important one, of the Russian military. Unlike the U.S. Air Force, which has responsibility not only for ICBM's but also for bombers and many tactical forces, the primary responsibility of the Strategic Rocket Forces is the Russian ICBM force; consequently this organization has every incentive to enhance its role in strategic planning. The Long Range Aviation command, which has responsibility for the Russian bombers, has never had the bureaucratic strength of the Strategic Rocket Forces, and the Russian navy has responsibility for a number of other forces besides missile submarines.

The strategic-planning emphases of the U.S. and the U.S.S.R. differ particularly on the subject of bombers. At present the U.S. has more
than 450 intercontinental bombers, about a fourth of which are kept on
"ready alert" at a large number of air bases (so that they can avoid
being destroyed even in case of surprise attack). The Russians have
about 140 long-range bombers. These are qualitatively inferior even to
the B-36 bombers deployed by the U.S. in the 1950s, are not kept at as
high readiness and are located at just a few air bases. Although a new
Russian bomber (named the Backfire by the Pentagon) is just beginning production, it seems primarily intended for targets on the periphery of the U.S.S.R. In any case it is not certain how many Backfires will
be built, and the plane appears to lack the critical range and low-
altitude capabilities of the B-52s.

As for SLBM's, the U.S.S.R. is building new missile submarines
and is allowed more boats and SLBM's than the U.S. under the terms
of the SALT agreements. In contrast to the active U.S. MIRV programs
for both ICBM's and SLBM's and the new Russian MIRV programs
for ICBM's, however, the Russians have not begun testing multiple
warheads on their new SLBM. The U.S.S.R., moreover, usually keeps
only five or six missile submarines on patrol at any one time, compared
with 40 percent of the 41 U.S. boats. In sum, the U.S.S.R. does not
seem to give missile submarines the same priority in strategic planning
as the U.S.

Schlesinger essentially hinges his denial that first-strike fears by
the U.S.S.R. would be enhanced by the planned U.S. improvement in
its capabilities against ICBM's on the relative invulnerability of the
Russian missile submarines. Compared with the U.S. missile submarines, however, the Russian boats are noisier—an important qualitative disadvantage—and must operate in ocean areas where it is
easier for the U.S. to locate and detect them. In addition the U.S. has
under way a large, aggressive antisubmarine-warfare program for tactical and strategic uses. It has been reliably estimated that U.S. expenditures in the fiscal year 1972 for antisubmarine warfare were $2.5
billion and that by 1974 they would rise to more than $4 billion. The
Russian leaders might well fear, at some future crisis point, that the
U.S. had developed a significant antisubmarine-warfare capability,
making Schlesinger's suggested ultimate reliance on their missile
submarines less than completely reassuring.

One "crisis scenario" that is often concocted to show the danger of
the growing Russian counterforce capability against Minuteman and to
justify developing improved U.S. counterforce capabilities is an attack
or threat of attack by the U.S.S.R. against U.S. ICBM's. The scenario
envisions the following chain of events: (1) a real or threatened Russian

238

attack against Minuteman; (2) a realization by the U.S. leadership that it is left or will be left with no more than a capacity to attack Russian cities; (3) major concessions or even surrender by the U.S.

This scenario has an obviously fantastic quality. Even if the internal logic of the scenario were accepted, it still does not justify improving U.S. counterforce capabilities. It does not matter whether the U.S. missiles destroyed are highly accurate or not. What matters is what other U.S. forces can do if these missiles are destroyed. Indeed, as we have seen, by presenting an increased threat to the U.S.S.R., U.S. development of highly accurate missiles might actually make the Russians more likely to attack, thus making the scenario less implausible.

More important, the underlying logic of the scenario is simply wrong, as should be evident to both the U.S. and the Russian leadership. First, the Russians would have to consider that Minuteman might be launched against Russian targets in the 30-minute warning time between the launch of the Russian ICBM's and their arrival at the Minuteman silos. Second, even if a surprised or reasonably cautious U.S. leadership did not launch on warning, a few Minutemen would survive even the most careful attack. Also surviving would be at least the bombers on alert and most if not all of the U.S. missile submarines in the water. (If the attack occurred after an initial crisis period, more bombers than usual would be on alert and more submarines would be in the water.) These combined forces would provide the U.S. with the capacity to carry out a number of limited strikes while still retaining an assured-destruction hedge.

Finally, some U.S. retaliation would seem very likely to the Russian leadership since tens of millions of Americans would be killed in any "Minuteman only" attack. In attacks against silos the bombs are set to explode as close to the ground as possible, thereby picking up much dirt and debris. The fallout from the explosion of thousands of megatons of nuclear weapons over the Minuteman fields would be tremendous, and winds would carry the lethal contamination over many major U.S. cities. Such calculations of fallout do not even include the possibility of a few Russian warheads going off course and directly hitting populated areas, nor the collateral damage by Russian attacks against other targets, such as bomber bases, many of which are near cities.

Even not assuming a crisis, the consequence of these new U.S. counterforce developments might be to push the U.S.S.R. toward accelerating or expanding existing programs, or starting new ones. The arms race is not as mechanically "action-reaction" as some have suggested, but a substantial new U.S. capability against the primary strategic offensive force of the U.S.S.R. will surely fuel justifications within the Russian bureaucracy for some kind of reaction. This should be particularly true when U.S. antisubmarine-warfare programs, noted above, are also considered.

If the U.S. counterforce programs are allowed to continue beyond the rhetoric of announcing them, these programs would operate to undercut any progress at SALT. Of course, if announcing these programs is just a short-term ploy designed to strengthen the U.S. bargaining position for the impending SALT II agreements, then little real harm will result. There is no evidence, however, that top Administration officials intend to turn these programs off quickly. And even if there are such intentions, new weapons programs tend to gain a momentum of their own once they are announced. High-level officials become publicly committed to rationales for them, rationales that include more than the systems' just being "bargaining chips." Bureaucracies are created with a vested interest in the continuation and expansion of these programs. Moreover, improvements in accuracy and yield would be particularly difficult to limit explicitly in SALT, making it harder to rationalize publicly any subsequent termination of the program.

Accuracy improvements are generally accepted as being among the most difficult weapons characteristics to limit in an arms-control agreement, because of problems of both definition and verification. Drafting a workable, direct limit on accuracy seems impossible, since the counterforce potential of a warhead depends on the accuracy-yield combination. Moreover, a simple numerical limit on accuracy would not be verifiable. A photograph of a silo or even the missile gives little clue to the kind of small but important differences in accuracy that are being considered here. Closer examination through on-site inspection, even if such inspection could be negotiated, would be insufficient. On-site inspection could indicate whether the warhead was a terminally guided MARV, but this would not establish any particular accuracy. Moreover, on-site inspection includes a heroic assumption that the latest warheads are on the missile and not stored nearby in an area excluded from the on-site inspection provisions.

Surveillance of Russian missile testing may give some indication of accuracy. The indication, however, is indirect and not conclusive. Test data tell one about the ballistic coefficient (or pointedness) of the warhead, its reentry speed and similar information, all of which helps in estimating accuracy. An outside observer, however, can never be sure what the actual target is. Similarly, course corrections by the warhead would indicate a maneuvering capability but not necessarily terminal guidance or particularly high accuracies.

An indirect way to limit or impede accuracy improvements

through SALT would be by placing a strict limit on the number of missile tests. This would make it more difficult to develop advanced guidance techniques and to test them often enough so that the military would have confidence in them. The low limits necessary seem non-negotiable, however, since they represent a direct challenge to all new strategic programs. Even without accuracy improvements the Pentagon will want to do extensive research and development and operational testing of the new Trident missile and further operational testing of the Minuteman and Poseidon missiles. Similarly, the Russians will want to flight-test extensively their four new ICBM's and their new SLBM as well as their existing arsenal of missiles.

Limits in SALT on the yield of warheads might be more possible, but they would be of uncertain significance. The two sides could limit yield by an agreement that warheads not be larger than a given yield or a given weight. The effect of any such limitation could be circumvented, however, by increasing the number of warheads and by inceasing their accuracy. Moreover, it would be difficult to verify the exact yield of a warhead. Even elaborate on-site inspection would not ensure that "advanced" warheads were not hidden nearby. Surveillance of flight tests only gives an estimate of the size of the warhead, and yield per pound of warhead can be varied by warhead design and the richness of the nuclear "fuel" used.

In short, the practical difficulties of fashioning limitations in SALT on the type of counterforce improvements now planned by the U.S. make such limitations unlikely and will instead presumably create strong pressures in the U.S.S.R. to expand old programs or to start new ones that either match or compensate for the U.S. programs. This in turn can only work against other limitations on strategic arms.

Allied concerns about the credibility of the U.S. deterrent are another reason offered for developing missiles with improved counterforce capabilities. Occasionally a specific scenario—a Russian attack in central Europe—is given as a justification for such improvements. Neither the scenario nor the more general invocation of allied claims is persuasive.

The European scenario supposedly demonstrates that the U.S. needs the ability to respond with nuclear weapons in order to show its resolve and to destroy some of the attacking Russian forces. There are, however, already sizable U.S. forces in Europe that could accomplish both of those objectives. Even if the U.S. decided to employ strategic weapons, existing U.S. forces could carry out a wide variety of selective attacks.

As for the broader claims of allied concerns, Morton Halperin, an authority on nuclear strategy, has remarked:

241

The credibility of the U.S. deterrent to an Ally is primarily a result of the overall U.S.-Ally relationship, which includes economic and political considerations as well as military. To the extent that Allied leaders evaluate U.S. military capabilities, they look especially to the U.S. conventional and nuclear forces in that particular theater of operations. Fine distinctions in the U.S.-Soviet strategic balance or in U.S. strategic policy are unimportant to Allied leaders. Among those Allied analysts who care, opinion is probably split between those who favor the U.S. possessing an efficient silo-kill capability and those who do not.

Among the European strategic analysts who oppose such deployments is Ian Smart, formerly assistant director of the London-based International Institute of Strategic Studies. Smart writes: "Producing and deploying much more accurate strategic missiles . . . is to be regretted and even feared since . . . it can only reduce the stability of the strategic balance in any period of acute tension." At least part of this European concern can be attributed to the fact that, in a strategic exchange, the industrialized European countries are very likely targets—if only because of the U.S. forces deployed in or near those countries.

Finally, even assuming that the allies (or even the American people) accord considerable political significance to fine distinctions in the "strategic balance," Schlesinger's proposed counterforce improvements are not very helpful politics. The supposedly important distinctions are usually visible ones such as the number of delivery vehicles, the number of warheads or the throw weight. Schlesinger's accuracy and yield improvements do not affect these indicators, except possibly in the counterproductive way of reducing the number of warheads in order to allow larger ones.

On balance, then, there seem to be strong arguments against developing missiles with improved counterforce capabilities. Collateral damage can best be minimized by shifting targets, not improving accuracies by a few hundred feet. The ability to destroy efficiently large numbers of missile silos in order to "match the Russians" seems not only unnecessary and expensive but also destabilizing. SALT might well be undercut, and the supposed concerns of our allies about the U.S. deterrent are not answered by such programs.

As one gets caught up in considering nuclear-war scenarios and nuclear-weapons capabilities there is a dangerous tendency to forget that the primary objective of nuclear strategy is to avoid nuclear wars, not to fight them.

Given the destructive power of nuclear weapons and the world's lack of experience in using them, crossing the "nuclear threshold" would be a profoundly destabilizing event. It is a delusion to believe one country could employ nuclear weapons, even on a limited scale, and have a high degree of confidence that the response by another nuclear power would be predictable and proportionate. The particular first use might be estimated by the opposing country's observers to be greater than it actually was, or the use might have created more damage than expected (for example through greater-than-expected fallout). The opposing country might not have readily available weapons of the same yield or similar targeting options and decide to escalate. The political reaction in the opposing country might lead to escalation. In short, the possible causes for matters getting out of hand are endless.

To make deterrence work, a country must carefully consider its public attitude toward nuclear war and cautiously select its retaliatory options. This does not mean that the U.S. should have only the single strategic option of massive retaliation against cities. This country already has ample capabilities for lesser options, and it seems appropriate to have the flexibility, at a minimum, for possible responses to accidental or limited launches.

The Nixon Administration, however, is going beyond this. It is seeking the additional capability to attack efficiently large numbers of Russian missile silos. Not only might this counterforce option be destabilizing in itself but also the Administration's promotion of the option and its general public advocacy of a counterforce strategy might have a pervasive, if subtle, tendency to reduce the inhibitions against the use of nuclear weapons—in effect, to lower the "nuclear threshold." New bureaucracies, with vested interests in the hardware and rationales of a counterforce strategy, are created. In trying to gain public approval of new policies and programs, leaders find themselves taking more simplistic positions than the uncertainty of nuclear warfare warrants. In this climate some of the risks of nuclear war are downplayed. Unrealistically precise calculations suggest that limited nuclear war can be kept limited and even result in positive gains.

There are some disturbing parallels here to the vogue of limited conventional war in the early 1960s. In pushing for changes in conventional strategy and new procurement, advocates of limited conventional war ignored some of the pitfalls and costs of such a strategy. The searing national experience of the war in Vietnam was needed to demonstrate these oversights.

Exactly where the line should be drawn on "selective targeting options" is not at all clear. It seems most inadvisable, however, to take the gamble of developing missiles with improved counterforce capabilities, whether this is to match a specific Russian capability or for any other reason.

Opponents of U.S. counterforce improvements, nonetheless, must recognize certain practical limits to their arguments. Even if Congress declines to fund the new and accelerated development programs Schlesinger is proposing, continued U.S. testing of strategic missiles and various research-and-development efforts already under way inevitably will lead to some improvements in missile accuracy. (As Schlesinger has pointed out, some refinements in existing guidance systems will occur almost as a matter of course—through better software, programs, greater purity in rocket fuel, better measurement of the earth's gravitational field and numerous other factors. The development of a terminally guided MARV, something further beyond the state of the art, requires more of a conscious bureaucratic decision to proceed.) Besides U.S. advances, moreover, Russian counterforce improvements are likely to continue, raising serious questions about Russian intentions.

Faced with these likely developments, the solution is still not to follow the Schlesinger approach. Rather, the solution should be to seek actively to negotiate for limits on MIRV's and for the reduction of vulnerable strategic forces.

Limits on MIRV's would be designed to slow the perceived threat to U.S. ICBM's, a Russian threat that many consider destabilizing. In return for the U.S. slowing certain of its strategic programs, for example, the U.S.S.R. might agree to limits on the deployment of the SSX-18, the "follow on" missile to the large SS-9. This would push at least a few years further into the future the time when analysts would estimate that only a particular level of Minuteman could survive a Russian counterforce attack.

Negotiating missile reductions represents another approach: to limit not only the threatening forces but also the threatened ones. This approach would essentially mean bilateral reductions in ICBM's, presumably in a way that would retire the more threatening ICBM's, so that the remaining ICBM's would be less vulnerable. Some asymmetrical reductions might also be considered. For instance, the U.S. could reduce its ICBM's, whereas the U.S.S.R. (having less to fear in the short run about the vulnerability of its ICBM's) could reduce some ICBM's plus other forces.

Reductions in the land-based missiles of both sides would reduce the importance of this strategic strike force. It would thereby undercut the rationale for an expensive contest of matching counterforce improvements. More important, it would reduce the greatest potential source of instability in a crisis. Both countries would have less incentive to adopt an unstable, launch-on-warning posture or to launch an attack out of fear of a preemptive strike.

The reductions approach has received support recently from such diverse sources as the Federation of American Scientists and Fred C. Iklé, director of the Arms Control and Disarmament Agency. It was even accorded the status of a possibility in Schlesinger's recent annual report.

Rather than focusing on how to match the U.S.S.R. in a particular. capability when such matching does not bode well for either country, the strategic debate in the U.S. . . . should focus on MIRV limits, force reductions and other measures designed to minimize the chances of nuclear war and to decelerate the arms race.

5

THE ROLE OF NUCLEAR WEAPONS IN THE PURSUIT OF NATIONAL OBJECTIVES

Although deterrence of nuclear attack continues to be the primary objective of America's nuclear arsenal, much of the current policy debate has centered on questions pertaining to the contribution of nuclear weapons to the achievement of national objectives. The role these weapons can play in periods of acute crisis and military conflict has attracted particular interest, as exemplified by the controversy surrounding the degree to which U.S. silo-based ICBMs are vulnerable to destruction by their Soviet counterparts, and whether the U.S. should adopt mobile ICBMs such as MX. Additional views on this subject can be found in the articles of Paul H. Nitze ("Assuring Strategic Stability") and Jan M. Lodal ("Assuring Strategic Stability: An Alternate View") reprinted from *Foreign Affairs* in Robert J. Pranger, ed., *Détente and Defense: A Reader*, American Enterprise Institute, 1976.

STRATEGIC VULNERABILITY: THE BALANCE BETWEEN PRUDENCE AND PARANOIA

John D. Steinbruner and Thomas M. Garwin

One of the issues most often debated in recent years is that of the vulnerability of silo-based ICBMs. Not only will the outcome of this debate have profound implications for strategic force postures through the end of this century, but similar implications will also determine the course of the Strategic Arms Limitation Talks.

Source: *International Security*, vol. 1, no. 1 (Summer 1976), pp. 138-70.
Editors' Note: The appendixes to this article, detailing technical aspects of the computer modeling employed by the authors, are not included in this volume.

Much has been written on both sides of this issue, and it is the thesis of the authors of the following article that a good deal of the debate has failed to recognize the uncertainties inherent in any calculus of ICBM vulnerability. Steinbruner and Garwin attempt to rectify this neglect by focusing on three factors which affect the operation of ICBMs and which are excluded from most calculations of missile performance and effectiveness. While it is not at all certain that our Minuteman missiles are vulnerable under standard calculations, the inclusion of these three factors in the calculus provides further evidence that any adversary contemplating a first strike would have little assurance of success. The authors conclude that the Soviet Union will not be in a position to threaten our Minuteman force with any confidence for some time to come, and that our attention could be more profitably focused on the vulnerability of the command, control, and communication systems necessary to maintain political control over strategic nuclear forces.

Among its many consequences, the basic agreement on strategic arms limitations announced at the Vladivostok summit in November 1974 seems destined to energize a long simmering debate over the vulnerability of the land-based missile component of the United States strategic forces. The decidedly permissive limit on multiple-warhead missiles, tentatively set at 1,320, means that each side will be able to allocate a relatively large number of separately directed warheads to each of the opponents' land-based installations. Since controls are imposed on current missile installations and since the Soviets have built larger silos for missiles with greater payload, they will be able to build a force with six or more warheads targeted on each silo in the American force—if they match American warhead technology and if they strain the limits of the agreement. Trends in accuracy and yield-to-weight efficiency are such that a force of this size according to standard, widely accepted calculations would appear to give the Soviets a decisive first strike advantage against one component of the United States' strategic forces—the one which contains most of our capacity for flexible nuclear retaliation. It has been authoritatively asserted and seems to be widely believed that such an apparent advantage would translate into diffuse but significant political advantages across the many international issues in which the two countries are involved.

There have been many attempts to deal with this issue of ICBM vulnerability by summary arguments designed to remove the problem a priori. Many have pointed out, for example, that strategic missile submarines remain invulnerable to a swiftly executed preemptive at-

248

tack, and they have argued that devastating retaliation from the United States submarines (or submarines and bombers in combination) would be so certain as to render a first strike completely irrational and therefore as unlikely as any deterrent policy can make it. Others have noted that various detection systems allow the United States to observe Soviet missile launchings and to plot their trajectories, and they have argued that this capability allows the United States to fire its land-based missiles after an attack on them has been launched but before the damage has been accomplished. Again the proposition is that any potential attacker would have to consider that we might launch a retaliatory attack on the basis of the unambiguous warning accompanying a massive first strike and that this realization would deter any government whose actions are at all determined by reason.

Of course, to these arguments there are summary rejoinders which have been offered by those who remain concerned with ICBM vulnerability. Submarines, some argue, may be far more vulnerable to sabotage than to direct attack; this possibility is difficult to evaluate and therefore difficult to eliminate. Similarly, the launch-on-warning tactic can be said to endanger crisis stability, and the systems which provide rapid warning are themselves vulnerable to attack. Some feel, moreover, that once he had calculated that war was unavoidable, a strategic opponent might disregard the possibility of launch-on-warning and, given adequate offensive capacity, might find it rational to preempt against a powerful but vulnerable force. For these reasons, it is argued that the vulnerable force would be destabilizing in a serious crisis since decisions as to whether war is avoidable would be affected by perceptions of vulnerability. Finally, many believe that the political effects of putative vulnerability are not proportionately diminished by low probability of an actual attack.

The issue of strategic force vulnerability has resisted resolution by means of summary arguments of this sort, in part because the arguments remain inconclusive, but far more because the roots of the issue go much deeper. Military preparedness, for example, has long been an important and at times explosive theme in American politics—an issue on which elections can be lost and careers can be ruined. Despite widespread disillusionment with the performance of the military over the past decade, the projection of American power abroad still has strong political resonance—particularly given the current importance and instability of the Middle East. As a result decision makers tend to be extremely cautious about allowing any apparent disadvantage to rise, and their caution one suspects is not so much intellectually as politically derived. In addition, pressure is being generated by the very large organizations which have been created to develop, to manufacture, and to operate the missiles in question. The ultimate disposition of the large investment which the United States has made in fixed land-based installations inevitably involves both jobs and profits in the aerospace industry as well as the status of major military commands. Vested interests and developing conflicts among these underlying forces powerfully affect the issues of arms control and defense management, and summary arguments are not penetrating enough to provide adequate guidance for the decisions which must be made.

But the problem is not simply one of political pressures and organizational momentum overwhelming clear thinking. The issue has deep intellectual roots as well, involving genuine difficulties in the fundamental conceptual structure of American defense policy. Fears about vulnerability of the land-based missile force are inherent in long established assumptions and habits of mind, derived from the theory of rational deterrence, which affect analysis of virtually all the major questions of defense policy; and it is at this level of fundamental assumption that the core problem regarding vulnerability is to be found. The conclusions reached about strategic vulnerability as well as other major force posture issues are substantially determined by the framework of assumptions applied, and the resulting analysis has unavoidably been the basis for attempts to exercise intelligent policy direction over the complex and recalcitrant process of weapons development and deployment.

Believing that well-established assumptions which determine major policy judgments cannot be shaken by a few bold strokes of the pen, we pursue in the discussion which follows some intricate details of the vulnerability problem. We do so in pursuit of broad purposes, however, which can be summarized by a few propositions: notably, that the beginning of wisdom on this issue is to be found in realization of the inevitability of ignorance and in acceptance of its consequences; that on the basis of technical information available—at whatever level of privileged access—calculations of vulnerability are indeterminate; that categorical assertions about vulnerability, which are frequently found in current political discourse, rest upon tacit assumptions more than technical fact; and, that the usual assumptions are not the only ones which ought to be made. More succinctly stated, vulnerability of the land-based missile forces, to paraphrase Wolfgang Panofsky,[1] is far more a state of mind than a physical condition; but, nevertheless, it is an extremely important state of mind, worthy of the most exacting analysis.

---

[1]W. K. H. Panofsky, "Roots of the Strategic Arms Race: Ambiguity and Ignorance," *Bulletin of the Atomic Scientists*, June 1971, p. 18.

The Conservative Basis of Strategic Analysis

The destructive energy of thermonuclear weapons is so great that scientific investigation of their characteristics must be severely constrained. Even before international agreements imposed controls, nuclear weapons could be tested only under conditions of strict security and physical isolation, and this has always limited quite directly the number of phenomena which could be investigated. Though weapons tests have provided a great deal of knowledge about the design of individual weapons and their basic physical effects, there are many critical features of the vulnerability problem which never have been and, one hopes, never will be subjected to either controlled experimentation or operational experience. Most notably no one has measured or experienced the effects of a large number of closely timed nuclear explosions on a United States missile base. Indeed there never has been and, one hopes, never will be any concentrated series of explosions even remotely approaching the requirements of full counterforce attacks.

Constraints apply as well to the testing of missile delivery systems. Intercontinental range missiles are so expensive, politically provocative, and inherently dangerous that there is much about their operation which we cannot learn by experiment or experience. The United States has never fired an intercontinental range missile at a target in the Soviet Union, has never exploded a nuclear warhead at the end of an intercontinental missile flight, has never fired a strategic missile on 15 minutes warning from an operational silo randomly chosen, and has never fired more than a very few missiles simultaneously or in close coordination. As far as can be known from the public record the Soviet test program has been similarly restricted.

As a result of these altogether desirable restrictions, calculations about overall force performance under actual combat conditions must be projected from data on single components under highly unrepresentative test conditions. What must be projected, moreover, is the overall technical performance of a missile force *the first time it is used*—not the performance which might result after many iterations. It seems obvious and compelling that technical estimates generated by such means must be treated as extremely uncertain and must be bounded by appropriately wide confidence intervals.

In line with the familiar logic of deterrence,[2] however, and with normal human tendencies to hedge against the worst, defense

[2] See J. Steinbruner, "Beyond Rational Deterrence: The Struggle for New Conceptions," *World Politics*, January 1976, pp. 223-45, for a discussion of the relationship between deterrence doctrine and force planning.

planners in the United States have focused almost entirely on the unfavorable extreme of the imagined distribution of Soviet strategic force performance. Believing the Soviet Union to be at least potentially malevolent, strategic planners have labored to estimate the worst damage that the Soviet forces might do on first strike; and it has become a major principle of force planning that the size and operational characteristics of the United States strategic nuclear forces ought to enable us to absorb a virtually flawless Soviet attack and still to exert massive destruction in retaliation. Although the intelligence services do make estimates of Soviet technical capabilities, it seems quite clear that conceptions of the worst attack we might encounter are very powerfully influenced by the best technical performance of United States missiles and warheads under test conditions, and even by the best performance *projected* for future American systems under such conditions.

The apparent vulnerability of the United States strategic forces is a consequence of this principle of conservative force planning and of the test procedures which provide the only empirical data available. If the best technical performance is projected for an entire Soviet force, modernized to the limits allowed by the Vladivostok guidelines, then the United States Minuteman and Titan II missiles (if not launched before destruction) could be reduced to a very few or theoretically eliminated by a massive Soviet attack which still held in reserve ample residual capacity to destroy the major American cities. Such a conclusion seems to follow from calculations of the type long familiar in the literature on strategic problems.

Conventional Calculations of ICBM Vulnerability

In the standard calculations used in public discussions, the strategic force balance is determined by a few parameters pertaining to components of the opposing forces—the number, accuracy and yield of attacking warheads, and the number and hardness of the targets being attacked. Using simple equations or readily available calculating aids, one derives from such data the probability of a given silo being destroyed by the attacking force, and this probability is then taken as the best estimate of the percentage of the overall force that would be destroyed. Such calculations allow assessments of the strategic balance to be done by hand on the back of the proverbial envelope and they do capture much of what is solidly known about the effects of nuclear weapons.[3]

---

[3]The standard calculations are presented in some detail by Lynn Davis and Warner Schilling, "All You Ever Wanted To Know About MIRV and ICBM Calculations But Were

The strategic balance as it is understood by the conventional calculations can be conveniently summarized by using the parameter, $NY^{2/3}/(CEP)^2$, where N is the number of warheads independently aimed, Y is the yield of the warheads expressed in megatons, and CEP (circular error probable) is the conventional measure of accuracy expressed in nautical miles.[4] This expression contains that part of the standard formula for probability of damage which concerns the properties of offensive missiles and thus is a convenient way of summarizing results obtained from standard calculating aids such as the Bomb Damage Effect Computer published by the Rand Corporation. It also has been a major justification for the concern for missile throw-weight as a strategic measure.[5]

Table 1 presents data on United States and Soviet forces essentially as they stood at the time the Vladivostok guidelines were first announced in late 1974. It includes published estimates of the yields and accuracies of the various missile systems. Since the table doubtless reflects some inaccuracies in the public record it should not be burdened with fine discriminations. Nonetheless, it does suggest that both military establishments had ample offensive capacity to carry out the assured destruction threat,[6] and that if either side had an advan-

---

Not Cleared To Ask," *Journal of Conflict Resolution,* vol. 17, no. 2 (June 1973), pp. 207-42. Vulnerability estimates done by the Defense Department for its own planning purposes use somewhat more complex calculations of silo hardness which are derived from data on pulse duration and dynamic overpressures and which take into account idiosyncratic characteristics of individual targets. Since critical elements of this analysis remain classified, however, and underlying assumptions therefore cannot be explicitly examined, we prefer not to use it. Moreover, an examination of the unclassified portions of the Defense Intelligence Agency's *Physical Vulnerability Handbook—Nuclear Weapons* (U) (AP550-1-2-60-INT) and its *Mathematical Background and Programming Aids for the Physical Vulnerability System . . .* (DI-550-27-74) indicates that the conventional calculations summarized by Davis and Schilling are more conservative than the DIA method of calculation—that is, the conventional calculations produce *smaller* estimates of the number of surviving silos. . . .

[4] The parameter, recently used by Kosta Tsipis in his widely noted (and widely debated) pamphlet, *Offensive Missiles,* Stockholm paper No. 5 (Stockholm: Stockholm International Peace Research Institute, 1975), has raised a great deal of controversy. It is true that some values of the parameter would be very misleading—e.g., a force with 50 warheads and a parameter value of 1,000 per warhead clearly would not be more threatening than a force of 1,500 warheads with a value of 30 per warhead. If warhead per target ratios are above unity, however, if reliability is ignored, and if the parameter is not extended to extreme values, then it provides a convenient summary of offensive capability for a large number of possible accuracy and yield combinations.

[5] See, for example, the appendix to "A Summary Study of Strategic Offensive and Defensive Forces for the U.S. and U.S.S.R.," prepared for the Director of Defense Research and Engineering, September 8, 1964; declassified on December 31, 1972.

[6] A level of 400 equivalent megatons (EMT $= NY^{2/3}$) is sufficient to destroy more than half the industrial floor space of either society and 1,000 EMT is well into the area of very sharply diminishing marginal effects of an attack on either side. See Alain Enthoven and K. Wayne Smith, *How Much is Enough: Shaping the Defense Program 1961-1969* (New York: Harper & Row, 1972), p. 207.

Table 1
UNITED STATES AND SOVIET FORCE COMPARISONS

Missile System	Number in Inventory	Warheads per Missile	CEP (n. mi.)	Yield (Mt)	$NY^{2/3}$ $(CEP)^2$ (to nearest 50)
U.S.					
Minuteman III	550	3	.2	.17	12,650
Minuteman II	450	1	.3	1	5,000
Titan II	54	1	.5	5	650
Poseidon	496	10	.3	.04	6,450
Polaris	160	1	.7	.6	250
Total US Missile Forces	1,710				25,000
U.S.S.R.					
SS-9	288	1	.7	25	5,050
SS-11	1,010	1	1	1	1,000
SS-13	60	1	.7	1	100
SS-8	109	1	1.5	5	150
SS-7	100	1	2	5	50
SS-N-6	528	1	1.5	1	250
SS-N-8	180	1	.8	1	300
Total 2nd and 3rd Generation Soviet Missile Forces	2,275				6,900

Source: Congressman Robert L. Leggett, "Two Legs Do Not a Centipede Make," *Armed Forces Journal International*, February 1975, p. 30.

tage it was the United States because of greater accuracy and more rapid deployment of MIRV systems. Table 2, which again reflects guesses inspired by the public record, suggests that neither side, as of the Vladivostok announcement, had sufficient offensive capability to destroy as much as 90 percent of the opponent's land-based force on a first strike.[7] A value of 52,350 on the summary parameter would be required to achieve 90 percent destruction of the United States missile forces whereas the value for the total Soviet missile forces was only [6,900; see Table 1]. Uncertainty about hardness makes the calculation more difficult for the Soviet Union; but, if we accept the higher estimate—as an attacker would have to do—43,450 would be required

[7] Note that it is entirely possible that actual Soviet silo hardness exceeds even the higher estimates of Table 2.

254

Table 2
ESTIMATED UNITED STATES AND SOVIET LAND-BASED FORCE VULNERABILITIES UNDER CONVENTIONAL CALCULATIONS

Missile System	Number in Inventory	System Hardness (PSI)	$NY^{2/3}$ $(CEP)^2$ (to nearest 50) required for:		
			$P_k=.9$	$P_k=.97$	$P_k=.99$
U.S.					
Minuteman III	550	1,000	28,150	42,850	56,250
Minuteman II	450	1,000	23,050	35,050	46,050
Titan II	54	300	1,150	1,750	2,300
Total Force	1,054		52,350	79,650	104,600
U.S.S.R. (Lower estimate)					
	140	(soft)	200	200	200
	1,000	1,000	9,300	14,200	18,600
	427	300	9,150	13,900	18,300
	1,567		18,650	28,300	37,150
U.S.S.R. (Higher estimate)					
	140	(soft)	200	200	200
	1,000	300	21,400	32,600	42,900
	427	1,000	21,850	33,250	43,700
	1,567		43,450	66,050	86,800

Source: *IISS Strategic Survey*, 1974, p. 50; Davis and Schilling, *All You Ever Wanted to Know*, p. 234f; SIPRI, Stockholm report #5, *Offensive Missiles*, p. 21.

for even the very lax 90 percent criterion while the United States offered only 25,000.

But what about projected vulnerability? What if the Soviet Union proceeds to use its payload advantage to deploy large numbers of independently targetable warheads each of which operates with the accuracy and yield efficiency which our own forces expect to be able to achieve under test conditions? Using official estimates of the force loadings and relative payload of the fourth generation of Soviet missiles now being deployed,[8] Table 3 projects aggregate characteristics of

[8] See, for example, *Report on United States Military Posture for 1975* by Admiral Thomas H. Moorer, USN, Chairman of the Joint Chiefs of Staff, p. 15, for an estimate of the number of warheads expected for each of the land-based missiles the Soviets now have under deployment. Updated assessments are provided by Secretary of Defense James R. Schlesinger, *Annual Defense Department Report FY 1976 and FY 197T*, Washington, D.C., February 5, 1975, pp. 11-16.

Table 3
SOME AGGREGATE CHARACTERISTICS OF SOVIET MISSILE FORCES MODERNIZED UNDER THE VLADIVOSTOK AGREEMENT

Missile Type	CEP in Nautical Miles	Y in Mega-tons	$\dfrac{Y^{2/3}}{(CEP)^2}$ per RV	No. of RVs	$\dfrac{NY^{2/3}}{(CEP)^2}$ per Missile	No. of Launchers	$\dfrac{NY^{2/3}}{(CEP)^2}$ Total
SS-18	.29	3	25 }	8	200	300	60,000
	.2	1	25 }				
SS-17/19	.2	1	25 }	3			
	.15	.2	15 }	5	75	1000	75,000
	.19	.3	12.5 }	6			
SS-N-8 and SS-13/16	.2	1	25	1	25	700	17,500
							152,500

the Soviet force resulting from these extreme assumptions. Though the accuracy/yield combinations of Table 3 are better than the Soviets are likely to achieve for operational systems, they are technically conceivable and clearly within the scope of the principle of conservative planning. (Alternative possible configurations with equal effect against targets of constant hardness are provided for the SS-17, SS-18 and SS-19 missiles.)

If the Soviets were to produce the force projected in Table 3, the conclusions from the conventional analysis would be reversed. Even assuming the entire United States missile force can withstand up to 1,000 pounds per square inch (psi) overpressure (but no more), it apparently could be destroyed with greater than 99 percent probability by an attack which totaled 105,000 on the parameter described.[9] The same result can be generated by using the more conventional measure of kill probability. The Bomb Damage Effect Computer suggests that 99 percent damage could be created by a force of one megaton (MT) yield, 1,200 feet CEP, and five warheads per target against a land-based force hardened to 1,000 psi. Under the conditions of Table 3 the Soviets could deliver such an attack and still hold in reserve a force with greater destructive power than their current strategic forces possess. This, in our inherently anxious world, would tend to be read as decisive vul-

---

[9] This number is derived using the standard formulas for kill probability given in Davis and Schilling, *All You Ever Wanted to Know*, pp. 211-13. For simplicity and because the numbers are only useful as indicators of rough magnitudes rather than exact values, the United States force is projected as 1,000 land-based missiles representing the Minutemen force. The 54 Titan II missiles which the United States still maintains are completely discounted.

nerability. In fact, Paul Nitze, a member of the United States delegation which negotiated the SALT I agreement, has invoked the standard calculations to project the vulnerability of the United States land-based forces and other officials have expressed fears in qualitative terms that a Soviet force of the sort projected by Table 3 could credibly threaten a decisive first strike.[10] The entire issue of vulnerability largely concerns such perceptions of threat and the political consequences drawn from them.

Well before the dangers of potential vulnerability can be affirmed and policy conclusions drawn from them, however, both the calculations themselves and the assumptions on which they are based must be called into question. When the simple calculations reach stabilizing conclusions—that a full counterforce first strike is neither physically possible nor politically rational—we properly ignore elements of the problem which have been left out because including them would only serve to strengthen results. The excluded factors cannot be ignored, however, when the standard calculations begin to make a first strike counterforce attack or, more important, the threat of it, appear more conceivable.

The Impact of Operational Factors: A Modest Simulation

The conventions with respect to force balance calculations have not been casually established, and it is impressively difficult to step beyond them into the great thicket of excluded effects without losing one's bearings. One can readily note missile reliability as an excluded problem, and most analytic discussions do take this into account. It is not easy, however, to establish what actual reliability might be in a massive first strike. Beyond that, the multitude of complex effects and imperfect knowledge create extreme uncertainty and even threaten to preclude clear conceptualization. There is immediate danger that the attempt to produce more penetrating calculations will be overwhelmed by arbitrariness, incoherence or both. The central problem, then, is to find a limited extension of the established calculations which does not abandon the advantages of simplicity, and in fact one which compromises simplicity only to a very modest extent.

In seeking to illustrate some of the complexities of the force vulnerability problem while still preserving at least conceptual simplicity we have focused on three interrelated phenomena not represented in Table 3.

---

[10]Paul H. Nitze, "Assuring Strategic Stability in an Era of Détente," *Foreign Affairs*, vol. 54, no. 2 (January 1976).

1. Reliability. This includes both the reliability of the missile up to the point where the rocket engines are shut off and the ballistic trajectory is substantially determined (boost phase), and the reliability of the warhead after the boost phase.[11] Since there are many more sources of failure in the boost phase of a missile flight, that component of reliability is more significant. It is quite possible, however, to detect failure in the boost phase and to replace the failed missile (although it has not been authoritatively stated that either the United States or the Soviet Union has actually acquired this capability). It is much more difficult to detect warhead failures after the boost phase and hence if failures of this kind are present at all they could be a more severe problem to the attacker.

2. Interference. Since the land-based missiles of the United States are concentrated on a few bases the Soviet Union could not conduct an approximately simultaneous attack with several warheads per silo without having some of the attacking warheads either deflected or effectively destroyed by previous explosions in the attack sequence— explosions resulting from earlier attacks on the same silo and on nearby silos.

3. Timing. Although measures can be taken to overcome at least partially the effects of reliability and interference, all of these measures cost the attacker in terms of time. An attack sequence in which missiles are still being launched, say, 40 minutes after the first ones have exploded could be subject to disruption by military action or by threats even if the victim chose not to retaliate massively and did not act on the basis of radar warning alone.

Clearly this is not an exhaustive list of all important but previously excluded effects. Most notably it does not include any direct calculation of the human element in missile command and control systems, a factor which would undoubtedly be of primary importance to anyone actually attempting to conduct a decisive first strike. The point, to reiterate, is merely to illustrate what lies beyond the accepted conventions.

We have constructed a model . . . which includes illustrative calculations of reliability, interference and timing and allows these dimensions of the problem to interact with the conventional factors of accuracy, yield, hardness, and the warhead-to-target ratio. In brief,

---

[11] In assessing the United States strategic forces an additional factor, labeled readiness, is included to reflect that portion of the missile force undergoing maintenance or modification and thus unavailable for response. Since we are assuming a premeditated first strike by the attacking force, however, we also assume that the attacker would successfully bring his entire force up to readiness at the planned time of attack. Under this assumption residual technical problems would be reflected in the two components of reliability.

the model programs an attack on the actual missile deployment at Malmstrom Air Force Base in Montana whose silo density falls in the mid-range for American missile bases in general. In addition to silo locations, the model accepts values for 20 variables describing the attack and for one variable—hardness—describing the targets. It traces the fate of each attacking warhead, and calculates both the timing of the overall attack and the cumulative damage over time done to the 200 silos at Malmstrom. While it would be possible to adjust the geometric coordinates in the model to represent the other American base, the results for Malmstrom alone are reported with the belief that they are roughly representative of the entire land-based Minuteman force.[12]

The model with its modest extension into the unknown also gives impetus to a second important challenge to convention, that is, a questioning of the predominant focus on unfavorable attack assumptions as mandated by the principle of conservative force planning. In considering some of the difficulties the attacker must confront, the model provides concrete reasons for examining the consequences of a technically mediocre attack and for taking these consequences seriously in making policy decisions.

In order to conduct this analysis we define what we will call a standard attack scenario in which the attacking force—the red force—has available a total of 6,100 warheads, each of which has a yield of one megaton with elliptically distributed range and cross-track errors comparable to a CEP of 1,200 feet (in effect, the assumptions of Table 3 including SLBMs [submarine-launched ballistic missiles]). Of these, 700 single warhead missiles are to be held as a strategic reserve, leaving 5,400 warheads carried on multiple-warhead launchers available to conduct the counterforce attack. The boost phase and post-boost phase reliability of the red force are assumed to be .75 and .90 respectively, values which might be exceeded on test ranges but would be quite respectable under combat conditions. It is assumed that the warheads of the red force are destroyed if they fly through the cloud stem of a nu-

---

[12]The density (number of missiles in a given land area) of the separate missile squadrons at Malmstrom vary as much as the missile densities of the other Minuteman bases. We have compared damage to least-dense and most-dense areas of Malmstrom for typical model runs and find the differences to be too small to affect the analysis advanced below.

Regarding the technical aspects of estimates of kill probability discussed in footnote 3, the model uses the conservative approximations of the damage function and of target hardness embodied in the conventional calculations. However, there is a further technicality which biases the results of *both* the conventional method of calculation and the DIA's new method in the direction of higher apparent vulnerability, but which we have corrected in the model. This is the fact that ICBM impact errors are known not to be circularly distributed and that the standard range errors (along the RV's intended path) are about three times the standard cross-track errors (across the RV's path). (See D. G. Hoag, "Ballistic Missile Guidance," in B. T. Feld, *et al.*, eds., *Impact of New Technologies in the Arms Race,* Cambridge: MIT Press, 1971, p. 43ff.). . . .

clear explosion within five minutes of detonation,[13] and thus it is assumed that the attack plan requires a delay of six minutes between the arrival of separate warheads at the same target.[14] We also assume that the red force experiences a timing error in his attack execution exponentially distributed with a mean of one minute.[15] The defending force—the blue side—is assumed to consist of 1,000 silo installations located at five bases of 200 silos each, with all bases being identical to Malmstrom Air Force Base. Each silo on the blue side is hardened to withstand up to 1,000 psi overpressure.

The results of these standard assumptions are summarized in Figure 1 in which damage to the blue force is plotted for various levels of attack. The variation in results indicated by the width of the band is produced by the stochastic effects of reliability, accuracy and timing. With this as the defined state of the world one can then investigate the various ways in which the attacker might view his problem.

One basic approach for the attacker is to set a criterion of damage to be achieved—say at least 90 percent destruction of the blue force[16]—and to allocate his attack in such a way as to give the best chance of meeting that criterion. As can be seen from Figure 1, the red force can approach but cannot achieve that criterion under the standard assumptions simply by throwing all his available 5,400 warheads against the blue missiles. It would require an improbably favorable break of chance to destroy 90 percent of the opposing silos with an attack level averaging 5.4 warheads per silo. Thus the attacker would presumably look for means of improving his results.

---

[13] This assumption is derived from calculations of the abrupt deceleration which would be experienced by reentry vehicles colliding with the debris sucked up from the ground and carried in the intense winds which accompany a nuclear explosion. . . . See Lt. Col. Joseph J. McGlinchley, USAF, and Dr. Jakob W. Seelig, "Why ICBMs Can Survive," *Air Force Magazine*, September 1974, pp. 82-85.

[14] There would be a brief time interval following the initial radiation pulse from a nuclear explosion and ending no more than 10 seconds later during which interference would be low because the cloud stem with its debris had not yet propagated sufficiently. An attacker might conceive of attempting to time an attack on a silo with such precision that, say, four or five warheads all detonated within this interval of low interference. Consideration of this possibility is being undertaken by Ron Siegel of the Massachusetts Institute of Technology. The consequences of slight mistiming for such an attack would be so devastating, however, that we assume an attacker would not attempt it. If he did attempt it at the scale required, one must expect misfortune for the attacker well in excess of what is projected in our standard scenarios.

[15] Though a fully automated strike would presumably achieve much more tightly confined timing, we assume that human factors are in fact present. The human part of the missile firing sequence, although operating according to specification, would nonetheless introduce some variation in timing.

[16] This presumably is a minimal criterion of damage for the attacker. If it were to be exactly achieved, blue would still have 100 land-based launchers available for retaliation. A force of that size, for example, actually delivered against urban industrial targets in the Soviet Union would probably kill over 35 million citizens and destroy well over half of their industrial capacity.

Figure 1
U. S. silos destroyed under basic attack and standard assumptions: mean values and 95%
confidence limits.*

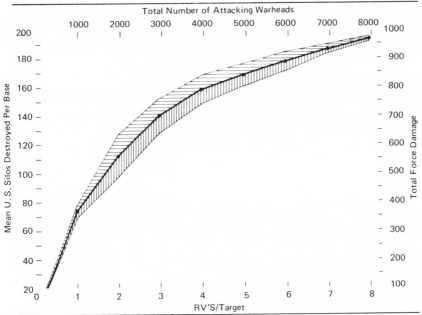

*The means and standard deviations in this and in the following figures pertain only to the results
of the model. They are not asserted to be estimates valid for the actual missile population.

There are three ways that red can attempt to improve his performance with the same force. He can develop procedures for detecting
launch failures in the boost phase and he can reprogram other missiles
to replace those which fail. At the cost of additional missiles this would
diminish the effects of imperfect reliability. Alternatively, at the cost of
time red could design his attack so as to begin with the southernmost
silos of each base and proceed northward with some planned delay,
thus minimizing interference between warheads attacking separate
silos. To avoid extreme increases in the total time required for the attack, this northward progression would be executed simultaneously
against as many different sections of the target complex as possible
given the path of the warheads through the atmosphere.[17] In order to

[17] In the model this is done by dividing the target complex into rectangular sections
whose longer sides are aligned with the warhead path. The sections need to be longer
than the horizontal distance the warheads will travel through the atmosphere. For immediate purposes we assume warheads with low drag coefficients entering the atmosphere at 22 degrees. This translates into section lengths of 45 miles. Section widths of 10
miles are large enough to minimize interference between adjacent sections.

avoid prolonging the attack for more than two hours we assume only a 30 second delay between the initiation of attack at one silo and initiation at the next one northward within the same section. As a third alternative, at the cost of both time and warheads, the attacker could both rollback and reprogram his attack.

Table 4 gives representative results for each of these attack options. It assumes an initially planned attack of four warheads per silo

Table 4
ILLUSTRATIVE FORCE BALANCES UNDER STANDARD
ATTACK ASSUMPTIONS

Assumptions	Attacking Warheads				Attack Duration After First Explosion (minutes)	Silos Destroyed		Residual Land-Based Forces No. of Missile Launchers	
	No. planned (1)	No. launched (2)	No. armed (3)	No. Exploded (4)	(5)	Full attack (6)	1st 40 min. (7)	U.S. (8)	U.S.S.R. (9)
1. Basic Attack	4,000	4,000	2,670	1,953	26	790	790	210	337–467
2. Reprogrammed Attack	4,000	5,312	3,604	2,575	59	887	834	113	21–29
3. Rollback Attack	4,000	4,000	2,670	2,377	51	868	779	132	337–467
4. Rollback and Reprogrammed Attack	4,000	5,312	3,604	2,856	81	922	802	78	21–29

Note: Tables 4 and 5 present results from model runs under various assumptions about the nature of the attack. The numbers are derived by totalling the results of the first five iterations of the model. This is equivalent to multiplying mean (n = 5) results for Malmstrom by five to represent the 1,000 silo Minuteman force.

Column 3 represents the number of weapons that would have exploded in the absence of interference. Regarding the residual force estimates of column 9, we assume that the Soviets would rely primarily on their land-based MIRV force for conducting the attack. The calculations assume the first of the possible configurations for the SS-17/19 force and thus an average force loading of 4.15 RVs per launcher for the Soviet MIRV forces of Table 3. A range for the Soviet residual force (excluding the strategic reserve of SLBMs and SS-13/16's) is derived by assuming (lower number) that an average mix of SS-18's and SS-17/19's is launched and by assuming (higher number) that the SS-18's are all used in the initial attack. The number of residual Soviet warheads (excluding the reserve) is constant across this range and can be obtained by subtracting the number launched (column 2) from 5,400.

These assumptions are more favorable to the Soviets than are current projections of their force by U.S. officials. The Pentagon, for example, estimates that the Soviet Union is in the process of deploying the SS-19 in a configuration with 6 warheads of 300 KT yield and 1/4-1/3 nautical mile CEP (see *New York Times,* January 15, 1975). Due largely to lesser accuracy than assumed in Table 3, this SS-19 would have an $NY^{2/3}/(CEP)^2$ value of 24-43 rather than 75.

which covers the rapidly rising portion of the damage curve in Figure 1 and still leaves 1,400 warheads available for reprogramming or for adding to the strategic reserve. The table indicates that under the standard attack assumptions it is more advantageous for the attacker to allocate four warheads per target in the initial wave and then reprogram for observed failures than it is to throw all available warheads against the blue side at the outset. At an attack level of four warheads per target with reprogramming, the attacker just achieves a 90 percent criterion leaving his strategic reserve intact; he would have to commit his entire force including the strategic reserve to achieve the same result with the

Table 5
ILLUSTRATIVE FORCE BALANCES UNDER
REPROGRAMMED ATTACK

Assumptions	Attacking Warheads				Attack Duration After First Explosion (minutes)	Silos Destroyed		Residual Land-Based Forces No. of Missile Launchers	
	No. planned	No. launched	No. armed	No. Exploded		Full attack	1st 40 min.	U.S.	U.S.S.R.
1. Standard Attack Assumptions	4,000	5,312	3,604	2,575	59	887	884	113	21–29
2. Degraded Reliability	4,000	8,098	3,188	2,394	94	876	820	124	0[a]
3. Degraded Accuracy	4,000	5,312	3,604	2,575	59	705	693	295	21–29
4. Mistiming in the Attack Plan	4,000	5,312	3,604	1,874	59	775	758	225	21–29
5. Execution Mistiming	4,000	5,312	3,604	2,407	150	871	800	129	21–29
6. Greater than Anticipated Hardness	4,000	5,312	3,604	2,575	59	839	827	161	21–29
7. Combined Degradation: Reliability, Accuracy, Plan Mistiming, Hardness	4,000	8,098	3,188	1,902	94	518	471	482	0[a]

[a] Denotes that under the assumptions of Table 3 the attacking force would be totally exhausted—including the strategic reserve—before the attack could be completed.

263

basic attack pattern. The rollback option is less attractive. It does produce a modest increase in damage but still leaves the attacker well short of his goal. This option also requires an attack sequence lasting over an hour, leaving it vulnerable to disruption in the later stages. The combination of rollback and reprogramming does produce the greatest effect but the cost in time would appear to nullify the marginal advantage. It seems then that the intelligent attacker committed to achieving a decisive level of damage would conduct a reprogrammed attack.

But what if he does not achieve the performance ascribed to him under the standard assumptions? Table 5 displays the results of a reprogrammed attack which has experienced a variety of technical problems. In row 2 the reliability has been degraded to .5 for the boost phase and .8 for the post-boost phase. The reprogramming procedure does compensate for this and leaves the damage essentially unchanged but under these circumstances it exacts a terrible cost. The attack sequence runs nearly an hour and 45 minutes and it requires more warheads than would be contained in the entire Soviet force under the assumptions of Table 3. The red side in other words disarms himself in conducting this attack and leaves blue with a residual force of over 100 launchers and 300 warheads on land alone. To provoke an enemy to this extent and then to leave him with absolute superiority would presumably lead either to the surrender or the destruction of the attacker or perhaps both.

The third row of Table 5 reflects the results of a 50 percent increase in range and cross-track errors of the incoming warheads (a net CEP of about 1/3 of a nautical mile). The result of this technical "failure" is that damage is reduced to the point that a quarter of the blue force survives; and red, although he retains his strategic reserves, has left blue with substantial counterforce superiority. The red war-fighting forces have been reduced to such a low level that they might be destroyed by the residual blue force if blue were able to undertake post-attack reconnaissance.

Rows 4, 5, and 6 of Table 5 show the isolated effects of more esoteric technical failures: respectively, a mistiming of the attack plan such that the delay between attacking warheads does not exceed the lethal time of the cloud stems of previous explosions, a mistiming of the attack execution such that the mean of the error distribution is five minutes, and a greater than expected resistance of blue silos to destruction (up to 1,500 psi). These degradations of red's performance have more modest effects on damage to blue but they do either extend the attack sequence to render it quite vulnerable to interdiction (as with execution mistiming) or reduce damage significantly below the criterion. All of these problems leave blue with a substantial counterforce superiority in the end, excluding the strategic reserve of both sides.

Finally row 7 of Table 5 shows the combined effects of degradation in accuracy, reliability, attack plan timing, together with increased hardness of the blue silos. The effects are obviously disastrous to red, leaving him completely disarmed and his severely provoked opponent, blue, with half his land-based force plus his strategic reserve still able to function.

In order to reach a final evaluation of the reprogrammed attack option, red would have to assign subjective probabilities to these possible outcomes and, of course, it is very difficult to guess what probability values a tempted attacker might choose. No matter what probabilities are ascribed, however, it is apparent that, under this analysis, a reprogrammed attack designed to achieve 90 percent destruction of the opposing force is more likely to disarm the attacker than the victim, and that the most probable outcome appears to be a substantial post-attack force superiority for the victim.

On the basis of this exercise red might reasonably wish to reexamine the attack options again, perhaps with a view to adjusting his objective. . . . The attacker, by withholding some forces, can be reasonably confident that the residual force balance will be approximately equal; and, of course, were the war to stop after the initial attack, all the explosions would have occurred on blue's territory. Does this latter asymmetry then constitute relative vulnerability of the blue force? There are at least two solid reasons to deny that it does. First, the rationality of this attack from red's point of view depends upon the ability of blue's political system to distinguish between it and a fully damaging attack. The latter perception would call forth full retaliation; the former, it is supposed, might not. Since a very large number of warheads are involved, and since the latest estimates of the United States government suggest that considerably more than 16 million deaths would result from an attack of the sort hypothesized, the ability of the victim to discriminate must be considered to be in question. Second, if the victim does distinguish the "limited" character of the attack, he could retaliate with a relatively small portion of his residual force against a relatively small part of the attacker's urban/industrial system in order to equalize the damage.[18] The significance of this possibility is that it allows the victim to remove the asymmetry in the scenario while still maintaining a residual force balance and still withholding retaliation from the major

[18] See "Analyses of Effects of Limited Nuclear Warfare," United States Senate Committee on Foreign Relations, September 1975, page 18 and passim. The 16.3 million estimate for a ground-burst attack of two one-megaton RVs per silo includes only early fallout deaths and not deaths due to disease or disruption of services. Note that blue could equalize the damage without "escalating" to direct urban/industrial strikes by exploding ground-burst weapons upwind of a few major cities.

portion of the attacker's urban/industrial targets (thus maintaining the post-attack deterrence situation). The entire scenario is very bizarre indeed, but as a hypothetical possibility it represents a parity of misfortune rather than relative strategic vulnerability.

. . . Red can improve his performance against blue and still have a substantial residual force if he conducts a rollback attack. The improvement is only marginal, however, and it doubles the time required to execute the attack sequence. This option does not differ significantly enough from the basic attack to affect any calculating decision maker's conclusion. Similarly, the rollback and reprogrammed attack . . . offers slight improvement over the simple reprogrammed attack and does not change the basic result.

The attacker's options then reduce to two, and both of them are very unattractive. He can attack with full force and in the process either disarm himself or leave his residual forces inferior to those of his opponent. Alternatively he can attack more cautiously, thereby preserving an equal residual force but achieving only a balance of misery, destruction, and residual deterrent capability.

But suppose red proposes to build the force of Table 3 with no intention of conducting an actual attack but, rather, trusting that appearances will be forever deceiving, for the purpose of realizing political returns. Before embarking on such a course red should consider the victim's perspective. . . . A low intensity attack—a single warhead against each silo—[might be] executed very swiftly at low cost to the attacking force. A target force arrayed in the fashion of the American forces would lose on the order of 25 percent of its capacity to such an attack. Although this is a very uninteresting result to a cold-blooded aggressor intent on executing the decisive first strike, it might be very interesting indeed to a nervous potential victim who had convinced himself that his opponent was about to attempt a devastating first strike. In other words, the potential victim facing a superior force might be tempted to preempt in order to deny red his advantage and to guarantee a post-attack parity of strategic forces.[19] The flaunting of apparent superiority for political benefit, to the extent that it is believed, could have highly unfortunate effects on crisis stability. At any rate limited preemption appears to be a counterthreat at least as credible as the threat of a full first strike itself.[20]

---

[19] The logic here requires an extension of the results based on the geographic coordinates for an American base to the Soviet base system. Obviously this is of questionable validity, but the effect of the error would not be very significant for a low intensity attack (i.e., one warhead per target). The roles of red and blue could be reversed from their usual assignment, of course, and we could consider the American force as a potential red force. . . .

[20] The efficacy of the counterthreat rests on the fact that the coordination of the full first strike would require elaborate planning and a reasonably extensive period during which

Because the background level of uncertainty is so high, the results just presented cannot be taken as adequate quantitative estimates of an actual strategic exchange. What they do indicate, however, is that even highly aggressive development of the Soviet forces under the Vladivostok regime—so that they actually possessed the number of warheads some American observers seem to fear—still would not render the Minuteman force vulnerable under reasonable assumptions, even setting aside the summary arguments. Those who project fearsome Soviet superiority based on multiple warheads are tacitly promoting a very restricted set of assumptions.

The Prospect of New Technologies

If the problem of strategic defense were constrained to that of making a projection of the actual Soviet threat, then one could reasonably halt the analysis at the point just reached. The Soviet Union does not have the forces projected in Table 3, and in all probability for a decade or more the Soviets will not be able to play even the unrewarding role assigned to red in the analysis.

The dynamics of force planning do not require an actualized threat, however, since the process is stimulated to a substantial extent by our own advanced weapons research. At the frontiers of the American weapons program, technologies are now being projected which promise drastic increases in the most sensitive variable, accuracy. Should those increases be realized, should they be extended to an operational force of the size projected in Table 3, then the complexities of reliability, interference, and mistiming might be overridden and the problem of relative vulnerability might be reestablished. Backed by the experience of three decades of rapid development of weapons technology, the established principle of conservative force planning allows policy planners to project with genuine conviction the possibility of the Soviet's deploying a decade hence extremely accurate missile guidance systems which are now little more than a designer's aspiration.

A particularly important variant of this argument posits a Soviet threat consisting of highly accurate warheads with yields far lower than the one megaton assumed in the previous analysis. The increased accuracy allows an allocation of fewer warheads to each target silo and

---

the attacking force was being brought up to full readiness. The limited preemption by contrast is far less demanding and could be prepared far more rapidly. Hence any breach in secrecy during the climb to full readiness would expose the would-be attacker to limited preemption. Since the entire argument deals with threats rather than actual attacks, it is sufficient to establish that the successful execution of limited preemption is reasonably judged to be at least as probable as the successful execution of the full first strike itself.

with each having a yield of only a fraction of a megaton the aggregate explosive power of the attack would be dramatically reduced. This would reduce residual radiation and the consequent damage to the victim's society. It is a widely held judgment that the decision to undertake a full counterforce attack becomes easier and the threat to do so more credible the more collateral damage from such an attack is reduced. Thus a plausible first strike threat from a Soviet force of low yield, highly accurate warheads would be interpreted in the United States as a particularly pernicious form of vulnerability (and presumably vice versa).[21]

Figure 2 provides some sense of the magnitudes involved in this argument. The curves show expected damage to blue at various levels of attack under the standard assumptions previously defined except that yield is reduced to 50 kilotons and the range and track errors are reduced, in the extreme case, by a factor of 10. If such accuracy is achieved with no serious degradation—that is, if accuracy were held to a comparable CEP of 120 feet, and no biased sources of error were present, then blue's land-based force could be virtually destroyed on first strike while red retained over 1,400 warheads in addition to his strategic reserve. An attack of this character planned at three warheads per target with reprogramming (following the highest curve in Figure 2) would still produce over 2,500 explosions with a total yield of over 125 megatons.[22] This is not a small attack but since it would be targeted predominantly in rural areas it might, in advance and in the abstract,

[21] Of course, such an attack by either side would be even more to be feared if it were possible to minimize early fallout by using warheads fuzed to explode at an altitude such that their fireballs would not touch the ground. The technical implementation of such a strategy is difficult, however. A 50 kiloton weapon has to be exploded above about 500 feet to prevent the fireball from touching ground. (See the DIA's *Physical Vulnerability Handbook* cited in footnote 3, Figure I-4.) It is essentially impossible to destroy a 1,000 psi silo if the detonation occurs above 750 feet (700 feet for a 1,500 psi silo) and the effective weapon radius decreases rapidly in the range between 600 and 750 feet. Thus a very accurate fuzing mechanism is needed if the weapon is to perform properly. (Note that if its fuze causes it to explode at the wrong altitude, this will produce a substantial added accuracy error.) A fuze which works on barometric pressure or on the drag encountered by the warhead will not do, since the necessary accuracy is less than one percent of the scale height of the atmosphere, and thus the density of the atmosphere differs by less than one percent over these distances. (Similarly discouraging results are obtained for all weapon yields.) Radar fuzing could not be used with any confidence because it would be susceptible to jamming and interference from other explosions. See R. L. Garwin, "Technology for the Enhancement of Military Capability," *International Security*, Fall 1976.

[22] When blast and thermal effects are being considered damage is assumed to be proportional to $NY^{2/3}$ because distances associated with particular intensities of these weapon effects are related to the cube-root of the yield which is then squared because damage is proportional to the *area* so exposed. (For yields over one megaton, $NY^{1/2}$ is often used instead, to adjust for the fact that most area targets are too small for such large yields to be efficient.) When long-term radiation effects are the primary concern, however, the total explosive yield is a more appropriate measure than such "equivalent megatonnage" formulae.

Figure 2
U. S. silos destroyed by high-accuracy, low yield attack: y = 50 KT

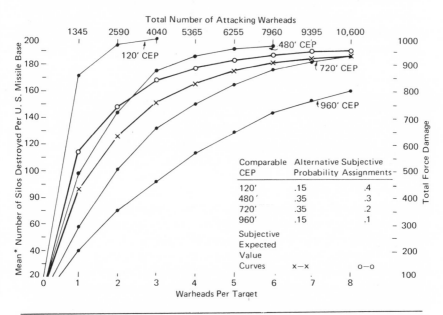

*The means were calculated over a number of model runs ranging from 5 to 10. For attacks of 2 warheads per target or more and mean values less than 180, the standard deviations ranged from 3 to 7. Outside of this area they ranged from less than 1 to 5.

be judged a limited enough provocation to be credible as a threat.

Again, though, one must consider the problem from the attacker's point of view, and the basic insight is that there is no practical test program a potential attacker can undertake which will provide much confidence that his forces will perform in the real event according to the required specifications. As seen from the lower curves of Figure 2, even slight slips in technical performance would reduce very substantially the damage done to the victim. An unexpected error of only one-tenth of a nautical mile (600 feet), even if unbiased, would allow more than 30 percent of the victim's force to escape fatal damage, and any serious evaluation of this force design and attack option must include the possibility of such failures. The attacker, red, can hedge against such degradation in planned accuracy by increasing the level of his attack but in doing so he depletes his own force. Moreover, if the unplanned accuracy error does approach or exceed one-tenth of a nautical mile, red would again risk disarming himself while leaving blue with decisive post-attack superiority. In other words, if the possibility of

269

even modest accuracy degradation is allowed, as suggested by the subjective expected value curves of Figure 2,[23] the high-accuracy, low-yield threat does not substantially differ in its effects on the blue missile force from those previously examined and thus the earlier conclusions would stand unaltered.

The technologies which would allow ballistic missiles to achieve accuracies of 120 feet CEP or better at intercontinental range are, of course, complex, diverse, highly classified, and at present only partially developed. This renders it impractical to evaluate in technical detail whether it is plausible to claim that advanced missile guidance systems will be so reliable and that they will be understood in such minute and exhaustive detail that the possibility of modest, previously unrecognized accuracy degradations under combat conditions can be excluded on the basis of test results. There are, however, very general reasons to doubt that such confidence is possible. It is apparent from the public record, for example, that high accuracies can be pursued by using stellar sightings and/or satellite communications to correct warhead trajectories in the post-boost phase and by using spin stabilized reentry vehicles (RVs), with ablative heat shields and low drag coefficients which traverse the atmosphere at high velocities. At 120 feet CEP or better most of the RVs from such systems with suitable attack timing would avoid the cloud stems of previous explosions during the five minutes or so within which abrupt deceleration resulting from the warhead hitting the debris in the cloud would be fatal to the warhead. Warheads arriving 10 minutes after the initial explosions in a missile field, however, would unavoidably encounter high altitude clouds with dust particles of sufficient density to cause significant errors in accuracy.[24] Also, although high velocity reentry vehicles would

---

[23] The assignment of subjective probability, in this situation, is constrained, of course, only by intuitive plausibility—not a very confining or precise criterion. The procedure is nonetheless useful as a means of structuring the personal judgments which must inevitably be made. The higher of the two aggregate curves in Figure 2 suggests that even if there is a 70 percent chance that the attacking missiles will achieve accuracies comparable to 480 feet CEP or better (with a 40 percent chance of 120 feet comparable CEP) nonetheless the residual chance of lesser technical performance would deny expectations of success to a reasonably calculating attacker. Even under this distinctly optimistic probability assignment the attacker must expect to exhaust his offensive war-fighting force without achieving total destruction of his opponent's force.

[24] Rough calculations suggest that more than 10 kilograms of heat shield might be worn away by such dust. If this wear occurs asymmetrically, then the spin axis may no longer coincide with the aerodynamic axis. Three mechanisms can then produce dramatic inaccuracies. First, both the effective frontal area and the drag coefficient of the RV will be increased, causing it to hit the ground short of its target. Second, the RV may fly at a different trim attitude, causing unpredictable aerodynamic lift. Third, if the center of mass moves with respect to the center of pressure, the RV may no longer be aerodynamically stable, with unpredictable effects.

As a rough guide to the possible magnitude of the first of these effects, we can calculate the effect of an unexpected decrease in the ballistic coefficient from 1,000 lbs./ft.^{2} to 900

traverse the atmosphere in a relatively short time, ambient winds of unusual intensity and unpredictable direction caused again by previous explosions would be likely to add another component of error. Particularly given the international treaty prohibiting atmospheric tests it appears very unlikely that such effects could be measured with sufficient precision that absolutely reliable and exact compensation could be built into the guidance system.

If, as seems likely, sophisticated analytic calculations designed into the missile guidance and reentry vehicle systems cannot really guarantee the accuracies required under the combat conditions of a massive first strike, then it is possible to approach the problem by means of active sensing systems which set up a direct data link or feedback loop between the target and the incoming warhead and allow the warhead to home in on the target. It is presumably systems of this sort which strategic analysts have in mind when they project accuracies on the order of tens of feet CEP or better and associated yields far lower than 50 kilotons. There is an intrinsic problem with such systems, however, in that their communications and sensing devices are vulnerable to interference, and disruptions in the feedback loop would degrade accuracy very seriously. Such disruptions can occur through jamming or other direct measures undertaken by the defender, and they can be produced by previous explosions in the attack sequence.

Moreover, quite apart from the technical approach adopted, it is reasonable to expect that the attempt to achieve extreme kill probabilities with low yield weapons will force system designers to deal with more recalcitrant and esoteric sources of error than have been encountered to date. The measure of missile accuracy, CEP, assumes that the miss distances of missiles (difference between aiming points and actual impact points) fall into a normal distribution and this can be true only if the sources of error are random. It is unlikely, however, that actual experience neatly follows a normal distribution, for a number of factors such as slightly substandard components or systematic errors introduced into the trajectory calculations could and undoubtedly do generate biased sources of error. Errors of this sort which would seem relatively small when compared with the destructive radius of a megaton yield weapon (lethal radius [LR] = 1,540 feet against 1,000 psi targets) or with a random error component on the order of two-tenths nautical miles might be significant for a 50 kiloton yield (LR = 570 feet against

---

lbs./ft.[2] caused either by a change in the drag coefficient or an increase in the effective area because of oscillation. Such a deviation would cause an ICBM on a minimum energy trajectory to hit the ground 1,000 feet short of its target. Maneuvering warheads with inertial sensing all the way to the point of explosion is a design approach which might mitigate these problems but at the cost of greater complexity and probably lesser reliability.

1,000 psi targets) and a random error component of only two-hundredths nautical miles. Since the United States is now undertaking very expensive improvements in the instrumentation of its missile test ranges in order to sort out the various sources of error for missile systems aspiring to accuracies only on the order of two-tenths nautical miles, it is a fair presumption that such sources of error are being encountered and that they have not yet been adequately measured.[25] As with any other area of human affairs, driving missile technology against the limits of perfection is likely to be increasingly expensive and frustrating.

In general it is not objectively valid for either the potential attacker or the potential victim to base major strategic decisions—the determination of force posture, the planning for actual attacks, or the political calculus of threats—solely on the claims of weapons system designers or even on limited test range results. If one takes into account just the most obvious complications that the attacker faces, the massive first strike at hardened land-based installations begins to look at least as dangerous to the attacker as to the victim. Though assumptions can be found at the favorable extremes of technical performance which would make a first strike apparently successful, modest changes in such assumptions reverse the conclusions. A categorical projection of impending vulnerability of the land-based missile force to a high-accuracy, low-yield force of the sort described cannot be made on the basis of objectively compelling analysis.

The High-Accuracy Medium-Yield Threat

If, ignoring all the sage insight that has been offered up to this point, an incorrigibly malevolent enemy were to design his forces for optimal performance in the hypothetical world defined by the particular strategic model we have been using, he would probably use intermediate-range yields and moderately improved accuracies. Yields on the order of 200 kilotons would mitigate (as compared to those of one megaton or greater) the interference effects of previous explosions and yet would not require that extreme accuracies be achieved and maintained.

---

[25] Two Navstar satellites were specifically authorized (beyond a program of four such satellites independently justified) in order to gather trajectory information for tests of the Trident C-4 missile. See "New Missiles Spur Range Instrumentation Advances," *Aviation Week and Space Technology,* November 3, 1975, and "DOD Weighs Navstar Schedule Advance," *Aviation Week and Space Technology,* December 2, 1974. For an official statement of the difficulty of achieving high confidence estimates of missile accuracy, see the testimony of the Deputy Director of Defense Research and Engineering in charge of Strategic and Space Systems, Senate Armed Services Committee FY 1976, Research and Development Authorization Hearings (part 4), pp. 2136-37.

Weapons designers sensitive to the variables we have been consider-ing might want to pursue greater ruggedness and greater operational reliability in their offensive warheads, and they might sacrifice a small decrease in optimal accuracy and a substantial increase in collateral damage in order to do so. For the sake of completeness, then, let us consider whether such a threat, which does at least vaguely resemble the current United States advanced warhead program, would reverse the impressions created by the previous analysis.

Figure 3 displays mean model results for a reprogrammed attack under the standard assumptions with the exception that yield is re-duced to 200 kilotons and accuracy increased to be comparable to a CEP of 720 feet. Figure 3 indicates that if the attacker, red, were willing to expend his entire offensive force (excluding his strategic reserve) he would be able to approximate complete destruction of the United States land-based force. Moreover, the cost to the attacking force may be less than indicated, since Figure 3 does not credit red with improved reliability for his design compromises.

Table 6 provides the basis for a detailed analysis of the medium

Figure 3
U. S. silos destroyed by a moderate yield, advanced accuracy, reprogrammed attack: mean model results and 95% confidence limits.

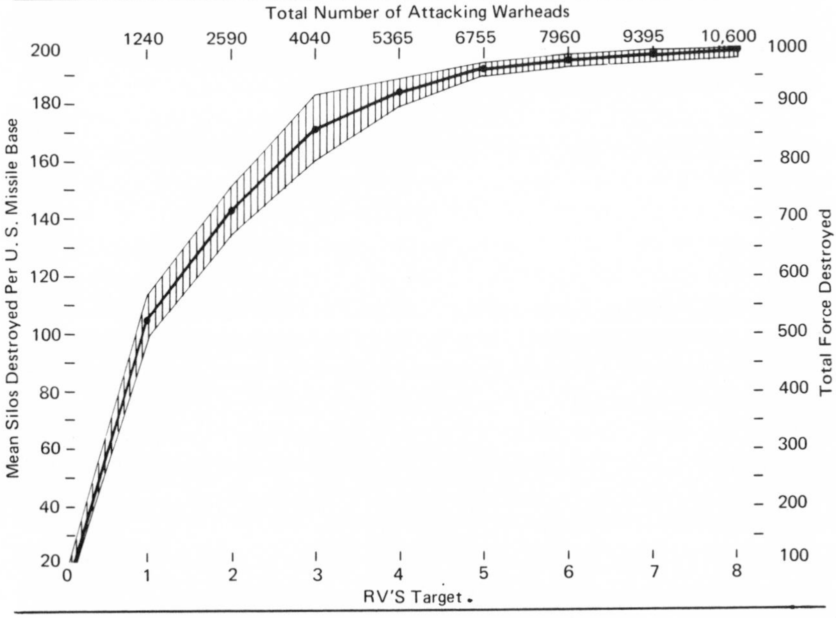

Table 6
UNITED STATES SILOS DESTROYED: REPROGRAMMED ATTACK AT FIVE WARHEADS/TARGET

Comparable CEP	Mean per Base (to nearest unit)	No. of Trials	Stand. Dev. (to nearest unit)	Alternative Subjective Probability Assignments		
				1	2	3
720 ft	192	21	3	.8	.5	.33
1200 ft	159	21	6	.15	.3	.33
1800 ft	112	21	5	.05	.2	.33
Subjective Expected Value for Entire Force				915	830	770
Residual Force Expected				85	170	230

Note: y = 200 KT; Reliability = .9, .95; Actual number of warheads launched = 1,109 for Malmstrom—equivalent to 5,545 for the 1,000 missile force.

yield threat. The attacking force in Table 6 allocates five warheads per target, and is credited with high reliability—.9 in the boost phase and .95 in the post-boost phase as compared to .75 and .9 respectively under the standard assumptions used previously. The accuracy attributed to the force—at slightly over one-tenth of a nautical mile—is outstanding in relation to current capabilities although it is of course not as good as the best projected accuracies. If that accuracy should hold without any degradation, then the Minuteman force would be reduced to less than 50 missiles, at the cost of 5,545 attacking warheads.

Under these conditions, red would have depleted his offensive force and would have reduced his strategic reserve to 555 single warhead missiles. Nonetheless, this situation approaches more closely the classic conception of vulnerability, and it is clear that any blue response would have to rely on the submarine force. The dual problem described earlier still applies; blue's ability to discriminate the character of the attack would still be in question and, at least in theory, blue would still have the capacity to conduct an equalizing retaliation while still withholding attack from some portion of the red urban/industrial system. Assuming that only half of the Poseidon/Trident force was ready to respond, blue would have a six to one warhead advantage in residual forces, although the residual blue force would have smaller yield per warhead. Blue would have received an attack of over 825 megatons targeted primarily in rural areas and would face the question of whether to equalize the damage created by this attack. Whether or not he would in fact do so, blue could equalize damage by means of a partial urban/industrial response using only a portion of his 3,600-3,700 warhead reserve. Nonetheless, those giving full thrust to conservative force planning principles might consider the outcome of this scenario to represent unacceptable vulnerability of the land-based force even though the attacker has had to expend all but his strategic reserve to achieve it.

The question then is whether that outcome can be legitimately projected as the only acknowledged result of an attack by such a highly reliable, highly accurate, medium-yield force. Again, if the uncertainties inherent in force operations are admitted, the answer to that question is negative. Table 6 projects some levels of possible accuracy degradations which would critically affect the result. That table suggests that if accuracy degradations, which are high as a percentage of the nominal design figure but very small in absolute values, are admitted to the analysis with any serious probability, then the attack could result in the same sort of disaster for red which was described previously. If only a small probability of substantial accuracy degradation is allowed (case 1) the medium-yield threat still leaves an expectation that there would be a surviving blue force on land approximating 100 missiles. As that possibility is increased (case 3), blue gains a decisive expected superiority over red in terms of residual offensive forces, excluding the strategic reserve.

On balance a threat consisting of highly reliable, highly accurate, medium-yield MIRVs, although it burdens the conclusions of the previous analysis, still does not appear sufficient to reverse them. Under these conditions the full first strike still can reasonably be said to be as dangerous to the attacker as to the victim. As long as United States decision makers appreciate these realities, any enemy attempting to use such a force to bolster some political demand would have to do so not on the basis of relative vulnerability of the United States force—according to theory the more powerful basis for threat—but rather on the basis of parity of potential misfortune, something that is already available at current force levels.

Implications for Strategic Policy

We come then to the critical matter—our collective state of mind.

It is apparent that dangerous and destabilizing vulnerability of the land-based missile forces of both the superpowers can be projected, even given full implementation of the Vladivostok guidelines. Strategic missiles probably will achieve—on test ranges—accuracies measured by CEP values of less than one-tenth of a nautical mile. If this figure is inserted into established conventional calculations, vulnerability

275

will be the apparent result; and to the extent that is believed in either the United States or the Soviet Union some destabilizing effect will occur as a self-fulfilling proposition.[26] But it is equally apparent that belief in the relative vulnerability of land-based missiles can be constructed only on the basis of a narrow and rigid criterion of analysis, one which requires that any technically conceivable threat to the missiles be covered—no matter how fantastic the conceived threat might be when viewed from the practical world in which an offensive force must operate. We have seen in the analysis above that under some plausible assumptions even rather modest shifts in the pertinent assumptions are sufficient to change the apparent advantage from the attacker to the defender if a full first strike on land-based missiles is attempted. Thus, the fundamental problem: Where is the line between prudence and paranoia to be drawn?

Under strict rules of evidence and inference this question cannot be answered with both precision and confidence. The full consequences of nuclear war cannot be calculated with much assurance, and, as far as objective validity is concerned, even the most exacting analysis is destined to be overwhelmed by uncertainty. The central parameters of ballistic missile performance must necessarily be established under restricted conditions which are very remote from the conditions under which a war would actually be conducted: the effect of human performance on missile reliability has not been tested under pertinent conditions,[27] nor have the various possible effects of dust, atmospheric turbulence and large-scale electromagnetic disturbances from previous explosions on warheads in the reentry phase. The coordination required to have even a serious chance at a successful first strike has not been attempted in actual practice and it is extremely unlikely that these forces have even been exercised at the levels of alert that would actually be required. Public information is less clear about the effects of unfavorable or even simply unusual weather, trajectories that have not been flown before, reentry stresses on warhead fuzing systems, and a host of other factors which could substantially affect the outcome; but it is very doubtful that all aspects of the problem have been adequately considered. They never are in other areas of human endeavor.

---

[26] That is not to assert that war would break out with the first serious crisis, but only that this firm belief on one side is all that is required for some destabilizing effect to occur.

[27] In the United States operational missiles tests are conducted by removing selected missiles and their operational crews to test ranges. It may be true that this process does not affect the missile, but it certainly affects the crew, and their performance under test conditions is not likely to be the same as it would be in severe crisis or actual combat. What the Soviets do is more of a mystery, but it is rather unlikely that they have been able to simulate the actual combat conditions of a first strike.

Massive uncertainty, however, is not a stable condition of a decision maker's mind. As a practical matter the simple, unrealistic but well-established calculations of the strategic balance have provided a clear structure for the many decisions on strategic force posture which modern governments have had to make. Similarly, perceptions of threat throughout the world and political judgments which derive from such perceptions have been and undoubtedly will continue to be influenced at least in professional circles by the results of highly imperfect analytic calculations. Men cannot and do not shrink from the implications of strategic analysis even if scientific inference cannot carry them to firm conclusions.

In duly humble spirit, then, we advance the following judgments which are inspired by the analysis conducted but admittedly not strictly compelled by it.

First, the strategic forces of the Soviet Union, even if very aggressively modernized, will not be sufficient to threaten with true credibility the decisive destruction of the United States Minuteman force. As far as the traditional parameters of accuracy, yield, reliability, warhead numbers, and silo hardness are concerned, the risk to the attacker and to the victim appear to be equally great across the operationally achievable ranges of values, and this should work to deny access to any new dimension of political threat. The greater total payload of the Soviet missile force can be translated into a serious strategic advantage only if overly restricted calculations maintain their established hegemony. This conventional analysis may be psychologically, organizationally, and/or politically so entrenched that a revision cannot be effected; but, if so, we should be clear that the real problem of relative strategic vulnerability lies more in that fact than in weapons technology.

Second, the entire focus on missile silo vulnerability which the conventional calculations have brought about is increasingly anomalous in technical terms. The most vulnerable elements of modern strategic forces are not the hardened, fixed-site missiles but rather the command channels and the communication and information processing systems which service the command structure. There are serious problems to be encountered in this latter area, but most of these have little to do with the traditional parameters which have been used to define the strategic balance. Attacks on political and military authorities do not require large numbers of weapons and for the most part not even particularly accurate or otherwise advanced weapons. Moreover, the value to either the attacker or the victim of large, single-missile payloads is diminished by the fact that targeting flexibility is reduced as the ratio of warheads to launchers increases. In general, although the true strategic balance is very substantially affected by the capabilities and vulnerabilities of systems designed to enable intelligent, authoritative command and effective operational control, conventional strategic analysis—even as adjusted in the calculations advanced above—is virtually blind to this dimension of the problem.

The implication, therefore, is that it would be more pathological than prudent to undertake major changes in the deployed strategic forces of the United States in order to solve the problem of vulnerability as defined by conventional analysis. A replacement of the Minuteman force, which presumably would involve mobile missile systems deployed either on land or in submarines, would cost many tens of billions of dollars in directly associated marginal costs. Such a program would run the risk of purchasing gains in the very elusive matter of political perception at a cost to safety and real military capability due to the burdens imposed on command and control arrangements. This is not the way in which national security ought to be pursued.

SOVIET-AMERICAN STRATEGIC COMPETITION: INSTRUMENTS, DOCTRINES, AND PURPOSES

Colin S. Gray

In a critical analysis of its strategic programs, Colin S. Gray concludes that the Soviet Union is seeking nuclear superiority over the United States. In the past, there was an incongruity between Soviet doctrine and Soviet weapons capabilities, but, the author believes recent Soviet weapon acquisitions and civil defense efforts have allowed that gap to be narrowed considerably.

Gray is concerned with two basic issues: the failure of defense analysts in the United States to recognize the trend in Soviet strategic programs for what it is, namely, an attempt by Moscow to exploit for political advantage both the asymmetries between its strategic capabilities and those of the United States and the vulnerability of silo-based ICBMs. Soviet doctrine maintains that a superiority in arms can be employed coercively in a crisis. Should war occur, such superiority, together with extensive civil defense preparations, would ensure victory. The author believes the asymmetrical relationship of the two superpowers' strategic potential must be rectified, and his immediate concern is for the vulnerability of U.S. ICBMs. Because these weapons embody unique qualities in their flexibility of use and their command and control, Gray argues that the United States should deploy mobile ICBMs with improved counterforce capabilities to replace its vulnerable Minuteman missiles.

Source: *Long-Range U.S.-U.S.S.R. Competition–National Security Implications*, National Security Affairs Conference, National Defense University, Washington, D.C., October 1976, pp. 36-53.

Of Capabilities and Intentions

A competition in armaments may serve many purposes for the participants, prominent among which is the forwarding of the foreign policy ambitions of the state. Specific weapon programs may be explained in terms of bureaucratic expediency, while the scale of particular procurement programs may invite very general stylistic explanation/ rationalization (e.g., "the Soviet Union always builds in large numbers" or "large rocket-boosters is simply 'the Soviet way' in missile technology"). Nonetheless, Soviet missiles and tank armies pose objective, latent threats to Western values, whatever the balance of true rationales may be for their deployment. It is easy to select explanations for Soviet developments which fit our doctrinal/political predispositions. A great deal of the Soviet military endeavor that has borne fruit in weapons deployed since the mid-1960s may reflect nothing more sinister than tangible side-payments by the Soviet political leadership to the Soviet military as the price exacted for acquiescence in detente. Also, one might argue that the scale and breadth of the Soviet commitment to enhanced military capabilities shows nothing more worrisome to the West than a pervading sense of insecurity and inferiority. By this latter line of reasoning, the stronger the relative military position of the Soviet Union, the more secure Soviet leaders will feel—and hence the more willing they should be to engage in what Western commentators would term "genuine" detente activity.

The above arguments, and others to the same comforting effect, are far from absurd; however, they do strain the evidence and lack any persuasive measure of logical dominance over rival, less comforting arguments. Whatever Soviet motives may be, it is difficult to find comfort in the record of Soviet strategic programs in the 1970s. The burden of the argument in this paper is to suggest that the Soviet Union is seeking to purchase military options that should provide it with not unreasonable prospects for (a) deterring crises, (b) winning crises, and (c) winning wars (at any level). It is not suggested either that Soviet leaders will seek confrontation—in order to road-test their military capability—or, still less, that they would welcome nuclear war. Furthermore, lest there should be any misunderstanding, it is not suggested (even implicitly) that Soviet foreign policy ambitions are rigidly cast, either as to place or timing. By its military efforts the Soviet Union appears to be seeking to buy freedom of action: to what precise ends no one, probably not excluding the Soviet leadership, can presume detailed knowledge.[1] However, because Western theorists have diffi-

---

[1] See Herbert Goldhamer, *The Soviet Union in a Period of Strategic Parity*, R-889-PR (Santa Monica: RAND, November 1971).

culty writing plausible scenarios wherein the Soviet Union could cash its military investment to good political effect, it does not follow that military investment should be discounted. It is only sensible to presume that the Soviet Union is not devoting 11-13 percent (which is probably the lowest defensible range) of its GNP on defense for frivolous reasons. For the first time in twenty years, Soviet strategic doctrine and Soviet strategic capabilities are beginning to betray an ominous congruence. The traditional Soviet endorsement of what Western analysts have chosen to term a "war-fighting" capability now shows plausible signs of being matched by military capabilities that might just yield *victory*. It is, perhaps, worth recalling that in 1973, the late Soviet Defense Minister, Marshal Grechko, claimed that in the event of a world war, "we are firmly convinced that victory in this war would go to us."[2] Such a declaration could be dismissed summarily as being purely hortatory, or even ideologically ritualistic, were it not for the defense capabilities that the Soviet Union is providing itself. Any Soviet attempt to road-test their strategic investment might well end in catastrophe for both principal parties, in part for the reasons cited by John Steinbruner and Thomas Garwin,[3] but there are persuasive grounds for taking Soviet strategic doctrinal utterances at face value.[4]

Whatever one may think to be the value of the strategic attitudes of an arms race adversary, it is only prudent (and not paranoid) to be sensitive to those indicators of strategic intent that he takes seriously. With respect to the Soviet Union, one is competing with a state which (a) views war (at all levels) as an instrument of policy;[5] (b) views a good defense as a good deterrent; and (c) views Western interest in detente processes as a fairly direct consequence of the rise in the relative military strength of the Soviet Union. There is no obvious doctrinal constraint upon the growth of Soviet military power. Soviet officials intend to perform as well as possible, should war occur. There is no evidence of note that would suggest a serious Soviet interest in the concepts of sufficiency, parity or stability (in common Western under-

---

[2] Marshal Grechko, Report at the Fifth All-Army Conference of Party Organization Secretaries, *Karsnaia zvezda*, March 28, 1973.

[3] John D. Steinbruner and Thomas M. Garwin, "Strategic Vulnerability: The Balance Between Prudence and Paranoia," *International Security*, vol. 1, no. 1 (July 1976).

[4] On Soviet doctrine, the following are particularly useful: V.D. Sokolovskii, *Soviet Military Strategy*, 3rd ed., edited by Harriet F. Scott (New York: Crane, Russak, 1975); Roger Barnett, "Trans-SALT: Soviet Strategic Doctrine," *Orbis*, vol. 19, no. 2 (Summer 1975), pp. 533-61; Benjamin S. Lambeth, "The Sources of Soviet Military Doctrine," in Frank B. Horton III et al., eds., *Comparative Defense Policy* (Baltimore: John Hopkins University Press, 1974), pp. 200-16.

[5] See "Foremost Soviet Military Journal Emphasizes Continuing Crucial Role of War and Military Might," *Soviet World Outlook*, vol. 1, no. 2 (February 13, 1976), p. 7.

standing). With the experience of 1941–45 still very fresh in their minds, Soviet officials take the prospect of war very seriously indeed—they appear to believe, even in 1976, that states can win or lose. One may not approve of, or even really understand, this point of view—but it is only prudent to take full account of it. A strategic posture that looks awesome *to us,* largely in terms of our ability to devastate the urban-industrial structure of the Soviet Union, may look considerably less forbidding to a state that designs its strategic forces largely with a counterforce focus, and which does not expect to have a large fraction of its urban population at nuclear risk in an intense crisis.

Strategic Superiority Revisited

On June 25, 1976, Secretary of State Kissinger issued the following dictum: "Increasingly, strategic forces find their function only in deterring and matching each other."[6] As a terse summary of much of Western opinion, the Secretary was very close to the mark. However, it is appropriate to wonder whether such an opinion is sensible for a superpower that has very extensive overseas interests which could require limited first-strike support from American strategic forces. Furthermore, one wonders how such an apolitical perspective will affect American performance in an arms competition with a state that does not obviously share it. On July 3, 1974, Kissinger asked the following set of questions: "What in the name of God is strategic superiority? What is the significance of it, politically, militarily, operationally, at these levels of numbers? What do you do with it?"[7]

These were good questions deserving good answers. They penetrate to the very heart of much of the strategic debate of recent years—though, thus far, they do not seem to have elicited any very direct and well-formulated replies. The answers offered here may not be as illuminating as Kissinger's questions, but they do, at least, confront the issues without evasion. Kissinger asked, "What in the name of God is strategic superiority?" In descending order of operational strategic significance, a three-tiered answer must be provided.

1. *Type A superiority:* the ability to prevail in World War III—at tolerable cost to your society. The concept of *victory* may be passé among most Western strategists, but—perhaps alas—acute international crises will not be conducted solely by those strategists.

---

[6]Henry Kissinger, Address to the International Institute for Strategic Studies (London), *New York Times,* June 26, 1976, p. 7.

[7]Henry Kissinger, "News Conference at Moscow, July 3," *The Department of State Bulletin,* vol. 71, no. 1831 (July 29, 1974), p. 215.

2. *Type B superiority:* the acquisition of major strategic capabilities, unmatched by the adversary, that should yield non-marginal military and political advantages. These capabilities, however, will be understood to fall well short of a plausible war-winning capability. Prominent examples, looking over the next decade, could be the leverage acquired (or perceived to have been acquired) by a working (though far from immaculate) civil defense program, and a major hard-target counterforce capability. Neither should enable the Soviet Union to be confident of victory at low cost, but—in combination—they should enable the Soviet leadership to take and keep the initiative.

3. *Type C superiority:* the acquisition of a strategic force posture which *looks* more substantial/capable than does that of the adversary. Even if military advantage could not be taken of such a posture, most interested observers of the strategic balance who were not professional defense analysts should perceive a marked tilt in that balance.[8] The public relations for a strategic superiority of this third variety could probably be left safely by the Soviet leadership to such willing instruments as *Aviation Week* and American presidential and senatorial "hopefuls."

The above tripartite answer to Kissinger's first question should be non-controversial. In theory, at least, there is little doubt as to what would constitute strategic superiority. Next, Kissinger posed the question: "What is the significance of it [strategic superiority], politically, militarily, and operationally, at these levels of numbers?"

Again, he deserves an answer. The mutual perception, by adversary crisis managers, of any type of strategic superiority should place the perceived inferior party at a severe psychological disadvantage. The expectation by the disadvantaged side that it would be assessed by the adversary as lacking a balancing measure of strategic weight could encourage rational but possibly reckless behavior in an endeavor to mobilize credibility in a hurry.

Should the "high threat" estimate of the danger to Minuteman presented by Secretary Rumsfeld develop,[9] then—by 1982-1983—it is not implausible that Soviet leaders might believe that they had achieved Type B superiority, and were well on the road to Type A. Deprived forcibly of all save 50 or so of the land-based missile force, and *possibly* having lost 40 percent plus of the SSBN [strategic missile-launching submarine] force in part and some proportion of the

---

[8] See Edward N. Luttwak, *The Missing Dimension of U.S. Defense Policy: Force, Perception and Power,* ARPA-T10-72-2 (Arlington, Va.: Defense Advanced Research Projects Agency (February 1976). Also of interest is Charles Wolf, Jr., *Perceptions of the Military Balance: Models and Anecdotes,* P-5402 (Santa Monica: RAND, March 1975).
[9] See Figure 1 below.

manned bomber fleet on its runways, the United States might find (a) that it could not effect anything even close to the assured destruction of Soviet urban-industrial values, and (b) that it was not strongly motivated to try. It is true that mass urban evacuation in the Soviet Union *should* occasion maximum alarm in the United States[10]—but what could the United States do in that circumstance?—seek to emulate?—launch a portion of the ICBM force?—put some bombers on airborne alert and disperse the rest?—send SSBNs to sea? While there are crisis measures that the United States undoubtedly could and would effect, it is difficult to deny the argument that mass urban evacuation in the Soviet Union would create a major (and possibly fatal—for the United States) strategic asymmetry. The Soviet civil defense program may not be as impressive in fact (or in prospect) as some commentators would have us believe, but its potential as a crisis and/or war winner does seem to be appreciated in the Soviet Union and resisted in the United States.

It is one thing to argue that a serious civil defense program in the United States is impractical, for reasons of political culture or urban geography, it is quite another to argue that civil defense *really* would make very little difference. One should be honest with oneself, even if the answers are unpalatable. The Soviet estimate that they could hold their casualties down to 10 million or so may be a considerable underestimate, but—in the light of Soviet experience—such a (prompt) casualty list is by no means unprecedented. Probably upward of 10 million Soviet citizens were sacrificed to the end of consolidating Soviet political power and modernizing the structure of Soviet society (on a "crash" basis) in the 1920s and 1930s, while the Soviet Union took close to 20 million casualties (from all causes) in the Great Patriotic War. Plausibly, one might suggest that even a very ruthless and desperate Soviet leadership would conclude "never again," but—no less plausibly—one might suggest that such a leadership would deem the price well worth paying (as it had been in the past). After all, the Soviet political objective in such a conflict would be the defeat of the United States (or, at least, its reduction to a fourth- or fifth-rate power), following which happy event, the Soviet Union would no doubt expect to resolve the outstanding problems in Sino-Soviet and Soviet-West European relations in a satisfactory way.

The above is not a prediction, but is intended as a warning of what might occur if the United States permits very substantial strategic asymmetries to develop in an arms competition with a strategically alien culture which does not eschew the old fashioned notion of victory.

---

[10] It might be understood as the functional equivalent of pre-1914 mobilization.

283

COLIN S. GRAY

Kissinger's third question, "What do you do with it [strategic superiority]?" is not difficult to answer. Depending upon the type of superiority attained, three categories of advantage can be specified.

1. To deter crises. In other words, perceptions of strategic superiority, and foreign expectations of the will and confidence that should flow therefrom, should induce preemptive political accommodation. The strategic historian has the problem of negative evidence. We can never know which crises did *not* occur in the 1950s and 1960s because of Soviet understanding of American Type A and, eventually, Type B strategic superiority.

2. To wage and win crises. Even Type C strategic superiority—of (some) appearances only—should yield some crisis-waging weight. It should be possible to so manipulate the perceptions of the adversary, and certainly of very interested third-parties, that others expect you to anticipate a favorable outcome. Hence, you are expected to press your claims with vigor, and to be prepared to take the crisis to a higher level for an improved outcome. Should one enjoy the benefits of Type B (major strategic asymmetries in your favor—of prospective military significance) superiority, then one has "escalation dominance." There should be major military use options to choose from for the effecting of a "knights' move" in the crisis if, say, a local passage of arms develops unsatisfactorily. Anticipating escalation dominance, a state with a superior strategic arsenal (Type B—perhaps approaching Type A) should be far more willing to engage in crisis—or to threaten to force a road-test of political will (and military competence, if need be).

3. To wage and win wars. Western strategic theorists, for excellent reasons, have devoted far more attention to the deterrence than they have to the conduct of thermonuclear war. Even when the theoretical veil masking actual nuclear use is lifted, discussion tends to focus upon "intra-war deterrence" and "war termination." One may applaud the reasoning and values behind this bias, but it behooves us to recognize that the attitude-set of the arms race competitor shows every plausible sign of being rather different. Specifically, one seeks to deter (though there are some linguistic problems here) war, and then—if deterrence fails—one moves smartly and, with good luck and judgment, preemptively (going first in the last resort) into the phase of war waging for the end of gaining victory.[11] Speculation on intra-war deterrence, and how wars might end, are prominent by their absence from the visible Soviet debate.

---

[11] See John Erickson, "Soviet Military Policy: Priorities and Perspectives," *The Round Table*, no. 256 (October 1974), p. 370; and Benjamin S. Lambeth, *The Evolving Soviet Strategic Threat*, P-5493 (Santa Monica: RAND, August 1975), pp. 7-11.

284

Under discussion here is not the merit of one or another strategic theory; rather it is the likely use that a politico-strategic culture very different from our own might choose to make of a strategic posture that it deemed to be usefully superior. Because *we* would be strongly disinclined to try to cash a probable Type B (or even Type A) superiority through a military road-test, it does not follow that Soviet leaders will reason similarly. It is prudent, and not paranoid, for American officials and legislators to so plan their strategic posture that the Soviet willingness to translate their rather muscular strategic theory into practice is never put seriously to the test.

The burden of this section has been to argue that strategic superiority, in all three types specified, is—in theory—attainable and usable. The key factor is whether or not one party alone to the arms competition would be able to reduce very, very substantially the proportion of its population that would be at immediate nuclear risk. Given the current American enthusiasm for (relatively) low-yield warheads that should minimize collateral damage—and for limited strategic options—the Soviet Union has every incentive to devote considerable resources (possibly $1 billion per annum and 72,000 full-time personnel) to civil defense and the protection of key industrial machinery (rather than buildings). A crucial asymmetry that one must reasonably presume is that the Soviet Union is willing to place a far higher figure upon the identification of "tolerable" casualties than is the United States. No civil defense program could keep casualties to less than 10 million against a determined (if ragged) assault, but the asymmetry in willingness to suffer pain should mean that a civil defense program is far more cost effective for the Soviet Union than it would be for the United States. There are, of course, ways in which the Soviet civil defense program could be offset. Indeed, should American officials begin to suspect that Soviet leaders felt convinced that their civil defense program yielded them a prospective war-winning edge, it would be sensible to specify, very publicly, that American counterpopulation options were being designed explicitly to offset the reduced vulnerability that should flow from urban evacuation. (This sounds easy, but in practice would be very expensive and difficult to accomplish.)

The Land-Based Missile Question

The question of the decade, for both superpowers in the 1980s with respect to the structure of their strategic forces, should be what to do about land-based ICBMs. Despite some valiant attempts to prove the

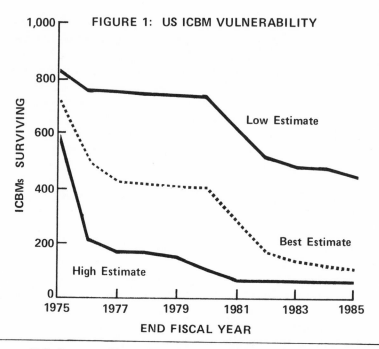

FIGURE 1: US ICBM VULNERABILITY

(y-axis) ICBMs SURVIVING

Low Estimate

Best Estimate

High Estimate

END FISCAL YEAR

Source: U.S. Congress, House Committee on Appropriations, Subcommittee on the Department of Defense, *Department of Defense Appropriations for 1977, Hearings,* Part I, 94th Congress, 2nd session, 1976, p. 560.

contrary,[12] it is implausible that either superpower will be able to rest confidence in its silo-housed ICBMs for *second-strike* missions, by the end of the decade of the 1980s. According to the "best" official American estimates, this condition of acute (theoretical, of course) vulnerability will afflict the United States as early as 1982. Figure 1 was presented by Secretary of Defense Rumsfeld early in 1976.

The "best" and "high" draw-down lines of Figure 1 *may* be grossly conservative, but skeptics should take note of the following points: (a) those who compiled and assessed the data for Figure 1 had no obvious interest in exaggerating the threat to Minuteman (the USAF and the CIA certainly have none); (b) these lines were not drawn as a consequence of "back of the envelope" arithmetic—nor taking simple readings from a "vulnerability assessment calculator"; (c) the detailed and even careful arithmetic of the skeptics rests upon a knowledge (and reasonable guess) base vastly inferior to those who drew Figure 1. "Monday morning quarterbacking" on the National Intelligence Esti-

---

[12]For example, Steinbruner and Garwin, "Strategic Vulnerability: The Balance Between Prudence and Paranoia."

mates (NIEs) may be a legitimate exercise for extra-official analysts, certainly it is an intriguing game to play, but it must not be allowed to obscure the fact that the only authoritative source of data on Soviet and American strategic weapon systems is the official intelligence community. Since university-based groups do not maintain missile-test monitoring equipment, nor reconnaissance satellites, it behooves us to treat their projections with some reserve—particularly when they are flatly contradictory of official estimates. Both official and extra-official estimates may be wrong (there can be no absolute authority on, for example, the degree of super-hardening of Soviet ICBM silos), but for much of the data that is critical to the silo-vulnerability question, one group (officials) knows the facts and semi-facts that are available, and the other group (extra-official) does not. To repeat, there are no independent, extra-official, sources of reliable data on the performance of weapons.

Prudently, one must presume that the Soviet Union will acquire a sufficient force of MIRV launchers, with reduced CEPs [circles of equal probability], to pose an all but annihilating threat to American ICBMs in the early- to mid-1980s. Presuming, probably unreasonably, that the common aggregate ceilings of Vladivostok are translated into a SALT II treaty, and that the Soviet Union elects to maximize its hard-target counterforce potential by MIRVing only land-based systems, a force of 1,000 SS-17-19s [200 and 800 respectively] and 303 SS-18 Mod 2s would be able to deliver 8,024 warheads of close to, or in excess of, 1 mt [megaton] (SS-17-900kt [kiloton]; SS-19-1-2mt; SS-18 Mod 2–2 plus mt.)[13] with CEPs of close to 0.1 nm [nautical mile] (608 feet) by the mid-1980s, ignoring reliability problems. Since the United States offers a hard-target structure numbering only a little over a thousand aim points, and since the CEP estimate cited above was provided by Representative Robert Leggett,[14] who is not exactly a friend to "paranoid" strategic calculations, it is easy to see why the Soviet Union should have an ample number of reentry vehicles to place the two on each silo required to offset reliability problems, yet meet the exacting launch-window requirement for the preclusion of serious fratricide problems.

The United States cannot acquire a matching high-confidence, hard-target killing capability until (and if) the MX-ICBM is deployed in

---

[13] See James Schlesinger's testimony in U.S. Congress, Senate Committee on Foreign Relations, Subcommittee on Arms Control, International Law and Organization, *U.S.-U.S.S.R. Strategic Policies, Hearing,* 93rd Congress, 2nd session, released April 4, 1974, pp. 6-7.

[14] In U.S. Congress, House Committee on International Relations, Subcommittee on International Security and Scientific Affairs, *The Vladivostok Accord: Implications to U.S. Security, Arms Control, and World Peace, Hearings,* 94th Congress, 1st session, 1975, pp. 12-13.

numbers. If one is serious about hard-target counterforce, the only candidate system in the existing American inventory, Minuteman III, simply does not carry the requisite number of reentry vehicles to place two warheads on each Soviet silo. Facing a Soviet hard-target structure of 1,500 plus aim points, 550 Minuteman IIIs carry only 1,650 warheads. Even if Minuteman's CEP was zero, instead of 0.15 that it probably is at present,[15] the United States would not have a high-confidence total, hard-target killing capability (because of reliability uncertainties). To summarize thus far: both superpowers face the problem of the total vulnerability of silo-housed missile forces in the 1980s; and the United States should be in this condition (at least) two or three years before the Soviet Union.

Intriguing questions flow from these conclusions. A selection includes the following:

1. What use, if any, might the Soviet Union make of a unilateral, major hard-target counterforce capability?

2. Should the United States seek to "match" the Soviet capability, "stuffing" its Minuteman III silos with a follow-on ICBM designed to be a hard-target killer?

3. Should the United States respond to the predictable Soviet hard-target killing capability by moving to a dyad of SSBNs and manned bombers/cruise missile carriers?

4. Should the United States learn to live with vulnerable silos—seeing ICBMs thus housed as of value for (a) limited (first-strike) strategic options; (b) their attack-timing complication merit—thereby providing cover for bomber and SSBN facilities?

5. Should the United States defend ICBM silos?

6. Should the United States deploy land/air mobile ICBMs?

7. Should the United States consider the firing tactics of launch on warning (LOW) or launch through attack (LTA)?

This author has addressed these questions at length elsewhere and will not seek to reproduce here the detail of that analysis.[16] Figure 2 presents the structure of the decision problem in bare outline.

The case for retaining a strategic triad is a substantial one—notwithstanding former Secretary Schlesinger's disparagement of

---

[15] See Jan M. Lodal, "Assuring Strategic Stability: An Alternative View," *Foreign Affairs*, vol. 54, no. 3 (April 1976), p. 465.
[16] In *The Future of Land-Based Missile Forces, 1976-1990*, Adelphi Paper (London: IISS, forthcoming).

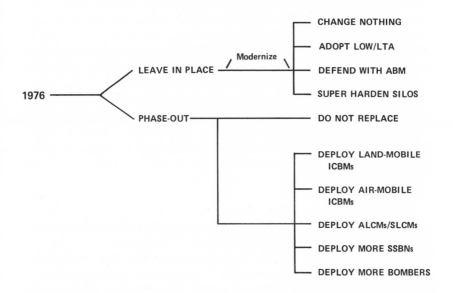

FIGURE 2: THE FUTURE OF LAND-BASED MISSILE FORCES

"the canonical logic of the Triad."[17] Specifically, a triad offers three distinctive warfighting problems to the adversary, it functions synergistically for enhanced survivability, and each of the three legs has quite characteristic strengths and weaknesses for the accomplishment of particular strategic missions. The SSBN force, out of port (and presumably not "trailed" in a dedicated fashion), is the most survivable of the strategic launching modes, but some CEP degradation results from small inaccuracies in the ships' inertial navigation system (which can be offset by stellar guidance), while reliable communication, at depth, is an as-yet unresolved problem. ELF *Seafarer*, if ever constructed (environmentalists willing), should greatly alleviate the problem of communicating with SSBNs at depth, but ELF [extremely low frequency] communication, by definition, has a very low traffic flow. Also, communication problems aside, SSBNs are not always where they should be for the launching of prompt missile strikes.

The manned bomber force, in principle, has problems of prelaunch survivability and of penetration. Furthermore, a manned bomber, however wondrously equipped with ECM [electronic countermeasures] and defense-suppressing ASMs [air-to-surface missiles], is (relatively) slow to target. Really high confidence in the

---

[17] In *U.S.-U.S.S.R. Strategic Policies*, p. 25.

prospective performance of a penetrating manned bomber force through the 1980s is possible only if land-based missiles (however deployed) maximize attack-warning time and a cloud of LRCMs [long-range cruise missiles] confuses and overloads air defense systems.

Land-based missiles, in silos or in pre-surveyed sites (possibly shelters), have the characteristics of very high accuracy, very secure communications, and symmetry of gross appearance with the land-based missiles of the other side. Force structure choice should be driven by doctrine. If the United States wishes (a) to avoid offering the Soviet Union a major, very lucrative, vulnerable military target system; (b) to pursue a major silo-killing capability; (c) to retain a near-instantaneous strategic capability to respond (or initiate) at the homeland-to-homeland level; and (d) avoid very prominent visible strategic disparities—then it is difficult to see how the option of purchasing a land-mobile ICBM system could be eschewed. If one is not very interested in "matching," and indeed offsetting and denying, Soviet hard-target killing potential, and if one decides that the requirement for near real-time strategic response is little more than dogma,[18] of no substantial strategic importance or political interest, then one should consider very seriously the option of phasing-out silo-ICBMs and not replacing them with a follow-on land-based system. What follows is a terse and summary commentary upon the options cited in Figure 2.

Leave Silo-Housed ICBMs in Place

1. *Change Nothing:* this amounts to saying that even a vulnerable ICBM force is cost-effective: bombers would receive maximum tactical warning, while one should have some sizeable first-strike options. Also, one could be expressing the belief that the vulnerability of silos is probably a myth. Lest a contrary impression [has been] given above, let it be understood that it would be no easy task to reduce the Minuteman force to 50 or 60 missiles, even in 1983 or 1984. Soviet reentry vehicles would have to "walk," very carefully, from South to North to avoid fratricide phenomena, while the attack timing would have to be excellent (*the first time!*) for the second RV on target to arrive prior to the critical and disabling environmental disturbance. Moreover, operational CEP degradation and reliability estimates would have to be within tolerable margins.

2. *Adopt LOW/LTA:* LOW has some value as an option that one does

---

[18] See Fred Iklé, "Can Nuclear Deterrence Last Out the Century?" *Foreign Affairs*, vol. 51, no. 2 (January 1973), p. 283.

not authoritatively eschew (the vague possibility of LOW should promote a healthy uncertainty in the mind of a potential first-striker), but
it has very serious drawbacks. Prominent among its limitations are the
following: (a) false warning might be received, processed and acted
upon; (b) the absence of time for attack assessment means that the response would have to be pre-programmed and indiscriminate; (c) it is
vulnerable to the degradation of warning facilities—e.g., does one
launch the entire ICBM force if one early warning satellite ceases to
function (for reasons unknown), or two? If one loses one's warning facilities, one cannot LOW. LTA calls for steady nerves and virtually invites an adversary to try to pin your forces down, pending the arrival of
the total hard-target killing force.

3. *Defend with ABM [anti-ballistic missile] (or other site defense hardware)*: this range of options, if more than token in scale, would require
the renegotiation of the ABM treaty of 1972. Also, the scale and sophistication of the Soviet threat has grown to such a degree since 1969, that
linear descendants of Spartan and Sprint would probably be over-
matched. Radical (both "exotic" and very "mundane")[19] anti-missile
systems, however, might be of interest.

4. *Super-Harden ICBM silos*: the Soviet Union is doing this, but the
arithmetic is not promising for its cost-effectiveness (e.g., an increase
in nominal silo blast resistance from 2,000 to 3,000 psi [pounds per
square inch of pressure] can be offset by an improvement in missile
CEP of 60 feet).

Phase-Out Silo-Housed ICBMs

1. *Do Not Replace*: one loses the distinctive advantages of land-
based missiles and, unless the process is conducted under the umbrella
of an arms control agreement, one risks political perceptions of a major
disadvantageous asymmetry (i.e., our ICBMs were coerced out of their
silos).

2. *Deploy Land-Mobile ICBMs*: the major options include the following: dispersed shelters; garage mobility; buried trench mobility;
off-road random crawling; road and rail mobility; canal/deep pond
mobility; lake bottom mobility. The problems of "public interface" effectively rule out any deployment mode away from military reservations. The interesting remainder promise survivability via deception
and the proliferation of aim points for the defeat of a saturation attack.
This notion of creating an "RV [reentry vehicle] sink" is attractive, pro-

---

[19] For example, high energy lasers and "gatling guns."

vided one is confident that it would prove cost-effective at the very high threat levels achievable by the Soviet Union in the 1980s and beyond. The shell-game of the dispersed shelter system is probably the least flawed of the land-mobile options, though it does pose (what appear to be) insurmountable problems in terms of arms control verification. At the present time, it is not at all certain that the Soviet Union could not offset any multiple-launch point system that involves (hard or semi-hard) shelter and roadway construction, by means of the fractionation of missile payload.[20]

3. *Deploy Air-Mobile ICBMs:* such a system could have serious pre-launch vulnerabilities, would be extremely expensive to procure and to maintain on an alert basis (particularly on airborne alert), and would have CEP degradation problems that could be expensive to solve with very high confidence.

4. *Deploy ALCMs/SLCMs* [*air/sea-launched cruise missiles*]: aside from their well-appreciated incompatibility with any viable arms control verification procedures, LRCMs have much to recommend them. They could serve as a *substitute* for silo-housed ICBMs in that, nuclear-armed, they could kill any hard-targets (conventionally-armed, they could not—TERCOM [terrain contour matching] promises to be an excellent guidance system, but the CEP it should provide will probably not be as good as many seem to assume), *but* they will be vulnerable at all stages of their missions and they are (relatively) slow to target. As a supporting element for a penetrating B-1 force LRCMs promise to be highly cost-effective. As a substitute for a penetrating bomber force, major questions arise. In their ALCM mode, they are vulnerable on runways, their carrier aircraft would have a slower escape speed than the B-1 and would be less resistant to nuclear effects, while the carrier aircraft—prior to LRCM release—would be large preferential targets. Also, it is not the case that LRCMs, flying at, say, 300 feet, subsonically, would be invulnerable to air defense attention (dogmatic claims to the contrary notwithstanding). A fleet of specialized ALCM-carriers would be very expensive to procure.

5. *Deploy More SSBNs/Manned Bombers:* to augment a dyad, in order to offset the military and political perceptual costs of the abandonment of land-based missiles, does not look very attractive. Transition to a strategic dyad should dramatically raise the cost-effectiveness of Soviet air defense and ASW [anti-submarine warfare] research. The distinctive limitations of submarines and bombers would remain,

---

[20] In 1974, Schlesinger speculated that a Soviet ICBM force with the payloads of the SS-18 and SS-19 could dispense 33,000 warheads. *U.S.-U.S.S.R. Strategic Policies*, p. 6.

while the vulnerability of the ground facilities of the dyad would necessarily be enhanced.

As of 1976, the Department of Defense wishes to proceed to engineering development of the MX ICBM, but the Congress is not convinced that the Department knows what it wants, nor why. The following points summarize this action:

1. The next generation of American ICBMs should not be placed in silos, though it should be recognized that deployment of a mobile silo-killer will probably drive Soviet ICBMs out of *their* silos.

2. On perceptual grounds, at least, an American dyad should not confront a Soviet triad.

3. On the substitute options for silo-housed ICBMs, a dispersed shelter system should prove the most attractive, but . . .

4. Critical to the decision on how to deploy MX must be very careful analyses of the probable cost exchange ratios of shelters to low-yield Soviet warheads.

What Value SALT?

The now-classical texts on arms control theory[21] proclaimed that arms control should (a) reduce the risk of the outbreak of war; (b) reduce the likely damage should war occur; and (c) reduce the burden of peacetime defense preparation. These were, and remain, impeccable objectives. Unfortunately, rarely has it been very clear which details of possible agreements would promote these objectives; while the history of the past sixteen years (taking 1960 as a critical year for the formulation of arms control theory) suggests that arms control processes conducted with an alien politico-strategic culture can be fraught with the dangers that flow from self-delusion. Succinctly, a persuasive case can be made to the effect that arms control as a process could not sustain the military and political traffic and that some would have it bear.

In passing largely adverse judgment upon the arms control history of the 1960s and 1970s in general, and SALT in particular, one need not assault the theoretical citadels of arms control itself. Indeed, could one favor arms race and instability, as opposed to arms control and stability? Superpower arms control processes have come to be recognized, for good and ill, as a continuous litmus-test for the state of superpower political relations. Far from SALT being a joint, substantially technical

---

[21] See, for example, Thomas C. Schelling and Morton Halperin, *Strategy and Arms Control* (New York: The Twentieth Century Fund, 1961).

enterprise, removed from the ebbs and flow of wider diplomatic considerations, it has proved to be both vulnerable to the deterioration in detente frameworks and a contributor to that deterioration. In the words of *Strategic Survey, 1975:* "Far from arms control promoting detente, detente would be needed to produce the trust required for arms control: yet the very process of arms control—with its concentration on military imbalances, weapons and the scenarios of conflict—tended to undermine what trust there was."[22] Moreover, to cite an argument that has been underappreciated in the United States, the elevation of SALT to its status as the diplomatic centerpiece of detente politics, is to risk public overappreciation of the strength of the Soviet Union. It is really only in military strength that the Soviet Union can be considered a serious competitor with the United States. Hence, the attention focused upon, and the importance attached to, SALT risks the encouragement of public misperceptions of the overall competitive strength of the Soviet Union. In broad competitive political perspective, it is not in the interest of the United States to accord first-class, superpower status to the Soviet Union—nor, logically, to emphasize in the rank ordering of its functional dealings with the Soviet Union, that one category (military power) wherein a very serious challenge is presented.

An obvious difficulty attendant upon an exercise in SALT-assessment is to specify criteria. At opposite extremes one may discover analysts disgusted either that SALT has not, thus far, terminated the arms competition, or that the Soviet Union has not been negotiated out of weapon developments that clearly were in its interest to pursue. In making the strongest case that he was able for the value of SALT, in an adverse domestic (and international) political climate, Kissinger has argued as follows:

> In an era of expanding technological possibilities, it is impossible to make rational choices of force planning without some element of predictability in the strategic environment. Moreover, a continuing race diverts resources from other needed areas such as forces for regional defense, where imbalances can have serious geopolitical consequences.[23]

These are not insubstantial arguments. As a consequence of SALT I, American defense planners knew that they would not have to plan to penetrate Soviet ABM defenses (save around Moscow—and provided the treaty endured), and that Soviet offensive forces could number no more than 1,618 ICBMs (they thought) and 740 SLBMs through 1977. SALT II, with its tentative common aggregate ceilings of

[22] *Strategic Survey, 1975* (London: IISS, 1976), p. 5.
[23] Address to the International Institute for Strategic Studies, *The New York Times,* June 26, 1976, p. 7.

2,400 (strategic offensive forces) and 1,320 (MIRV launchers), should similarly build a useful certainty into the next decade.

However, since SALT I was, in substance, little more than a registration of Soviet progress—a recognition of facts (somewhat generously interpreted with respect to the SSBN count)—set in a context where the Soviet Union was on the threshold of a major qualitative upgrading of its forces, the strategic worth of the Interim Agreement is open to serious question. The United States paid in the (possibly counterfeit—given domestic political objections) coin of a much superior ABM technology, for what? The appearance of the constraint of the Soviet silo-killing threat? In fact SALT I yielded no alleviation of the threat to Minuteman silos worthy of note.

One can, and probably should, note that SALT was innocuous in that while it was devoid of obvious strategic merit, in itself, it did not disadvantage the United States. If Safeguard (and a Site-Defense follow-on) had not been arrested by the ABM Treaty of SALT I, it would almost certainly have been stopped by the United States Congress. Also, while the Soviet SS-16 through 19 ICBM series, with its much increased (and MIRVed) payload over the SS-9s, 11s, and 13s, was not constrained by SALT (save in a way that the Soviet Union might have found attractive anyway—the necessity to phaseout less capable systems), neither can its deployment be laid at the door of SALT. One can argue that SALT *failed* to preclude the modernization of the Soviet ICBM force in the directions of greatly increased payload and (independently targetable) payload fractionation, but that argument is fatally vulnerable to the judgment that the modernization program was not negotiable.

While, in general, Henry Kissinger's assertion of the value of "predictability in the strategic environment" sounds reasonable, in practice it is not obvious that SALT I and (possibly) SALT II offered predictability that was worth purchasing. ICBM launcher numbers were frozen by the Interim Agreement, but that kind of five-year certainty was of little, if any, worth—given the very extensive freedom to modernize that was agreed. Also, it is perhaps useful to know that Soviet strategic offensive forces can number no more than 2,400 under the terms of SALT II, with 1,320 MIRV launchers, but since those numbers are way beyond the necessary numerical zone for the posing of a (near) total hard-target counterforce threat—where is the comfort in that certainty?[24] In the absence of a SALT II, the Soviet Union could elect simply to add the SS-16 through 19 ICBM series to the existing deployment—in keeping with its traditional practice of not retiring ob-

---

[24] That certainty is somewhat eroded if Backfire, the SS-X-20 and LRCMs are excluded from precise numerical regulation.

solescent systems. However, such a tactic would have political perceptual, rather than strategic, significance (not that one should minimize
the importance of the former; nor deny that a quantitative American
arms race response might have been triggered thereby).

In terms of the three classic goals of arms control, SALT, thus far,
has been either an unambiguous failure, or does not lend itself to sufficiently precise discussion. In order:

1. Has SALT reduced the risk of the outbreak of war? This is difficult to answer unless one has a reasonably concise theory of the causes
of war. In the sense that the somewhat apolitical American arms control establishment tends to believe that technical instabilities can promote conflict, SALT has been an irrelevance. SALT has arrested
stabilizing silo-defense options, and has legitimized the deployment of
destabilizing (limited) first-strike capabilities. In fact, the Soviet view
that technical instability need not promote political instability probably
has a great deal of merit.

2. Has SALT reduced the likely damage that would be suffered
were war to occur? Not at all, must be the cautious answer. SALT has
not involved, at least on the Soviet side, the discussion of strategy—let
alone the negotiation of rules for homeland-to-homeland engagement.
The LSO [limited strike option] theme in American strategy evolved
contemporaneously with SALT, but it was a planning process almost
totally removed from SALT considerations. If the Soviet Union has revised its SIOP [single integrated operations plan] as a consequence of
SALT-related developments, that fact remains a very well-guarded secret.

3. Has SALT reduced the burdens of peacetime defense preparation? Yes, if one chooses to believe that either superpower was willing
and able to proceed to full-scale ABM deployment. No, if one believes
(in company with this author) that neither side wanted (Soviet Union),
or would be permitted (the United States), to proceed with deployment. It is not certain that SALT, thus far, has had more than a very
marginal impact upon Soviet offensive forces programs (any "arms
control dividend" from quantities not deployed has been instead in the
quality and quantity of successor systems); while SALT-bargaining
considerations increased the attraction of early MIRVing and lent
diplomatic-rationale weight to the B-1, Trident and LRCM developments in the United States.

To be fair to the SALT process, the discussion immediately above
probably speaks as much to the shallowness of arms control theory as it
does to the deficiencies of SALT and its negotiations. The litany of the

goals of arms control has become so familiar that few people have stood back and observed that those goals have no operational value. Perhaps those who debate the merits of SALT—both as a process and as a series of outcomes—are guilty of not making explicit first what it is reasonable to expect. After all, one could set one's sights so low that almost any SALT-related activity is deemed to be valuable, or so high that no degree of negotiable progress would warrant ascription as success. It might be felt that SALT is in need of no specific justification, provided it does not occasion harm to Western security interests. Where one feels the burden of proof to lie, on those who would justify the continuation of SALT, or upon those who would effect its swift demise, is very much a matter of individual political preference. Views on the worth of the SALT enterprise are driven by one's assessment of the nature of Soviet foreign policy goals, the enduring character of Soviet strategic doctrine, and the relative competence of Soviet and American negotiators. This last point refers not merely to the style and capacity of individuals, but to the characteristic negotiating habits of two very different political-social-bureaucratic systems.[25] Before turning to a line of assessment of SALT according to some very different criteria, it is useful to present thumb-nail sketches of the typical approaches to arms control negotiations of the two superpowers.

Relevant Soviet Attitudes

1. Arms control is a form of political struggle, wherein victory or defeat may be registered.

2. Arms control is primarily a political, rather than a technical, exercise. Arms control is *not* a process concerned with the joint solution or alleviation of technical strategic problems (e.g., surprise attack anxieties); rather does it record the facts of changing political relationships in the coin of (preferably sparse and *general*) technical strategic detail.

3. Arms control involves a protracted test of will, skill and resources. Rigidity, patience, linguistic manipulation, ambiguous "technical" breaches of past agreements—all play a part in what is seen essentially as a conflict process.

4. Arms control can contribute to the psychological disarmament of the adversary.

---

[25] See William R. Van Cleave, "Political and Negotiating Asymmetries: Insult in SALT I," in Robert L. Pfaltzgraff, Jr., ed., *Contrasting Approaches to Arms Control* (Lexington, Mass.: Lexington Books, 1974), Chapter 2.

5. Arms control is genuinely sought. Items 1-4 do *not* indicate disinterest—they are simply "the Soviet way"—the manner in which Soviet officials believe the best result (for the Soviet Union) for the cost can be secured.

Relevant American Attitudes

1. Arms control is about the promotion of stability defined largely in technical strategic terms.

2. Arms control, particularly with respect to strategic armaments, is so important and is so obviously a common superpower interest, that it should, and can, be promoted apart from considerations of day to day politics.

3. Arms control is about the *fixing* of particular strategic problems (in important respects the United States gives the appearance of being a nation of engineers).

4. Arms control processes should produce prompt and visible results—preferably in the terms of 3 above. Quadrennial domestic defense-debating excess means that the timetable for negotiations has to be influenced strongly by domestic political considerations.

5. Americans tend to be impatient—a cultural characteristic of a credit-card society which North Vietnamese, as well as Soviet, negotiators understood very well indeed.

6. Arms control, though primarily technical in focus, should promote improved political relations.

7. Arms control processes should allow for the strategic education of retarded foreigners (who do not understand their own best interests).[26]

The above contrasting selections, with the danger of some exaggeration admitted, do point to the probable fact that arms control negotiations between the superpowers are as unlikely a process for the promotion of better political relations as they are for the improved management of the arms competition. The sharply divergent strategic doctrines and political styles of the two countries could hardly fail to ambush the SALT process: even should major extra-SALT political developments not poison the negotiating climate fatally.

An obvious constraint in the discussion of the value of SALT in

---

[26] On the subject of "raising the Russian learning curve," see John Newhouse, *Cold Dawn: The Story of SALT* (New York: Holt, Rinehart and Winston, 1973), pp. 3-4.

1976 is that one is talking about an existing structure in diplomacy. The very fact of SALT is, in and of itself, important. If it did not exist, a prudent man might hesitate long before seeking to create it, but any very substantially negative assessment of the past and prospective value of SALT could lead one to the conclusion that SALT should be terminated. Whatever the narrow strategic basis of the assessment that SALT was of little or even negative worth, to take steps for termination would be viewed, worldwide, as a major political decision intended to provide a very broad-gauged signal to the effect that Soviet-American relations had deteriorated dramatically. In fact, it might not be too strong to say that the termination of SALT would be judged to be the end of the detente cycle that began in earnest in 1969. Of course, one can conceive of circumstances wherein that is precisely the signal that one would wish to transmit.

Although analysts and commentators will disagree about the appropriate answers, it is useful to approach the issue of the value of SALT by means of the provision of a set of relevant questions upon which most can agree.

1. Has SALT promoted political detente?

Comments: Yes and no, but largely no. Very strong motives for the appearance of better relations made possible SALT I in 1972. But, SALT I was a "false dawn" in that it sidestepped the more difficult and substantial strategic questions, and its dependence upon a unique political climate was not widely appreciated. As a general rule, detente promotes arms control, and not vice versa. The consideration of arms (im)balances is not likely to promote trust, good-will, and a willingness to take chances. It follows that the negotiation of a severely flawed agreement package (SALT I) is not likely to lead to the negotiation of more substantial and equitable agreements. Stylistic divergences must intrude strongly into the follow-on negotiations, (a) as each party monitors the manner in which the other complies with the agreed-upon terms, and (b) as those subjects upon which the negotiators of the initial round had agreed simply to disagree cannot be evaded any longer.

2. Has SALT promoted a benign convergence of strategic theories and attitudes (in the direction of what Western analysts understand by stability)?

Comments: The evidence of Soviet strategic programs developed and deployed since November 1969, and particularly since 1972, lends no support to the benign convergence thesis. The Soviet Union, no doubt for good reasons of its own, is deploying a family of ICBMs (and developing a successor ICBM series) that should compel the evacua-

COLIN S. GRAY

tion of American ICBM silos. There has been no noticeable evolution of Soviet strategic doctrine in directions identified as stabilizing by Western arms controllers.

3. Has SALT had any traceable impact upon the action-reaction mechanisms that characterize competitive activity?[27]

Comments: Very definitely not. The Soviet Union seems to be locked into a weapons development and procurement rhythm that is largely independent of American arms race moves. It is the United States that is the "reacting" party in the 1970s. Aside from the need to demonstrate comparable technical prowess, had the Soviet Union shared the assured destruction preference of many Western theorists, the ABM Treaty *should have* removed the necessity of its moving to MIRVed systems. SALT I and, prospectively, II place a premium upon the qualitative upgrading of strategic forces (and, of course, increase the attraction of systems that are not covered by agreement). In terms of the control of the arms race, SALT has been an irrelevance.

Not infrequently, one encounters the assertion that "SALT is essential for detente, there is no alternative to detente, therefore SALT must continue." Leaving aside the question of the proper character and objectives of detente, as understood in Moscow and Washington, the assertion is vulnerable to the argument that there are many alternatives to detente, as practiced and expressed rhetorically since 1969. We are the victims of simplistic era-mongerers. Eras of Cold War and of detente, as identifiable periods, are largely fiction (perhaps convenient and plausible fiction, but fiction nonetheless). Superpower interest in avoiding crises and wars that they would not expect to be able to prosecute to satisfactory conclusions will continue, with or without SALT and what is referred to as detente. The SALT skeptic should not be intimidated by the (apparent) dilemma of the non-existent alternative.

The most that should be expected of the SALT process is that it brings forth agreements that are not disadvantageous. The SALT process cannot "control the arms race" or reduce potential crisis instabilities very markedly, because SALT pertains to an arms competition, one of the participants in which has a (blurred and possibly unrealistic) concept of victory. The Soviet Union wants to achieve as superior a relative strategic position as it is permitted by American defense activity. The political roots of this ambition are quite beyond the competence of arms-control and detente-process attention. The degree to which the driving force of the Soviet-American arms competition should be laid at the door of ideology, as opposed to geopolitics, is

---

[27] See Colin S. Gray, *The Soviet-American Arms Race* (Lexington, Mass.: Lexington Books, 1976), particularly Chapter 4.

300

as uncertain as it is uninteresting. The scope for arms control interdiction of that competition is extremely limited. All that one can ask is that American negotiators function competently, and that the defense community recognize the character of the long-term strategic challenge that it must meet.

6

NATO'S EVOLVING NUCLEAR STRATEGY

NATO'S DOCTRINAL DILEMMA

Richard Hart Sinnreich

In 1967 the NATO allies adopted the doctrine of "flexible response" to guide their defense efforts should war occur in Central Europe. The author of the following article provides a brief historical overview of the policies followed by the United States in order to de-emphasize the role of nuclear weapons in defending against aggression from the Warsaw Pact countries.

Although flexible response received the consent of all NATO countries, Richard Hart Sinnreich argues that the doctrine is sufficiently imprecise in terms of its actual implementation to encompass divergent views of what constitutes effective deterrence. Of particular importance is the question of how nuclear weapons will serve to deter, or defend against, an invading army. As such, the doctrinal debate within NATO is closely related to that taking place in the United States over the function of strategic nuclear weapons: Are nuclear weapons merely to deter war, or are they to be employed in actual combat? And, if they are solely for the purpose of deterrence, what characteristics must they embody in order to deter most effectively?

The dilemmas encountered in defining a role for nuclear weapons in the defense of the United States are further exacerbated by the extension of its nuclear umbrella over the security interests of the NATO countries. According to Sinnreich, the United States sought to circumvent these dilemmas by

Source: *Orbis*, vol. 19, no. 2 (Summer 1975), pp. 461-76.

improving NATO's conventional forces and enhancing the deterrent capability of strategic nuclear weapons. While questions as to when and how nuclear forces might be employed have yet to be explicitly answered, American policy has been designed to avert a situation that would require such answers.

Few foreign policy problems present as great a political challenge as that of adapting strategic doctrine to changes in the international environment. Difficult even for a single government, it is still more difficult for an alliance, in which doctrine must satisfy simultaneously the strategic objectives and domestic constraints of all the member states, even when those objectives and constraints diverge or conflict.

In its twenty-five year history, the North Atlantic Alliance has been uniquely successful in meeting this challenge, though success has had its price for the member states and—as in the case of France—for the alliance as a whole. Each requirement for doctrinal redefinition inherently risks unraveling the fabric of mutual confidence that binds the alliance together. The danger is still greater when the threat against which the alliance is principally directed declines, or is perceived to do so.

The last five years have witnessed a major effort by the United States to adjust NATO military policy to new environmental conditions, in the face of unusually vexing alliance schisms. This article seeks to describe and assess this effort.

I

The basic statement of current NATO military doctrine is contained in Military Committee document MC 14/3, "Overall Strategic Concept for the Defense of the NATO AREA," adopted by the Defense Planning Committee in ministerial session in March 1967. Popularly known as "flexible response," MC 14/3 commits NATO to (1) meet initially any aggression short of general nuclear attack with a direct defense at the level—conventional or nuclear—chosen by the aggressor; (2) conduct a deliberate escalation if aggression cannot be contained and the situation restored by direct defense; and (3) initiate an appropriate general nuclear response to a major nuclear attack.

So defined, flexible response is perhaps most meaningful in comparison with the massive retaliation doctrine it replaced, a doctrine that (at least rhetorically) relied almost exclusively on the threat of U.S. strategic nuclear retaliation to deter any but the most limited threats to the Atlantic Alliance. In contrast, flexible response clearly postulates an initial conventional response to a significantly broader range of provocations. Beyond this, however, the operational implications of the doctrine are obscure. NATO and U.S. spokesmen defend this ambiguity on the grounds that it complicates Soviet planning. But a more plausible explanation for the ambiguity lies in the origins of flexible response.

First, it was primarily a U.S.-inspired doctrine—a "McNamara strategy," although its roots go back before the Kennedy Administration to the Gaither Report and earlier. It was so much an American strategy, in fact, that by the time of its formal adoption, NATO merely ratified what unilateral U.S. force posture decisions had virtually accomplished.

Not only was flexible response a U.S.-developed doctrine, it was also largely a U.S.-*imposed* doctrine. Fully six years elapsed between the effective decision by President Kennedy and Defense Secretary McNamara to seek strategic revision and the doctrine's formal ratification by the European allies. The intervening debate was so bitter that it contributed significantly to the military defection of France, and is still recalled with extreme discomfort by American officials then in government. The bitterness resulted only partly from the relatively high-handed way in which Washington approached the issue. For the most part, it reflected acute European awareness of the reason for the U.S. initiative, for however explicated by its defenders, flexible response clearly played to a U.S. problem: the emerging vulnerability of the United States to survivable Soviet strategic forces.

It was already clear by the late 1950s that the threat of massive retaliation was too blunt an instrument to deter reliably the sorts of limited provocation represented by the Berlin crisis. By the 1960s, Soviet delivery capabilities had improved to the point where the strategic nuclear threat was not only too blunt but too dangerous. U.S. initiation of strategic nuclear war in response even to a serious attack in Western Europe risked an equally devastating Soviet riposte against the United States itself. American analysts reasoned logically that under these conditions a deterrent posture relying primarily on U.S. strategic nuclear power would become increasingly incredible. Predictably, many Europeans viewed this argument as a thinly-disguised attempt to hedge American risks, a suspicion which deepened as the United States, in response to the demands of the Vietnam war, began to cannibalize the deployed ground forces upon which flexible response nominally depended.

All things considered, it was surprising that the allies bought flexible response at all. They did so largely in response to what was already an American *fait accompli,* and in tacit recognition of the fact that no alliance defense posture whatever was conceivable without a substantial U.S. contribution. More important, however, adoption was achieved by framing the doctrine in terms sufficiently ambiguous to enable all parties to interpret it as they pleased. The extent of this ambiguity was nowhere more marked than in the role accorded so-called tactical nuclear weapons. Both the United States and the allies agreed on their importance, but for precisely opposite reasons—the allies because tactical nuclear weapons represented the best assurance that a European war would threaten the U.S.S.R. with general nuclear war by escalation, and the United States because they offered the best hope of limiting a land war short of that catastrophe. MC 14/3 and subsequent NATO nuclear guidelines could readily accommodate either view; needless to say, however, the inherent contradiction effectively foreclosed any attempt to derive from declaratory doctrine precise guidance concerning the way in which theater nuclear weapons might ultimately be employed.

At the heart of this ambiguity, and the debate over flexible response in general, lay a fundamental disagreement between the United States and her allies regarding both the nature of deterrence and how its risks should be apportioned. At issue were two polar approaches to the deterrence problem. The first, manifested in its pure form by massive retaliation, grounded deterrence in the threat of punishment. Its foundation was the willingness of the United States to apply her nuclear power directly against the Soviet homeland. The second, implicit in the U.S. interpretation of flexible response, sought deterrence in the denial of objectives. Its foundation lay in maintaining a conventional capability adequate to deny Soviet arms physical access to NATO territory, or at least to make such a penetration intolerably expensive to the Soviet Union.

From the U.S. viewpoint, deterrence-by-threat-of-punishment suffered from two drawbacks. Since it postulated a maximum-risk response to any provocation, it risked being incapable of deterring anything less than outright, massive aggression. On the other hand, if the Soviets nevertheless believed the escalatory threat, such as posture implied enormous instability in a local crisis, for there would be considerable incentive for them to preempt an anticipated NATO nuclear initiation. The United States would therefore risk thermonuclear war over what might in reality be a minor confrontation.

Both arguments seemed to U.S. strategists to point clearly to the need for a substantial capability to contain aggression without resort to the ultimate nuclear response. Unfortunately, deterrence-by-denial posed equally severe drawbacks from the European standpoint. It threatened to undermine deterrence by reducing the aggressor's risks;

the very existence of a substantial conventional capability, it was argued, would lessen the credibility of the United States's willingness to engage her strategic forces. At the same time, deterrence-by-denial translated into land war on NATO territory. It therefore promised to make Western Europe a battlefield once again, while the two principal powers of the contending alliances escaped essentially unscathed.

Fortunately for NATO, the theoretical distinction between these competing deterrence postures is not easily maintained in practice. In the continuum between local conventional and strategic nuclear war it is difficult to specify the precise point at which efforts to deny become indistinguishable from efforts to punish. This is especially true given the possession by both sides of a wide diversity of theater nuclear capabilities. As it finally emerged from intra-alliance debate, flexible response attempted to make a virtue of this ambiguity. In effect, by asserting the continuity of the conflict spectrum, and grounding deterrence in the risk that any confrontation, however small, might—but need not—escalate to total war, flexible response satisfied both European insistence on the centrality of the strategic nuclear deterrent and the U.S. desire to hedge the risk of its use.

II

At the outset, the tolerance of flexible response to widely divergent interpretations posed a number of more or less severe practical problems. The inability to define with any precision the guidelines for employing theater nuclear weapons has already been mentioned. Equally vexing ambiguities beset the conventional force posture. For example, it was not clear at what point NATO might escalate the land battle. Europeans choose to interpret MC 14/3 as calling for conventional defense only against a limited Warsaw Pact attack of the sort represented by the "Hamburg Grab" scenario familiar to European defense analysts. In the event of a massive invasion, they visualized rapid escalation to general nuclear war. Such an interpretation was consistent with the European preference for deterrence-by-threat-of-punishment, and served the additional purpose of foreclosing any necessity to maintain substantial—and increasingly expensive—conventional ground forces.

In contrast, the United States interpreted flexible response to require maintenance of a conventional capability adequate to contain even a massive Warsaw Pact attack for a substantial period—the longer the better. Few even in the U.S. military establishment were comfortable with this requirement, and their discomfort grew as the Seventh Army deteriorated as a result of Vietnam levies. But the net effect was to produce serious asymmetries in such areas as ammunition stockage, the United States maintaining levels adequate for several weeks of combat while the allies maintained hardly a one-week supply.

Another bothersome difficulty concerned the definition of forward defense, to which all parties were nominally committed. For the Germans, forward defense meant defense at the frontier. Germany's shallow geographic depth, lack of natural barriers, urbanized demography and proximity of major industrial areas to the border made anything less politically intolerable. Since few European planners believed NATO would be able to conduct such a defense successfully against a serious Soviet thrust, given any economically feasible level of conventional military effort, this interpretation once again argued for a declaratory willingness to escalate rapidly across the nuclear threshold. In response, Washington complained insistently about the irrationality of tying escalation to the defense of "scenery," and chose for its part to interpret forward defense considerably more loosely. The disagreement over the meaning of forward defense, like that over its duration, produced a variety of force posture inconsistencies.

These were by no means the only problems confounding flexible response in its practical application. But they suffice to demonstrate the extent of the real disagreement that underlay apparent doctrinal consensus from the beginning. Thereafter, developments in the strategic environment exacerbated the problem.

The most immediate of these was Vietnam. Expanding American involvement cut deeply into the U.S. commitment to NATO. A few figures help to illustrate the magnitude of the impact. As the war soaked up trained manpower, U.S. divisions deployed to or earmarked for NATO dropped from fourteen to nine. More significantly, even the remaining deployed divisions were heavily cannibalized; all told, U.S. deployed manpower declined from 416,000 in 1962 (the first year of Kennedy force posture decisions) to 291,000 in 1970 (the last Johnson year). The raw figures tell only part of the story, however, for the drawdown inevitably impinged most heavily on the critical middle-management level—officers, NCOs and specialists—as experience and skill were siphoned off for service in Southeast Asia.

Meanwhile, the resources available in Europe to support training and maintenance—fuel, ammunition, spare parts—evaporated as combat in Vietnam intensified. The real degradation in combat readiness of NATO-deployed units was accordingly far greater than numerical reductions alone might suggest. Since Soviet conventional strength in Europe increased markedly during the same period, with manpower rising from 475,000 to well over 500,000 the effect was to undermine the U.S. argument for greater NATO reliance on the conventional option. Under the circumstances, it is hardly surprising that efforts to secure the allies' acceptance of flexible response met with bitter incredulity.

On the other hand, there was no turning back to massive retaliation. U.S. strategic forces peaked in terms of deliverable equivalent megatonnage in 1964. Thereafter, as Vietnam absorbed funds that might otherwise have gone toward strategic weapons, the Soviet Union steadily closed the gap, and by 1969 U.S. strategic superiority was manifestly ended. From a technical point of view, this development probably meant little; certainly it was of far less consequence than the original Soviet attainment of a survivable retaliatory capability. But even if its practical consequences could be dismissed, its psychological implications could not. At the least, parity was bound to intensify both the United States's desire to avoid a strategic exchange and the Europeans' sensitivity to any U.S. action that appeared to do so at their expense. Parity thus reinforced both sides in their already divergent interpretations of the common doctrine, and rendered still more perilous any effort to reconcile them.

In the face of these difficulties, the theater nuclear capability held things together (an achievement largely ignored by contemporary critics of the deployed nuclear posture). By the late 1960s there were over 7,000 U.S. nuclear weapons in Europe, ranging in yield from less than one kiloton to over 100 and capable of delivery by cannon, missile and aircraft, or of emplacement as giant land mines. Together, these weapons allowed NATO to maintain the fiction of a flexible response capability despite manifest conventional weakness. That the theater nuclear posture was supported by no viable employment doctrine, that the conventional forces it presumably supported were neither trained nor equipped to operate in an intense nuclear environment, and that in any case the use of these weapons and their Soviet counterparts would almost certainly leave a good deal of NATO territory in ruins was only too well known by both American and European planners. These inconvenient facts were nevertheless ignored by general consensus— the Europeans refusing to entertain the notion of a purely local nuclear conflict, and the United States fearing that any attempt to redress these deficiencies would serve only to demolish once and for all the argument for a strong conventional option.

By 1969, in sum, the gap between NATO's declaratory strategy, however vague, and the military capabilities that presumably gave it effect had grown dangerously wide. The risk existed that at any time the fragile doctrinal consensus might rupture altogether, lending its own contribution to the political and economic disarray already afflicting the alliance.

III

The Nixon Administration entered office with a public mandate to extricate the United States from Vietnam and a strong pre-election commitment to revitalize the Atlantic Alliance. At first blush, these two objectives would appear to have been highly compatible. Most of the strains in alliance relations seemed to derive directly or indirectly from U.S. preoccupation with Southeast Asia. An end to the war might reasonably be expected to free attention and resources for reallocation to a suffering NATO.

In reality, the problem facing the Administration was far more complicated. In addition to the direct effects already described, Vietnam produced a number of trends whose long-term consequences for the alliance promised to be still more serious. Most of these are by now too familiar to require lengthy description. They included a general American dissatisfaction with the scale of U.S. overseas commitments—dissatisfaction directed primarily at commitments in the Third World, but from which even NATO was not exempt; a growing domestic crisis urging revision of national spending priorities; mounting pressure from an overextended economy, manifested by rising inflation and large trade and monetary deficits; and finally, a deep weariness with all things military, fed by the apparent inability of America's massive military power to produce foreign policy successes. By 1969, some of the implications of these diffuse trends for U.S. NATO policy were already evident: mounting opposition to defense spending, itself burdened by escalating equipment and personnel costs; strong political pressure to end conscription; and—most immediately related to NATO—increasing Congressional support for a U.S. troop reduction, symbolized by the consecutively larger minorities polled by the Mansfield Amendment. Together, these developments served notice on the Administration that even a swift conclusion of the Vietnam war would produce no sudden or magical solution to NATO's malaise.

Accordingly, one of the first tasks assigned to the revitalized National Security Council system was examination of the United States's worldwide defense posture. From this examination, completed early in 1969, two salient conclusions emerged. The first, concerning the U.S.-Soviet strategic balance, merely confirmed what was by then apparent to most observers: that U.S. recapture of strategic nuclear superiority in any meaningful sense was not a feasible objective, politically or economically. From this followed the decision to accept "sufficiency," in effect ratifying the parity condition, and the further decision to seek negotiated arms limitations at the earliest appropriate opportunity.

The second conclusion concerned the general-purpose forces—those central to the flexible response concept. Manifestly, conventional forces had to be reduced; upward pressure on the defense budget was staggering, and a major cause was increased personnel costs. Moreover, the Nixon Administration was already committed to ending the draft; a volunteer force implied additional costs to bring military compensation in line with civilian levels, and to provide the additional incentive needed to attract volunteers to military service. Manpower must therefore be cut, and the bulk of the cut had to come from the manpower-intensive conventional forces, especially the army.

So much was obvious. How the cuts were to be apportioned regionally, however, was not so clear. One solution was to reduce conventional forces across the board. This approach had the virtue of retaining maximum flexibility to meet threats worldwide, and promised to minimize regional dislocations that might result from U.S. drawdowns. Yet an across-the-board reduction in deployed strength would leave the remaining forces dangerously undermanned, rendering them incapable of sustained operations in the event of a really serious contingency. To choose this option meant in effect to revert to a mobilization strategy, at the price of the very readiness for which the forces were maintained in the first place. Finally, such an approach clearly implied the demise of flexible response in Europe—at least in its U.S. interpretation.

The alternative was to contract the regional responsibilities to which U.S. conventional forces must be committed, and the obvious place to do so was in Asia. With counterrevolution bankrupted by Vietnam, and a new strategic balance emerging from the three-way relationship among the United States, the U.S.S.R. and China, a lower American profile seemed as desirable politically as it was necessary militarily. There was also an institutional incentive, for the military services were not unhappy to revert to their traditional preoccupation with Europe. The result was the Nixon Doctrine, and a corresponding shift from a "2½ war" to a "1½ war" capability. Clearly, the "one" in "1½" referred to Europe.

While these decisions were being reached, the NATO defense issue lay dormant, apparently because it was decided to defer attention to the European security problem until the broader force posture question had been settled. In the meantime, several stop-gap programs were undertaken, largely to ward off both Congressional pressures to reduce U.S. troops in Europe and the Europeans' attempts to make similar cuts in their own forces. U.S. troop levels were stabilized at a little over 300,000, and the President promised that no further reductions would be made except in the context of a negotiated

East-West agreement, provided the allies maintained their own forces. At the same time, strong efforts were made to persuade the latter to improve their conventional capabilities; as an inducement, they were encouraged to satisfy burden-sharing requirements by upgrading their forces and NATO's common infrastructure. Finally, the Administration attempted to rebuild confidence in NATO's conventional option (and stave off Congressional charges that U.S. troops were merely a trip-wire) by advancing the concept of "total force," in which all European and U.S. forces—active and reserve—would be counted in assessing the conventional East-West balance (at least, in public).

These efforts, it was apparent, were palliatives for a problem which required more radical treatment. The Alice-in-Wonderland redefinition of NATO capabilities implied by "total force" persuaded neither the Congress nor the allies; nor were the latter anxious to expend greater effort on increasingly expensive conventional forces while the United States restricted its efforts to mere exhortation. If flexible response were to survive more than rhetorically, Washington would have to lead the way.

Consequently, in 1970, having settled the relative priority of European and Asian commitments, the Administration began a major effort to revitalize the NATO deterrent. This effort had two components: to refurbish the conventional posture, and to find a way to restore some deterrent value to the U.S. strategic nuclear umbrella.

The immediate requirement was to halt the erosion of the conventional posture. This involved the shaping of a U.S. commitment tailored to budget and manpower realities, defensible in Congress, and capable of stimulating similar allied improvements. In the process, a major hurdle had to be overcome: the general belief, shared by American as well as allied planners, that NATO was simply incapable of defending conventionally against a serious Warsaw Pact attack. From this belief flowed another, that such an attack must quickly lead to nuclear war. Together, these two beliefs produced a "Catch-22" situation: if escalation was inevitable, conventional force improvement would be a waste of effort. Without such improvement, however, escalation *would be* inevitable. Between them, pessimistic U.S. planners and Europeans opposed to deterrence-by-denial thus neatly squared the circle.

In response, the Administration attacked on several fronts. First, it attempted to show that the threat on which the argument depended was overstated. Part of the job had already been done by McNamara, whose systems analysts had demonstrated that simple division comparisons between NATO and the Warsaw Pact greatly inflated the latter's apparent advantage. Less than half of the Soviet divisions committed to Europe were considered to be combat-ready. The remainder would require reserve augmentation—in short, mobilization. Such a mobilization, the Administration argued, could not take place instantaneously or without detection by NATO intelligence and appropriate countermeasures. Specifically, U.S. planners were ordered to assume that the Warsaw Pack would require at least a month to prepare for a serious conflict, and that NATO mobilization would lag behind by only a week. The Europeans were not likely to applaud such an assumption, and neither were U.S. planners. But the former were not consulted, and the latter had little choice but to accept political guidance whose validity could neither be verified nor disproved.

The Administration also attacked other aspects of NATO's threat analysis. For example, it argued that the Pact's quantitative superiority in tactical aircraft was more than compensated by qualitative NATO advantages in loiter time, payload, all-weather capabilities and aircrew training. It contended that the massive Soviet advantage in tanks was partially offset by greater NATO antitank capabilities—an argument subsequently enhanced by the October 1973 Arab-Israeli war. It also pointed out that Soviet supply capabilities were vastly inferior to NATO's, so that if the alliance could simply contain a Pact thrust for ninety days or so, the Soviets would run out of steam. The trick, in short, was to "outlast the Pact." Obviously, this was not an objective calculated to appeal to the professional soldier raised in the MacArthur tradition. Nor was it likely to appeal to the Germans, who knew only too well where the "outlasting" would take place. But the postulation of a ninety-day war was nevertheless an extremely useful device, enabling the Administration at one and the same time to exhort the allies to increase their war reserve stocks and U.S. planners to trim the logistical tail.

Eventually the examination of relative sustaining capabilities led to a handle on still another controversial issue—the high ratio of support to combat elements in NATO forces, especially U.S. forces. With the help of RAND analysts, the Administration was able to demonstrate a curious contradiction between the argument of NATO planners that the conventional phase of a European war would be short, and a "tooth-to-tail" ratio apparently anticipating a much longer conflict. This inconsistency, it was maintained, produced the paradoxical result that greater aggregate NATO manpower nevertheless translated into less front-line fighting strength than that mustered by Warsaw Pact forces.

Throughout these efforts to prove that the Soviets were not ten feet tall, Administration spokesmen had to proceed with some care. To overstate the argument would be as dangerous as to understate it. It would not do to convince either the allies or the U.S. Congress that NATO and the Pact were in balance, or worse, that NATO was superior. Nor would such a conclusion help NATO in its effort to negotiate East-West reductions weighted in its favor.

Fortunately, the Soviets themselves provided a way out of the dilemma. In the wake of the 1968 Czechoslovakian invasion, they had undertaken substantial improvements in conventional weapons, to include new armored vehicles and artillery, and a new fighter and medium bomber. Consequently, the Administration could—and did—argue that NATO's conventional deficiency was largely qualitative, and that specific improvements in such areas as antitank weapons, active and passive air defense and close air support would go far toward resolving the problem—*provided* that existing manpower levels were maintained.

There remained the problem of redressing the tooth-to-tail imbalance. Here the Administration drew on institutional self-interest. After demonstrating that both budget and volunteer recruitment prohibited a net manpower increase, it offered to allow each service to increase its combat capability, within limits, if the necessary manpower could be obtained by cutting support and headquarters units. The response of the three services varied widely, but the army—the critical service in this case—responded vigorously. By 1974 it was building another division from support spaces, and looking forward to building two more. At the same time, planning began to make "total force" a reality by integrating reserve with active units on a periodic basis.

Overall, by 1974, the Administration was well on the way to turning NATO's conventional situation around (though for the reason already suggested, it was muting its claims). It was helped no little in this process by the desire of the U.S. military to rehabilitate itself in the wake of Vietnam, by extraordinarily good management on the part of successive Secretaries of Defense, and—inadvertently—by the Soviet Union, whose support of the October 1973 Arab attack led Congress to take a relatively benign view of the fiscal 1975 defense budget.

Paradoxically, in winning allied acceptance of this entire program despite its unpleasant doctrinal implications, the greatest help may have come from Congress itself. Faced with Congressional threats to cut the U.S. deployment to NATO, the Administration could argue persuasively with the Europeans that the shortest route to an American drawdown lay in failure to demonstrate a satisfiable conventional need. Without some demonstration that a conventional option was desirable and attainable, even the possibility of a negotiated withdrawal would probably be insufficient to stave off a unilateral U.S. reduction.

Even so, this argument alone was unlikely to assuage allied concern that renewed U.S. emphasis on conventional forces implied nuclear decoupling, especially in the light of SALT I. Also, there was always the danger that the conventional force improvement effort might unravel, leaving NATO with no deterrent at all. To handle the first problem and forestall the second, the Administration turned to the second part of its program: the re-establishment of an extended strategic deterrent.

In the process, it drew once again on a McNamara idea—the notion of intra-war deterrence. Simply stated, the argument was that even though vulnerable to nuclear retaliation, the United States could use her strategic forces to deter Soviet aggression, provided she could demonstrate a willingness and capability to use those forces selectively. By threatening to employ strategic weapons discriminately and at a carefully regulated pace, she could raise the costs of aggression beyond any benefit Soviet decision-makers might hope to gain. If implemented, of course, such a program of deliberate punishment would not be without its costs; equal or greater Soviet counterattacks must be expected. But as long as the United States retained the ultimate capacity to destroy Soviet society in its entirety, Soviet decision-makers would have an incentive to restrain their own use of strategic weapons. The incentive could be enhanced by targeting U.S. weapons, not against Soviet cities, but against military targets carefully selected to avoid collateral civilian damage.

This program became known as the counterforce strategy, and the Administration did not expound it in the terms just described. Instead, Secretary of Defense Schlesinger described it as a retaliatory policy, and justified it by the need for a less-than-catastrophic response to a hypothetical Soviet attack on American Minutemen. Other Administration spokesmen offered similar scenarios, each involving a U.S. response to a limited strategic attack.

Such arguments were not persuasive. With no hope of disarming the United States, a limited strike on U.S. strategic forces would offer the Soviets no conceivable benefit worth the risk of escalation. Nor would it be likely, given Soviet conventional preponderance, that such an act would be forced on them. Only as an initiatory doctrine could counterforce make sense, and only in Europe could a threat be found of the proportions justifying such a dangerous counterthreat.

It is not difficult to understand why the Administration avoided the latter formulation. Even expounded as a retaliatory policy, counterforce was immediately deluged with criticism—some of it sound, some of it bordering on the hysterical. Much of the criticism concerned the procurement implications of the doctrine, alleging that the need for discriminate weapons implied a new round of weapons purchases. This was not necessarily true, however; the key technical requirement for selective employment—the Command Data Buffer System allowing rapid retargeting of weapons—was already under construction, and added not a single megaton to the nuclear stockpile. Other developments—reduced warhead yields, maneuverable re-entry vehicles, terminal guidance systems—might well facilitate selective employment but are not critical to it.

Another criticism—even less persuasive—was that counterforce might wreck strategic stability by threatening the U.S.S.R. with a disarming first strike. Such a charge ignored the invulnerability of Soviet missile-launching submarines. It also failed to explain how selective employment might destroy the Soviet land-based force, when by Defense Department admission even a massive attack could not reliably do so.

Perhaps the most persuasive criticism of the doctrine attacked its fundamental premise—that nuclear war, once begun, could be controlled by an act of will. Skeptics pointed out that such a claim imputed substantial self-restraint to Soviet decision-makers, and ignored the mentally destabilizing effects of fear, anger and uncertainty that a nuclear attack, however limited, might produce.

Finally, nearly all critics pointed out that selective employment increased the risk of nuclear war by lowering its perceived potential costs. In one sense, this was quite true; the doctrine's utility as a deterrent depended on reducing the apparent inhibition against initiating a strategic attack. In the sense that any war would be more likely to become nuclear, therefore, counterforce lowered the threshold. In defense, the Administration argued that making the nuclear option more viable decreased the likelihood of any war at all, and thus *raised* the threshold. The force of this argument, unfortunately, was largely undercut by the Administration's simultaneous insistence on the retaliatory function of the new doctrine.

However debatable the premises of the counterforce strategy, from the Administration's point of view it apparently had the desired effect. The allies were pleased by the reassertion of the nuclear deterrent; the Soviet Union was impressed, as its sharply negative reaction indicated; and the Administration was satisfied that it had re-anchored the upper end of the deterrence ladder.

Together, then, the reconstruction of the conventional posture and the enunciation of counterforce represented an impressively vigorous response to NATO's military weakness. All things considered, the Administration in five years achieved something of a strategic miracle; the McNamara strategy, in its doctrinal essentials, was resurrected like Phoenix from the ashes of a decade of neglect.

IV

Regardless of one's opinions about the Nixon Administration generally, it is hard not to admire the achievement represented by its NATO defense policy. In the space of five years the military posture of the alliance has been virtually refabricated. Conventional forces have been upgraded—their weapons modernized, supply levels increased, combat-to-support ratio improved, and most important, manpower levels maintained. At the same time, the strategic nuclear deterrent has been revitalized by the simple expedient of redefining its operational function. All this has been accomplished in the face of political strain within the alliance, a highly unfavorable budgetary environment, a major domestic crisis of confidence in the United States, and widespread public weariness with—if not antipathy toward—overseas commitments generally. Moreover, it has been accomplished in the name of a strategic doctrine whose original formulation was the source of nearly a decade of alliance discord.

That, however, is precisely the problem, for despite its success in rebuilding a military posture which by 1969 had risked collapse through neglect, the Administration has evaded rather than resolved the ambiguity at the heart of flexible response. Nor has the evasion been accidental. Scarred by the earlier McNamara experience, U.S. policymakers have deliberately avoided discussion of the doctrinal implications of U.S. NATO policy initiatives. Thus, conventional force restructuring has been sold as a cost-effectiveness measure, European defense improvement as a means of satisfying Congressionally-imposed burden-sharing requirements, and counterforce strategic options as a hedge against Soviet limited nuclear aggression.

None of these justifications comes to grips with the central strategic issue: how far NATO should be prepared to rely on nonnuclear forces to deter and, if necessary, defend against aggression from the East. Instead, while insistently asserting NATO's conventional defensibility, the Administration has advanced a strategic nuclear doctrine whose only logical presumption is conventional failure. At the same time, it proposes to modernize a deployed theater nuclear stockpile whose military value is obscure, diverting attention from the conventional force improvement effort, lowering the nuclear threshold, and thus still further undermining the credibility of its own alleged confidence in NATO's nonnuclear capability.

It is easy enough to understand—and sympathize with—the political difficulties that prompt this ambivalence. In the absence of some attention to the nuclear posture, conventional force improvement risks being perceived by the allies as the prelude to nuclear decoupling. And even if this were discounted, explicit commitment to conventional defense implies a no-first-nuclear-use policy to which the alliance has been inalterably opposed. It thus asks the allies to accept an interpretation of flexible response to which they have never subscribed, and which would require them to prepare for a war they do not want to fight, risking intense alliance friction at a time when there is more than enough to go around.

There is thus a persuasive political argument for retaining a visible NATO nuclear commitment, notwithstanding its questionable military utility. And doubtless some capability to respond to a Soviet first use must be retained, however unlikely such an event might be. But the danger increases that technological pressures will convert what is presently an essentially political concession into an active drive for a NATO nuclear war-fighting posture, with broad and almost certainly undesirable ramifications for both deterrence stability and alliance relations. Recent proposals to modernize theater nuclear weapons suggest that such pressures are already at work.

The failure to resolve the nuclear-conventional dilemma constitutes the greatest present danger to the success of an otherwise impressive U.S. effort to rationalize NATO's defense posture. It threatens political support for conventional force improvement by undercutting the best justification for it; it complicates the negotiation of balanced mutual force reductions; and—most dangerous—it risks miscalculation in a crisis by those to whom the credibility of alliance intentions is most critical: the Soviet Union and its allies. One can hardly avoid the conclusion that such risks far outweigh the political costs of addressing the nuclear issue directly, and that, accordingly, a basic rethinking of NATO's defense concept is overdue.

A CREDIBLE NUCLEAR-EMPHASIS DEFENSE FOR NATO

W. S. Bennett, R. R. Sandoval and
R. G. Shreffler

Economic and political constraints on national defense budgets are likely to persist for some time to come. The authors of this article, taking this into account, along with their belief that NATO's present conventional forces may be inadequate to defend against a Warsaw Pact attack, propose an alternative

Source: *Orbis*, vol. 17, no. 2 (Summer 1973), pp. 463-79. This article was written by three members of the staff of the Los Alamos Scientific Laboratory of the University of California. It reflects their own studies and discussions as well as exchanges with experts who have participated in seminars held at the Los Alamos Laboratory, but they accept sole responsibility for the opinions expressed.

defense posture for the alliance. Retaining the present strategy of forward defense, this posture would consist of low-yield tactical nuclear weapons and discriminate delivery vehicles that would not threaten the Soviet Union. The authors maintain that an initial theater nuclear defense of Western Europe would prove to be a more credible deterrent to attack, would result in less damage than a protracted conventional conflict, and would minimize the probability of escalation to strategic nuclear exchanges. In addition, such a nuclear defense posture would allow the United States to reduce its level of ground forces in Europe without jeopardizing NATO's defense capabilities.

This is a proposal of long-term goals toward which changes in NATO's defense posture should be directed. Its primary aim is to increase the effectiveness of NATO defense against Warsaw Pact aggression and to make that increase manifest and credible to both NATO and Warsaw Pact decision-makers. Negotiation of the issues dividing East and West in Europe could then be approached by the NATO governments, secure in the knowledge that the West's military posture was adequate to repel any invasion.

An effective defense threatens nothing but the ambitions of an adventurous aggressor. If a similar posture were acquired by the Warsaw Pact, no harm would be done to NATO's defense. Instead, the parties would enjoy a mutual state of confident deterrence, or stalemate—a situation even more stable than that now existing between the U.S. and U.S.S.R. strategic forces.

The primary aim of making NATO's defense effective, and therefore credible, cannot be achieved without careful consideration of the prevailing political, military, economic and technical conditions affecting both NATO and the Warsaw Pact. The necessary changes must be planned and accomplished deliberately to avoid disturbing the foundations on which the North Atlantic alliance is built. In particular, positive attitudes toward the existing NATO political and military posture must not be weakened during the conversion to an effective defensive posture. Finally, it is assumed that the configuration of a credible NATO defense must result in a decreased economic burden.

Approach

NATO's military posture has always been regarded as a counter to a formidable Warsaw Pact threat—a threat inferred as much from Soviet ambitions as from pure military capability. In the mid-1950s, our NATO allies concurred in U.S. plans to deploy nuclear weapons in

Europe to offset the disparity between conventional forces on the two sides. Since then, the Soviet Union has acquired intercontinental nuclear capabilities that have changed the strategic context in which the United States views its worldwide relationships. Furthermore, the Soviet Union has acquired and fielded nuclear weapons in the Warsaw Pact framework that more than suffice to deter any attack by forces based in Western Europe. These weapons also provide a de facto capability to destroy most of Europe should the Soviet Union choose to do so, for whatever reason. Meanwhile, the conventional forces of the Pact, characterized by large numbers of armored and mechanized units, provide a disturbingly credible instrument for Soviet adventurism ranging from political pressure to massive invasion.

Flexible response, NATO's declared strategy for coping with these various contingencies, attempts to combine military and political measures to contain the more limited forms of aggression and to deter the wider forms by threatening to inflict damage that the Soviets would find either unacceptable or out of proportion to any prospective gains. To many analysts, including the present authors, there is something illusory about this strategy. First, the ability of the NATO force to defend effectively against a massive attack is seriously questioned. Second, actual use of the nuclear deterrent component of the force would result in unacceptable damage to both NATO and the Warsaw Pact. The result is NATO's reliance on a military instrument inadequate for effective defense and unusable if it fails to deter. Faced with this dilemma, how do our allies hope to prevent a war in Europe from proceeding beyond a defensive engagement on the battlefield to an exchange of high-yield nuclear weapons on a theater-wide scale? They see no alternative but to rely on the mutual restraint imposed by the possible involvement of the United States and the Soviet Union in a war of mutual destruction. So far, Washington appears to have resigned itself to this formulation, which it actually helped to devise.

Several factors currently tend to deny stability to the situation just described. Political discussions that may result in a reduced NATO military structure have already begun. All alliance members are feeling economic pressures to reduce forces. Another factor, inherent in NATO's nuclear weapons and in the procedures prescribed for their use, is the enormous potential for collateral or unintended damage even if NATO fights only a defensive war. All these factors suggest the need for a detailed examination of the NATO military posture.

The most obvious deficiency of the NATO posture is the limited ability of present defenses to deny territory to a determined Warsaw Pact attacking force. To stop an invasion and retake lost territory, NATO would be forced to depend on mobilization and reinforcement.

This buildup would take time, during which an invading force could be expected to have penetrated deep into the Federal Republic of Germany. West Germans thus face the prospect, if the Pact attacks in force, of a prolonged war fought over their territory, quite possibly involving the use of nuclear weapons by both sides. Our other NATO allies, fearful of their fate in such a conflict, join the FRG in the hope that the Pact will be deterred from attacking by the threat of our use of nuclear weapons, including strategic weapons. There is, however, little hope among our allies that defensive action against a massive ground attack would be effective enough to forstall escalation to theater-wide use of nuclear weapons. Understandably, then, they would want the destruction of the United States and the U.S.S.R. indissolubly linked to their own demise through our commitment of intercontinental strategic nuclear capabilities.

Discriminate use of nuclear weapons from the outset would enable NATO to conduct a successful defense. Western policymakers should aim to replace, in Pact calculations, the uncertainty of an irrational NATO response with the certainty of an immediate, effective response to attempts to take NATO territory. Dealing with threats of irrational attacks to destroy all or part of NATO is a problem for our European allies to face without counting on U.S. strategic nuclear weapons. It is their survival that such attacks threaten. However, they should recognize that the existence of European retaliatory forces cannot be ignored by the Pact, and might provide an otherwise absent incentive for a pre-emptive disarming attack. It is true, after all, that retaliatory forces can also be used pre-emptively.

The strategy proposed in this article departs radically from present plans to try first to defend conventionally in Europe: it calls for immediately engaging an attacker with low-yield nuclear weapons for all but the most trivial incursions. Yet this concept would require no change in NATO's accepted strategy of forward defense, only in its interpretation. We admit there is no place in our proposal for any U.S. forces whose useful purpose in a defensive role on the battlefield cannot be defined. We acknowledge the utility of an undeclared reliance on the U.S. Single Integrated Operational Plan (SIOP) for an indeterminate contribution to the deterrence of high-intensity theater war in Europe. We hold that a NATO force optimally configured to employ nuclear weapons defensively would require a smaller U.S. investment and would accommodate the many constraints that now prevent NATO from mounting a realistic deterrent to Warsaw Pact pressures.

First, we will address the political, military, economic and technical factors bearing on this proposed solution to NATO's defense under the following headings:

(1) Our perspective of nuclear weapons.
(2) U.S. courses of action with respect to NATO.
(3) Defensive capability and deterrence.
(4) Escalation of a nuclear war in Europe.
(5) The NATO force and its interactions with the threat.

Then we will identify the general characteristics of a future NATO force posture consistent with our analysis of these factors. Finally, we will indicate some directions that development of the future NATO force structure should take to reflect the recommended posture, and suggest ways to adapt the alliance's present force.

Some aspects of our proposal are extremely controversial. A number of strategic analysts have warned that our suggestions could undermine NATO. In particular, some critics feel strongly that Europeans do not want a defense of any kind, that they rely on the fact that any conflict on their territory would rapidly involve a U.S.-U.S.S.R. intercontinental exchange, and that this fact is the only deterrent that protects NATO. Whatever the merits of that position, it strikes us as a holdover from the days of unquestioned faith in U.S. strategic superiority. This argument has been overtaken by the conditions of strategic parity, so we believe NATO must take a new look at its own defenses. If it can find a credible defense posture for its European members, military aggression will be deterred. And if the Europeans gain confidence in this posture, it will give them the courage to resist the more likely threat of political coercion. Conjecture of this kind is clearly subjective, but our aim is to strengthen NATO and to make the U.S. contribution meaningful rather than illusory.

Factors Bearing on the Problem

In some instances, the following factors are little more than definitions; in others, they are matters of substance that can severely restrict our choice of realistic solutions to the problem. All must be understood, however, if a dialogue on this complex subject is to be intelligent.

Our Perspective of Nuclear Weapons. The numerous complex parameters required to define nuclear weapons and the infinite set of political-military situations their existence influences make them difficult to classify. Are they defensive, retaliatory, or both? Confusion is especially evident in this period when the United States is obliged to formulate its world position accurately.

For example, the 7,000 U.S. weapons in Europe would be regarded by many as a stockpile of defensive nuclear weapons. One would do better, however, to take the opposite view and acknowledge that, although the NATO General Strike Plan (GSP) is directed against military targets, its execution with NATO's present high-yield weapons would cause widespread collateral damage in Warsaw Pact homelands. This situation arises because we usually consider the GSP in the same context as the U.S. SIOP—i.e., as a deterrent only. But because the Warsaw Pact perceives the GSP to be coercive (or even pre-emptive) in intent, weapons assigned to the plan cannot be regarded as relating solely to the defense of NATO. Only those weapons put to use directly on the battlefield can be properly described as defensive.

One reason for the present confusion (and we must recognize that some of it flows from deliberate decisions) is our past practice of designing weapons systems and forcing them into the existing military structure. A more rational approach is to decide what political and military needs exist, develop an accommodating force structure, and then call on the technical community to build weapons that support that force structure. Each theater has different demands. The political-military confrontation between the U.S.S.R. and the United States varies from one part of the world to another; for example, the NATO-Warsaw Pact confrontation differs from the situation confronting the United States in Asia. When we evaluate a nuclear weapon or a nuclear arsenal, weapon characteristics should be chosen to ensure that they best meet the demands of a particular theater, or even a particular area within a theater.

Let us consider how some of these characteristics relate to our assessment of political acceptability and military utility. The first essential is what might be called weapon controllability. To be politically acceptable as an instrument of national policy, a nuclear weapon must be capable of manufacture, deployment and use under conditions that make unauthorized detonation virtually impossible. Deployment and use, in particular, must unquestionably support the achievement of a clearly defined objective, and, in the case of defensive weapons, must be carefully limited. On the other hand, if a weapon is to be militarily useful, the control apparatus must be responsive to military exigencies and must not impose an inordinate security, storage and maintenance burden on the force.

Another important characteristic is the destructiveness of the weapon. NATO's political leadership wants no weapon explosion to expose people or their cultural heritage to indiscriminate destruction. This collateral damage can be largely controlled by the choice of target area and target damage criteria. The military commander, however, should have weapons whose use can effectively attain military objectives. Delivery accuracy, range and responsiveness of the delivery system, weapon yield and fuzing, target acquisition, damage assessment, and battlefield survivability of the system all play an obvious role in assuring effectiveness.

Economic considerations involved in developing a new stockpile which can best meet these effectiveness criteria include (1) the transition from a present force representing sunk costs; (2) the resources already committed to, and the costs still to be paid for, weapons in development; and (3) the relationship of these factors to other costs of fielding and maintaining forces, all of which have a profound influence on the defense decisions of NATO leaders. Ultimately, as experience has shown us, military planners will probably have to settle for less than they feel is enough; but they will still want to make sure that the force structure we can afford has military utility.

Other weapon characteristics affecting political acceptability are the image the weapon projects into the minds of our allies and adversaries and the weapon's ability to conform to constraints explicit in policy or implicit in the doctrine of use.

U.S. Courses of Action with Respect to NATO. Before addressing the NATO defense problem, it is appropriate to consider a range of future U.S. military linkages with Western Europe. At the risk of oversimplification, one might consider four courses of action: (1) Complete removal of U.S. military forces from Europe as quickly as possible. (2) Complete removal of U.S. military forces from Europe according to a schedule set by the U.S. government. (3) Retention of present U.S. military forces in Europe indefinitely into the future. (4) Retention of a reduced U.S. military presence in Europe indefinitely into the future.

If any of the first three courses is pursued, there is no need to develop a rationale to support refurbishing stockpiles of nuclear weapons or redesigning the U.S. contribution to the military force. The action required to follow the fourth course is less clear. U.S. international responsibilities and domestic considerations should induce us to choose the fourth course, but drastic revisions of the U.S. force will be necessary to make this a feasible course to follow. Associated revisions of the NATO force as a whole would likewise be mandatory to ensure the military compatibility of its components. Our proposal addresses this problem.

U.S. political decision-makers can hardly choose intelligently unless they are given carefully evaluated military options from which to select. In February 1971, President Nixon documented his frustration in developing these options:

> The basic problem was not technical or esoteric. It was an absolute necessity to devise a sensible posture of defense we

can plausibly ask our peoples to support. Many voters, legislators, and officials in Western countries have raised questions about the continuing burden of defense budgets—not because they did not see the need for security, but because they did not see a clear rationale for the forces proposed. Our armies are not ends in themselves, or merely tokens of a commitment. They have a function to perform: to aid in deterrence and to defend if deterrence fails.[1]

As the leader of the NATO alliance and the Free World, the United States should play a leading role in developing the required military solutions. In addition, Washington has by far the greatest potential for resolving these issues, particularly when the options may depend on the essential defensive use of tactical nuclear weapons—weapons over which the U.S. government may feel obligated to retain control.

Whatever military solution is selected, the obvious principal goal is to create a deterrent force posture that minimizes the possibility of war. The issue is how to develop such a deterrent force consistent with the other constraints previously identified.

Defensive Capability and Deterrence. There is a great deal of discussion and confusion over whether and how deterrence is associated with a war-fighting capability, which we prefer to call a defensive capability. The following argument is presented for consideration: First, we hypothesize that deterrence is a function—possibly some product—of how an adversary views the military potential of your force and your willingness to use that force. It is not hard to associate this definition of deterrence with a conventional or a defensive nuclear force. For either force, one associates military potential with defensive capability, and the close connection is understandable if you assume willingness to commit the nuclear force. We maintain that the U.S. President would encounter great reluctance, and therefore great difficulty, in releasing defensive nuclear forces in NATO as long as the NATO stockpile contains so many high-yield, indiscriminate weapons. The present NATO force accordingly has little or no real deterrent value beyond that attributed to the uncertainty of its use.

The situation is not so clear with respect to strategic forces. The military potential of the U.S. or the Soviet strategic force can be placed near infinity on any scale. Even as willingness to use the force approaches zero, deterrence can be large, or at least indeterminate. Not only is the military potential enormous, but it has an impersonal and unreal character—a far cry from the concrete features that define a

---

[1]*United States Foreign Policy for the 1970's: Building for Peace.* A Report by President Nixon to the Congress, February 25, 1971, p. 33.

conventional or defensive nuclear force. U.S. strategic forces, however, constitute the only significant deterrent we have in Europe—a deterrent conceived before the advent of strategic parity.

Escalation of a Nuclear War in Europe. There is a puzzling ambivalence in current attitudes toward escalation. On the one hand, it has been contended that any use of nuclear weapons introduces a qualitative change in the nature of the battlefield. Allegedly, one side or the other will find this change intolerable and attempt to redress it by widening the conflict in some fashion that will initiate an irreversible escalatory process ending inevitably in the intercontinental strategic exchange, an unthinkable denouement. On the other hand, once the introduction of nuclear weapons is postulated, escalation is viewed by the same people as the only credible threat one can hold over an adversary to restrain him from taking escalating steps himself. The positive feedback potential of this scheme is self-evident. If war should occur while we possess our present strategy and military force, the intercontinental strategic exchange may well come to pass. But if our security needs are to be truly met, it is essential that a war fought with nuclear weapons should not escalate out of hand. Any employment doctrine must be fashioned to this end.

Escalation is defined as an extension or amplification of a war in one or more of the following directions: (1) The war might become intense. More yield would be delivered in a given engagement area. (2) The area over which the war is fought might be expanded. (3) The distance from which weapons are launched might be increased.

To minimize the possibility of a nuclear war escalating out of hand, the following steps must be taken:

(1) We must construct a defensive force that can use low-yield nuclear weapons to stop the enemy before he becomes irreversibly committed through seizing a significant part of NATO territory, or through suffering nuclear retaliation that forces him to escalate.

(2) In conducting and terminating a conflict, the NATO objective must be to preserve or re-establish the pre-conflict border. Insistence on wider goals in an engagement supported by the U.S.S.R. and the United States can lead to escalation involving a release of their strategic forces.

(3) We must exclude the planning option of using U.S. nuclear forces in Europe—primarily our Quick Reaction Alert (QRA) aircraft—which are capable of striking the territory of the U.S.S.R. To this end, such forces now in Europe should be removed. The United States should dissociate itself from allied forces possessing a compara-

ble capability, and discontinue its declared policy of promising to defend NATO with U.S. CONUS [continental U.S.]-based and otherwise strategically-oriented nuclear forces. The importance of an undeclared policy in this regard is vital. Under these conditions, the President's options for defending NATO can be weighed separately from the problem of releasing forces meant only for deterrence, not for defense.

(4) Other steps doubtless need to be taken to relieve the President's concern over escalation, but they are more tenuous. For example, we should consider advertising the ground rules by which NATO would fight a war. These rules could cover such matters as number and yield of nuclear weapons in stockpile. In this regard, NATO could consider a low maximum yield (in the neighborhood of a kiloton). The rules could also specify the policies under points (1), (2) and (3) above. In short, NATO could advertise its constraint policy.

By taking the foregoing steps, we would avoid the enormous risks of depending on a controlled, but possibly uncontrollable, escalation to halt a Pact invasion and then retrieve lost ground. With the suggested approach, planning for NATO's defense becomes a much simpler problem: we would be able to meet aggression at the border with only the requisite nuclear force to bring it under control. This concept is compatible with accepted NATO strategy, except that current interpretations stress a conventional-emphasis phase while ours relies on immediate nuclear emphasis. Current fears about escalation are warranted, but they result from the commingling of defensive and offensive (even if called counteroffensive) nuclear forces in Europe. Removing U.S. offensive forces allows us to rely on the defensive forces.

We see no possibility of effective military action in defense against an irrational attack on Europe: for example, Soviet release of IRBM/ MRBM [intermediate-range/medium-range ballistic missile] weapons to destroy all or part of it. There can only be suicidal retaliation for such an act, authority for which is present in the President's ability to release the SIOP. This capability provides strategic deterrence based on the balance of terror. It is more a political counter than a military one. The danger is that political adventurism by the Soviets, combined with military thrusts for limited objectives, could escalate uncontrollably. Nothing can guarantee that this will not happen, but we believe the purely defensive force we propose will minimize the risk. If, in addition, the NATO force lacked offensive capability, the chances would be minimized that the Soviets would fear the force to the point where they felt they had to strike first to blunt our threat to them.

The NATO Force and Its Interactions with the Threat. The character of the NATO force has varied little since shortly after its origin. Briefly, NATO relies on a large conventional army, air force and navy; the protection of the U.S. SIOP, if necessary; and nuclear weapons deployed in the European theater, both as an ill-defined backstop of the conventional force and as a coercive deterrent, deliberately implying a trigger to the SIOP.

This combination of forces would seem unrealistic in light of the previous discussion and the following points in particular:

(1) The inflexibility the current NATO force causes in addressing problems that arise in debates on SALT, MBFR [Mutual and Balanced Force Reduction in Europe] and other security matters.

(2) The lucrative targets offered to Warsaw Pact nuclear weapons by a conventionally deployed NATO force.

(3) The consideration of nuclear weapon use *in extremis,* particularly if the conventional force has insufficient time to mobilize.

(4) The difficulty concerning Presidential release of nuclear weapons in the theater, where the stockpile and delivery systems include threats to the territory of the Soviet Union.

(5) The absence of suitable military doctrine for using nuclear weapons in a purely defensive war.

(6) The fundamental difficulty of warping a conventional-force structure to meet the demands of nuclear war and the associated difficulty of structuring a sensible stockpile of defensive nuclear weapons.

(7) The probable Soviet intention to expand Moscow's influence without a major war—certainly without a strategic nuclear exchange.

It is frequently asserted that the Soviets still view our NATO force with considerable apprehension and respect. Quite the reverse may actually be true. They may dismiss our NATO deterrent force as a noncredible planning option. They may well attempt to extend their influence into Western Europe against a defensive force they consider a facade—a military force in which NATO pretends confidence but which the Soviets fear very little. Given time, and merely flexing the muscles of their massive force, they might expect to accomplish their goals with little risk of reaction.

A decision to retain the present NATO force has the attractive feature of requiring no change in current political or military posture. This factor alone is probably sufficient to argue for continued endorsement. The additional fact that there has been no conflict in

Europe in over two decades of East-West antagonism encourages some to extrapolate the present state of affairs into the indefinite future. Also, recent negotiating efforts to resolve East-West differences at the diplomatic level are used as a basis to argue in favor of maintaining the present posture, i.e., "don't rock the boat." We can only reply that, should the Warsaw Pact countries, particularly the Soviet Union, choose to invade Western Europe either with or without nuclear weapons, the political leadership of our alliance would have distressingly few choices of response, with widespread destruction almost certainly the only alternative to humiliation. Moreover, the present force provides a poor bargaining position from which to resist Soviet political pressures.

The Characteristics of a Future NATO Force Posture

NATO should be extremely cautious in considering any change in its military force without first giving careful consideration to its long-term goals. Although the present force posture is not altogether rational and cries out for revision, it still has some value. We contend, however, that if Warsaw Pact forces were to attempt to seize Western Europe, as opposed to an attack intended to devastate it, our force could be decimated. If NATO's purpose is to be fulfilled in the future, it follows that the present conventional-emphasis force posture should be changed drastically over the long term. Because of the early decisions to be made at SALT, MBFR and CSCE [the Helsinki Conference on Security and Cooperation in Europe], and because of possible force reductions, it is essential that NATO adopt a military design which gives direction to the necessary changes in force posture.

The foregoing leads us to visualize the desirable characteristics of a future military posture predicated on the following considerations:

(1) The U.S. SIOP has some indeterminate residual value in deterring irrational forms of Warsaw Pact aggression or escalation, but this role should not be articulated in declared policy.

(2) No U.S. capability for other than defensive war should be retained on European soil.

(3) Any NATO forces deployed in Europe that are solely deterrent (i.e., punitive or retaliatory) should be provided and controlled by Europeans.

(4) The defensive capabilities of the NATO force should be tailored to the characteristics of each prospective battle area in which these capabilities may be exercised. The force should be constructed in

each case around U.S.-supplied and U.S.-controlled nuclear weapons and should be designed to defend NATO at its borders.

(5) The design of the force should accommodate to economic pressures to reduce the cost of acquiring and maintaining forces. In particular, the size of the U.S. manpower commitment in Europe should be reduced. Since the NATO force will depend largely on nuclear weapons to defeat massed attacks by Warsaw Pact armor, our goal should be eventually to restrict the U.S. role to command and control of these weapons. The Europeans should be left to provide those elements of the force that would cope with other than massed armor attacks. This goal seems to be a clear application of the Nixon Doctrine to the defense of Europe. Also, emphasis should be placed on procuring weapons that minimize acquisition and maintenance costs.

(6) The force must be usable and effective without exceeding collateral-damage constraints. We offer two thoughts on the control of collateral damage, defined as unintended destruction which should be minimized or avoided if possible: (a) To make a nuclear-emphasis defense acceptable to our allies, the goals for minimizing expected collateral damage must be set at levels at least equal to and preferably even lower than would be associated with a conventional defense. (b) Concern about collateral damage stems largely from the presence of high-yield weapons (greater than a few kilotons) in our NATO stockpile and from vivid memories of wars as long engagements that ravaged the continent. We contend that a nuclear-defensive war by NATO, fought in proximity to the border with low-yield weapons and discriminating delivery systems, would result in a short conflict. Under such conditions, collateral damage is far less an issue, and the criteria set forth in (a) are reasonable.

(7) We are fated to pursue the brinkmanship game of strategic deterrence (assured destruction) in the NATO theater until NATO adopts this new defensive stance. The problem is far more one of policy and doctrine—and U.S. leadership—than it is one of technology. There are advantageous changes possible in both weaponry and forces, but the first step is a recognition that a new approach is necessary. As NATO comes to this realization, there is much to trade the Warsaw Pact in MBFR negotiations: our theater-range weapons for theirs, for example. We need not develop expensive new "bargaining chips"; both sides have many of them already. Because Europe is the issue, this is a problem for the multilateral MBFR talks, not for bilateral SALT II negotiations. In any case, our negotiating position does not become worse by NATO's acquiring an effective defense.

If plans for the force proposed here were generated by the United

States and clear steps were taken toward ultimate implementation, a number of benefits would result:

(1) The inevitable changes to be made in the present force could be planned to advantage for political bargaining power in such matters as SALT and MBFR talks.

(2) Internal pressures to reduce the U.S. contribution to NATO forces could be accommodated.

(3) The deterrent value of NATO's defensive force would be enhanced if the President were confident that release of weapons for defensive purposes would not inevitably be followed by execution of the SIOP. He would also be far more likely to establish peacetime consultation procedures with our NATO allies for the release and employment of defensive nuclear weapons.

(4) The United States and its NATO allies could possess a truly effective defensive force and supporting arsenal that would take maximum advantage of nuclear weapons as the dominating presence on the battlefield. Planning for the use of this force would be uninhibited by the dogma associated with the present force and the deployment of U.S. strategic capabilities in the theater.

(5) The United States could initiate the creative development and implementation of the political, military and technical elements of command and control systems required for nuclear defense. These difficult tasks become more tractable when divorced from their strategic counterparts.

(6) The Soviets would be far more cautious in dealing with an alliance whose deterrent would be a credible nuclear defensive force marked by high confidence and resolve. At the same time, the stage would be set for detente through military stalemate, and ultimately for further, major mutual force reductions.

Several problems are doubtless associated with proposing such a force: (1) The force has yet to be defined in detail. (2) The existing force structure would certainly have to be reoriented and, possibly, drastically changed. (3) Definition of the force and transition from the present force to the new one would take a number of years.

The United States should—and apparently intends to—remain in Europe indefinitely, though at lower force levels. This necessitates that serious consideration be given to adopting a NATO military posture having the characteristics identified above. If we can configure a force clearly capable of conducting a nuclear defense of NATO's borders for as long as the Warsaw Pact forces can mount an invasion attempt, we will have removed the one Warsaw Pact option most dangerous to Europe's future, namely, the extension of Soviet hegemony over the entire continent. Of course, it must be reiterated that the Soviet Union can maintain indefinitely the capability to destroy Europe.

*   *   *

Future Courses of Action

We have searched for a new configuration for a NATO defensive force. This force, hypothetical at present, would derive its credibility from a manifest capability (lacking in the present force) to deny success to any Warsaw Pact attempt to seize NATO territory. In the preceding sections, we identified what might be regarded as a set of conditions to be satisfied by such a force. We then derived the general characteristics of the military posture NATO should assume in preserving its territorial integrity. What remains to be done to lend form and substance to this concept is outlined as follows:

(1) Development of alternative force structures, each conforming to the new posture. These will be designed specifically to engage in defensive nuclear operations. They will include an evident capability for accurate, responsive, low-yield nuclear weapon delivery. Battlefield survivability will also be a prominent characteristic. The design of such forces is an appropriate task for military agencies already engaged in configuring force structures to support national objectives. It can also be addressed usefully by others having a special interest and knowledge.

(2) Extension of the methodology for evaluating force structures to permit the selection of optimal forces for the nuclear battlefield, subject to appropriate constraints. Provisions for objective testing would include: (a) Scrutiny equaling that accorded in the cost-effectiveness analyses to which force proposals are now subjected. Among the tests to be applied should be one for compatibility with the factors we have set forth, arranged in some order of priority. In this way, appropriate trade-offs can be identified. (b) Field exercises to evaluate organizations, doctrine and tactics successively in the U.S. military CONUS base, in the U.S. NATO component, and in NATO as a whole.

(3) Review of the present force to identify elements that could be used in configuring the kind of defensive capability we are seeking. Those weapons and delivery systems capable of engaging battlefield targets with appropriate (no larger than necessary) yields and at ap-

propriate distances would have obvious utility. Similarly, some conventional elements of the force would have relevant tasks in the nuclear environment. The review should assess realistically the capability of the present force to conduct nuclear defense. In particular, the analysis should proceed without the complications arising from consideration of an initial conventional phase of battle and the attendant difficulties of a transition to the nuclear phase.

The essence of our proposal is the substitution of an effective forward defense for a NATO force which, if attacked, would today pin all its hopes on a questionable ability to counterattack after trading space for time until mobilization could be realized. Hovering in the background in this unlikely scenario are panoplies of nuclear power possessed by both sides. For too long we have depended on U.S. strategic power based in this country and around the world to frustrate Soviet expansionism. It is increasingly evident that those forces are mutually deterred by similar Soviet capabilities, so that neither can be used in times of crisis. For either nation to seek the attainment of any political objective at the risk of destroying both is nearly inconceivable. For either to declare that it would do so seems naive.

The matter of greatest priority to the U.S. national security interest, short of survival itself, is the preservation of a healthy NATO Europe sharing its essential goals with America. We urgently need decisions at the highest political level to direct the configuration of a military force which can indefinitely maintain an effective defense against encroachments of NATO territory. Further, that force must be releasable by an American President, mindful of the risks of escalation. If those decisions are not forthcoming, present pressures to reduce forces will lead to further diminution of an already inadequate defensive strength. Should the decisions we advocate be made soon, however, U.S. force reductions can be implemented without distrubing the present shaky military equilibrium in Europe. Most important, our NATO allies will acquire a renewed confidence in the efficacy of NATO's defenses.

SENATE DEBATE ON THE NEUTRON WARHEAD

On July 1, 1977, after a closed session during which classified information was discussed, the Senate began a public debate over funding production of enhanced radiation warheads for tactical nuclear artillery and Lance missiles.

Source: *Congressional Record*, 95th Congress, 1st session, vol. 123, no. 115 (July 1, 1977), pp. S11429-S11439; and vol. 123, no. 118 (July 13, 1977), pp. S11742-S11768.

Commonly known as neutron warheads, they became the subject of a heated controversy, which, in turn, attracted public attention to the more general issue of qualitative changes in weapon systems.

For a number of days, the debate centered on the implications of enhanced radiation warheads for deterring war in Europe, for NATO's nuclear doctrine, and for arms control. Another subject the Senate considered was the manner of making decisions pertaining to the acquisition of nuclear weapons. Referred to as a procedural question, the issue arose from the Carter administration's request that the Senate approve funding for the warheads in the Fiscal Year 1978 Public Works Appropriations Bill before the President had made his final decision on their procurement and deployment. Although the Senate eventually voted to fund production of the warheads, an amendment sponsored by Senators Robert C. Byrd (Democrat, West Virginia) and Howard H. Baker (Republican, Tennessee) reserved the right of Congress to deny funding by concurrent resolution of both houses within forty-five days of the President's determination that their production would be in the national interest.

Included in the following excerpts is the "Arms Control Impact Analysis" provided by the Carter administration for the enhanced radiation warhead of the Lance missile system.

July 1, 1977

Mr. CLARK: Any program—with respect to nuclear armaments—shall include a complete statement analyzing the impact.

Surely, Mr. President, a weapon of the nature of the enhanced radiation warhead unquestionably falls in this category, and, the congressional requirement for an arms impact statement is fully justified, for it demands of the Executive a thoughtful and reasoned analysis of the overall significance of the weapon under consideration.

The executive branch submitted no such impact statement on the Lance enhanced radiation warhead. . . .

Mr. President, the requirements of the law are clear. Before we appropriate money for a system, we must know what that system will do. We must have this impact statement. The lack of this alone, it seems to me, justifies withholding Senate approval at this time.

*   *   *

Mr. President, beyond these procedural questions are fundamental questions involving our commitment and interest in arms limitation, our national security requirements, and our foreign policy interests. On the surface, it appears attractive to develop and deploy so-called "clean" nuclear weapons. But what are we really talking about?

The nuclear warheads under discussion are "clean" only to the extent that they will do less damage individually to the physical surroundings than the weapons they were designed to replace. But even according to newspaper accounts, we know that the weapon to be carried by the Lance warhead will destroy buildings and bridges and houses for a great radius around the explosion—far greater than any conventional weapon we possess. Let us make no mistake: this is a nuclear warhead. The fact that it manages to reduce blast and thermal impact while maintaining the same level of lethal neutron radiation hardly qualifies it as a "clean" weapon, except, I guess, to those among us nowadays for whom the words "kilotons" and "megatons" seems to have lost their terrible meaning.

But, let me concede for a moment that the enhanced nuclear weapon is marginally less destructive when used singly than a regular nuclear warhead, and that it might be possible to destroy an advancing enemy armored column through neutron bombardments with somewhat less destruction to the surroundings than possible with other nuclear weapons. This has, it seems to me, very ambiguous ramifications for arms control.

On the one hand, it is argued that it makes the nuclear deterrent more credible. Potential attackers, we are told, would more readily believe that we would use a warhead of this nature, particularly in allied areas, because it would be less destructive of the surroundings.

I have to accept that. I have to agree that commanders would be more inclined to use such a weapon than a similar weapon which would blow up more of the surrounding landscape.

But just for that reason I think the enhanced radiation warhead might be an incredible threat to our own security. For I find it hard to believe that a nuclear exchange is going to remain confined to just a couple of our "clean" bombs.

For one thing, who is going to guarantee that the Soviets are so thoughtful as to reply with enhanced radiation "clean" bombs?

So far as we know, they do not even have them at this time. But why should they necessarily forego the additional blast and thermal effects?

But more than this, I find the concept of a "limited" nuclear exchange—clean or not—extremely dubious. I cannot really imagine that when a nuclear exchange takes place everyone—including ourselves—will limit it to "clean" bombs. In a nuclear exchange it is awfully hard to see the sign "clean" on incoming nuclear warheads.

Indeed, I think it is vitally important to retain the distinction between conventional and nuclear war. I think nations and leaders must be aware that when they go nuclear, they are introducing an entirely new dimension into the conflict. Nuclear war must remain so clearly a step into the terrible unknown that nobody will venture to try it. The introduction of supposedly "clean" weapons, the illusion of some sort of benign nuclear exchange, threatens to blur that distinction, and as such is potentially a dangerous trigger to nuclear holocaust.

It would, as the *Washington Post* described it,

> Set NATO's nuclear force on more of a hair trigger, when sound strategic doctrine demands a reliable safety catch; and it would commit NATO more deeply to the dangerous premise that a small nuclear exchange can be conducted without serious risk of expanding into a general nuclear war.

Mr. President, I would like to note that two recent directors of the Arms Control and Disarmament Agency emphasized the importance of maintaining just that distinction. In an exchange in 1976 the distinguished former disarmament subcommittee Chairman Stuart Symington was emphasizing the dangers of developing "mini-nukes" of limited yield which would blur this dividing line. ACDA head Fred Iklé replied,

> I agree with the importance of preserving the dividing line between nuclear weapons and conventional ones.

And back in 1974, a well-known and respected private commentator on arms control issues, Paul C. Warnke, told a Foreign Relations Committee Subcommittee that the prospects of developing smaller, neater and cleaner tactical nuclear weapons, the so-called mini-nukes, appalled him. "To the extent that mini-nukes blur the distinction between conventional weapons and nuclear weapons," said Mr. Warnke, "they lower the nuclear threshold." They would, Mr. Warnke went on,

> . . . make the consequences of use of tactical nuclear weapons less dire in the minds of the potential attacker and, as a consequence, they would not constitute to the same extent the degree of deterrent that a weapon which is clearly different in kind now presents.

Mr. Warnke, as we know, is now head of ACDA. And his conclusion as to what the use of those smaller, cleaner weapons would mean was simple and direct:

> And once the nuclear threshold is crossed the process of escalation could become irreversible.

To quote Secretary of Defense Harold Brown on this issue at the time of his confirmation hearings:

I do not think it at all likely that a limited strategic nuclear exchange would remain limited. I would be very cautious about structuring the force and expending a great deal of effort on making the force able to engage at length in a limited strategic nuclear war.

That Mr. President, makes a lot of sense. . . . I come to this discussion without any preconceptions. I honestly have not yet formed a final opinion on whether the additional "credibility" of the enhanced radiation weapon justifies the extent to which it might lead to "going nuclear," and trigger with it a full nuclear exchange. But I am convinced that the question is serious enough that it should be thoroughly explored in hearings and in a public discussion. And that is why I feel that appropriating these funds now is premature, and should await the results of our inquiry.

*   *   *

Mr. NUNN: Mr. President, many times in this debate, proponents and opponents have tended to overstate their arguments and confusion has been the result. I, therefore, feel that I should state what this weapon will not do.

First, it will not totally redress the military balance in Europe.

Second, it does not obviate the need for strong conventional defense.

Third, it does not make our entire tactical nuclear posture in Europe credible.

Finally, it does not make absolutely credible the U.S. strategic guarantee to Europe.

It is, however, a step toward restoring the credibility of our present tactical nuclear posture.

The central issue we face relating to the neutron warhead is who is going to be deterred—we or the Soviets?

The essence of the argument against the neutron warhead is that we should not develop nuclear weapons that we can use; rather that we should keep these weapons so dirty and destructive in blast and heat effects that there will be great reluctance on the part of the President, the NATO chain of command, and our European allies to use them.

Both proponents and opponents can agree on the basic premise that we hope we will never have to use nuclear weapons of any type. Where, then, do we disagree?

Opponents believe that weapons whose use is credible become weapons whose use is more likely. I submit, however, that weapons whose use is credible become weapons whose use is less likely. The likelihood of our being compelled to use tactical nuclear weapons increases as the credibility of their use decreases.

The opponents' basic premise leads to the conclusion that the deterrence they seek is a self-deterrence, whereas the deterrence I seek and which NATO must seek is a deterrence of the Soviet Union and the Warsaw Pact.

Opponents seek to convince our chain of command that our tactical nuclear weapons must not be used. I seek a posture which demonstrates to the Soviets that we have weapons which we are willing to use should they invade.

Those who oppose the warhead apparently believe in self-deterrence; that is to say, that we should keep the weapons so destructive we would never use them or if we did use them, it would be only under the most desperate of conditions. The fault with this argument is that if the Soviets perceive this to be our posture, then deterrence is weakened, and by extension, the likelihood of Soviet aggression is increased. Thus, if we deter ourselves, we encourage the very war we seek to avoid, and we make more likely the necessity to use weapons which we hope never to use.

I do not state to my colleagues in the Senate that a Soviet invasion of Western Europe is inevitable, nor do I state that it is likely. I do state, based purely on a military analysis, that it is the least unlikely of the possible scenarios of Soviet military aggression. By deterring ourselves from using tactical nuclear weapons except weapons which would destroy the territory we are pledged in NATO to protect, the advantages which the Soviets now maintain in conventional forces are greatly magnified, and the least unlikely scenario becomes even less unlikely.

I remind my colleagues that the purpose of deterrence in Europe is to deter Soviet aggression, not to deter ourselves from responding to that aggression. The Soviets are not deterred by NATO weapons which the alliance probably cannot use. They are deterred by weapons whose use is credible. If we do not have usable weapons, then we do not have deterrence, and if we do not have deterrence, then we may end up being forced to use unusable weapons or to capitulate. We must not invite the very aggression we seek to deter.

*   *   *

Mr. STENNIS: . . . It has been thoroughly gone over here that this small warhead, I call it, for the Lance missile, on which we rely in Western Europe, is a step forward in that it carries, more or less, the radius of a pistol shot, as compared to the radius of a shotgun shot, in the spread of its effect.

If it is used—which God forbid—it can be centered on the adversary and the military part of the adversary far, far, better—far better—than the regular warhead. These things come and go, but the idea of having this weapon under this amazing control, with a limited application, is the best news that I have heard in years to relieve the situation as to a probable human kill and reduce greatly the chances. At the same time, it carries a tremendous deterrent force—and that is what we want, a deterrent force—to the adversary. Here is the message that this technology permits the perfection of this little warhead to this very limited area and, therefore, is better able to concentrate its great destruction upon the adversary's military units.

In that way, I think it is a tremendous factor. It carries its deterrence in a greater way, carries a probable kill of fewer innocent human beings and bystanders and people of Western Europe, including the great number of dependents of our own people that we have there.

*   *   *

Mr. HATFIELD: One of the things that has become most apparent throughout both the closed session and now the open session this afternoon has been that this is an issue that has not been thoroughly discussed. It is the first time when this issue has really been gone into in great depth. I have indicated before that, according to my investigation, very few of the staff or members of the committees seem to be fully aware of the existence, let alone the implications, of this particular weapon.

We have attempted today not to make a final determination on the weapon, because of the magnitude of the question. Because of the far-reaching implications involved if we should adopt this as part of our arsenal, we simply ask the Senate to delay its final decision on this matter until procedures have been complied with which were set into law. . . .

The procedure to which I refer most specifically today and most frequently is the arms limitation impact, which very clearly states that this statement shall be made available to Members of Congress, through committee requests. On this weapon, we have information as late as this morning that such a statement has not been made . . . that the preliminary information has been gathered but the final determination has not been made; and, in fact, they are not going to make this impact statement until after President Carter has made a determination on whether he wants the weapon or not.

Mr. President, I should like to review briefly the sequence that has brought us to this point.

When this matter was first revealed through the press by a very diligent, accurate, and well-known reporter, it was brought to my attention as a member of the subcommittee. I was very alarmed at the time by the report in the press, and I wanted to find some answers to my questions. It became very apparent that those questions were not easily answerable, not because of classification as much as because of lack of knowledge, lack of information, or lack of awareness. That was true on the part of some of the staff of the committee as well as the members.

I am not standing here this afternoon being critical of the fact that this was one of those rather interesting exercises where one item more or less appeared in the budget by some way, some method, but certainly not one that was well known or understood.

Rather I am today suggesting that, perhaps, this system we are following does not always bring to light the full implication or the impact of the decisions we make or the actions we take.

When it became apparent that this was in the budget, and some of the elementary and rather cursory facts became known concerning this weapons system, I called the White House and I asked to talk to Mr. Stu Eizenstat, who is, as Senators know, a very close adviser to the President in his administrative family. I asked Mr. Eizenstat the question: "Simply what is the President's position on this weapon?"

At the time it was apparent by comments made in response that Mr. Eizenstat was not aware that the President had a position or that the issue even had been raised. He said he would get back to me and indicate what the President's position was. This was in the first part of June.

In a few days we had another conversation and it was then related to me that the President would be provided with a memorandum on this weapons system and, upon reading and studying the memorandum, the President would make known a position.

Then a few days more passed, and I got another call from the White House that indicated they would not be able to get the response to me as soon as they had anticipated, but that the whole question was in the machinery and that there would be a response made.

As time went along, our subcommittee became very concerned, because we had marked up our bill, with a few exceptions, and this was one of the exceptions. It soon would be necessary to refer the bill to the full committee. At that time it was suggested that we perhaps should refer this question, then, to the full committee rather than have the subcommittee attempt to make a determination, because we had not heard from the White House. This we did.

After we referred the question to the full committee, I received a letter from Mr. William J. Perry, Director of Defense Research and Engineering. On behalf of President Carter, he stated, and I refer now to the key paragraph in the letter, that "to afford the President maximum flexibility in his final decision on production, particularly if he chooses to authorize the presently proposed schedule, we respectfully recommend that adverse funding actions should not be taken by the Congress."

. . . it seems to me, if this logic is to prevail, and if it were applied to the rest of the bill, we would appropriate full funding of all the items under consideration in order to give the President maximum flexibility to spend only the money he wants. In so doing, we would effectively remove the Congress from a legitimate, and what I consider a responsible, role of shared decision making.

*   *   *

Were this a matter of extending some weapons system into a more sophisticated area, as it has been alleged, then I suppose technically it could be justified and defended. That is a separate issue. I think we have to look at this in a little broader scope than just the technological context. That is, we are talking about a weapons system now, a warhead—I say system, corporately, but warhead, specifically—that does introduce a whole new dimension to warfare and, particularly, to conventional warfare.

In my opinion, it invites use, because of the arguments that have been used that this weapon is a very precise weapon, that it has the capacity to hit a very constricted target, and that it does not destroy great areas of land or of property or buildings, but it is concentrated on meeting the enemy. The enemy here is defined as personnel, and it has been argued that this is a deterrent for its use.

But I would suggest that the logic is reversed. I would say that one of the great deterrents today, as far as utilizing the Lance warhead as presently constituted in the NATO arsenal, is the concern that it could destroy our allies and it could destroy broad areas beyond merely the target of the enemy.

This weapon, its supporters note, can be brought to bear on a more specific target. Therefore, I suggest the rationale is that we could use it with greater possibility of maintaining a restricted nuclear engagement.

Mr. President, this, of course, begs the entire issue, because this introduces again an old conundrum that we have heard many times over, from various and sundry sources, as to whether we could embark upon a limited nuclear war. I think that is a myth to begin with.

* * *

So to say that this weapon lends itself to a limited nuclear attack and that somehow it could prevent an expanded nuclear war I think is fallacious; and furthermore, any time that one argues the question of nuclear war or limited nuclear war one is assuming that one can predict the response of the enemy.

I think that again is a totally fallacious assumption, because one cannot predict, nor can one anticipate what the enemy response would be. . . .

Therefore, in effect, it is introducing nuclear weaponry into conventional warfare for the first time in our history.

It would, in effect, bring us into a new era of warfare, because where we now delineate between conventional war and nuclear war, it would not be only the potential of introducing a nuclear weapon in a conventional war, but it certainly, at the minimum, would create a fuzzy undefinable situation.

Also, in our Foreign Relations Subcommittee 3 years ago Mr. Warnke, who is now in the role of negotiator for limitation of arms, made a statement which I think is very appropriate to recall. He said:

A new generation of tactical nuclear weapons would be an absolute disaster.

Then, Mr. President, Mr. Warnke went on to say that—

New weapons with lower yield and greater accuracy and presumably few collateral consequences would erode. . .

And I underscore the word "erode"—

rather than strengthen the deterrence, and could at worst increase the prospects of eventual all-out nuclear war.

Of course Mr. Warnke now is in a role of trying to negotiate some kind of an agreement on arms limitation. May I point out that this really is the focus that we should be stressing, as well as the procedural question. Of course, we also must address the moral issue of introducing nuclear weaponry into conventional warfare. The issue is simply this: We talk about deterrence, but who is going to be deterred?

* * *

July 13, 1977

Mr. HATFIELD: Now, Mr. President, there also has been a fundamental issue raised by these enhanced radiation weapons as to whether the concept of limited nuclear warfare is valid.

I believe we all naturally have a great interest in peace. I believe the interests of everyone in this Chamber is basically for peace. But I also believe that that great goal of peace is ill served by making nuclear exchanges more likely.

I think we also tend to lose sight in this debate of one of the most significant priorities of this nation today. That is the goal of striking a deal with the great powers, particularly the Soviet Union, and I shall restrict my comment only to the Soviet Union at this point, but eventually, we hope to bring all the great powers into some arms limitation agreement.

Secretary of Defense Brown and the ACDA Director Warnke have stated that they know of no way of keeping a nuclear conflict limited. As recently as yesterday's news conference, President Carter said:

> My guess is that the first use of atomic weapons might very well lead to a rapid and uncontrolled escalation in the use of even more powerful weapons, with possibly a worldwide holocaust resulting.

Just how President Carter squares that statement with his letter to Senator Stennis about the potential for discreet use of enhanced radiation weapons is difficult to fathom. I quote from the letter to Senator Stennis, dated July 11. The President of the United States said to Senator Stennis—the same President who spoke to this issue at yesterday's press conference—that:

> It must be recognized that NATO is a defensive alliance which might have to fight on its own territory. For these purposes the capability for discreet application of force—

Let me report for emphasis the phrase referring to the capability for discreet application of force—

which the ER—

Enhanced radiation—

weapons may provide present an attractive option.

I repeat:

> For these purposes, the capability for discreet application of force which the ER weapons may provide present an attractive option.

I cannot reconcile those two statements, made by the same President barely a day apart.

Mr. President, there was an interesting editorial on July 8 in the *Washington Star*, which I think certainly put a proper light on this issue. I read into the *Record* a portion of that *Washington Star* editorial:

> If the neutron warhead is thought to be a genuinely tactical or battlefield scaled nuclear weapon, it will be the first such weapon to qualify unambiguously. No strategist that we know of, from Dr. Kissinger on, has convincingly shown that a reliable distinction is to be drawn between tactical and strategic nuclear warfare. Any weapon that promotes the illusion, short of absolute certainty, is to be viewed with the utmost suspicion, even if it does promise to spare civilians and their life support systems the side effects of the big bombs.

One further quote, I think, is worthy of attention today, as we again discuss this matter. In a column in yesterday's *New York Times*, Herbert Scoville, Jr., former technial director of the Defense Department's special weapons project, and former deputy director of the CIA, said:

> Our security depends on strengthening, not breaking, the barrier between nuclear and conventional conflict. The neutron bomb should be put back on the shelf and we should, instead, concentrate on developing ways of deterring aggression by conventional means.

*   *   *

Mr. President, I also happen to have been one of the first into Hiroshima after the bomb had been dropped, and I saw the devastation of that bomb. . . .

One who walked into that city and found bodies yet unburied and found the devastation that I saw and the survivors who were able to survive that bomb at Hiroshima and smelled the stench of the dead cannot escape reality. What I am saying here today is simply that, even though we could discuss the moral dimension and the ethical dimension of embarking further on this mad dash to extinction which nuclear warfare can only lead to, let us disabuse our minds of any myth that, somehow, we can use an instrument of war of this kind in such a precise target manner that we can restrict nuclear war, that we can have all the advantages of nuclear weaponry and use them on such a limited base. That is a myth. To me, those who propagate that myth in our minds are far more guilty of impracticality and lack of reality than those of us who are trying to limit this nation in its headlong pursuit of nuclear destruction.

*   *   *

So I suggest the Senate today make very carefully a decision that could lead us into a great holocaust strictly on the myth that somehow we can use this—and it invites use because of its precision, or, in the words of the President, that it presents an attractive—an attractive—option.

I cannot accept that. I cannot accept that belief.

*   *   *

Mr. NUNN: . . . when the Senator [Mr. Hatfield] describes, as has been described in the past few days, the horrible effects of radiation, about the horrible effects of fallout, about the fact that nuclear weapons kill people and that they are lethal, dangerous, and dirty, this is the argument that perhaps should have been made before the first one was exploded in World War II. I say that it is irrelevant to this particular discussion except as we distinguish between the existing inventory and this particular weapon. That is what the argument should be about.

Unfortunately, that is not what it is about. I have read lengthy articles in the last few days about the effect of radiation as if this new weapon is the only weapon that has radiation. We have something in the neighborhood of 7,000 tactical nuclear weapons in NATO. Each one of them generates radiation. Each one of them kills people. Each one of them has a blast effect and thermal effect of probably about 10 times that of the neutron warhead.

The American people are confused about this argument, and they have every right to be confused because we have in this Chamber and in the news media in the last few days suddenly discovered radiation, and we have suddenly discovered lethal nuclear weapons. So I submit: Let us focus this debate on the difference between this proposed weapon and what we already have, not on the self-evident proposition that nuclear weapons kill people and are dangerous to mankind. I would certainly stipulate nuclear weapons are dangerous; they kill people; they are lethal; and we hope and pray that we will never have to use them.

Mr. HATFIELD: I appreciate the Senator's question.

I only say that I would have to reject the implication of the philosophy that is included in the Senator's comments that somehow we are on a machine or we are on a wheel where we have no capacity to redirect, to restrict or to stop. The idea that we should have made this decision before Hiroshima is irrelevant, too, in the sense that the question is—

Mr. NUNN: I am not saying that.

Mr. HATFIELD: We can still make decisions and determinations. I think we have some control over our destiny.

Mr. NUNN: We certainly do. We have control whether we produce this weapon. That is a perfectly legitimate question.

What I hate to see is a dialog on the issue of nuclear weapons in general and rather than one which addresses itself to the difference between this nuclear weapon and the approximately 7,000 that we already have sitting over there in NATO. This is unfortunate because the misperceptions regarding this particular weapon are more widespread than those surrounding any other weapon I have seen since I have been in the Senate.

Mr. HATFIELD: I appreciate the Senator's comments, and I would agree in part. I would also like to say that the Senator in recent debate indicated certain characteristics of the bomb. The very able and well-informed Senator from Georgia said on many occasions about weapons systems, about the residual impact, and I would only say since that last debate we now have the questions raised about carbon 14 which would totally reverse the argument used by the Senator from Georgia before that somehow this was so precise and controllable we did not have the residual impact. I am saying there are these questions.

Mr. NUNN: I wish to have the Senator from Oregon point out where the Senator from Georgia said this bomb did not have residual radiological effects. The Senator from Oregon does not realize there are such residual effects with any nuclear weapon. We call it fallout. It is a function related to how far that weapon explodes above the ground. That is the case of every weapon in the inventory today.

I have never described this as being a clean weapon. I have never said there was no fallout. What I have said is that it reduces the collateral damage by minimizing the thermal blast and fallout effects.

Every weapon that produces nuclear radiation produces fallout. The amount of fallout is dependent on how far it is above the ground when it is exploded. This weapon is just like those we have in inventory in Europe. It can cause fallout and it will cause fallout if it is exploded on or near the ground; it picks up particles, the particles go in the air, and there is where you get your fallout. But that is no different from weapons in the existing inventory. What the Senator has described for the last 2 or 3 days by the term "fallout" applies to every single weapon we have today.

*   *   *

Mr. STENNIS: On the 12th of July, yesterday, I received this letter from the President of the United States. It says:

> In reply to your July 6, 1977 letter, let me bring you up to date on my thinking with regard to the enhanced radiation (ER) weapons.
>
> I have requested that the Department of Defense provide me a study of such weaponry by August 15, 1977; it will be accompanied by an Arms Control Impact Statement (ACIS). I intend to make a final production decision shortly after receiving these two documents.

Could anything be simpler, or more logical, or more positive, and more natural than the statement there that he intended to make a final production decision shortly after receiving these two documents?

> If the production decision is an affirmative one, I will send the Congress the ACIS at the time my decision is announced.

My goodness alive, Mr. President, as long as it takes to get items of this kind into production, there is plenty of time—plenty of time—for the Congress, even in extended debate, to take such action as it might see fit with reference to the President's decision.

Continuing with the letter:

> In the interim, the Department of Defense has prepared for me an initial assessment of these weapons. It is my present view that the enhanced radiation weapon contained in the ERDA budget is in this Nation's security interest. I therefore urge Congress to approve the current funding request.

There is nothing more positive nor more certain than this, Mr. President. It is possible, of course, that is an erroneous decision, but I do not think it is erroneous. I think it is real and anything not acted on in this field now, looked at and acted on by whomever is President, would be a mistake. But that is beside the point.

The point is that the President is coming right down on these things, answering the question that the Congress asked him and giving his reasons therefor.

Continuing:

> We are not talking about some new kind of weapon, but of the modernization of nuclear weapons.

So true. So true. This is nothing new. This is nothing that has come out or leaked out or certainly conceived of and going to destroy the world.

This is just a part of the family of weapons that we have been making all these years, praying at the same time we never have to use them, making them first for their deterrent effect—and we need not doubt, Mr. President, that is their main purpose.

As I have said before, man has not outlawed war, but weaponry itself has virtually outlawed and stopped wars on a large scale because of the terrible consequences of an all-out battle of this kind. But a deterrent is what we have in mind, primarily.

Now, continuing:

> In the absence of satisfactory agreements to reduce nuclear weapons we must retain and modernize our theater nuclear capabilities, especially in support of NATO's deterrent strategy of flexible response. Tactical nuclear weapons, including those for battlefield use, have strongly contributed to the deterrence of conflict in Europe.

How could anything be more true and how could any deterrent be more effective than these nuclear weapons that he is talking about? And he said he does not want to see them run down or lacking in proper supply.

I emphasize that sentence again and read again from his own words:

> . . . have strongly contributed to deterrence of conflict in Europe.

I think it is highly probable that if we had not had them, Western Europe already would have been overrun. Everyone knows that the Soviets have an outstanding superiority in that field, in that area of the world. The U.S. troops never can be there in such volume as to destroy that preponderance of weight in favor of the Soviets and their allies.

So I think the President is correct, without any doubt, that these weapons have contributed strongly to deterrence of conflict in Europe.

Continuing with his words:

> I believe we must retain the option they provide, and modernize it.

That is exactly what virtually every Member of this body has run on for more than 30 years, a determination not to go to sleep at the switch but to have the weaponry and keep it modernized.

*   *   *

The next sentence:

> These weapons are not strategic and have no relationship to SALT.

As I understand, he means they are not involved in any prospective agreement in the so-called SALT talks.

Continuing with his letter:

> It must be recognized that NATO is a defensive alliance which might have to fight on its own territory.

We all know that. The charge is made against us that this is all put together and we are looking for a chance to go on the offensive, that we want to obliterate someone, that we want somebody else's territory. We know that is not true, and we maintain that position.

However, we went into this defensive alliance for the very purpose of holding off the aggressor, should one develop.

Continuing with the letter:

> An aggressor should be faced with uncertainty as to whether NATO would use nuclear weapons against its forward echelons. For these purposes, the capability for discreet application of force—which the ER weapons may provide—present (at least in this sense) an attractive option. Whether or not the weapons have significant destabilizing aspects requires and will receive study in the ACIS.

That is the arms control impact statement.

> The ER weapons, then, would be designed to enhance deterrence . . .

There is the emphasis again—deterrence.

> . . . but if deterrence fails to satisfy dual criteria:
> First, to enhance NATO's capability to inflict significant military damage on the aggressor.
> Second, to minimize damage and casualties to individuals not in the immediate target area, including friendly troops and civilians.
> The decision to use nuclear weapons of any kind, including ER weapons, would remain in my hands, not in the hands of local theater commanders.

There never has been any authority in the hands of any local theater commander. It "would remain in my hands"—in the hands of the President of the United States.

I continue reading from the letter:

> A decision to cross the nuclear threshold would be the most

agonizing decision to be made by any President. I can assure you that these weapons would not make that decision any easier. But by enhancing deterrence, they could make it less likely that I would have to face such a decision.

Mr. President, whether the name is Carter, Ford, or whatever—any President—is there anything that goes to his innermost soul more than having to live with this decision process that may land in his lap at any moment, day or night, all the time, 24 hours in every day and every day of every year, as to what he would do if faced with this decision? This man is pouring out, as an individual and as an official, the innermost part of his mind, heart, and soul, and I commend him for the very fine way he has answered these questions and put them out here for all to see and to judge—his innermost sentiments and purposes.

*   *   *

. . . this particular weapon . . . brings into view and to thought the horrors of nuclear weapons, but that has been true all the time, and it will continue to be true. Would anybody suggest that we just abolish them unilaterally? I do not believe a Member of this body, not a single one, would suggest that we abolish them.

Well, does anyone seriously object to modernizing? That is the key word here.

*   *   *

Mr. HEINZ: Mr. President, we have debated the neutron bomb now for many hours. But we are talking not just about a weapons system, not just about our need for a strong national security, not just about the need for a good defense with and for our NATO allies. We need all of those, and I have always been a strong and consistent supporter of a national defense second to none. The fact is, though, we are also talking about the very way we are making our decision. I want to make it clear at the outset that I do not at this time oppose in principle the neutron bomb. I want to make that very clear. What I do oppose is a rush to judgment, and what I seek is much more careful consideration of an enormously important issue.

Mr. President, statements the President made at his news conference yesterday have only reinforced my opposition to funding the neutron bomb program at this time.

*   *   *

There is simply no urgency to the matter. Before we give the go ahead to what could ultimately cost the taxpayers billions of dollars, the President has an obligation to make a solid case, and we have the obligation to debate it thoroughly. Congress just does not know enough to be plunging into this new weapons technology. Even Mr. Carter, who prides himself in having been a nuclear engineer, is still studying the matter. Yet most Congressmen had never even heard of a neutron bomb a few weeks ago. This is no way to run a government.

*   *   *

Mr. President, in one of my accompanying statements, I note that it is bad enough that this weapon seems akin to chemical warfare, not only because it targets people rather than property, but because it will subject them in many instances to excruciating death by radiation.

But even on the level of hardheaded strategic argument, the neutron bomb remains a big question mark. Consider the following . . . First, the effectiveness of the weapon in certain circumstances is unclear; second, the biological effects are speculative; third, the Russians may be able to devise countermeasures; fourth, the immediate impact of the neutron radiation may actually be counterproductive; fifth, in some cases, policymakers may not in fact be likelier to use the weapons as proponents of the bomb claim; sixth, even neutron weapons will be capable of wreaking enormous havoc, especially if the fireball hits the ground—something that can be affected by human variables—or if the Soviets retaliate with old-fashioned weapons; seventh, there is still a question of the bomb's long-term radioactivity—both in the soil, and, as Senator Hatfield argued earlier, in the air via carbon 13 and carbon 14; eighth, the bomb might siphon off money that could be spent on a better conventional defense of Europe which would accomplish the same objective; and ninth, the attitude of our allies to the use of these neutron bombs on their territory is not clear.

Mr. President, I think it is significant that Senator Hart, as he said a few moments ago, has never been briefed on any neutron weapon in his 2 years as a member of the Armed Services Committee and as a member of the Intelligence Committee. I think it is significant that most of the relevant committees, the authorizing committees, and the appropriations committees, have not had any serious hearings on this matter.

Mr. President, I for one, am not willing to commit what could be a $5 million expenditure without one very, very thorough investigation of the effectiveness of this weapon, our policies as to its deployment, the implications for deterrence, and a very clear idea of what the Pentagon ultimately intends.

*   *   *

Mr. THURMOND: The proposed neutron, or enhanced radiation warhead merely complements our nuclear missiles already in place. If our troops are forced to retreat, then it would be necessary to retake land once held by friendly nations. In the event of a nuclear attack by the Soviets the neutron warhead would enable us to accomplish this task with minimum damage to life and property.

While the radiation effects of the neutron warhead and the current Lance nuclear weapons are similar, the blast and thermal effects are greatly reduced. We have already developed "clean" nuclear warheads for other weapons, why deny their development for tactical weapons?

Mr. President, I do not believe the neutron warhead lowers the nuclear threshold. Just because it is a cleaner weapon will not make us more likely to use it.

The only time this country would use nuclear weapons in Europe would be if the enemy had already done so. If the world ever reaches that horrible moment, this weapon would enable us to fight back in the least devastating manner.

Mr. President, the President of the United States has written the chairman of the Senate Armed Services Committee a letter on this subject dated July 12, 1977. I want to read a few excerpts from this letter by President Carter as I feel it is important that the Senate gain the advantage of the information he has provided in his letter.

In this letter, President Carter stated:

> It is my present view that the enhanced radiation weapon contained in the ERDA budget is in this Nation's security interest.

Now, who is that speaking, Mr. President? That is the President of the United States, President Carter, and he says that in his view this enhanced radiation weapon is in this Nation's security interest.

The President is in a better position than anyone else to know the jeopardy which this country might face. He is the Commander in Chief as well as the President of the United States, and when the President says that a weapon is in the Nation's security interest, how can we turn him down?

*   *   *

Mr. President, the President of the United States is simply saying this: We better have this weapon on hand, it will help to deter war, it will not bring on a war, it will help deter war.

Then, if it answers that purpose, the main purpose in having a defense force has been accomplished, as we would rather deter war than have to fight a war.

This just puts another element in the nuclear arsenal which the enemy knows must be faced if he starts aggression in NATO.

*   *   *

In other words, the President is saying that if we have such weapons as this, it will make it less likely we will ever have to use such weapons because it will help to deter aggression and help to deter war, and that is what we want to do.

Mr. President, I simply say that those statements by the President of the United States, I think, are very strong statements. I do not know of any better argument that anyone can make on the subject.

I also state that the Defense Secretary supports this position. I also say that the President has already twice sent Congress budget requests for production of this weapon. The President has approved the underground tests of the neutron warhead held last month, June 29.

Mr. President, all weapons kill people. That is the purpose in building weapons. Somebody said, "Well, this weapon will kill people and will not damage property."

The purpose in weapons is to destroy the enemy. Primarily, I would envision these weapons would only be used in friendly territory because we will not use nuclear weapons unless we were attacked first, and then the President of the United States would have to give the order. The President of the United States would have to say when they could be used, if they are to be used at all.

I think a better descriptive term for this weapon would be "diminished destruction weapon," because the present Lance warhead is not as clean as the neutron warhead. The current nuclear Lance warhead has more blast; it has more thermal effects. This weapon has less blast and less thermal effects. It has more radiation, yes, and that is the purpose of it—to provide more radiation, but at the same time to save all the property possible in friendly territory.

*   *   *

Mr. President, something has been said about Mr. Paul Warnke's position, I believe. Mr. Paul Warnke has disavowed news reports that the Arms Control and Disarmament Agency opposes this warhead. He has termed the report "inaccurate and misleading." So any statement along that line is inaccurate.

Mr. President, a sensible position on the neutron warhead has been taken by one of America's greatest scientists and patriots, Dr. Edward Teller, of the Hoover Institution at Stanford University. If I had any doubt about which position to take in this matter, I do not know of anyone in this Nation we could go to in order to consult for sounder scientific advice than Dr. Teller. Dr. Teller is known as the father of the H-bomb. He is one of the most astute scientists in this Nation today.

In essence, Dr. Teller proposes a public policy that the neutron bomb would be used only in defense of invaded territory. He says the enemy, so advised, would weigh more carefully any attack and the dangers of escalation would be reduced. That is Dr. Teller's position. He thinks that it will help to deter war.

Unfortunately, Mr. President, all weapons in our defense arsenal are designed to kill people and destroy property. That is the terrifying and shameful consequence of war.

My position has always been that by being prepared to fight with the most advanced weapons, we are much less likely to ever face the decision of having to use any of them.

* * *

Mr. CLARK: The President is asking the Senate to act without benefit of time to study and hold hearings on this issue. In fact, the President is asking the Senate to approve this funding before he, as he has publicly confirmed, has decided on the production and deployment of this weapon. Therefore, my question: Why then must the Senate decide at this juncture? What sense does it make to approve funding for production of a weapon, before the President has decided on its deployment.

The case for going slowly was, in my judgment, given further support yesterday by the findings of the distinguished Senator from Oregon. According to his report, a prominent scientist, J. Carson Mark, for 30 years head of the theoretical division at the Los Alamos research center, has now challenged claims that this warhead is all that "clean."

"Clean" is a very relative term, and for those persons—and buildings—within the immediate range of the weapon, it is just as "dirty" as a normal nuclear weapon. For that matter, though it may be "clean" for those victims "lucky" enough to get a lethal dose of 8,000 to 10,000 rads and die almost immediately, many other persons at varying distances would get a progressively lesser dose, leaving many to die a slow and, I suggest, "dirty" death.

But now we are told, by Professor Mark, that there is serious concern about the impact of the neutron radiation on the surrounding area. The neutron radiation apparently reacts with the carbon and cobalt in the soil in ways about which we know very little. It is claimed, for example, that the radiation creates a radioactive carbon isotope with a half-life of 5,720 years.

I would not pretend to have the technical competence to judge whether this is accurate. But I do find it significant that a leading figure in the nuclear weapons business raises the question. And, in my judgment, it is the unanswered questions such as this which should cause us to hold off funding a weapons program on which we are not sufficiently informed to judge the impact. Why can we not afford to at least find out what it is all about?

Perhaps the most vital point which it seems to me deserves to be clarified is the impact of this weapon on the likelihood of nuclear war. Some of the supporters of this weapon inside this administration are on the record stating flatly that they doubt that "clean" nuclear weapons or "mini-nukes" can be used without provoking a strategic nuclear exchange.

Let me quote Paul C. Warnke, now the head of the Arms Control and Disarmament Agency, and our principal SALT negotiator, back in 1974: "to the extent that mini-nukes blur the distinction between conventional weapons and nuclear weapons they lower the nuclear threshold."

I see no way that sentence can be interpreted other than to assume that the neutron bomb could lower the nuclear threshold.

Such weapons, Mr. Warnke continued, would "make the consequences of use of tactical nuclear weapons less dire in the minds of the potential attacker and, as a consequence, would not constitute to the same extent the degree of deterrent that a weapon which is clearly different in kind now promises." What would this mean? Mr. Warnke concludes: "and once the nuclear threshold is crossed the process of escalation could become irreversible."

*   *   *

. . . I think one of the greatest deterrents to a nuclear exchange is the awareness that "going nuclear" is an enormous new order of magnitude—that it is a step toward the possible destruction of the world as we know it. I think it is extraordinarily dangerous to have policy planners think that they can go halfway, and have a nice, clean, tactical limited nuclear exchange.

That is why we must retain, as much as possible, a high nuclear

355

threshold, a clear demarcation line between conventional and nuclear weapons.

Now, I realize that the Senator from Georgia, and others, has argued that the bomb has to be clean in order for it to be credible that we would use it, and therefore it can serve as a credible deterrent. I appreciate this argument. This is the fundamental argument made in favor of this weapon. "Make nuclear weapons just clean enough," it is argued, "to insure that they will be used."

I think our security depends upon convincing the Soviet Union that to "go nuclear" means to provoke a strategic exchange. The illusion that we could—as some Pentagon planners are apparently proposing—use some clean warheads and some standard warheads, not fired alone, but in a package of 30 to 50 nuclear shells and warheads, and not provoke a general nuclear exchange, is a faulty argument to the extreme.

In this regard, Herbert Scoville, Jr., among the most respected and experienced men in the arms control field, points out that "the Russians have shown little interest in low-yield battlefield nuclear weapons. Their doctrine has called for massive responses in the event that we initiate the use of nuclear weapons at any level. Therefore, our attempt to save European cities by relying on low-yield neutron bombs is most unlikely to succeed."

I find that very persuasive, Mr. President, and I see a lot of merit, as Scoville argues, in strengthening, not breaking, the barrier between nuclear and conventional conflicts.

*   *   *

Just in conclusion, let me add one comment on the broader significance of this debate. The Senate would not even be discussing this issue today had it not been for the fortuitous declassification of the fact that these funds were even in this bill.

Up until now we did not even know about enhanced radiation weapons, or at least the overwhelming majority of us did not. We did not even know they existed and indeed did not even know they passed in the authorization measure. We had no idea what some of the funds we were appropriating were even to be used for. It may well be that a small group of Senators did know about this weapon system and knew a considerable amount about it. The vast majority of us did not. It makes one wonder what else is in these appropriations bills. It prompts me to wonder what sort of activities and what kind of projects are routinely approved without our really knowing what is involved.

Mr. NUNN: Mr. President, there has been a great deal of discussion in the last couple of days about the relative dangers of this particular weapon as compared to the weapons we already have in our inventory. At least that is the context in which the discussion should have taken place. It unfortunately has not.

In terms of trying to clarify some of the misunderstandings I have a letter, dated July 13, 1977, that I have just received at my request from Dr. F. C. Gilbert, Deputy Director of Military Applications of the Energy Research and Development Administration.

*   *   *

I think the Senate would be interested in the information in this because this letter is in response to my request to clarify some of the technical details. This represents a comparison of the current nuclear Lance warhead with the enhanced radiation warhead that we are now discussing, and I quote this letter:

> In response to your question concerning the relative effects of the Enhanced Radiation Lance Warhead and the Standard Nuclear Lance Warhead, the table below gives a comparison of radiation (neutron) output, C^{14} production, fallout potential, thermal (heat) output, and blast output.
>
> As you can see from the table, in terms of neutron output, lethal radiation radius, and Carbon^{14} output, the differences between the current and proposed enhanced radiation Lance Warheads are negligible. Most significant, however, . . .

And I would ask my colleague from Oregon to listen to this particular part:

> Most significant, however, is the fact that the neutron warhead produces less than 1/10 of the fallout, heat, and blast which the present Lance Warhead generates.

*   *   *

I believe, Mr. President, that this should in very simple fashion allow the Members of the Senate, and for that matter the public, to begin to put in perspective what has not been put into perspective, and that is the comparison between our existing warheads and the proposed nuclear warhead. This may not change anyone's mind about deterrence. Deterrence is a separate argument, but I think at least this should clarify the scare stories that have been going on around about carbon 14 fallout potential.

*   *   *

We have tactical delivery systems with very short ranges, which means that if there was an invasion by the Warsaw Pact with little warning time, then it would mean that our military commanders in NATO would feel a strong compulsion to ask for the quick release of authority to use tactical nuclear weapon authority because, in the position we are now in, there would be a rapid fallback from the border.

The further we get back from the border the more likely it is that our weapons will be used on NATO territory. This is the posture we are in now.

What we are talking about now is, that instead of having a high nuclear threshold, at least as far as the military is concerned—and, of course, the decision would not be military—we have an incentive system based on the horrible destructive weapons which are there now, which would obliterate the territory we have sworn to defend. We have a system which lends itself to an early request for an early release of tactical nuclear authority. If that authority is not given early, then the weapons will fall on almost exclusively West German territory.

That is the situation we are in now.

*   *   *

One of the things which amazed me was to read just recently that the administration and the Pentagon were advocating this weapon because it was cheaper than conventional weapons to knock out tanks. I contend that is erroneous. I contend the Department of Defense does not have that position. Anyone who has that position, and I do not believe the White House does, does not realize that NATO's firm policy is not to use nuclear weapons as a substitute for conventional weapons, but to use them only as a last resort.

. . . We need to build a conventional defense in Europe which creates parity with the Warsaw Pact. We do not have that kind of parity now in conventional arms, and we have lost the nuclear advantages we once enjoyed.

I believe these matters have to be put into context before we talk about the whole concept of deterrence. The situation has changed in NATO. We no longer have nuclear advantages there, either strategically or tactically, in the opinion of the Senator from Georgia. If we do not give more credibility to our present tactical nuclear deterrence in NATO, then we increase, as days go by, the likelihood that we will have aggression in some form.

*   *   *

Mr. HUMPHREY: Now, part of the law known as the Arms Control and

Disarmament Act was not fulfilled insofar as the so-called neutron bomb authorization or appropriation, which is now before us. The previous administration did not get an impact statement nor did this administration. When the President was informed of this matter, he asked, of course, that the impact statement be prepared, and it was accomplished or it was undertaken by the Arms Control Agency.

We were informed—and when I say "we," the members of the Committee on Foreign Relations and the Committee on Armed Services, Senator Hatfield and others were informed—that there was such an impact statement.

I took the liberty, at the suggestion of our esteemed colleague, Senator Claiborne Pell, to call the Secretary of Defense, Mr. Brown, and suggest to him that the impact statement should be forwarded at once to the committees that had requested it, and the Senate Armed Services Committee had made the request, through the chairman, Senator Stennis; the Senate Foreign Relations Committee had made the request through Senator Sparkman.

That request of mine was made this morning at around 11 o'clock. I was informed that the Secretary of Defense would discuss this with the President, which he did, and the order was given to present to these committees at once the impact statement, and that means that this statement is before us even before the National Security Council has had full time to analyze all of its significance.

The impact statement was delivered to the respective committee chairmen about 3 hours ago. In the meantime, the Senate Foreign Relations Committee, at the order of our chairman, met. We, as individual members of that committee, have had an opportunity to discuss in concert with our colleagues this arms control impact statement.

I am taking the liberty, Mr. President, since the National Security Council has indicated that this statement is unclassified, to ask unanimous consent that the entire text of the statement be placed at this point in the *Record*, and I so ask unanimous consent.

There being no objection, the statement was ordered to be printed in the *Record*, as follows:

Arms Control Impact Analysis

Program Title: W-70 Mod 3 (Lance) Warhead

I. Program synopsis:

A. Descriptions:

The W-70 Mod 3 is being developed to satisfy an Army requirement for a low-yield enhanced radiation (ER) warhead for the Lance missile system.

Enhanced radiation is achieved by fusion reactions that produce high energy neutrons. When these neutrons are produced in connection with relatively low-yield fission reactions, the range of effect of the neutrons is greater than the range at which blast or thermal effects are lethal. At higher yields, blast and thermal effects predominate over both neutron and gamma radiation effects of any type. By employing ER as the target damage mechanism, a reduction in collateral damage is achieved since lower yields are required when personnel are the targets rather than equipment. For example, a 1KT [kiloton] ER warhead gives the same approximate damage expectancy of tank crew incapacitation through radiation effects as a 10KT fission warhead does through radiation effects.

The Lance is a highly mobile surface-to-surface, ballistic missile system which can provide tactical nuclear artillery support to the battlefield through attacks on either fixed targets or non-fixed targets (e.g., tank battalions in staging areas). The nuclear Lance missile has a maximum range of 130 kilometers with a CEP (Circular Error Probable) of 400-450 meters. Lance has replaced the Honest John and Sergeant missile systems in the U.S. forces in Europe and is replacing the Honest John and Sergeant in most NATO countries (UK, FRG, Belgium, Netherlands, Italy) in both cases on a less than one-for-one basis, thus reducing the number of forward-deployed nuclear systems and weapons. (A total of 92 Lance launchers are now programmed for Europe.) Additionally, two Lance Battalions will be based in the U.S. with one presently earmarked for deployment in the Pacific should the need arise. The Lance system is more survivable and more responsive than the systems it replaces, and it has a selectable yield capability. Its longer range allows it to remain further behind the forward edge of the battle area (FEBA) and thus contributes to its survivability. The longer range also facilitates targeting across Corps boundaries.

B. Rationale:

An ER warhead provides increased kill capability, principally against personnel, and reduced collateral effects (blast and thermal). It has less effect on standard military equipment than a fission weapon of the same yield. With this weapon armored vehicles, which are relatively unaffected by blast effects except at close range, can be temporarily neutralized by radiation casualties of crew personnel. Requisite effects can still be achieved at much greater ranges, with less collateral damage, than could be expected from blast predominant weapons.

C. Funding:

ERDA's total projected direct costs are $32.1 million for FY-77 through FY-80.[1]

II. Analysis:

The ER warhead will kill tank crews by nuclear radiation. In covering the same intended target area with a non-ER fission weapon, casualties to civilians and damage to property from blast and thermal effects in a congested region would be greater.

It can be argued that the improved warhead may make initial use of nuclear weapons in battle seem more credible which might enhance deterrence. However, by the same token, it can be argued that it increases the likelihood that nuclear weapons would actually be used in combat. In any event, the escalating potential is the same for this weapon as for any other nuclear weapon.

The political effects of deploying enhanced radiation warheads relate to characteristics which may be imputed to the entire class of enhanced radiation weapons rather than to the Lance warhead alone. Potential effects on the nuclear threshold lie more in the gray area of perception—U.S. public, Allied, Soviet, and third world—than in judgments based on hard analytical criteria or weapons characteristics. This class of weapons is more dependent on radiation than on blast or thermal yields, but not entirely so. It is designed primarily against personnel and less against material and sheltering structures. Some will see this class of weapons as more plausible for battlefield use than other kinds of nuclear weapons and might infer a greater U.S. willingness to engage in nuclear war.

Soviet perceptions are difficult to analyze. There is no evidence that the development of this system would have any effect on Soviet doctrine for the initiation of nuclear war or that the Soviets would be less likely to escalate a nuclear exchange if ER weapons were used by the U.S. rather than standard fission weapons. They would presumably follow their own doctrines whether or not this weapon is introduced. The fact that the W-70 Mod 3 warhead may cause less collateral damage to civilians and property in NATO

---

[1]Cost data provided by Energy Research Development Administration. The ERDA Budget Estimate (as amended for FY-78) supplied to Congress cites a figure of $43.3 million for FY-78, of which $14.4 million are direct costs.

territory cannot be expected to moderate Soviet response. Its use would be no less likely than the present warhead to evoke Soviet retaliatory use of tactical nuclear weapons. Unless the Soviet forces are supplied with a comparable warhead, their response would create the kind of devastation that this warhead is designed to prevent.

Thus, the President would be faced with a decision of the same nature whether or not this class of weapons or other tactical nuclear weapons are used.

If ER weapons are deployed, the Soviets will continue to accuse the U.S. of contributing to the arms race in Europe. There is little doubt that the Soviets would seize on publicized materials alleging that U.S. development of ER weapons make nuclear war more likely by lowering the threshold.

In the U.S. case, the prospect of escalation would remain a central component of a U.S. decision to use nuclear weapons regardless of the performance characteristics of this or other classes of nuclear weapons. Thus, any U.S. decision to use nuclear weapons is in all likelihood insensitive to whether or not ER weapons were deployed.

There is no evidence that NATO governments would be particularly concerned about Lance deployment with this warhead. Nevertheless, public discussion of the sort now taking place here could affect NATO attitudes.

The W-70 Mod 3 development and deployment would not be affected by the TTBT [Threshold Test Ban Treaty] since the underground testing of warheads under 150 KT is not prohibited.

A CTB [comprehensive test ban] would pose limitations on the further development of this class of weapons since over the long term further testing would be required. Conclusion of a test ban treaty with no PNE [peaceful nuclear explosion] exception during the next few years would limit the development and refinement of such weapons by both sides.

With regard to MBFR [Mutual and Balanced Force Reduction], the Western proposal does not affect Lance launchers. Neither does the Western warhead proposal select specific types of warheads for removal. Development and deployment of the W-70 Mod 3 could, however, be cited by the Soviets as evidence that the U.S. proposal would involve elimination of obsolete weapons while actual capability is being upgraded.

Some governments might couple a decision to deploy ER weapons with perceptions that U.S. doctrine has changed so as to make the use of nuclear weapons more likely in a tactical situation;

such a coupling could have an adverse effect on U.S. efforts to prevent further nuclear proliferation.

In conclusion, this weapon system has no arms control advantages.

To the extent it has any impact on ongoing arms control negotiations, the impact would be marginally negative.

A decision to cross the nuclear threshold would be the most agonizing decision to be made by any President. These weapons would not make that decision any easier. But by enhancing deterrence, they could make it less likely that the President would have to face such a decision.

Mr. HUMPHREY: Mr. President, I think it should be noted that the statement is one that really fits the description of "on the one hand," and "on the other hand." It has statements that individual Senators can select that would, in a sense, buttress their respective positions.

The first part of the statement gives the description of the weapon. I think it should be noted that the weapon, while it is alleged to be a new weapon is, in a sense, a technological development and improvement of the existing weapon that is used in the Lance missile. The current weapon is a fission weapon, the weapon we are talking about here becomes a fusion weapon.

I am sure that some of my colleagues who have served in this body for some years can remember back in the 1950's when we used to talk about the so-called dirty bomb, the fission bomb, and then what we called the clean bomb, the fusion bomb.

The real truth is that bombs are destructive, whether they are dirty or clean, however one wishes to label them.

This weapon is a destructive vehicle. It is nuclear. The fact is that while it may be an advanced technology, it is still a nuclear weapon that has all of the nuclear capabilities. The difference is that the so-called neutron bomb has less radioactivity and less fire blast than the current weapon used in the Lance missile.

We had yesterday a meeting with the technicians and specialists of ERDA in the field of nuclear weaponry. As Senators know, under the current organization of the Energy Research and Development Administration, the Atomic Energy Commission was folded into that body, and there is what we call the military applications section. We had representatives of the military applications section come before Members who wished to attend a meeting to discuss all of the technical and engineering aspects of the weapon under discussion in this appropriation. This is described in the impact statement which I have now printed in the *Record*.

*   *   *

I call to my colleagues' attention that ACDA is not very positive on anything here. What they are really pointing out is what the Senator from Georgia (Mr. Nunn) has pointed out before, that we have in a very real sense, to use the metaphor, blown this weapon out of all proportions, that it is not a major weapon as such. It is an advanced technology of an existing weapon, and it is not a weapon that just kills people and does not damage buildings. It is a weapon that will kill people, damage buildings, destroy tanks and armies, just as any other weapon will.

The difference is that, based on the fact that NATO is a defensive alliance, this weapon could be used in a more selective way without having the danger of radioactive fallout upon friendly forces and upon villages and civilian population in a friendly territory. From that point of view, if you wish to extrapolate and in a sense really exaggerate, you could say in a sense it is a more humane weapon. I do not think any weapon is humane. I do not know where one would ever find one that is called humane. What I am getting at is looking back over the days when I first served in this Senate, when we came to what we called the hydrogen bomb, the fusion bomb, we had a great deal of talk about how it was a cleaner weapon than the old fission bomb. I remind my colleagues that clean or dirty it kills, destroys, blasts, burns.

The argument you will find that will be made, and I think with considerable justification, is that this weapon could possibly encourage the use of nuclear weapons more readily than the current weaponry. That is one argument.

Second, as one of our esteemed colleagues has pointed out, the present system of deterrence in NATO works quite well. Why modify it? Why change it?

The third possibility is the argument that can be made that the Soviets will undoubtedly launch a propaganda offensive saying this is a buildup in the arms race, that it represents escalation of the arms race on our part.

I think that the truth would be that what it really is is a replacement weapon for one that is currently deployed, that is, it is essentially the same size, has practically the same capacity for destructive power, but, as I pointed out from the analysis that we have here and that we heard yesterday, it has the features of being less destructive to collateral areas.

But I repeat again it is a powerful weapon.

The conclusion is one that does not give much of a conclusion, I regret to tell my colleagues, and it says as follows:

> In conclusion, this weapon system has no arms control advantages. To the extent it has any impact on ongoing arms

control negotiations, the impact would be marginally negative. A decision to cross the nuclear threshold would be the
most agonizing decision to be made by any President. These
weapons would not make that decision any easier.

And then it comes down on the other side and says:

But by enhancing deterrence, they—meaning these weapons—could make it less likely that the President would have
to face such a decision.

Namely, the decision of using nuclear weapons.

The logic of that statement is that there is some additional deterrent effect with this weapon which is debatable, but the argument is
made that there is such a deterrent effect, but I think you have to
balance it off by saying that the Arms Control and Disarmament
Agency also said it could have a marginally negative effect upon arms
control negotiations.

*   *   *

Mr. CHURCH: First of all, I fail to see any evidence that the existing mix
of weapons has not proved to be adequately credible.

I might say, no evidence has been brought to this Chamber, no
compelling reason has been given to us, why such a new weapon
should be so hastily approved.

It is puzzling, Mr. President, and I think we ought to look to those
who want the new weapon to carry the burden of proof. It should be up
to them, not up to us who have misgivings, to demonstrate how our
military position will be improved, or the likelihood of war lessened,
by beginning to produce and deploy a nuclear warhead that can be
more readily used.

I suppose, if the burden of proof lies with the proponents, and it
usually does, that we should look to the documents which have been
supplied by the executive branch.

I refer to the letter signed by the President, sent to the distinguished manager of the bill, Mr. Stennis, and read the paragraph
which undertakes to justify this new neutron bomb. The paragraph
reads as follows:

It must be recognized that NATO is a defensive alliance
which might have to fight on its own territory. An aggressor
should be faced with uncertainty as to whether NATO would
use nuclear weapons against its forward echelons. For these
purposes, the capability for discreet application of force—
which the ER weapons may provide—present (at least in this
sense) an attractive option.

Listen to the argument once more:

> The capability for discrete application of force—which the ER weapons may provide—presents an attractive option.

Of course, there is only one way this sentence can be read and understood. The President is saying it would be nice to have a weapon which can be more readily employed, should an attack ever occur in Western Europe. But even as he makes that argument, he recognizes the counterargument. So his next sentence is:

> Whether or not the weapons have significant destabilizing aspects requires and will receive study in the ACIS.

Mr. President, I have the ACIS in my other hand. It has just been furnished. I would like to call the Senate's attention to the analysis which the President said would be contained in this impact statement on the question of whether or not neutron weapons might have a significant destabilizing effect.

I will read the paragraph:

> It can be argued that the improved warhead may make initial use of nuclear weapons in battle seem more credible which might enhance deterrence. However, by the same token, it can be argued that it increases the likelihood that nuclear weapons would actually be used in combat.

We are given nothing, no meat at all, nothing has been added by the impact statement except a restatement of the two possible arguments, one favorable to the weapon and the other against it.

The impact statement concludes:

> In any event, the escalating potential is the same for this weapon as for any other nuclear weapon.

What does that mean? It means, if you do use the weapon, that its escalating potential to convert the war into a general nuclear exchange, or even a global holocaust, is the same for this weapon as for any other nuclear weapon.

I must say that is the least convincing argument imaginable for the party bearing the burden of proof as to why we should start to manufacture and deploy the neutron warhead.

There is little else in the impact statement, except certain concessions which cause me to pause.

For example, on page 6 of the paper, I read:

> Some governments might couple the decision to deploy ER weapons with perceptions that U.S. doctrine has changed so as to make the use of nuclear weapons more likely in a tactical

situation. Such a coupling could have an adverse effect on U.S. efforts to prevent further nuclear proliferation.

In conclusion, this weapons system has no arms control advantages. To the extent that it has any impact on ongoing arms control negotiations, the impact would be marginally negative.

So we are presented with a statement from the executive branch which balances almost perfectly the arguments for and against this weapon, but suggests that it might have some possible negative impact upon our efforts to control proliferation and make progress in the ongoing SALT talks.

There is no case here—certainly none that you would ever submit to a jury. If this were a case that had to be decided on the rules of evidence, any judge would return a directed verdict against the administration.

Yet, we are asked, all at once, without really having any opportunity to reflect upon it, to jump to judgment. The President is not going to jump to judgment. He has reserved for himself the right to wait until the middle of August to make up his mind. Is it not reasonable, then that Congress should also reserve to itself a few more weeks before we make up our minds?

7

CIVIL DEFENSE

CIVIL DEFENSE IN LIMITED WAR—A DEBATE

Arthur A. Broyles, Eugene P. Wigner, and Sidney D. Drell

The adoption of the strategy of flexible response with limited nuclear options has revived interest in the role of civil defense in national security planning. In the following article, three scientists debate efforts to protect the population of the United States from the effects of limited nuclear war and the possible implications for strategic stability.

Broyles and Wigner argue that the Soviet Union does not subscribe to the notion that deterrence is strengthened by allowing populations to be hostage to an adversary's nuclear weapons. Citing evidence of extensive Soviet and Chinese civil defense planning, the authors contend that the United States should not allow the current asymmetry in population protection to continue, since it could prove destabilizing in a nuclear crisis.

While agreeing with Broyles and Wigner that population evacuation procedures and blast shelters could provide significant protection to noncombatants, Drell maintains that the social, economic, and political costs of such efforts would be excessive. American society would have to become regimented in attitude and lifestyle, and in a nuclear crisis, a series of population evacuations could prove destabilizing.

Source: *Physics Today*, April 1976, pp. 44–57.

In Favor

Arthur A. Broyles and Eugene P. Wigner

Should the American people be protected from the effects of nuclear war? Let us first narrow that intensely studied question[1] to one that lies within the realm of physics to answer—namely, can such protection be effective? Evaluations of various evacuation and shelter systems show that they can greatly reduce the number of casualties in a nuclear encounter. Our response thus agrees entirely with the statement by V. Chuykov in the *Civil Defense Handbook* of the U.S.S.R.: "Although the discussed means of destruction are called mass means, with knowledge and skillful use of modern protective measures, they will not destroy masses of people, but only those who neglect the study, mastery and use of these measures."[2]

The question then broadens into one with psychological and political aspects and cannot be answered precisely or completely. Nevertheless we feel that our nation's civil-defense preparations may determine the balance of power in some future nuclear crisis. Civil defense is more important than ever at a time when other nations have extensive civil-defense plans and when the balance of terror that has reigned to date is being upset by the development of new types of weapons.

The protective measures against nuclear explosions and their effectiveness can be evaluated on the basis of a wealth of data gathered by the Atomic Energy Commission in its nuclear testing program. Besides making quantitative measurements of such phenomena as blast-wave pressures, fall-out intensity patterns and heat-ray intensities, the AEC constructed buildings and other structures in the vicinity of nuclear explosions and observed the resulting damage.[3] This information has been used by the AEC (now ERDA [Energy Research and Development Administration]) laboratories, Stanford Research Institute, RAND Corporation, the Hudson Institute, the National Research Council and other institutions to devise and determine the effectiveness of methods for protecting people. Their results are in surprisingly close agreement.

---

[1]*Civil Defense*, A Report to the Atomic Energy Commission by a Committee of the National Academy of Sciences (Washington, D.C., 1968); T. L. Martin and D. C. Latham, *Strategy for Survival* (Tucson: University of Arizona Press, 1963); C. M. Haaland, *Systems Analysis of U.S. Civil Defense via National Blast Shelter Systems*, Oak Ridge National Laboratory (ORNL), Oak Ridge, Tennessee, Report ORNL-tm-2457, 1970.

[2]*Civil Defense*, ed. N. I. Akimov (Moscow, 1969), translated by S. J. Rimshaw, ORNL-tr-2306 (1971).

[3]S. Glasstone, *The Effects of Nuclear Weapons*, rev. ed. (Washington, D.C.: Government Printing Office, (1974).

Unfortunately the general public is not well informed about such studies, probably because a large fraction of the physics community as a whole is not aware of them. . . . A clear presentation of the facts is essential because it is possible, as we shall see, that a nation's civil-defense preparedness may determine the balance of power in some future nuclear crisis.

The principal sources of danger and the most effective measures against them are listed in Table 1. . . . Because of the short time available for action to protect against effects of nuclear weapons, survival depends very heavily on previous planning and preparation. The effectiveness of all the protective measures would be much increased if the population were familiar with them well before the attack. The stockpiling of relatively simple tools can also help in the long term recovery effort. Because this subject is complicated and requires extensive considerations, we shall limit our discussion to the problems of survival of the initial effects of the attack that are listed in the table.

The most obvious way of protecting against all these effects is to prevent the bombs from exploding. For example, the U.S. might attack the enemy launch site before the missile leaves it. . . . Or, the U.S. might destroy the incoming missile with its own missile—the Anti-Ballistic Missile. Despite extensive debate over the ABM, it cannot be generally implemented now. As a result of the SALT I treaty, the ABM is restricted, as far as nonmilitary defense is concerned, to Moscow (with a population of 4.5 million) and Washington, D.C. (population of 1.5 million). Nevertheless, even a small ABM system could be very effective. By destroying the first wave of incoming missiles, it can give time to the people to enter shelters or to protect themselves in other, although less effective, ways.

Once a bomb does strike, the first effect is the electromagnetic pulse. This pulse threatens electric power transmission rather than human lives, although the disruption of radio transmission is of concern during an emergency.

The protection against the other effects of nuclear explosions can be provided in two ways—evacuation and shelter. Evacuation takes very much longer than the missile flight time and hence cannot be considered to be a truly defensive measure. If evacuation is undertaken during a crisis, it will greatly aggravate the situation. It can be effected before provoking a showdown and serve as an aggressive move. Hence, since the advent of missiles, our country did not seriously propose it until the elaborate evacuation preparations of the U.S.S.R. became known. Now it is being seriously planned as a "counterevacuation," that is, as a response to a possible evacuation of the cities of the U.S.S.R. The Ponast study, which was organized by the National

Security Council,[4] considered a nuclear attack in which the U.S.S.R. aimed two thirds of its destructive force at civilian targets. This attack would destroy 45 percent of the U.S. population under present circumstances. The preparation for the "counterevacuation" would cost about $500 million—one day's welfare expenditure— and would reduce the population loss to 11 percent. Because the U.S.S.R. population is less crowded into cities than ours, their losses would be smaller yet—less than 5 percent according to our calculations.[5] This loss is half of that experienced by the Soviets in World War II.

Shelter Design. The defense measure advocated in the U.S., and installed by the Chinese, is the provision of shelters. The technical problem is to design a shelter with maximum blast resistance, minimum access time and minimum cost. The Chinese appear to have conquered the problem. . . . U.S. scientists, during a 1970 study at the Oak Ridge Civil Defense Project,[6] estimated that effective shelters could be built at a cost of $23 billion. In similar conclusions four years later, the Ponast study found that a $35 billion investment—very much larger than that needed for preparation for counterevacuation and one tenth of one year's federal expenditures—would reduce the casualties caused by an attack by the U.S.S.R. to 5.5 percent.[7]. . . Actually, as we have just described, the effectiveness of shelters should not be surprising: if shelters were ineffective, the expenditure on their construction by the government of China, the government of a nation much poorer than ours, would be entirely unjustifiable.

A third intermediate arrangement for defense, also indicated already in the Soviet handbooks on civil defense,[8] is to move most city dwellers away from densely populated areas but not as far as the pure counterevacuation proposes. Instead, the Soviets would build "expedient shelters" using materials at hand. Rather ingenious designs, which can be built by untrained prospective occupants, give a blast resistance of 30 pounds per square inch. . . . Such a system, not significantly more expensive than the simple evacuation plan (not much over $500 million, according to the Ponast study) could reduce

[4]R.H. Sandwina, "Ponast II," *Proceedings of the Radiological Defense Officers Conference,* South Lake Tahoe, October 23-25, 1974, State of California Governor's Office of Emergency Services.

[5]E. P. Wigner, "The Myth of Assured Destruction," *The Journal of Civil Defense (Survive),* July-August 1970.

[6]D. L. Narver, Jr. and D. T. Robbins, *Engineering and Cost Considerations for Tunnel Grid Blast Shelter Complex,* ORNL-tm-1183 (1965); D. T. Robbins and D. L. Narver, Jr., *Engineering Study for Tunnel Grid Blast Shelter Concept for Portion of City of Detroit, Michigan,* ORNL-tm-1223 (1975).

[7]State of California Governor's Office of Emergency Services, *Proceedings.*

[8]*Civil Defense* (ORNL translation).

Table 1
H-BOMB MAJOR IMMEDIATE EFFECTS

Effect	Cause	Damage	Defense
ELECTROMAGNETIC PULSE	Expanding charged particles from bomb explosion	Damage to electronic equipment up to hundreds of miles; power stations at shorter ranges	Special protective equipment related to lightning security devices; no effects on humans
PROMPT NUCLEAR RADIATION	Nuclear reactions during bomb explosion	Normally less than blast	(Normally negligible compared to blast)
HEAT RADIATION	Radiation from the hot fireball generated by the explosion	Fires ignited a few tens of miles but greatly reduced by clouds or smog and dampness	Eliminating exposed inflammable material; shelters including large public buildings
BLAST WAVE	Expansion of hot bomb material pushes air into a wave of wind and high pressure	Destruction of buildings as well as serious injuries to people from flying objects and falling buildings from five to ten miles	Evacuation blast shelters; reinforced public buildings
FALLOUT	Radioactive products of nuclear fission mixed with vaporized earth	Heavily wind dependent; can be the order of one hundred miles	Sheltering by large public buildings or special shelters for a few days or weeks until the radiation level has died down

373

the fatalities as well as does the elaborate and rather expensive shelter system referred to above. However neither one can provide protection against a sudden attack.

In the design of shelters, prompt nuclear radiation can generally be ignored in comparison with the blast wave unless the blast protection is very good or the weapon is very small. The reason is that prompt-radiation effects decrease much more rapidly with distance than do blast effects. To see this, note that the blast pressure in pounds per square inch from a W kiloton explosion at a distance r in kilometers is given approximately by

$$p = \frac{1.6 \ W^{2/3}}{r^2}$$

The intensity of the prompt radiation decreases more rapidly than $1/r^2$ because of the absorption by air. Thus, according to the equation, blast shelters designed for 100 psi will be effective against a 1-megaton weapon for distances greater than about 1¼ km. The area within which the pressure exceeds a given amount is inversely proportional to this pressure. Thus the area where the pressure exceeds 5 psi—the pressure often considered as the survival pressure for unprotected people—is twenty times the area for 100 psi.

The effects of blast decrease more rapidly with bomb yield than do those from prompt nuclear radiation. For very small nuclear weapons, prompt radiation can be more harmful than the blast. Thus for a 1-kiloton bomb, neutron and gamma radiation at 750 meters are 700 and 400 R if no protection is provided. The blast pressure at that distance is 5 psi—quite tolerable. Indeed the mid-lethal blast pressure for a well instructed person, who knows how to protect himself from flying objects, is well in excess of 30 psi.

Blast shelters are designed not only to diminish the air pressure to which a person is subject, but also to protect him from flying objects. A properly designed blast shelter will also place sufficient mass between a person and the outside fallout particles to shield him adequately from the radiation. One foot of earth cover reduces radiation perpendicular to it by a factor around ten, and more than that for slanting rays. Shelters also provide cover against heat radiation and external fires. Two feet of earth will provide adequate protection from actively burning fire.

Global Consequences. Worldwide effects from the detonation of a nuclear explosion naturally demand as much concern as the immediate effects. Many wonder whether the global consequences such as fallout might not be so severe as to deter any nation from even precipitating an attack. The most recent investigation of this question, the Nier report by the National Academy of Sciences,[9] verified previous conclusions that worldwide fallout produced in a nuclear attack would not be sufficient to deter the attack. It found, however, that the depletion of the ozone layer could be more serious. Increased radiation might force people to adopt special protection against sunburn, and it would lead to an increase in the skin-cancer rate by a factor of almost two. The depletion of ozone would also upset some ecological systems in important ways. Although this study calls for additional research to answer some remaining questions regarding worldwide effects, Philip Handler, President of the National Academy, makes the following statement in his letter accompanying the Nier report:

> At the same time, the governments of the United States and of other major nuclear powers should be alert to the possibility that a geographically distant, populous other nation might determine that the degree of short-term damage to itself in this report, would be "acceptable" and that, since long-term recovery would be highly likely, might conclude that its own self-interest is compatible with a major nuclear exchange between other powers.

In other words, we cannot count on global effects in themselves as deterrents.

Even though civil-defense measures can be effective as population protection, the U.S. lags behind many nations of the world in building such systems. The Chinese have installed extensive blast shelter systems; the Russians have preferred an evacuation procedure that removes the city population to outlying areas where hasty shelters are to be constructed from materials at hand. . . . Admittedly, this system would lose effectiveness if another nation initiated the war: it takes two or three days to evacuate cities and to build emergency shelters. However, if such time is available, the U.S.S.R. system is cheaper and probably more effective than the Chinese blast shelters. The Chinese, however, can occupy their shelters in a very short time and thus be prepared for an attack with very little warning. Evidently the Chinese are afraid that someone will attack them with little notice, while the Russians believe that they are in a position to determine when the nuclear exchange will come and that they can carry out their evacuation and construction in time.

---

[9] *Long-Term World Wide Effects of Multiple Nuclear-Weapons Detonations*, The National Research Council (Committee Chairman, Alfred O.C. Nier), the National Academy of Sciences, Washington, D.C. (1975).

Political Aspects. The United States, on the other hand, has essentially no civil-defense system. This lack is deliberate, and the reasoning behind it is clearly evident in the hearings before Congress on military matters.[10] Our leaders recognize that, if the nuclear powers have the capability of destroying the opposing nuclear attack forces, they will be tempted to strike first. If they wait, their own weapons may be destroyed first and they would be defenseless. Thus the U.S., until quite recently, carefully designed its nuclear strike force to be effective against the population of an opponent but ineffective against his weapons. We also did not protect our people. This inaction assured him that we would not attack first and therefore, that he need not strike a preventive blow.

The trouble with our strategy was that the Soviets, and more recently the Chinese, have not accepted this "balance of terror." The Soviets' large missiles are effective against our land-based missiles and their killer submarines can attack our Polaris submarines. In addition, our population is so exposed that it is doubtful we would accept the casualties required to participate in any stage of nuclear war through a second, third, or any strike with our missiles. Perhaps such considerations led Secretary of Defense James R. Schlesinger to propose the addition to our arsenal of missiles that would be effective against sheltered enemy ICBM's.[11] However we are disappointed that Washington has not given strong support for measures that will protect the U.S. population from the effects of a nuclear war.

As a final remark we wish to add that it disturbs us greatly that passionate opponents of the protection of our own civilians against nuclear attack do not oppose, and do not even mention, the elaborate preparations of the U.S.S.R. in this direction. The Soviet handbook on civil defense is circulated in millions of copies. (It has been carefully studied at the Oak Ridge National Laboratory.) The U.S.S.R. gives instruction on civil defense in the high schools, they carry out exercises in their factories and, most distressingly, they have made elaborate preparation to evacuate their cities preceding a confrontation. If the opponents of civil defense feel that these preparations are not even worth mentioning, why do they consider the protection of our own civilians objectionable and even provocative?

---

[10]*Analyses of Effects of Limited Nuclear Warfare,* prepared for the Subcommittee on Arms Control, International Organizations and Security Agreements, of the Committee on Foreign Relations, U.S. Senate, September 1975; and Hearings before the Subcommittee on International Organization and Disarmament Affairs of the Committee on Foreign Relations, U.S. Senate, 91st Congress.
[11]Ibid.

Opposed

*Sidney D. Drell**

The strategic doctrine of "limited nuclear counterforce strikes" has been revived in the United States during the past few years. This return to a policy that was discarded more than a decade ago is accompanied by a renewed interest in extensive and organized civil defense programs, which would require massive relocation and evacuation of populations during crises. Official government statements during the past two years allege that this combination offers the prospect of low levels of fatalities and casualties resulting from the immediate blast, thermal, radiation and subsequent radio-active fallout effects. In particular the former Secretary of Defense, James R. Schlesinger, in the Annual Defense Department Report for FY 1976 stated that "relocation of the population from high risk areas near key military installations and the protection of the rest of the population against fallout could reduce nationwide fatalities due to fallout from a limited Soviet counterforce attack to relatively low levels well under 1 million—provided that the people in the communities that would be most exposed by fallout from such an attack make effective use of the shelters available."

The conclusion drawn from these claims and analyses is that limited nuclear war may be palatable and need not escalate to the level of an all-out nuclear exchange, which would cause unimaginable horror. In fact, on September 11, 1974, Secretary Schlesinger testified[1] to a subcommittee of the U.S. Senate Committee on Foreign Relations that "the likelihood of limited nuclear attacks cannot be challenged on the assumption that massive civilian fatalities and injuries would result."

Because the basis for this change in strategic doctrine is the relatively low fatality level, we must examine not only the total civil defense implications of this doctrine but also the assumptions about the nature and effectiveness of the weapons used in the attack.

Civil defense in the larger context of an all-out nuclear strike against population centers will not concern us here, not only because it is not being proposed at present but also because most who have studied the financial and societal costs, not to mention the technical challenges, of such a program have concluded that it is not practical.

---

*This text is adapted from testimony presented on September 18, 1975, to the Subcommittee on Arms Control, International Law and Organization of the U.S. Senate Foreign Relations Committee.

[1] *Analyses of Effects of Limited Nuclear Warfare,* prepared for the Subcommittee on Arms Control, International Organizations and Security Agreements, of the Committee on Foreign Relations, U.S. Senate, September 1975.

But how practical and how effective is civil defense in a limited counterforce context?

The resurgence of the doctrine of limited nuclear counterforce has been spurred by progress in weapons technology—in particular, the development of accurate and reliable MIRV's (multiple independently targetable reentry vehicles), which enable a single missile to attack several different targets with high accuracy. These MIRV's can selectively attack hardened military targets such as underground silos containing the fixed land-based ICBM forces and at the same time can cause relatively low casualty levels. Indeed this combination of factors forms the basis for the military value and strategic credibility that are claimed for such an attack.

Of course the effect of weapons against both military targets and civilians depends critically on such factors as the numbers and yields of incoming warheads, their height of burst and the level and extent of civil defense protection. One example described by Secretary Schlesinger in his Senate testimony envisioned an attack against all the fixed ICBM's—1,000 Minutemen and 54 Titan missiles—with a single one-megaton warhead incident on each silo and with the warhead fuzed to detonate in air at the optimum height of burst. The attack would result, he claimed, in fewer than 800,000 dead and 800,000 injured or ill from radioactive fallout.

The fatality levels for such an attack are calculated by making certain assumptions about the civil defense protection provided in terms of the protection factors of various shelters. These numbers are the reciprocals of the fraction of radiation that penetrates the shelter. Thus the existing civil defense program requires that, for a shelter space to be identified as such and stocked, it must have a protection factor of 50-100. That is, it must shield against all but 1-2 percent of the radioactive fallout. This factor is equivalent to a dirt cover of approximately two feet or a concrete wall of about 16 inches. By comparison, a single-story residence has a protection factor of three, and a residential basement, a factor of 25.[2]

In the attack described by the Secretary, the Department of Defense assumed that for 30 days roughly 35 percent of the U.S. population remained in designated shelters with protection factors of 50-100, that 20 percent sought residential-basement protection and that the remaining 45 percent were protected by the average residential protection factor of 3. These calculations were stopped after this thirty-day period and thus do not include the final 6 percent of the fallout nor the long-range effects.

---

[2] S. Glasstone, *The Effects of Nuclear Weapons*, rev. ed. (Washington, D.C.: Government Printing Office, 1974).

However, the Secretary did not describe the military effects of this attack, which was designed to cause such low civilian casualty levels. Straightforward calculations show that the nuclear attack assumed in the above calculations would destroy well under one half of our fixed ICBM force if carried out by missiles with the targeting accuracies projected for the Soviet ICBM force. This conclusion follows even if we assume that the Soviet missile systems have a perfect 100 percent reliability, which is surely a gross overestimate, particularly when you recall that we are talking of a massive attack coordinated in time so that all 1,054 U.S. ICBM silos are hit essentially simultaneously. I can see no practical military value to such an attack. On the contrary it would surely invite lethal retaliation.

In response to these and other DOD calculations on collateral civilian damage related to counterforce attacks, the Senate Foreign Relations Committee in September 1974 asked Congress's Office of Technology Assessment to review the DOD analyses. A panel convened by OTA for this purpose raised questions about the sensitivity of the DOD analyses to various assumptions, including a range of possible weather conditions, civilian protection factors and parameters of the incoming attack.[3] The DOD responded with more calculations, which showed that the expected fatalities are indeed very sensitive to the nature of the attack and can vary by large factors. In particular, the DOD now finds that fatalities in the range of 10 to 20 million will result from prompt effects and fallout alone if the attack is delivered by the nuclear weaponry of today or of the near future and is designed to destroy the majority of the attacked ICBM force.[4] Figure 1, which is based on DOD calculations, illustrates the fatalities as a function of the percentage of ICBM silos destroyed. (Note that the DOD reduced the civil defense protection factors assumed for the last two attacks by 25 percent relative to that described earlier; otherwise, with identical protection factors, one would expect the one-megaton ground burst to cause more fatalities than two 550-kiloton bursts—one in air and one on the ground.) Even at the highest level in Figure 1 a healthy retaliatory force of some 210 ICBM's would remain as well as all the SAC [Strategic Air Command] bombers and missile submarines.

Naturally the predictions of Figure 1 are subject to such uncertainties as the weather and winds at the time of attack, and are sensitive to the degree of civil defense protection and to the ability to provide medical care to the ill or injured. Nevertheless, one can clearly not contemplate an effective strategic attack designed to decimate our ICBM force in terms of casualty levels of one million civilians, but

[3]*Analyses of Effects of Limited Nuclear Warfare.*
[4]Ibid.

rather must consider it in terms of upwards of tens of millions, even assuming extensive protection of the population.

The Price of Civil Defense. The most recent DOD reports also make clear that civil defense would be a central element of our policy of flexible response, with emphasis on limited nuclear counterforce. Indeed the justification for the civil defense budget was expressed in the report for FY 1976 largely in terms of its role as a necessary adjunct of our policy emphasis on flexible response. The DOD report also argues that we must have the same population-evacuation options as the Soviet Union for two reasons:

- "to be able to respond in kind if the Soviet Union attempts to intimidate us in time of crisis by evacuating population from its cities," and

- "to reduce fatalities if an attack on our cities appears imminent."

This position marks a major shift in emphasis of the civil defense program since the 1974 Annual DOD Report, when it was largely justified by Secretary of Defense Elliott Richardson to help recovery from peacetime disasters. I personally endorse this previous objective and furthermore I support the existing program of identifying and stocking shelters as a prudent insurance program against a wide range of incidents, including the accidental launch of nuclear weapons, a severe nuclear-reactor accident or natural disasters such as hurricanes. However, a comprehensive civil defense program involving both sheltering and evacuating the population on a very large scale is a different thing. Undoubtedly it can be demonstrated to have a great lifesaving potential in the event of a nuclear attack against specific military targets. But the issue is in essence an issue of the price one has to pay for a civil defense program in relation to the degree of protection one buys against specified attacks: What price in our priorities, values and style as a society? What price in dollar costs?

Investment in a civil defense program could, as one function, protect the population from the blast, thermal and radiation effects in the immediate vicinity of a nuclear explosion—roughly within a radius of four miles for a blast of one megaton. Such protection against the close-in effects is either impossible or tremendously costly.

Another function of civil defense is to reduce casualties from fallout generated at distances well beyond several miles. This effect of dangerous fallout levels, extending many hundreds of miles downwind from nuclear explosions, plus the long-range effects of radioactive contamination to extensive areas, differentiates nuclear war from all other previous experience. The range and extent of the threat to life of radioactive fallout depends critically on many factors including the height of burst (that is, whether or not the fireball from an explosion near Earth's surface scoops up and spreads an enormous cloud of radioactive debris); the fraction of fission yield in the bomb design and the weather.

The biological effect of fallout is measured in terms of the standard dosage unit of the roentgen-equivalent mammal (the rem). Whole-body exposures to less than 100 rems cause blood changes but no disabling illness. Experience following the Hiroshima and Nagasaki blasts shows that doses of 100 to 200 rems cause a certain amount of illness including fatigue and perhaps some nausea, but are rarely fatal. However, levels of about 450 rems of whole-body exposure can cause severe illness and produce a 50 percent fatality rate. This scale is the basis for assessing how much protection must be provided for an effective civil defense. . . . An unsheltered person as far away as several thousand miles downwind from an attacked missile field or military base would be exposed to an expected 600 rems.

The time scale of the radioactive fallout is also of great importance in considering protection. For how long a period of time after an explosion must one be sheltered from fallout in order to survive? For

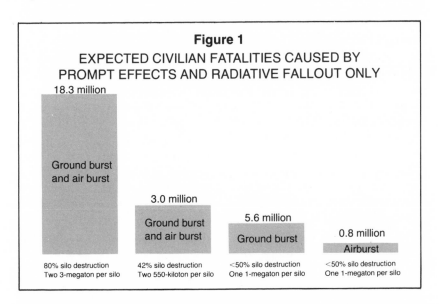

Figure 1
EXPECTED CIVILIAN FATALITIES CAUSED BY
PROMPT EFFECTS AND RADIATIVE FALLOUT ONLY

18.3 million

Ground burst
and air burst

3.0 million

Ground burst
and air burst

5.6 million

Ground burst

0.8 million

Airburst

| 80% silo destruction | 42% silo destruction | <50% silo destruction | <50% silo destruction |
| Two 3-megaton per silo | Two 550-kiloton per silo | One 1-megaton per silo | One 1-megaton per silo |

Casualty toll varies with the type of nuclear attack, among other parameters. All the calculations were done by the DOD in its analysis "Sensitivity of Collateral Damage Calculations to Limited Nuclear Scenarios," sent to the Senate Foreign Relations Committee on 11 July 1975, except for the two with asterisks, which are by the author.

typical burst altitudes in the atmosphere a human body totally and completely shielded from fallout during the first hour immediately following a nuclear explosion will still receive 45 percent, or almost half, of the total fallout if exposed thereafter. Twenty percent of the total dose is deposited after the first day, and a person emerging after four weeks of complete protection from fallout will still be subject to 6 percent of the total dosage. The decrease in rate of fallout follows a $1/T^{1.2}$ law, and evidently the required time scale for protection is measured in weeks.

This discussion of fallout effects shows the required physical parameters of civil defense shelters. Few dispute the technical facts concerning the means to protect large populations for one to four weeks after an attack from the physical effects of blast, fire, radiation and fallout. However, major social parameters and costs are also involved because identified shelter spaces and evacuation plans do not by themselves make an effective civil defense program, in my judgment. A total system must be organized and interwoven extensively into civilian life through training programs, rehearsals, and volunteer activities. The pre-attack shelter organization envisioned by the 1962 Office of Civil Defense Guide planned that a shelter accommodating 100 civilians would require an operating cadre of 25, of which 10-12 would need prior training. This number constitutes 10 percent of the sheltered or 20 percent of the adult population.

To recruit the required large cadre of trained personnel the government would have to look beyond existing community safety personnel such as policemen and firemen. Perhaps the military reservists and National Guard units could play a central role in organization and training, but they would still have to rely on a large functioning organization involving a much larger number of trained civilians.

One task of trained personnel would be to operate communications systems over large distances in order to deal with shortages of food, water and medical supplies. They would also have to know how to use radiation dosimeters, because in the immediate post-attack period the fallout levels can vary greatly from one locale to another. Like the snow, radioactive debris accumulates where driven, depending on wind and weather conditions as well as on the location and shadows of tall buildings. Local pockets of relative safety may exist amid areas with lethal levels of radioactivity. Finally the trained cadre would have to provide leadership in the long period of extreme social duress after the attack and would have to reestablish requisite services for a society with a large proportion of ill and injured citizens.

Beyond the training of these special leaders, the plans for massive population relocation and evacuation out of high-risk areas near the possible counterforce target system require a heightened level of public awareness and concern, and a willingness to rehearse the evacuation plans. Without them, surely a chaos spawned by panic will ensue at the time of implementation. How can one draw public attention, much less commitment, to such plans without "overselling" them by a sustained escalation of apprehensions from the mood of today vis-à-vis the dangers of nuclear exchange between the U.S. and the Soviet Union? Is not such an escalation of apprehensions more to be feared than desired as the U.S. and Soviet Union move further from the brink of a nuclear conflict due to misunderstanding, misapprehension or mistake and strive mutually at SALT for a more stable nuclear balance at lower levels of nuclear armaments? Indeed one of the lessons of the civil defense shelter exercises in 1961 and 1962 was that the large expenditures for civil defense and the general dislocations accompanying a major shelter program could only be sold to the American public by presenting the very real threat of nuclear war.

Strategy. Consideration of civil defense as an element of strategy has been given renewed importance by the new emphasis on fighting a limited nuclear war. This policy changes our nuclear doctrine of the past decade, which has been dominated by the recognition that once a nuclear weapon is detonated on U.S. or Soviet territory there would be substantial probability that nuclear exchanges could not be terminated before both nations were destroyed and the casualties numbered hundreds of millions. The new strategic doctrine raises the issue of whether this unpleasant "balance of terror" and mutual hostage relationship might be changed by the adoption of new tactics and the development and purchase of new weapons for fighting limited nuclear wars at acceptably low casualty levels. I believe such a policy would cause the following deleterious effects:

- Harm to strategic stability. The development of a new missile force designed specifically as hard-silo killers would fuel concern on both sides about the vulnerability of the fixed ICBM's to a preemptive first strike. It would emphasize the importance of striking first and could thereby destabilize a crisis situation. Furthermore the development and rehearsal of civil-defense plans involving evacuation and relocation of large populations could be viewed with alarm by an opponent as preparation for executing a first strike.

- Harm to SALT talks. The development and testing of the required new missiles will create pressures against quantitative reductions in the numbers of strategic forces and against such verifiable qualitative restraints as missile test-flight quotas and limits on the rate of deployment of new systems that would slow down the pace of progress in the arms race.

- Waste of resources. The plans justified by this year's rhetoric may materialize into the multibillion-dollar weapons systems of the next decade unless the rationale behind them is rejected.

- Shift of values. Implementation of an extensive civil defense system through massive training will affect the priorities of our society and will require heightened concern about nuclear war, which would counter the progress that has been made toward reduced international tensions.

Finally, what will prevent the eventual escalation of an initially limited nuclear war to an all-out nuclear holocaust? Once nuclear weapons are used in war at all it will be very difficult, if not impossible, to verify yields, sizes, numbers and types of the nuclear explosions on both sides. However, the one technically unambiguous fact is whether or not nuclear weapons have been used at all. Therefore it is wisest for the U.S. to adopt as a national policy the highest possible nuclear threshold. We should maintain a gap between nuclear and non-nuclear warfare that is as clear and wide as possible, and resist the temptation to develop doctrines and civil defense programs that understate, on dubious technical and strategic premises, the collateral damage and the casualty levels of nuclear conflict.

Broyles and Wigner Reply to Drell

Our own discussion is principally concerned with the technical question of whether defense against nuclear weapons is possible. We feel that as physicists we should be able to judge the extent to which such defense is possible and we also feel that the physics community at large should have a degree of familiarity with this problem. Sidney Drell's article is less concerned with the physical problem than with the more important but less precisely ascertainable one concerning the political implications and consequences of a vigorous civil defense effort—a subject to which only the last section of our own article refers. Nevertheless, we would like to comment, first, on a problem of physics concerning which our opinions differ.

We differ with Drell in our estimation of the radiation danger from fallout after a reasonably long sojourn in shelter, let us say two weeks. First of all we calculate that the total radiation dose from the fallout after two weeks amounts to less than 7 percent of the total radiation of the fission products from 1 minute on to infinity. In addition, the radiation becomes softer as time goes on, so that it becomes easier to protect against it. More importantly, the radiation after two weeks is stretched out over a rather long period—six months or so. Although the damage done to man by 10 percent of this radiation is not reversible the damage done by the remaining 90 percent appears to decrease by 2½ percent per day. As a result, by the end of the half year, the effect of the radiation received in the early period after emergence from the shelter has decreased to 11 percent of its initial magnitude. Altogether, the damage caused by the radiation received after the two-week sheltering period hardly exceeds 4 percent of the damage that a person outside would receive in the initial two-week period. Even more importantly, because the radiation intensity after two weeks is only one thousandth of its intensity at one hour after the explosion, after two weeks the shelter can be abandoned for reasonably long periods. Thus survivors can possibly clean up surroundings or, in extreme cases, move to a less contaminated location. We conclude that the danger from the fallout radiation can be easily guarded against after a period of two weeks from the time of the explosion and that the emergence from the shelter after that period produces much less difficulty than indicated in Drell's article. We do not wish to deny, of course, that it is even better if no nuclear explosion takes place.

The second, still somewhat technical, point to which we wish to take exception is the statement that "Protection against the close-in effects (blast and heat) is either impossible or tremendously costly." The gross national product per person of China is a small fraction of ours, yet most visitors to their land return greatly impressed by the very effective and easily accessible civil defense shelters that were proudly shown to them. More concretely, the implementation of the counter-evacuation plan would cost $2.50 per person and the Chinese-type shelters $175 per person (or $35 per person per year, because their construction may take about five years). Surely, neither of these figures can be called "tremendous"; yet they would really buy each of us a great deal of security and would discourage attacks or threats of attacks—an equally important accomplishment. In fact, the Swiss civil defense book says that the most important accomplishment of civil defense preparations is that they will never have to be used.

On the other hand, we agree with Drell that an unlimited nuclear exchange between the U.S.S.R. and the U.S. would result in more than one million casualties on both sides. But in our opinion, we must strive for an approximately equal casualty rate—not 2 or 3 percent in the U.S.S.R. and about 45 percent here. We also note that as Drell points out, the U.S. Secretary of Defense believes that nuclear attacks on military targets may be feasible. Unfortunately the Soviet government may share this view.

Our last objection to Drell's statement is nontechnical and is in the spirit of his own article. He says, "Furthermore, the development and rehearsing of civil defense plans involving evacuation and relocation of large populations could be viewed with alarm by an opponent as preparation for executing a first strike." If that is so (and we believe it is) we do not understand the failure of his article to mention the U.S.S.R. development and rehearsal of civil defense plans involving evacuation and relocation of large populations. Evidently, he is not concerned by these plans and does not view them with alarm; he does not even think that they are worth mentioning. What he sees with alarm is that we may duplicate these efforts, that we put an end to the situation in which we may have to face an enemy who can destroy fifteen times more citizens in the U.S. than we can destroy of his. Frankly, this current situation is what alarms us and is what we wish to terminate.

Drell Replies to Broyles and Wigner

Although Arthur Broyles and Eugene Wigner frequently allege that the Soviets have extensively interwoven a civil defense program into their society, to the best of my information no evidence exists that they have in fact exercised a civil defense system capable of massive population relocation or evacuation. A large number of emigrés from many parts of the Soviet Union have been received in the West; had there been any widespread civil defense rehearsals in the Soviet Union we surely would have heard about them by now. The Soviets have indeed written much on the subject and have given their population a more intensive exposure to civil defense. Apparently they have spent much more money on plans and organizations and involved small numbers of people with key skills in exercises. However, I believe that in view of the unprecedentedly large scale of the nationwide disaster we are considering, an effective civil defense program must also include, as one of its essential components, full-scale rehearsals and survival living exercises involving the population.

Selective quotations from civil defense manuals are not reliable guides to the effectiveness of a civil defense program. If it were, we might cite from their manuals the removal of anti-Western polemics in the 1974 edition. We might also cite the fact that their civil defense manuals for 1970 and 1974 . . . contain elementary substantive errors such as the translation, from U.S. sources, of miles directly to kilometers without the conversion factor of 1.6 in giving ranges of destruction from given bomb yields. Furthermore, the Soviet analysis of minimum requirement for air supply in shelters has not changed from old manuals. Thus the U.S. editor of the translation is led to comment, in the preface, that "the Soviet Union has not conducted mass shelter living experiments or even simulated ones as has been done in the U.S." The editor then comments further: "We believe that this is the most serious flaw in the whole Soviet Civil Defense planning." In my judgment, plans and manuals, on one hand, and an effective operating system, on the other, are very different things!

In referring to the Nier report Broyles and Wigner stated that it "verified previous conclusions that worldwide fallout produced in a nuclear attack would not be sufficient to deter the attack." In fact the report contains no such conclusions, nor does it address questions as to what will or will not deter war. Its task was the much more narrow one of considering the consequences of nuclear conflict "by examining, independently, possible effects upon, respectively, the atmosphere and climate, natural terrestrial ecosystems, agriculture and animal husbandry, the aquatic environment and both somatic and genetic effects upon humans," as remarked by Handler in his letter of transmittal. In my reading of the Nier report I was more impressed by how extensive are the unknowns that will determine the scale of the disaster resulting from a major nuclear conflict and by how little can be predicted with confidence.

I believe there is no basis in fact for the statement by Broyles and Wigner that "the Soviets' large missiles are effective against our land-based missiles and their killer submarines can attack our Polaris submarines." This allegation is also at variance with assessments given by our civilian and military leaders. To quote Secretary Schlesinger, for example, in the Annual Defense Department Report for FY 1976, "Our sea-launched ballistic missile force provides us, for the foreseeable future, with a high confidence capability to withhold weapons in reserve."

PART THREE
IMPLICATIONS FOR
ARMS CONTROL

8

ARMS CONTROL: OFFICIAL DOCUMENTS AND STATEMENTS

JOINT STATEMENT ON STRATEGIC OFFENSIVE ARMS ISSUED AT VLADIVOSTOK, NOVEMBER 24, 1974

In November 1974, President Gerald R. Ford and General Secretary Leonid I. Brezhnev met in the Soviet city of Vladivostok to establish guidelines for further negotiations to limit strategic arms. Influenced by a number of political and military considerations, the two leaders agreed to the principle of equal aggregates as the basis for a SALT II agreement. It was subsequently disclosed that this successor to the Interim Agreement on Offensive Arms of May 26, 1972, limited national force levels to 2,400 strategic launchers. No more than 1,320 of these launchers could be equipped with MIRVed warheads.

Joint U.S.-Soviet Statement

During their working meeting in the area of Vladivostok on November 23–24, 1974, the President of the U.S.A. Gerald R. Ford and General Secretary of the Central Committee of the CPSU L. I. Brezhnev discussed in detail the question of further limitations of strategic offensive arms.

They reaffirmed the great significance that both the United States and the U.S.S.R. attach to the limitation of strategic offensive arms. They are convinced that a long-term agreement on this question would be a significant contribution to improving relations between the U.S. and the U.S.S.R., to reducing the danger of war and to enhancing world peace. Having noted the value of previous agreements on this question, including the Interim Agreement of May 26, 1972, they reaffirm the intention to conclude a new agreement on the limitation of strategic offensive arms, to last through 1985.

Source: *Department of State Bulletin*, vol. 71, no. 1852 (December 23, 1974), pp. 879–81.

As a result of the exchange of views on the substance of such a new agreement, the President of the United States of America and the General Secretary of the Central Committee of the CPSU concluded that favorable prospects exist for completing the work on this agreement in 1975.

Agreement was reached that further negotiations will be based on the following provisions.

1. The new agreement will incorporate the relevant provisions of the Interim Agreement of May 26, 1972, which will remain in force until October 1977.

2. The new agreement will cover the period from October 1977 through December 31, 1985.

3. Based on the principle of equality and equal security, the new agreement will include the following limitations:

a. Both sides will be entitled to have a certain agreed aggregate number of strategic delivery vehicles;

b. Both sides will be entitled to have a certain agreed aggregate number of ICBMs and SLBMs [intercontinental ballistic missiles; submarine-launched ballistic missiles] equipped with multiple independently targetable warheads [MIRVs].

4. The new agreement will include a provision for further negotiations beginning no later than 1980-1981 on the question of further limitations and possible reductions of strategic arms in the period after 1985.

5. Negotiations between the delegations of the U.S. and U.S.S.R. to work out the new agreement incorporating the foregoing points will resume in Geneva in January 1975.

November 24, 1974.

Joint U.S.-Soviet Communiqué

In accordance with the previously announced agreement, a working meeting between the President of the United States of America Gerald R. Ford and the General Secretary of the Central Committee of the Communist Party of the Soviet Union L. I. Brezhnev took place in the area of Vladivostok on November 23 and 24, 1974. Taking part in the talks were the Secretary of State of the United States of America and Assistant to the President for National Security Affairs, Henry A.

Kissinger and Member of the Politburo of the Central Committee of the CPSU, Minister of Foreign Affairs of the U.S.S.R., A.A. Gromyko.

They discussed a broad range of questions dealing with American-Soviet relations and the current international situation.

Also taking part in the talks were:

On the American side Walter J. Stoessel, Jr., Ambassador of the U.S.A. to the U.S.S.R.; Helmut Sonnenfeldt, Counselor of the Department of State; Arthur A. Hartman, Assistant Secretary of State for European Affairs; Lieutenant General Brent Scowcroft, Deputy Assistant to the President for National Security Affairs; and William Hyland, official of the Department of State.

On the Soviet side A. F. Dobrynin, Ambassador of the U.S.S.R. to the U.S.A.; A. M. Aleksandrov, Assistant to the General Secretary of the Central Committee of the CPSU; and G. M. Korniyenko, Member of the Collegium of the Ministry of Foreign Affairs of the U.S.S.R.

I

The United States of America and the Soviet Union reaffirmed their determination to develop further their relations in the direction defined by the fundamental joint decisions and basic treaties and agreements concluded between the two States in recent years.

They are convinced that the course of American-Soviet relations, directed towards strengthening world peace, deepening the relaxation of international tensions and expanding mutually beneficial cooperation of states with different social systems meets the vital interests of the peoples of both States and other peoples.

Both Sides consider that based on the agreements reached between them important results have been achieved in fundamentally reshaping American-Soviet relations on the basis of peaceful coexistence and equal security. These results are a solid foundation for progress in reshaping Soviet-American relations.

Accordingly, they intend to continue, without a loss in momentum, to expand the scale and intensity of their cooperative efforts in all spheres as set forth in the agreements they have signed so that the process of improving relations between the U.S. and the U.S.S.R. will continue without interruption and will become irreversible.

Mutual determination was expressed to carry out strictly and fully the mutual obligations undertaken by the U.S. and the U.S.S.R. in accordance with the treaties and agreements concluded between them.

II

Special consideration was given in the course of the talks to a pivotal aspect of Soviet-American relations: measures to eliminate the threat of war and to halt the arms race.

Both Sides reaffirm that the Agreements reached between the U.S. and the U.S.S.R. on the prevention of nuclear war and the limitation of strategic arms are a good beginning in the process of creating guarantees against the outbreak of nuclear conflict and war in general. They expressed their deep belief in the necessity of promoting this process and expressed their hope that other states would contribute to it as well. For their part the U.S. and the U.S.S.R. will continue to exert vigorous efforts to achieve this historic task.

A joint statement on the question of limiting strategic offensive arms is being released separately.

Both Sides stressed once again the importance and necessity of a serious effort aimed at preventing the dangers connected with the spread of nuclear weapons in the world. In this connection they stressed the importance of increasing the effectiveness of the Treaty on the Non-Proliferation of Nuclear Weapons.

It was noted that, in accordance with previous agreements, initial contacts were established between representatives of the U.S. and of the U.S.S.R. on questions related to underground nuclear explosions for peaceful purposes, to measures to overcome the dangers of the use of environmental modification techniques for military purposes, as well as measures dealing with the most dangerous lethal means of chemical warfare. It was agreed to continue an active search for mutually acceptable solutions of these questions.

III

In the course of the meeting an exchange of views was held on a number of international issues: special attention was given to negotiations already in progress in which the two Sides are participants and which are designed to remove existing sources of tension and to bring about the strengthening of international security and world peace.

Having reviewed the situation at the Conference on Security and Cooperation in Europe, both Sides concluded that there is a possibility for its early successful conclusion. They proceed from the assumption that the results achieved in the course of the Conference will permit its conclusion at the highest level and thus be commensurate with its importance in ensuring the peaceful future of Europe.

The U.S.A. and the U.S.S.R. also attach high importance to the negotiations on mutual reduction of forces and armaments and associated measures in Central Europe. They agree to contribute actively to the search for mutually acceptable solutions on the basis of principle of undiminished security for any of the parties and the prevention of unilateral military advantages.

Having discussed the situation existing in the Eastern Mediterranean, both Sides state their firm support for the independence, sovereignty and territorial integrity of Cyprus and will make every effort in this direction. They consider that a just settlement of the Cyprus question must be based on the strict implementation of the resolutions adopted by the Security Council and the General Assembly of the United Nations regarding Cyprus.

In the course of the exchange of views on the Middle East both Sides expressed their concern with regard to the dangerous situation in that region. They reaffirmed their intention to make every effort to promote a solution of the key issues of a just and lasting peace in that area on the basis of the United Nations resolution 338, taking into account the legitimate interests of all the peoples of the area, including the Palestinian people, and respect for the right to independent existence of all States in the area.

The Sides believe that the Geneva Conference should play an important part in the establishment of a just and lasting peace in the Middle East, and should resume its work as soon as possible.

IV

The state of relations was reviewed in the field of commercial, economic, scientific, and technical ties between the U.S.A. and the U.S.S.R. Both Sides confirmed the great importance which further progress in these fields would have for Soviet-American relations, and expressed their firm intention to continue the broadening and deepening of mutually advantageous cooperation.

The two Sides emphasized the special importance accorded by them to the development on a long-term basis of commercial and economic cooperation, including mutually beneficial large-scale projects. They believe that such commercial and economic cooperation will serve the cause of increasing the stability of Soviet-American relations.

Both Sides noted with satisfaction the progress in the implementation of agreements and in the development of ties and cooperation between the U.S. and the U.S.S.R. in the fields of science, technology and culture. They are convinced that the continued expansion of such cooperation will benefit the peoples of both countries and will be an important contribution to the solution of worldwide scientific and technical problems.

The talks were held in an atmosphere of frankness and mutual understanding, reflecting the constructive desire of both Sides to strengthen and develop further the peaceful cooperative relationship between the U.S.A. and the U.S.S.R., and to ensure progress in the solution of outstanding international problems in the interests of preserving and strengthening peace.

The results of the talks provided a convincing demonstration of the practical value of Soviet-American summit meetings and their exceptional importance in the shaping of a new relationship between the United States of America and the Soviet Union.

President Ford reaffirmed the invitation to L. I. Brezhnev to pay an official visit to the United States in 1975. The exact date of the visit will be agreed upon later.

For the United States
of America:

GERALD R. FORD

*President of the United
States of America*

For the Union of Soviet
Socialist Republics:

L. I. BREZHNEV

*General Secretary
of the Central Committee
of the CPSU*

November 24, 1974

TEXT OF SECRETARY OF STATE HENRY A. KISSINGER'S BACKGROUND BRIEFING ON VLADIVOSTOK, DECEMBER 3, 1974

In a background briefing for reporters on December 3, 1974, Secretary of State Henry A. Kissinger provided details of the arms accord reached by President Ford and Secretary Brezhnev at Vladivostok. Kissinger commented on the history of negotiations preceding the agreement and provided insights into the attitudes and perceptions of American policy makers on the question of nuclear superiority.

The significance of the agreement, according to Kissinger, lay in the fact that for the first time in the history of arms control equal numerical limits would be placed on the size of the strategic nuclear arsenals of the United States and the Soviet Union. With this principle of parity of forces established, the prospects for future negotiations on actual reductions of forces were seen to be much improved. In addition, the agreement was expected to reduce the element of uncertainty that had plagued intelligence estimates upon which force planning is, to a large extent, predicated.

Source: Department of State, Bureau of Public Affairs.

Acknowledging that the Vladivostok accord did not solve all problems pertaining to the arms race, Kissinger noted that had an agreement not been reached a relatively unrestrained expansion of nuclear forces and a serious deterioration in U.S.-Soviet relations might have resulted. By eliminating the incentives for further expansion of force levels, and by providing incentives to channel efforts toward less vulnerable weapons systems, a more stable political and military relationship could be realized.

Secretary KISSINGER: Let me sum up what can be said about the agreement. The President stated yesterday that the ceiling on strategic delivery vehicles is 2,400; the ceiling on MIRVs is 1,320. The number of land-based silos will remain constant, though they are subject to the same modifications that are permitted in the Interim Agreement—which is to say that their dimensions can be increased by 15 percent and that airborne missiles of a range of more than 600 [kilometers] will be counted as individual missiles, though not as MIRVs.

I think these are the essential elements of the agreement—which means that each side is free to compose these 2,400 in any way it wishes, except that it cannot add land-based silos. It can add land-based mobiles; it can move land-based missiles to sea.

The numerical limitations of the Interim Agreement with respect to submarines, as well as to the total numbers of submarine-based missiles, will not be in effect. The only number of the Interim Agreement that will remain in effect is that of the land-based silos; and those are, of course, the most vulnerable part of the strategic forces. Those are the essential elements of the agreement.

*   *   *

QUESTION: Mr. Secretary, do the silos remain so that they're limited to 15 percent in size, even though there's not anything specifically said?

Secretary KISSINGER: Well, that does not happen to be exactly true because the United States, either because of great foresight—as the Russians believe—or for other reasons—as some others believe—designed its silos in such a way that they can take a considerably larger missile than is presently in them, so that it is within our capability, even without increasing the size of the silo substantially, to reduce Soviet throw-weight advantage, and, if we increase the silos by 15 percent, to come close to eliminating Soviet throw-weight advantage—if that's the decision that we want to take.

But . . . I believe that the throw-weight issue has been vastly overstated and the decision of whether we will attempt to close the throw-weight will be taken by us for our reasons and not simply because the Soviet Union has heavier missiles than we do.

Q. Mr. Secretary, since the Soviet Union has not deployed any MIRV missiles and since the United States does not plan as many as 1,320 MIRV missiles, why couldn't you get a lower MIRV figure?

Secretary KISSINGER: We could have probably gotten a slightly lower MIRV figure: One thousand three hundred and twenty is slightly above the American MIRV plan and, therefore, gives us some degree of flexibility. We could have gotten a slightly lower MIRV figure; it wouldn't have made any real difference.

Q. Where did you get the 1,320? How did you arrive at that figure?

Secretary KISSINGER: We arrived at the figure of 1,320 by taking some of the planned programs and, in effect, adding to them the Trident force—which is twenty-eight missiles. [Deleted material.]

*　　*　　*

Secretary KISSINGER: Let me make a general statement of what the significance of this agreement is before we get lost in a lot of technicalities.

First, in terms of the negotiating history of this agreement, there were the following items throughout the negotiations:

(1) Total aggregates.

(2) Limitations on MIRVs—for which the code name was "qualitative restraint."

(3) There was the issue of forward bases.

(4) There was the issue of the British and French nuclear forces.

(5) There was the fact that the Soviet Union claimed compensation for a more vulnerable geographic position—the fact that some potential enemies were geographically closer to it than to us—or, to put it into less complicated language, that China would have nuclear weapons aimed at the Soviet Union.

Therefore, these were the paramaters of the negotiations as they had been going on for several years until this summer.

What we attempted to do is approve immediately a comprehensive agreement that would take care of all of the issues simultaneously. Therefore, until this summer, we attempted to bring about an extension of the Interim Agreement, in which the Soviet Union had a differential in missiles and for which we wanted to compensate by obtaining a differential in MIRV vehicles. Even though we were prepared to give them a differential in total missiles until the end of 1979, the differential in missiles for which we asked was not to be negotiable during the time of the summit [meeting between President Nixon and Secretary Brezhnev in July 1974].

Secondly, as we analyzed the problem at the time of the summit, it became clear that this was really a very precarious agreement—that you extended the Interim Agreement for a number of years at a time when the production program of both sides of MIRVs would reach a certain peak—that, therefore, the breakout potential was very substantial—and where the Soviet Union, or we, simply by deferring the deployment of one year's production, would have a massive breakout potential at the precise moment that the agreement ended.

Therefore, it was decided at the summit meeting . . . that we would, in July, aim for a ten-year agreement, in which it would be easier to catch several cycles of the program and to attempt to bring about a negotiation in this manner.

As far as the United States is concerned, we had a number of preparatory Verification Panel meetings, out of which emerged five to eight options which were presented to the President and to the NSC [National Security Council] meeting which took place in October. . . .

These options range from some that were extraordinarily simple to others of great esoteric complexity. Out of these options, the President chose not one of the options but a combination of two of the simpler ones and asked me to present those in Moscow when I was there in October.

We had two days of very difficult and very inconclusive meetings, which then led to a meeting of the Politburo on the last day that I was in Moscow . . . at which, apparently, some fundamental decisions were taken by the Soviet Union, because that evening they made a proposition to us, which I made clear afterwards brought the issue within negotiating range.

Now, what brought it within negotiating range was the Soviet Union accepted then the principle of equal aggregate at some stage of the ten-year problem. They, nevertheless, still insisted on compensation for the British and French nuclear forces and some compensation for forward based missiles.

The reason why equal aggregates become more important in a ten-year agreement than a five-year agreement was that if we gave up on the principle of equal aggregates in a ten-year agreement following [the] five-year [Interim Agreement on Offensive Arms], it would mean that [in] the period of 1972 through 1985 the United States would have accepted a position of numerical inferiority in strategic delivery vehicles, which whatever it actually invites strategically—which I never thought was much—nevertheless, symbolically, could have had some political impact on the potential of other countries. This was the situation when I left the Soviet Union at the end of October.

On the basis of the proposal that the Soviet Union made to us in October—which they also put in writing to us—we formulated a counterproposal, in which equal aggregates were to be achieved earlier, sometime during the 1975 to 1985 period, and in the interval before the United States achieved total equal aggregate, there would be a MIRV differential in our favor.

. . . This, more or less, was the situation in Vladivostok. I brought it out only to make clear that there was not a precooked agreement that was simply ratified in Vladivostok. The negotiations were, roughly, as I had described them to you upon our arrival in Vladivostok.

Saturday evening we had an extended negotiation on what differentials in total numbers and what differentials in MIRV numbers for what period of time might be acceptable, and this is where it stood about midnight, when we adjourned.

It was the next morning that General Secretary Brezhnev made his proposal on moving to equal aggregates immediately—not asking for compensation for the British and French nuclear forces. And out of this developed a more extended discussion having to do with bomber armament and the position of heavy missiles—the limitation of heavy missiles, the agreement which we have discussed. . . .

I have heard it said that the United States gave the Soviet Union rather large figures. Now, I think the fact of the matter is quite the contrary. The overall total is below the figures which the Soviet Union has today . . . We hope that the Soviet Union will be forced to reduce numbers to achieve the agreed level by 1977.

Secondly, before we went to Vladivostok—and not necessarily connected with Vladivostok—we asked the intelligence community to give us three projections of Soviet development, both in the MIRV field and in the missile field—and in the total strategic delivery field. Those estimates were made by people who had no idea of the figures that we were debating.

The intelligence estimates were made in three estimates—a low estimate, a medium estimate, and a high estimate.

All three estimates . . . [were] considerably above the figures [finally agreed upon for] both the MIRVs and the delivery systems. . . .

So with all due respect, it is total nonsense to say that the United States gave the Soviet Union figures that were granted to them by us.

The United States agreed with the Soviet Union on figures below their present figures in total numbers of missiles, and well below our estimate of where they would be—well below their lowest estimate of where they would be without an agreement—and substantially below our estimate, our most likely estimate, of where they would be without an agreement. And all of this was done without counting the British and French nuclear forces, without counting the forward based systems, and without any of the other frills. . . .

The second argument, [that] all we are doing is continuing the race . . . is not true. If the Soviet Union had built to the level that was what our intelligence estimate predicted—and I repeat that our intelligence estimate projected without any knowledge of the figures we were discussing with the Soviet Union—if the Soviet Union had built up to those figures, we would have been faced with the following problem: We would have been faced with the problem of whether we wanted to match all those, or exceed all those figures, or whether we were going to permit, as a result of an arms race, a gap to exist, which many in our countries considered intolerable, though it was ratified as part of a SALT Agreement.

In other words, the gap which we had permitted to arise without an agreement before 1972—which we had frozen as a result of the Interim Agreement—would have grown against us as of 1977.

Therefore, the only way the United States could have responded is either to let the gap grow or to make a massive effort in order to close it. So our expenditures on the strategic forces would have had to go up rapidly, and would have had to go up now.

Now if we had permitted the gap to grow—in other words, if we had kept our strategic expenditures down—our capability of bringing the arms race under control would have declined substantially, because what arguments could we have used against the Soviet Union in order to induce them to accept figures even roughly comparable to the ones we have accepted? If we had gone into an arms race of our own, the consequences would have been quite unpredictable.

We had constantly felt that one of the primary objectives of these negotiations would be not to bring about a level in which the destruction of human life was not possible—that is beyond our ability—but rather to get the perceptions of both sides into a framework in which they are not a series of self-fulfilling prophecies—a fuel wasting arms race which can be sustained only by the argument of "an imminent surprise attack" which, in turn, then makes political accommodations more and more difficult.

Now whether the level of forces is 2,400, 2,200, or 2,000 has some financial difference. But in terms of the capacity to destroy human life, it is almost irrelevant.

Therefore, the arguments that the levels before us are not uninteresting, but they do not go to the center of the issues—to reduce the strategic forces to a level where they cannot destroy human life—the reductions would have had to be to level[s] that are inconceivable today.

Now I would like you all to remember that in 1962 at the time of the Cuban missile crisis, the United States was at something like 1,500 warheads, maybe 2,000 warheads. The Soviet Union possessed something like seventy ICBM warheads.

But in the records of the deliberations at that time, the policy makers had the perception to see that the delivery of even a fraction of those Soviet warheads on the United States would present quite unmanageable problems for the United States.

We are now in a period where, with MIRVs and with the proliferation of strategic nuclear weapons, the level at which human life—or at least civilized life as we now know it—could be substantially reduced is not affected by whether the total ceiling is 2,400, 2,200, 2,000, or any of the ceilings that anyone has talked about.

In fact, if you want to make a sophisticated argument, you can make the argument that at certain levels of MIRV, the fewer the aimpoints, the more precarious the situation becomes, because if one of the risks of the contemporary situation is disparity between warheads and aiming points, so that a first strike again becomes a possibility. . . .

And therefore, from the point of view of either the destructiveness or the destruction of human life, I see no significant difference between the figure of 2,400 and any of the other figures that have been talked about—even though we would have preferred lower figures.

The significance of this agreement is that a ceiling has been put on the total number for a ten-year period, so that the argument can no longer be made that the other side is racing into newer and newer fields.

In this respect, incidentally, the argument that this isn't saving any money is also incorrect, because if the Soviet Union had built to our expectations of its program . . . we would have had to expend a substantial additional sum to that which we now face.

Q. Were these intelligence estimates based on intentional capability?

Secretary KISSINGER: These intelligence estimates were based on the best judgment—well, on a combination of both, really. We know, for example, that they have recently converted a certain number of their SS-11 missiles to a newer type. We are, therefore, subtracting those, and we are assuming that they wouldn't go through the expense of converting those to a new, and non-MIRV type—and then immediately replace them with MIRVs—so we deducted those from the total number, and assume that the remaining number were candidates for

MIRVs. Also, we have some information about some other activities—so it is a combination of capabilities and intentions.

But it is certain all of these estimates were well within their capabilities. Indeed, if we are talking about total numbers, the Soviet Union is modernizing its force now because of the constraints of the Interim Agreement by rebuilding the existing silos. That process is at least as difficult and at least as costly as the building of new silos.

Therefore, the Soviet Union would have an almost infinite capability of expanding its force by leaving the existing missiles in the silos and building new silos—and the expense to us of attempting to match this program would have been substantial.

Now let me say a word about throw-weight. I believe, as I have said before, that throw-weight is not an important part of the issue, because throw-weight is not an entity in itself. Throw-weight is a means to an end. Throw-weight is significant if it is translated into numbers of warheads and accuracy—and that, in turn, matters if you have specific targets against which to use them.

As I pointed out earlier, to the extent that the United States considers throw-weight significant, there is nothing in the agreement to prevent us from building things a bit larger. On the other hand, there is no point in building up a larger throw-weight just for a theoretical quality.

The danger that is seen by us in the Soviet throw-weight is that it will enable them to multiply numbers of warheads on their missiles, and thereby threaten our land bases. This danger is not very probable in the existing generation of MIRVs which we are now testing, because the numbers of warheads they have on theirs is not significantly larger than the numbers of warheads we have on ours; and in some categories, it is smaller than the numbers we have now.

However, if you try to analyze throw-weight, you also have to analyze the vulnerability of the target.

The Soviet Union has 85 percent of its throw-weight in the most vulnerable target, that is to say, in its land-based missile. The United States has only about 25 percent of its throw-weight in its most vulnerable targets—that is, our land-based missiles.

In the 1980s the greater flexibility of our force, and the greater vulnerability of their force, is very likely to bring about a situation in which the threat to their forces is likely to be much greater than the threat to our total force—regardless of what the weight of the individual warhead is.

So we believe that this agreement has, for the first time in the nuclear age, established a ceiling—for the first time in the nuclear age, enabled both sides to plan without the fear of an escalating numerical arms race in both the overall numbers and the numbers of those vehicles which have multiple warheads.

For the first time, it gives us the base from which to negotiate for our reduction and it has eliminated from the negotiations those items that were most divisive within the Alliance.

So if we are worried about the arms race, not only about the numbers, but about the self-fulfilling prophecies about the perceptions by each side of the other—and about the arguments that will have to be used to continue this—then I believe that the achievements of this ceiling will turn out to have been of considerable historical importance.

Now this is particularly true if you look at the alternative: The alternative to making this agreement was for the United States to begin a substantial additional building program of its own. Certainly, the Soviet Union was not likely to reduce its numbers. . . . Therefore the realistic choice for the United States was either a substantial build-up now, beginning now, after which, perhaps, somewhat lower levels might have been possible—or to settle for what was achieved. Our judgment was that the risk of this escalating to an arms race—not to speak of the probability of obtaining it from the Congress—all combine to argue for making this preliminary settlement now.

Q. Mr. Secretary, how did it come to pass that the Soviets became unconcerned about the matter of compensation for the British and French and the Chinese missile sites? Was that a throw-weight point with them, in the first place, or were they really——

Secretary KISSINGER: Well, I can only tell you that [U.S. SALT negotiator U. Alexis] Johnson used to say to us that there are two points on which the Soviet Union would never give ground: One is equal aggregates. And the other was forward based systems.

So I must say that we had all expended an enormous amount of ingenuity trying to figure out ways of bending these issues, and we were unprepared for the position of the Soviets. We had no advance warning, and, in Moscow, the last word I heard from the Soviet Union was that they were giving us theoretical equality, but they wanted us to deduct from that the British and the French [forces].

*　　*　　*

Q. Mr. Secretary, when you speak of the 25 percent of the U.S. throw-weight being land-based, are you speaking of the present configuration or future configuration?

Secretary KISSINGER: That is the present configuration. That is likely to be less.

Q. Well, we have 1,054 land-based missiles—

Secretary KISSINGER: This includes our bombers.

Q. So if you take the 450 bombers, plus the 600-odd submarine missiles—that amounts to 75 percent of our throw-weight?

Secretary KISSINGER: Give or take a few percent, yes.

Q. Mr. Secretary, the President seemed to hint last night that the forward based systems that you mentioned a few moments ago might be entered into the MBFR [Mutual and Balanced Force Reduction in Central Europe] talks. Is that likely to—

Secretary KISSINGER: Well, this depends on the evolution of the MBFR talks. They have received no such proposal up to now. [Deleted material.]

Q. Mr. Kissinger, you indicated in Vladivostok that you felt that the agreement would meet the approval of Senator Jackson. Had you had some previous discussion with him?

Secretary KISSINGER: I may have been a little bit hasty, because it seemed to me that since he criticized the previous agreement for setting levels too low, that I was not quite prepared for having disagreement attached for setting the levels too high.

And secondly, since Senator Jackson had always insisted that the major fault of the previous agreement was the absence of equality—and since this agreement achieved an equality in all of the categories and excluded all of the items that he had always said should be excluded—I got carried away by the heady atmosphere of Vladivostok.

* * *

Q. If I have the content of this straight, if I understand it correctly, on the basis of generally understood publications, we have had about 800 deployed MIRVs. We have had publicly announced plans for something in the neighborhood of a thousand. And this agreement sets a level of 1,320. The Soviets, at this point, as far as we know, don't have any MIRVs.

Secretary KISSINGER: That is right.

Q. So the agreement in ten years would permit them to build up to this 1,320. And each one of these missiles would have a certain number of warheads.

Now the thing that I'm having difficulty with here is, obviously, it would cost billions of dollars for them to build up to the level where we are now, and it would take a great period of time to do it, too. And this is a catch-up for them, as far as the MIRVs are concerned.

Secretary KISSINGER: Yes.

Q. And what you are saying is that we have set this number "high," if I understand correctly—or the number has been set high—or we have been satisfied with the number set this high—because of our fears that they might have wanted to go way beyond where we are now. Is that right?

Secretary KISSINGER: Way beyond—

Q. 1,320?

Secretary KISSINGER: Way beyond the 1,320, that is right.

Q. So we actually believe that they not only were prepared to spend the billions of dollars to catch up with us, but to go way beyond?

Secretary KISSINGER: That we believe that this might well be the case, yes.

Q. How long have you had that conception? About a year and a half?

Secretary KISSINGER: I think any of you who have heard me speak about this problem have heard me speak with a great sense of urgency, that if the MIRV development were not brought under control, that it would drive both sides in a direction which would become unmanageable.

And it was based on these intelligence estimates plus the fact that if the Soviet Union had decided, after the expiration of the Interim Agreement, to put its MIRVs into new holes, rather than into the old holes—then if you assumed that they were aiming to give any number—1,500 missiles—1,500 MIRVs—we might have faced a missile force of 4,000 rather than 2,400—if that had been their decision. I am not saying it would have been their decision, but it was certainly their option.

Now it is not true that our [MIRV] program was only 1,000. Our program was well above 1,000.

Q. Our program is publicly announced.

Secretary KISSINGER: Well our program is publicly announced, whatever it is—we have set the level at roughly our program.

Q. It speaks—the intention of our program was about 1,320.

Secretary KISSINGER: Give or take . . . You add the Tridents, the Poseidon, the Minutemen, and you will come to the figure [of 1,320].

Q. Mr. Secretary, on the same question, how does one logically reconcile the fact that the Soviet Union, which you say was going to be far beyond any of these projections last October or last June, was talking with us about a figure half the size of the 1,320? What is the logical rationale there?

Secretary KISSINGER: First of all, the Soviet Union did not accept the figure—which was a little higher than half—for a five-year period. Here we are talking about a ten-year period. Since the Soviet Union did not accept the figure, which was somewhat larger than half of what we settled for for a five-year period, which was the beginning of their MIRV program, you have a rather good estimate that in the second five-year period they would have done at least as much again, and, therefore, in a ten-year period you would have been well above 1,320.

Q. Who wanted the 1,320? Is that the Russian figure or the American figure?

Secretary KISSINGER: It's substantially our figure. I'm not saying we couldn't have had a hundred less.

Q. Mr. Secretary, we could have had 300 or 400 less, wouldn't you say?

Secretary KISSINGER: I doubt it.

*   *   *

Q. As you look back at it now are you sorry you went ahead with the MIRV?

Secretary KISSINGER: Well, that's a good question. And I think this is the same question that people faced when the hydrogen bomb was developed. And it raises the issue whether your development of MIRVs or of a weapon produces the development on the other side, or whether by not going ahead you then simply give an advantage to the other side.

I would say in retrospect that I wish I had thought through the implications of a MIRVed world more thoughtfully in 1969 and 1970 than I did. What conclusion I would then have come to I don't know. . . .

Q. I wanted to ask about what appears to be a conflict between what you and the President are saying about putting a cap on the growth of weapons development and what this agreement actually provides to the extent that I understand it.

Secretary KISSINGER: It puts a ceiling on the numbers of weapons in certain categories.

Q. Right. And you have always said, if I understood correctly, that warheads are in many respects a key figure simply because one is killed by warheads and not by vehicles.

Secretary KISSINGER: That is true.

Q. Now, since numbers of warheads are not limited and throw-weight is not limited—indeed, we have said that we maintain the option to build up our throw-weight—isn't it misleading to say that a ceiling has been put on the numbers of weapons?

Secretary KISSINGER: In the sense that you argue that the number of warheads can be increased.

Q. Yes.

Secretary KISSINGER: Well, we have a good estimate—in fact, we have a certain estimate—of the number of warheads that the Soviet Union had deployed on their present missiles because we have some idea of their testing program. And they are not likely to deploy a warhead that they hadn't tested. That's axiomatic. So to all practical purposes we have an estimate of the total number of warheads that are going to be deployed at that period. And they have a rather good estimate of the total number of warheads that we are likely to deploy in that period.

Now, it is, of course, possible that the two sides, within the total limit of 1,320, could develop . . . MIRVs which have [a] larger number of total warheads on them than the MIRVs that are presently designed. The question will soon have to be raised. In fact, it is a question that will have to be raised now: What is the advantage in multiplying the number of warheads beyond a certain point? As all of you know, I have never taken the view of numerical equality as seriously as some other people.

First of all, our estimate is that in the number of warheads, we will remain ahead in this ten-year period, for a variety of reasons, including the greater sophistication of our MIRVs. But in any event, we will reach a total number in which whether we build more warheads or not it seems extremely unlikely to give us a decisive, or even significant, superiority. We have that theoretical capability within the 1,320 limit.

And, moreover, I would like to point out that we intend as soon as this agreement is ratified and begins to operate to begin negotiations on the reduction.

Q. Does this agreement as it now stands commit both sides to enter into negotiation for reduction at some point, and, if so, at what point?

Secretary KISSINGER: It permits both sides to enter into negotiations for reduction no later than 1980.

Q. As I read it, you are not committing yourself to begin the negotiations before December of 1981.

Secretary KISSINGER: In 1980 or 1981.

Q. Right, but it could begin as late as December 1980 as I read the agreement. The question really is, realistically do you have any expectation that such arms reduction talks will begin seriously long before that?

Secretary KISSINGER: That will be our effort. And I think that once proposals on both sides have stabilized—you see, the Soviet Union will have to reduce their forces to get to the level of 2,400. If they deploy some of their new forces, some of the land-based mobiles that people are talking about, they will have to reduce even more forces. I think once the equal aggregates have been reached—or to put it another way, once the Soviets have gone down to the level that is required—I think we will certainly urge the beginning of talks on reduction. And I have great hopes that we will succeed.

Q. How long will it take them to MIRV up to a point where they will be willing to enter into arms reduction talks?

Secretary KISSINGER: Well, supposing the arms reduction brings about a reduction in the number of MIRVs and they haven't yet reached that level. So what? Then they would just not build up to the [number] presently permitted and only build up to the newly permitted levels. I think it will be easier to have reduction talks once you are not in an open-ended arms race in which both sides are watching production programs of the other, whose scope they cannot assess.

Q. Mr. Secretary, you described here, if I get it correctly, a process over these last months in which the Soviet Union point by point gave in to us while we resolutely held our ground. I guess I have two questions. What did we give up to them? And if you did not yield at some point in the last month anything to them, what's your reasoning on why this came about?

Secretary KISSINGER: I believe that one of the difficulties of the previous negotiations was the uncertainty of our domestic situation. Conversely, I think that they confronted a new President as an individual with whom they might have to deal for a six-year period. Secondly, they dealt with a President unencumbered by past history, who, therefore, if he failed to get an agreement could go back to his original defense orientation and really pick up the arms race. Thirdly, I believe that they probably attempted to vindicate the significance of détente by getting off on the right foot with a new President or with a new administration.

I think it was a combination of all, plus, fourthly, they probably analyzed what I believe any thoughtful analyst of the strategic situation would have to do—that in the field of strategic forces superiority is an illusive concept. And I think it was a combination of all of these factors that produced rather significant movement between July and December—and I must tell you quite candidly, rather unexpectedly.

Q. How many warheads do you foresee on each side in 1985?

Secretary KISSINGER: Well, I would expect us to have somewhat above 10,000, and I would expect the Soviets to have less.

Q. Do your figures work out to about 11,000, Mr. Secretary?

Secretary KISSINGER: That sounds reasonable to me. I haven't multiplied it out. I expect the Soviets to be below that.

Q. Somewhat less?

Secretary KISSINGER: Maybe 9,000. It depends how many warheads—

Q. Mr. Secretary, you say the Soviets would have to reduce their force level—

Secretary KISSINGER: Could we put all the figures on Deep Background? All the figures I give I would like to put on Deep Background so that you multiply it out.

Q. You mentioned the Soviets would have to reduce their forces. You mean the forces they actually have deployed?

Secretary KISSINGER: The Soviet Union under SALT I is permitted, and would reach, something like 950 [SLBMs] plus 1,401 [ICBMs]. [That equals] 2,350.

Q. But they are not at that level now?

Secretary KISSINGER: Well, it depends. If you count the SS-7, they are at that level now because what they are doing now is to trade in SS-7s and 8s for submarine-launched missiles. So if you count the 210 SS-7s and 8s, they are in the area between 2,300 and 2,400. And if you add the 150 bombers that they have, they are about at a total level of 2,500 right now. So they will have to give up probably their bomber force.

Q. Mr. Secretary, what's your estimate of the Chinese nuclear capacity five years from now at a time when the reduction talks are supposed to start between here and Moscow?

Secretary KISSINGER: Insignificant.

*   *   *

Q. Dr. Kissinger, just on the subject of throw-weight again, you conceded here this afternoon that, at least theoretically, the Soviets have the potential of increasing the number of warheads that a given missile could deliver, given their greater throw-weight, theoretically.

Secretary KISSINGER: So do we. We could increase the number of warheads on our missiles at least as fast as the Soviet Union could, because you have to assume that the Soviet Union is going to deploy the warheads which they have recently tested. You cannot assume that they are going to deploy a larger number of warheads than those they have tested. Therefore, you have to assume that this generation of Soviet MIRVs is going to use the number of warheads that they have tested. That number is comparable to the number of warheads that we carry on smaller missiles because of our superior technology. . . .

We could, if we wanted to, put more warheads even on our existing missiles. We have the additional option, if we wanted to, to design a larger missile to put into the existing holes which could carry many more warheads. So if you are asking about who could expand the number of his warheads more rapidly, the Soviet Union or we, I would say that over the period of the agreement I would bet on us.

Q. What I was really asking is what is to prevent there being, in effect, another arms race in that given area?

Secretary KISSINGER: The fact that it doesn't make a great deal of sense to increase the number.

Q. Yes, but you have frequently told us that what is important is the perception that each side has of the other. And I can easily see this becoming a political football in this country.

Secretary KISSINGER: The capacity of this country to develop political footballs seems to me to be unlimited. [Laughter.] But I'll tell you what my recommendation to the President would be. It would be that we would not go into wild multiplication until we see the Soviets actually testing something.

Q. On this question of policing the MIRVs, Mr. Secretary, would you dwell briefly on that? Isn't that an area we are going to have to go into now, and isn't it tough and intricate, a major issue?

Secretary KISSINGER: The major issue in the negotiations now is going to be the verification issue. And it is because of an accident of Soviet design, luckily not as difficult as it might easily be. Let me explain.

The Soviets have developed missiles to carry their MIRVs which do not fit into the existing silos—in other words, which require extensive modifications of the existing silos. Therefore, we will assume that any silo that is being substantially modified will be carrying a MIRV missile. Therefore, we will be able to count the number of their missiles by the number of silo modifications of that type, with which we are very familiar and which are undisputed.

Or to put it in another way, any missile that has been tested in a MIRV mode successfully will be counted by us as being MIRVed. In other words, we will not permit the Soviet Union to claim that they are deploying an SS-17 or 19 with the argument that it will only have a single warhead, since we believe that the [MIRV] testing program on the SS-17 and 19 has been substantially successfully concluded. Any silo that we see modified to take an SS-17 or 19 we would count as being MIRVed.

This is one of the issues that will have to be discussed in the verification. Otherwise, there is almost no other way of verifying because you could not accept the unsupported statement of the Soviet Union that certain silos have only single warheads.

*   *   *

Q. Might we not have to go to on-site inspection to make certain that they are obeying the limit?

Secretary KISSINGER: No. There may have to be certain collateral restraints, into which I do not want to go now. But I believe that it is quite possible—we have gone over this in the Verification Panel on innumerable occasions—that if we can obtain the position that any silo that accepts a SS-17 or 19 missile—and we have already told the Soviets that this is going to be our definition—and after the SS-18 program is completed, which it is not yet, any silo that accepts SS-18 missiles will be treated as MIRVed. I think we have a largely foolproof method of inspection, with a few collateral restraints.

On submarines, the problem is going to be somewhat more complicated because we have not yet seen any [MIRV] tests of their submarine-based missiles. Therefore, we don't know what the characteristics will be. But on the whole we would have to again assume that any submarine capable of carrying a MIRVed missile, once the missile has been tested, likely will have to be counted as MIRVed, just as all of our submarines will have to be counted as MIRVed.

Q. Well, could they have SS-17s and 19s in silos that haven't been modified?

Secretary KISSINGER: No.

Q. All those that have the new missiles have been modified?

Secretary KISSINGER: That's right. And on that we have no question.

And they have never rejected it. They've also never accepted it. But it's the only possible—if that is rejected, I see no other basis for inspection. When you talk of on-site inspection, we went through that drill in '69 and '70 when we didn't understand the MIRV problem well enough and thought you could simply screw a MIRV warhead on an existing missile. And actually, on-site inspection wouldn't help you very much because you would have to have a random inspection, you couldn't inspect every missile every day. With the time delays that would be involved until you get to the site, they could easily take off the MIRV warhead and put on a single warhead, have a MIRV storage, and when you leave put the MIRV back on the missile.

*   *   *

Q. Would it be fair to say that if they rejected the verification formula there is no deal?

Secretary KISSINGER: If they reject the verification formula, unless there is enormous ingenuity in which we come up with another one, I really wouldn't know where to begin. I think if they reject verification it will be very hard to conceive how there can be a deal.

Q. What is your feeling? Do you think they will accept it?

Secretary KISSINGER: I think they will accept it. I cannot conceive that they have gone this far in order to blow up the agreement now when verification is used, when it was very easy to blow it up on numbers.

Q. Unless they are buying time.

Secretary KISSINGER: What time are they buying? Maybe one cycle of the defense budget. If we find out by next April that they are stalling on verification, and if they are worried about us going into a bigger defense program, I think we would have a much better chance with Congress having in good faith accepted these numbers and then finding that the numbers evaporate because they won't agree to really the only reasonable inspection system that can be designed. And there is no alternative to this inspection.

*   *   *

Q. Mr. Secretary, given the psychology of the arms race up to now, why do you think that pressures won't develop to keep improving the weapons that are agreed on?

Secretary KISSINGER: Well, but to say that you haven't got anything because you haven't got everything is a very dangerous course.

Q. I'm saying for the future, spending for example.

413

Secretary KISSINGER: Well, whether you are improving weapons within an accepted ceiling or whether you are driving the ceiling while you are improving the weapons seems to me two different problems. It's quite possible that some improvements within the existing weapons [ceilings] would be possible. Again you have to distinguish two categories. The improvements in the Soviet force after they reach their ceiling will be composed of 1,320 MIRVs and 1,080 unMIRVed vehicles. My guess is that most of them will be ICBMs. The improvements that you can make in single-warhead weapons in relation to the strategic utility are relatively marginal. We have greater flexibility making improvements because our force is going to be composed of bombers and other elements. Now, the area of improvement is likely to be, therefore, in MIRVs. Now, you can improve accuracy, and you can improve yield. Then you have to ask yourself again, why?

The strategically unsettling effect of improvement in accuracy and yield is not as large when it is constricted within fixed numerical limits as it is when it is also driven by larger numbers. I find it conceptually very hard to see how you could get a decisive advantage by technological innovations that are now foreseeable in the offensive forces over the period of this agreement. I may be wrong, but I think that by limiting the numbers of both the qualitatively worrisome and the overall figures you have put some very significant constrictions on the arms race.

*   *   *

Q. Mr. Secretary, is it fair to say at this stage that the agreement in Vladivostok rules out the possibility that either side could achieve in the next ten years a first-strike capability?

Secretary KISSINGER: I would say that, yes. With the limitation you can say that there is a first-strike capability against certain categories of weapons. I would think that the land-based missiles on both sides are going to become increasingly vulnerable. And that is in any case going to happen, with or without this agreement. Then it is up to each side to compose its forces so that the land-based forces are not the most significant element in its force. And this I must say is a bigger problem for the Soviets than for us because over that ten-year period our land-based force is not going to be the most significant element in our force.

Q. How are we going to verify that there is not an increase in their land-based mobiles?

Secretary KISSINGER: The factor of confidence we have with respect to land-based mobiles is, of course, much less than it is with respect to land-based fixed. In land-based fixed, we have almost 100 percent confidence. In land-based mobile, we could be off by some 25 percent.

You have to remember now that any land-based mobile of any quantity will have to come out of either the submarines or the land-based fixed. . . .

*   *   *

Q. Mr. Secretary, can I go back to the reduction thing just once because of the importance that Senator Jackson, amongst others, at least professes to attach? From what level, at what point, do we hope again to negotiate reductions?

Secretary KISSINGER: From the level agreed in these numbers.

Q. Before they are attained?

Secretary KISSINGER: We are perfectly prepared to discuss them before they are attained.

I must say [something about the argument] that this agreement is inadequate because it doesn't reduce defense spending, and that what we should have done was to get lower numbers. The only way we could have even talked about lower numbers was to drastically increase defense spending and to hold the increase for a larger number of years—long enough to convince the Soviets that we were going to drive the race through the ceiling with them. At that point, getting the vested interests in this country to accept even the figures that we were going to talk about seems to me an argument that I find very difficult to deal with. . . .

If we had gone back to Geneva, when obviously the Soviets attach great symbolic importance to the first meeting between Brezhnev and President Ford in light of all the pressures that had existed against détente—and if this agreement in which the Soviet Union made very major concessions should suffer the fate of some other negotiations—then we must ask ourselves whether on the other side the whole process of détente may not have been drawn into the most serious question. Because here they met every point that all the critics of détente had consistently made—actually quite unexpectedly—in which equality is achieved in all significant categories, in which the arms race in terms of numbers is at least limited and even qualitative improvements will have to be affected by the fact that they cannot be translated into quantity. I believe that, really, as a country we should not denigrate this thing.

TEXT OF ANDREI GROMYKO'S PRESS CONFERENCE
FOR SOVIET AND FOREIGN CORRESPONDENTS

In one of his rare press conferences, Soviet Foreign Minister Andrei Gromyko presented Moscow's case for rejecting the arms control proposals which Secretary of State Cyrus R. Vance conveyed in March 1977. Essentially, Gromyko called for a speedy conclusion to negotiations relating to the Vladivostok accord of November 1974. Acknowledging that the United States and the Soviet Union disagree whether cruise missiles were included in the Vladivostok force ceilings, Gromyko stated that these ceilings must cover all "nuclear weapons carriers" capable of striking targets within the opponent's borders.

The Soviet foreign minister took exception not only to the substance of the American proposals but also to the manner in which they were presented and to the political atmosphere surrounding the talks. Both the American comprehensive reduction proposal and the "fall-back" option of concluding an agreement based on the Vladivostok accord were rejected because they differed sharply from Moscow's conception of the 1974 understanding. They were seen as allowing the United States to gain "unilateral advantages" to the detriment of Soviet security. Aside from divergent perceptions of what would constitute an adequate level of arms and capabilities for national security, another impediment to successful conclusion of an agreement was the alleged failure of the Carter administration to comply with understandings reached by the previous administration. Despite these problems, Gromyko expressed Soviet willingness to continue the search for a new strategic arms limitation agreement to replace the 1972 Interim Agreement, which expired in October 1977.

Foreign Minister GROMYKO: In connection with the visit of U.S. Secretary of State Cyrus Vance in Moscow, rumors appeared abroad, chiefly in the United States, as well as all sorts of versions in regard to the outcome of the talks held.

It will be recalled that U.S. President Carter also made a statement without even waiting for the Secretary of State's arrival in Washington. I must say that the rumors do not accord with the actual state of affairs. What is more, some of them distort the actual situation, and that is why there is need for appropriate explanations and clarifications from our side.

One of the main questions discussed during the talks held by Leonid Brezhnev with U.S. Secretary of State Cyrus Vance, and also during my own meetings with the Secretary of State, was the question of concluding a new agreement on the limitation of strategic arms, since the agreement now in force expires in October of this year.

Source: Soviet Embassy Information Department, *News and Views from the U.S.S.R.*, March 31, 1977, pp. 1-11.

What is the essence of the Vladivostok accord? For example, what is the essence of the main question which was considered? It would not be out of place to recall this.

Way back in Vladivostok [November 24, 1974], an accord was reached that the Soviet Union and the United States will each have 2,400 strategic arms carriers, including 1,320 MIRVs. This is the main content of the Vladivostok accord.

You know that there were many reports—both official and semi-official—saying that there was progress after Vladivostok. There were also more moderate reports. But, in general, it is true that quite a few steps forward have been made. There were opportunities to bring things to completion. This, however, did not happen. Then all of a sudden the question arose of the so-called cruise missiles. What does this mean? There is hardly need to dwell on the technical aspect of the matter. They tried to prove that the Vladivostok accord did not refer to the cruise missiles, that these missiles . . . are generally not subject to any limitations and that the Vladivostok accord concerns ballistic missiles only. We resolutely objected to this attempt. At Vladivostok the question was posed differently. No green light was given there to the cruise missiles. The question was posed thus—to achieve such an agreement that would shut off all channels of the strategic arms race and reduce the threat of nuclear war.

The United States of America and the Soviet Union exchanged relevant official documents which sealed the Vladivostok accords. Everything, it seemed, was clear and it remained to carry the matter forward to the signing of an agreement. Working on some of the questions, including the juridical wording of the agreement, were the delegations of the U.S.S.R. and the U.S.A. at Geneva. At first, things were moving. But all of a sudden, a wall had risen and everything was frozen. Apparently somebody, some influential forces in the U.S., found all this not to their liking. And you know that great difficulties arose and these difficulties have not been removed. If one is to speak frankly, of late these difficulties have increased. What should we call this situation and this kind of position, which certain people in the United States began taking after Vladivostok? This is the line of revision, a line of revising the commitments taken in Vladivostok.

We are categorically opposed to this. We are all for the edifice that was built by such hard work in Vladivostok, an edifice on which such intellectual and other resources were spent, not only to be preserved, but that things should be brought to a conclusion and a new agreement on limiting strategic arms should be concluded between the U.S.S.R. and the U.S.A.

We were told, and it was said to us even in the last days when the talks were on in Moscow, that one of the obstacles is the Soviet Union's possession of a certain type of bomber (it is called "Backfire" in the United States) which, it was said, can be used as a strategic weapon and that this plane absolutely must be taken into consideration in the agreement. We categorically rejected it and continue rejecting such attempts. Time and again, Leonid Brezhnev personally explained to President Ford, specifically during the meeting in Helsinki [during the European Security Conference, July 30 to August 1, 1975], and later, to President Carter, that it concerns a medium-range bomber and not a strategic bomber. Nevertheless, this question was tossed at us once again. Somebody evidently needs to artificially create this additional obstacle. It is better known to the Americans at what level these obstacles are being created. We note that this question is being artificially introduced to complicate the situation along the road of concluding an agreement.

During the first talk with Mr. Vance, Leonid Brezhnev set forth our position on all the basic questions of limiting strategic arms and concluding a new agreement. In several public statements, Leonid Brezhnev furthermore set forth the Soviet Union's policy on that question, underlining its readiness to work for this agreement. It was emphasized that this agreement accords with the interests of the United States and the Soviet Union, as well as with the interests of the whole world. Throughout the talks here in Moscow, our side emphasized the main idea that the foundation for a new agreement, that has been built up, should not be destroyed, but that it should be preserved at all cost.

And truly, what will happen if the arrival of a new leadership in some country will scrap all the constructive things that were achieved in relations with other countries? What stability in relations with other countries can be talked about in such a case? What stability can be talked about in relations between the U.S.A. and the U.S.S.R. in this case? We, our side, would like to see precisely stability in our relations, and that these relations should be as good as possible and based on the principles of peaceful coexistence and, even better, that they should be friendly. This is our stand and we would like to see similar actions in reply from the other side, that is, the United States of America.

A version is now being circulated in the U.S.A., alleging that the U.S. representatives at the Moscow talks proposed some broad program for disarmament, but that the Soviet leadership did not accept this program. I must say that this version does not accord with reality. This version is essentially false. Nobody proposed such a program to us.

I am dwelling on some facts from which you, certainly, will draw for yourselves some conclusions. For example, it is proposed to us now to reduce the total number of strategic arms carriers to 2,000 or even to 1,800 units, and MIRVs to 1,200 - 1,100. What is more, it is simultaneously proposed to liquidate half of those rockets in our possession which are simply disliked by somebody in the United States. They are described differently: sometimes "too heavy" or "excessively effective." They dislike these rockets and that is why the Soviet Union must be deprived of half of these weapons. So the question is whether such a unilateral way of putting the question is a way to agreement? No, it only damages the Vladivostok accord, breaks the balance of limitations concerning which agreement was reached in Vladivostok. What changed after Vladivostok? Nothing, absolutely nothing changed.

Call this as you like, but this is no way of solving problems. It is a way of piling one unresolved problem on another unresolved problem. Unfortunately, there are quite a few such problems as yet, especially if we take the broad area of the arms race. Here too, we are all for the accord earlier reached between the U.S.A. and the Soviet Union being meticulously observed as it was intended when this accord was achieved.

*　　*　　*

Next, in the talks with Cyrus Vance it was suggested that we revise the right of the two sides to modernize existing missiles as laid down in the present agreement, just as in the Vladivostok accord. This was taken for granted. No problems arose here. But no, it is now proposed to break up the agreement also in this respect, and to do so in a way that would give advantages to the United States, with the Soviet Union finding itself in a worse position. Clearly, we shall not depart from the principle of equality also in this respect. And to put forward such demands is a dubious if not a cheap move.

One more fact. It was proposed to us to include in the agreement a clause prohibiting the development of new types of weapons. At a first glance, it would seem that there is nothing wrong with this. But I would like to recall that the Soviet Union itself has long ago made the proposal on banning the manufacture of new types and new systems of weapons of mass extermination. Moreover, we have submitted to the United Nations a draft of the relevant international treaty. And what was the response? Maybe the U.S. Government supported this treaty? No, it did not say a single word in support of this treaty.

Indeed, at the Moscow talks too, only the most general words were uttered to the effect that such a clause should be included into the agreement, in a "package" at that, or geared to other obviously unacceptable proposals. All this made a very dubious impression. If there is a serious intention in this matter then, as I have already said, there is a concrete proposal. At first, when we raised the question of banning new types of weapons we were asked: What do you have in mind? Can one really invent a new nuclear weapon? When we cited relevant facts, and they are known not only to us but also to scientists of other countries, the attitude to our proposal somewhat changed. That is why I cannot say that our proposal met with a negative attitude on the part of all other states. No. But unfortunately, it did not enlist support from the big states, from the U.S.A.

Let us speak frankly. If both our countries stand for banning new types of weapons of mass extermination, then let us discuss the draft treaty we have. If you have amendments to the Soviet draft, put them forth. Let us discuss these amendments. If you have no amendments, then let us conclude this treaty. I repeat, our draft treaty is in the hands of the U.S. Government. And would it not be better to reply concretely to the question: Is the U.S. Government ready to sign such a treaty or is it not ready? And to attach this idea to other questions and to propose that all this be considered in the single "package" means to bury both the "package" and to bury the idea together with the "package." This, of course, is no new method. It has long been practiced by somebody. It seems to us that in international affairs in general, including relations between the U.S.A. and the Soviet Union, it would be better to examine relevant problems on a more realistic, on an honest basis. The more attempts there are to play a game in this matter, to tread on the foot of the partner, the more difficulties there will be. This will not promote an improvement in Soviet-American relations, the cause of detente, consolidation of peace. This should be said especially in connection with recent statements appearing in the United States in newspapers and, unfortunately, not only in newspapers.

I should like to add a few more words. If the U.S.A. is prepared to ban new types of weapons, why then is the need to produce the "B-1" strategic bomber, so beloved by some people in the U.S.A., defended all that much? The same is true of the manufacture of the "Trident" atomic submarine. Leonid Brezhnev spoke of these new American weapons systems both in his public speeches and in his remarks during the official negotiations with the American side, and did so repeatedly. So what we have is that certain declarations by the American side do not tally with the actual readiness to ban new types of weapons of mass extermination.

One would rather not speak on this theme, but one has to. In his last statement, the President of the United States used the word "sincerity" when referring to the Soviet leaderships' attitude to questions of strategic arms limitation. I would like to say: We do not lack sincerity. We have plenty of it. It is on this basis that we are building all our policy and would want all to build their policies on the same basis, so that the deeds would not differ from the words.

U.S. representative Cyrus Vance described his proposals as the basis for a broad and all-encompassing agreement. But it is easy, after an objective study of these proposals, to draw the conclusion that they pursue the aim of getting unilateral advantages for the U.S.A. to the detriment of the Soviet Union, its security and the security of its friends and allies. The Soviet Union will never be able to agree to this. This was openly said by Leonid Brezhnev to the U.S. Secretary of State during the first talk. He said the same during the last talk which was held yesterday.

Reading some of the statements made in the U.S.A. you probably noticed that not only what some people call all-encompassing proposals, but also an alternative "narrow proposal" has been made to us. But what is the essence of this "narrow proposal"? Here it is: We are simply told, let us conclude an agreement that will concern ballistic missiles and strategic bombers. At the same time, it is proposed to leave aside the cruise missiles and the Soviet bomber referred to as "Backfire" which, as I have already mentioned, is not strategic at all. It looks as if a concession is being made to us, but this is an extremely strange concession. We are offered what does not belong to the United States. A nonstrategic aircraft was named a strategic one, and then they say: We are ready not to include this bomber in the agreement now, if the Soviet Union consents to give a green light for the manufacture and deployment of the U.S. cruise missiles. So according to this narrower agreement, the cruise missiles would be totally excluded from an agreement. Such a decision would mean that, while plugging one gap—the ballistic missiles—a new gap, maybe an even wider and deeper one, would be simultaneously opening—nuclear weapons carriers.

I stress nuclear weapons carriers. But it is our objective to prevent an outbreak of a nuclear war, to deliver mankind from nuclear war. Is it not the same for a human being to die of a weapon from a cruise missile, as from a weapon from a ballistic missile? The result is the same. Apart from it, the manufacture of cruise missiles will swallow up no less funds, dollars, pounds sterling, rubles, francs, lire, et cetera. Do people stand to gain from it? One cannot help asking what such an agreement will give for security? And is it going to be security in general? No, it will not be security, which peoples sincerely want. It will not even be a semblance of security. That is why we rejected, frankly speaking, this so-called narrow agreement too. We declared that it does not present a solution to the problem and does not even come close to solving this problem. This is what the U.S. Secretary of State took back when he left Moscow.

We do not know how all this will be presented to public opinion in the U.S.A. Judging by the first symptoms, the actual state of things is distorted. The results of the exchange of opinions and the statements that were made to the U.S. Secretary of State were also distorted. Leonid Brezhnev's statements were distorted too.

All this does not help towards a productive solution of problems, though we would sincerely wish so. But we are ready to continue talks on all these problems. The Soviet leaders have enough patience. We would like the discussions, regardless of where they are held—here in Moscow, in Washington or in other places—to finally come to a favorable conclusion.

Leonid Brezhnev strongly emphasized: We firmly stand for good relations with the United States just as with other countries in the world. We stand for relations based on the principles of peaceful coexistence, for friendly relations. And the possibilities for it are far from having been exhausted. They have not been exhausted because the point at issue is the United States and the Soviet Union.

We do not intend to belittle the substantial differences that now exist between the stands of the U.S.A. and the Soviet Union. The Secretary of State was told about it frankly. But does this mean that there are insurmountable obstacles? No, it does not. We would like to express the hope that the leadership of the United States will take up a more realistic stand, that it will give greater consideration to the interests of the security of the Soviet Union and its allies and will not strive for unilateral advantages.

*   *   *

During the session of the Political Consultative Committee in Bucharest [November 26, 1976], the Warsaw Treaty member-states jointly proposed that the participating countries of the [Helsinki] All-European Conference take commitments not to be the first to use nuclear weapons one against the other. One cannot help asking: Is there anything bad in that proposal?

As if nuclear weapons are not used first, there will be no state that would be second and, consequently, third, fourth and fifth to use it. This would mean a removal of the threat of a nuclear war. It is one of the most effective proposals aimed at a strengthening of peace and easing of tension.

The NATO member-states, however, without any particular discussions, although they say there was a difference of views, declared their negative attitude to this proposal. We do not regard the discussion of this matter to be over. This question may not officially be on the agenda of NATO, but it remains in life, and it will be discussed until the problem of non-use of nuclear energy for military purposes is resolved.

*   *   *

The Soviet Union is pursuing a consistent policy of peace, the easing of international tension, the policy of curbing the nuclear arms race, the policy of disarmament. It is a Leninist peace-loving policy. You heard about it from the rostrums of our Party congresses, the Plenary Meetings of the Party Central Committee. It is our basic line and we will pursue it persistently and nobody will be able to sidetrack us from this road. But we will also give a rebuff to those who are trying to mend their affairs to the detriment of our interests, the interests of our friends and allies.

It is precisely on such a just basis that we are dealing and would like to further deal with the United States.

Do not think that the critical remarks addressed to the U.S.A., in particular in connection with the question of strategic arms, diminish to some degree our wish to see the relations between the U.S.A. and the Soviet Union to be good, and what is even better, friendly. But this does not depend only on us. We will be covering and will cover our part of the way. But there is also the other part of the way that must be covered by the United States. I would like to believe that they will cover their part of the way.

I shall touch on two more questions. Some people pretend that they are not directly concerned with the problem that was discussed as the basic one during the stay of the U.S. Secretary of State in Moscow. But it is far from being so.

I would like to formulate the first question thus: This is the question of not handing strategic weapons over to third countries and of taking no actions whatever to evade the agreement, the signing of which we are now concerned. On this question we formulated a concrete proposal. It was discussed. At any rate, we put it forward in Geneva in the course of the talks between the U.S. and Soviet delegations. But our representatives as a matter of fact received no substantive reply.

We attach no small importance to the solution of this matter.

The second question is about the advance deployment of U.S. nuclear weapons in Europe, around Europe and in other areas, from where the Soviet territory is within reach.* In concluding the first agreement on the limitation of strategic weapons we made official

---

*Editors' Note: Foreign Minister Gromyko is referring to nuclear weapons deployed in the European Theater and commonly called forward-based systems (FBS).

statements to the effect that we must return to this question. In the interests of reaching an agreement, we did not propose in Vladivostok that the provision of liquidation of U.S. nuclear weapons of advance deployment be included into an agreement as a compulsory term. But now we have a different view of this issue in the light of the latest U.S. proposals. This is a matter of our security and the security of our allies. We are entitled to pose the question of liquidating U.S. advance deployment means. This concerns atomic powered submarines, bombers capable of carrying nuclear weapons and aircraft carriers in the corresponding region of Europe. . . . Call it what you may: a toughening of position, a change of position. But I have to say it again: This question now faces us in connection with the latest U.S. proposals.

*   *   *

We will never cede our legitimate interests and our security. We can do business only on the basis of equality, including the transaction of business with the United States of America, with no damage to our legitimate interests. If the other side does the same, I think that both sides can look into the future with optimism.

*   *   *

[Mr. Gromyko then answered the following questions submitted by correspondents.]

Q. What can you say about the statements from the White House that, in case of a failure of the talks on the limitation of strategic arms, the U.S.A. will create and deploy new strategic weapons?

Mr. GROMYKO: I can say only one thing: If anyone takes this road, he would assume the whole responsibility for the consequences of such actions. In our opinion, every effort must be made to curb the arms race, to achieve positive results in the talks.

Q. What other questions of arms limitation and disarmament were examined during the talks with Cyrus Vance, and what is the U.S.S.R.'s stand on this score?

Mr. GROMYKO: I gave a sufficiently full list of questions that were examined. I can only add, concerning some issues that remain open at the present time—and the U.S.A. has objections on most of them—we agreed that our representatives will evidently have to meet, and maybe more than once, in order to remove the existing disagreements. Such meetings can prove to be useful. This is a positive side of Cyrus Vance's visit.

Q. Does the line by the U.S. President on the question of "human rights" affect resolving of the strategic arms problem? Don't you think that the campaign being waged in the U.S.A. by certain circles on the far fetched "human rights" question is a deliberate building up of tension?

Mr. GROMYKO: The second question helps me to answer the first one. I will not say that, in discussing any aspect of the problem of preparing a new agreement on the limitation of strategic arms, we talked about "rights." Of course not. But the thing is that all that is lately said in the U.S.A. about "human rights" . . . naturally poisons the atmosphere and aggravates the political climate. But does this help to solve other issues, including those related to strategic arms? No, it does not. On the contrary, it hinders it. And speaking on the essence of the matter, I would like to say as follows: We do not claim to be teachers of anybody since the domestic affairs of states are concerned and only the states themselves can decide on their domestic affairs. I stress "domestic affairs." But we will not allow anybody to assume the pose of teachers and decide how to solve our internal affairs, I stress "our internal affairs."

*   *   *

Q. Can you say what was, in your view, the use of the meeting with the U.S. Secretary of State Mr. Vance, meaning the use for a better understanding between the U.S.S.R. and the U.S.A.?

Mr. GROMYKO: I would answer the question as follows: The visit of the Secretary of State was necessary and indeed useful because we must know each other well. I mean not a superficial acquaintance, but the knowledge of positions, the knowledge of the policies of the countries on the problems concerned. We also diverge on questions, and important questions they are. I have already spoken about it and I don't think that there is a necessity to repeat it. Some agreement was reached to continue discussions of unsolved matters, on which we could not find a common language with the U.S.A. An exchange of views may be held, not necessarily at a high level, but, say, at the level of experts, counsellors. Then we will be able to see where we stand. We hope that the U.S. side will show a serious attitude to these efforts. On our part we guarantee this.

PRESS CONFERENCE OF DR. ZBIGNIEW BRZEZINSKI, NATIONAL SECURITY ADVISER, APRIL 1, 1977

Following Secretary of State Cyrus R. Vance's visit to Moscow in March 1977, National Security Adviser Zbigniew Brzezinski held a press briefing to outline the strategic arms limitation proposals the Carter administration had put before the Soviet government. Dr. Brzezinski's remarks revealed a continuing concern over the destabilizing consequences of qualitative improvements in weapon systems, especially as they affect the survivability of land-based ICBMs.

As explained by Brzezinski, the American proposals were designed both to codify the principle of strategic parity and to maintain a stable political and military relationship between the United States and the U.S.S.R. By limiting the number of missiles capable of threatening an opponent's land-based ICBMs, by proscribing future improvements in existing land-based missiles, and by placing restrictions on the Backfire bomber and cruise missile, both countries would be relieved of some of the anxiety inherent in the nuclear arms competition and inhibiting the development of better political relations.

Brzezinski concluded by stating that the Carter administration's comprehensive reduction proposal is "in many respects the first truly, genuinely disarmament-oriented proposal" ever made within the context of SALT. Despite the initial Soviet rejection, the United States would continue to seek Soviet approval of such a proposal.

Mr. BRZEZINSKI: What I would like to do is essentially give you as much information as I legitimately can on the proposal that we made in Moscow [on March 28, 1977]. In so doing, I don't propose to engage in any recrimination, but would merely like to lay out for you the kind of proposal we made and the thinking that went into that proposal. For I believe that the thinking that the proposal reflected is almost as important as the proposal itself.

What we were trying to accomplish and what we intend to accomplish is to move forward to genuine disarmament; that is to say, to obtain a significant reduction in the level of the strategic confrontation.

We believe that SALT agreements should not only set the framework for continued competition, but that they should indeed limit that competition, reduce its scope, introduce greater stability into our relationship.

Our proposals were thus designed to accomplish two basic purposes: to give both sides the political and the strategic parity to which

---

Source: Office of the White House Press Secretary, April 1, 1977.

each of them is entitled, and this means that there should be no self-evident advantage in the agreement which would be either of a strategic character or which would be susceptible to political perceptions as an advantage; and secondly, it was our basic purpose to seek an agreement which would provide to both sides again political and strategic stability. Parity in the first instance, stability in the second instance.

By this, I mean a proposal which would take into account the fact that if you only have certain kinds of limits but do not anticipate technological dynamics, what may seem stable in 1977 or 1978 could become very unstable in 1980 or 1985. It was therefore felt that genuine strategic arms limitations, indeed, a genuine strategic arms reductions agreement, ought to take both of these elements into account.

The proposal that we made was therefore very finely crafted. We attempted very deliberately to forgo those elements in our strategic posture which threaten the Soviets the most, and we made proposals to them that they forgo those elements in their strategic posture which threaten us the most. We felt particularly by concentrating on the land-based ICBMs that are MIRVed we would take into account the greatest sources of insecurity on both sides.

I truly believe that this proposal, if accepted, or when accepted, could serve as a driving wedge, as a historical driving wedge, for a more stable and eventually more cooperative American and Soviet relationship. It is thus a proposal which is not only strategic but political in its character, and Secretary Vance, in his remarks in Moscow, placed a great deal of emphasis on the political significance of this proposal.

It was a proposal which has strategic as well as political intentions very much in mind. Because of that, it was also a proposal which was accompanied by a series of other proposals designed to place the American-Soviet relationship not only on a more stable basis, but to make the cooperative elements in that relationship more comprehensive. This is why we have deliberately matched or accompanied the SALT proposals with initiatives in regard to such matters as the Indian Ocean, and the desirability of achieving mutual restraint in regards to our respective military presence in that part of the world.

This is why we proposed that we hold further discussions on conventional arms transfers to third parties. This is why we suggested that it would be in our mutual interest as a stability-producing initiative to . . . discuss our respective civil defense programs. This is why we suggested that we talk about a comprehensive test ban. This is why we suggested that there be controls on antisatellite capabilities and on prior notification of missile test flights.

All of that cumulatively was designed to produce greater mutual stability, to widen areas of cooperation, to indeed offset the competitive elements in our relationship by a widening pattern of cooperation. And we are encouraged by the fact that eight working groups were set up on the basis of these proposals, as well as some that the Soviets made, in order to move forward on these issues.

I should have added, incidentally, that we also proposed meetings on nonproliferation. That was part of our proposal.

It is in this context that we proposed a comprehensive package with negotiating flexibility inherent in it in order to structure [a] rather different and more stable and more equitable U.S.-Soviet strategic relationship.

That package has two key elements in it.

First of all, it called for reductions which were of a greater scope than just symbolic. And the second equally important part of the package involved a proposal for a freeze, for a halt on the modernization of ICBMs; and I will talk about that in more detail.

You can well see how these two key fundamental elements are interrelated. We proposed the reduction so as to lower the level of the competition and we proposed a freeze in order to halt it qualitatively and quantitatively. Thus, it is in many respects the first truly, genuinely disarmament-oriented proposal introduced into the Strategic Arms Limitations Talks.

We proposed more specifically that the present strategic aggregates which were set [at Vladivostok on November 24, 1974] at the high level of 2,400 [delivery vehicles] for each side be reduced to a range between 1,800 and 2,000, and here again is a demonstration of the inherent flexibility of the package because this is something which we were prepared to discuss.

We proposed, moreover, that within that framework the present level of MIRVs, which is set at 1,320, be reduced to something between 1,100 and 1,200. And we also suggested that in that context it would be desirable that the total number of the so-called Soviet modern large ballistic missiles, particularly the SS-9 and SS-18, be reduced because, within the framework of lowered aggregates, these large missiles with their potential for numerous MIRVing (indeed the SS-18 can be MIRVed up to 8 to 10 warheads), become increasingly significant and introduce an asymmetrical aspect into the relationship.

On that basis we proposed that both sides freeze the deployment of all of their ICBMs, and ban modifications on existing ICBMs, and indeed limit the number of annual flight tests for ICBMs, thereby reducing the likelihood of significant modifications; and also ban the development, testing, and deployment of new types of ICBMs and particularly ban the deployment, testing, and development of mobile ICBMs, a factor, again, which if not checked, could introduce very major uncertainty into the U.S.-Soviet strategic relationship.

This more specifically meant that on the U.S. side we were prepared to freeze our Minuteman III deployment—that is to say, the MIRVed ICBM—at 550, which is where it is currently. And we would forgo further improvements in all U.S. ICBMs, and we would abandon the MX program, both for silo and mobile basing. And we would forgo any plans for any other ICBMs.

On the Soviet side we proposed that the Soviets freeze the number of their strategic ICBMs, the SS-17s, 18s and 19s at a number not in excess of 550, which actually means that they could still go up because they are below that number and these would be the Soviet MIRVed missiles. Given the size of some of them (this is an important point to bear in mind for it raises the issue of equity), their total number of warheads eventually could be greater than our land-based ICBMs would provide. And we would expect that the MLBM, or the modern large ballistic missile component within the context of the 550 would not be greater than 150. This is important because this would provide for a reduction.

Q. Could you repeat that?

Mr. BRZEZINSKI: We also proposed that the total number of the modern large ballistic missiles, which we would expect would be the SS-18s because they are the most modern Soviet ballistic missiles that are large, would not be greater than 150 and that would be a reduction from the present total, but that will be an important element of stability because that large number of the modern large ballistic missiles introduces the destabilizing potential inherent in large throw weight, and many, many warheads.

Q. Do they currently have 320 [heavy ICBMs]?

Mr. BRZEZINSKI: Three hundred and eight. We would also expect the Soviets to abandon the development and deployment of the SS-16, which is their mobile ICBM, just as we would abandon the MX.

Q. How about the SS-20; would that also be abandoned?

Mr. BRZEZINSKI: The SS-20 in its precise configuration is not a strategic weapon and we would want, in the course of the agreement, to develop arrangements which would permit us to have the needed assurance that the SS-20 is not being upgraded into the equivalent of the SS-16 because, as some of you clearly know, the SS-20, with a third stage, could be, in effect, the equivalent of the SS-16. We would therefore want to have some arrangements whereby we could clearly differentiate between the two.

Finally, we would propose to make an arrangement with regard to the Backfire which would give us some assurances that it would not be used as a strategic weapon by the Soviet Union, and this is something that would be negotiated more fully within this framework. We would propose to ban all strategic cruise missiles, and that, again, is something which would be negotiated. In that context, though, it is to be noted that the Soviet side has insisted that the Backfire is not a strategic weapon, though it has a radius of over 2,000 miles. We would presumably define the cruise missile as being strategic at the level lower than that in the context of our negotiations.

I would say that if one analyzes this proposal in detail, I think one is justified within the limits of human reason, within the confines of one's own background, tradition and concerns, which necessarily confine our ability to be absolutely certain about our judgments, that this was a genuine effort at an equitable arrangement.

We would constrain those aspects of our strategic programs which are threatening to the Soviets. We would want the Soviets to adjust similarly in those regards which are most threatening to us.

We would cap the arms race, we would impose a limit on the numbers through a reduction, significant reduction, and we would impose restraints of a qualitative type on offensive systems. Thus, we would both take a giant step forward. I see a certain analogy between the situation in which we find ourselves today and the late 1960s. At that time, some of you might recall, we proposed to the Soviets that ABMs [anti-ballistic missile systems] be banned because ABMs introduce an inherent element of instability into the relationship.*

The first Soviet reaction to that proposal by Prime Minister Kosygin was very negative, given their backgrounds, their traditions, their ways of looking at the strategic relationship. Yet, over time, through a continuing discourse, the Soviet side came to recognize the fact that indeed in the age of highly advanced strategic systems the introduction of the ABM element into the equation was truly destabilizing and the most important accomplishment of SALT I was precisely that which the Soviets earlier had so indignantly rejected, namely, a ban on the ABM systems. We are thus in the first phase of an ambitious and far-reaching search for a significant American-Soviet accommodation.

We believe in some respects we are in the earlier educational part of the process in which both sides have to think through the implica-

---

*Editors' Note: President Lyndon B. Johnson and Secretary of Defense Robert S. McNamara first proposed banning ABM systems at a summit conference with Soviet Prime Minister Alexei N. Kosygin in Glassboro, New Jersey, June 23 and 25, 1967.

tions, both of an unchecked arms race and of the benefits of reductions and a freeze. We are going to continue these talks with the Soviets. . . . We are hopeful that the search for something truly significant will bear fruit.

I don't think anyone in this house or in this city engaged in this process expected the Soviet Union simply to accept these proposals instantly.

We went [to Moscow] in order to present to them our views regarding what might constitute a truly creative and historically novel framework for our strategic relations. We will persist in that effort and we are hopeful, on the basis of prior experience and given the overriding interest that both sides have in stability and accommodation, with patience and with persistence, and with good will on both sides, there will be significant progress made towards what could be a very significant turn in the American-Soviet relationship.

Q. Would you please clarify two points? Your definition of the American definition of the strategic cruise, and would you go over again . . . the MIRV idea? Were you talking simply about MIRV equivalency or was this—

Mr. BRZEZINSKI: In regard to the cruise missile, our position is that a cruise missile which is not capable of employment either in a transcontinental operation or which doesn't have a range in excess of weapons systems that are typically considered to be strategic is nonstrategic. And since there has been an ongoing discussion with the Soviets as to what is and is not a strategic weapon, we would want to reach a more precise definition of that in the course of the negotiations, banning those cruise missiles which have as themselves a strategic range, and retain for both sides flexibility for those that are not.

I should add also that if any of the cruise missiles that would be retained by both sides were to be placed, for example, on the bombers, these bombers would then count as a MIRV weapon and would therefore be counted within the MIRV aggregate.

Specifically talking about the MIRVs, our proposal is to freeze the land-based ICBMs that can be MIRVed at 550 and to reduce [to 150] particularly the number of those very large Soviet ICBMs which can be MIRVed into very numerous warheads, given their throw weight, because that, in the long run, could introduce an element of instability for both sides.

We would, at the same time, in that context, forgo those systems which are particularly threatening to the Soviet land-based ICBM force. It is to be remembered in this context that, at least for the time being, the Soviet strategic forces are heavily dependent on their land-based ICBMs. Those American systems which could threaten these land-based ICBMs are naturally and understandably particularly threatening to the Soviets.

*   *   *

Q. Doctor, you didn't talk about the so-called data base and I have a question about it.

The President, at his press conference here in this room, spoke of some form of verification of the data base material once it was submitted by either side to the other side, I guess. Can you elaborate on what verification we are talking about?

Mr. BRZEZINSKI: I don't want to go into too many specifics . . . but, specifically with regard to the data base, let me limit myself to this observation.

We would hope and we would expect that in the context of this increasingly more stable and more accommodating relationship that we feel ought to develop between us and them in the strategic realm, the Soviet Union would become increasingly more forthcoming with regard to data base.

Many of you know about this SALT relationship as much as, and I am sure in quite a few cases much more than, I do and therefore you will remember that throughout much of SALT I the data base on which these negotiations was based was largely American-provided, and the pattern of the negotiations typically involved a situation in which we would provide information about our systems, numbers, dimensions, characteristics, and then we would say to the Soviets: "And with regard to your systems, which we estimate at being at so many and to possess the following dimensions and to have the following characteristics, we would propose the following."

And the Soviets would respond and say: "With regard to the strategic information which you have provided us about yourself, our position is as follows. And with regard to the information that you have given us—the alleged information you have given us—about our systems, our position is as follows." And they could comment on it, but without a truly equitable data base.

I would hope and we would expect that in a symmetrical strategic relationship, which it has now become, the Soviet Union would provide us with all of the necessary data, just as we provided them with the necessary data, and we would each have and retain the needed means for verifying the accuracy of that data.

Q. How?

Mr. BRZEZINSKI: For one thing, through satellites, which are very important sources of information, but beyond that, with regard to the cruise missile, we would have to perhaps explore some additional ways of verification. I don't want to be too specific, because that is something which again would have to be negotiated, but let me merely note the difficulty with which, again, many of you are familiar.

It is very difficult to differentiate between the cruise missiles which are strategic and nonstrategic—their sizes, dimensions, are the same. It is very difficult to differentiate between a cruise missile which has a nuclear warhead and those which do not. So we would have to have some additional, more comprehensive arrangements to give both sides the assurance that they need to have on this issue.

Q. I am really not asking for details but is this an on-site inspection proposal, basically?

Mr. BRZEZINSKI: I don't think we have yet reached the stage in which direct on-site examination of all weapons systems is feasible. But certainly, if the Soviet side were prepared to accept some on-site verification, it would be a giant step towards mutual confidence, and we would certainly welcome on-site Soviet inspection of some of our weapons systems, so that this in itself would be something which would be a great contribution to mutual stability. And I would hope that as Soviet confidence grows, as Soviet preoccupation with secrecy declines, that they will find this idea less and less abhorrent.

Q. You talked about the Soviet concern for their land-based weapons, and there has always been a lack of symmetry between their perception of their defense needs and the U.S., which is why they came up with a freedom of choice within their weapons systems.

Your proposal, the American proposal—according to what you say—would appear to take away a lot of their freedom of choice, and, at the same time, it doesn't say anything about sea-based missiles, which also are a threat, or the Soviets perceive them as a threat to their land-based systems.

Therefore, can you explain why, in your perception, this is equivalent, a third thing that they have to cut back from 308 to 150 in their super-launch missiles and we don't have to cut back any land-based?

Mr. BRZEZINSKI: First of all, as far as the freedom to mix is concerned, that would still be retained by both sides, though there would be upper limits set on what you can do, particularly in regards to land-based [MIRVed] ICBMs. That limit indeed would be set at 550. But each side, or one of the sides, could decide that it prefers to have fewer of these and more sea-based. So, in that sense, there is some freedom to mix, no doubt about it.

As far as the Soviet throw weight or large ballistic missiles are concerned, their reduction is a necessary concomitant of mutual stability, because if they are not reduced in numbers, then by MIRVing them, the Soviet Union would gain, particularly within these lower aggregates, a very significant advantage.

I think one has to recognize the fact that if you have fewer total numbers, then any asymmetry becomes increasingly significant, and the Soviets do have that asymmetry to their advantage in the possession of the large ballistic missiles which can be MIRVed up to eight or ten warheads.

In addition to that, there is this other problem, which I don't want to exaggerate, but which has to be taken into account when we think of equity at the lower aggregates, namely, the Backfire. We were prepared to consider special arrangements for the Backfire. But again, the Backfire—however one defines it, whether it is a strategic or nonstrategic weapon—becomes more significant if you have lower aggregates than if you have higher aggregates.

If these aggregates are high, then you can say, well, it is more marginal, but if you go down at 1,800, then the introduction of the Backfire, at some number which is in excess of 100, becomes a factor. And yet we are prepared to accommodate on that, too.

I am not going to argue . . . that this was an infallible package which has to be taken in toto. All I am going to say is that we made the damnedest effort to produce a package which, within the limits of our own intelligence—and by intelligence, I not only mean information, I also mean what is in our heads—we could say was reasonably equitable for both sides. We did our best to define it that way and will be glad to discuss it, and we intend to discuss it. We would like to find out what aspects of this are particularly troubling to the Soviets, because that is what negotiations are about and conceivably, if the case is persuasive, this or that adjustment could be made in return for this or that adjustment.

Q. What was the Soviet reaction to the package in the general sense? Did they reject it out of hand or say that certain things were difficult?

Mr. BRZEZINSKI: To say that the Soviets rejected it out of hand gives it a dramatic and categorical quality which I really do not think the circumstances justify.

The sequence was essentially as follows: prior to the Vance mission, we did indicate to the Soviets that we will be making proposals for significant reductions. We did that deliberately because we wanted the Politburo to think about these issues.

As you know, the Soviets do not have an arms control agency. The

Soviets do not have influential groups in their society that are concerned with arms control. Arms control proposals are assessed in the Soviet Defense Ministry, which has certain interesting implications, and we felt it would not be particularly constructive to send in a detailed proposal which then is staffed out in the Soviet Defense Ministry and goes up to the Soviet Politburo with a categorical critique. We wanted the top Soviet leaders to focus on this issue.

Therefore, we drew their attention to the fact that we will be making proposals that call for reductions that we think would have a significant impact on the broader nature of our relationship. And then Secretary Vance presented that and, as I said earlier, not only in its strategic setting but also in its political context, when he made his opening statement to the Soviets.

The Soviet leadership then expressed a preference for the discussion of other issues . . . and then in the final or the pre-final session, I forget which, Secretary Brezhnev informed Secretary Vance that this proposal was not acceptable to the Soviet Union. But he coupled it, at the same time, with a clearcut indication that it is the Soviet expectation, which is matched by us, that these talks, including the SALT aspects, will continue and that, indeed, the Gromyko-Vance meeting will be resumed directly in Geneva in May.

So, it is in this context that I think one ought to assess where we are and, again, I would like to draw your attention to the analogy that I made before, namely, to the initial reaction by Prime Minister Kosygin when, for the first time, he was confronted at the top level, and not through bureaucratic channels, with the arguments why an ABM is mutually destabilizing. This was a new argument for him. It was not a convincing argument initially, even though it was made very persuasively when he met in Glassboro with President Johnson and Secretary McNamara. And then subsequently it became clear that such an arrangement was indeed in mutual interest.

Q. Dr. Brzezinski, in Mr. Vance's news conference in Moscow, he alluded to a Soviet counterproposal based on the 1976 discussions with Dr. Kissinger. I am interested in why that counterproposal was not negotiable?

Mr. Brzezinski: I don't want to engage here in a critique of the Soviet position because, as I said at the beginning of my remarks, I am really not going to engage in recriminations or a kind of side dialogue on their proposals versus our proposals, but really to try to explain the rationale and the content of ours.

Let me limit myself, therefore, to one comment. It is OUR broad feeling that, 27 years after the beginning of the nuclear race, the time is right in our relations for doing something more than just creating frameworks for continued competition. It is our feeling that the framework defined by Vladivostok is so high in its numbers, so open-ended in its consequences, so susceptible to quantitative as well as qualitative improvements, that in some respects it comes close to a misstatement to call any such arrangement arms limitations. All it is, really, is an arrangement for continued arms competition, and we have gone to the Soviets with a proposal which we crafted as best we could in order to convince them that maybe the time is right to take a significant step toward reductions.

We gave them ranges so they could pick either the more ambitious or the less ambitious part of it, depending on their estimate of the strategic consequences of cuts. They have very good analysts. They should be able, and I am sure they are able, to assess whether 2,000 is better for them, or 1,800, whether 1,200 MIRVs is better for them, or 1,100, and so forth. So we weren't very categorical about it.

Q. Dr. Brzezinski, you placed heavy stress at the beginning on the political aspect of this, as well as this strategic aspect of the proposal. You said that no one expected them to accept it out of hand, but neither was there widespread expectation of the kind of fierce reaction from the Russians, including the press conference yesterday by Mr. Gromyko. Politically speaking, do you feel that the reception of the proposal and what has happened has set back Soviet-American relations, or were you surprised at what happened, and, if you weren't, was this a miscalculation?

Mr. BRZEZINSKI: If I wasn't, then it couldn't be a miscalculation. It would be a miscalculation if I was. No, we did not expect the Soviets to accept this total framework on the basis of three days' talks. We expected them to consider it. Our judgment . . . was that the discussions were generally conducted in business-like fashion, that the Soviets' side, through little gestures, went out of its way to indicate that this is an ongoing relationship. They did not hide the fact that they took a negative view of this proposal, and they were quite explicit on it, but there were no nasty polemics in the meeting.

You are absolutely right in saying that some of the statements, maybe even some of the gestures that were made in the press conference by the Soviet minister, were of a more assertive type. But I would describe that perhaps as a reaction to the political perception that indeed the United States has come up with a proposal which, if accepted, would have a significant contribution to disarmament.

The Soviets, over the years, have prided themselves on being in the forefront of the disarmament proposals, and perhaps there was just a tiny touch of defensiveness, therefore, in some of these gestures and some of these comments. I don't think that these gestures and these comments are really that important. What is important is that the relationship involves continued negotiations, that agreements were read in Moscow to develop working groups on a large number of highly sensitive issues . . . and that, therefore, the negotiating process continues. And in the negotiating process you expect to be turned down, to be pressed, to be asked to make accommodations and concessions, but that is part of the game.

Q. Doctor, what did we offer to forgo that they would have found most threatening to their land-based missiles? I am not clear on that.

Mr. BRZEZINSKI: Particularly the MX, which in its consequences, given its accuracy and so forth, by the early eighties, could be extremely, extremely threatening to them and, in that sense, I think that in itself would [be] a source of considerable assurance to them.

Beyond that, if we were to limit the cruise missiles merely to tactical cruise missiles, this, too, in the longer run, would be a significant assurance to them. Beyond that, we would have to make some accommodations, given the total numbers in Minutemen I and II and in the Poseidons.

Basically, what it would give them is the sense of security that the United States is forgoing, as a basic strategic option, the acquisition of first-strike capability against their land-based systems.

9

NUCLEAR PLANNING AND ARMS CONTROL

SOVIET NUCLEAR PLANNING—A POINT OF VIEW ON SALT

Lewis Allen Frank

While much has been written on what the United States should seek to achieve in the Strategic Arms Limitation Talks, relatively little public attention has been given to Soviet objectives. In the following excerpt, an American analyst attempts to illustrate the type of advice Soviet political leaders might receive from their defense planners.

Viewing SALT as a logical and necessary extension of détente from the political to the military sphere of U.S.-Soviet relations, a Russian defense planner would have to take into account the possibility that leadership changes in the United States might result in a reversal of the détente process. Prospects for successful arms limitation negotiations could thereby be jeopardized. In addition, the evolution of technology and its application to weapons development programs could further complicate military détente. These factors, together with existing Soviet strategic doctrine, are employed by the author to gain insight into the objectives which political leaders in the Kremlin might seek to achieve in future rounds of SALT.

Introduction by a Soviet Planner

The recent evolution of Soviet-U.S. relations has resulted from a shift in the correlation of forces between the Socialist and capitalist countries in favor of the Socialist camp. The U.S.A. has been suffering a

Source: Lewis Allen Frank, *Soviet Nuclear Planning: A Point of View on SALT* (Washington, D.C.: American Enterprise Institute, 1977), pp. 1-43. The author has written this paper as if he were a Soviet defense planner. The attitudes and style throughout are therefore characteristic of the hypothetical planner.

439

LEWIS ALLEN FRANK

series of shocks as a consequence of high expenditures on arms, inflation, unemployment, imperialist gambles, such as the involvements in Vietnam and Angola, and economic competition with other capitalist countries.[1] President Gerald Ford, like Richard Nixon before him, has therefore been forced to become more flexible on matters relating to arms limitation and arms reduction. In the call for the Twenty-fifth Congress of the Communist Party of the Soviet Union (CPSU), which was scheduled to begin on 25 February 1976, the party plenum of 16 April 1975, under the leadership of General Secretary and Chairman Comrade Leonid I. Brezhnev, reaffirmed the policy of peaceful coexistence and urged continued international solidarity to make the satisfactory progress of détente irreversible and consistent with the improved world situation.[2]

Arms limitation and reduction measures serve to supplement political détente with military détente.[3] This fundamental and correct approach, which reflects the peace program of the Twenty-fourth Congress of the CPSU, has yet to take total hold within the U.S.A. The peace program made possible the conclusion of the Interim Agreement on Certain Measures with respect to the Limitation of Strategic Offensive Arms of 26 May 1972, the Treaty and Protocol on the Limitation of Antiballistic Missile (ABM) Systems of 26 May 1972 and 1 July 1974, and the Vladivostok Accord of 24 November 1974 on the further limitation of strategic arms. Those agreements evolved as a result of the positive changes in the correlation of forces and the atmosphere engendered by the Basic Principles of Mutual Relations between the Union of Soviet Socialist Republics and the United States of America [of 29 May 1972] and the Agreement on the Prevention of Nuclear War [of 22 June 1973].[4] Those changes produced a new alignment of forces

---

[1]M. Suslov, "Remarks on 105th Anniversary of the birth of V. I. Lenin," *Radio Moscow,* North American Service in English, 23 April 1975; Academician N. Inozemstev, *"Kapitalism 70-kh godov: obostrennye protivorechiy"* ["Capitalism of the Seventies: An Intensification of the Contradictions"], *Pravda,* 20 August 1974, translated in U.S. Air Force, AF/IN, *Soviet Press Selected Translations,* no. 74-10 (1 November 1974), p. 8. Suslov is a Politburo member and Secretary of the Soviet Communist party. Inozemstev is director of the Institute of World Economics and International Relations.

[2]*"Politika yasnaya, uveryennaya"* ["Clear and Confident Politics"], *Izvestiya,* 18 April 1975, broadcast by *Radio Moscow,* North American Service in English, 20 April 1975.

[3]Colonel V. V. Larionov, *"Razryadka naprashennosti i printsipi ravnoy bezopasnosti"* ["The Relaxation of Tension and the Principle of Equal Security"], *Krasnaya Zvezda [Red Star],* 18 July 1974, translated in *Strategic Review,* Winter 1975, p. 106. Colonel Larionov is a leading instructor and theoretician on politico-military affairs at the Armed Forces (Voroshilov) Academy of the General Staff in Moscow, the U.S.S.R.'s highest military school. It functions at approximately the same selection level as the U.S. National War College.

[4]N. D. Turkatenko, *"Vazhnyy etap v razvitii sovetskoamerikanskikh otnosheniyakh"* ["Significant Stage in the Development of Soviet-American Relations"], *SShA: Ekonomika, Politika, Ideologiya [USA: Economics, Politics, Ideology],* no. 1 (1975), p.8.

440

reflecting the political, economic, social, and military growth of the U.S.S.R. and other Socialist countries. Nevertheless, it must be realized that a resumption of the arms race is possible because of the attempts by U.S. military-industrial leaders to undermine détente and create tensions and hotbeds of war throughout the world.[5]

The Soviet Planner Discusses Strategic Nuclear War Doctrines and Soviet Force Development

Recent Strategic Nuclear War Doctrine of the U.S.A. There are noticeable asymmetries between the U.S.S.R. and the U.S.A. with respect to the basis for the development and use of strategic nuclear weapons. In contrast to the dialectical-historical Soviet approach to such matters reflecting the principles of Marxism-Leninism, the U.S. government's policy follows the rigid capitalist, aggressive, military-industrial line. This line calls for furthering the designs of the imperialist camp against the Socialist countries with military means, which can only undermine the spirit of détente.

This narrow approach, as exemplified by statements to the U.S. Congress of Secretary of Defense James Schlesinger and Chairman of the Joint Chiefs of Staff General George Brown, incorporates a long-held desire by the military-industrial circles to preserve certain areas of military-technical superiority over the U.S.S.R.[6] Should these desires form the basis for the development of future U.S. strategic nuclear forces, they would result in the creation of additional weapons. Such an eventuality could threaten détente by undermining the principles of reciprocity and equal security between the two countries, which are based upon mutual respect for sovereignty, noninterference in internal

[5]General-Lt. M. A. Mil'shteyn and Colonel L. S. Semeyko, "The Limitation of Strategic Armamemts: Problems and Perspectives," *USA: Economics, Politics, Ideology* [*SShA: Ekonomika, Politika, Ideologiya*], December 1973. The authors are strategic specialists affiliated with the Institute of the U.S.A. and Canada of the Academy of Sciences in Moscow. *USA* is its house organ. Text of Vladivostok understanding from "Joint Soviet-American Statement on Strategic Arms Limitation," *Survival*, January-February 1975, p. 32. See also essay by Colonel F. Ovsyuk, "Weapon of Aggression and Brigandage: Political Training on Imperialist Aggression," *Znamenonosets* [*The Standard-bearer*], no. 2 (February 1975), translated in U.S. Joint Publications Research Service, *Translations in USSR Military Affairs*, no. 1131 (8 April 1975), p. 54; A. Bovin, "Polozheniye razryadki naprashennosti" ["Facets of Détente"], *Izvestiya*, 6 February 1975, p. 4; condensed translation in *Current Digest of the Soviet Press*, vol. 27, no. 6 (5 March 1975), p. 11; G. Ratiani, "*Mezhdunarodnaya Nedelya: Obozreniye*" ["World Week: Survey"], *Pravda*, 25 May 1975, p. 4.

[6]U.S. Department of Defense, *Annual Report by Secretary of Defense James R. Schlesinger, FY 1976 and Transition* (Washington, D.C.: 5 February 1975) (referred to subsequently as *Schlesinger Report*); U.S. Congress, House, Committee on Armed Services, *United States Military Posture for FY 1976 by Chairman of the Joint Chiefs of Staff Gen. George S. Brown, USAF*, 94th Congress, 1st session, 7 February 1975 (referred to subsequently as *Brown Posture Statement*).

affairs, peaceful competition in economic spheres, and relationships of mutual advantage.[7]

The current U.S. economic situation reflects the contradictions between various groupings of the ruling classes of the capitalist countries, particularly that between industrialists and workers.[8] It is well known that wars and preparations for war are a stimulant to economic activity in the U.S.A. and other imperialist countries. Thus, we take a negative view of the expanding parameters for weapons which may be used by the U.S.A. to threaten the U.S.S.R. and friendly Socialist countries. Such aims have been alluded to by Schlesinger, Brown, Deputy Secretary of Defense William Clements, and the Director of Defense Research and Engineering, Malcolm Currie.[9]

Taken together, these statements of high U.S. government officials reflect a desire by the U.S.A. to retain its lead in certain aspects of strategic rocketry and bomber aviation, particularly in accuracy, restrike, and multiple retargetable warhead (RGCh or MIRV) capabilities. At the same time, the U.S.A. acknowledges the Soviet lead in rocket payload (or "throw weight") capability.[10]

The growth of Soviet strategic rocket and other nuclear forces, and their impact on what the West calls the "strategic balance," continues to form a significant part of the basis for relations between the U.S.S.R. and the U.S.A. The means of waging war are growing both qualitatively and quantitatively.[11] Numerous U.S. spokesmen, such as Clements, consider this an acceptable practice for their country, but hypo-

---

[7]Larionov, *"Razryadka naprashennosti,"* p. 106; L. I. Brezhnev, general secretary of the Central Committee of the CPSU, "In a Friendly Atmosphere," address at Kremlin dinner, 15 October 1974, quoted in *Pravda,* 16 October 1974, pp. 1-2, and translated in *Current Digest of the Soviet Press,* vol. 26, no. 42 (13 November 1974), pp. 1, 20.

[8]B. N. Ponomarev, address to European Communist and Workers Party meeting, Warsaw, 17 October 1974, quoted in *Pravda,* 18 October 1974, p. 4, and translated in *Current Digest of the Soviet Press,* vol. 26, no. 42 (13 November 1974). Ponomarev is a candidate member of the Politburo and secretary of the Central Committee of the CPSU.

[9]*Schlesinger Report,* pp. II-18-57; *Brown Posture Statement,* p. 7; William P. Clements, Jr., deputy secretary of defense, address before the Institute of Electrical and Electronics Engineers, Los Angeles, 6 February 1975, excerpted in *Aviation Week and Space Technology,* 17 February 1975, p. 20; U.S. Congress, House, Committee on Armed Services, *Statement by Dr. Malcolm R. Currie, Director of Defense Research and Engineering,* 94th Congress, 1st session, 21 February 1975, pp. V-1-V-52 (referred to subsequently as *Currie Statement*).

[10]The Soviet term for missile accuracy is *Kvo or Krugovaџr veroyatnaya oshibka,* which is roughly equivalent to the Western term *CEP,* or *Circular Error Probable.* The Soviet term for what is known in the West as a MIRV is *RGCh* or *Razdelyayushchiyesya golovnyye chasti individual'nogo navedeniya.* What is known in the West as "throw weight" refers to the weight of the part of a rocket that lies above the last boost stage. The Soviets calculate throw weight on a slightly different basis than does the West.

[11]Colonel V. V. Larionov, "Arms Limitation and Its Opponents," *Pravda,* 7 April 1974, p. 4, translated in *Current Digest of the Soviet Press,* vol. 26, no. 14 (1 May 1974), p. 3.

critically charge that Soviet improvement programs undermine the strategic balance.[12]

At present, the U.S.A. is proceeding to develop more sophisticated strategic means of warfare, which incorporate new launch techniques, penetration techniques, and quantum improvements in accuracy. While leading Soviet theoreticians correctly admit that there is an enormous distance between intention and reality in the complex spheres of military science and military art, there is also a corollary link between the development of military doctrine and the development of new weapons.[13] The U.S.A. attempts to justify its latest nuclear war doctrine—flexible strategic response—on the grounds that it needs forces that are (1) operationally equal to those of the Soviet armed forces ("essential equivalence"), (2) tactically equal to Soviet forces in crisis ("crisis stability"), and (3) capable of influencing the politico-military behavior of the U.S.S.R. and the North Atlantic Treaty Organization (NATO) countries ("perceived respect").[14]

There is no unanimity in the U.S.A. about these objectives. "Essential equivalence" is a Pentagon-inspired argument for weapons which could maximize suspected U.S. strategic nuclear advantages. But the Department of State under Henry Kissinger and some committees of the Congress favor the term *crisis stability* in order to promote political détente, avoid wars by miscalculation, and prevent nuclear war. Kissinger recently admitted that domestic divisions in the U.S.A. have undermined its alliance system by creating doubts about its willingness to defend Western Europe.[15] In contrast to Kissinger's view, the Department of Defense, reflecting the military-industrial line, favors more provocative, narrow military measures to attain crisis stability.

The third basis of the new U.S. strategic nuclear parameters—that of perceived respect—is apparently contrived simultaneously to overcome increased internal opposition by workers to higher arms spending, to shore up the crumbling imperialist alliance system by assuring the NATO countries that existing and planned U.S. strategic forces can defend them, and to cover up the Vietnam disaster. In a secret briefing, now published, Schlesinger assured a Senate Foreign Relations Subcommittee in September 1974 that "limited response options" and

---

[12]William P. Clements, Jr., address before the American Defense Preparedness Association, Washington, 16 May 1974, reprinted in *National Defense*, July-August 1974.

[13]Larionov, "Arms Limitation," p.3.

[14]See *Schlesinger Report*, pp. II-4, II-8, and II-9.

[15]Henry A. Kissinger, U.S. secretary of state, "US Foreign Policy: Finding Strength through Adversity," address before the American Society of Newspaper Editors, Washington, D.C., U.S. Department of State, *Press Release No. 204*, 17 April 1975, p. 5.

LEWIS ALLEN FRANK

"rapid retargeting" capabilities are now sufficient to eliminate any "doubts about the coupling of U.S. strategic forces with the defense of Western Europe."[16]

If U.S. forces were roughly equal to Soviet strategic forces in terms of payload accuracy, "yield-to-weight" (a measurement of nuclear weapon efficiency) warhead ratios, and systems reliability, the U.S.A., according to a Schlesinger presentation, could selectively wage nuclear war against Soviet forces and destroy hardened military control sites, "soft" undefended cities, and troop concentrations with precision. At the same time, Schlesinger promised that the U.S. population would be suitably evacuated and sheltered against reprisal.[17] Such bellicose plans may anticipate the use of forward-based aircraft, Polaris and Poseidon ballistic rocket-launching submarines, and Sixth Fleet carrier aviation—a clear contradiction between essential equivalence objectives and those of political and military détente. The Pentagon's drive for some kind of "permanent" strategic nuclear advantage over the U.S.S.R. through the adoption of one-sided military definitions of strategic balance amounts to stepping up the arms race.[18]

As presented, the Pentagon's narrowly based strategic nuclear war doctrine promotes the possibility of nuclear war between the imperialist and Socialist spheres by undermining political détente between the U.S.A. and the U.S.S.R. The official "Limited Response Options and Rapid Retargeting" nuclear attack plan, announced by Schlesinger on 10 January 1974, was recognized in leading Soviet commentaries as a spurious attempt to regulate the means of conducting a nuclear war, and could threaten the June 1973 Soviet-U.S. Agreement on the Prevention of Nuclear War.[19] This doctrine rests on the assumption that under conditions of nuclear war, the U.S.A. would be able to retain its nuclear strike capability for the purpose of destroying Soviet rocket complexes and control centers.[20] Such an assumption must not go unchallenged.

The Schlesinger doctrine aroused stormy and continuing controversy in the U.S. Congress and among specialists in the U.S.A.

---

[16]U.S. Congress, Senate, Subcommittee of the Committee on Foreign Relations, *Briefing on Counterforce Attacks*, 93rd Congress, 2nd session, 10 January 1975, p. 44.

[17]*Schlesinger Report*, pp. I-13 and I-14.

[18]Georgii A. Arbatov, "Soviet-American Relations in the Seventies," Vandenberg Lecture at University of Michigan, Ann Arbor, quoted in *SShA: Ekonomika, Politika, Ideologiya*, May 1974. Dr. Arbatov is director of the Institute of the U.S.A. and Canada of the Soviet Academy of Sciences and a vice-chairman of the Soviet-U.S. Institute in Moscow.

[19]Larionov, "Arms Limitation," p.1.

[20]L. Tolkunov, "Serious Turn," *Izvestiya*, 22 June 1974, pp. 3-4, translated in *Current Digest of the Soviet Press*, vol. 26, no. 25 (17 July 1974), p. 4.

Among its opponents are Fred Warner Neal, a former State Department advisor on Soviet affairs, and nuclear scientist Wolfgang Panofsky. Appearing before a House Foreign Affairs Subcommittee in 1974, Neal said that such measures are "highly contradictory to the spirit of détente" and reflect a deeply ingrained "cold war psychology" in the U.S.A. sustained by pressures from many sources.[21] In a similar vein, Panofsky told a Senate Foreign Relations Subcommittee in 1975 that strategic initiatives would be "escalatory."[22] This confusion in the U.S.A. has coincided with a time when the possibilities for avoiding war are strengthened, as the correlation of forces in the world grows more favorable to the U.S.S.R. and the Socialist countries—not just in the military sphere, but also in economic, social, political, and psychological aspects.

Influential U.S. congressmen and senators perceive the defeat of imperialism in South Vietnam as a signal to revamp U.S. foreign policy. Henry Reuss, chairman of the Banking, Currency, and Housing Committee of the U.S. House of Representatives was quoted in the press as saying that the U.S.A. should get its economy "in order at the expense of the military budget" and reduce its foreign bases in Korea, Taiwan, and Italy. Even a Pentagon supporter, Senator John Stennis, argued that it was time for a "new situation in the Pacific" and a more independent role for Japan.[23]

The confusion in the U.S.A. reflects a point recently made by Comrade Marshal Andrei A. Grechko, Politburo member and minister of defense. He said that the question of solving the problems of war and peace no longer solely depends on the actions of imperialist circles. Now the solution can be influenced by the forces of socialism.[24]

The Basis for Qualitative Change in Soviet Strategic Nuclear Forces. The CPSU Central Committee reported to the Twenty-fourth Party

---

[21] Testimony of Professor Fred Warner Neal in U.S. Congress, House, Subcommittee of the Committee on Foreign Affairs, *Détente*, 93rd Congress, 2nd session, 1974, pp. 12, 14 (subsequently cited as *Détente Hearings*).

[22] Testimony of Professor Wolfgang K. H. Panofsky in U.S. Congress, Senate, Hearings before the Subcommittee on Arms Control, International Organizations and Security Agreements of the Committee on Foreign Relations, *Non-Proliferation Issues*, 94th Congress, 1st session, 16 April 1975, p. 12. Ambassador Gerard C. Smith, former delegation chief on arms limitation-reduction (SALT I), similarly disagrees with counterforce notions of Schlesinger in his statement before the same U.S. Senate Subcommittee, 16 April 1975, p. 8.

[23] Interviews with Congressman Henry Reuss and Senator John Stennis in the *Washington Post*, 21 April 1975, p. A4.

[24] Marshal A. A. Grechko, *"Rukovodyaschaya rol' KPSS v stroitelstve armii razvitogo sotsialist'cheskogo obshchestva"* ["The Leading Role of the CPSU in Building the Army of a Developed Socialist Society"] in *Problems of the History of the Communist Party*, May 1974, abridged translation in *Strategic Review*, Winter 1975, p. 89.

Congress that"... to strengthen the Soviet state means to strengthen its armed forces."[25] In this connection, each service must develop its operational art to the highest possible degree. This reinforces the Leninist objective of equality and equal security in international relations, without which there could be no progress on either arms limitation-reduction or other, broader, aspects of international relations.[26] Consequently, it is important to continue the expansion of military-scientific potential in all phases of the revolution in military affairs.[27] The development of military cybernetics is of particular importance for achieving effective automation and force control throughout the chain of command, including the functions of targeting, planning, and weapons selection.[28] The extent of this expansion will help form the basis for resolving complex combat tasks by harnessing computer, inertial guidance, and radio-electronic warfare technologies in order to find such solutions.[29] Indeed, the growing role of science in military construction has been one of the decisive factors in modern warfare since the time of Lenin.[30]

---

[25]*Materialy XXIV S'yezda KPSS* [*Materials of the Twenty-fourth Congress of the CPSU*] (Moscow: Politizdat, 1971), p. 81, cited in introduction to General-Colonel N. A. Lomov, ed., *Nauchno-teknicheskiy progress i revolyutsia v voyennom dele* [*Scientific-Technical Progress and the Revolution in Military Affairs*] (Moscow: Voyenizdat, 1973), translated in U.S. Air Force, *Soviet Military Thought*, no. 3 (Washington, D.C., 1974), p.3.

[26]Larionov, "*Razryadka naprashennosti,*" p. 106.

[27]*The revolution in military affairs* is a Soviet term for the fundamental reorganization of the Soviet armed forces that was brought about by the invention of nuclear weapons, the development of military cybernetics, and the introduction of nuclear missiles and other modern means of combat.

[28]See introduction by General S. M. Shtemenko, first deputy chief of the general staff of the armed forces, in General-Colonel V. V. Druzhinin and Colonel-Engineer D. S. Kontorov, *Ideya, algoritm, resheniye* [*Concept, Algorithm, Decision*] (Moscow: Voyenizdat, 1972), translated in U.S. Air Force, *Soviet Military Thought*, no. 6 (Washington, D.C., 1975), p. 5; also B. Bely et al., *Marxism-Leninism on War and Army*, 1st English language edition (Moscow: Progress Publishers, 1972, reproduced in Washington, D.C.: U.S. Government Printing Office, 1974), pp. 232-33.

[29]These radio-electronic technologies include radar, radio, telemetry, over-the-horizon, infrared, and electronic surveillance (ERO) techniques and methods. In 1975 it was reported in the West that the air defense armed service, PVO-Strany, was the largest military user of automation, with the most sophisticated installations tied to the operation of the Moscow antirocket (PRO) defense system. See Colonel William Scott, "Soviet Aerospace Forces and Doctrine," *Air Force*, March 1975, pp. 37-38. A Western computer expert, Dr. E. Callen, claimed that the U.S.S.R.'s computer systems trailed those of the U.S.A. in language sophistication, time-sharing capability, and interactive programming technique. See testimony in *Détente Hearings*, p. 185.

[30]Colonel V. Bondarenko, "*Sovetskaya nauka i ukrepleniye o oborony strany*" ["Soviet Science and Strengthening of the Defense of the Country"], *Kommunist vooruzhennikyh sil* [*Communist of the Armed Forces*], no. 18 (September 1974), pp. 22-30, translated in U.S. Air Force, AF/IN, *Soviet Press Selected Translations*, no. 75-2 (February 1975), p. 4. Colonel Bondarenko is a leading instructor and writer on military science and is on the faculty of the Lenin Military Political Academy in Moscow. The Lenin Academy is the highest school for political officers and is run by the Main Political Administration. See also

Qualitative change in the strategic means of attack may follow different paths in coming years, with emphasis on various parameters depending on the levels of operational art required for waging war, initiating war, crisis-bargaining, or deterrent purposes. The choices among objectives will in turn be altered by shifts in the correlation of forces over time, and by the growing potential for development, testing, and deployment of decisive strategic means of attack.

Comrade Marshal Grechko has written that the necessary conditions are being created for a new qualitative leap ahead in the development of arms and combat equipment.[31] These qualitative changes can significantly enhance the operational art of controlling and employing our forces in wartime—including a strategic nuclear war—through a variety of means. In his 8 May 1974 address to military academy graduates, Comrade Marshal Viktor G. Kulikov, chief of the general staff of the Soviet armed forces and first deputy minister of defense, stated the six basic force effectiveness parameters subject to the processes of qualitative change. In summary, these are: (1) firepower of weapon systems, (2) striking power of weapon systems, (3) mobility of weapon systems, (4) tactical skills of personnel, (5) political maturity of personnel, and (6) military-scientific training of personnel.[32] Of the above, practical steps to improve firepower, striking power, and mobility are of particular importance for successfully implementing Soviet strategy.

Improvements in Soviet firepower would enhance the strategic means of conducting group nuclear strikes or massed nuclear strikes by long-range ballistic rocket weapons or other weapons against specific objectives. Those means include usable payload, warhead characteristics, destruction techniques (nuclear, high-energy laser, chemical, et cetera), and guidance and control techniques.

Improvements in Soviet striking power would enhance the strategic means of launching group or massed nuclear strikes conducted or assisted by:

(a) Intercontinental ballistic rockets (MBR/BRSN) on alert in the Strategic Rocket Troops (RVSN) and the intercontinental ballistic

---

Colonel V. G. Kozlov's chapter entitled "V. I. Lenin on the Material Prerequisites for the Military Power of the Socialist State" in General-Major A. S. Milovidov and Colonel V. G. Kozlov, *Filosofskoe nasledie V. II Lenina i problemi sovreminnoi voyny* [*The Philosophical Heritage of V. I. Lenin and Problems of Contemporary War*] (Moscow: Voyenizdat, 1972), translated in U.S. Air Force, *Soviet Military Thought*, no. 5 (Washington, D.C., 1975), p. 149.

[31] Grechko, "*Rukovodyaschaya rol'*," p. 93.

[32] General of the Army (now Marshal) V. G. Kulikov, "The Invincible Force of Socialism," *Krasnaya Zvezda*, 9 May 1974, p. 1.

rockets (MBR/BRPS) on board the nuclear rocket-firing submarines of the navy (VMF);

(b) Early-warning, radar-tracking, antibomber, antirocket (PRO) and anticosmic (PKO) defense installations of PVO-Strany;

(c) Heavy bombers of long-range aviation (ADD) units and other armed reconnaissance, antisubmarine, and early warning aircraft or pilotless vehicle units attached to the air force (VVS) or the aviation forces of the navy; and

(d) Military construction complexes, control posts, radio-electronic installations, and cybernetic (computer) systems contributing to survival, command, and retargeting of all forces under attack conditions.[33]

Improvements in mobility would enhance Soviet prelaunch capability for executing group or massed nuclear strikes, including the placement of strategic rockets and other weapons aboard various platforms, such as wheeled, floating, surface effect, rail, or tracked transporter-launchers, nuclear submarines, orbiting space stations, orbiting satellites, or long-endurance air-refuelable (wide-body) aircraft.

Table 1 summarizes Western estimates of the latest models of Soviet strategic-nuclear rockets (having ranges beyond 2,700 kilometers) in strategic rocket troops and naval units as of mid-1975. Table 2 summarizes the kinds of scientific-technical progress required in three areas of qualitative change, firepower, striking power, and mobility, according to our latest estimates.

The Soviet Planner Relates the Military Science of the U.S.S.R. to War Conduct and SALT

The Military-Scientific Basis for New Forms and Methods of Strategic Nuclear War Conduct. The tasks of the Soviet armed forces in nuclear war are determined by the strategy laid down by the CPSU. Table 3 may be used as a guide to possible combat tasks, combat task priorities, and related objectives for strategic nuclear units in the conduct of a nuclear war. This table reflects official military doctrine concerning operations enunciated in 1971 by Comrade Marshal Grechko and recently simulated in the combined global tactical exercise *Ocean-75.*

---

[33]The radio-electronic installations include Electronic Warfare, Electronic Countermeasures, Electronic Counter-countermeasures, nucleonic, sonar, acoustic, Magnetic Anomaly Detection, radar, radio, propagation, and guidance-related facilities.

Table 1

SOVIET STRATEGIC ROCKET LAUNCHERS, 1975

Type	Reentry Vehicles	Throw Weight[a]	Launchers	Total Force of Reentry Vehicles	Total Throw Weight[a]
Strategic Rocket Troops (RVSN)					
SS-7	1	5.0	190	190	950
SS-8	1	5.0	19	19	95
SS-9 Series	1	15.0	280	280	4,200
SS-11 Series	1–3[b]	2.0	962	1,094	1,924
SS-13	1	1.2	60	60	72
SS-17	4[c]	5.0	40	160	200
SS-18	6–8[c]	15.0	30	180–240	450
SS-19	6[c]	7.5	10	60	75
Subtotal Strategic Rocket Troops			1,591	2,043–2,103	7,966
Navy (VMF)					
SS-N-6 Series	1–3[b]	0.7	544[d]	640	381
SS-N-8	1	1.8	156[e]	156	281
Subtotal Navy			700	796	662
Total Force			2,291	2,839–2,899	8,628

[a] In thousands of pounds.

[b] MRV.

[c] MIRV.

[d] Tubes on 34 "Y" type submarines.

[e] Tubes on 13 "D" type submarines.

Note: Early in 1976 the U.S.A. acknowledged the operational status of the single-warhead version of the SS-18 ICBM, while at the same time contending that any Soviet systems previously tested in a MIRV configuration "are presumed to be deployed with MIRVs." Such a presumption is incorporated in this and succeeding tables dealing with numbers of reentry systems accorded the U.S.S.R. by Western sources. See report of Secretary of Defense Donald H. Rumsfeld, in U.S. Congress, Senate, Committee on Armed Services, *Hearings on S. 2965* (FY 1977 Defense Authorization), 94th Congress, 2nd session, part I (Washington, D.C.: U.S. Government Printing Office, 1976), pp. 65-67.

Sources: Reentry vehicles carried by each system constructed from *Brown Posture Statement,* pp. 10, 21. Gross and system throw-weight estimates constructed from International Institute for Strategic Studies, *The Military Balance 1974–1975* (London: I.I.S.S., 1974), pp. 3-4; Edgar Ulsamer, "The Soviet Drive for Aerospace Superiority," *Air Force* (March 1975), p. 45; John W. R. Taylor, "Gallery of Soviet Aerospace Weapons," *Air Force* (March 1975), pp. 72-73; and Clarence A. Robinson, Jr., "SALT Proposals Facing Hurdles," *Aviation Week and Space Technology* (9 December 1974), p. 14. Numbers of launchers and tubes in place or under construction based on *Brown Posture Statement,* pp. 10-18, 28; *The Military Balance 1974–75,* pp. 8-9; Address by Clements, 6 February 1975; and John Newhouse, *Cold Dawn: The Story of SALT* (New York: Holt, Rinehart and Winston, 1973), p. 203.

Table 2
TASKS IN STRENGTHENING SOVIET
STRATEGIC NUCLEAR FORCES, 1975–1985

Category	Keep or Increase Lead over U.S.A.	Stay Abreast or Pass U.S.A.
Firepower		
Payload	X	
Number of MIRVs		X
Yield-to-weight ratios[a]		X
Nonnuclear kill		X
Accuracy		X
Striking Power		
Number of strategic rocket launchers	X	
Ballistic missile and space defense		X
Silo-launch control hardness		X
Command and control systems (including retargeting)		X
Warning and surveillance systems (including radar)		X
Booster efficiency		X
Solid propellant technology		X
Antisubmarine warfare systems		X
Radio-electronic warfare systems		X
Advanced long-range aircraft		X
Mobility		
Wide-body aircraft technology		X
Land-mobile strategic rockets	X	
Ballistic-cruise rocket-launching submarine technology		X
Military space operations—manned	X	
Military space operations—satellite		X
Aerial refueling operations		X

[a] A measurement of nuclear weapons efficiency.

The priorities in Table 3 indicate needs for increased long-range, very accurate weapons that can survive an initial strike, a requirement dictated by the character of modern war. Moreover, any war involving direct engagements between the Soviet Union and the U.S.A. will most likely become an all-out nuclear war, in which events are fast

Table 3

SOVIET OBJECTIVES AGAINST U.S. FORCES IN A NUCLEAR WAR

Targeting Priority	Objective	Combat Tasks
1	Destruction of enemy nuclear attack capability	Early warning sites and antisub ships in U.S.A. and United Kingdom; U.S. TRIAD (ICBM, SLBM, bombers) U.S. national command links, North American Defense Command and SLBM communications U.S. forward-based air carriers U.S.-West German Pershing rocket bases United States Air Force Europe, West German and British strike command nuclear-capable aircraft bases Nuclear rocket sites in People's Republic of China Tanker bases in France British and French ballistic rocket submarines Nuclear storage sites in West Germany
2	Destruction or disruption of enemy troop basing system	U.S. Seventh Army bases and casernes in West Germany Major ports of entry and supply, for example Antwerp, Belgium (port) Wiesbaden, West Germany (base) Hamburg, West Germany (port) Charleston, S.C. (port and base) Dover, Del. (base) Rota, Spain (port) Holy Loch (Scotland), United Kingdom (port) Rhein-Main, West Germany (base) Fayetteville, N.C. (base) Fort Hood, Tex. (base)
3	Destruction of enemy military-industrial support facilities	Tank farms in northeast U.S.A., United Kingdom, Chicago and Los Angeles areas Nuclear power reactors in United Kingdom, Belgium, West Germany Oil refineries in Sicily, Virgin Islands, southeast U.S.A., United Kingdom Thermal-electric generating plants in northeast U.S.A., Pacific coast, midwestern cities

(Continued)

451

Table 3 (continued)

Targeting Priority	Objective	Combat Tasks
4	Destruction or disruption of enemy control of state and other military activities	U.S. capital region, alternate command posts, communications transmitters
5	Destruction and disruption of enemy rear services and transport	U.S. and NATO highway, rail, barge "choke points," nuclear storage sites in U.S.A.

Note: Combat tasks and targeting priorities developed from objectives cited in Marshal A. A. Grechko, "On Guard for Peace and the Building of Communism," 2 December 1971, translated in U.S. Senate, Committee on the Judiciary, *Staff Study*, p. 61.

moving and largely automated.[34] Soviet planning must therefore take these conditions into account as well. . . .

The waging of a successful, decisive, nuclear war requires the development of operational art to fulfill strategic objectives and tactics which can destroy, immobilize, or diminish the aggressor's military-industrial centers and forces. The objective analysis of prestrike and poststrike conditions of a scientific-technical and military-geographical nature are vital to proper force and target planning.

Let us now make some observations about the contemporary nature of strategic problems facing the U.S.A. They consider themselves quite vulnerable to nuclear attack should "deterrence" fail. Their military bases and economic control centers would have to survive a long period of warfare, even after the initial exchange. Defense Secretary Schlesinger said: "The United States has more to lose from a nuclear war than any other country."[35]

It would not be easy for the Soviet Union to defeat the U.S.A. in a nuclear war. We Russians would have to solve many complex problems in force retargeting, direction, and control beyond the initial exchange. Until the third stage of the revolution in military affairs, military cybernetics, is fully implemented, the Soviet armed forces

[34]Marshal I. I. Yakubovskii, first deputy minister of defense and commander-in-chief of the joint armed forces of the Warsaw Pact nations, stated in March 1971 that "the time of entry into combat depends increasingly less on the subjective capabilities of man and is determined more by the functioning of stable and reliable systems." See his "Under the Combat Colors of the Homeland," March 1971, translated in U.S. Congress, Senate, Subcommittee of the Committee on the Judiciary, *Staff Study: Soviet Disarmament Propaganda and the Strange Case of Marshal Grechko,* 93rd Congress, 2nd session (Washington, D.C., 23 April 1974), p. 99.
[35]*Schlesinger Report,* p. II-6.

must continue to have more strategic launchers than the U.S.A. to compensate for any suspected operational deficiencies in new automated systems.

Battlefield and battlespace asymmetries can influence the outcome of a nuclear war between the United States and the Soviet Union. Large land mass may create more problems for the U.S.S.R. than the U.S.A. in command-control and undersea operations. On the other hand, large land mass may permit the U.S.S.R. more favorable opportunities vis-à-vis the U.S.A. for adding ground or air mobility prior to attack.

At present, Soviet forces continue to require thousands of command-control sites on our national territory, linked by duplicate air-, space-, or sea-based command posts and message links. We do so in order to avoid the pitfalls of over-relying on a single communications system, which the enemy may target, and to protect ourselves against possible operational failure of a system under attack conditions.[36] Fortunately, all of our Molniya communication satellite systems, including *Molniya IV* in stationary orbit, are capable of military command and control, and we could definitely add to this capability, as demonstrated by our success in orbiting multiple as well as single payloads.[37]

We face certain problems in securing deep ocean access. The character of such operations in a global setting restricts much of our strategic rocket submarine operations. Should the U.S. Navy be able to target these operations at sea, we would have to develop further techniques to protect our fleet, change its operational art to stress firing from home waters, or reduce operations in favor of additional land- and air-based rockets.

In more specific terms, the U.S.S.R. probably has a two-to-one advantage over the U.S.A. in usable strategic rocket payload.[38] This advantage should be protected. We also have a current advantage of 1.3 to 1 over the U.S.A. in available numbers of strategic launch silos and launch tubes.[39] This can be of great use to us. We are at a disadvantage compared with the U.S.A. in numbers of single, multiple, and RGCh (MIRV) rocket warheads—perhaps by as much as 3.4 to 1, though this difference may be reduced over the next few years by the production of our new land-based rockets with RGCh and range

---

[36] This is realized in the West. See *Brown Posture Statement*, pp. 166-67.

[37] See *Brown Posture Statement*, pp. 168-70.

[38] Estimate based on Western throw-weight data in Table 1, which is consistent with statement of Joint Chiefs of Staff Chairman General Brown in early 1975: "Notwithstanding a 2 to 1 advantage, the USSR appears to be building an even greater advantage. It may be that this superiority will exceed even 3 to 1." See *Brown Posture Statement*, p. 37.

[39] Estimate from Western sources based on launcher-tube numbers in Table 1 and *Brown Posture Statement*, pp. 19-21, 23.

capability exceeding 10,000 kilometers. We are now developing other types of new rockets as well.[40] In addition, the Soviet government is well aware of the tremendous U.S. nuclear stockpile in Europe: Western sources say there are 7,000 nuclear warheads under U.S. custody in NATO's European command, and over 2,000 aircraft, rockets, and howitzers capable of delivering them located in all NATO countries except Luxembourg.[41] In the coming decade we will require the means to equal and surpass the quantity of arms in this vast arsenal if progress in arms limitation and reduction is not forthcoming.

The Relation of Military-Scientific Potential to Progress in Arms Limitation and Reduction. Since the peace program of the Twenty-fourth Party Congress set in motion the progress of events in favor of the Socialist bloc, the U.S.A. and the Soviet Union have concluded a significant series of agreements to reduce the possibility of nuclear war, halt the arms race, and obtain equality and equal security through limitation of strategic offensive and defensive systems. Both sides recently agreed to implement the results of the Vladivostok meeting of 24 November 1974 between Comrade Chairman Brezhnev and President Ford, which will eventually specify mutual quantitative and qualitative limitations on the number of defined strategic systems and RGCh and MIRV systems.[42]

Current Soviet-U.S. relations are relaxed and fairly stable despite outstanding obstacles to furthering the implementation of détente, such as the Middle East question. . . . However favorable this process might be for continuing the relaxation of tensions, actions by military-industrial leaders in the arena of strategic initiatives will always threaten détente and risk starting a new war. Realizing that the proper approach to forces development results in part from an accurate appraisal of such politico-military intentions, we must at all times keep abreast of U.S. decisions that may result from adherence to the strategic initiatives (or Schlesinger) doctrine or a return to cold war revisionism.

So long as these and similar policies are advocated, and so long as imperialist military-industrial circles continue to rule the U.S.A. and

---

[40]Contemporary estimates based on Western sources for reentry vehicle numbers in Table 1, *Military Balance 1974-1975* (see sources note to Table 1), p. 3, and *Brown Posture Statement*, pp. 19-21, 23. These data reveal that by mid-1975 the U.S.A. will have between 7,594 and 9,578 RVs of all types, including 1,650 on Minuteman III, 450 on Minuteman II, 4,960-6,944 on Poseidon (depending on force loading), 480 on Polaris A-3 and 54 on Titan II. Minuteman III and Poseidon are "MIRVed" systems with three and ten to fourteen warheads per rocket, respectively. Polaris A-3 is a three-warhead MGCh (MRV) system. . . .

[41]*Military Balance 1974-1975*, p. 16.
[42]K. Borisov, "Important Stage in SALT Talks," *New Times* (Moscow), no. 12, (March 1975), pp. 18-19.

the Western bloc, there is an inevitable threat of nuclear war. Since the U.S.S.R.'s security can only be guaranteed by our own efforts in the face of still unlimited, though currently thwarted, aims of imperialism, reaction, and chauvinism, there is consequently no upper limit to the preparations which might have to be taken to counter future aggressive ambitions, as well as the kinds of weapons and strategies which the U.S.A. in particular might use in light of its advanced military-industrial base. Because of the shift in the correlation of forces, the imperialist sphere is being reduced, and this reduction may lead to substantial progress in diminishing the parameters of the arms race. Yet there remain those in powerful positions in the U.S.A. and other Western nations who still want another chance at turning back the clock to the days of cold war.

The full flowering of U.S. strategic initiatives—a policy that would call for increased "counterforce" lethality, concealment of new rockets on giant Trident submarines, and new B-1 bombers and rockets recently approved by some committees of the Congress would mean that the U.S. government has not freed itself from the approach to foreign policy advocated by the military-industrial complex. The more so-called strategic initiatives the U.S.A. is allowed under these or similar guises, the more will it obstruct détente and increase the temptation by military-industrial circles to start a new war.

*   *   *

There is likely to be divided opinion in the U.S.A. over the desirability of future arms limitation and reduction measures vis-à-vis the Soviet Union. Such divisions could be advantageous to us. A refusal by the Americans to accede to significant Soviet proposals could be cited as another example of their fanning the arms race, which threatens détente. The internal divisions of the U.S.A. are also beneficial because they operate to reduce the strength and authority of its negotiating teams.[43]

Thus a scientific appreciation of the conditions of waging war, of its class basis, and of the contradictions inherent in Western society forms the foundation for negotiating successfully with the U.S.A. Even if the U.S. government should become more willing than it is now to cooperate with the Soviet Union in implementing military détente along with political détente, the threat of war will not be eliminated so long as military-industrial intrigues and espionage oper-

---

[43]Paul Nitze, a former high U.S. government official, described some of the contradictions and weaknesses of the narrowly based American negotiating approach to arms limitation-reduction since 1969. See his testimony and statement of 2 July 1974 to the U.S. Congress, House, Subcommittee of the Armed Services Committee, *Review of Arms Control and Disarmament Activities*, 93rd Congress, 2nd session, 1974, pp. 57-71.

ations increase tensions. The path of détente and the highly favorable correlation of forces in the world would operate in the direction of dismantling the imperialist NATO, Southeast Asia Treaty Organization (SEATO), and Central Treaty Organization (CENTO) alliances, making it more difficult for the U.S.A. to initiate new wars in the world.

* * *

A U.S. cold war revisionist stance would inevitably transform the arms limitation and reduction process. No longer would Soviet-U.S. discussions focus on aspects of broad-scale arms reduction as they do now. Instead we would be fighting a rear-guard action to hold the U.S.A. to its previous commitments to arms limitation-reduction and lessening the threat of war. Washington's abrogation of the 1972 Trade Agreement, caused by Senator Henry Jackson's attempt at interfering in purely internal Soviet matters regarding Jewish emigration by means of the Jackson-Vanik amendment, has already set a very bad precedent. We realize, of course, that the U.S.A. became committed to arms limitation-reduction only recently, not through a basic change of heart, but because of a fundamental change in the Soviet-U.S. strategic nuclear balance and in the correlation of forces in the world that has made one-sided "damage-limiting" strategies obsolete.[44]

Should the U.S.A. hark back to the days of the cold war, it would seek maximum diplomatic advantage while planning for nuclear war.[45] A cold war revisionist administration would make unacceptable, nonnegotiable demands to try to deprive the Soviet Union of its main deterrent to imperialist escalation, our land-based strategic forces, while trying to conserve for itself forces of greatest advantage and greatest relative invulnerability, especially the almost silent Trident submarines and rockets. But these systems, as powerful as they are, cannot alone carry out the aims of the strategic initiative set. They need much bigger and more accurate boosters in harder or more mobile launchers even to plan such a suicide mission. Hence the clamor for the M-X program, the B-1 bomber, and the air-launched cruise missile (ALCM) heard in U.S. military-industrial circles.

As its military-industrial leaders realize and admit, without these

---

[44] General-Lt. M. A. Mil'shteyn and Colonel L. S. Semeyko, "*Problema nedopustimosti yadernogo konflikta: O novykh podkhodakh v SShA*" ["The Problem of the Inadmissibility of a Nuclear Conflict: On New Approaches in the USA"], *SShA: Ekonomika, Politika, Ideologiya*, no. 11, 1974, pp. 1-12, translated in U.S. Air Force, AF/IN, *Soviet Press Selected Translations*, no. 75-1 (1 January 1975), pp. 11-12.

[45] General-Colonel A. Altunin, chief of civil defense, and deputy minister of defense of the U.S.S.R., "*Idti vpered, dal'she*" ["Move Forward, Onward"], *Voyennyye znaniya* [Military Knowledge] no. 10 (October 1974), pp. 2-3, translated in U.S. Air Force, AF/IN, *Soviet Press Selected Translations*, no. 75-2 (1 February 1975), p. 27.

strategic initiatives weapons, they could not calculate (except on a purely theoretical basis) how they might attempt to defeat the Soviet Union and the Socialist world in another war. With strategic initiatives weapons in the hands of a cold war revisionist administration, however, these same leaders might think the unattainable is attainable, and that theory can be put to the test even if it means U.S. national suicide. Thus, further arms limitation reduction processes will be significantly affected by the force development needed to confront either a cold war revisionist U.S.A. or a détente-minded U.S.A.

For its part, a cold war revisionist U.S.A., bent on stepping up the arms race, increasing tensions, and reestablishing an imaginary nuclear superiority in the world, would attempt to negotiate on the basis of the one-sided equivalence theory, using the Pentagon-invented "throw weight" category to allow the U.S. land-based rocket force to increase its threat to the U.S.S.R. by imposing size limitations on Soviet rockets. The U.S.A. has attempted to achieve this objective by publicizing its trial launchings of an intercontinental rocket from a large transport, and by advertising the various ways in which a rocket can be hidden or moved about. The contradictions of this policy are obvious: it would make it impossible to verify any negotiated limits on MIRV systems and delivery systems by purely national means. By the mid-1980s the U.S.A. will have already deployed more rockets and newer systems, including miniature radars even more difficult to verify than present models.[46] So again, the phony strategic initiatives gambit fails to meet legitimate criteria for arms limitation and reduction matters. Indeed, should the U.S.A. deploy more forces according to this concept, it might well create unprecedented contradictions and insuperable barriers for the arms limitation-reduction process.

Cold war revisionist policies might also lead to related attempts at extracting unilateral advantages in newer areas of weaponry. For example, the U.S.A. might re-deploy a substantial number of its forward-based air and anti-aircraft defense systems back to continental North America, particularly if the processes that are spurring its withdrawal from certain foreign areas increase in momentum and begin to include tactical bases and aircraft carriers. A North American anti-aircraft defense, including F-14 and F-15 aircraft and air-to-air rocket systems combined with improved automation and airborne radar control systems (AWACS), might tempt the escalationists and interventionists once again to think that their country can be made safe from a

---

[46]In a recent address to weapons developers at Los Alamos Scientific Laboratory, Nitze estimated that new "site defense" radars might be only one-twenty-fifth of the volume, less expensive, and more capable than current models now around the U.S. ABM site at Grand Forks. See his "Soviet's Negotiating Style Assayed," *Aviation Week and Space Technology,* 17 February 1975, pp. 40-41.

total counterblow—a reversion to the now discredited damage-limiting strategy.[47] This could amount to abrogation by the U.S.A. of the 1972 ABM Treaty. . . .

In still another area of arms limitation-reduction, land-based silo rockets, certain opportunities may appear. Several hundred of the lighter (1.2—5.0 kilopounds) and older Soviet rockets—appropriate for their time—are even now being replaced by more contemporary, advanced systems. Additional hundreds of these older systems could be retired with no detriment to the Soviet Union if the U.S.A. would do likewise with its comparable systems. Given these conditions of equality, the same principles of equal security could be applied to reduce some of our older aircraft and submarine rockets vis-à-vis those of the U.S.A. Of course, mutual reductions, if furthered in a détente setting, provide equality and equal security consistent with Marxist-Leninist principles. Since the Soviet Union devotes a higher percentage of its national product to science than does the U.S.A., we can be confident that equal reductions accompanied by understandings on qualitative improvement will benefit the Soviet Union.

From every perspective, it is essential for us to continue to retain a firm basis for the development, testing, and ultimate production of the means of warfare applicable to counter aggressive tactics in either détente or cold war revisionist periods in the 1970s and 1980s. Détente provides a firmer basis for Soviet initiatives and peace proposals to blunt aggressive weapons development by the U.S.A. Because of the foresight of our CPSU leaders, we have been able to achieve parity in deployed overall strength. Because of the unity between our defense programs and society as a whole, we have been able to continue to test and develop new systems that may be needed in the future at a rate which the U.S.A. is forced to admit exceeds its own. We therefore have enough systems already in advanced or deployed stages to assure equality and equal security in the arms limitation-reduction process.

The Soviet Planner Projects Future Strategic Nuclear Force Levels of the U.S.S.R.

The Marxist-Leninist principles of the U.S.S.R. preclude those contradictions found in capitalist states between the aims of fighting forces and the aims of the people. The revolution in military affairs has created in the minds of Western bourgeois theoreticians (like Thomas Schelling, Henry Kissinger, Raymond Garthoff, Robert Osgood, Her-

---

[47]Lomov, *Nauchno-tekhnicheskiy progress*, p. 95.

man Kahn, Maxwell Taylor, Klaus Knorr, and Morton Halperin) an illusory contradiction between political-strategic conditions and military-strategic thresholds of weapons use, notwithstanding the theoretical and practical absurdity of trying to regulate the conduct of nuclear war. Notions of a small and painless nuclear skirmish constitute a myth which in no way corresponds to the realities of nuclear war.[48]

While the revolution in military affairs has created new conditions for high rates of response in the course of battle, there is also no lack of unity between our Soviet leaders and those performing combat tasks. Comrade Marshal Kulikov points out that the principle of one-man management—responsibility at all command levels—remains constantly viable, and with the appearance of modern means of destruction this principle increases the determining role of political policy in relation to strategy and troop control. Consequently, the taking of new and improved practical steps in the strengthening of strategic nuclear forces, which our previous analysis shows is dictated by present and possible future policies of the U.S.A., would be consistent from both a political and a military point of view.[49]

Bourgeois ideologues in the West make the mistake of assuming that there will be no victor in a thermonuclear world war.[50] Therefore, successful preparation to fight such a war, as well as successful war conduct, derives ultimately from an understanding of the class nature of warfare, which takes into account the aggressive character of imperialism. The comprehensive appraisal of all aspects of the situation—social, political, and economic, as well as military—is essential in preparing for battle. This "gnoseological" (multibased) maturation approach to the creation of material means of warfare involves the efforts of all the sciences, disciplines, machine-building ministries, and laboratories of the Soviet Union.[51] The revolution in military affairs has intensified this process and has placed unprecedented demands on soldiers and the modern technology at their disposal to assess and respond effectively to the quickly changing character of wars and battlefield situations. As Comrade Marshal Kulikov has indicated, this

---

[48] Mil'shteyn and Semeyko, "*Problema*," p. 16.

[49] Marshal V. I. Kulikov, "*Mozg armii*" ["The Army's Brain"], *Pravda*, 13 November 1974, p. 1, translated in U.S. Air Force, AF/IN, *Soviet Press Selected Translations*, no. 75-1 (1 January 1975), pp. 27, 30.

[50] Colonel V. F. Khalipov, "The Problem of War and Peace in the Present Era," in General-Major A. S. Milovidov and Colonel V. G. Kozlov, eds., *Filosofskeo naslediye V. I. Lenina i problemi sovremennoi voyny* [*The Philosophical Heritage of V. I. Lenin and Problems of Contemporary War*] (Moscow: Voyenizdat, 1972), translated in U.S. Air Force, *Soviet Military Thought*, no. 5 (Washington, D.C., 1974), p. 17. Colonel Khalipov, a leading Soviet theoretician, died in 1975.

[51] Colonel V. Bondarenko, "*Sovetskaya nauka*," p. 6.

LEWIS ALLEN FRANK

process applies even to those situations which may emerge prior to the initial exchange.[52]

The practical steps we have thus far taken in strengthening our armed forces have reduced the threat of war by forcing the U.S.A. to back away in recent years from the more strident aspects of the counterforce policy. This development, however encouraging, has not prevented Messrs. Schlesinger and Currie, and Senators Jackson, Strom Thurmond, James Buckley, Barry Goldwater, Gordon Allott, and their kind from advocating a return to the cold war.[53] One of them (Senator Jackson) became an avowed presidential candidate in the 1976 elections, and others representing the forces of reaction and imperialism (ex-Governor Ronald Reagan, Governor George Wallace) also sought the office. The coming to power of such individuals would be a likely "green light" for strategic initiatives, which in turn would threaten détente and raise the threat of a new war.[54]

The more these ominous developments proceed, the more must our military-scientific potential be devoted to curbing aggressive appetites. The U.S.A., NATO, and other chauvinistic powers squeezed by the economic crisis in the capitalist countries, could once again raise tensions in the world and start new wars in the Middle East, Europe, Asia, and Africa against the interest of Socialist peoples. Any one of these results of imperialist aggression might escalate into a nuclear war that could result in a crushing defeat for the aggressors. In preparing for this situation we have long realized that the counterblow to U.S. aggression might well be all-out in character, as described by Comrade Marshals Grechko and Ivan Yakubovskiy. The evolution of these conditions and the class character of the struggle would, of course, determine the weapons and tactics that would be used by the Soviet Union. A successful course of action in situations that might involve escalation depends on blunting the impact of the aggressor's tactics as early as possible, either by coercing him from escalating, or, in the event escalation arises from the aggression, by defeating his forces swiftly, using all means available.

In responding to the peace program of the Twenty-fourth Party Congress, which correctly interpreted and continues correctly to inter-

---

[52]Kulikov, "Mozg armii," p. 30.

[53]G. A. Trofimenko, "Na strezhnevom napravlenii" ["On a Pivotal Course"] Mirovaya ekonomika i mezhdunarodnyye otnosheniya [World Economy and International Relations], 1 February 1975, p. 3, translated in U.S. Air Force, AF/IN, Soviet Press Selected Translations, no. 75-4 (1 April 1975), p. 3. Trofimenko is a senior researcher at the Institute of the U.S.A. and Canada.

[54]Governor Wallace was quoted in the foreign press as having favored a U.S.-Fascist alliance with Japan and opposed Allied efforts against Nazi Germany in World War II. Washington Post, 8 May 1975, pp. A1, A28.

460

pret the world situation, we have taken practical steps to insure that our strategic nuclear forces can survive even the most powerful of blows and smash the aggressor. In the U.S.S.R. we have taken this condition into account by widely and carefully dispersing our land-based rockets, submarine rockets, and anti-aircraft forces. Should the processes of détente continue, the overall threat of war and even the threat of overt U.S. escalation from aggression to nuclear war could be reduced. Our forces would be able to survive and overcome an attempted surprise attack—even if the U.S.A. should be so foolhardy as to try one.

While the possession of identical weapons and methods of weapons operation may be theoretically attractive, it is impractical, since it constitutes a highly dangerous invitation to aggressors such as the U.S.A. to attempt to destroy our forces in a surprise attack. The peace program of the Twenty-fourth Party Congress correctly anticipated this development at a time when the U.S.A. was still attempting to base its foreign policy on a from-a-position-of-strength policy. In accordance with CPSU directives, our forces were simultaneously designed and implemented in a variety of ways so as to nullify aggressive temptations. No longer do U.S. forces carry out operations with impunity in the world. The dreams of its interventionists have turned out to be nightmares.

In order to defeat a U.S.A. armed with newly powerful strategic-initiatives weapons by the 1980s, it would be necessary for our forces to be able to strike decisively against enemy front-line forces and rear-area reserves at the earliest possible moment. This tactical-operational requirement embodies what Comrade Marshal Tolubko has called "the optimization of prepared proposals and solutions."[55]

In a global war, we would be faced with a single overriding threat: massed nuclear strikes against us by the U.S.A., either separately or in conjunction with its NATO partners or other chauvinistic powers. To thwart the aims of the U.S.A., we will therefore continue to require the military-technical and military-scientific capacity for either group nuclear strikes or massed nuclear strikes by our strategic forces units in conjunction with other units.

Group Nuclear Strikes. Soviet military science defines a group nuclear strike as one that is launched simultaneously by several nuclear weapons under either of two basic tactical conditions:

---

[55] Interview with Marshal V. F. Tolubko, *"Poveliteli raket"* ["Sovereigns of the Rockets"], *Izvestiya,* 19 November 1974, translated in U.S. Air Force, AF/IN, *Soviet Press Selected Translations,* no. 75-1 (1 January 1975), p. 31. Marshal Tolubko is deputy minister of defense and commander-in-chief of the Strategic Rocket Forces.

(1) When the situation will not permit a single nuclear weapon to attain the assigned degree of destruction of an important objective; or

(2) When the situation will not permit a single strike by a more powerful nuclear weapon.[56]

It is not hard to see that practical steps on our part to deliver group nuclear strikes would be needed to deal a convincing blow against the U.S.A., NATO, or other powers should they initiate a massed nuclear strike against the Soviet homeland, a strike that might simultaneously destroy or disable hundreds of our larger land-based rocket weapons and other installations in a short period. To compensate for these losses, our surviving land- and sea-based rocket units as well as available aircraft must be able to bring an equivalent amount of firepower to bear against objectives in the enemy's front and rear areas.

Our increased potential for intercontinental group nuclear strikes is derived from a substantially increased number of nuclear weapons placed in a force which will become more closely balanced between silo- and submarine-based ballistic rockets over the 1975–1985 period. During this period, the nuclear weapons count will increase over three and a half times that of mid-1975—from over 2,800 to well over (a mean figure of) 10,000 by 1985—if military-scientific development proceeds at a moderate pace.

*   *   *

Our successful use of group nuclear strikes to counter U.S. massed nuclear strikes puts a premium on strategic nuclear force survival beyond the strike: each surviving unit of striking power must have a maximum amount of firepower with which to carry out strenuous combat tasks under the most demanding conditions. Hence the almost decisive importance of RGCh [MIRV] systems and booster payload in this type of force. It should also be noted that the U.S.A. can only acquire a massed nuclear strike capability providing the present alignment of forces in the world takes a sharp turn for the worse, including principally a turn to cold war revisionism.

To dissuade the U.S. leaders from producing such means requires that we carefully, skillfully, and continuously make political use of our force-strengthening measures so as to gain the maximum advantage from the arms limitation-reduction process in which the U.S.A. now has a sizable political stake. Favorable developments in the arms

[56]Colonel A. A. Sidorenko, *Nastupleniye* [*The Offensive*] (Moscow: Voyenizdat, 1970), translated in U.S. Air Force, *Soviet Military Thought*, no. 1 (Washington, D.C., 1973), p. 111. Colonel Sidorenko is on the faculty of the Frunze Military Academy in Moscow. This academy is the U.S.S.R.'s advanced school for combined arms warfare instruction of Soviet officers and officers of the Warsaw Pact and other Socialist countries.

limitation-reduction process can help forestall the time when the U.S.A. can acquire such a massed nuclear strike capability. . . .

In this regard, it is equally important to note that the U.S.A. is still highly dependent on a sizable land-based rocket force to carry out a sudden, precise, massed nuclear strike. Thus, our force strengthening tactics, in combination with a favorable arms limitation-reduction atmosphere, could potentially erode the will of the U.S.A. to maintain its Minuteman force at present levels and forestall strategic initiatives in any sphere—land, sea, air, or space. Developments of this kind, involving corresponding reductions . . . would redound to our advantage by diminishing the threat of massed nuclear strikes being launched against us by the U.S.A. . . .

Massed Nuclear Strikes. Soviet military science defines a massed nuclear strike as one that is inflicted simultaneously or within the shortest possible period of time by a large number of nuclear weapons under three basic tactical conditions: (1) when the situation requires the destruction of enemy means of nuclear attack that have been discovered; (2) when the situation requires the inflicting of destruction on the main formations of his troops; and (3) when the situation requires disorganization of the enemy's rear, economy, and troop control.[57]

In such cases, practical steps on our part to effect massed nuclear strikes would be needed to devastate the U.S.A. and its allies so that their armed aggression against the Socialist camp would not escalate into a massed nuclear strike against us. Our strategic forces must therefore be sufficiently reactive, accurate, and powerful to satisfy the above tactical conditions after U.S. aggression has commenced, with the uppermost requirement again being to bring the appropriate amount of firepower to bear in order to achieve a favorable outcome based on CPSU priorities.

*   *   *

Our successful use of massed nuclear strikes to forestall a massed U.S. nuclear strike places a premium on powerful and accurate land, multibased, and land- and air-mobile rocket weapons and aerial platforms to achieve simultaneous as well as successive destruction of objectives. It again should be noted that a U.S. massed nuclear strike capability obtained via strategic initiatives schemes is a virtual military precondition for a reversion to a cold war political stance by the U.S. government.

Consequently, the achievement of a massed nuclear strike capabil-

---

[57]Sidorenko, *Nastupleniye*, p. 111.

ity by the U.S.A. would severely restrict and endanger the processes which are now pressing to supplement political détente with military détente, and would therefore undermine the associated arms limitation-reduction process. . . .

*   *   *

[A force posture capable of massed strikes] has apparent advantages for blunting any U.S. attempts to plan with high confidence a massed nuclear strike. It would make extremely difficult the enemy's attempts at verification, intelligence-gathering, and pretargeting of our forces. [In addition, it] could also give us a firm politico-military basis for furthering limitation and reduction of rocket-launching submarines, intercontinental bombers, and associated air and space defense systems. . . .

Should a cold war revisionist policy prevail in the U.S.A. over the forces of détente, its harmful effect on the arms limitation and reduction negotiations could require the Soviet Union and the Socialist nations to undertake a variety of military, political, social, and economic steps to force the U.S.A. once again to reject the path of war. This means that many things must take place, which we have been able to mention in only a brief fashion. Even the most rabid nuclear escalationists in the U.S.A. and NATO would have to be brought to understand the impossibility of avoiding a crushing blow, even in the initial exchange. Should they initiate war, there must be no "threshold" available to them to initiate a nuclear strike in the course of that war.

Therefore, we must have a sufficient number of powerful, land-based rockets with RGCh systems and long-range aircraft with penetrating rockets to strike the U.S.A. and NATO while they are attempting to escalate an imperialist war caused by U.S. policy. Our reserve weapons must be safe from any attempts by the U.S.A. and NATO to effectuate a group nuclear strike on the homeland by rockets that have survived the initial strike, especially Tridents, or by B-1s or cruise rockets. Even if we are forced to expand our antirocket defense in the face of U.S. provocations, we must expect heavy, though by no means unbearable, casualties. If the population is promptly sheltered during a nuclear attack it will be possible to hold losses to a minimum and to implement evacuation and relocation procedures.[58] Casualties to our Soviet people should be relatively less costly than the amount of destruction that we can inflict on more concentrated U.S. objectives.

---

[58]General-Colonel A. Altunin, *"Vazhniye polozheniye nastavlennie"* ["Important Aspects of Instruction"], *Uchitel'skaya Gazeta* [*Training Gazette*], 24 August 1974, p. 3, translated abstract in *Current Digest of the Soviet Press*, vol. 27, no. 5 (26 February 1975), p. 18.

THE RACE TO CONTROL NUCLEAR ARMS

Paul Doty, Albert Carnesale, and Michael Nacht

The authors of this article contend that the ability of political leaders and institutions to maintain stable deterrence and arms control has been outpaced by technological advances in nuclear weapons. In short, "the race to control strategic arms is being lost."

The SALT process has failed to address itself to a number of important considerations: qualitative improvements in nuclear weapons, the Chinese, French, and British strategic forces, and the theater nuclear forces of the United States and the Soviet Union in Europe. The authors identify four major obstacles to arms reductions under the SALT regime and suggest an alternative approach to the control and reduction of nuclear arsenals. This approach would entail numerical reductions of delivery vehicles, restrictions on their qualitative improvements, and limitation of nonstrategic nuclear systems through negotiations as well as unilateral initiatives of restraint.

As the nuclear age lengthens and the opportunity for viewing it in perspective grows, its essential features seem increasingly related to successive eight-year American presidential administrations. Measures to control nuclear weapons have been seriously considered in each of the first four postwar "octades," and there has been an acceleration in the number of agreements reached—most notably in limiting nuclear tests, slowing nuclear proliferation, restraining the quantitative growth of the Soviet and American nuclear arsenals, and restricting defenses against nuclear weapons.

Yet, as the nuclear age enters its fifth octade, the race to control strategic arms is being lost. Numerous obstacles have arisen to block further progress in the Strategic Arms Limitation Talks (SALT), thereby creating the danger of a new escalation in "vertical" arms proliferation. And the spread of nuclear weapons to other countries—"horizontal" proliferation—appears to have been rekindled, attributed by some to the stagnation of SALT. Moreover, new weapons systems likely to be deployed within the next few years are certain to exacerbate the arms control problem, for the already shaky SALT process appears inadequate to the task of bringing them under control. Clearly, a major change in our approach to arms control is necessary—one that addresses more decisively and more urgently the interrelated problems of vertical and horizontal proliferation.

Source: *Foreign Affairs*, vol. 55, no. 1 (October 1976), pp. 119-32.

The present commitment to joint Soviet-American negotiations to preserve the nuclear balance at progressively lower numerical levels of armaments is wise and prudent, but it is not the only course. If this approach does not produce meaningful limitations and reductions, and if it means the neglect of the growing threat of horizontal proliferation, then it is possible that a reversion to non-negotiated management of nuclear forces and unilateral initiatives offers more hope of restraint than the deceptive pursuit of "arms control" that does not bring control.

II

Each of the four postwar presidential administrations has left its distinctive imprint on the nuclear age. The Roosevelt-Truman years, 1945–1952, the first octade of the nuclear age, comprised the development period of nuclear weaponry, stretching from the first explosion in 1945 to the thousand-fold greater yield of the first thermonuclear device in 1952. At the outset, Secretary of War Henry Stimson saw relations with Russia being "dominated by the atomic bomb" but no agreement was reached on mutual management of the new force. Instead, the cold war became dominant. In 1952, the United Kingdom became the third member of the nuclear club.

The Eisenhower octade, 1953–1960, saw the full flowering of nuclear weapons systems. Both sides developed thermonuclear weapons and built large bomber forces for their delivery. With the United States in the lead, massive retaliation became its official strategic doctrine. Meanwhile, planning shifted to second-strike forces, ballistic missiles were born, and the octade closed with the deployment of the first Polaris submarine. American and Soviet arms control plans became more realistic and showed some convergence, but fell short of agreement. In 1960, France exploded her first atomic bomb.

The Kennedy-Johnson octade, 1961–1968, saw the completion by the United States of a modern nuclear force based on about 2,000 delivery systems consisting of intercontinental ballistic missiles (ICBMs), submarine-launched ballistic missiles (SLBMs) and bombers (mostly B-52s). The Soviet buildup lagged by nearly a decade, finally producing by 1968 about half as many modern delivery vehicles as the United States. Anti-ballistic missile (ABM) systems developed to the point where claims for their practicability were taken seriously, generating concern that second-strike effectiveness might be compromised, and that the underlying premise of deterrence—mutual assured destruction—was jeopardized. The growing radioactive contamination from fallout catalyzed the first substantive Soviet-American arms control agreement, the Limited Test Ban Treaty of 1963. The nuclear club expanded to include China, and the U.S. entrapment in Vietnam showed vividly how impotent nuclear weapons could be. Interest in a worldwide effort to prevent the spread of nuclear weaponry grew and became more focused throughout the 1960s, culminating in the signing of the Nonproliferation Treaty (NPT) in mid-1968. Despite the intensity of the Vietnam War, serious approaches to arms control, stimulated by the pressures of ABM developments and growing assurances on verification promised by reconnaissance satellites, pyramided in the summer of 1968 only to be disassembled in August by the Soviet invasion of Czechoslovakia.

This brings us to the fourth octade, which is now nearing its end. During this period, nuclear arms control has for the first time become a central focus of Soviet-American relations; yet its progress has been disappointing, its value increasingly questioned, and its future, and the ability of the superpowers to restrain proliferation, in doubt. If this central focus is to be marked by failure, what then is to become of the overall relationship? While the fundamental causes of this condition surely derive from various sectors of the unique Soviet-American experience, it is important to focus on those sources of difficulty inherent in the arms control enterprise itself in order to suggest goals and measures appropriate to the nascent fifth octade.

III

The Strategic Arms Limitation Talks have served throughout the Nixon-Ford octade as the primary forum for negotiation of limits on American and Soviet strategic weapons systems. As a result of SALT I, the two parties signed in May 1972 and ratified six months later the Treaty on the Limitation of Anti-Ballistic Missile Systems and the Interim Agreement on Strategic Offensive Arms. The ABM Treaty, with its protocol of July 1974, prohibits either party from deploying ABM systems outside of one small area, while the Interim Agreement limits the numbers of launchers for ICBMs and SLBMs. Unlike the ABM Treaty, which is of unlimited duration, the Interim Agreement is scheduled to expire in October 1977. Guidelines established at Vladivostok in November 1974 would, if converted into a formal SALT II treaty, take the place of the Interim Agreement. These guidelines call for a limit of 2,400 on the total number of strategic delivery vehicles—ICBMs, SLBMs, and heavy bombers—each side could deploy through 1985, as well as a ceiling of 1,320 on the aggregate number of ICBMs and SLBMs which could be equipped with multiple independently targetable reentry vehicles (MIRVs).

Further progress toward limiting the testing of nuclear weapons has also been accomplished. The Threshold Test Ban Treaty signed in July 1974 would limit the yield of underground tests of nuclear weapons to 150 kilotons (KT). (The Limited Test Ban Treaty of 1963 prohibited all nuclear tests in the atmosphere, in outer space, and underwater, but did not restrict tests underground.) In May 1976, the United States and the Soviet Union signed a companion treaty on underground nuclear explosives for peaceful purposes, which would limit to 150 KT the yield of any individual peaceful nuclear explosion (PNE) and to 1,500 KT the combined yield of any group of PNEs detonated in rapid succession. Special verification procedures, including on-site observers, are provided for the group explosions and for some individual explosions over 100 KT. The Threshold Test Ban Treaty and the treaty on PNEs have not yet been ratified: some opposition is expected on the grounds that the 150 KT limit is too high and that the agreements would "legitimize" the PNE path to nuclear proliferation. (India justified her May 1974 nuclear explosion by calling it a PNE.)

Measured by diplomatic activity, numbers of agreements, and the extent of national armaments affected, the Nixon-Ford era undoubtedly represents a profound shift from the episodic contacts of earlier years to an acceptance by each side that its national interest is served by continuing mutual efforts to limit nuclear weaponry. The issue, however, is not whether serious problems have received serious attention in a sustained and comprehensive manner—they have—but that the rate at which limitations are being imposed, even assuming a successful conclusion to SALT II, falls far short of the rate at which the forces are being improved. The race to control strategic arms is being lost.

The accomplishments of SALT to date, including the Vladivostok guidelines, will leave the Soviet and American strategic forces at extraordinarily high levels through 1985. Paradoxically, the limit of 2,400 strategic delivery vehicles agreed to at Vladivostok is not very different from the total number of delivery vehicles in the U.S. arsenal in the early 1950s, before the age of intercontinental ballistic missiles, when the strategic inventory was comprised solely of propeller-driven bombers! But the number of deliverable warheads has increased dramatically and continues to do so, with both superpowers likely to pass the 10,000 mark by the end of the decade.

What is and is not included in SALT remains a problem. The Chinese, French and British forces are excluded from limitation, and the Soviets, viewing these as potential threats, cite them as justification for a Soviet nuclear force greater than that of the United States. On the other hand, the Americans insist that their forward-based systems, including fighter bombers based in England, on the European continent, and on aircraft carriers are theater forces and should be excluded from consideration in SALT, despite the fact that they can carry out nuclear attacks on the Soviet Union, at least on one-way missions. A recently developed Soviet bomber, known in the West as the Backfire, presents a comparable problem, and hundreds of intermediate range ballistic missiles in the Soviet Union targeted on Western Europe—and now being MIRVed—have been left totally untouched by negotiations.

The listing here of what is not covered by the SALT agreements and the Vladivostok guidelines suggests that if strategic arms are to be brought under control, the achievements of the Nixon-Ford era can only be considered the essential stage-setting for what must follow.

IV

Considering the comprehensiveness of approach and the continuity of effort one must ask why it took seven years of SALT to reach even this point. Had this been accomplished in half the time there would have been ample opportunity to grapple with the problems of real control —reductions, restraints on improvements and new systems, improved command and control arrangements, and limitations on weapons systems of intermediate range. Of course, the 1973 war in the Middle East and its aftermath, as well as Watergate, were unusually disruptive diversions. But the real impediments to progress in SALT lie deeper. In retrospect, four obstacles stand out.

The first obstacle has been the mismatch in strategic conceptions of the two sides. When one side may see an advantage—even a mutual advantage—in proceeding with some arms control measure, the other side may not, and over time each side may reverse its position and remain out of phase with the other (as occurred in the negotiations leading to the Limited Test Ban Treaty and the ABM Treaty). A coincidence of some perceived interests is a prerequisite for any meaningful agreement. It is a function of diplomacy to see that opportunities are identified and brought to the attention of the other side.

It is likely that each side bases its weapons requirements on two strategic conceptions: that of maintaining secure second-strike forces and that of maintaining a nuclear war-fighting capability. The acceptance of a virtual ban on ABM systems at SALT I implies that both sides accepted the view that the assured destruction of the attacker is the primary deterrent against an attack; however, this stability is threatened if either side perceives that a major portion of its deterrent force may be vulnerable. Hence, the development of high accuracy, reliable, counterforce missiles and their deployment in large numbers are destabilizing. A major requirement of future SALT agreements should be the removal of this threat.

Both sides consider that strategic weapons are also needed for use against fixed targets of military value other than strategic forces. This targeting doctrine justifies the development of high accuracy weapons, but it is precisely this development that can threaten the stability of second-strike forces. Moreover, since target lists can be generated almost without limit, the numbers of warheads required can be inflated to very high levels. Thus, the superpowers must find sufficient common ground in their strategic doctrines to justify diminishing requirements for nuclear weapons.

The second obstacle to further progress in SALT is the difference between Soviet and American perceptions of strategic parity. A decade ago it was obvious that the United States had a considerably superior nuclear capability. It was not so obvious that this brought much advantage, because the Soviet forces were capable of inflicting unacceptable damage on the United States in a retaliatory attack. In the decade that followed, the Soviets have matched approximately our level of strategic delivery vehicles. Indeed, the buildup has been sufficiently aggressive to indicate that they will not stop at parity unless restrained by SALT agreements.

Nevertheless, that the preservation of parity, or essential equivalence, must be a central aim of SALT is unquestioned. But unfortunately, the virtue of parity preservation as a final goal does not ensure its usefulness at every step in the negotiating process.

How is it to be decided that a certain proposal for limiting the strategic forces of both sides meets the criteria of equality—or rough equality? One approach would be to ascertain whether panels of experts on each side would reach the same consensus that the military capabilities of the two forces were approximately the same. Considering only static indicators of weapons systems performance, such a judgment could be made despite the many asymmetries involved. But would this judgment be meaningful? Probably not, for most informed analysts would argue that it is the ability of the weapons to perform important missions that is decisive, not the numbers, placement and characteristics of the hardware itself.

Yet it would hardly be possible to reach a consensus on what missions are to be chosen, on the criteria by which success is to be measured, and on other elements of the scenarios that are relevant (such as effectiveness of command and control, and likely actions and reactions of the adversary). Thus, the search for a test of parity flounders in the complexities and uncertainties of war-gaming. It would seem more prudent to admit that parity can be claimed to exist only within rather wide bounds and that many changes are possible within the bounded area without upsetting the overall judgment of parity. The important consequence of such an approach is that the asymmetric forces of the two sides can be subjected to symmetric constraints while parity is maintained.

The third obstacle to arms control is the view widely held on both sides that the effectiveness of nuclear weapons in actual use would be roughly proportional to their megatonnage or numbers. This is surely not the case. In an exchange against urban-industrial complexes, the delivery of a few hundred low-yield weapons would destroy so much of the target areas on both sides that additional weapons would be of little effect. And a credible war-fighting exchange might involve tens, hundreds, or even a few thousand warheads. Because individual warheads in a given missile can now be directed to any of a number of different targets by simple adjustments prior to firing, deliverable warheads in excess of a few thousand are largely superfluous even though the list of possible targets may be much larger. In all cases, then, military utility is not proportional to the number of warheads but reaches a plateau beyond which further increases in the number of warheads provide virtually no increase in military effectiveness. Therefore, experimentation with mutual reductions and restraints involves much less risk than is generally alleged.

The fourth and perhaps most decisive obstacle to bringing strategic weapons under control lies in the profound differences in cultural attitudes and military traditions of the United States and the Soviet Union. In any negotiated schedule of reductions and restraints both sides would naturally attempt to preserve forces considered most vital, maintain certain war-fighting options, retain military postures thought capable of yielding political advantage, and keep open the possibility of introducing new weaponry. However, the culture and tradition of each side strongly influence its patterns of force structure and modernization, making difficult the adoption of common limits and reductions.

Most striking is the contrasting emphasis placed on numbers and new technology by the two powers. Despite much progress the Soviet Union continues to lag technologically and has had its attitudes molded by a long heritage of inferiority in technological innovation. In its wars its survival has been due largely to numbers—numbers of weapons or numbers of men. Because numbers have saved it in the past, it still gives priority to numbers in seeking security and in projecting political power. With few exceptions, the traditions of the United States give priority to technological innovation and quality of weaponry in order to achieve the same ends. It is not surprising, therefore, that even in a state of parity the United States seeks to maintain an image of strength by continuing to innovate and introduce sophisticated weaponry, while the Soviet Union relies on the maximization of numbers and sizes to project its power image.

To cope with this divergence of national outlooks it is, of course, essential to deal with the two proclivities together: to negotiate reductions in numbers, and perhaps in sizes and ranges, together with restraints that limit the rate of improvement and the rate of introduction of new systems.

V

The approach to overcoming these four obstacles which has been attempted repeatedly in the past seven years is to extend the time allotted to negotiations. Experience demonstrates, however, that this does not work. The dynamics of the arms competition will not be stilled. The rates of improvements of old systems and development of new ones set a pace that negotiations have not been able to match, and that threatens to overwhelm the modest repertoire of verification measures that makes negotiated arms control possible. (Nuclear-armed cruise missiles illustrate this latter point.) Consequently, the ultimate challenge to arms control now confronts the Soviets and the United States. Either ways must be found to cope with the obstacles and negotiate comprehensive agreements within a very few years, a period considerably shorter than the development time of major improvements and new systems, or the whole process seems destined to become obsolete and futile.

New weapons systems already on the horizon will only complicate the arms control problem further. Soviet systems include a new submarine designed to carry 16 missiles of 5,000-mile range; a new missile, the SS-20, that may attain intercontinental range and be fired from mobile launchers; and the Backfire bomber, that may or may not be considered as strategic. Emerging U.S. systems include a new larger missile designed for mobile land and air basing, the MX; a new strategic bomber, the B-1; and a new submarine, the Trident, with 24 missiles, initially of 4,600-mile range. Both sides are developing long-range cruise missiles, and recent developments increase the likelihood that space-based laser weapons may lead to a new generation of strategic weapons.

It is under this pressure of a new generation of weapons systems and the approaching termination of the Interim Agreement in October 1977 that the United States and the Soviet Union must decide whether or not to commit themselves to an accelerated negotiation of arms control agreements. Failure to step up the pace of negotiations, and continuance at the slow rate of the Nixon-Ford era, mean not attaining the rate necessary to experience a turning down in the growth of strategic capabilities. If this is not attained and its benefits tested, the justification for the whole enterprise comes into question.

Moreover, superpower arms control is, of course, linked to the problem of "horizontal" nuclear proliferation—a problem which has been exacerbated by the global rush to nuclear energy following the 1973 oil embargo. The lack of progress at SALT is used as a rationale, sincerely or otherwise, by spokesmen in non-nuclear states who advocate the acquisition of an independent nuclear capability. Nuclear proliferation, if it continues unabated, will produce substantial pressures within the United States and the Soviet Union to modify or abrogate the ABM Treaty and to deploy at least "thin" anti-ballistic missile systems to defend themselves against nuclear attacks by third countries. Thus, progress toward the goal of controlling vertical proliferation reinforces efforts to control horizontal proliferation, and vice versa. Similarly, a lack of progress in one area undermines efforts in the other. Both challenges must be met if either goal is to be achieved.

VI

What then is to be done? Policies to be adopted during the next octade must necessarily support the dual objectives of placing meaningful controls on the Soviet and American nuclear arsenals and minimizing the proliferation of nuclear weapons to other states.

The most immediate problem lies in converting the Vladivostok Accord into a longer term SALT II treaty. This conversion apparently has been delayed for well over a year by disagreement over the manner in which strategic cruise missiles and the Soviet Backfire bomber are to be treated. Because constraints on the cruise missiles are sought by the U.S.S.R. while constraints on the Backfire are sought by the United States, these weapons systems have become linked in the negotiating process. But there is no logical connection in military terms between the two systems; termination of the stalemate will require a purely political compromise. The October 1977 expiration date of the Interim Agreement heightens the urgency of resolving this deadlock.

From an American perspective, an agreement should inhibit the capability of the Soviet Backfire force to attack the United States. This can be achieved if a SALT II treaty prohibits both the deployment of tanker aircraft for in-flight refueling of the Backfire and the deployment of Backfire at Arctic and other forward bases. Such an agreement would, for all practical purposes, limit the Backfire to its designed role as a theater weapons system, eliminating the need for it to be classified as a strategic weapon in SALT II. Moreover, when SALT turns to negotiating controls on non-central systems, i.e., those of less than intercontinental range, the Backfire will naturally become a candidate for limitations.

Because older generation cruise missiles of short range already have been deployed, it is unrealistic to expect that a complete ban on cruise missiles can be achieved. But the extraordinary potential flexibility of new cruise missiles to perform strategic and tactical missions, to be launched from a variety of land-, sea- and air-based platforms, and to be deployed in large and unverifiable numbers, is such that only negotiated limitations promise to inhibit their wide-scale deployment. A preferred formula would be (a) to ban the testing and deployment of cruise missiles with ranges greater than 2,500 kilometers, and (b) to prohibit the deployment of cruise missiles with ranges between 600 kilometers and 2,500 kilometers on platforms other than manned strategic bombers, counting against the 1,320 MIRVed launcher limit those strategic bombers on which cruise missiles were deployed. (There would be no limits on the deployment of cruise missiles having ranges less than 600 kilometers.) Because short-range attack missiles (SRAMs) have better payload capabilities than do cruise missiles, it is unlikely that, under such an arrangement, large numbers of cruise missile-equipped strategic bombers would be deployed. Such limitations on the deployment of cruise missiles in the strategic mode would retard their development and inhibit the spread of this technology to other nations, thereby helping to prevent the proliferation of a strategic weapons capability to many other states. While it is true that the verification procedures presently available cannot guarantee that all violations would be detected, a combination of testing and development limitations is sufficient to ensure that any undetected violations could not be great enough to be of military significance.

Following the completion of a SALT II agreement, nuclear arms control should be pursued along five fronts: reductions in strategic delivery vehicles, qualitative constraints, limitations on non-central strategic systems, unilateral initiatives, and nonproliferation measures.

As argued earlier, numerical reductions and limits on qualitative improvements must proceed together. The most attractive approach is that of phased reductions—perhaps as much as ten percent of the remaining number of strategic delivery vehicles each year for ten years, with freedom to mix among systems. This would reduce the permitted number of vehicles from 2,400 initially to 836 at the end of ten years. A similar reduction formula should be imposed on MIRVed vehicles, thus reducing that ceiling from 1,320 to 460. This step, perhaps more than any other, would demonstrate the seriousness of Soviet and American arms control policy and be conducive to stemming the tide of nuclear proliferation.

Qualitative constraints on new systems and on the improvement of existing systems are also essential if the competition in strategic arms is to be halted. A principal means of decreasing the likelihood of nuclear weapons use, particularly in a first strike, is to reduce the confidence which political leaders and military staffs have in the performance capabilities of the delivery vehicles carrying these weapons. These confidence levels can be reduced by imposing graduated limitations on the flight tests of strategic delivery vehicles. Given the first-strike threat posed by highly accurate land-based ICBMs, a negotiated limitation on the frequency of full-range ICBM flight tests is especially worth achieving. The available verification techniques are sufficient to provide substantial confidence that violations would be detected.

Limiting the rate at which major new strategic weapons systems could be deployed to one every five years, for example, would be an additional qualitative constraint of significant value. Though the problems inherent in negotiating a mutually acceptable definition of "major new systems" would be sizable, they should not be insoluble. If such an agreement were reached, the pace of weapons system modernization could be seriously slowed, and the element of surprise in strategic deployments would be greatly reduced. Qualitative restraints inevitably restrain technological developments, but they do not constrain all technologies. Development of those technologies which promise greater stability or improved verification should be permitted under agreements and should have priority. Under these constraints, the research and development process itself would bear a heavier burden than otherwise, since only a few, rather than many, of the systems developed could be carried through the deployment stage.

Related to this constraint on new systems and applicable to existing systems as well is the matter of deployment schedules. Often it is the uncertainty aroused by the pace of deployment, rather than the qualitative attributes of particular systems being deployed, which is the source of concern. This uncertainty can be alleviated by the establishment of pre-announced deployment schedules, perhaps on a yearly basis, which would map out the rate at which specific kinds of delivery vehicles would enter and leave the strategic forces. These schedules, by adding a highly desirable element of predictability, would help reduce the reliance on "worst case" assumptions in the force planning activities of both nations.

Non-central systems—those nuclear-capable delivery vehicles other than ICBMs, SLBMs, and strategic bombers—should be added to the agenda of nuclear arms control negotiations. Reaching agreement on limitations and reduction in this area will be extraordinarily difficult because of the multiplicity of systems involved (e.g., medium-range and intermediate-range missiles, land- and sea-based tactical aircraft), because of geographical asymmetries between the superpowers, because alliance considerations may require multilateral rather than bilateral negotiations, and because of verification problems. But if both nations are serious about nuclear arms control and seek to block potential channels for redirection of the arms competition, it would be logical and desirable to pursue such negotiations.

Inasmuch as future negotiations will encounter difficulties and delays, it is useful to consider a separate, parallel counterpoise: reciprocal unilateral initiatives. The United States should be prepared to undertake one or several initiatives in restraint for a limited period of time, proposing that they would be continued if matched by comparable Soviet restraints. This posture would demonstrate that nuclear arms limitations are a significant element in American foreign policy, would support the arguments in non-nuclear states against "going nuclear," and would apply pressure on the other nuclear powers, particularly the Soviet Union, to exercise similar restraint. It is time that the strategy of reciprocal unilateral restraint be activated in American arms control policy.

Exercising prudence in the discussion of nuclear weapons policies is one relatively simple unilateral action which can contribute substantially to the goals of arms control. Regardless of the degree of success achieved in halting vertical and horizontal proliferation, it is crucial that the use of nuclear weapons be inhibited and, in the event of their use, that further use be halted as rapidly as possible. To discourage initial use, the firebreak between conventional and nuclear weapons must be preserved and indeed reinforced. This can be achieved in part by adopting a declaratory policy in which the possibility of using nuclear weapons is raised only by the President and is treated invariably with the awe it deserves. A balance should be struck in which allies are reassured of the strength of American security guaranties, including the use of nuclear weapons, without conveying in a cavalier fashion the notion that limited nuclear war is a readily feasible option.

Finally, stemming the tide of nuclear proliferation is a challenge which requires aggressive and imaginative action. For of all the elements that can contribute to a less stable world, that of horizontal nuclear proliferation is perhaps the most threatening, and at the same time, the most diplomatically demanding. In concert with other nations, the United States could do much to slow proliferation and to make that which does occur less threatening. The first step is to terminate the testing of nuclear weapons worldwide. With the United States and Soviet Union so far in advance of other states, they could best take the initiative by joining in an agreement not to test for at least five years, and by inviting all other nations to join. At the end of five years the agreement would be extended unless continued adherence somehow threatened the vital interests of the parties.

If handled with diplomatic skill, such an agreement would, in time, apply pressure on France, China and India to halt their testing programs. On balance, the contribution to nonproliferation, coupled with the knowledge that testing could be resumed in short order if deemed necessary, far outweigh the often-cited disadvantages of such an agreement (e.g., slowing American development of advanced weapons, reducing the reliability of these weapons, weakening the guard against technological breakthroughs by potential adversaries, and accelerating the flow of highly skilled manpower away from weapons research and development work).

A number of additional measures could also be part of the orchestration of an aggressive stance to stem the spread of nuclear weapons. On a case-by-case basis, the United States should apply unilaterally or, where possible, in concert with other nuclear powers, the wide range of incentives and disincentives at its disposal to prevent threshold countries from exercising their nuclear option. Such actions, of course, should not contravene existing treaties or guaranties of reactor fuel supplies, but renewals of alliance commitments and future guaranties of fuel supplies should be contingent upon adherence to nonproliferation policies.

Security guaranties and pledges to non-nuclear states can also play vital roles. Guaranties provided by the superpowers through alliance systems have undoubtedly served to diminish the incentive for client-states to develop separate nuclear capabilities—while also constraining their ability to do so. The recently demonstrated ability of the United States to dissuade South Korea from purchasing a nuclear fuel-reprocessing plant from France illustrates that political leverage within alliance structures can be an effective tool to inhibit proliferation; the threat to withdraw security guaranties can be as powerful in this context as the guaranties themselves.

But pledges not to use nuclear weapons against non-nuclear-weapons states should be viewed with caution. There is a danger that such pledges could undermine the coherence of alliances. For example, the credibility of the NATO alliance structure and American security guaranties to South Korea rests in large measure on the continued deployment of tactical nuclear weapons in Western Europe and on the Korean peninsula. These weapons serve an important role in the "tripwire" strategy of nuclear deterrence. Should the United States make a no-use pledge generally or even in a regional context, it would substantially diminish German and South Korean confidence in the credibility of American security guaranties and, ironically, add to the pressures in both of these states for development of independent nuclear capabilities. The kind of no-use pledge that might advance the cause of nonproliferation, while requiring the least modification of existing alliance commitments, is that in which nuclear-weapons states pledge not to use nuclear arms against any non-nuclear-weapon party to the NPT unless the non-nuclear-weapons state is engaged in armed aggression in concert with a nuclear-weapons state. But if the United States must choose between maintaining strong alliance structures and issuing no-use pledges, the former choice is preferable.

These suggested measures to rescue arms control from a marginal role and to direct it toward reducing the strategic nuclear capabilities of the superpowers and decisively slowing the spread of nuclear weapons are complex and demanding. It cannot be otherwise. This contrasts with the much simpler arms control prescriptions of two decades ago, when nuclear weaponry was itself simple, albeit revolutionary. Twenty years of the most intensive technological development the world has ever seen, at a cost of more than half a trillion dollars, have made the difference. To control the products of this effort cannot be simple, elegant, or easy; at best it will be complex, messy, and unbearably difficult. But in a world in which the two superpowers are just learning to control their competitive impulses while their nuclear arsenals continue to grow, and the number of independent fingers on nuclear triggers threatens soon to increase beyond manageable bounds, the alternative to nuclear arms control is simply unacceptable.

TECHNICAL INNOVATION AND ARMS CONTROL

Harry G. Gelber*

Recent experience in the negotiations to limit strategic arms has shown that a critical feature of any future SALT agreement will be the control of qualitative aspects of weapon systems. In this article, Harry G. Gelber examines the military research and development process as a "major area of strategic competition" between the United States and the Soviet Union.

The increasing complexity and sophistication of nuclear weapons, together with the rapid pace of scientific discovery, have served to broaden

Source: *World Politics*, vol. 26, no. 4 (July 1974), pp. 509-541.

* I am greatly indebted to Yale University and Nuffield College, Oxford, where most of the work on this paper was done. I am especially grateful to Peter A. Busch, Raymond D. Duvall, Charles E. Lindblom, Merton J. Peck, Derek de Solla Price, Bruce M. Russett, Aubrey Silberston, and Raymond Vernon who offered helpful comments on earlier drafts. Any remaining errors and omissions are, of course, my own.

traditional concepts of national power and the manner in which they are factored into assessments of the strategic balance. Because technical innovation is incremental in nature and its implications for strategy and arms control often unpredictable, Gelber believes the major challenge for SALT lies in finding ways whereby political leadership can provide more precise control over the direction of military research and development. After examining various proposals for restraining qualitative improvements of strategic arms, and the advantages and disadvantages of each approach, the author concludes that whatever method is adopted should not impair technological advances which actually further the prospects for arms control.

The Soviet-American strategic arms limitation discussions and agreements have been widely welcomed not only as important steps toward tighter arms control but as a symbol of the entire process of East-West détente. For the first time since 1945, the two superpowers have shown themselves willing to put agreed limitations on their central strategic armaments. The SALT I talks imposed rough numerical ceilings on deployment. One of the major difficulties in the attempt to extend these limitations in SALT II is the formulation of qualitative restraints. Each side is under pressure to create improved weapons systems. Each is concerned lest the other should achieve a breakthrough which would render its own systems ineffectual. Each needs to hedge against the possibility that the other might design around any particular set of arms control arrangements. In this paper I will examine the desire for innovation and the difficulties of control, and suggest a general framework within which the question of limitations might be further examined. In the first part, I will discuss the meaning of innovation and the ways in which it is organized and promoted. In the second, the reasons are examined why the two great powers seek advantages over each other in the area of R & D [research and development]. Finally, I will look at some of the difficulties of achieving restraint by agreement and under verifiable conditions.

I. R & D and Technical Advance

The innovatory process covers a very wide spectrum of activities. I propose to try to discuss it in terms of the following classification: discovery, invention, innovation, development, technological drift, and testing. By discovery I mean the discovery of new ideas about the physical universe or its organizing principles. By invention I mean the creation of new things, which may or may not be based on new discoveries. By innovation, I mean the creation of new systems from previous inventions[1] or known components, or improvements in products or processes whose essential characteristics are known and remain unchanged. There is an obvious but probably insoluble ambiguity about the point at which improvements of detail begin to change the essential characteristics of the product. Development covers the process of engineering refinement from laboratory development to the final elaborations that precede and accompany testing. Technological drift is the useful term, coined by J. P. Ruina, to denote processes which do not, or need not, result from the decisions of higher authority or the formal R & D machinery at all. It involves minor improvements in systems and components, to cope with minor snags which have appeared during development, marketing, deployment, or servicing, but whose cumulative impact can amount to or make possible substantial system changes.

These or any other divisions are of course an arbitrary way of dividing what is in reality a continuum. And although discovery at one end of the spectrum and technological drift at the other are relatively clear-cut notions, invention, development, and especially innovation involve two quite separate kinds of change. One is a change or set of changes in policy, doctrine, or strategy for production or use. Changes here may or may not involve changes in the materials or equipment available. They may concern new processes, or new ways of organizing old processes, or new ways of using available items of hardware, or a combination of them. The other is a change in systems or products which might involve inventions which in turn may or may not be based on new discoveries, or innovations which may or may not incorporate new inventions.

These difficulties in defining types of change are naturally reflected in the categorization of activities designed to achieve them. A rough division between basic research, applied research, and development seems to be accepted both in the literature and in budgetary practice.[2] But this, too, has its difficulties. An attempt to achieve an invention may call for an effort to develop the results of some previous innovation; a development process may be held up pending the attempt to invent or innovate among subsystems or components.

---

[1] Edwin Mansfield, *The Economics of Technological Change* (London 1969), 131.

[2] The definitions used in the literature differ in detail, but this kind of division seems widely accepted. The U.S. National Science Foundation distinguishes between basic research, or original investigations for the advancement of scientific knowledge without specific commercial objectives; applied research, or investigations to try to discover new scientific knowledge with specific commercial objectives in mind; and development, or the translation of research findings into products or processes. See also John Jewkes,

Perception and Causes of Discovery, Invention, and Innovation. There are certain conceptual difficulties about trying to decide what "discovery," "invention," and "change" are, how they can be recognized, and how their implications can be perceived. Discoveries and inventions may be of two kinds. One is accretion to existing knowledge. The other comes through criticism, "by a method which destroys, changes, and alters, the whole thing including its most important instrument, the language in which our myths and theories are formulated."[3] Discoveries and particularly inventions can be "made to order" in the sense of being a response to some external demand. Or they can come without external and organizational stimuli. Either way, they often result from a highly imaginative and individualistic approach to a problem and the gift of seeing unusual associations and ideas. For this quality Derek Price has coined the term "mavericity."[4]

A judgment on a discovery or its quality must, like other judgments, depend upon the framework of assumptions within which perception and evaluation take place. Assessment will therefore depend upon the rapidity with which the unfamiliar idea is recognized as being not merely unfamiliar but fruitful, or the changed approach as more powerful than existing ones. Often this presents no problem. An accretion to existing knowledge can be comparatively easily recognized. An invention in response to a demand presents minimal problems of recognition and classification. Even for less expected changes there are established testing procedures. These are strongest within a well-defined scientific field. The validity of a new theory or proposition is likely to be apparent to the discoverer's fellow professionals. Views about its power and significance are usually formulated by the collective judgment of scientists in the field concerned. But these procedures are not free from difficulty. It usually takes time to formulate a collective judgment.

The immediate reaction to claims of discovery or invention is typically dispute and debate rather than unanimous recognition. Even when formulated, collective judgments are fallible. Nor is a professional opinion on "power" and "significance" necessarily relevant to a

---

David Sawers and Richard Stillerman, *The Sources of Invention*, 2nd ed. (London 1969), 26ff. Sir Frederick Dainton has suggested a further subdivision of the non-development segments of these activities into basic science, or pure research: strategic science, or a general effort to maintain the vigor of the scientific disciplines on which innovation and development are based; and tactical science, undertaken in support of immediate aims of product creation or improvement. See his report, "The Future of the Research Council System," in *A Framework for Government Research and Development*, Cmnd. 4814 (London, November 1971), 3-4.

[3]Karl Popper, *Conjectures and Refutations*, 4th ed., rev. (London 1972), 129.

[4]Derek de Solla Price, *Big Science, Little Science* (New York 1963), 107.

political or administrative decision-maker.[5] The judgment of a man's professional peers is, however, usually the best available. Difficulties can therefore increase in a situation where there is nobody of precisely relevant scientific expertise. That can happen when a judgment has to be made outside a well-defined and established field, perhaps in relation to some new area of knowledge. In such a case established professional opinion may be unavailable or irrelevant. Here, even more than elsewhere, recognition—not just of the value of a discovery but of the fact that one has been made—may depend upon the subtlety of an observer's mind and the bias of his whole character.

How are such discoveries and inventions—as well as more easily recognized innovations—caused? There are, broadly speaking, three schools of thought. The first regards them as the result of personal inspiration which cannot be planned or predicted but merely discerned and accepted. The second argues that they are responses to social (often economic) needs. The third argues that they are the cumulative results of many previous or simpler innovative steps. Some evidence can be found to support each of these views, which relate to different parts of the innovative process in different ways. Roughly speaking, the first seems to have most validity at the discovery and invention end of the spectrum, while the second and third apply more clearly to development and parts of innovation. Certainly the underlying factor in all innovatory processes, whether in basic science or applied technology, is the motivation and creativity of individuals. The motivation can range from simple curiosity, or research done because it's fun, to the desire for career advancement, professional standing, or simply to serve mankind. Creativity, on the other hand, is a mysterious quality which can wax and wane over time within an individual and the direction of whose results can neither be predicted nor taken for granted.

The idea of discovery, invention, and innovation as a response to social or economic need also has something to be said for it. It seems likely that much the greater part of governmental and industrial expenditure on technical innovation is spent on "made-to-order" innovations and on product improvements where administrative and economic stimuli are primary motivating forces. A better can opener can be designed and produced in response to direct market pressures. A new anti-tank missile can be developed and deployed in response to the appearance of a new and faster tank in the opponent's order of battle. The research and development machineries of consumer goods

---

[5] The scientist is concerned with explanatory power in the field concerned, the decision maker with the question, "what difference does it make in the world of affairs?" The answer, even for a very powerful theory, may be, "none."

and defense departments are geared to the need to respond to such challenges. It is also true in a broader sense that problems cannot be solved before they have arisen and been defined.

The third argument, that innovation results from a cumulative process, largely excludes those additions to knowledge which result from criticism and changes of theory. Within its sphere of reference, the argument can mean two things. If it means that new knowledge tends to emerge, not in isolation but in the form of addition to existing knowledge, and that new technology usually develops from old, it seems sensible. It is an ancient idea that we all stand on the intellectual shoulders of our predecessors. If, however, it means that there is something automatic about the way in which old knowledge breeds new, it is more suspect. The simultaneity of discovery in many areas lends color to the idea. But the differences in phasing, pace, and direction of progress in different areas seem to deny its mechanistic or deterministic basis.

Exploitation and Management. It is clear, however, that there is no direct or linear relationship between discovery and innovation on the one hand and practical exploitation on the other. Scientific knowledge at or near the discovery end of the innovative spectrum circulates quickly and internationally, both through the professional literature and through person-to-person contacts. At the highest level, scientific expertise appears to be inseparable from membership of the transnational professional groups within and between which information flows much more quickly than the printed literature would suggest.[6] It seems a plausible hypothesis that scientific ideas in some respects behave like money: the quantity available may for many purposes be less important than the velocity of its circulation. If so, attempts to maintain secrecy at the level of basic science may not merely lead to, but define, a state of relative deprivation, since they must produce a less than optimal velocity of circulation of ideas.

Scientific knowledge is therefore something like a public good. But its relationship to exploitation is indirect. Conceptual breakthroughs and fundamental discoveries are comparatively rare, though they can be of the utmost importance when they occur. At lower levels of invention and innovation the supply of new ideas often greatly exceeds the demand. Moreover, practical system changes for commercial or strategic purposes usually rest on several innovations—often accomplished many years before—and only rarely on a single technical

---

[6]Keith Pavitt has pointed out that copying hardware or blueprints is no effective substitute for the exchange of know-how and close person-to-person contacts. "Technology, International Competition, and Economic Growth," *World Politics*, xxv (January 1973), 186.

advance. In the weapons field, especially, programs are not usually begun until the feasibility of a practical system has begun to emerge.[7] Indeed, the larger and more complex the system, the safer it is to keep innovation to a minimum. As Sir Hermann Bondi has remarked: "It is an essential feature of any major project in advanced technology, be it concerned with space exploration, a particular missile system, or a special aeroplane, that it does not contain any very advanced parts. The problem with these systems is that they are extremely complex and accordingly very expensive. Therefore, these are not systems in which to try out devices or pieces of gadgetry that have not been tested before—one does not innovate, if one can possibly avoid it."[8]

It seems, therefore, that exploitation relies on three related processes: the selection or combination of already available ideas and innovations, the planned promotion of particular additions to the stock of ideas (usually in the more predictable areas of innovation and development), and the most rapid recognition and analysis of unexpected new ideas. There is an action-reaction relationship between existing ideas and technology and new knowledge, whether expected or not. At the same time, the availability of new ideas is not the only or even the principal motive force behind a move to exploit. Even if an invention or innovation is recognized to be exciting, it may not be economically or politically or strategically viable. Many inventions, especially those whose adoption would involve major departures from existing practice, must await changes in ancillary technology, or factor costs, or fashion, before they can be utilized. The claims of science and the pressures for a marketable technology may therefore contradict each other in some situations as much as they reinforce one another in others. The process of innovation may be, and in practice very often has been, separate in time from the changes of administrative attitude or economic circumstance which permit particular innovations to be applied for industrial or strategic purposes.

The rate of utilization of an innovation[9] is governed by the extent of uncertainty when the innovation first appears and the expected rate of reduction of that uncertainty. In each case, the uncertainties involve three categories: feasibility and performance of the end product, cost, and the extent and duration of the expected competitive or strategic advantage. Insofar as judgments involve the future, they involve economic and technical prediction. This concerns not just the performance

[7]Merton J. Peck and Frederic M. Scherer, *The Weapons Acquisition Process: An Economic Analysis* (Boston 1962), chap. 8.

[8]Sir Hermann Bondi, "International Collaboration in Advanced Technology," *The World Today*, xxix (January 1973), 16-23.

[9]This categorization is partly derived from Mansfield (fn. 1), 119.

of the product or the advantages which it confers, but predictions about what ordinary production and operating teams can be trained to do routinely. It follows that the greatest innovations tend to have the least predictable effects, and that useful technical change is often due to a number of minor and hence more manageable changes rather than to discoveries and inventions. Technological forecasting itself is better at predicting the diffusion of available knowledge than the appearance of something new. And the results of research are, *ex hypothesi*, unknown. Some of the objectives of an R & D program may be met by other research programs or invalidated by some other advance. Especially at the discovery and invention end of the spectrum the interaction between disciplines and research projects "is quite unpredictable both in its nature and in the nature and extent of its consequences, which may be the emergence of an entirely new area of scientific activity or the application of a particular scientific technique to an entirely different field of science."[10] Many of the more valuable results of an R & D effort, in fact, turn out to be externalities or spin-off benefits.

The probability that a particular aim will be achieved, or can even be defined at the start of a research project, is not always high.[11] Unexpected problems and opportunities often arise during development and testing. As a result, the product which finally emerges is apt to differ substantially from the original concept. One method for managing such uncertainties is to use prototype hardware items emerging from advanced development as building blocks in the development of a variety of possible systems: to develop a technological catalog from which end items can be procured comparatively cheaply and quickly.[12]

The question of resources for basic research is therefore, as Richard Nelson has pointed out, the classic problem of external economies.[13] Altogether, the financing of R & D presents serious analytical problems. It is true that, for both firms and industries, the rate of technological change seems to correlate directly with the rate of growth of cumulative R & D expenditures. Mansfield suggests that a 0.1 per cent increase in the first correlates with a 1 per cent change in

---

[10]Dainton (fn. 2), 11, para. 33.

[11]Some ways of dealing with these probabilities are discussed in Robert L. Winkler, "The Consensus of Subjective Probability Distributions," *Management Science,* xv, No. 3 (1968), B61-B75.

[12]See, for example, Thomas K. Glennan, "Research and Development," in Stephen Enke, *Defense Management* (Englewood Cliffs, N.J. 1967); Burton M. Klein, "Policy Issues Involved in the Conduct of Military Development Programs," in Richard A. Tybout, ed., *The Economics of Research and Development* (Columbus, Ohio 1965).

[13]Richard R. Nelson, "The Simple Economics of Basic Scientific Research," *Journal of Political Economy,* lxvii (June 1959), 306.

the second. But, as he also points out, correlation does not necessarily prove causation.[14] In any case, there is no very precise measure of the rate of technical change. There is no measure for R & D in terms of inventions, or any measure for the relationship between invention and application. We know very little, in detail, about what we get in return for R & D expenditure.[15] The problem of externalities alone not merely makes it difficult to quantify the benefits of past research, but probably makes it impossible to use estimates of the future economic gains expected to accrue from any basic research program as a criterion for decisions on that program.[16] In practice, R & D funding is probably decided less on grounds relating to scientific proof than for a number of reasons, including public faith in the progress of science, general political and economic need, managerial instinct, a willingness to gamble on a man or a project and, not least, the wishes of a scientific community, carrying much public and political clout, for an appropriate slice of the public resource cake.

The forms of organization pose further problems. One would expect the independent inventor to be relatively prominent in low-cost areas calling for great personal initiative and ingenuity. It is such people who are likely to score highly on "mavericity." But even when researchers work in teams, there seems to be a preference for tightly knit groups with a high degree of autonomy and initiative. This may help to account for the suggestion that small firms or groups are better at making discoveries and inventions—especially important ones—than large organizations. Quantification in this field is extremely difficult, but studies which have attempted to distinguish between major and minor inventions do indicate that individuals and small groups play a disproportionately important role.[17] Hamberg has suggested a number of possible reasons: the desire of large organizations for quick, reliable, quantifiable, and predictable results; their desire to concentrate on extensions of work or processes which have already proved their worth; the type of individual attracted to work in large, organized laboratories; and the fact that team research necessarily involves compromise.[18] Larger organizations, on the other hand, are often excellent in the larger and costlier areas, those of innovation and development

---

[14]Edwin Mansfield, *Industrial Research and Technological Innovation* (New York 1968), chap. 4.

[15]Richard M. Byrd, "Public Finances and the Technological Revolution—Comments," *Public Finance*, xxvi, No. 2 (1971), 160.

[16]Dainton (fn. 2), 9, para. 24.

[17]See, for example, Jewkes, Sawers, and Stillerman (fn. 2).

[18]D. Hamberg, "Invention in the Industrial Research Laboratory," *Journal of Political Economy*, lxxi (April 1963), 95-115.

on the basis of existing knowledge. They can therefore play an essential part even in the development of innovations originally made by small groups. It is the large organizations which provide the coordinating and development teams and the resources required to bring an invention to fruition as a commercially or strategically deployed system.

Irrespective of the size of the organization, the processes of invention, innovation, and development are in essential ways processes of trial and error, and of piecemeal adjustment. As suggested earlier, in developing a system it is usually not possible to predict the precise mix of performance characteristics which will emerge or the problems of component production which will crop up. Nor is it possible to be sure when a particular mix will be capable of production or deployment. Indeed, in important ways no system is ever finished and complete, if only because the requirements in response to which the system is produced are themselves constantly changing. . . .

The best way to organize the development or the execution of a project in applied technology—such as the moon landings—may be through a massive and centralized organization. But, for R & D, too much stress on coordination, planning, and efficiency can be counterproductive. The best way to organize technical change may be an untidy and apparently contradictory one. Since one cannot predict the optimum result from paper planning, development may actually be less costly and more efficient if there is some duplication, internal competition,[19] and confusion, if at times several people seem to be doing the same job, and no one is sure (or cares) who is the boss—provided always that management remains adaptable and flexible. The emphasis, then, is less on form and structure than on the ability of managers to coordinate and encourage their scientific and technical people, to promote fruitful interaction, to recognize novel factors and potentially important insights and the need to amend goals in a constant process of reaction between ends and means. In sum, by traditional standards the innovative organization is not organized.

The spectacular technological successes which have occurred in fields ranging from moon exploration to agricultural technology and oceanography appear, therefore, to be based on several factors. There has been a conscious and partly successful attempt to reduce the impact of uncertainty, even within the research side of R & D. Governments and management have used the machinery of comparatively impersonal peer-group evaluation of scientists by scientists, both to choose research personnel and to encourage successful work. They have encouraged promising men as well as promising projects and,

---

[19]Charles J. Hitch and Roland N. McKean, *The Economics of Defense in the Nuclear Age* (Cambridge, Mass. 1960), 249-51.

having chosen them, made maximum administrative, logistic, and instrumental support available. They have devised ways of monitoring details of projects as well as projects as a whole. There are sanctions in case of failure, or at least of repeated failure. And research administrations have reinforced any tendencies to concentrate on "manageable scientific questions," defined by Harvey Brooks as: "[ones] which are answerable either out of the existing body of scientific knowledge or through a search for new knowledge guided by existing understandings and involving only limited extensions of the current conceptual structure of science."[20]

Discovery and invention are, in any case, often less important than innovation and development in bringing technological success about. Development is not only the greatest source of improvements; it is also the most expensive and the most easily quantified segment of the R & D process, and the one which is easiest to steer in terms of expected end demand, whether by a commercial consumer or a Department of Defense. The development phase tends to be controllable in accordance with comparatively well-understood principles of industrial management. Questions about the cost-effectiveness of a particular process of production can be answered with some precision. Engineering developments may offer results which are relatively predictable in character and timing and whose impact on one's existing structure of doctrines, means, and ends seems both marginal and controllable. Even its nonlinear effects seem (sometimes mistakenly) easier to judge. And financial control of this element seems almost equivalent to financial control of the R & D process as a whole since, as a rule of thumb, development spending is to research spending as ten to one.

Overall, then, the management of R & D calls for particular skills in coordination, the integration of various innovations or disciplines or levels of scientific activity, the identification and combination of existing or feasible concepts or components, the recognition and quick exploitation of innovation, and the direction of these processes toward existing or possible end demands. At the same time there must be no stifling of the autonomy of research or developmental groups or of that initiative on the part of working scientists and technologists which is essential to the success of the enterprise. In this sense, R & D is a man-management problem rather than simply a technical one.

Management also influences or controls what may be the most important links of all: the communication links between technical groups as well as between scientists, administrators, outside groups,

[20]Harvey Brooks, "Knowledge and Action: The Dilemma of Science Policy in the '70's," *Daedalus*, cii (Spring 1973), 128.

and the government. The possession of knowledge is meaningless unless it can be communicated to those who need it. Communication is therefore vital not merely to the internal workings of the R & D process, but to the development outside it of that end demand toward whose fulfillment the process is principally directed.

The role of governments in these matters is, of course, substantial and often decisive. Both the scale and the long-term nature of R & D investment, especially in very large projects such as space exploration or the production of airliners, make participation or underwriting by the state essential. No less important is the state's role as an underwriter of smaller risks, or its role in encouraging or imposing longer-term judgments in some areas than normal commercial criteria would suggest. The state, as the embodiment or carrier of the will of society, can define not merely the general direction of overall science and research policy, but the proportion of national resources which can be devoted to that end. In the weapons field, especially, where ordinary commercial tests do not operate, it sets the requirements and constitutes the sole customer. Within society at large, the state can and does encourage and influence research even in areas which it does not control directly. This can be done in a multitude of ways, ranging from research contracts awarded to industry, or grants to universities, to methods of partial support like tax concessions. The R & D process, like other areas of social policy, is therefore subject to the overriding political judgments that motivate state action.

Limitations. It is necessary to recognize the limits of the attempt to minimize uncertainty both in R & D and its practical exploitation. The incidence of innovation in large social aggregates may be predictable, as a matter of statistical probability, within quite narrow margins of uncertainty. But the magnitude of innovation and its precise direction are not, nor is the relationship between the scale and costs of innovative activity and the value of its results. Least of all can the particular be inferred from the statistical aggregate. All innovative work rests, in the end, not on aggregate but on individual creativity. And in planning research or development projects there are irremovable uncertainties about the assumption that some particular man or team will be creative; that, even if he or they have been creative in the past, they will go on being so in the future and under the conditions of some project which has not yet begun. Judgments here concern the largely subconscious processes that appear to underlie all genuinely creative activity.[21] Even if creativity were a static property of individuals rather

[21]Anthony Storr, *The Dynamics of Creation* (London 1972). I suppose that even Skinnerians would not argue that laws governing creative activity have yet been discovered.

than a quality which can wax and wane over time, and even if creativity were randomly distributed within populations (which seems unlikely), it would still not be true that the form of its expression could be calculated as a function of the distribution patterns of that property.

If, moreover, scientific and technological progress relies particularly upon unexpected conjunctions of ideas, it relies by definition upon the unpredictable. For prediction implies that, at least at the conceptual level, the predicted idea or circumstance already exists. R & D is much more a matter of organized serendipity. Technology does not follow science directly or by predictable paths; nor is it always clear beforehand from what disciplines or combinations usable answers will emerge. Most R & D does not result in useful products; many of the results achieved lead to quite unpredictable utilities, and in trying to solve one problem it not infrequently happens that the answer to quite a different one turns up.

Even when new ideas do emerge, the pattern of their adoption bears only a partial relationship to the pattern of their appearance. In part this is because, as suggested earlier, there is a disjunction between ideas and their economic utility. More broadly, there seems little evidence for saying that discoveries and inventions produced at a time when they were immediately needed would not have been produced but for that need; or that the most interesting and fruitful discoveries and inventions of any period relate to its salient social or economic needs; or that the emergence of a social need has customarily been followed by the discovery or invention required to fill it. Inventions often occur in the absence of social challenges. And social and economic challenges often remain unmet, whether by inventions or otherwise.

These uncertainties of the R & D process help to account for the large errors that are so often made in estimates prior to the development of commercial and especially of military systems. Other factors include unexpected problems which arise during development, and the alterations in system requirements caused by market changes or changes in an opposing order of battle. There is also the matter of technological drift. It has been argued, for example, that the increases in range and payload between the early model B-52's and the B-52H's, and the increases in SLBM [submarine-launched ballistic missile] ranges from the 1,200 miles of the Polaris A-1 to the 2,800 miles of the Polaris A-3 were achieved largely in this way. It is not only that some of the small changes involved may be relatively inexpensive and others not. It is that the costs and the development are unrelated to the recognized administrative and budgetary categories of R & D, may not become apparent until after they have happened, and even then, though apparent in the aggregate, seem difficult to identify in detail.

There are further difficulties about the relationship between R & D effort and public authorities or political decision-making. To begin with, many and perhaps most R & D decisions take place deep within organizations or technical teams and do not become apparent to top management or the government until after they have been taken. Most of them, indeed, do not crop up in a " yes-no" form at all. But even at higher levels there is no clear line of division between governmental and non-governmental effort, if only because of the sheer variety of institutional and financial ways in which R & D is promoted, in which governmental and non-governmental efforts are intertwined, and in which the complementary and conflicting interests of various groups are reconciled. It is true that research contracts can be audited and that the behavior of officials is influenced by the fact that they may have to explain themselves to some parliamentary or congressional committee. Rough controls, at aggregate levels, are imposed. Nevertheless, it is not always clear what the relationship is between any organization's innovative effort and the ends of public policy, or indeed whether those ends have been operationally defined.

It would in some cases be equally difficult to demonstrate a clear correlation between any particular form or quantity of public support or direction and the results achieved. It is not even always possible to be sure that a particular piece of governmentally encouraged work would have remained undone but for that encouragement. Equally, work done in military establishments or under military contracts is usually (but not always) of greater military value than work done elsewhere. The line between military and non-military technology is proverbially difficult to draw. One of the classic cases is that of nuclear energy. Though the military applications of nuclear energy may be definable and controllable, the capacity to achieve such applications is in practice not clearly separable from work on nuclear-energy technology as a whole.

In view of these uncertainties, what is it that large nations try to achieve by their R & D efforts, especially in the military field?

II. The Requirement for Military R & D

The idea that technical innovation and development are important in defining strategic balances is of course not new. The whole history of war testifies to the role which improvements, whether of weapons or of tactics, have played in the relationships between states. If the nature of this role tended to change, and if its importance increased to some extent in the period after 1945, this was probably for two reasons. One was the growing complexity not only of weapons technology but of

HARRY G. GELBER

many other components of national power and influence. The other was the speed of technical change, which made assessment in general more difficult and even good assessments short-lived. These circumstances have altered the role of defense R & D in subtle but important ways. Innovative effort has always been an auxiliary in the production and perfection of the weapons systems which largely determine the military aspects of relations between powers. It has now become a major area of strategic competition in its own right. The possession of technical superiority in some field, and the perception by others of one's technical superiority, can produce political and strategic advantages even in the absence of deployed weapons.

The United States and the Soviet Union have over the years emphasized the technical and qualitative competition between them. Between 1969 and 1973, for example, the U.S. seems to have devoted approximately 10 per cent of its defense budget—or about 0.8 per cent of GNP—to defense RDT & E.[22] The Russians have spent more, both in absolute and relative terms, in order to narrow the American technical lead.[23] The precise balance has been difficult to determine because, among other things, the distinction between military and non-military R & D is not exact. But as SALT II began, it seemed clear that though the Soviet Union had achieved a technical lead in some areas, the United States retained advantages in a number of crucial fields including multiple warhead technology, computer science, telecommunications, and some other areas of electronics. U.S. Administration spokesmen were, however, unanimous in arguing in 1972 and 1973 that the nation's security would be endangered if this technical lead was not maintained, and that increased funding was needed to maintain it.

---

[22]Melvin R. Laird, *National Security Strategy of Realistic Deterrence,* Statement before the House Armed Services Committee on the FY 1973 Defense Budget and FY 1973-77 Program (Washington, D.C., February 17, 1972), 189, Table 1; John S. Foster, Jr., *The Department of Defense Program of Research, Development, Test, and Evaluation, FY 1974,* Statement before the Defense Subcommittee of the Senate Appropriations Committee, 93rd Cong., 1st sess. (Washington, D.C., March 28, 1973), 1-3.

[23]Between 1963 and 1971, U.S. total spending on R & D declined from 2.9% to 2.6% of GNP (1972: 2.4%), while Soviet R & D spending during the same period rose from 2.3% to 3.0% of a much smaller GNP. (A different computation suggests that total Soviet research expenditure rose from 1.6% of the national income in 1950 to 3.7% in 1968. See V. P. Dyatchenko and S. A. Sitaryan, "Problems of Public Finance in the Field of Research and Technical Development," *Public Finance,* xxvi, No. 2 [1971], 117.) Between 1961 and 1969, the proportion of U.S. governmental R & D expenditure going to defense declined from 65% to 49% (1972: 54%); see *Science Indicators 1972,* Report of the National Science Board, 1973 (National Science Foundation, Washington, D.C. 1973), 2-3, 20-25. In sum, American defense R & D spending rose somewhat during the 1960's in current dollars, declined in constant dollars, and declined somewhat more sharply as a proportion of total R & D spending and of government expenditure in the field. . . .

In analyzing what the two superpowers hope to gain by such efforts, the following ten categories of real or potential advantages might be suggested.

1. The first aim is one of the two that have the greatest traditional importance: the urge to know. Each side has sought to refine its understanding of scientific principles and know-how in defense-related areas, whether as a prerequisite for management forecasts about the probable future course of scientific or strategic developments or as a means for deciding what systems, with what characteristics, to produce and deploy. In certain fields—for example, electronics and communications—increasing systems sophistication has made it more difficult to design around some remaining areas of ignorance.

2. The other traditionally important aim is the production of more effective and efficient weapons than those of the opponent. Security requires deployed weapons, not merely technology. The effort to achieve this aim, as well as the first, is of course subject to various limitations. The principal ones are the character of one's strategic planning, the fiscal and budgetary constraints of the national economy, the skills and creativity of the national scientific and technical community, and the need to relate R & D not just to one's own preferences but to specific deployed or expected systems in the hands of an opponent. Within such constraints, each side has sought qualitative improvements in both existing and projected weapons and support systems. Improved aircraft, whether the Soviet Backfire or the American B-1, clearly fall under this heading. So do the improved missile submarine (FBMS) systems on both sides and various improvements in warhead or missile boost and guidance systems.

3. Each side can also hope to develop weapons likely to avoid particular sets of legal or political inhibitions. That could mean developing alternatives to napalm or new forms of bomb guidance which, by improving accuracy, limit collateral damage. It might mean using laser-based systems for guidance and, eventually, as part of a defensive system against bombers or (given the ambiguities of the SALT I arrangements), perhaps even against missiles. Indeed, the creation of any system of static limitations, especially one resting on rough numerical criteria like SALT I, seems sure to increase rather than to decrease the incentive to search for new techniques not subject to those prohibitions.

4. Not only can political leaders expect their R & D programs to refine the weapons and deployment possibilities among which they can choose; they can also expect their freedom of maneuver to be

increased in other ways. By shortening the lead-times for alternative forms of deployment, R & D can increase a nation's political and strategic flexibility. And, in case unexpected technical possibilities were suddenly to appear on one side or the other, an administration able to adjust quickly to the new circumstances would have an obvious advantage.

5. The possession of technical initiative—which in practice means an advantage in lead-time—also offers increased possibilities for influencing, even manipulating, the decisions of an opponent. He can be faced with the possible deployment of weapons or equipment in such a way as to compel him to react even before the threat has materialized, with a consequent diversion of his resources and efforts. He would face additional difficulties if he could not estimate precisely at what stage of development a deployment decision of one's own was likely to be taken, and where additional time on development might result in the deployment of a system with significantly different operating characteristics, requiring different countermeasures. Insofar as an opponent, especially a technically inferior one, could not avoid trying to hedge against various forms of one's own possible deployment, he could be compelled to divert increased development efforts and resources. He could, for example, be compelled to replicate a suspected system before he could construct an effective counter. Or he might decide to increase his inventory in some category of weapons so as to compensate for certain kinds of qualitative inferiority. One side possessing tanks which had become increasingly vulnerable to the anti-tank equipment of the other might, at least pending the development of an effective anti-anti-tank system, build more of the old tanks as a hedge against force erosion. It is possible to view Soviet qualitative inferiority as one reason for the large increases in Soviet long-range missile launcher numbers during 1968–72.

6. Technical advantage is therefore also an increasingly important element of national intelligence efforts. It can permit estimates of the probable methods and timing of development by others which are essential to the effort to avoid technological surprise by an opponent. Dr. Foster has claimed that, "As long as we retain technological superiority, we can make meaningful measurements of relative strength without fear of surprise. We can estimate their progress because we've already been there. . . . Once we appear to have lost that superiority, we lose our ability to measure our relative strength and to compete efficiently, and in due course we should lose confidence in the realism of our deterrence." Moreover, "In those areas where we acknowledge technological parity or inferiority, we cannot have high

confidence in our estimates of Soviet capability, nor can we predict with confidence what their next steps forward will be."[24]

Though Dr. Foster's formulations may have had as much to do with his budget requests as with a dispassionate analysis of his achievements, as a statement of aims this is plausible enough. R & D was thus regarded as permitting a closer estimate of the future capabilities of others. It provided hypotheses which could later be examined and validated by the normal means of collecting hard intelligence. It was, and is, much easier to find significant data and evidence if one knows what one is looking for—a fact which is bound to have repercussions not only on assessments of capabilities but on estimates of intentions. R & D programs can also, as Dr. Foster implied, suggest comparatively cost-effective methods of hedging against technological surprises. The R & D community might even in some cases be able to devise a counter to a system which the opponent had not yet deployed but was trying to develop to counteract one's own existing and deployed systems. This would be possible in cases where technical ascendancy enabled one to judge, within acceptable tolerances, along which technical route the opponent would have to go at what pace in devising his counter.

7. It may also be possible to influence an opponent's strategic perceptions and his resource-allocation decisions at minimal cost. Under conditions of uncertainty, information becomes a commodity. The management and reduction of uncertainty are essential parts of any model of strategic behavior. They relate both to hardware and to information, and to the balance between them. Insofar as the R & D machinery on both sides produces more complex systems, the assessment of which requires more detailed and complicated information, progress in R & D is likely to increase the difficulty, for opposing strategic managers, in achieving a satisfactory trade-off between expenditure on hardware and expenditure directed to the acquisition and processing of information.

A side possessing a technical lead will have an advantage in its attempts to decrease the opponent's uncertainties in some respects. It may wish to do so for two reasons. One is to indicate the general nature of its own deployed systems and strategic purposes as a means of restraining the opponent. Deterrence requires that the opponent should know what one has and what one may do. A side having a technical advantage may also find it easier to convey information in

---

[24]Dr. Foster's testimony on the fiscal year 1973 Defense RDT & E Program before the Armed Services Committee, House of Representatives, 92nd Cong., 2nd sess. (Washington, D.C., February 29, 1972), 1-13, 14, 15.

ways which maximize the deterrent effect but minimize the opponent's opportunities of using the information to further his own programs. The second reason might be to try to decrease the opponent's uncertainties so that, in reducing his need to hedge against them, one also reduces one's own need to respond to these hedging measures. To this extent, it may be possible to influence the feedback from an opponent's program upon one's own scientific efforts or force structures.

8. R & D management can also pursue aims of strategic deception, and indicate and exploit political advantages emerging from technical possibilities. One can employ tactics such as deceptive budgetary allocations to different R & D categories, or the leakage of misleading information on R & D, possibly through the press, or deception in the management of testing. In each case it might be possible to mislead others (including, upon occasion, domestic critics) about the major thrust of one's own research or developmental work. It would not always be necessary that the deception be sustained for long, for an advantage in lead-time is an advantage in substance. This would be the case especially if the deceiver could rely on the inability of the other side's management to move swiftly from the acquisition of knowledge, whether of intelligence matters or scientific principles, to the development and deployment of suitable weapons systems. It might then be possible to indicate political and military ways of exploiting any deficiencies in the opponent's management. To this extent, it may be possible to blunt the effect of his R & D program.

9. There are also the diplomatic effects vis-à-vis allies. For a superpower, R & D cooperation with smaller allies can result in additional work done relatively cheaply but—an important aim—without any impairment of the greater power's independence of strategic decision. In 1972, for example, Dr. Foster called for increased integration of R & D within the Western alliance and, speaking before the Senate Armed Services Committee, claimed significant advantages in terms of cost-sharing and the production of mutual understanding. He added: "Any candidate considered for U.S. participation [i.e., in joint projects] also requires a prototype test and evaluation program, as well as the transfer of data and expertise for U.S. production. This will assure that the U.S. retains technological know-how, maintains a favorable balance of payments, sustains industry employment and remains independent of foreign sources for critically needed hardware."[25]

*   *   *

---

[25]*Ibid.*, 2-14. In 1973 he expressed similar views. See his testimony of March 28, 1973 (fn. 22), 1-13, 3-18.

10. In terms of domestic politics, R & D effort has over a number of years proved to be much less open to challenge than the deployment of weapons systems. Even in the U.S.S.R., the fragmentary evidence indicates that the groups opposing larger strategic forces have hesitated to try to cut R & D. In the U.S., congressional criticism of R & D has over the years been notably less significant than criticism of production, procurement, and deployment. Whether this can remain so is not entirely clear. It seems possible that the political debates surrounding SALT II, and the talks themselves once they delve more deeply into problems of technical innovation, could make R & D a subject of greater controversy. During 1972 and 1973 there were signs that this might happen in the case of the development process—especially engineering development—partly on the grounds that it can establish a dynamic which may spill over into procurement and deployment. But by the end of 1973, neither innovation nor exploratory development had come under serious and sustained criticism.

The desire for technical improvement is not related merely to administrative or governmental decisions about knowledge, or weapons, or political tactics. It is connected, both for individuals and groups, to the very meaning of concepts like "effort" and "success." The desire for national prestige is complemented by the fact that individual prestige can depend on the ability to design better components, systems, and techniques. The man who designs a better way to insulate wire or a quicker way to transmit information, or who can give a faster rate of climb to an interceptor aircraft, is successful in his profession in a way in which others are not, even if appreciation of his success is confined to his own team or firm. Not only do these pressures of individual and social psychology militate in favor of innovation, but there appear to be few directly competing, let alone contradictory, psychological pressures.

Institutional pressures frequently operate in a similar direction. They can range from inter-service competition or the desire to keep a particular contractor in business to the need to remedy some strategic or systems weakness for which one is responsible. This is a large subject, and one in which slogans like "bureaucratic imperialism" are unhelpful. It is not necessary to assume that service officers are other than patriotic, or officials other than carefully and properly concerned with their public duties, in order to explain why a service will seize the opportunity to perform some strategic task more quickly or cheaply or effectively than has been possible hitherto, or why the case for the elimination of identifiable weakness can be incontrovertible in committee, or why officials and businessmen alike adopt positions designed, among other things, to shield them from criticism or budgetary difficulty. Given the character of nation-states as the foci of political and institutional loyalties, the elimination of real or apparent national security risks ranks very high among the motivating forces of these institutions.

III. Approaches to Restraint

Why Restraint? The pressures to restrain military R & D are nevertheless considerable. The most important arise from the wish to make war less likely, to make it less destructive if it should occur, to strengthen political controls over technical and strategic processes, and to diminish the cost of military preparedness. It has been argued, for instance, that there exists a weapons-technology spiral which can make the strategic competition more vulnerable to mutual overreaction or technical accident.[26] Such a spiral is destabilizing in that it increases the technical uncertainties of each side's estimate of the other, and therefore the number and severity of the risks against which each side will feel compelled to hedge. Technical development can lead to further increases in the destructiveness of an already unbearably destructive form of warfare. It can also weaken political controls, whether by making technical matters harder to understand or, more importantly, by creating facts or defining risks to which statesmen have no choice but to react.

Research and development programs are increasingly expensive and produce ever more complicated and costly types of equipment. Worst of all, at both the scientific and economic levels, the R & D process has a built-in tendency to proliferate. The solution of one scientific problem, or the creation of a new technology, as a rule produces as many new difficulties as it resolves and as many new requirements as it satisfies. And since most technical advantages are relatively short-lived, the achievement of one merely creates fresh impulses to search for its successor. The solution of one R & D problem therefore often means pressures for further, and usually more, R & D. The creation of new information technologies, for instance, has made it possible to contemplate a large variety of new and much more complex technical tasks. Requirements may be increased in two ways. One stems from the fact that, as previously suggested, once the competing R & D processes on both sides increase technical complexity, each side requires larger, more complex, and more expensive means of obtaining

---

[26]The idea of a spiral usually assumes that the U.S. and the U.S.S.R. have been engaged in an "arms race." I ought, perhaps, to say that, for reasons going beyond the scope of this paper, I believe this idea is at best a dangerously oversimplified model of reality and at worst simply wrong.

adequate information. Increased R & D expenditure therefore tends to compel additional increased expenditure in adjacent fields. The other way in which requirements may expand lies in the fact that increasing technical complexity may encourage the adoption of strategies which are optimal under conditions of maximum technical uncertainty. The R & D process therefore influences the formulation of basic strategic doctrine in ways which also frequently imply greater costs.

The level of defense R & D activity, moreover, ultimately rests on comparatively arbitrary political judgments. Government-supported R & D is usually directed to areas where normal commercial notions of costs and profit will not induce spending by private or even state-owned corporations, or where corporate effort needs to be supplemented or coordinated in the interests of non-commercial aims. It follows that standard economic and market criteria alone cannot be decisive in judging R & D spending. Rather, the decision on what level of effort is appropriate rests on a combination of strategic doctrine and political attitude. But insofar as these attitudes and judgments are arbitrary, they are also vulnerable, either to alternative strategic doctrines, or to different political ideas, or to general social arguments for lower research- or arms-spending.

These propositions are not free from difficulty. The wish to make war less likely can, and often does, conflict with the wish to make it less destructive if it should come. And either aim can be promoted rather than obstructed by the results of R & D programs. One can produce *less* destructive weapons, for instance, rather than *more* destructive ones. R & D can also create arms-control possibilities which did not previously exist—for example in the field of surveillance mechanisms. It can help to prevent technical accidents—as was done during the early 1960's by work designed to strengthen the control devices on U.S. strategic weapons. . . .

Major Constraints. It is more complicated and difficult to restrain technological development than to try to encourage it. There are several reasons. First, how can one restrain ideas? The penalties for even trying to restrain them can be severe, including as they do a decline in the number and morale of research staff and engineers, and increasing sterility in a wide range of teaching and research. Even the ability to monitor advances elsewhere can atrophy. Second, how can one know that a piece of knowledge which one has refrained from acquiring will remain undiscovered and dispensable? To quote Harvey Brooks once more: "The questions we begin by asking are not those which we end by answering and an insight that initially appears to have little relevance may rather suddenly turn out to be the key to further progress towards a practical goal."[27] The importance of externalities means that any particular measure of restraint may prove in retrospect to have had quite unpredictable and undesirable side effects. At the same time, given the international character of science, knowledge which one has refrained from acquiring may turn out to have been acquired later by someone else and under conditions which confirm one's relative disadvantage. Third, restraints or limitations might take one of two forms: they could be very broad, embracing whole categories of research, or they could be selective and finely tuned. In the first case, they would create very large gaps, not just in capability but in knowledge. Such gaps are unlikely to be politically or scientifically acceptable, if only because of their effects on adjacent areas of knowledge and the difficulties of designing around large areas of deliberate ignorance. In the second case, how could one design limitations save on the basis of technical definitions which require prior knowledge of that which is to be limited? Fourth, in an important sense the thrust of developmental work is less toward the creation of "better systems" *per se* than toward the identification and definition of deficiencies in existing policies, structure, and weapons inventories.[28] From this perspective, a limitation of R & D implies acceptance of a permanent set of deficiencies in one's defense structure—deficiencies, moreover, whose character and consequences no one can clearly predict.

To design mutually understood and accepted restraints as between two opposing parties is harder still, for it introduces additional conditions, those of verification and assurance. It has so far been a principal requirement for abstention by either side that the opponent be known to be abstaining in related or affected areas. From this point of view there are, it seems, a number of things which cannot be done. One cannot give either side assurance that the other is not having interesting scientific or technological ideas, or that it is refraining from developing those ideas to whatever extent may be consistent with the avoidance of detection. In the absence of inspection of a sort which both sides have so far regarded as unacceptably intrusive, it is not possible to obtain satisfactory assurances about the processes by which scientific and technical possibilities emerge. In fact, it is very difficult to be sure whether any particular improvement is due to movements toward known production boundaries or to the expansion of those boundaries through an increase in knowledge. Nor is it possible to establish a clear line of separation between military and civilian

---

[27]Brooks (fn. 22), 129.

[28]The point has been clearly put by Dr. Foster. See his address of January 10, 1973, to the American Institute of Aeronautics and Astronautics in Washington (Department of Defense Press Release, no date).

technology at any stage prior to development, testing, and procurement. It is not possible to draft formal agreements to limit any technology whose essential characteristics have not become definable by the time the agreement is drafted. Indeed, since the danger of a scientific advance or technical breakthrough by the opponent cannot be removed by changes in any one parameter condition for innovative effort, any particular measure of "less R & D" will leave open the possibility of circumvention. Nor are evasion and circumvention the sole difficulties. Any agreement incorporating defined and static limitations will leave open to either side the possibility of research and development work that is consistent with its terms but will shorten the lead-time for any subsequent progress and therefore create a position of relative advantage if the agreement should be broken or abrogated. In other words, it is not easy to design a treaty which will not create disparities in the event of sudden abrogation by either party.

Approaches. Some things, on the other hand, seem possible. Most of them rest on notions of a common interest within the adversary relationship of the two sides,[29] and the impossibility or undesirability of limiting advances in knowledge and associated research and exploratory development programs.

In the first place, security considerations are always a function of the general political relationships between the powers concerned. Strategic planning rests upon threat perceptions and estimates of the balance of risks which are not immutable. Security problems sometimes come to seem less important, either because the political relations between the countries concerned improve, or because a possible conflict seems so cataclysmic that the prospect of its occurrence is less credible, or simply because attention comes to be focused on other problems, making security matters apparently less urgent. For any or all of these reasons, military effort, including R & D, can become less important and pressing. Sometimes the pressures can be indirect: energy, pollution, and environmental problems, for example, can divert attention and resources from defense matters or change the circumstances in which defense can be organized. Management of pressures and incentives in this area is clearly a matter of overall political intentions and leadership.

There are also the statements of strategic doctrine and intentions from which requirements for weapons systems are often derived. The relationship between weapons and strategy is of course a two-way affair: the appearance of a new system can affect strategic planning as

---

[29] Or more than two, as and when the development of nuclear forces by additional states makes it feasible and desirable to draw them into such discussions.

much as planning affects the search for new systems. Nevertheless it may be possible to change the strategic intentions of both sides in such a way as to facilitate arms control rather than to make it more difficult. This could happen in two ways. First, one side or both might choose to emphasize the deployment of systems capable of inspection and verification rather than systems which make it difficult; to improve national means of verification; to emphasize systems permitting more time for decision making rather than those requiring instant reaction; systems less sensitive to variations in strategy or tactics by either side; systems with greater accuracy and therefore less potential for direct and collateral destruction; and systems which potentially facilitate further arms-control measures. This last might be done by increasing the incentive for either side to eliminate older weapons systems and by designing systems so as to limit possible instabilities in the event that both sides agreed to move to lower numerical levels. Both sides might, for example, agree to abstain from the deployment of land-mobile ICBM's with very heavy-yield warheads. Or they might develop smaller-yield and more precise strategic systems, or ones with characteristics specific, and seen to be specific, against some third party.

Second, it may also be possible to redefine the areas in which both sides require assurance, as well as the degree of assurance needed. It may be true, for example, that an opponent could shorten his lead-time for potential deployment by clandestine or other non-observable forms of development. But it might be more fruitful to ask how close he could get, not to any new systems or technologies, but to drastically destabilizing ones, without giving adequate warning that he was doing so. It may be true that not all tests can be observed or their nature unambiguously established. But it might be enough to ask whether an opponent could reasonably plan for, say, a first strike against a land-based missile force unless he had tested his attack systems in an actual operational configuration and in ways which were bound to be observed.

Any such strategic changes would be quickly reflected in the procurement of weapons and therefore in the management of R & D efforts. Those efforts are highly sensitive to consumer expectations; it is the prospect of procurement which gives incentives and a sense of mission to R & D personnel. Changes in strategy and procurement can therefore change the very concept of what constitutes "success" in R & D. It is not always necessary to affect the views of all scientists and technologists. If the views and judgments of the professional leaders of the R & D community—of those who pass upon the efforts of others—can be influenced, the whole tenor of the R & D enterprise may be affected. To do so deliberately is, however, not free of risk.

Attempts to influence can be counterproductive. Competing strategic and procurement views will continue to be held both within and outside most segments of the defense community, and will find reflection among R & D people. Mangement which is too tight and centralized, however laudable its aims, can render much R & D effort sterile. And, of course, any attempt to limit R & D may prove incompatible with other forms of arms control. If, for example, a limit on R & D means an increase in the risk of qualitative inferiority in some categories, it may be less tolerable at reduced deployment levels than at high ones.

If verified controls are to be added to changes of incentive, they are likely to be most effective if imposed in the area of advanced development and prototype testing. Such a procedure would avoid the apparently insoluble difficulties of trying to combine the necessary freedom of scientific work with tight administrative control and the varied and often obscure ways in which research is done with the needs of verification. It would allow, indeed encourage, senior scientists to help control the results of their own work. It has been estimated that half of the technology events which contributed to the production of new weapons systems in the United States during the 1950s and 1960s arose from advanced development work, and a further 20 per cent arose in the engineering development phase. It is during these stages that the results of R & D can begin to become sufficiently visible to make verification possible.

One method for changing incentives which has been much favored by critics of the military and, for obvious institutional reasons, by legislatures, is to cut research and development funds and to decrease the rate of return from investment in these areas. This has obvious attractions. It is easy to accomplish, popular with competing agencies or firms, avoids careful definition of terms, and operates with some effectiveness at gross or aggregate levels of activity. There may even prove to be usable direct correlations between development spending and the rate of growth of particular technologies. If so, any method for limiting development spending which an outsider felt able to monitor with confidence would also provide confidence in his estimate of the rate of growth of the technology or technologies concerned. Moreover, budget limitations inevitably create trade-off problems, or make them more acute. Arms controllers can exploit this. There is, for instance, the trade-off between information systems and weapons procurement. A tighter budget might compel the spending of a greater percentage of the defense dollar on information rather than weapons. At the same time there would be pressures to slow down changes in deployed systems. Slower changes would mean greater learning-curve reductions in unit costs for production and servicing, as well as improvements in systems reliability. Both these pressures could operate in the direction of decreased emphasis upon, or at least speed of, changes in weapons systems.

The limitations of this approach are, however, severe. If, as suggested earlier, a 0.1 per cent increase in the rate of technological change correlates with a 1.0 per cent change in the rate of growth of cumulative R & D expenditure, then—even assuming that correlation shows causation, which is by no means certain—a 20 per cent decline in the rate of growth of funding would entail a mere 2 per cent reduction in the rate of technological change. This hardly seems very cost-effective. In any case, the internationality of science and technology, and the steadiness of its gross growth curves over time, suggest that the breeding of new knowledge is not greatly affected by increases or slowdowns in expenditures for research and development by any single nation. If decreased R & D spending is intended to limit knowledge and know-how, therefore, it would have to be accompanied by effective, and perhaps verifiable, measures to deprive the country concerned of access to the science and technology of others. That seems impractical, except at quite exorbitant social and scientific costs.

Nor can the argument be usefully turned around to say that if a 20 per cent decline in the rate of growth of funding leads to so small a reduction in the rate of technical change, technical development would not be seriously damaged by a levelling-off of spending and a reallocation of resources to more popular social purposes. Technological change does not have a direct and immediate relationship to research. But research provides the basis for the most interesting and far-reaching technological changes over the longer term. A small percentage reduction in the rate of change might, therefore, conceal a substantial alteration in its direction and character. Moreover, as we have seen, only a small percentage of R & D costs goes into research. Though the rule of thumb is that research is to development as one to ten, other categorizations are sometimes used. The U.S. National Science Foundation, using its division of defense R & D into categories of basic research, applied research, and development, suggests that, in 1965 for instance, the expenditure percentages for these categories were 4 per cent, 22 per cent, and 73 per cent, respectively.[30] It seems highly probable that across-the-board budget cuts would principally damage research rather than development—the more so because the political and administrative justifications for such cuts would be likely to emphasize the short-term rather than the long-term payoff. Any attempt to cut budgets in discriminating and detailed fashion, on the other

---

[30]*Federal Funds for Science*, xiv, National Science Foundation (Washington, D.C. 1965).

hand, would be administratively difficult and cumbersome, and would almost certainly require large increases in the bureaucracy of science administration, with adverse effects on its subsequent speed of operation and reaction-capacity to new ideas. Since there are no precise and essential correlations between expenditure and the character of R & D results, it would still not be certain that lower funding would necessarily lead to less weapons development, let alone less weapons development of a particular kind.

One other consideration must be borne in mind. If R & D budgets were to be considered vital measures for the observance of international agreements, they would become even more politicized than they are. Budgets can be drained of effectiveness as decision-making tools once the terms in which they are drawn up, and the criteria in accordance with which information is presented, have themselves become the subject of political dispute. Funds can be channeled in ways that are difficult to detect, even by careful auditing. It is a matter on which public accounts and control committees have tales to tell.

There are other senses in which attempts to limit funds might be counterproductive. As a consequence of heavy developmental expenditure, numbers of able people are tied down to development. Many of them might turn to basic and comparatively inexpensive research work if these funds were cut. That might increase the rate of discovery and innovation, and thereby pave the way for even swifter technical development at some point in the future. If, as is sometimes suggested, high labor mobility among scientific and technical personnel is correlated with increased inventiveness and innovation, this result would be even more likely to occur because scientific advances owe much to the introduction of techniques and insights from one field of research to another.

It is also possible to take measures relating to the flow of information. Since detailed information about developments on an opposing side can help, by narrowing uncertainties, to limit the risks against which each power feels compelled to hedge, it can also encourage restraint. The obvious difficulty is that too greatly asymmetrical a flow of information, or information which reveals the existence of a unilateral advantage, can encourage attempts to exploit it. Four means of managing the information flow seem to be available: unilateral and invulnerable systems of surveillance and verification, tacitly tolerated surveillance, management of the information flow, and the removal of restrictions on information flow in some areas.

Surveillance and verification are the principal methods on which both sides have so far relied. They operate at the point at which weapons systems and major components become visible. Each side is likely to seek maximum efficiency and accuracy for its monitoring and reconnaissance mechanisms, part of the so-called national means of verification. Infra-red and visible light photography already have for-midable capabilities, and it must be assumed that satellite-borne cameras can achieve ground resolutions of 0.5 feet.[31] Both sides are likely to continue R & D work in these fields. But the point at which new systems become visible may itself to some extent depend upon the willingness of each side to accept monitoring and inspection. The SALT I provisions, by which each side has granted immunity to the other's surveillance satellites from interference by its own anti-satellite systems, are highly significant here. They clearly imply mutual accept-ance of this form of inspection. Though the qualitative gap between on-site inspection and satellite surveillance has been narrowed by the increasing accuracy of satellite photography, there are some things photography cannot do. It cannot, for example, detect all forms of work being done under cover, or whether a missile nose cone contains MIRV's. One of its substantial utilities lies in permitting each side to gather enough information to be deterred from risking conflict. But it may also be that the traditional Soviet reluctance to accept close inspec-tion is being eroded, and that the results of this process may become exploitable for additional forms of inspection. A managed flow of mutual information also has possibilities. In the SALT negotiations and in the Joint Consultative Commission set up under SALT I, both sides have shown themselves willing to go some way to use mutual informa-tion for the purposes of strategic reassurance. Perhaps this can be taken further. Though it might in theory be possible to slow down the requisite flow of information within any national R & D system, it is difficult to see how reassurance on such a point might be conveyed by one party to the other.

There is also the idea that some kinds of scientific and technical information might simply be allowed to flow more freely between the two sides. This is likely to have a limited application. I have already argued that scientific knowledge is something like a free good, and that the velocity of circulation of ideas is a vital element in determining the rate of scientific and technical discovery, invention, and innovation. If so, the openness of Western information channels, and the quicker and freer circulation of ideas through them, is in many ways an asset. The relative slowness of Soviet and Chinese access to such informa-tion, and their comparative lack of person-to-person contacts, are liabilities; encouragement of freer exchanges of information and of people could be to their advantage. To some extent, improved contacts

---

[31]See Ted Greenwood, "Reconnaissance and Arms Control," *Scientific American*, ccxxviii (February 1973), 14-25.

have indeed been promoted. But the remaining obstacles are formidable. Exchanges of scientific information do not easily translate, for either side, into reduced uncertainties about opposing weapons programs. For both sides, the importance of externalities means that the nonlinear effects of any information exchange cannot be easily planned for. In any case, governments are traditionally concerned with maintaining the flexibility and relative advantage that a monopoly of information can provide. On the Soviet and Chinese side, especially, proposals for easier and more uncontrolled exchanges between scientists could easily prove politically embarrassing.[32] At the levels of applied technology, where knowledge is not a free good, and which are of especial importance for arms control purposes, there are different complications. The United States, with its internal freedom of information, regards itself as being at a permanent disadvantage compared to the Soviet Union or China. Though the Russians argue that the multiplicity of American information sources results, for outsiders, in a degree of confusion whose effects are not dissimilar to those of their own misinformation policies, it is difficult to see how the U.S. could make even more detailed information available in defense-related areas without a large Soviet *quid pro quo*—or how, for the time being, the Russians could give it.

It is understandable that, in view of these ambiguities and uncertainties, both sides have seemed willing to explore the possibility of moving from ideas of limitation by treaty to limitation by an ongoing process of negotiation. The basic notion is that since science and technology progress in dynamic fashion, any system of limitations must itself be dynamic and not static. Many variations are possible here, ranging from the idea that the process of negotiation can itself exercise a restraining influence on both parties to the possibility of a series of partial and interim agreements. To some extent, SALT performs the task of just such an arms control conference in semi-permanent session and symbol of a will to cooperate. The Joint Consultative Commission has taken the idea further. So have the various ideas about following up the SALT I Interim Agreement on Limiting Offensive Weapons not by a treaty, but by another Interim Agreement which could eventually be succeeded by a third. Clearly such a process would have many advantages, one of them being an ongoing exchange of information, including information about specific points of doubt. But there are drawbacks. Arms negotiation in this context becomes just

---

[32]Suggestions for freer movement of persons have already proved embarrassing in the framework of discussions about European security. For the Russians to permit such free movement could, of course, pose grave dangers to the entire apparatus of political control.

another, technical branch of diplomacy. Limitations depend upon the continued willingness of the two governments to cooperate amid the continuing flux and play of political and economic pressures. That must mean a willingness, at need, to subordinate a variety of other domestic and foreign interests to the overriding requirements of cooperation with each other on strategic arms. But that desire for political cooperation could wane for any number of reasons, particularly in an era strongly marked by intolerant neopopulist politics. If it does, it is hard to believe that open-ended arms-control discussions will continue, or be effective if they do.

The final possibility which deserves mention is that of non-verified arms control. This can mean one of two kinds of activity: agreements not subject to verification or inspection, or unilateral actions by either side. Examples of each have occurred. During the middle and later 1960s, the United States refrained for some time from developing and deploying ABM systems, and tried to use that unilateral restraint to secure countervailing Soviet restraint. The numbers of U.S. land- and sea-based launchers have remained stable since 1967. And both sides have limited their CBW [chemical and biological warfare] weapons by unverified understanding. But to apply such a principle to the whole of defense R & D presents difficulties. Precisely because science and technology move quickly, any advantage which either side possesses will be evanescent. Advantage therefore permits no slowdown in further research. A lead implies an advantage in lead-time and strategic substance; once it is lost, it may be irrecoverable. To slow down R & D in uncontrolled fashion may therefore be to incur strategic costs of an entirely unexpected magnitude and—given the role of externalities—character. Moreover, the greater a sudden and unexpected advantage promises to be for an opponent, the greater the probability that he will regard it as compensating for the risks he incurs by going to development and deployment.

A unilateral slowdown in R & D might be attempted by other means, for example by a damping-down of domestic inter-service or bureaucratic competition. But since the competition relates to real problems of political and strategic substance, eliminating it at the inter-service or inter-agency level without any alteration of the strategic balance or the attitudes of either party would merely lead to its reappearance in a new bureaucratic form somewhere else.[33] In any case such competition is, among other things, society's protection against bureaucratic or service secrecy and inertia. Even if it were possible to eliminate competition, therefore, it might be unwise to try.

---

[33]This idea is hardly new. *Natura furcam expellas, tamen usque recurret.*

In sum, acceptance of restraints without verification is merely the acceptance of greater risks. Such acceptance might be justified in conditions of improved political relations between the parties, or with respect to less important military systems,[34] or even because one's forces had become so large and sophisticated that the chances of sudden major changes in the overall strategic balance were thought to have measurably declined. Whether such risks are regarded as acceptable will continue to depend for both sides not only on perceptions of how far they have in fact been reduced, but on the answer to the question: if the bet fails, who will be held responsible and with what consequences?

IV. Conclusion

This analysis suggests that R & D is unlikely to be limitable by any single or static measure, whether of monitoring or spending. What may be needed is the injection of the idea of control of weapons R & D into the political and strategic process at all levels and in a continuing way. Arms control, and its R & D control component, are rightly becoming permanent features of the diplomatic and military scene. If action is to be taken, it must be not just on R & D but on the strategic and political setting in which R & D decisions are made.

There is a considerable possibility that the larger interests of arms control may, in fact, lie not so much in limitations on R & D as a whole, but in much more intensive R & D in at least some novel directions. These will include not only verification and inspection mechanisms, or methods for avoiding accidents or the failure of control, but the development by both sides of new kinds of strategic weapons outside the field, and therefore also outside the politics, of long-range, heavy-yield nuclear warheads. Several possibilities seem to be becoming available. One is for altogether more accurate and smaller-yield classes of warheads. Another may be for novel methods of air and anti-missile defense, possibly based in part on radiant energy.[35] Another may be climate control. The possibilities are many. But it already seems clear that what might emerge is nothing less than the separation of two concepts which, since 1945, have seemed inextricably linked and whose linkage has given the strategic problems of the 1950s and 1960s

---

[34] They might be less important for any one of several reasons: because they were less effective in relation to some particular mission, or because their effects were less controllable (as in the case of biological warfare), or because their use was subject to insurmountable political objections.

[35] Whether the development of such anti-missile systems would or would not be prohibited under the SALT I ABM Treaty is a matter of interpretation on which different views are possible.

their particular character. They are the concepts of "strategic weapons" and "mass destruction."

If and when one power or another develops strategic weapons which are not weapons of mass destruction, and possibly not even nuclear, a great many of the assumptions which underlie the present structure of security may require fundamental reevaluation. The character and direction of R & D will necessarily follow, where it does not already precede, these changes. Not only will the question of control over the R & D process then need to be reexamined as to both aim and method, but it will also be clear that although SALT I and II may have changed some of the conditions for strategic competition, they could not remove the perennial problems of the control and management of power, or prevent the emergence of novel dangers which need not be less than those which SALT was designed to meet.

CONTRIBUTORS

ROGER W. BARNETT is commander, U.S. Navy and formerly served on the JCS staff and the U.S. delegation to the Strategic Arms Limitation Talks.

W. S. BENNETT is a member of the systems analysis staff of the assistant director for weapon planning, Los Alamos Scientific Laboratory, University of California.

ARTHUR A. BROYLES is professor of physics and physical science at the University of Florida, Gainesville.

ZBIGNIEW BRZEZINSKI is assistant to the President for national security affairs.

ALBERT CARNESALE is associate director of the Program for Science and International Affairs at Harvard University and coeditor of the quarterly journal *International Security.*

BARRY CARTER served on the staff of the National Security Council and is now practicing law in California.

FRANK CHURCH is a U.S. senator from Idaho (Democrat).

DICK CLARK is a U.S. senator from Iowa (Democrat).

PAUL DOTY is director of the Program for Science and International Affairs at Harvard University and chairman of the editorial board of the quarterly journal *International Security.*

SIDNEY D. DRELL is deputy director of the Stanford Linear Accelerator Center and professor of physics at Stanford University.

LEWIS ALLEN FRANK is a consultant on arms control and other issues for Analytic Services Inc. of Falls Church, Virginia.

THOMAS M. GARWIN is a graduate student in the John F. Kennedy School of Government at Harvard University.

HARRY G. GELBER is on the economics and politics faculty at Monash University, Melbourne, Australia.

COLIN S. GRAY is a member of the professional staff of the Hudson Institute.

ANDREI GROMYKO is minister of foreign affairs of the Soviet Union.

MARK O. HATFIELD is a U.S. senator from Oregon (Republican).

JOHN H. HEINZ, III is a U.S. senator from Pennsylvania (Republican).

HUBERT H. HUMPHREY is a U.S. senator from Minnesota (Democrat).

FRED CHARLES IKLÉ was director of the U.S. Arms Control and Disarmament Agency and is now a private consultant in Washington, D.C.

HENRY A. KISSINGER was secretary of state and is now professor of diplomacy in the School of Foreign Service at Georgetown University.

ROGER P. LABRIE is a research associate specializing in defense policy at the American Enterprise Institute.

MELVIN R. LAIRD was secretary of defense and is now senior counsellor for national and international affairs with *Reader's Digest* and chairman of the advisory council of the American Enterprise Institute's public policy project on national defense.

MICHAEL NACHT is assistant director of the Program for Science and International Affairs at Harvard University and coeditor of the quarterly journal *International Security*.

RICHARD M. NIXON was thirty-seventh President of the United States.

SAM NUNN is a U.S. senator from Georgia (Democrat).

514

WOLFGANG K. H. PANOFSKY is director of the high energy physics laboratory, Stanford Linear Accelerator Center.

ROBERT J. PRANGER is director of foreign and defense policy studies at the American Enterprise Institute, adjunct professor in Georgetown University's School of Foreign Service, and professorial lecturer at The George Washington University.

DONALD H. RUMSFELD was secretary of defense and is now president of G. D. Searle & Co.

R. R. SANDOVAL is a staff member of the systems analysis group, Los Alamos Scientific Laboratory, University of California.

JAMES R. SCHLESINGER was secretary of defense and is now secretary of energy.

R. G. SHREFFLER is a member of the director's staff, Los Alamos Scientific Laboratory, University of California.

RICHARD HART SINNREICH is captain, U.S. Army and assistant professor of national security affairs at the U.S. Military Academy, West Point.

JOHN D. STEINBRUNER is associate professor of political science in the School of Organization and Management at Yale University.

JOHN C. STENNIS is a U.S. senator from Mississippi (Democrat).

STROM THURMOND is a U.S. senator from South Carolina (Republican).

A. TROFIMENKO is chief of the foreign policy department and senior strategic analyst at the Institute of the United States of America and Canada in Moscow.

WILLIAM R. VAN CLEAVE is associate professor and director of the Defense and Strategic Studies Program in the School of International Relations at the University of Southern California.

EUGENE P. WIGNER is professor emeritus in the department of physics at Princeton University.

Cover and book design: Pat Taylor